*Part One*

# The National Experience

Fourth Edition

*A History of the United States
to 1877*

## Part One

# The National

### John M. Blum
*Yale University*

### Edmund S. Morgan
*Yale University*

### Willie Lee Rose
*The Johns Hopkins University*

### Arthur M. Schlesinger, Jr.
*The City University of New York*

### Kenneth M. Stampp
*University of California, Berkeley*

### C. Vann Woodward
*Yale University*

# Experience

### Fourth Edition

## A History of the United States to 1877

HARCOURT BRACE JOVANOVICH, INC.

New York / Chicago / San Francisco / Atlanta

*The National Experience, Fourth Edition*

**John M. Blum**
**Edmund S. Morgan**
**Willie Lee Rose**
**Arthur M. Schlesinger, Jr.**
**Kenneth M. Stampp**
**C. Vann Woodward**

Hardbound ISBN: 0-15-565680-5

Paperbound ISBN, Part One: 0-15-565681-3

Paperbound ISBN, Part Two: 0-15-565682-1

Library of Congress Catalog Card Number: 76-13664

Printed in the United States of America

*Cover illustrations:*
Hardbound: Airview of Nebraska wheatfield by Georg Gerster from Rapho/Photo Researchers
Paperbound, Part One: Keystone from Photoworld
Paperbound, Part Two: from NASA

# A note on the paperbound edition

This volume is part of a variant printing, not a new or revised edition, of *The National Experience*, Fourth Edition. Many of the users of the Third Edition found the two-volume paperbound version of that edition useful because it enabled them to fit the text into the particular patterns of their teaching and scheduling. The publishers have continued that format in preparing this printing, which exactly reproduces the text of the one-volume version of *The National Experience*, Fourth Edition. The first of these volumes begins with the discovery of America and continues through Reconstruction. The second volume, repeating the chapter on Reconstruction (Chapter 15, "The Aftermath of War"), carries the account forward to the present day. The variant printing, then, is intended as a convenience to those instructors and students who have occasion to use either one part or the other of *The National Experience*. Consequently, the pagination and index of the one-volume version, as well as its illustrations, maps, and other related materials, are retained in the new printing. The difference between the one-volume and the two-volume versions of the book is a difference only in form.

# *Preface*

Men and women make history. Their ideas and their hopes, their goals and contrivances for reaching those goals, shape all experience, past and present. The Indians, the first Americans, had to decide, by deliberation or by default, how to use the continent and its extraordinary resources. So have the successors of the Indians and the children of those successors—the early European settlers, the English colonists, the men and women of the new United States, and the generations that have followed them. Each generation has committed the nation to a complex of policies, some the product of thought and debate, others of habit or inadvertence, still others of calculated or undiscerning indifference. As the nation has grown, as its population has diversified, its economy matured, and its responsibilities multiplied, questions of national policy have become more difficult to understand but no more troubling. It took long thought and hard debate to settle the issues of independence, of democratic reform, of expansion, of slavery, of union itself, of control of private economic power, of resistance to totalitarianism across two oceans. All those issues and many more have made up the national experience.

This book endeavors to recount and explain that experience. It examines both the aspirations (often contradictory among themselves) and the achievements (often less grand than the best hopes) of the American people. It examines, too, the ideas, the institutions, and the processes that fed hope and af-fected achievement. It focuses on the decisions, positive and negative, that reflected national goals and directed national purposes, and consequently it focuses continually on the men and women who made those decisions, on those who made history. The book emphasizes public policy, but the history of public policy perforce demands continuing discussion of the whole culture that influenced it.

The authors of this book believe that a history emphasizing public policy, so conceived, reveals the fabric and experience of the past more completely than does any other kind of history. They believe, too, that an emphasis on questions of public policy provides the most useful introduction to the history of the United States. In the light of those convictions they have agreed on the focus of this book, on its organization, and on the selection and interpretation of the data it contains. The structure of the separate parts and chapters is now chronological, now topical, depending on the form that seemed most suitable for the explanation of the period or the subject under discussion. The increasing complexity of public issues in the recent past, moreover, has persuaded the authors to devote half of this volume to the period since Reconstruction, indeed more than a third to the twentieth century.

The authors have elected, furthermore, to confine their work to one volume so as to permit instructors to make generous supplementary assignments from the abundance of excellent monographs, biographies, and "problems" books now readily and inexpensively available. Just as there are clear interpretations of the past in those books, so are there in this, for the authors without exception find meaning in history and feel obliged to say what they see. The authors also believe that, especially for the beginning student of history, literature is better read than read about. Consequently, in commenting on belles-lettres and the other arts, they have consciously stressed those expressions and aspects of the arts relevant to an understanding of public policy. Finally, they have arranged to choose the illustrations and the boxed selections from contemporary and other sources in order to enhance and supplement not only the text but its particular focus.

This is a collaborative book in which each of the six contributors has ordinarily written about a period in which he or she is a specialist. Yet each has also executed the general purpose of the whole book. Each section of the book has been read and criticized by several of the contributors. This revision has profited from the assistance of many historians who were kind enough to review portions of the book before it was revised. These include: David Brion Davis, Yale University; Sidney Fine, University of Michigan; Michael Holt, University of Virginia; Howard R. Lamar, Yale University; Robert Middlekauff, University of California, Berkeley; James T. Patterson, Brown University; Bradford Perkins, University of Michigan; Edward Pessen, Baruch College; and Morton Rothstein, University of Wisconsin. As in all previous editions of this text, so in this one, Everett M. Sims has assisted all the authors with his perceptive and gentle criticisms.

Not even a collaboration as easy and agreeable as this one has been can erase the individuality of the collaborators. Each section of this book displays the particular intellectual and literary style of its contributor; all the contribtors have been permitted, indeed urged, to remain themselves. The ultimate as well as the original responsibility for prose, for historical accuracy, and for interpretation remains that of the author of each section of this book: Edmund S. Morgan, Chapters 1–6; Kenneth M. Stampp, Chapters 7–12; Willie Lee Rose, Chapters 13–15; C. Vann Woodward, Chapters 16–21; John M. Blum, Chapters 22–26; Arthur M. Schlesinger, Jr., Chapters 27–29, revised for this edition by John M. Blum; and Arthur M. Schlesinger, Jr., Chapters 30–33 and Epilogue.

JOHN M. BLUM, *Editor*
*New Haven, Connecticut*

# A note

## On the suggestions for additional readings

The lists of suggested readings that follow the chapters of this book are obviously and intentionally selective. They are obviously so because a reasonably complete bibliography of American history would fill a volume larger than this one. They are intentionally so because the authors of the various chapters have tried to suggest to students only those stimulating and useful works that they might profitably and enjoyably explore while studying this text. Consequently each list of suggested readings points to a relatively few significant and well-written books, and each list attempts to emphasize, in so far as possible, books available in inexpensive, paperback editions—books whose titles are marked by an asterisk.

Use of the suggested readings, then, permits a student to begin to range through the rich literature of American history, but interested and energetic students will want to go beyond the lists. They will profit from the bibliographies in many of the works listed. They should also consult the card catalogs in the libraries of their colleges and the invaluable bibliography in the *Harvard Guide to American History*, rev. ed. (Belknap). For critical comments about the titles they find, they should go on, when they can, to the reviews in such learned journals as the *American Historical Review*, the *Journal of American History*, the *Journal of Southern History*, and the *William and Mary Quarterly*.

Those students who want to acquire libraries of their own and who want also to economize by purchasing paperback editions will find the availability of titles in paperbacks at best uncertain. Every few months new titles are published and other titles go out of print. For the most recent information about paperbacks, students should consult *Paperbound Books in Print* (Bowker), which appears quarterly.

The reading lists refer to very few articles, not because articles are unimportant, but because they are often rather inaccessible to undergraduates. There are, however, many useful collections of important selected articles, often available in inexpensive editions. So, too, students will have no difficulty in finding collections of contemporary historical documents that add depth and excitement to the study of history. A growing number of thoughtful books organize both contemporary and scholarly materials in units designed to facilitate the investigation of historical problems.

The problems books, documents books, and collections of articles will whet the appetite of engaged students for further reading in the fields of their interest. They can serve in their way, then, as can the lists of suggested readings in this volume, as avenues leading to the adventures of the mind and the development of the understanding that American history affords.

# Contents

CHAPTER **1**

## Making use of a new world  2

# Maps

*Part One*

# The National Experience

Fourth Edition

*A History of the United States
to 1877*

CHAPTER **1**

# *Making use of a new world*

The first American was an immigrant. Although anthropologists disagree about where man first appeared on earth, no one claims the honor for the Western Hemisphere, which had probably never been seen by human eyes until twenty or thirty or at most forty thousand years ago. Presumably the earliest immigrant came by way of the Bering Straits and was followed by hundreds, perhaps thousands, more who trickled slowly southward, spreading out across North America and funneling through Mexico into Central and South America, venturing across the water to the Caribbean islands and perhaps much farther to the South Pacific. The immigration may have gone on for centuries, and it probably included people from various parts of Asia, Africa, and Europe.

For these early arrivals America was no melting pot. The people we lump together as Indians, or Amerinds, were divided into hundreds of tribes, enormously varied in physical appearance, language, and civilization. Those who made their homes south of the present United States were unquestionably the most numerous and the most skillful in exploiting their territory. They were the inventors of Indian corn (maize), as efficient a method of transforming earth into food as has ever been devised. Corn is so civilized a plant, so highly bred, that botanists have only recently been able to track down the wild ancestors from which the Indian plant-breeders developed it. The early inhabitants of Mexico and South America were skilled in other ways too. They built great cities of stone, richly carved and ornamented. They knew enough mathematics and astronomy to construct a calendar that required no leap year and to predict eclipses of the sun. And they knew enough political science to construct strong governments under which they worked out an advanced division of labor. In central Mexico their economy supported a population of several million and a city (Tenochtitlan, now Mexico City) that ranked in size with those of Europe.

By contrast, the Indians who lived north of Mexico were primitive. They made less effective use of the land, and it supported far fewer of them, probably not many more than ten million in the present area of the United States. They grew some corn and other vegetables but also relied on nuts and berries, game and fish, and starved when these were unavailable. In parts of the Southeast they organized governments with real authority, the Powhatan Confederacy in Virginia and the Creek Confederacy in the Gulf Plains. But most often they joined together only loosely in tribes or clans under leaders or chiefs whose authority depended on the respect that their fierceness in war and their wisdom in peace could elicit from the other members of the tribe. They had dignity in abundance, self-reliance, and self-control—it was rare for Indians to show anger or even to raise their voices. Indeed they were so self-reliant, so individualistic, that even in war it was apt to be every man for himself; and in peace they did not achieve the cooperation and organization, the division of labor, needed to make the most of the country's resources or to defend it against strangers better organized than they.

3

# Exploration

Such strangers began to arrive shortly after 1492. There had been earlier visitors in the eleventh century, when some wandering Norsemen from Iceland, led by Leif Ericson, spent a winter in what they called Vinland, probably in Newfoundland. A few years later other Icelanders attempted to establish a settlement. But the Norsemen had no real need for this vast continent and went home, leaving behind only the ruins of their encampments to show that they had been there.

**The rise of kings and commerce.** If Columbus had sailed when the Norsemen did, his voyages would probably have had as little effect as theirs on the course of history. By 1492, however, Europeans were ready for new worlds. During the intervening centuries two important historical developments had prepared them. One was the rise of a large merchant class hungry for foreign trade. Spices, dyestuffs, and textiles from India and the Far East traveled overland by slow,

*Caravel—*
*faster and more seaworthy*

expensive caravan through Asia or partly by sail through the Red Sea or the Persian Gulf, passing from one dealer to another along the way until they finally reached the marketplaces of Europe. The prices people were willing to pay for these exotic imports were enough to send fifteenth-century sailors in search of sea routes to the source of the treasures. A direct sea route would permit importation in greater volume at less expense and would net the importer a huge profit.

Portugal took the lead in maritime exploration with a new type of vessel, the caravel—faster, more maneuverable, more seaworthy than any formerly known. Portuguese explorers, encouraged by their kings and by Prince Henry the Navigator (1394–1460), discovered the Azores and pushed their caravels farther and farther south along the coast of Africa. At first they were probably seeking only new trading opportunities in Africa itself, but by the 1480s they were searching for a way around the continent to the greater riches of the Orient. In 1488 Bartholomeu Diaz rounded the Cape of Good Hope. Ten years later Vasco da Gama reached India.

The rise of kings was the second great development that prepared Europeans to use a new world. At the time of Leif Ericsson's voyage Europe was divided into tiny principalities, usually owing nominal allegiance to a king but actually dominated by local magnates who levied tolls on all trade passing through their territories. Even towns and cities tended to be autonomous, bristling with local regulations that discouraged trade with the outside world. The rise of kings meant the reorganization of society into larger units, into national states more wealthy and more powerful than any one of the towns or cities or principalities of which they were composed. A state organized under a king had the power and resources to cut through the strangling web of local trade barriers, to sponsor exploration for new lands to trade with, and even to seize the lands and their riches when the natives were not strong enough to resist.

During most of the fifteenth century Portugal far outran the rest of Europe in pursuit of foreign trade and of new lands to conquer. Other countries were still too troubled by domestic feuds and foreign wars to offer much competition. The first to emerge as a serious rival was Portugal's neighbor, Spain. And, as luck had it, Spain was also first to find America and first to find a use for it.

**Columbus and the Spaniards.** Christopher Columbus, the son of a Genoese weaver, was a man with a mission. He wanted to reach the Orient by sailing west, and he was convinced that the distance was no more than three or four thousand miles. Columbus was wrong, and when he tried to sell his idea the

Voyages of Columbus

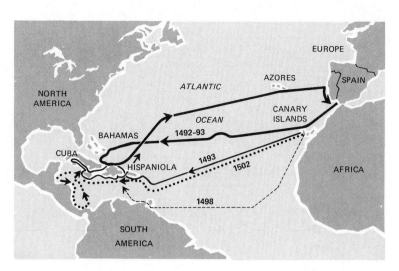

experts told him so. The experts had known for centuries that the world was round, and they had a much better notion of its size than Columbus did. The king of Portugal would have none of his scheme, and neither would anyone else until Queen Isabella of Spain, who was not an expert, decided to take a chance. In the very year that the consolidation of the Spanish monarchy was completed by the conquest of Granada from the Moors, she persuaded her husband, Ferdinand II, to pay for an expedition of three ships and to give Columbus authority, under Spain, over any lands he might discover on the way.

Armed with this commission and with a letter to the emperor of China, Columbus made his magnificent mistake. He failed to deliver the letter but found America (so named after his death for a later explorer, Amerigo Vespucci), at the island of San Salvador, on October 12, 1492. From here he threaded his way through the other Bahamas to Cuba and Hispaniola. By March 15, 1493, he was back in Spain. In succeeding years he explored the rest of the Caribbean area, still looking for China and Japan. Though he did not find them, he did find gold; and everyone in Europe knew what to do with that.

But for the gold, Europeans would probably have looked upon America as a mere obstacle on the route to the Orient. Even after Ferdinand Magellan carried out Columbus' original intention by sailing around the tip of South America (1519–22), explorers continued for two centuries to probe hopefully up American rivers in search of the Pacific. But the Spaniards recognized at once that Columbus' substitute for China might have advantages surpassing the original. With approval of Pope Alexander VI they joined the Portuguese in the Treaty of Tordesillas (1494), dividing the world by a line drawn north and south, 370 leagues west of the Cape Verde Islands (between the present

forty-sixth and forty-seventh meridians): Spain was authorized to take possession of all the heathen lands she found to the west of the line; Portugal could do the same to the east. Thereafter Spaniards swarmed over the Caribbean islands and onto the mainland of North and South America.

By comparison with the natives, the invaders were few in numbers, but they were courageous, unscrupulous, and armed. They wanted gold, and they were ready to take what the natives had and make them dig for more. The Indians were no match for them. In the West Indies the first Spaniards killed or enslaved wherever they went, and slavery was only a slower form of killing. After working the Caribbean natives to death, they brought in black slaves purchased from the Portuguese, the beginning of an involuntary migration that ultimately carried nearly 10 million Africans to the New World. In the Caribbean islands the Africans died, too, but not before they had earned their purchase price many times over. When the supply of gold ran out, the Spaniards turned them to planting sugar, which in the long run proved even more lucrative—and no less deadly—than digging for gold.

On the mainland, where the Indians were more numerous, small armies led by private adventurers, the conquistadors, subdued whole countries. Hernando Cortez with fifteen hundred men conquered Mexico (1519–21), and Francisco Pizarro with still fewer men conquered Peru (1531–35). The extraordinary conquests made by these small forces were possible because Spanish firearms and cavalry seemed irresistible to men who had never seen either guns or horses before—the Indians frequently took a man on horseback to be some superhuman quadruped. But even with this enormous advantage the Spaniards could scarcely have subdued such large and populous

*Mainland Indians:
the earliest depiction*

areas if the Indians had not been divided among themselves and if most of them had not already been living as subject peoples. To many Indians the Spaniard was only a more powerful and exacting master than the Aztec or Inca ruler whom they had served before.

The conquistadors were quick to seize the gold and silver with which the native palaces abounded, but the people themselves were the greatest treasure of Spain's new possessions. Spain in the sixteenth century had a population of about 9 million. The native population of Spanish America probably amounted to many more than that, and they all could be put to work for Spain. In the course of the century, thousands of Spaniards came to the new land, most of them to profit from the immense supply of cheap labor that Columbus and the conquistadors had delivered to them.

The Spanish government did what it could, from a distance of three thousand miles, to protect the rights of its Indian subjects, and the Church sent countless priests, friars, and bishops to look after their souls. Devoted Spanish clerics never ceased to denounce the way in which their countrymen relentlessly overworked the Indians. But everyone agreed that they ought to work, and neither church nor state was able to prevent the new lords of the land from exacting the utmost from every Indian who came within their reach.

Indians who resisted the Spanish advance were enslaved. Others, technically free, were parceled out in *encomiendas,* at first to the conquerors but later to nearly every Spaniard who appeared on the scene. From the Indians of his *encomienda* the *encomendero* could demand labor at token wages and also an annual tribute. When the government finally brought this form of exploitation under control in the middle of the century, the settlers devised other forms of forced labor.

The Spanish colonists made use of the Indians in mining the great deposits of silver ore that were discovered in both Mexico and Peru and in manning huge ranches and farms (haciendas). While the labor supply lasted, many settlers made fortunes, and the Spanish treasury welcomed the silver that poured in from its numerous taxes, which included a fifth of the proceeds of privately owned mines. But within a century the boom had ended, because overwork, despair, and disease destroyed the Spanish empire's basic resource. In the century after the conquest the native population of Mexico declined from several million (some scholars say 25 million) to little more than a million. A comparable decline is thought to have occurred in Peru.

Of the acknowledged causes for this catastrophic loss, probably the most lethal was the unavoidable introduction of European diseases against which the Indians had no natural resistance. Many of those who did survive were of mixed ancestry, mestizos as they were called. They, together with the creoles (people of European descent born in Spanish America), the Africans, and the few remaining Indians, furnished a base from which Spanish America in succeeding centuries was to recover its population and perpetuate the advanced civilization that Spain, at whatever cost, had brought to the New World.

North of Mexico the Spaniards at first found little to interest them. Ponce de León cruised along the shores of the Florida peninsula in 1513, and Pánfilo de Narváez and Hernando de Soto both explored the western side of the peninsula and the Gulf Plains before the middle of the sixteenth century. But there was no visible gold or silver about and no extensive population to exploit. Both expeditions marched on across the continent to Mexico without finding anything on the way that made them want to stay. In a futile search for seven legendary cities of gold, Francisco Vásquez de Coronado circled through present Arizona, New Mexico, Texas, Oklahoma, and Kansas (1540–42). He too thought the country not worth taking and returned to Mexico.

During the second half of the sixteenth century the Spaniards began to take a more lasting interest in the northern areas. They established a fort at St. Augustine, Florida (1565), and carried on missionary activities as far north as Port Royal (South Carolina) and for a few years even up to Chesapeake Bay. By the end of the century they were settling into present New Mexico and Arizona, planting missions to benefit the peaceable natives and *presidios* (military outposts) to hold back hostile ones. The mission was an ambitious undertaking, a nucleus from which Spanish civilization might grow in the borderlands of the empire. The mission gathered Indians (often nomadic in this section) into settled communities where, under supervision of the Church, they were taught Christianity along with techniques of farming and handi-

crafts. During the seventeenth century Spain sowed missions in Texas and during the eighteenth in California. But long before this, the force of the Spanish thrust had spent itself, and other countries were ready to make use of the vast and lonely North American continent.

***The Europeans in North America.*** Columbus never saw the shores of North America, nor do we know what European was the first to do so. Perhaps other sailors had happened on it just as the Norsemen had. There may even have been fishermen walking the streets of St. Malo or Bristol or Plymouth who could have told Columbus of a distant coast where pines were tall and codfish plentiful. If so, no chronicler set down their discoveries until in 1497 John Cabot, like Columbus a Genoese, sailed west for the king of England and returned to report a new land. Henry VII gave Cabot £10 and an annuity of £20. Cabot undertook another voyage the next year, but he and other Europeans thought of the new land as a barrier, not an opportunity.

In 1524 the king of France, Francis I, sent a Florentine navigator, Giovanni da Verrazano, along the Atlantic coast from North Carolina to Nova Scotia in search of a passage through the barrier to the Pacific. Ten years later the king sent Jacques Cartier on the

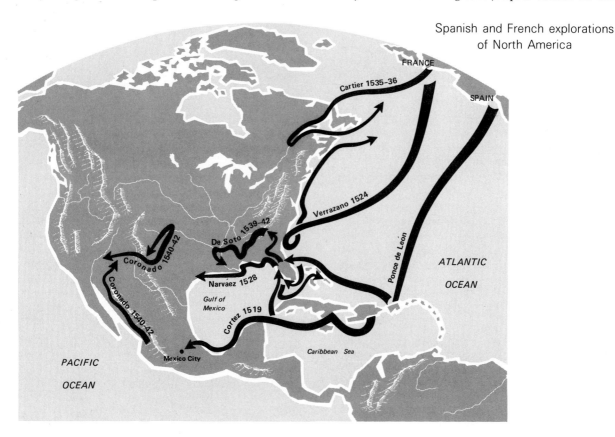

Spanish and French explorations
of North America

same errand. Cartier, encouraged by the promisingly large entrance of the St. Lawrence River, sailed inland as far as the first rapids before giving up. He was sufficiently impressed by the surrounding country, however, to attempt a settlement there in 1541. Since Spain had found riches in the southern continent, it seemed reasonable to expect them in the north as well. When Canadian gold proved to be fool's gold, Canadian diamonds quartz, and Canadian winters terrible, the colonists returned home, and France forgot about North America for the rest of the century.

The first Europeans to find a lasting use for the continent were summer people, who liked the fishing there. Every spring in the ports of France, England, Portugal, and Spain fishermen piled aboard their precarious craft and headed for the Grand Banks, where the continental shelf of North America lies submerged at a depth that codfish find congenial. They set up docks and drying stages ashore and assembled knocked-down dories and other small boats carried in the holds of their ships. They killed a few auks or netted some minnows for bait, rowed far out to the deeper waters, and fished all day with hand lines. Each night they brought in their catch to be dried, salted, and packed for sale in the markets of Europe. Caring little for the doings of their remote monarchs, they lived together in little international communities in Newfoundland and Nova Scotia—sleeping aboard their ships or in rough cabins ashore, planting gardens, and visiting one another of an evening—until the approach of winter sent them and the cod to friendlier climates. None of them seems to have contemplated permanent residence.

As the years passed, more and more Europeans sailed west to cruise along the coasts of North America, catching its codfish, prying into bays and rivers, kidnaping an occasional Indian to show off at home. Gradually they became aware that the country had more to offer than fish and pine trees. Behind the coast lay rivers and lakes teeming with beaver, otter, and other fur-bearing animals, which the Indians were adept at trapping. When Indians and Europeans met, the Indians demanded metals, whose superiority to stone they were quick to recognize. The furs they offered in exchange brought a good price in Europe—especially beaver, which was turned into felt for hats.

Early in the seventeenth century the French, the Dutch, and the Swedes all set up permanent fur-trading posts in America. The great French explorer Samuel de Champlain, after reconnoitering the New England coast and the St. Lawrence region, founded Quebec in 1608. Henry Hudson, an Englishman working for a Dutch company, in 1609 sailed up the river

*Champlain encounters the Indians*

he named for himself; the Dutch planted trading posts there in 1624, on the Delaware River in 1623, and on the Connecticut River in 1633. A Swedish company also maintained posts on the Delaware from 1638 until the Dutch seized them in 1655.

The French and the Dutch came to trade with the Indians, not to subjugate them. Neither in New France nor in New Netherland, as their settlements were called, did the Indians become slaves. Instead they lived on in their customary manner, roaming the woods they had roamed before, though trapping beaver in unaccustomed numbers. Contact with the Europeans inevitably meant new things for them: Christianity, comfort, progress, guns, hatchets, deadly drinks, deadlier diseases, sharper rivalry with other tribes, and a weakening of tribal customs. But the continent was still theirs. In the course of time both the French and the Dutch did try to transform their trading posts into larger settlements of Europeans, who would supplant rather than suppress or exploit the Indian, but this was only after the English had arrived on the continent and begun to fill it with their children.

# Tudor England and the New World

Before England could turn its interests to America at all, before its merchants could support expensive and risky overseas expeditions, it had to experience the same political consolidation under a powerful king that Spain and Portugal had undergone a century earlier. Henry VII, who sent John Cabot to America in 1497, began the job; his son Henry VIII and his granddaughter Elizabeth I finished it. In the process they transformed England from a Catholic country into a Protestant one, a fact that would affect profoundly the land that John Cabot had found across the seas.

**Henry VIII and the Reformation.** Soon after Martin Luther launched the Reformation, which split the monolithic west-European Church into Protestant and Roman Catholic segments, Luther's teachings reached England. Perhaps no Englishman was less receptive to them than the king, Henry VIII, who demonstrated his devotion to Rome by writing a book against the German heretic. The pope rewarded Henry by conferring on him the title "Defender of the Faith."

Before many years passed Henry found himself, if no friendlier to Luther, a good deal less friendly to the pope. Henry was the most powerful king England had ever known, so powerful that no baron or lesser local potentate could oppose him. Only one set of men in England dared challenge his authority: the priests and bishops, the monks and abbots, who acknowledged a higher power than Henry not only in the heavens but on earth, in Rome. Moreover, the Church owned about one-fourth of England and collected a yearly income of more than £320,000, much of it from the rent of lands owned by monasteries. When Henry needed funds to meet the cost of England's new and growing governmental machinery, the wealth of the monasteries caught his eye. In 1539 he found an opportunity to lay hold of it.

In 1509 Henry had married Catherine of Aragon, daughter of Ferdinand and Isabella, and in twenty years she bore him no son who lived. Henry desperately wanted an heir, and besides he had grown tired of Catherine. In 1529 he asked the pope for a divorce. When the pope refused, Henry defied him, married Anne Boleyn, severed England's ties with Rome, made himself head of the English Church—and in 1539 confiscated the monastic lands.

**The results of Henry's break with Rome.** Although Henry never showed the slightest interest in the New World, his divorce and his defiance of the pope had enormous consequences for both England and America.

The first and simplest consequence was that his new wife bore him a daughter, Elizabeth, who was to become England's greatest monarch. Elizabeth became queen in 1558 and ruled for forty-four glorious years—years in which Englishmen triumphed on land, at sea, and in the human spirit. Under her direction England became strong enough to begin the building of a North American empire.

Second, by divorcing his Spanish queen, Henry touched off over a hundred years of intermittent hostility with Spain. Spain, the spearhead of Catholicism and the headquarters of the Inquisition, gradually became synonymous in Protestant England with the antichrist. Englishmen attacked the Spaniard most successfully at sea not only by outright war but by privateering against Spanish shipping. The English privateers (or sea dogs, as they came to be called) resembled the earlier conquistadors in their daring, toughness, unscrupulousness, and flair for the spectacular and heroic. But the sea dogs operated on water rather than on land, scouring the Atlantic and the Caribbean for Spanish vessels laden with gold and silver from the New World. Under Queen Elizabeth privateering against Spain reached its height and drew England's attention to the riches of America.

Third, Henry's break with Rome gave impetus to a Protestant movement in England that had been covertly under way for some years. Its adherents in-

9

*Queen Elizabeth I:
England's greatest monarch*

selling land to make ends meet. The turnover of so much real estate had widespread repercussions: in some places rich men got richer and poor men poorer, while in other places the rich were getting poor and the poor rich. The sale of monastic lands was certainly not wholly responsible for this upheaval, but it was a step in the chain of events that destroyed the social and economic security of large numbers of Englishmen and helped to make the fortunes of others, especially the merchants. Whoever lost from the rise of prices and the sale of lands, it was not they. As the sixteenth century wore on, they accumulated more and more capital, enough to finance overseas expeditions, while men who lost their homes or fortunes began to think of regaining them, perhaps in another part of the world.

***Gilbert finds a use for North America.*** The historical developments that were set in motion by Henry VIII's break with Rome became significant for America only gradually. After the voyage of John Cabot in 1497, Englishmen showed very little interest in the New World until 1576, when the Cathay Company (Cathay was another name for China) was formed to trade with China by way of North America. The company sent Martin Frobisher to find a way through the continent. He probed the northern waters and found Baffin Land and Frobisher's Bay, where glittering gold-flecked rocks diverted his attention from further search. With the usual captive Indian and a case of ore samples, he hurried back to England. The assayers declared that the ore was indeed gold, and he returned to North America for more. When the twelve hundred tons he brought back turned out to be worthless, the Cathay Company folded. For years thereafter Englishmen with capital to invest were wary of risking it in America.

Although the Cathay Company had planned to establish a small permanent settlement in America, it was intended to serve merely as a supply station for voyages to the Orient. The first Englishman, possibly the first European, to have a glimmering of the northern continent's colonial future was a soldier of fortune named Humphrey Gilbert. Gilbert had served the queen in Ireland, where his skill in exterminating the natives won him a knighthood. While there he concocted a scheme for settling Ireland with Englishmen. But then his interest shifted. North America was a larger Ireland. Englishmen planted there could exploit the natives (the counterpart of the wild Irish), forestall Spanish settlement, catch codfish, and search for a passage to the Pacific (Gilbert wrote a tract in 1576 to prove that there must be one). When the passage was found, they could supply ships passing through. What was more immediately attractive, an American colony would serve as a base from which

terpreted Henry's defiance of the pope as a total repudiation of Roman hierarchy, ritual, and doctrine. Henry himself would have been content to serve as England's pope without substantially altering the internal organization or doctrines of the Church. But he could not wholly control the forces he had unleashed. The ideas of Luther and of the French reformer John Calvin became increasingly popular during the next 125 years; and, as their numbers grew, the extreme Calvinists—the Puritans—became increasingly discontent with the incomplete reformation of the English Church. Many of them would come to America with a view to completing the Reformation there.

Finally, Henry's confiscation of the monasteries set off a train of unexpected events that indirectly provided still more Englishmen willing to people a new world. Henry, not content with the income from the lands he had confiscated, began to sell them; succeeding monarchs continued the process, selling other royal lands as well. They were led to do so partly by a steady rise in prices during the sixteenth and seventeenth centuries (the so-called Price Revolution) that was induced or accelerated by the flow of Spanish gold and silver from America. Other people felt the pinch, especially landlords whose rents were fixed by custom and unalterable. They too began

sea dogs could raid the Spanish treasure fleets that sailed every year from the Caribbean. In every way America was more attractive than Ireland.

Gilbert, impelled by greed and chauvinism, had vision: he was the first to see America as a place for Englishmen to live. In 1578 he induced Queen Elizabeth to grant him a charter empowering him to discover and take possession of North American lands not claimed by any other Christian monarch. Within six years he was supposed to settle a colony over which he would exercise absolute authority, provided he made no laws contrary to the Christian faith, and provided he gave the queen one-fifth of the gold and silver he mined (a provision generally inserted by subsequent monarchs in such charters).

Gilbert made two attempts to found his colony. The first attempt, in 1578, is a mystery. No one knows where he went or what he found, but there is a strong suspicion that he went not far and found a number of ships not his own—in short, that piracy, for the moment, proved more attractive than colonization.

Gilbert's second attempt, in 1583, was a larger undertaking, for by this time he had managed to sell his idea to other Englishmen: noblemen who felt the pressure of inflated prices and the loss of lands and power their fathers had had; merchants who scented opportunities for trade in the new land; discontented religious minorities, privateers, pirates, paupers, and fools. Drawing men and money from these divergent sources, Gilbert was able to launch an expedition. He got underway in June 1583, with two hundred sixty prospective settlers and five ships, one of which he stole from a pirate just before departing and took along, pirate crew and all. Before reaching America one ship turned back for lack of provisions. The pirate ship had no such trouble: she simply plundered another vessel encountered along the way.

In August the expedition reached Newfoundland, where Gilbert came upon a sizable international community of summer fishermen. He probably did not intend to establish his colony this far north (though it should be remembered that Newfoundland

English explorations of the New World

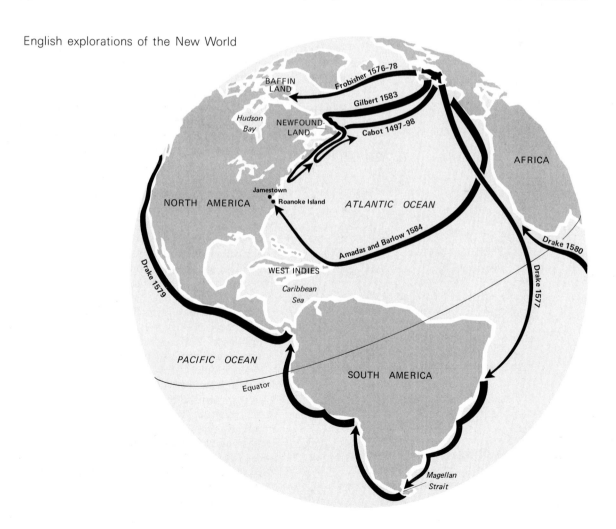

*Tudor England and the New World*

is south of England), but he made a great ceremony of taking possession of the settlement. The fishermen humored him and even agreed to pay rent for their fishing stages. They probably calculated, rightly, that no one would come to collect it.

After two weeks in Newfoundland, the men on one of the ships decided they had had enough of America and sailed for home. Gilbert, with the other three, cruised southward, filled with enthusiasm by the splendor of the uninhabited coast. He lost another ship with eighty men on a reef and shortly thereafter was obliged to turn the two remaining ships back to England for supplies. In mid-ocean they ran into an alarmingly heavy sea, but Gilbert demonstrated his nonchalance by sitting on the afterdeck of his small vessel reading a book. At one point he shouted across to a friend in the other ship: "We are as near to heaven by sea as by land." That night, as the others watched, the lights of his vessel went out. No more was ever heard of the man who first envisaged England's American empire.

**Raleigh and Roanoke.** Although Gilbert's ventures accomplished nothing concrete, he had stirred the imagination of other Englishmen: the kind of men who backed him would back other expeditions to the New World. Before his last voyage, he had enlisted the

Indian woman, by John White

talents of his younger half-brother, Sir Walter Raleigh. Raleigh equaled Gilbert in daring and exceeded him in polish. He was a favorite with Queen Elizabeth, who gave him nearly everything he asked for. After Gilbert's death, Raleigh asked her for a charter to found a colony in the New World.

Raleigh was as interested as Gilbert in piracy against Spanish treasure fleets, and like Gilbert he wanted his colony to be more than a base of operations. From the beginning he planned it as a permanent settlement, and he enlisted his friend Richard Hakluyt to write propaganda persuading Englishmen to emigrate. Hakluyt was already fascinated by the idea of colonization and developed into England's greatest advocate of overseas expansion.

Raleigh got his charter in 1584 and immediately sent out a reconnoitering force under Philip Amadas and Arthur Barlow. They made their landfall a couple of thousand miles south of Newfoundland—perhaps in order to be closer to the Spaniards—and explored the coast south of Chesapeake Bay. When they returned with glowing descriptions of the region, Raleigh named it Virginia in honor of Elizabeth, the Virgin Queen.

In 1585 Raleigh fitted out an expedition to settle Roanoke Island, near the present boundary between Virginia and North Carolina. The group, under the command of Ralph Lane, included John White, an artist; Thomas Cavendish, who later sailed round the world; and Thomas Hariot, a noted mathematician. White made some excellent drawings of the American Indians, the best executed during the whole colonial period; Hariot took notes from which he later prepared the first detailed description of any part of the present United States. The settlers themselves, instead of digging in, spent their time searching Virginia's rivers unsuccessfully for the Pacific and its shores unsuccessfully for gold. In June 1586, when Sir Francis Drake called to visit them after searching successfully for gold in the Spanish fortresses of the West Indies, the settlers all climbed aboard with him and went home.

Raleigh tried again the next year, 1587, sending one hundred twenty persons under the command of John White. White spent a month getting the new Roanoke settlement started and then returned to England for supplies, leaving his daughter, her husband, and their new-born child with the settlers. A supply fleet commanded by Sir Richard Grenville was prepared, but the Spaniards chose this moment for an all-out attack on England (the great Spanish Armada), and Grenville and his ships were pressed into service for defense. Not until 1590 could White sail back to Roanoke, and when he got there his colonists had completely vanished. Someone had carved the name of a neighboring island, CROATOAN, on a post. But no trace of the colonists was ever found there. Presumably, hostile Indians had overwhelmed them, but to this day no real clue to their fate has been found.

The sixteenth century closed without an English colony in North America. Raleigh turned his attention to South America. Richard Hakluyt sang the praises of England's explorers and published accounts of their great voyages in *The Principall Navigations, Voiages, and Discoveries of the English Nation* (1589). But no one else with the vision of a Gilbert or a Raleigh stepped forward to lead Englishmen to new homes.

Actually Gilbert and Raleigh were as wrong, in their way, as Columbus. He expected to find China and found America. They expected not only to settle North America but to make a profit out of it. They failed, and even if their settlements had succeeded there would almost certainly have been no profit, unless from piracy. But Gilbert and Raleigh were not the last to be mistaken about the New World. In 1606 another group of Englishmen risked their money, and lost it, in an enterprise from which in the fullness of time grew the United States.

# The founding of Virginia

While Elizabeth reigned, men of daring in England enjoyed risking their money and their lives for her by attacking Spain. Her successor, James I, was so different from the great queen that he has always suffered by comparison. Elizabeth knew everything about power and kept her own counsel. James knew everything about everything and told everybody. One of the things he knew was that the war with Spain had gone on long enough. In 1604, the year after his accession, he made a peace that lasted twenty years.

James was probably right in ending the war, but Englishmen did not love him for it, especially after he told them that raids on Spanish shipping must cease. During the sixteenth century the line between legitimate privateering and piracy had been left conveniently thin, and hijacked Spanish bullion had poured into England. Francis Drake alone picked up close to a million pesos (over £300,000) worth of loot from Spanish ships he met during his dramatic voyage around the globe (1577–80). Elizabeth knighted Drake for his exploits and cheerfully collected a share of the profits. But James forswore such profits for his subjects as well as himself. As a result, men with spare lives and money began to think again about getting gold where the Spaniards got it. Efforts to find it in North America had so far been unsuccessful, but no one had tried very hard. Even if no gold was found, the conti-

*Sir Francis Drake: knighted for his exploits*

nent might hold other things of value. After the Roanoke venture of 1586, Thomas Hariot had described some promising native commodities, including sassafras, a root that the Spaniards were selling in Europe at high prices as a cure for syphilis. And piracy itself, now that the king had pledged his protection to Spanish shipping, might still be carried on from a base out of royal reach on the other side of the Atlantic. And so the tantalizing possibility of riches from America again lured Englishmen to try to plant a colony there.

*Jamestown.* In 1606 a number of noblemen, gentlemen, and merchants joined to petition the king for authority to establish colonies in America. Merchants had discovered a means of undertaking large and dangerous enterprises without risking financial ruin. Their scheme was the joint-stock company, in which participants profited or suffered in proportion to the number of shares they purchased. By investing modestly in a number of companies a man would gain only modest profits from successful ventures, but he would also avoid heavy losses from unsuccessful ones. In this way, through many small contributions, it was possible to accumulate the large amounts of capital necessary for undertakings that were beyond the range of private fortunes. The joint-stock company became the principal instrument of England's overseas expansion.

The men who petitioned the king in 1606 were divided into two groups, one from London, the other from Plymouth; and the king gave them a charter incorporating two companies for the colonization of North America: the Virginia Company of Plymouth was to operate in the northern part of the continent,

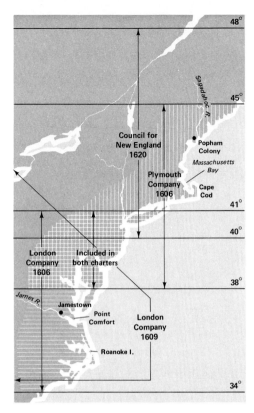

Virginia and New England grants

sitting in Virginia. The Virginia council consisted of seven men with a president who presided over its meetings but who had no authority to give orders of his own and no power to enforce orders transmitted from the king's council in England. Government by council proved to be no government at all. The members of the council in the colony quarreled with one another; and the colonists, undisciplined and disorganized, neglected the elementary tasks of plowing, planting, and building.

Fortunately, one man had the nerve to take command. John Smith, twenty-seven years old, of humble background but no humility, was not popular with the other members of the council, all men of greater age, importance, and indecision. Smith had spent four years fighting the Turks in Hungary, where he had been captured, sold into slavery, and rescued by fair maidens. In Virginia, by his own account, when the other members of the council proved fools, knaves, or cowards he took control of the colony, explored it, mapped it, overawed the Indians (and was again rescued by a maiden, Pocahontas), and obtained from them the corn that kept the settlers from starving. He stopped the disorganized scramble for gold, built fortifications, planted Indian corn, and cut a cargo of cedar wood to send back to the investors as the first tangible evidence of the colony's worth. He later told about it with such relish for his own role that readers ever since have suspected his veracity. Nevertheless, wherever his account can be checked, it holds up. Moreover he prepared a surprisingly accurate map of the region—a map that could only have been the product of first-hand observation.

In London, however, the armchair colonizers were not pleased. Smith, they heard, was unkind to the Indians. He had failed to find either gold or the Pacific Ocean. And some of the other members of the Virginia council, returning to the mother country, described his leadership as tyranny. The company did recognize, however, that the colony needed stronger direction. In 1609 it obtained a new royal charter establishing a new governing council (resident in London) composed entirely of company members and empowered to appoint an all-powerful governor or governors in the colony. The council decided on a single governor, who should choose a council of Virginians to advise him. To prevent a repetition of the colony's earlier squabbles over leadership and to ensure that the governor's council understood that its function was limited to advice, the London council specified that the Virginia councilors "shall not have, single nor together, anie bindinge or negative voice or power." The post of governor went not to Smith but to a nobleman, Lord De La Warr.

Under the new charter the company launched an elaborate campaign to sell Virginia to the English

and the Virginia Company of London in the southern part. The companies planned to send out settlers who would agree to relinquish the fruits of their labors to the investors for the first seven years; after that the settlers could enrich themselves. Anyone willing to pay his own passage was free to begin getting rich at once.

Both companies got off to a quick start. The Plymouth group dispatched an exploratory expedition in 1606 and in 1607 founded a colony at the mouth of the Sagadahoc River in Maine. The colony survived only one winter. The Virginia Company of London, in December 1606, sent over its first settlers, a hundred men and four boys crammed aboard three small ships, the *Susan Constant*, the *Godspeed*, and the *Discovery*. In May 1607 they sailed up a river they called the James and landed on a peninsula they called Jamestown. Swampy and forested, the site was well situated for defense but a haven for mosquitoes and microbes. The colonists made almost every possible mistake in their new environment, but they also corrected their mistakes; and they had the vision, the courage, or the foolhardiness to stick it out.

Their first big problem was leadership. In the charter granting authority to settle the colony, the king had retained authority to govern the colony himself, and he exercised it through a council sitting in England. This council in turn acted through another

*Making use of a new world*

public. With the proceeds of stock sold at £12 10s. a share, it fitted out a fleet of nine vessels to carry some six hundred emigrants. Some were servants who had agreed to work for the company for seven years in return for their passage. The rest paid their own way (passage was worth about £6) and received a share of stock as a bonus. All would work together until 1616, at which time the servants would be freed, the profits would be divided among the shareholders both in England and in America, and every shareholder would receive at least a hundred acres of land.

The expedition set sail from Plymouth in June 1609. Though one of the ships was wrecked at Bermuda, at least four hundred settlers reached Virginia that summer. Unfortunately Lord De La Warr was not among them. His departure from England had been delayed, and his substitute, Sir Thomas Gates, was on the ship lost at Bermuda. John Smith, injured in a gunpowder explosion, returned to England in the fall of 1609, and from then until the arrival of Governor Thomas Dale in 1611 the colony was without effective government and fell into worse disorder than before. Men starved; fortifications fell to ruins; at one point the entire colony had embarked, prepared to abandon the settlement, when a relief ship arrived. After 1611, Governor Dale and Governor Samuel Argall, who succeeded him, imposed rigorous disciplinary laws and resumed the course set by John Smith. Once again the colonists began to plant corn, erect and repair fortifications, and build houses.

*People were smoking for fun, to the distress of those who knew better*

But the men who left England for Virginia wanted more than corn bread and a place to lay their heads. To them survival was a means to an end, and they kept looking for a way to wealth, a way to live better in Virginia than they had in England. Since they had found no gold or silver, they had to find some other commodity of high value that they could produce in sufficient quantity and with sufficient ease to make the long voyage to English or European markets worthwhile. They tried cedar. They tried sassafras. But the market for both was quickly satisfied. The directors of the company had high hopes at different times for wines, silk, iron, tar. But in 1612, though they were not at once aware of it, the Virginians discovered their future—in smoke.

Tobacco was native to America. The Indians had taught the Spaniards to use it, and the Spaniards had taught the rest of Europe. At first it was valued only as a medicine, said to cure any affliction from the waist up. But by the end of the sixteenth century people were smoking for the fun of it, much to the distress of those who knew better, including King James, and much to the joy of Spanish tobacco merchants. The Indians of Virginia smoked a native variety, coarse and unpalatable. John Rolfe, who later gained greater fame by marrying Pocahontas, tried planting the West Indian species in 1612, just as other settlers were experimenting with other Spanish products. The West Indian variety grew extraordinarily well in Virginia, and the settlers turned enthusiastically to growing it. By 1617 they were able to ship twenty thousand pounds to England.

***The Virginia Company's great effort.*** The stockholders of the Virginia Company were pleased to have their faltering confidence in the colony reconfirmed by the promising shipments of tobacco. Hitherto they had received nothing but a few tons of sassafras,

*Ætatis suæ 21. Aᵒ. 1616.*

*Pocahontas*

cedar, and other trifles in return for an investment of approximately £50,000. In fact, when they sat down to divide up their profits in 1616, they had found nothing to divide except the land itself, and to many of them it hardly seemed worth dividing. Moreover, most of the servants they had sent over to work for the company had served out their time and had become free to work for themselves. To hire more men to produce so little would be to throw good money after bad.

Although the colonists' success with tobacco rekindled the expectations of the investors, they did not suppose that the colony could prosper with that product alone. But if Virginia could grow tobacco there must be other things it could produce too. They must keep the settlers experimenting until the right products were found, and then everyone could sit back and reap the profits of perseverance. While this new burst of enthusiasm was upon them, the members of the Virginia Company decided to revitalize and expand their venture by means of a reform program, which they inaugurated in 1618 under the leadership of Sir Edwin Sandys, a prominent figure in the English House of Commons. The program contained four points designed to entice more adventurers (investors), more planters (settlers), and more servants:

1. By overhauling its land policies the company made both investment and emigration more profitable. Henceforth anyone who paid the fare to Virginia for himself or anyone else received a "headright" of fifty acres on which he would pay a "quitrent" of a shilling a year to the company. Wealthy investors could thus acquire large tracts (called "particular plantations") simply by sending men to cultivate them on a sharecropping basis. The company in turn, with almost unlimited acreage at its disposal, would gain a perpetual income from quitrents.

2. To make life in Virginia more like life in England, the company relaxed the severity of its discipline and assured actual and potential settlers that henceforth the colony would be governed by English law and that the colonists would have the rights of Englishmen.

3. Even more important, the company decided to give the settlers a voice in the management of the colony. The planters were allowed to elect representatives to an assembly, which, along with the governor's appointed council, would have power to make laws for the colony. And to relieve the settlers of taxes, the cost of government was to be borne by assigning lands (and tenants to work them) to each government office.

4. The final point in the new program called for an all-out effort to diversify the colony's activities. The company itself took responsibility for sending over various craftsmen: vintners, ironworkers, brickmakers, glass-blowers. Somewhere among these skills, it was hoped, would be the right ones to give Virginia a healthy and profitable economy of which tobacco-growing would be only one part.

For five years and more, new settlers streamed into the colony. By the end of 1618 the population,

*In those twelve years of Sir Thomas Smythe his government, we aver that the colony for the most part remained in great want and misery under most severe and cruel laws sent over in print, and contrary to the express letter of the king in his most gracious charter, and as mercilessly executed, often times without trial or judgment. The allowance in those times for a man was only eight ounces of meal and half a pint of peas for a day, the one and the other mouldy, rotten, full of cobwebs and maggots, loathsome to man and not fit for beasts, which forced many to flee for relief to the savage enemy, who being taken again were put to sundry deaths as by hanging, shooting and breaking upon the wheel, and others were forced by famine to filch for their bellies, of whom one for stealing 2 or 3 pints of oatmeal had a bodkin thrust through his tongue and was tied with a chain to a tree until he starved.... Many through these extremities, being weary of life, digged holes in the earth and hid themselves till they famished.... So lamentable was our scarcity that we were constrained to eat dogs, cats, rats, snakes, toadstools, horse-hides and what not; one man out of the misery that he endured, killing his wife, powdered her up to eat her, for which he was burned. Many besides fed on the corpses of dead men, and one who had gotten insatiable, out of custom to that food could not be restrained, until such time as he was executed for it.*

**From "The Tragical Relation of The Virginia Assembly," 1624.**

which was only 400 in April of that year, had risen to 1,000. Between 1618 and 1624, about 4,000 more arrived. To judge by the number of ships landing passengers in Virginia, the colony was a success. To judge by the number of graves dug there, it was not. In spite of the heavy immigration, the population in 1625 stood at only 1,210 by official count. Some of the settlers had doubtless returned to England, but for most of them the colony had been a death trap. Sandys (who never set foot in Virginia) had sent shipload after shipload of settlers without supplies. Ill fed, ill clothed, and ill housed, they sickened and died. In 1622 the Indians rose up and killed 347.

Those who survived found themselves subjected to ruthless exploitation, unlike anything known in England. From 1618 until about 1629, Virginia tobacco brought prices ranging from a shilling to three shillings a pound. Since a man could produce 500 to 1,000 pounds a year, his labor was worth at least £25 and might be worth over £100 a year. As a result, those who had the nerve, the strength, and the authority (legal or illegal) to control the labor of other men could make small fortunes in a short time. In the scramble for the servants and tenants who arrived each year, the governor and members of his council were among the most successful in laying hold of large numbers. As long as tobacco prices held up, they made handsome profits—but for themselves, not for the company. While they grew rich on the labors of the men the company sent, the company itself was going bankrupt; and rumors reached England that

men and boys were sold back and forth in Virginia like horses. In 1624 when James I appointed a commission to investigate, the commissioners reported such shocking treatment of the settlers that the king dissolved the company and resumed control of the colony himself.

Thus ended the Virginia Company of London. At the cost of several thousand lives and perhaps £100,000 it had in the course of eighteen years established only twelve hundred Englishmen in America. But in spite of its wretched beginning, the colony was there to stay.

After the king took over, the population gradually rose as ships that came to carry away the tobacco every year continued to bring new supplies of men and some women. But, because English women were not used for field work, the planters imported many more men than women, giving Virginia a lopsided sex ratio throughout the century. While the bonanza prices lasted, the newcomers were exploited as ruthlessly as their predecessors. The king's authority at three thousand miles' distance was no greater obstacle to the local labor barons than the company's had been. But in 1630 tobacco dropped to a penny a pound and then, after a few wild fluctuations, settled for about twenty-five years at a little more than two pence a pound. At that price it still offered reasonable rewards but did not excite the kind of cupidity that had made Virginia in the 1620s a scene of misery, profiteering, and peculation. Men began to settle down and to think of the colony less as a labor camp and more as a home. They built houses, grew more corn, raised more cattle, went to church, and stopped working each other quite so hard. But they kept on growing tobacco.

In the cultivation of tobacco the Virginians had found a way to use America. And, in spite of all efforts to turn them to other occupations, they persisted in growing tobacco. They demonstrated, indeed, a certain headstrongness that England was to find characteristic of Englishmen living in America. In 1619 (before any other permanent English settlement had even been launched) Virginians met in their first representative assembly and passed their first laws. When James I took control of the colony in 1624 he did not provide for the continuance of a representative assembly; nor did his son Charles I, who became king in 1625. Charles was having enough difficulties with his own Parliament in England. But the governors he appointed found it impossible to rule Virginia without the help of Virginians. Though Charles refused them recognition until 1639, annual assemblies of representatives began making laws again in 1629 and have been doing so ever since.

# The founding of New England

James I stopped the Virginia Company but not the flow of Englishmen to America. The social, religious, and economic forces that had made their appearance in the time of Henry VIII were still at work, upsetting the lives of an increasing number of people. Prices were still rising; lands were changing hands; and sheep were grazing where men once drove their plows. To make matters worse, a depression settled over the woolens industry in the 1620s and lasted through the next decade. The land seemed "weary of her inhabitants," and the new king made it seem wearier by levying taxes without the consent of Parliament and by repressive measures against religious dissenters. The result was the Great Migration, in which perhaps as many as fifty thousand people left for the New World. The exodus lasted until 1640, when Englishmen began to see a more hopeful future for their own country. By that year Virginia's population had risen to eight thousand; Maryland had been founded; and so had the Bermudas, Barbados, St. Kitts, and other West Indian islands. About twenty thousand of the emigrants came to that northern part of Virginia now called New England.

After the failure of its Sagadahoc settlement in 1608, the Virginia Company of Plymouth had shown only sporadic interest in its territory. The company's most important action was to send Captain John Smith to explore the country in 1614; Smith named the place New England and first described its attractions. But his backers were not sufficiently impressed or not sufficiently affluent to support him in attempts to colonize it, and in 1620 they surrendered their rights to a more distinguished group of forty men who were impressed with New England but not with Smith.

The new group, made up of a duke, two marquises, six earls, a viscount, three barons, nineteen knights, the dean of a cathedral, and seven esquires, had visions of organizing feudal estates on a grand scale. Led by Sir Ferdinando Gorges, a Devonshire man who had also been the leading spirit of the Plymouth group, they gained from the king a charter establishing them as the Council for New England and granting them proprietary and governmental rights over the whole area from the fortieth to the forty-eighth parallels and from the Atlantic to the Pacific. In addition they were to have a monopoly of fishing in the offshore waters.

Cut up forty ways, the region would have provided each member of the council with a huge estate, a whole new England larger than the old. But the future of New England was to be less grand than gritty. In the very month in which the Council for New England was created, a band of humble but determined men and women put ashore below Cape Cod and began to use the country in their own way. Their way was called Puritanism.

***Puritanism.*** Puritanism has come to mean prudishness, cruelty, fanaticism, superstition, Philistinism, and hypocrisy. Actually, the Puritans who settled New England had no greater share of these human qualities than did their contemporaries or their descendants. What they did possess in stronger measure than other men was John Calvin's belief that God is omnipotent and good and that men are evil and helpless, predestined before they are born either to salvation or to eternal torment. Critics of this doctrine of predestination have always charged that it leads to moral indifference: if a man's present behavior does not affect his future salvation, why be good? But the facts belie the criticism: those who accept Calvin's doctrine have always outdone their neighbors in efforts to follow God's commandments as given in the Bible. The Puritan, knowing his efforts to be futile, nevertheless took a holy joy in them. They made him feel close to God's transcendent purpose. They also helped to ease his agonizing concern over whether he was headed for heaven or hell. Even though good behavior could not alter a man's predestined fate, it was observable that religious conversion (a personal experience by which God let a saved man know he was saved) often befell those who did try to live godly lives. Moreover, conversion manifested itself outwardly in renewed and intensified efforts to obey God's commands. A man's striving might thus be a sign that he was saved.

Not content with their own striving, the Puritans also felt responsible for their fellow men. Indeed they were certain that any society that failed to honor God by punishing infractions of his commands would meet with his sudden wrath, not in the next world but here and now. Governments, they thought, existed for the purpose of enforcing obedience to God.

The Puritans' ideas of what God required were less rigorous than many people have supposed. God did *not* require his people to wear drab clothes, live in drab houses, or drink water when something stronger was available. He *did* require that they refrain from drunkenness, theft, murder, adultery, and breaches of the Sabbath. Puritans were vastly uneasy about the English government's indifference to these evils. They were even more concerned because the Church of England—supported by the government—retained corrupt practices inherited from Rome and not sanctioned by God in the Bible. They thought the Church should abolish bishops and ecclesiastical courts and such other relics of Catholicism as kneeling and the use of priestly vestments and altars.

Puritans all agreed on what was wrong with the English Church, but they disagreed on how to make it right. Though they all relied on the Bible for guidance, they extracted different opinions from it about how God wanted his churches to be run. Those who settled New England belonged to a group that came to be known as Congregationalists. They differed from the other principal group of Puritans, the Presbyterians, in two beliefs: first, that there should be no general church organization with authority over individual churches; second, that a church should admit to membership only those who gave visible evidence of their Christian beliefs. Persons who openly flouted the laws of God should be excluded or expelled. Congregationalists wanted to change the structure and practices of the Church to conform with these beliefs.

Their dissatisfaction with the Church of England led them to the problem of all reformers: whether to remain inside a corrupt institution and try to reform it from within or to separate from it and start a pure new one. In 1583 an early Congregational leader, Robert Browne, advocated the latter course in a pamphlet appropriately titled *Reformation without Tarrying for any.* His followers, known as Separatists, deserted the English Church to meet in little churches of their own—of necessity in secret because the government did not acknowledge or permit any church other than the established one. But most Congregationalists were

*John Calvin (as drawn by one of his students)*

not Separatists. They did not think the Church of England was a hopeless case, and they believed the chances of reforming it were better from within than from without.

***The Pilgrims.*** The men and women who began the settlement of New England at Plymouth in 1620 were Separatists, part of a group that originated in 1607 at the village of Scrooby in Nottinghamshire. The English government did not look with favor on Separatists. Under Elizabeth two had been executed and many more imprisoned for long periods. Although the members of the Scrooby group were not seriously molested, they were distressed by the hostility of the government and the contempt of their neighbors. In 1608–09 they made their way, not without many hardships, to Holland, where the Dutch were known to be more tolerant. But as the years passed in Leyden they were still unhappy: their children were becoming Dutch; the only work they could get was day labor, poorly paid; and the weak among them were being tempted by the other religions that flourished

under Dutch tolerance. They thought of Virginia, a place where they might remain English and work for themselves, a place isolated from contagious heretical religions and far enough from government control so that they could have a church of their own design.

Since they were poor people, without funds to finance their passage, they proposed to set up a "particular plantation" in Virginia for a group of English merchants. As in other such ventures, they would work together for seven years as a community, and then the profits would be divided between them and their sponsors. They evidently intended to establish themselves some distance north of the other settlements (the claims of the Virginia Company extended as far north as the present site of New York City) and at one point even considered seeking a grant from the Council for New England, which was then being formed. In the end, one hundred two persons boarded the *Mayflower*, bound for Virginia. But after making their landfall at Cape Cod and exploring the coast, they decided to stay. In late December 1620 they began a settlement, which they named Plymouth after the English port from which they had embarked.

These "Pilgrims," as Americans have come to call them, were as poorly equipped in everything but courage as any group that ever landed in America. They had guns but knew little about shooting. They planned to become fishermen but knew nothing about fishing. They expected to settle in Virginia but landed in New England without enough supplies to last the winter. Like their predecessors and contemporaries in Virginia, many of them sickened and died. But the living stuck it out and justified their own estimate of themselves: three years earlier they had written to the men they hoped would sponsor their emigration, "It is not with us as with other men, whom small things can discourage, or small discontentments cause to wish themselves at home again." Since New England was outside the jurisdiction of Virginia's government, the Pilgrims established a government of their own by the *Mayflower* Compact, which forty-one adult males subscribed before going ashore. For governor they elected John Carver; and upon his death in 1621 they chose William Bradford, who recorded the colony's struggles in an eloquent history and was reelected nearly every year from 1621 to his death in 1657. Under his leadership the Pilgrims liquidated their debt to the English merchants (who had failed to send them the supplies they expected) and established for themselves a self-supporting community.

The Pilgrim settlement was important as a demonstration that men and women could live in New England. It remained, however, a small and humble community, attracting few immigrants. The great Puritan exodus did not begin until ten years after the landing of the Pilgrims. It engulfed, but did not greatly expand, the Plymouth colony.

### The Massachusetts Bay Company.

While the Pilgrims went their way outside the Church of England first in Holland and then in America, other Puritans, both Congregational and Presbyterian, continued the struggle to reform the Church from within. While James I reigned, the struggle did not seem hopeless. Although James scolded them, and even married his son to a Catholic princess, he did not "harry them out of the land," as he once threatened to do. If he had tried, they would have had enough strength in Parliament to stop him. But when Charles I became king in 1625, he quarreled incessantly with Parliament and finally announced in 1629 that he intended to rule henceforth without it. At the same time he befriended a group of aspiring churchmen who were as eager to suppress Puritanism as the Puritans were to make it prevail. Under the leadership of William Laud, whom Charles made Bishop of London in 1628 and Archbishop of Canterbury in 1633, these friends of the king deprived Puritan ministers of their pulpits and moved the Church of England ever closer to Rome in its ceremonies, vestments, and doctrines.

As the prospects of reform grew dim and the sins of the land grew heavy, the Puritans feared that God was preparing England for some great purging catastrophe. In despair and hope they, too, turned their thoughts to America, where they might worship in purity and escape the wrath both of God and of the king.

In 1628 a number of prominent congregational Puritans bought their way into a commercial company that was being organized in London. Called the New England Company, it took over the rights of a defunct group, the Dorchester Adventurers, which in 1623 had tried to plant a farming and fishing settlement at Cape Ann. From the Council for New England, the new company obtained a charter authorizing settlement in the area known as Massachusetts Bay, to the north of Plymouth. A year later, on March 4, 1629, the New England Company reorganized as the Massachusetts Bay Company and had its proprietary and governmental rights confirmed by a new charter obtained directly from the king.

In the shuffle the Puritan stockholders gained control of the company, and they had something more than commerce in mind. The royal charter bestowed on the company full authority to govern its own territory and made no mention of where company meetings were to be held. In 1629 the Puritans simply voted to transfer the company to Massachusetts. This meant that if Puritan company members emigrated, they would have full control of the government under which they would live. Thus in one bold stroke the Puritans won for themselves the opportunity to do in Massachusetts what Puritans for nearly a century had been yearning to do in England.

To act as governor, the company elected a solid Puritan squire, John Winthrop of Groton Manor, Suffolk. He and perhaps a dozen other company members, all Puritans, crossed the ocean in 1630, accompanied by a thousand like-minded men and women, who preferred a wilderness governed by Puritans to a civilized land governed by Charles I. Before the year was over they had planted settlements around Massachusetts Bay at Dorchester, Roxbury, Watertown, Newton (Cambridge), Charlestown, and Boston. During the next ten years, as Charles ruled without Parliament and Laud grew increasingly powerful, fifteen or twenty thousand more followed and their towns stretched out in all directions.

Winthrop and the handful of other company members had authority from the king's charter to govern this whole body of settlers. But Winthrop and his friends wanted a broader base for their government. And so, shortly after their arrival in New England, they transformed the Massachusetts Bay Company from a trading company into a commonwealth. In 1631 they admitted more than a hundred adult males as members, or "freemen," of the company eligible to vote at its meetings. The term "freeman" in seventeenth-century England generally meant a voting member of a business corporation or of an incorporated city or borough. In America the word came to mean a man who had the right to vote for representatives to the assembly in his colony. In Massachusetts, when the company and colony were blended, the freemen of the company became the freemen of the colony. The increase in their numbers did not remove the colony from Puritan control, because most of the new freemen (who must have been a majority of the heads of families then in the colony) were probably Puritans; moreover, it was specified that, in the future, members of Puritan congregational churches (and only such) should be eligible to become freemen.

The charter, which had envisaged only a trading company with limited membership, provided that company members assemble as a General Court four times a year to make laws. Between the meetings of

21

## Massachusetts: a contented view

*I prayse God, we haue many occasions of comfort heer, and doe hope, that our dayes of Affliction will soon haue an ende, and that the Lord will doe vs more goode in the ende, then we could haue expected, that will abundantly recompence for all the trouble we haue endured. yet we may not looke at great thinges heer, it is enough that we shall haue heaven, though we should passe through hell to it. we heer enjoye God and Jesus Christ, is not this enough? What would we haue more? I thanke God, I like so well to be heer, as I doe not repent my comminge.... I neuer fared better in my life, neuer slept better, neuer had more contente of minde, which comes meerly of the Lordes good hande, for we haue not the like meanes of these comforts heer which we had in England, but the Lord is allsufficient, blessed be his holy name, if he please, he can still vphold vs in this estate, but if he shall see good to make vs partakers with others in more Affliction, his will be doone, he is our God, and may dispose of vs as he sees good.*

**From John Winthrop, Letter to His Wife, 1630.**

the General Court a governor (or his second in command, a deputy governor) and a council of eighteen "assistants," elected annually, were to manage the company. When Winthrop and his associates opened freemanship to all church members, they foresaw that the number of freemen would soon become too large to assemble and work together as a legislature; and they decided to leave lawmaking to the council of assistants, who were still to be elected annually by all the freemen. But in 1634 the freemen insisted that the lawmaking powers assigned to them by the charter be delegated to "deputies" elected from each settlement. Henceforth the General Court consisted of the governor, the deputy governor, the executive council of assistants, and a body of deputies, or representatives. All were elected annually by the freemen. Since the company had power to govern the colony, this General Court was in reality both the legislature and the supreme court of the colony. Here, in truth, was a self-governing commonwealth, a Puritan republic.

**Puritan New England.** The freedom to do as they pleased posed many new problems to men who had not hitherto wielded the powers of government. Reformers and idealists are notoriously prone to dissipate their energies wrangling with one another. And there were disagreements in New England, though not so numerous or severe as has sometimes been suggested. The New England Puritans agreed on a great deal. They wanted congregational churches. They did not want bishops, church courts, or hierarchy. They wanted a government that would take seriously its obligation to enforce God's commandments and to support pure religion. Accordingly they confined voting to church members and levied taxes to pay ministers' salaries. But, contrary to common assumption,

they did not want their clergy to take any hand in government. For a minister to exercise political authority of any kind seemed to the Puritans a dangerous step toward Roman Catholicism. Compared to the clergy of England and Europe the New England minister, though highly influential, had little authority even within his own church. He taught, prayed, preached, and admonished; he commanded respect—else he lost his job—but he did not rule his church. Admissions to membership, censures, pardons, and excommunications were all decided by vote of the church members.

Neither the leaders of the Massachusetts Bay Colony nor the great majority of settlers were Separatists. Though they organized their own churches in the congregational manner, they took pains to affirm their love and friendship for the churches of England. Some even thought that the churches of Rome were not beyond redemption. But among the thousands who stepped ashore at Boston every year were substantial numbers of Separatists and other extremists, full of zeal and eloquence, full of impatience with anyone who disagreed with them. John Winthrop, whom the freemen elected governor year after year during most of his life, was good at turning away wrath and directing zeal to constructive ends. But during the three years from 1634 to 1637, when lesser men sat in the governor's chair, Massachusetts all but succumbed to the denunciations of a brilliant, saintlike, intractable man and a brilliant, proud, magnetic woman.

Roger Williams, who arrived in 1631, was a Separatist. He wanted everyone to repudiate the wicked churches of England. Moreover, he insisted that the royal charter of Massachusetts contained a lie (in claiming that England first discovered the region) and that the king had had no right to grant the charter or

*Making use of a new world*

*her cam ouer xxv passeingares and thare cume backe agayn fouer skore and od parsones and as maney more wolld a cume if thay had whare withe all to bringe them hom.... We may liue if we haue suppleyes euerey yere from ould eingland other weyse we can not subeseiste I maye as I will worck hard sete an ackorne of eindey wheat and if we do not set it withe fishe and that will cost xxs and if we set it witheought fishe they shall haue but a por crope so father I pray consedre of my cause for her will be but a uerey por beinge and no beinge withe ought Louinge father youer helpe withe prouisseyones from ould eingland I had thought to a cam home in theis sheipe for my prouisseyones ware all moste all spente but that I humbley thanck you for youer gret loue and kindnes in sendinge me s[o]me prouissyones or elles i sholld and myne a bine halef famiuyshed but now I will if it plese god that I haue my hellthe I will plant what corne I can and if prouissey-ones be no cheper betwein theis and myckellmes and that I do not her from you what I wase beste to do I purpose to c[o]me hom at myckellmes*

**From John Pond, Letter to His Father, 1631.**

the people to accept it without first purchasing the land from the natives. If word got back to England that the Massachusetts government allowed the expression of such subversive ideas, the king might be prompted to take control of the colony and end the Puritan republic. Williams also tried to persuade people that no government had authority over religious matters, not even the right to punish breaches of the Sabbath. In a community which believed that the prime purpose of government was to enforce God's commandments, his teachings were rank sedition.

Williams was a man whom everyone loved on sight; even John Winthrop became his good friend. But he propagated his inflammatory ideas so insistently, first as assistant to the minister and then as minister of the church at Salem, that the unity of the colony was endangered and the government finally felt obliged to banish him in 1636. He went to Rhode Island, where he was joined by those who believed him. There, while retaining his conviction that the state had no authority over religious matters, he reached the conclusion that in the existing phase of human history God authorized no organized churches at all. In spite of this view, which few of his followers could share, he retained the love and respect of his neighbors and lived out a long and useful life as the leading citizen of the new colony.

Scarcely had Williams been banished when a new threat to the civil and religious security of Massachusetts appeared: Anne Hutchinson, the wife of a merchant whom Winthrop described as "a man of a very mild temper and weak parts, and wholly guided by his wife." An amateur theologian, Mrs. Hutchinson took to elucidating her minister's Sunday sermons in informal gatherings of her neighbors. As the circle of her listeners steadily widened, her discourses be-

came more original, for her keen and imaginative mind could not be contained within the standard doctrines of Puritanism. Starting from the accepted principle that God grants salvation without regard to human merit, she denied (what other Puritans affirmed) that good conduct could be a sign of salvation and affirmed (what other Puritans denied) that the Holy Spirit in the hearts of true believers relieved them of responsibility to obey the laws of God. So, at least, her enemies charged, and she gave substance to their accusation by asserting that all the New England ministers except her favorite, John Cotton, and her brother-in-law, John Wheelwright, were preaching unsound doctrines. By emphasizing morality, she said, they were deluding their congregations into the false assumption that good deeds would get them into heaven. The clergymen hotly denied what was virtually a charge of heresy, and Mrs. Hutchinson herself protested that she had intended no insult. Nevertheless, a host of devoted Bostonians hung on every word she uttered and refused to conceal their contempt for her opponents. The colony split into hostile camps, and finally Mrs. Hutchinson was brought before the authorities. After they had cross-examined her for two days, she made the mistake of claiming that she had received an immediate revelation from God. To Puritan ears, this was blasphemy. So Mrs. Hutchinson too was banished and went to Rhode Island, which thus became the refuge for Puritans with too much originality.

After Charles I was forced to resummon Parliament in 1640, Roger Williams applied to that body (which was overwhelmingly Puritan) for a charter for his colony. The charter, granted in 1644, gave the Rhode Islanders a government much like that of the colony from which they had been expelled: they elected annually a representative assembly, a council of assistants, and a governor (at first called a president), but they did not confine voting to church members or collect taxes to support the clergy. In 1663 the existing government was confirmed by a royal charter that also guaranteed the "liberty in religious concernments" which had been the colony's distinction from the beginning.

Meanwhile another part of New England was filling up with Puritans who differed from those of Massachusetts primarily in their desire for more elbow room. In 1636 Thomas Hooker, the minister of Newtown (Cambridge), led an exodus overland to the fertile Connecticut Valley, where the small garrison of a Dutch trading post at Fort Hope (Hartford) was unable to prevent them from settling. They formed a government by a simple agreement among themselves (called the Fundamental Orders). The model, once again, was Massachusetts (but voting was not confined to church members), and again the existing arrangement was confirmed by royal charter (1662). The charter also joined to Connecticut the colony of New Haven, initiated in 1638 by a group of Londoners who could find no lands in Massachusetts to suit them.

The settlers of New Haven, beginning with a good supply of capital, had been disappointed in their expectations of a thriving commerce; but they had succeeded in establishing a somewhat stricter government than existed elsewhere in New England, and they were not altogether happy about the union with Connecticut.

There was, nevertheless, no serious difference between New Haven and the rest of New England. In New Haven as in Plymouth, Massachusetts, Rhode Island, and Connecticut, the population was predominantly Puritan. Puritans directed public policy, and the only serious resistance came from other Puritans. Although some of the inhabitants may have been indifferent or hostile to Puritanism, they were never strong enough or discontented enough to challenge Puritan control.

Settlers who wanted nothing more from the New World than an opportunity to make their fortunes or to live more comfortably than in England had little reason to object to Puritan control anyway. The government frowned on private cupidity when it threatened the public welfare, but Puritans saw no virtue in poverty. They had not traveled three thousand miles simply to starve in a holier manner than in England. They had come in order to build a society that would win God's favor, and they meant it to be a success, economically as well as religiously.

So long as the Great Migration lasted, the colonists prospered by selling cattle and provisions to the newcomers each year. When the Migration ended in 1640, New England had its first depression. The leaders looked hard for some native product they could sell to the outside world. Fortunately for them, they found no single product such as the Virginians' tobacco, and they consequently developed a more balanced economy. They caught fish, raised corn and wheat, bred cattle, cut lumber, and built ships. Before many years had passed, New England vessels were prowling the Caribbean and the Mediterranean, peddling their assorted wares, transporting other people's, and bringing home the profits. By the middle of the seventeenth century New England had laid down its economic as well as its religious foundations.

## Proprietary ventures

During the years that Puritans were building their republics in New England, non-Puritans were trying to establish private domains there and elsewhere. Three years after the Pilgrims landed, Sir Ferdinando Gorges, the most active member of the Council for New England, had backed a settlement at Wessagusset (Weymouth) in the Massachusetts Bay region, but it broke up after a year. Its failure discouraged the rest of the council from further efforts, and they apparently raised no serious objections in 1628 when the Earl of Warwick, president of the council, took it upon himself to grant the Puritans permission to settle the Bay area. In 1637 the Council for New England finally dissolved, leaving behind a host of shadowy claims. Only one claim was perfected: that of Ferdinando Gorges to the region north of the Merrimac River. Gorges divided the area with another would-be New England lord, John Mason, and in 1639 obtained a separate royal charter for his own share. He died in 1647, with no feudal retainers in his New World barony except a few hardy fishermen who pledged allegiance to no one. Massachusetts annexed the whole region in 1651.

The king authorized other ambitious gentlemen to colonize Newfoundland, Nova Scotia, and the Carolinas, but to no effect. The first English nobleman to realize the aristocrat's dream of founding a New World domain for his family was George Calvert, Lord Baltimore. A notable figure in the court of James I, Calvert had become interested in America first as a member of the Virginia Company and later as a member of the Council for New England. In 1620 he purchased rights in southeastern Newfoundland from another noble dreamer and started a settlement there. When he visited the place himself, he found that "from the middle of October to the middst of May there is a sadd face of wynter upon all this land."

Deciding to leave Newfoundland to the fishermen, he asked the king for a grant farther south. The charter, which was in the making when Calvert died in 1632, was finally issued to his son Cecilius. It conveyed to him 10 million acres on Chesapeake Bay, where the Calvert family was to have complete powers of government. The colony was to be known as Maryland, in honor of the queen of Charles I.

The name was appropriate, for both the queen and the Calverts were Catholics. Maryland was to be a feudal seigniory and at the same time a religious refuge. As a feudal seigniory it came nearer to success than any other attempted in America. Though the Calverts did not live there, they governed the colony (sometimes through a younger son), owned all the public lands, granted small estates or "manors" to their friends, and collected rents from the settlers. Because Virginia, Plymouth, and Massachusetts lent a hand, the settlers of Maryland were spared the early days of starvation that had been suffered by other colonists. Tobacco grew as readily in Maryland as in Virginia, and the two colonies became identical in their economic pursuits and interests.

As a religious refuge Maryland also succeeded. Although official hostility to Catholicism had relaxed in England under Charles, Catholics were still required by law to take oaths and to attend religious services that conflicted with their beliefs. In Maryland they would be free to worship as they chose, and so would other Christians. As it turned out, more Puritans came to the colony than Catholics. The Calverts welcomed both, and from the time of the first settlement in 1634 tried to prevent either group from oppressing the other. When the Jesuits threatened to become too powerful, Baltimore, in 1641, forbade them to hold land in Maryland. The Puritans were harder to handle, especially after 1640, when their friends gained the upper hand in England, but Baltimore did his best to restrain them. By the terms of his charter he was obliged to obtain the consent of the "freemen" (presumably in this case the term meant all adult males not bound as servants) to all legislation. As the population increased, the freemen deputed a few individuals to act for them in this matter, and thus arose a representative assembly similar to those which developed in the other colonies. This assembly in 1649 consented to the famous Maryland Toleration Act, securing freedom of worship for all Christians, whether Protestant or Catholic, who believed in the Trinity. The Calverts upheld the act through successive generations and thus made their colony, like Rhode Island, a model of what the rest of America was one day to become.

By the middle of the seventeenth century England had seeded North America. Many more immigrants were to come, from England and elsewhere, but

The colonies in 1650

the future was already visible on the coasts of New England and of Chesapeake Bay. Englishmen had moved in, and whether they favored toleration, as in Maryland and Rhode Island, or intolerance, as in Massachusetts, whether they caught fish or grew tobacco, the continent was effectively theirs.

A good account of the American Indians before the coming of the white man is Kenneth MacGowan and J. A. Hester, Jr., *Early Man in the New World** (1950). H. E. Driver, *Indians of North America* (2d ed., 1970), is more comprehensive. W. E. Washburn, *The Indian in America** (1975), incorporates new anthropological data and insights. G. B. Nash, *Red, White, and Black: The Peoples of Early America** (1974), surveys the development and relationships of all three races during the colonial period. And A. W. Crosby, Jr., *The Columbian Exchange: Biological and Cultural Consequences of 1492* (1972), traces some of the consequences of the discovery of America for the peoples of both the Old World and the New.

Anyone interested in the age of exploration should give first attention to S. E. Morison's great biography of Columbus, *Admiral of the Ocean Sea* (1942), and to his lively and authoritative *European Discovery of America: The Northern Voyages, 500–1600* (1971), and *The Southern Voyages, 1492–1616* (1974). J. H. Parry, *The Age of Reconnaissance** (1963), covers voyages to all the continents. A penetrating and succinct study of Spanish exploits and problems is Charles Gibson, *Spain in America** (1966), which contains a good bibliography of the subject. On the English voyages there is no substitute for Richard Hakluyt's collection of first-hand accounts, *The Principall Navigations, Voiages, and Discoveries of the English Nation* (1589, 1599), reprinted in Everyman's Library, *Hakluyt's Voyages,* 8 vols. Hakluyt's work has been carried on in the voluminous publications of the Hakluyt Society. Among these, see especially the volumes edited by D. B. Quinn, *Voyages and Colonising Enterprises of Sir Humphrey Gilbert,* 2 vols. (1940), and *The Roanoke Voyages, 1584–1590,* 2 vols, (1955). In *England and the Discovery of America, 1481–1620* (1974), Quinn summarizes a lifetime of work on the subject.

M. M. Knappen, *Tudor Puritanism** (1939), and Patrick Collinson, *The Elizabethan Puritan Movement* (1967), are the best accounts of early Puritanism. Two challenging interpretations are C. H. and Katherine George, *The Protestant Mind of the English Reformation* (1961), and Michael Walzer, *The Revolution of the Saints** (1965). For social conditions in England see Carl Bridenbaugh, *Vexed and Troubled Englishmen, 1590–1642** (1968), and Peter Laslett, *The World We Have Lost** (1965); for economic conditions, Joan Thirsk, ed., *The Agrarian History of England and Wales, 1500–1640* (1967); for political and legal institutions, Wallace Notestein, *The English People on the Eve of Colonization, 1603–1630** (1954). Keith Thomas, *Religion and the Decline of Magic** (1971), is a massive study of English folk religion and beliefs in the sixteenth and seventeenth centuries. Mildred Campbell, *The English Yeoman under Elizabeth and the Early Stuarts* (1942), is well matched by Lawrence Stone's monumental *Crisis of the Aristocracy** (1965).

On the first permanent English settlements in America, the most convenient and the most authoritative account is still C. M. Andrews, *The Colonial Period of American History,* Vols. I–III* (1934–37). For the Southern colonies this should be supplemented by W. F. Craven, *The Southern Colonies in the Seventeenth Century** (1949). J. E. Pomfret and F. M. Shumway, *Founding the American Colonies* (1970), incorporates recent research. Captain John Smith tells his own story in *Travels and Works of Captain John Smith,* 2 vols. (1910), ed. by Edward Arber and A. G. Bradley. The fullest modern account is P. L. Barbour, *The Three Worlds of Captain John Smith* (1964), but Alden Vaughan, *American Genesis: Captain John Smith and the Founding of Virginia** (1975), is a perceptive shorter biography. W. F. Craven, *The Dissolution of the Virginia Company* (1932), is a masterful study of the internal divisions that impaired the company's efforts in America. E. S. Morgan, *American Slavery American Freedom: The Ordeal of Colonial Virginia** (1975), shows how experience in Virginia eroded the original intentions of the founders.

The New England Puritans have been subjected to the scrutiny of historians, sympathetic and unsympathetic, from the time the settlers first stepped ashore. William Bradford, governor of the Plymouth Colony, told the story of the Pilgrims in *Of Plymouth Plantation,* an American classic that can best be read in S. E. Morison's edition (1952). A thorough history by a modern scholar is George Langdon, *Pilgrim Colony: A History of New Plymouth, 1620–1691** (1966). In his *Journal,* Governor John Winthrop did for Massachusetts Bay what Bradford did for Plymouth. The best edition is that of James

*Available in a paperback edition.

Savage, 2 vols. (1853), but this is hard to come by. The only edition in print is the modernized and expurgated one of J. K. Hosmer, 2 vols. (1908). For a contrast with Bradford and Winthrop, read Thomas Morton, *New English Canaan* (1637, 1883).

S. E. Morison, *Builders of the Bay Colony*\* (1930), is by all odds the best modern introduction to the history of New England. Morison continued his study of the Puritans in his works on Harvard, *The Founding of Harvard College* (1935) and *Harvard in the Seventeenth Century,* 2 vols. (1936).

New England Puritanism is also the subject of the most profound study of intellectual history yet written by an American, Perry Miller, *The New England Mind: The Seventeenth Century*\* (1939) and *The New England Mind: From Colony to Province*\* (1953). These volumes were preceded by his briefer study, *Orthodoxy in Massachusetts, 1630–1650*\* (1933), the subject of which falls chronologically between the two. He explores other aspects of New England history in a brilliant collection of essays, *Errand into the Wilderness*\* (1956). Some of Miller's conclusions are modified in Robert Middlekauff's sensitive study, *The Mathers* (1971), and by David Hall's examination of the New England ministry in *The Faithful Shepherd*\* (1972). Larzer Ziff, *Puritanism in America: New Culture in a New World*\* (1973), though less comprehensive than it purports to be, also contains some fresh insights. Puritan domestic life and social relations are examined in E. S. Morgan, *The Puritan Family*\* (1966), in John Demos, *A Little Commonwealth*\* (1970), and in D. H. Flaherty, *Privacy in Colonial New England* (1972). P. J. Greven, *Four Generations*\* (1969), traces the demographic changes over a century among the families that founded Andover, Massachusetts. Stephen Foster analyzes Puritan social thought in *Their Solitary Way* (1971). The conduct of church affairs is treated in Ola Winslow, *Meetinghouse Hill*\* (1952); the Puritan conception of the church in E. S. Morgan, *Visible Saints*\* (1963), and in R. G. Pope, *The Half-Way Covenant* (1969). The best biography of Roger Williams is Ola Winslow, *Master Roger Williams* (1957). E. S. Morgan, *Roger Williams: The Church and the State*\* (1967), analyzes Williams' ideas. Emery Battis, *Saints and Sectaries* (1962), gives a provocative psychological interpretation of Anne Hutchinson, and Kai Erikson gives a sociological interpretation in *Wayward Puritans*\* (1966).

For early New England economic history see Bernard Bailyn, *The New England Merchants in the Seventeenth Century*\* (1955). E. S. Morgan has dealt with some of the political problems faced by the founders of Massachusetts in *The Puritan Dilemma: The Story of John Winthrop*\* (1958). R. E. Wall, *Massachusetts Bay: The Crucial Decade, 1640–1650* (1972), stresses the rivalry of magistrates and deputies. Later Puritan problems as exemplified in the Winthrop family are treated in R. S. Dunn, *Puritans and Yankees: The Winthrop Dynasty of New England* (1962). G. L. Haskins, *Law and Authority in Early Massachusetts*\* (1960), describes political and social as well as legal institutions, and T. H. Breen, *The Character of the Good Ruler*\* (1970), treats the development of Puritan political thought during the first century of settlement. E. S. Morgan, *Puritan Political Ideas*\* (1966), is a collection of source materials.

\*Available in a paperback edition.

CHAPTER **2**

# *The pattern of empire*

**T**he first settlements in America, which cost Englishmen dearly in lives and money, cost the English government nothing. But in authorizing settlement the government did expect to gain something more than an outlet for disgruntled Puritans, misguided merchants, and adventurous fortune-seekers. Every European government, during the sixteenth, seventeenth, and eighteenth centuries, followed an economic policy that has been known since 1776, when Adam Smith coined the word, as mercantilism.

## Mercantilism

Mercantilism meant that the state directed all economic activities within its borders, subordinating private profit to public good. In particular, the government sought to increase national wealth by discouraging imports and encouraging exports. The English government let its subjects go to America because it was persuaded that their presence there would further this end.

*Shipbuilding in the seventeenth century*

Long before the settlement of Jamestown, Richard Hakluyt had explained how the mother country could profit from American colonies: they would furnish England with supplies such as lumber, tar, and hemp, which it was buying from other countries, and they would offer a market for the woolens that were England's principal export. "It behooves this realm," Hakluyt wrote in 1584, "if it mean . . . not negligently and sleepingly to slide into beggary, to foresee and plant [a colony] at Norumbega [a name for northern North America] or some like place, were it not for anything else but for the hope of the sale of our wool." What England wanted from America was what Hakluyt said it would get: a market for its woolen cloth and other manufactures and a source of supply for raw materials that it had to import from other countries.

What England wanted was not incompatible with what the colonists wanted: a ready market for the raw materials they had to sell and a cheap source for the manufactures they had to buy. During the years of settlement, the shortage of labor in North America made manufacturing unfeasible. England, on the other hand, had a surplus of labor and a low wage scale that made for cheap manufactured goods. It was mutually advantageous for the colonies to buy manufactures from the mother country and for the mother country to buy raw materials from the colonies.

The British empire in America was based on this compatibility of interests. But, while the interests were compatible, they required guidance to make them coincide. Left to themselves, the colonies might peddle their produce in France or Holland instead of England and take home French textiles instead of English ones, or they might produce materials not needed in England. In order to make the system work, it was necessary for the mother country to maintain continuous supervision and control over the economic activities of the settlers just as she did over the activities of Englishmen at home. The English government never doubted its right to exercise such control, but it was slow to develop consistent directives or effective machinery for carrying them out.

**England's imperial delay.** In the early years, before the colonies began to fulfill Hakluyt's glowing predictions, economic regulation probably did not seem urgent. Although the English government in 1621 ordered all Virginia tobacco to be brought to England, the order was not enforced, perhaps because English authorities considered it a mixed blessing for the nation to have its own private supply of smoke. But other regulations, adopted from time to time, also went unenforced. One reason was distance. Three thousand miles of ocean made a formidable barrier in the seventeenth century. Although it was faster and easier to travel long distances by water than by land, even over water three thousand miles was space enough in which to lose messages, orders, and interest.

A more serious obstacle to English control than either the distance or the seeming unimportance of the colonies was politics. During the seventeenth century, when most of its American colonies were founded, England was torn by a struggle for power between king and Parliament. In the 1630s Charles I ruled without Parliament, but by 1640 he needed it to pay his bills. He called it, dismissed it, called it again, and then found that he could not dismiss it any more. In 1642 the members raised an army to make war on him; in 1649 they cut off his head, and for eleven

**The use of America: opportunity**

years England had no king. In his place from 1649 to 1658 stood Oliver Cromwell, the soldier who had defeated him.

When Charles II, son of the old king, was placed on the throne in 1660, the acts passed by Parliament in the preceding eleven years were declared null and void. But Charles had the good sense to realize that English kings henceforth must work with Parliament or not at all. His brother and successor, James II, had no sense, and within three years of his accession in 1685 he had to flee the country. Parliament quietly replaced him with William and Mary in the bloodless Revolution of 1688. After 1688 the king was still no cipher in government, but everyone understood that he was subordinate to Parliament.

All but one (Georgia) of the thirteen colonies that later became the United States were founded before 1688, during the years when the ultimate location of sovereignty in England was uncertain. They were all founded under authority of the king, and their relationship to Parliament remained ambiguous. Parliament sometimes passed legislation affecting them, but even after 1688 it did not do so regularly. Yet if the king had denied the authority of Parliament in the colonies, Parliament would doubtless have brought him up short.

Distance, indifference, and the uncertain location of authority in England conspired to delay the development of a consistent and continuous colonial policy. From the founding of Virginia in 1607 until the middle of the seventeenth century the colonies interested king and Parliament only as a minor prize

in the contest for sovereignty. In 1633, when Charles I was trying to rule without Parliament, he appointed a commission headed by Archbishop Laud to govern the colonies. But the commissioners were too busy in England to do anything about America. During the English civil wars of the 1640s, Parliament and king both claimed authority over the colonies, but neither was able to exercise it.

Oliver Cromwell was the first ruler of England sure enough of his position at home to think seriously about fitting the colonies into a general imperial

*Charles I: he needed Parliament to pay his bills*

*New Englanders away from home:* Sea Captains at Surinam, *by John Greenwood*

scheme. In 1650 and 1651 he secured legislation to keep foreign shipping out of the colonies. He also planned a great expansion of the empire in the Caribbean and tried to persuade New Englanders to move to the West Indies, where the cultivation of sugar and other tropical products promised rich rewards. But his legislation against foreign shipping led to war with the uncooperative Dutch; his large military and naval expedition to the West Indies in 1655 captured only Jamaica; and his powers of persuasion proved insufficient to lure New Englanders from their rocky soil. They suspected, perhaps, that Puritanism would not work well in the tropics.

**The Navigation Acts.** When Charles II came to the throne in 1660, the colonies, in spite of Cromwell's failures, had grown enough to require attention. Virginia and Maryland were exporting over 7 million pounds of tobacco yearly, much of which never reached England, and New England harbored a group of merchants whose ships were already familiar in the markets of the world. English merchants, awakened to the potentialities of colonial trade, pressed the government for measures to prevent the profits from leaking into the pockets of foreign rivals. What they wanted was not merely to exclude foreign shipping from the colonies (as Cromwell had attempted in the acts of 1650 and 1651) but to direct colonial trade into channels profitable to the mother country. King and Parliament, in the first flush of Restoration harmony, agreed on two acts to take care of the matter.

These so-called Navigation Acts (1660 and 1663) were modified from time to time during the ensuing century, but their basic principles remained the same: (1) they forbade all trade with the colonies except in ships owned and constructed there or in England and manned by crews of which at least three-quarters were English or colonial; (2) they forbade the transportation *from* the colonies *to* any place except England or another English colony of certain "enumerated commodities," namely sugar, cotton, indigo, dyewoods, ginger, and tobacco; and (3) with a few exceptions they forbade the transportation of European goods *to* the colonies *from* any place except England.

Subsequent modification of the Navigation Acts consisted mainly of additions to the list of enumerated commodities (rice in 1704, naval stores in 1705, copper and furs in 1721) or specific limitations on, or encouragement of, colonial products. The act of 1705 that enumerated naval stores (pitch, tar, turpentine, masts, spars) also placed bounties on their production. The Wool Act (1699) forbade export from the colonies of certain textiles manufactured there. The Hat Act (1732) forbade export of colonial-made hats. The Iron Act (1750) removed all duties on English imports of colonial pig and bar iron (thus encouraging their production) but forbade the erection of any new colonial iron mills for manufacturing raw iron into finished products.

The Navigation Acts were ostensibly intended to ensure that the mother country would benefit from the economic activities of the colonies. But, in passing the original acts and in modifying them over the years, Parliament was not immune to the wishes of special groups. Adam Smith, in coining the very name "mercantilism," was charging that English policies were dictated by merchants at the expense of the rest of the community. And indeed particular acts were often opposed by one group as much as they were favored by another. The Iron Act, for example, represented a victory of English iron-manufacturers over English iron-miners and smelters; and in 1733 the Molasses Act, which placed a heavy duty on foreign molasses imported into North America, was a victory for one group of colonists, the West Indian sugar-planters, over another, the New Englanders who distilled molasses into rum.

Besides serving such private interests, and besides subordinating colonial trade to English trade, the Navigation Acts aimed at increasing the revenue of the English government, at least indirectly. Although the acts of 1660 and 1663 levied no taxes, the government from the beginning had collected duties in England on imports from the colonies. By requiring enumerated commodities to be brought only to England, the government expected to step up the volume of dutiable goods. The expectation was not unrealistic. Revenue obtained from duties on tobacco imports alone may have amounted in the 1660s to as much as £100,000 annually, which was more than the planters themselves made from the crop.

The Navigation Acts transformed the hopeful predictions of Hakluyt into specific legislation that told the colonists what they could and could not make, where and how they could trade. But the colonies were still three thousand miles from the lawmakers. If England was to receive the full benefit of the acts, they had to be enforced against foreign nations on the one hand and against refractory colonists on the other.

**The Dutch.** The principal foreign threat to England's emerging mercantilist empire in the seventeenth century came from the Dutch. This was their century; they seemed on the way to running the world. After shaking off Spanish domination, they built the largest merchant fleet ever known. Dutch captains nosed out rival vessels everywhere, took over most of the Portuguese empire in the East Indies, opened trade with Japan. Dutch privateers led the pack in raiding Spanish treasure fleets. Dutch merchants controlled the lumber trade from the Baltic and made Amsterdam the sawmill of Europe. Dutch fishermen dominated the North Sea. Dutch textile-workers finished and resold woolen cloth imported raw from England. When England tried to stop the export and save the valuable finishing process for her

own workers, the Dutch simply boycotted English cloth, and depression settled over the whole English woolens industry. This was the century of Rembrandt, Vermeer, Hals, Hobbema, DeHooch, the century of Huygens and Spinoza. Man for man, no people has ever matched the seventeenth-century achievement of the Dutch.

In North America the Dutch had not extended themselves with the vigor they showed elsewhere, probably because North America offered fewer prospects of immediate reward. Nevertheless, Dutch ships every year appeared in Virginia's great rivers to carry tobacco to Holland instead of England. Dutch textiles were sold in the shops of Boston. And the region that the Dutch had chosen for their settlements and trading posts in North America was strategically and economically the most important on the continent. The Hudson River commanded access to the interior by the only water-level route through the Appalachian Mountains. From the Hudson, it was possible to reach the Mississippi Valley along the Mohawk River Valley (or with greater difficulty by Lake George, Lake Champlain, and the St. Lawrence). Economically the Hudson River was the principal outlet of the fur trade south of the St. Lawrence; strategically it was an avenue along which an ambitious nation could strike for control of the inner continent. The Dutch were not that ambitious, but they did find New Netherland a convenient base from which to attack the Spaniards, drain off the continent's fur supply, and collect profit from England's settlements to the north and south. They used their West Indian colonies similarly to annex much of the trade of the English sugar planters there.

When Charles II set about enforcing the Navigation Acts, he took care of the Dutch problem in North America in the simplest possible way. He made a gift of the Dutch territories to his brother James, the Duke of York. To the seemingly formidable task of delivering the gift he assigned four commissioners, with four frigates and four hundred men. The commissioners arrived in 1664, a time when the Dutch settlers had been demoralized by arbitrary and incompetent governors. To everyone's surprise, the colony surrendered without resistance, and the commissioners took possession for the duke of the entire region from Maryland to Connecticut.

The Dutch in Holland, already at odds with England, declared war and continued to violate the Navigation Acts wherever willing colonists and the absence of the British navy made it possible. In the long run, the problem of enforcement could be solved not by foreign war but only by effective administrative machinery within the colonies themselves. That problem became at once more difficult and more urgent as a new burst of colonizing activity increased the dimensions of the empire.

# The Restoration colonies

The colonies founded in the second half of the seventeenth century were "proprietary," that is, they were founded by proprietors who exercised government over them and initially owned all the land in them. The proprietors, generally friends or relatives of the king, hoped to grow rich from the sale of their lands and from the annual fees, or quitrents (usually a shilling per fifty acres), that they charged the settlers. They kept the quitrents low enough not to deter prospective immigrants but high enough to guarantee themselves a tidy permanent income when the colony should be fully populated.

The new colonies all resembled Maryland in their proprietary origin (see p. 24); they differed from Maryland and the other old colonies in the sources from which they drew their actual settlers: comparatively few came directly from England. Some were on the spot already, like the Dutch and Swedish settlers in New Netherland. More came from Scotland, Ireland, Wales, France, and Germany. Still more came from America itself, men and women who had grown discontented with the part of the New World they already occupied and wanted to try a new place.

This search for greener pastures was to become one of the abiding characteristics of American life. Once uprooted, a man might wander long before he found a spot where he could remain content. After a few months or years in a new home, one morning he would turn his back on surroundings that had scarcely become familiar and be off to the promised land beyond the horizon. From this restless breed of men the new proprietors hoped to draw tenants for their feudal domains. Tenants less likely to pay feudal rents would have been hard to find, but that fact was not immediately apparent.

***New York.*** The most important of the new colonies was New York, whose settlers and problems the Duke of York had inherited from the Dutch. New Netherland had been primarily a series of riverside trading posts, located at Swaanendael (Lewes), Fort Nassau (Newcastle), and Fort Casimir (in Gloucester County, New Jersey) on the Delaware, and at Fort Orange (Albany) and Esopus (Kingston) on the Hudson. But New Amsterdam (New York City) at the mouth of the Hudson and a few other areas had more advanced settlements. The merchants of New Amsterdam were no longer mere Indian traders, and their flourishing overseas business supported a sizable and diversified community. In the Hudson Valley a number of well-to-do Dutchmen had tried to found agricultural settlements, known as patroonships, of the very kind that English proprietors were hoping to establish. One of these, belonging to Kiliaen van Rensselaer, had approached success. Though Rensselaer himself had gained little profit from it, his tenants still occupied the lands. On Manhattan, on the western end of Long Island, and in the lower Hudson Valley there were a few villages of Dutch farmers; and in eastern Long Island a number of New England Puritans had transplanted themselves and their way of life. The Dutch, finding them difficult to cope with, had left them much to themselves.

The Dutch West India Company had governed these sprawling settlements (probably totaling no more than seven or eight thousand persons at the end) through a director-general. Of the men who held the post, Wouter van Twiller (1633–38) and Willem Kieft (1638–47) had been disastrously foolish; and Peter Stuyvesant (1647–64), who surrendered the colony to the English, was little better. All had governed without benefit of a popular assembly. English rule brought no immediate changes, except in the quality of the governors. The terms of surrender confirmed the old settlers in their property rights. The Duke of York, by the charter that conveyed the area to him, was given full authority to govern as he saw fit. Since the duke had no fondness for representative assemblies, he appointed a governor to rule in the same manner as the old director-general.

Though the Dutch were not happy about rule by Englishmen, they submitted peacefully to the governors James sent: Richard Nicolls (1664–68), Francis

*New York, ca. 1720*

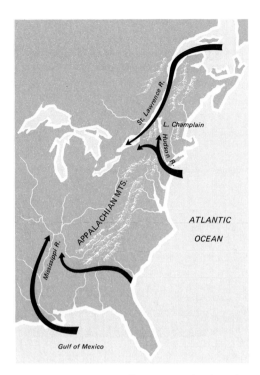

Routes to the interior
of North America

Lovelace (1668–73), Edmund Andros (1674–81), and Thomas Dongan (1683–88). The New Englanders on Long Island were less docile. They showed the familiar unfriendliness of Englishmen toward governments in which the governed had no representation. Governor Nicolls tried to appease them at the outset by compiling a special set of laws for them, drawn in part from the New England laws, which they presumably liked. This code, known as the Duke's Laws, was presented to a meeting of representatives from seventeen towns in 1665, but the meeting was not allowed to alter or add to it. The inhabitants accepted it, but not gratefully. During the ensuing years they objected continually to paying taxes without representation and, instead of being happy about their rescue from the Dutch, complained that they were now "inslav'd under an Arbitrary Power."

Perhaps because of the noisy discontent of these New Englanders, New York attracted comparatively few new settlers. There was consequently little profit from rents for the Duke of York. His governors told him of the demand for a representative assembly and hinted that the colony might be easier to govern with one than without. In 1683 he gave way, and on October 17 the first assembly was held at New York with eighteen representatives elected from the various areas of the duke's propriety. One of the assembly's first actions was to pass a Charter of Liberties stating

the right of the inhabitants to all the traditional political and civil liberties of Englishmen, such as trial by jury and representative government. Though this charter received the duke's assent, he repudiated it in 1686, after New York had been transformed from a proprietary to a royal colony by his accession (1685) to the throne of England as James II.

***New Jersey.*** New York in 1685 was not as large as New Netherland had been. Three and a half months after receiving his grant of the area, James had transferred the part later called New Jersey to two friends: John, Lord Berkeley, a privy councillor much interested in naval affairs, and Sir George Carteret, Vice-Chamberlain of the Royal Household and Treasurer of the Navy (James himself was Lord High Admiral, in charge of the navy). There followed a comedy of errors that was never entirely straightened out.

James' governor in New York, Richard Nicolls, did not learn of the transfer to Berkeley and Carteret until after he himself had granted lands in the New Jersey region to a number of New England Puritans from eastern Long Island. Nicolls, who was anxious to get the land settled and producing revenue, offered the Puritans the right to govern themselves through their own assembly. They in turn agreed to pay quitrents to James. Nicolls actually had no authority to offer such terms, but the Puritans accepted them and moved in.

When Berkeley and Carteret gained possession, they too offered liberal terms to settlers. They too wanted quitrents and promised a representative assembly to make laws. More Puritans, this time from New Haven, accepted the offer and moved in.

James, in transferring New Jersey to Berkeley and Carteret, gave them only property rights over the colony. His own governmental authority was not transferable. Berkeley and Carteret, therefore, had no authority either to hold a representative assembly or to appoint a governor. Yet they did both, and neither James nor his brother the king objected.

But the cantankerous transplanted New Englanders, who had accepted grants from Nicolls, did object. They held their own assembly and refused to accept the authority of the government established by the proprietors. The vehemence of their protests and their carelessness in paying rents were not diminished by subsequent developments. Berkeley and Carteret divided the province in two in 1674. Berkeley, who had taken the western half, sold it that same year to a Quaker, who resold shares to other Quakers. In 1680, after Carteret died, the eastern half, where both groups of Puritans were located, was sold at auction to another group of Quakers. Quakers were dissenters from the Church of England who carried a number of Puritan doctrines much farther than the Puritans did,

35

*Charles Town grew into a city*

and who thereby earned the anger and contempt of Anglican and Puritan alike. The fact that the proprietors were now Quakers did not endear proprietary government to the Puritan settlers. They continued to protest until the English government awoke to the fact that the government of New Jersey rested on a false assumption of power by the original proprietors. In 1702 East and West New Jersey were united as a royal colony with a single representative assembly and with the proprietors retaining only their property rights.

**The Carolinas.** Before Berkeley and Carteret received the grant of New Jersey, they had already become involved with several highly placed friends in a project for another colony in the region directly south of Virginia, known as Carolina. The moving spirit in this enterprise was probably Sir John Colleton, an old royalist soldier. After Charles I lost his head in 1649, Colleton had gone to Barbados. There he found that the Great Migration had deposited thousands of hopeful immigrants, who had carved the island into small farms. After 1640, however, as sugar gradually became the dominant crop, the land was absorbed into ever larger plantations worked by increasing numbers of imported black slaves. Many of the settlers had been squeezed off their farms and were now ready to move to the continent, where land was more plentiful.

When Colleton returned to England in 1660, he realized that this ready-made population for a new colony lay waiting, and he was probably already interested in the Carolina region. In London he met Sir William Berkeley (brother of John), the royal governor of Virginia (1641–52 and 1660–77). The governor knew that the Virginians had occupied much of their own tidewater land and were ready to expand down the coast into Carolina. Before long, he and Colleton had assembled a blue-ribbon board of would-be proprietors for the new colony. Besides themselves there were Berkeley's brother John; Sir George Carteret; Anthony Ashley Cooper, later Earl of Shaftesbury; George Monck, Duke of Albemarle (who had engineered Charles II's return to the throne); William, Earl of Craven; and Edward Hyde, Earl of Clarendon. To such men the king could not say no even though they were asking for the whole area extending from the present Atlantic border of the states of North Carolina, South Carolina, and Georgia westward to the Pacific.

The proprietors received the territory by royal charter on March 24, 1663, and they moved at once to fill it with footloose farmers from Virginia, New England, and Barbados. From the beginning they proposed two distinct centers for settlement. The region of Albemarle Sound in the northernmost part of their grant was already sparsely occupied by settlers who had drifted in from Virginia. The proprietors gave them a governor in 1664; a popularly elected assembly met for the first time by June 1665. At the end of the century this colony of North Carolina had a popula-

*The pattern of empire*

tion of four or five thousand. They engaged in subsistence farming and also grew enough tobacco to prompt enterprising New England merchants to go after it every year with shallow-draft vessels that could clear the shoals of the area.

Farther south, where the Cape Fear River offered a better harbor than did Albemarle Sound, the proprietors intended to plant a second colony. New Englanders had already tried living here without authorization from England but had pulled out after tacking up a sign at the mouth of the river, warning future settlers that the country was not worth occupying. This may have been an early piece of Yankee shrewdness, for the proprietors found a continuing interest in the region among New Englanders—not enough, however, to induce many Puritans to move there and pay quitrents to absentee proprietors (there were no quitrents in New England). The first authorized colonists were mainly Barbadians, who came in 1665 and dispersed in 1667—to Virginia, to the Albemarle region, to New England, or back to Barbados. A successful settlement, sponsored primarily by Anthony Ashley Cooper, was finally made farther south. Well equipped with provisions, an expedition set out from England in 1669 and picked up reinforcements at Barbados and other islands en route. The settlers located themselves at first on the south bank of the Ashley River about twenty-five miles from the sea. In 1680 they moved to the present site of Charleston (called Charles Town until 1783), where, as later Carolinians would have it, the Ashley and Cooper rivers join to form the Atlantic Ocean.

The proprietors had provided the settlers with a constitution designed to strike a balance between aristocracy and democracy. Drafted presumably by Cooper's secretary, John Locke, the Fundamental Constitutions of Carolina were based more on the political philosophy of James Harrington than on the philosophy for which Locke himself was to become famous (see p. 67). Harrington believed that the structure of government should match the distribution of property among the governed. The proprietors proposed to people three-fifths of their property with ordinary settlers (who would pay an annual quitrent) and to keep the rest in seigneurial and manorial estates for a hereditary nobility. The government was to consist of a governor appointed by the proprietors and a legislature in which the upper house would represent the nobility, the lower the commoners. The upper house was to have the sole right to initiate legislation (another idea of Harrington's).

The settlers of South Carolina, by accretions of Barbadians, Huguenots (who were the French equivalent of Puritans), New Englanders, Englishmen, Scots, and black slaves, increased to eight or ten thousand by the end of the century. They worked at turning the pines of the area into pitch and tar and turpentine (naval stores) and in producing rice. It was probably the slaves who taught the Carolina planters to grow rice, which was a familiar crop in Africa but not found in the areas from which the other settlers had come. Eventually it became South Carolina's most valuable export, cultivated extensively in the lowlands around Charles Town. Beyond the rice plantations frontiersmen outflanked the Appalachian Mountains, pushed back Spanish missions, and penetrated the interior of the continent to open a brisk trade with the Indians in deerskins and in slaves captured from other tribes. Charles Town grew into a city, the only one in the South. In spite of hurricanes, Indian attacks, and internal quarrels, South Carolina succeeded.

The Fundamental Constitutions did not. As in other colonies, the representative assembly—the lower house of the legislature—was impatient of restrictions: it claimed and took the right to initiate legislation, quarreled with the governor and the upper house, and generally got its way. By 1700 the Fundamental Constitutions were a dead letter, and proprietary rule was faltering. In 1719 a rebellion in Charles Town overthrew the last proprietary governor, and two years later a provisional royal government was organized in the colony. The proprietors finally surrendered their charter in 1729, and royal governments were provided for both North and South Carolina, each with a governor and council appointed by the king and an assembly elected by the landowners.

**William Penn's holy experiment.** The last English colony to be founded in the seventeenth century was also the private property of a friend of the king. It would be hard to imagine a more unlikely friend for Charles II than William Penn, Quaker, commoner, and enemy of royal prerogative. The association, a tribute to breadth of character in both men, began in the career of Penn's father, who was no Quaker. William Penn the elder started life as an ordinary seaman and by sheer ability worked his way to the rank of admiral. He was in charge of naval operations in Cromwell's grandiose expedition to the West Indies. When the expedition captured nothing but Jamaica, the admiral retired in disgrace to Ireland, where he remained until Charles II took the throne.

Disgrace under Cromwell was no bar to preferment under Charles. Admiral Penn was on hand to see the new king crowned in 1660 and took the occasion to present his son, then aged sixteen. In the ensuing years, while the father headed the navy office under the Duke of York, young Penn did the things that sons of gentlemen were expected to do. It was conventional that he should attend Oxford and almost conventional that he be expelled after two years

*[August 26, 1664] This day my wife tells me Mr Pen, Sir William's son, is come back from France, and come to visit her. A most modish person, grown, she says, a fine gentleman.*

*[August 30, 1664] ... after dinner comes Mr. Pen to visit me, and staid an houre talking with me. I perceive something of learning he hath got, but a great deale, if not too much, of the French garbe and affected manner of speech and gait.*

*[December 29, 1667] At night comes Mrs. Turner to see us; and there, among other talk, she tells me that Mr. William Pen, who is lately come over from Ireland, is a Quaker again, or some very melancholy thing; that he cares for no company, nor comes into any: which is a pleasant thing, after his being abroad so long, and his father such a hypocritical rogue, and at this time an Atheist.*

*[October 12, 1668] So to supper, and after supper, to read a ridiculous nonsensical book set out by Will. Pen, for the Quakers; but so full of nothing but nonsense, I was ashamed to read in it.*

**From the *Diary of Samuel Pepys.***

and sent on the grand tour of the Continent by a worried father. It was conventional, too, that he should spend some time at the Inns of Court studying law, but without becoming a barrister. As he reached maturity, Penn had the standard qualifications of a young courtier: high spirits, ready wit, skill as a swordsman. He cut a dashing figure at the court of the king. But he had one quality that was not quite conventional, one that kings, courtiers, and fathers of young gentlemen have often found embarrassing: he took ideas seriously.

What was worse, the ideas he took most seriously were of the most embarrassing kind: radical, offbeat, faintly ridiculous. The early Quakers (later called

Friends) were drawn from a wide spectrum of English society, including a substantial number of gentry and merchants, but they seemed to be the lunatic fringe of the Puritan movement. They heard voices; they insulted their betters; they appeared naked in church. One of them, James Nayler, thought he was Jesus Christ and entered the city of Bristol riding on an ass, with his admirers singing holy, holy, holy before him.

The authorities dealt with Nayler: they bored his tongue with a hot iron, cut off his ears, and branded his forehead with the letter *B* for blasphemer—thereby demonstrating what might have happened to Christ if he *had* reappeared. Respectable Englishmen thought that madmen like Nayler were typical of

The Restoration colonies

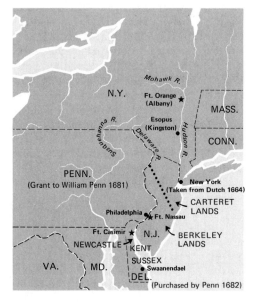

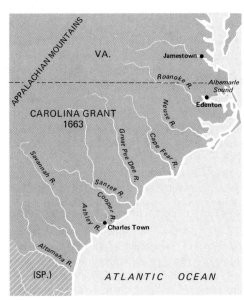

**William Penn on William Penn**

Quakerism. But by the 1660s, Quakers had shaken free of these eccentricities and were challenging the world by practicing what they preached.

What they preached was not far different from what other Christians had always preached. What others had variously called conscience, revelation, or saving grace, Quakers called the Inner Light. The Inner Light, they said, glowed in every man. He had only to live by it in order to be saved. Quakers tried to live by it.

All Christians believed that humility is a virtue. But the Quakers studiously, almost fanatically, avoided pride and the institutions that pride erected: they wore conspicuously plain and out-of-date clothes; they refused to honor one another—or anyone else—by bowing or kneeling or taking off their hats, or by using the second person plural when addressing an individual (ultimately they forgot the nominative and used only "thee"). All Christians professed brotherly love; but the Quakers refused to make war. They also refused to give or take oaths, partly because they believed the imposition of an oath implied distrust of one's fellow men.

Ideas of this kind first attacked William Penn as a student at Oxford and may have been responsible for his expulsion. One reason for the grand tour was to get them out of his head and something more fashionable into it. The tour worked, too, but only until Penn encountered a Quaker named Thomas Loe, whom he may have known earlier. In 1667 Samuel Pepys, a diarist who worked in the navy office, recorded the sad fact that Sir William Penn's son was "a Quaker again, or some very melancholy thing."

From this time forward, Penn was Quakerism's most energetic and effective supporter. He knew enough theology to argue with priests, enough law to argue with judges. He was so friendly with the king that no one dared ignore him, and he had such courage that he never allowed his friendship to weaken his arguments against the king's policies. He fought not only for Quakerism but for the right of all Englishmen to worship as they pleased and to run their own government.

The "golden days of good King Charles" were nevertheless hard times for Quakers. The Anglican Church was doing its best to limit and control dissent. Quakers, because they refused to hold their meetings in secret, spent more time in jail than other Dissenters. Penn joined with other Quakers in the purchase of New Jersey, which for a time served as a Quaker refuge. But eastern New Jersey was full of Puritans, always unfriendly to Quakers, and western New Jersey had poor soil. Penn heard that the land across the Delaware was better and that no one was there but wild Indians, who would be easier to live with than English bishops or New Jersey Puritans. The king owed him £16,000, a debt contracted to his father (who died in 1670) for back pay and loans to the royal exchequer. In 1680 Penn asked the king for the land and, after many protests from the king's advisers, got it. Charles named it Pennsylvania after the admiral. In addition, Penn later bought from the Duke of York the region that is now the state of Delaware, which was already populated by a few Dutch and Swedish settlers.

According to the terms of his charter, issued in March 1681, Penn was specifically required to enforce the Navigation Acts, to submit laws to the king for approval, to allow appeals to the king from Pennsylvania courts, and to provide an Anglican minister

*Quakers:
an eighteenth-century
meeting*

whenever twenty or more colonists asked for one. He was also required to obtain the approval of the free-holders (the male owners of land) for any laws that he imposed. Otherwise he had a free hand to govern the colony as he saw fit.

Penn saw fit to govern in a manner that he hoped would demonstrate the virtues of Quakerism and of political and religious liberty. Though, like other pro-prietors, he hoped to profit from his colony by quitrents on land, his primary purpose was to conduct a holy experiment in popular government and Chris-tian living. He served as governor when in the prov-ince and appointed a deputy when absent, but neither for himself nor for his deputy did he retain extensive powers. The people, he made plain in a statement issued a month after he received the charter, "would be allowed to shape their own laws." In the Frame of Government that he worked out to embody this prin-ciple, Penn placed the legislative power in a council and an assembly, both elected by the freeholders. He probably assumed, however, that the freeholders would choose the more successful and well-to-do among them to the council, while the assembly would be composed of more ordinary men. And Penn, who retained some traditional ideas about the prerogatives

of the well-to-do, made the council the more powerful of the two bodies, with the sole right to initiate legis-lation.

Attracted by the prospect of good land, free gov-ernment, and religious liberty, English, Irish, Welsh, Dutch, and German Quakers flocked to the colony. It prospered from the start and attracted many non-Quakers as well, partly because Penn advertised its advantages in pamphlets that were circulated widely. By the end of the century the total population was close to twenty thousand. Penn himself went to the colony in 1682 but had to return to England in less than two years to defend his southern boundary in a legal dispute with Lord Baltimore. The dispute was not fully settled until the 1760s, when Charles Mason and Jeremiah Dixon surveyed their famous line. Liti-gation, losses, and revolution kept Penn in England for fifteen years. During that time his friend King Charles died and his friend the Duke of York ascended the throne, only to flee from it in 1688.

In Pennsylvania, Quakerism in power fulfilled many but not all of Penn's anticipations. It brought religious peace (other sects found complete freedom), economic prosperity, and political quarrels. Although the council, where power was concentrated, was elected by the same people as elected the assembly, just as the United States Senate and House of Representatives are today, the assemblymen acted as though their lack of the right to initiate legislation was a denial of popular rights. The council and the assembly joined in attacking the governors whom Penn sent over, even though the executive power in Pennsylvania was weaker than in any other colony. It is true that Penn, who could never believe ill of any man, often sent incompetent, or at least inappropriate, governors, such as the old Cromwellian soldier, John Blackwell. Blackwell left the province saying that Quakers prayed for their neighbors on Sundays and preyed on them the other six days of the week.

After the fall of James II, Penn was for a while suspect in England because of their long-standing friendship. His province was temporarily taken from him and, from 1692 to 1694, was under a royal government, which gave the assembly the right to initiate legislation. Upon recovering the colony, Penn recognized that right, but by then the assembly was in pursuit of still larger powers. In 1699 he finally returned to the province and told the members of the assembly, since they did not like his plan of government, to draft one of their own. They did so, eliminating the legislative authority of the council altogether (it retained only the function of advising the governor), and leaving the proprietor with only the ownership of ungranted land and a veto power over legislation, normally exercised through his appointed governor.

The new plan, known as the Charter of Liberties, was established in 1701, with Penn's approval, by an act of the assembly. Pennsylvania thus became the only colony with a unicameral legislature. The same Charter of Liberties gave the counties of Newcastle, Sussex, and Kent (later the state of Delaware) a separate representative assembly, though they retained the same governor as Pennsylvania. In 1701 Penn returned to England, where the brotherly love that had founded Pennsylvania eventually landed him in prison for debts incurred by dishonest agents whom he had trusted. No quitrents arrived from Pennsylvania to extricate him. He died in 1718.

# Problems of enforcement

The settlement of Pennsylvania completed English occupation of the Atlantic coast from Spanish Florida to French Canada. All the colonies had been founded under authority of the king, but without his active participation or financial support. The government of each had been uniquely shaped by the varying purposes of the founders and settlers, not by an overall imperial policy. When, with the Navigation Acts of the 1660s, the king and his Parliament began to apply an imperial policy to America, they found that most of the machinery of colonial government by which the acts might have been enforced lay beyond their immediate control. Only in Virginia (through the royally appointed governor and council) did England exercise any voice in colonial government.

Even as the Navigation Acts were passed, Charles II was furthering this dispersion of power. In 1663 he gave Rhode Island a royal charter (to replace a similar parliamentary charter of 1644), authorizing the settlers to choose their own governmental officers. In 1662 he had given the same charter privilege to Connecticut (including New Haven, which would have preferred a separate charter). By these charters and by the others he granted, Charles, perhaps thoughtlessly, distributed authority that might have been used to enforce imperial policies.

At the same time, Charles strengthened another element in colonial government that was to make imperial control difficult. In each of his charters, except the one given to the Duke of York, he required the consent of the settlers to local legislation. The requirement was met by popularly elected representative assemblies like those already existing in older colonies. Assemblies had demonstrated their usefulness: to operate effectively, a colonial government had to obtain the advice and cooperation of the actual settlers, especially where they were Englishmen, used to having their laws made by their representatives. But the assemblies had also demonstrated a truculence, not unlike that of Parliament in England, which promised trouble for policies imposed from above. Nowhere was the threat greater than in New England.

**Recalcitrant colonists.** New England, of all the regions in the empire, fitted least well into the mercantilist scheme of supplying needed raw materials to the mother country. Its farmers and fishermen produced enough provisions to help feed the West Indies sugar plantations. But it had nothing in quantity that the mother country wanted. Since furs from the interior of the continent came out by way of the Hudson or the St. Lawrence, the New England fur trade lasted only until the local animals had been depleted. Lumber and lumber products, such as pitch and tar, were a minor resource. But mostly New England grew rocks, and even these contained no valuable minerals or ores. Because their resources were limited, New Englanders went into the business of distributing what the rest of the world produced. In plying their trade wherever the best price was offered, they competed— all too successfully—with the merchants of the mother country.

They could still have carried on a successful trade in obedience to the Navigation Acts, but disobedience was more profitable. The merchant who bought French silks and laces in France and carried them directly to Boston could undersell one who bought the same goods in England, because English prices included the extra cost of English duties and of transportation from France to England. The same advantage accrued to a merchant or captain who illegally carried enumerated commodities, such as sugar or tobacco, directly from the colonies to Europe.

New Englanders, therefore, had good economic reasons for resisting or evading directions from England. And, as was often the case in New England, economic interest coincided with religious interest. The New Englanders were Puritans, and they had come to New England to live as Puritans. Charles II, whatever else he may have been, was notoriously not a Puritan. New Englanders consequently looked with suspicion on his government and were wary of any move to bring them under its control. Their fathers had struck this defensive attitude almost as soon as they set foot in New England. According to Governor Winthrop, the Puritans had "hastened" their fortifications in 1633 when they heard that Charles I had appointed a commission under Archbishop Laud to govern them. Fortunately the fortifications did not have to be manned against the archbishop. Thereafter New Englanders had easily withstood the halfhearted efforts at control made by Parliament and by Oliver Cromwell. When Charles II came to the throne, they still had the royal charter of Massachusetts intact and did not hesitate to remind the new king of the privileges granted by his father (even though they were secretly harboring the men who had passed the death sentence on Charles I).

Charles II knew that New England was full of Puritans, whom he abhorred, and that Massachusetts in particular had passed laws that did not fully satisfy the requirement, stated in her charter (as in other colonial charters), that all laws conform to those of England. In 1662 he sent a letter commanding revisions. The assembly ignored it. And so, in 1664, when Charles sent his commission of four to capture New Netherland from the Dutch, he assigned them the additional task of investigating New England. They were empowered to adjust boundaries, hear appeals from colonial courts, redress grievances against colonial governments, and report to the king on how well New England was obeying the Navigation Acts.

The commissioners, who went to New England fresh from their triumph over the Dutch, made a discovery that was to be repeated often in the history of the British empire: England could govern Dutchmen (and Frenchmen, Spaniards, Egyptians, Indians, and Chinese) more easily than it could govern Englishmen. The commissioners were treated well enough in Rhode Island, Connecticut, and Plymouth, all of which were looking for improvements in their boundaries. Plymouth had no charter and perhaps hoped to get one by good behavior. But when the commissioners appeared in Boston they met with a reception the coolness of which has seldom been matched even in that city. The officers of government referred them to the charter of 1629 and ostentatiously refused to recognize their authority. A herald

*As long as* Plum Island *shall faithfully keep the commanded Post; Notwithstanding all the hectoring Words, and hard Blows of the proud and boisterous Ocean; As long as any Salmon, or Sturgeon shall swim in the streams of* Merrimack; *or any Perch, or Pickeril, in* Crane-Pond; *As long as the* Sea-Fowl *shall know the Time of their coming, and not neglect seasonably to visit the Places of their Acquaintance; As long as any Cattel shall be fed with the Grass growing in the* Medows, *which do humbly bow down themselves before* Turkie-Hill; *As long as any Sheep shall walk upon Old Town Hills, and shall from thence pleasantly look down upon the River* Parker, *and the fruitfull* Marishes *lying beneath; As long as any free and harmless Doves shall find a White Oak, or other Tree within the Township, to perch, or feed, or build a careless Nest upon; and shall voluntarily present themselves to perform the office of Gleaners after Barley-Harvest; As long as Nature shall not grow Old and dote; but shall constantly remember to give the rows of Indian Corn their education, by Pairs: So long shall Christians be born there; and being first made meet, shall from thence be Translated, to be made partakers of the Inheritance of the Saints in Light.*

**From Samuel Sewall, Phaenomena, 1697.**

appeared before the house where the commissioners were staying and, after a blast from his trumpet, in the name of the king formally forbade anyone to appear before them. Frustrated at every turn, they went back to England to report that the Massachusetts government was making no effort to enforce the Navigation Acts. They also recommended to the king that he revoke the Massachusetts charter, a suggestion echoed by every royal official to visit the colony in the next twenty years.

The king could not revoke the charter at will. It was a contract, binding both grantor and grantee. But the terms required that Massachusetts make no laws contrary to those of England. If it could be shown that Massachusetts had done so, a court of law would declare the charter void, and the king would recover all governmental powers.

After the experience of his commissioners, Charles decided to continue the investigation in England and demanded that Massachusetts send agents to account for its behavior. The General Court (as the Massachusetts assembly was called) sent masts for the king's navy, money for the sufferers in the great fire of London, provisions for the fleet, but no agents. The leaders of Massachusetts knew that many of their laws did violate England's, especially their laws about religion. It was precisely these laws that they wished to keep, even more than they wished to escape the Navigation Acts. So they tried every means to avoid a showdown, relying heavily on distance to support them in one delaying action after another. For ten years they got away with it and grew ever more prosperous and powerful.

In England the king paid only sporadic attention to them and made no effective move against them. But Parliament, in 1673, passed an act to make smuggling to foreign countries less profitable. It levied export duties, known as "plantations duties," on any enumerated commodity shipped to another colony instead of to England. Now, if a shipper pretended to be taking tobacco from Virginia to Boston but took it instead to Holland, he would already have paid a tax equivalent to that levied in England, and he would be unable to sell his cargo in Holland at a price much lower than that of tobacco reshipped legitimately from England. The act of 1673 made smuggling more difficult but did not stop it. As before, the most persistent evaders were the New Englanders, and the governors of other colonies complained that the example of Massachusetts undermined their own attempts to enforce the Navigation Acts.

The main reason for Charles II's failure to act decisively against Massachusetts during these years was that he had no administrative body devoted primarily to colonial affairs. At last, in 1675, he appointed a special committee of the Privy Council known as the Lords of Trade, which set about pulling together the strings of empire. The members quickly realized that England could not rely on the colonial governments to enforce her policies. She must have her own means of enforcement in the colonies. The first step, the Lords of Trade decided, was for the king to take a hand in governing them.

The earliest opportunity came in New Hampshire, into which Massachusetts had extended its authority beyond the boundaries set by its charter.

Robert Mason, who had inherited a claim to the region from the Council for New England, complained to the king about this encroachment, and in 1679 Charles took New Hampshire away from Massachusetts and gave it a royal government. Massachusetts was in danger of losing Maine as well, after an English court had declared its title to that area invalid. But Massachusetts managed to purchase the title of the counterclaimant, Ferdinando Gorges (who was the heir of the original Ferdinando), before the king could act.

The Lords of Trade took over Charles' fight against the Massachusetts charter by renewing the demand that the colony send agents to London. The General Court finally did so, but it gave them no authority to answer the questions the Lords wanted answered. The Lords insisted that the Massachusetts government enforce the Navigation Acts. The General Court, hardened by thirty years of ignoring and defying orders from England, loftily retorted that it was legally endowed by the king's own charter with full powers to govern the province and that therefore Parliament had no authority to pass laws affecting Massachusetts. But, in order to avoid a head-on collision, the General Court formally ordered enforcement of the Navigation Acts. Without waiting to see if Massachusetts would actually carry out the order, the Lords sent an imperial customs officer, Edward Randolph, to do the job; the General Court refused to recognize his commission, set up its own customs office, and imprisoned the deputies appointed by Randolph. The Lords demanded that Massachusetts show cause why its charter should not be revoked; again the General Court sent agents with insufficient powers and inadequate answers. In 1683 legal proceedings were begun, and in 1684 the charter was revoked. In 1685 the Duke of York became King James II.

*The Dominion of New England.* The accession of James II, which made New York a royal colony, together with the revocation of the Massachusetts charter, cleared the way for a scheme the Lords of Trade had long had in mind: a reconstruction of the American empire from New Jersey northward. The scheme shows that they had identified clearly the immediate sources of trouble; it also shows that they had learned little about political realities in either England or America. They proposed to place New Jersey, New York, Connecticut, Rhode Island, Plymouth, Massachusetts, New Hampshire, and Maine under one governor. And in this whole area, to be called the Dominion of New England, there would be no troublesome representative assembly. The royally appointed governor would be assisted by a council whose members would also be appointed by the king. It apparently did not occur to their lordships that the people, deprived of any share in their own government, might prove more troublesome than the assemblies had been.

When news reached Boston that the Massachusetts charter had been revoked, men talked of resistance, as their fathers had fifty years before when threatened with the rule of Archbishop Laud. But their fathers had never been put to the test and had had less to lose in ships, houses, and money than the Bostonians of 1685. Boston was no longer a mere beachhead on an unsettled coast. It was a prosperous city of some seven thousand people with a fleet rivaling that of any English city except London. Most Bostonians held to the faith of their fathers, but they and other New Englanders were perhaps a little more prosperous than Puritan. They allowed their General Court to be dissolved and submitted reluctantly to the interim government of a council appointed by the king. In 1686, when Sir Edmund Andros arrived to establish the Dominion of New England, he faced

*James Martin:*

*I received a wrighting from you by Mr. Shippin wherein you say you have a message from god to deliver to the people of Boston. Well, were it soe indeed, it is meete you should be heard: but for as much as I beleeve the contrary and that it is but a delution or suggestion of satan their is noe reason for me to grant your request for by your behaviour and wrighting you seame to be a professed Quaker and in reason to be thought to be of the same principals and perswations of the cheefe of the Leaders som of whose boocks I have seane and Red and Judg such to be as pernitious hereticks as ever was whose cheaf if not only rule for life and maners is imediate revelation and denying the trew Christian faith and salvation by believing in the Lord Jesus Christ god man and soe no cristians and theirfore that which you call Reasonable I conseave most unreasonable and unsafe and unlawfull as to permit a Jesuit or popish preest to preach or prate to the people and theirfore doe advise and Require you forthwith to depart out of this towne and jurisdiction without giving us any further trouble or disturbance.*

**From Simon Bradstreet, Governor of Massachusetts,
Letter to James Martin, March 27, 1683.**

hard looks and sullen words but no manned fortifications. Although the charters of Rhode Island and Connecticut had not been revoked, Andros extended his government over them without difficulty and in 1688 completed his domain by taking over New York and New Jersey, which he ruled thereafter through a lieutenant-governor. In each colony he dissolved the assembly.

Andros was not a happy choice to inaugurate the new system. An administrator of proved ability, he had already served successfully as governor of New York and would, in the years ahead, serve as governor of Virginia. But the present task called for diplomacy and tact as well as administrative skill. A blunt, outspoken man, Andros made decisions more easily than he made friends. He and the Lords of Trade believed, not without reason, that in order to establish imperial authority in New England the grip of the Puritan leaders must be broken and room made for a party of moderation. But it would have required a man of moderate temper and winning ways to organize and lead such a party.

The Lords of Trade, encouraged by the reports of Edward Randolph, supposed that the Puritans were a minority and that the majority of the population was tired of Puritan intolerance toward Quakers, Baptists, Anglicans, and customs officers. Nothing could have been further from the truth. Enemies of the old government were few, and Andros, by following the instructions of his superiors in England, succeeded in alienating what few there were. He levied taxes for the support of government, necessarily without the consent of a representative assembly. And when the inhabitants objected and pleaded their rights as Eng-

lishmen, he told them they had no rights. Massachusetts had parceled out lands to individuals through the agency of incorporated towns; Andros maintained that the Massachusetts Bay Company had no authority to create corporations and that all titles to land granted by towns were therefore invalid. Anyone who wanted to own the land that he or his fathers had carved out of the wilderness had to ask for a new deed from the governor, pay a fee for it, and agree to pay quitrents ever after.

Andros, with the help of customs officers sent from England, enforced the Navigation Acts, and Randolph later claimed that this was the real cause of

The Dominion of New England

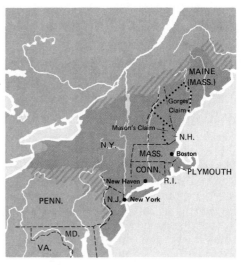

45

opposition to him. But the fact was that the Lords of Trade, in their zeal to establish imperial authority, had assigned Andros an impossible task. They required him to violate long-established rights and privileges and, without the support of an army, a police force, or a political party, to rule arbitrarily over a people who for more than fifty years had ruled themselves. Whether Puritan, non-Puritan, or anti-Puritan they could not be expected to like it. As Andros spelled out the dimensions of his immense authority, they began to have second thoughts about the wisdom of their submission.

**The Revolution of 1688.** Fortunately for New England, the rule of Andros coincided with the reign of James II. Although James could not dispense with Parliament as he had with the New England assemblies, he made it appear that he would have liked to. By exercising his power of pardon he effectively suspended the operation of many parliamentary enactments. He was, besides, a Catholic and made no secret of it. The political patience of Englishmen was as thin in old as in New England. In 1688 they welcomed William of Orange and chased James out of the country.

In Boston the Puritans did not wait for the fall of James to liquidate the Dominion of New England. After they had heard of William's landing in England, but before they had learned of his success in ousting James, they carried out a tidy, bloodless revolution of their own. Spurred by rumors that Andros and James were plotting to hand New England over to the pope, the inhabitants of Boston seized and imprisoned the governor and his council, restored the old government, and waited to hear how William was faring in England. The colony's most eminent minister, Increase Mather, had gone to London the year before to plead the colony's cause against Andros. Mather did his best to persuade the new monarchs, William and Mary, that the Dominion of New England was part and parcel of James' tyrannical policies in England and that the Glorious Revolution ought to include a glorious restitution of the Massachusetts charter. William gave orders for the recall of Andros and authorized Massachusetts to proceed temporarily under her old government, but he refused to restore the charter until he and his advisers should have time to investigate the situation.

Plymouth, Rhode Island, and Connecticut quietly resumed their old governments, and New Jersey returned to anarchy. But New York had its own revolution, which was not entirely bloodless. Andros' lieutenant-governor there, Francis Nicholson, was left in an anomalous position as the appointee of a deposed officer who was in turn the appointee of a deposed king. Nicholson was, besides, young and headstrong, a

*Increase Mather: eminent minister*

professional military officer with an unconcealed scorn for popular rights and liberties. When rumors of popish plots alarmed the population, he did nothing to quiet them.

At the end of May 1689 a party of local militia seized the fort that commanded New York harbor and took control of the government. The party was led by Jacob Leisler, a successful German immigrant who had married into a prominent Dutch family. After Nicholson departed for England in June 1689, a meeting of delegates from different parts of the province chose a committee of safety, which in turn named Leisler as commander in chief of the province. Leisler proclaimed the accession of William, and when ambiguously addressed letters arrived from the new king authorizing a continuation of government, Leisler claimed them.

Basing his authority on the letters, Leisler governed the colony arbitrarily but effectively for nearly two years. New York, thinly settled by people of differing nationalities and religions living in widely differing circumstances, was a long way from political maturity. To maintain order, Leisler had to rely heavily on his followers among the militia. When King William finally got around to appointing a regular governor in 1691, Leisler hesitated before surrendering authority to him and thereby gave the new appointee

*The pattern of empire*

the pretext for an accusation of treason. Leisler and his son-in-law, Jacob Milborne, were convicted and hanged on May 16, 1691. Four years later Parliament reversed the sentence.

### The reorganization of 1696.

The downfall of the Dominion of New England, together with the revolution in England, brought to a halt the efforts to consolidate the empire. After William mounted the throne, he was kept busy defending England in war against France and trying to shore up what was left of the royal prerogative. The new men he appointed to the Privy Council were unfamiliar with colonial problems, and the Lords of Trade had been turned into a committee of the whole, charged with new and broader functions. Once again nobody in the government devoted himself exclusively to colonial policy. The result was seven years of neglect.

In the colonies merchants and shippers ignored the Navigation Acts, and pirates brazenly pursued their prey in and out of harbors. Edward Randolph, now trying to enforce the acts in Maryland, found himself again thwarted by New Englanders who were buying tobacco from the planters and taking it to Scotland instead of England. Though Scotland had the same king as England, the two countries remained separate until 1707. Under the Navigation Acts, Scotland, like nations on the Continent, was excluded from the benefits of trade with England's colonies.

Scottish competition for the tobacco trade raised such a howl of protest from English merchants that the king and Parliament were driven to act. In 1696, guided by Edward Randolph, Parliament in one extensive enactment constructed machinery for enforcing the Navigation Acts. Henceforth the governors of all colonies, whether royal, proprietary, or corporate (Rhode Island and Connecticut), were to take an oath to enforce the acts. Failure to do so meant forfeiture of office. In place of the occasional peripatetic customs officer, a regular customs service subject to the English Treasury was established in each colony. The customs officers were authorized to take out "writs of assistance" from local courts entitling them to open buildings by force in search of smuggled goods. The officers were also empowered to prosecute violators of the Navigation Acts in admiralty courts, which the Privy Council ordered to be established in the colonies. Admiralty courts operated without juries, and it was expected that the judges, who held office only as long as they pleased the crown, would give short shrift to colonial offenders.

While Parliament was passing this measure, it also considered, and then rejected, a bill to create a council of trade and plantations to develop and administer colonial policy. The Privy Council, which had already planned a similar body, now swung into action to keep control of colonial policy under the king. In May 1696, by royal order, a new bureau was established to replace the old Lords of Trade. The Lords Commissioners of Trade and Plantations, as it was called, or more simply the Board of Trade, resembled a national chamber of commerce. It was appointed by the king and was charged to furnish him with information and advice on all colonial matters. Although the board included some members of the Privy Council, ex officio, the eight working members were not councilors and had no authority to issue orders. Their function was purely advisory. But, since they constituted the only body directly concerned with the colonies, their advice was seldom ignored.

Although the king retained control of colonial policy and administration, the circumstances of William's accession affected the kind of control that he and his successors were able to exert in the colonies. After the unhappy experience with James II, Parliament would have looked with suspicion on any move by the king to do away with a representative assembly, even in America. Parliament did not object, however, to the introduction of royal governors in colonies that had not formerly had them. Nor was there serious objection from the settlers, for in almost every case the advent of royal government relieved an intolerable internal situation. Maryland was converted to royal government in 1689, after a local rebellion against the proprietor. (It returned to proprietary government in 1715 after the fourth Lord Baltimore turned Anglican.) As we have seen, New Jersey became a royal colony in 1702 (see p. 36), South Carolina and North Carolina in 1729 (see p. 37). In the new charter that William granted Massachusetts in 1691 (which incorporated Plymouth and Maine as parts of Massachusetts), the king retained power to appoint the governor. Thus most of the colonies reverted eventually to the king.

Wherever a royal government was introduced, the king gained more direct control over his subjects. He appointed the governor, and he appointed the governor's council (except in Massachusetts). Although in each royal colony a representative assembly of freeholders retained legislative authority, the governor's council served as the upper house of the legislature, and its approval was necessary before any act passed by the lower house became law. Even an act passed by both houses was subject to veto by the governor, and even an act approved by the governor might be disallowed by the king. During the eighteenth century, usually on the advice of the Board of Trade, some 5½ percent of the acts passed by colonial assemblies were disallowed by the king, though no act of Parliament was ever vetoed after 1708. Moreover, in the eyes of the mother country the king's instructions to his governors were supposed to bind the assembly

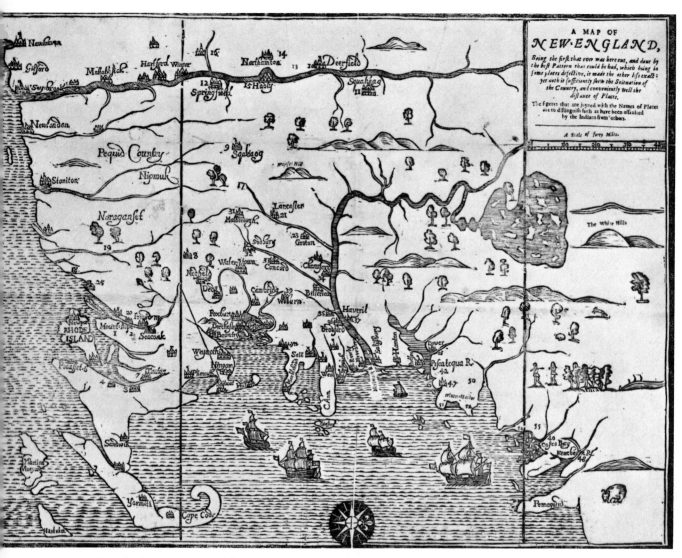

*New England: woodcut, 1677*

as well as the governor. But in spite of royal theories the popularly elected lower house of the assembly remained the most powerful branch of government in every colony. It enjoyed sole authority to levy taxes, and by threatening to withhold them it was often able to get its own way against both king and governor.

**The Old Colonial System.** Of the three agencies England now had for enforcement of the Navigation Acts, the admiralty courts proved unable to exercise jurisdiction because of ambiguities in the act of 1696; the customs service was ill paid and susceptible to bribes and could not operate effectively without the support of the local government. England's control of her colonies depended most heavily on the success of

her royal governors in working with the colonial assemblies. Since every legislative act required the assent of both the governor and the assembly, the needs of neither the mother country nor the colonies could be satisfied if the two refused to cooperate.

Thus in the last analysis the Old Colonial System (embodied in the Navigation Acts and in the act of 1696) rested on the harmony of English and colonial interests. Although occasional discord developed, especially at points of contact between royal governors and assemblies, the harmony was real and the system worked. Enriched by her colonies, England grew to be the world's most powerful nation. And, protected by England, the American colonies grew, each in its own style, toward a new way of life.

*The pattern of empire*

**Suggestions for reading**

Eli Heckscher in *Mercantilism,* 2 vols. (1935), sets the economic policies of the seventeenth and eighteenth centuries in historical perspective and thus furnishes the best introduction to an understanding of the Navigation Acts. For the acts themselves and the thinking behind them, the pioneering works of G. L. Beer are still valuable: *The Origins of the British Colonial System* (1908) and *The Old Colonial System,* 2 vols. (1912). On the administration and interpretation of the acts, see L. A. Harper, *The English Navigation Laws* (1939), C. M. Andrews, *The Colonial Period of American History,* Vol. IV* (1938), and T. C. Barrow, *Trade and Empire* (1967). Special aspects of British policy are well treated in Curtis Nettels, *The Money Supply of the American Colonies Before 1720* (1934), and A. C. Bining, *British Regulation of the Colonial Iron Industry* (1933). Michael Kammen, *Empire and Interest** (1970), analyzes the pressure groups that affected policy, and A. G. Olson, *Anglo-American Politics, 1660–1775* (1973), traces the effect of party politics on colonial administration.

On New Netherland and on the Restoration colonies the fullest general account is again C. M. Andrews, *The Colonial Period of American History,* Vols. II and III*. W. F. Craven, *The Colonies in Transition, 1660–1713** (1968), incorporates more recent research. T. J. Wertenbaker, *The Founding of American Civilization: The Middle Colonies* (1938), stresses social and cultural history. J. E. Pomfret has untangled much of New Jersey's early history in *The Province of West New Jersey, 1609–1702* (1956) and *The Province of East New Jersey, 1609–1702* (1962). For the Carolinas see Verner Crane, *The Southern Frontier, 1670–1732* (1929), M. E. Sirmans, *Colonial South Carolina* (1966), and C. L. Ver Steeg, *Origins of a Southern Mosaic* (1975).

There is no definitive biography of William Penn, but C. O. Peare, *William Penn** (1956), and H. E. Wildes, *William Penn* (1974), are adequate. M. M. Dunn has made a scholarly study of his activities in *William Penn: Politics and Conscience* (1967), and M. B. Endy of his religious ideas in *William Penn and Early Quakerism* (1973). J. E. Illick, *William Penn the Politician* (1965), treats his relations with the English government. Rufus Jones, *Quakers in the American Colonies** (1911), is a standard work, but see also F. B. Tolles' eloquent essays in *Quakers and the Atlantic Culture* (1960). The early history of Pennsylvania is treated in F. B. Tolles, *James Logan and the Culture of Provincial America* (1957), and G. B. Nash, *Quakers and Politics: Pennsylvania, 1681–1726* (1968).

Efforts of England to enforce the Navigation Acts are dealt with in Michael Hall, *Edward Randolph and the American Colonies, 1676–1703** (1960). Viola Barnes, *The Dominion of New England: A Study in British Colonial Policy* (1923), is the classic account of that episode, exonerating Andros of blame. Kenneth Murdock, *Increase Mather* (1925), treats fully Mather's role in seeking the overthrow of the dominion and in securing a new charter for Massachusetts. The long-range causes and consequences of Leisler's Rebellion are discussed in J. R. Reich, *Leisler's Rebellion* (1953), and in L. H. Leder, *Robert Livingston and the Politics of Colonial New York, 1654–1728* (1961). David S. Lovejoy, *The Glorious Revolution in America** (1972), is now the standard account.

On the reorganization of colonial administration in 1696, see again C. M. Andrews, *The Colonial Period of American History,* Vol. IV*, and I. K. Steele, *Politics of Colonial Policy: The Board of Trade in Colonial Administration, 1696–1720* (1968). The standard works on the Board of Trade are O. M. Dickerson, *American Colonial Government, 1696–1765* (1912), and A. H. Basye, *The Lords Commissioners of Trade and Plantations, 1748–1782* (1925). On the activities of the board in securing the disallowance of colonial acts of legislation, see E. B. Russell, *The Review of American Colonial Legislation by the King in Council* (1915). The role of colonial governors in administering British policy is the subject of L. W. Labaree, *Royal Government in America: A Study of the British Colonial System Before 1783* (1930). Finally, Lawrence Gipson, in fifteen volumes, surveys *The British Empire Before the American Revolution* (1936–1970).

*Available in a paperback edition.

# Patterns of existence

Americans moving across their continent have faced three questions again and again: how to live, how to live with one another, how to live with the outside world. They first learned how to live by tobacco, rice, furs, and fish. England told them, in the Navigation Acts, how they must live with the outside world. How did they live with one another?

A few simply did not. When the Puritans explored Boston harbor, they came upon an Englishman at Beacon Hill living alone among the blueberries. William Blackstone was company enough for himself. After the Puritans moved in, he moved out. For nearly three centuries the continent afforded room for men like Blackstone, American hermits who felt crowded when they could see the smoke from their neighbor's campfire.

Most Americans have been more gregarious. They have asked *how*, rather than whether, to live together, and they have answered partly from the heritage of ideas and institutions carried from Europe, partly from their own ideas evoked by the opportunities and limitations of their strange new environment. Each generation has solved the problem a little differently from the preceding one, but the first settlers, moving from an old established world to an empty new one, had the biggest problem and made the biggest change. Many of them came to America primarily for a chance to live together in a new and, they hoped, a better way. All of them had to adapt ideas made in Europe to existence in America. The results differed

# CHAPTER 3

# The first American way of life

*Virginia wharf, 1750*

from time to time and from place to place. But before the end of the colonial period most Americans were living together in one of four distinct patterns: the Southern plantation, the New England town, the loose collection of individual farms, or the coastal city.

**The plantation.** Plantations developed in colonies where the majority of people lived by growing a single crop for export: tobacco in Virginia and Maryland, rice or indigo in South Carolina, sugar in the West Indies. Originally "planter" meant simply a settler, and "plantation" a settlement—Jamestown was the London Company's plantation. Gradually the term plantation came to be attached to individual holdings and then to holdings where substantial numbers of men worked for the owner. Gradually too the term came to imply that the workmen were slaves, the

property of the man for whom they worked.

The plantation manned by slaves originated in the West Indies, but within the present United States it developed first in Virginia. It was the most novel way of living that colonial Americans devised for themselves. It was also the most productive, if we may judge by the exports of the thirteen colonies. And it was the most violent and oppressive, a way of living that required the continuous coercion of unwilling and unrewarded labor. In order to understand the role it played in American life, we shall have to look into its beginnings.

The first steps were taken during Virginia's tobacco boom of the 1620s, when everyone was scrambling for labor. A number of successful Virginians at this time were able to gather crews of ten, twenty, even thirty-odd men to grow tobacco for them. The

51

*Patterns of existence*

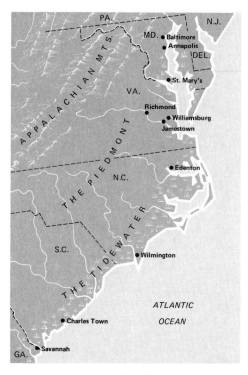

The tidewater and the piedmont

men were mostly Englishmen who had agreed to serve for up to seven years in return for passage across the ocean to the new land of opportunity. They themselves constituted an opportunity for the planters who bought them, sold them, traded them, and even won or lost them in card games. The planters would buy the labor of any man delivered to them, and Dutch traders delivered a few from Africa bound to serve for a lifetime. But you could buy an Englishman for seven years cheaper than you could buy an African for life; and in early Virginia seven years was more than most immigrants were likely to live anyhow. The death rate was comparable to that reached in England during years of the plague. The cause is not clear. Probably it was a combination of malnutrition with malaria and typhoid fever. Between 1625 and 1640 some fifteen thousand immigrants increased the population of the colony from around thirteen hundred to only seven or eight thousand.

In spite of the heavy death rate, servants were cheap enough to be worth importing even after the price of tobacco dropped to around 20 shillings a hundred pounds (2.4 pence per pound) in the 1640s and 1650s. By then the Virginians' increasing skill with the crop enabled a man to grow from one to two thousand pounds of tobacco a year, together with enough corn to feed himself. At that rate his output was still worth between £10 and £20—while he lived. And beginning somewhere around the middle of the

century people in Virginia evidently started living longer. The population rose to about fifteen thousand by 1653 and about twenty-five thousand by 1660.

Most of those who made up these numbers arrived in the colony as servants. As more and more of them lived to complete their period of service, the added years of labor meant added profits to their masters (who could thus acquire still more servants to operate still larger plantations). And the ex-servants themselves could at long last begin to enjoy the opportunities they had been helping to bring to others. They could start small plantations, grow tobacco for export, and import servants of their own.

For a number of reasons the opportunities diminished sharply after 1660. The increase in population brought an increase in the labor force and a consequent increase in the production of tobacco. Since the rise in production was accompanied by passage of the Navigation Act of 1660, restricting the market for Virginia and Maryland tobacco, the price fell to a penny a pound and sometimes less. At the same time the cost of production went up, especially for beginners, because land was more in demand and hence more valuable. Farsighted planters began acquiring huge tracts and by the 1670s had engrossed most of the best land in the tidewater, the area cut by great rivers and bays along which ocean-going ships could collect tobacco as much as a hundred miles inland. A new freedman looking for a place to plant either had to rent from the big owners or else settle for a location in the interior, cut off from river transportation, or far up one of the rivers, where he would be exposed to Indian attack.

As a result Virginia and Maryland (where the same conditions prevailed) acquired a growing class of indigent freedmen. They wandered from county to county, living from hand to mouth, dodging the tax collector, renting a bit of land here, squatting there, sometimes working for wages, sometimes trying to live from the land, hunting, stealing hogs, and enticing servants to run away with them. They were mostly young, because planters imported young servants; they were mostly single, because planters imported far more men than women; and they were mostly armed, because guns were a necessity of life in Virginia and Maryland, where dwellings were widely separated and a man had to be ready to shoot it out if attacked by Indians.

The established planters became increasingly uneasy about the band of wild bachelors in their midst. William Berkeley, who had been governor of the colony from 1641 to 1652 and became governor again in 1660, clearly saw danger ahead. When the Dutch made war against England and raided the James River in 1673, Berkeley led the militia against them with considerable trepidation, for he estimated that a large

*The first American way of life*

percentage of the men at his back were poverty-stricken freedmen, who "upon any small advantage the Enemy may gaine upon us, would revolt to them in hopes of bettering their condition by Shareing the Plunder of the Country with them."

Berkeley's fears were justified. Three years later, sparked by an Indian attack on the frontiers, a band of self-appointed Indian-fighters turned from an unsuccessful pursuit of the elusive enemy to attack their much less elusive rulers. Led by Nathaniel Bacon, a well-to-do sympathizer, the freedmen of the frontier found ready allies in nearly every part of the colony. In the largest popular uprising before the American Revolution they burned the capital settlement at Jamestown and drove the governor and his friends in flight to the Eastern Shore, the only loyal stronghold in the colony. Before it was over, the rebellion had swept up servants as well as freedmen in plundering forays against everyone who offered resistance.

Then, after they had redistributed as much of the wealth as they could lay their hands on, the rebels gave up as quickly as they had risen. Their leader, Bacon, had died of a fever; and he left them with no long-range solution to the problems that faced them, no revolutionary program, not even any revolutionary slogans. Old Governor Berkeley exacted a savage revenge by hanging the remaining leaders, though the king had sent a general pardon. For the rest of the century Virginians continued to eye one another uneasily, alert for new Bacons in their midst. Though

the rebellion had subsided, its causes had not. Servants were still arriving every year to man the plantations; they were still becoming free every year in large numbers; and they still could not afford the land on which to sustain their freedom. They had crossed the ocean to a wilderness and sold away seven years of their lives only to face the prospect of working out the remainder on another man's plantation. Their continuing discontent posed a real and present danger to the established planters.

It was under these circumstances that the traders who had been supplying the West Indies with slaves began delivering them in larger numbers to the tobacco colonies. A slave cost only about twice as much as a servant, around £20 instead of £10 at the close of the seventeenth century. With the decline in Virginia's death rate, slaves became a more profitable investment than servants, and for that reason alone the planters bought all the traders could bring. But the unsought social benefits to Virginia's big planters were larger than the economic benefits. Although every planter worried about taking into his household men and women who had good reason to hate him, slaves proved to be less dangerous than servants who had become free. No slave rebellion in American history ever approached the success of Bacon's Rebellion.

Slaves remained permanently under the control of their masters. They could safely be denied rights that Englishmen, servant or free, could legally demand. They could be subjected to harsh punishments without recourse to the courts. They could be kept unarmed, unorganized, helpless to resist. And the fact that they happened to be black announced their probable status and made escape difficult.

By importing permanent black slaves instead of temporary white servants for their plantations, Virginians ceased to add to the band of indigent freedmen, which gradually diminished. As the competition for land stopped escalating and the interior became safer for settlement, a man could once again get a foothold on the ladder that led up in the world. Slavery enabled the planters to go on growing ever larger crops without, on the one hand, creating a dangerous class of poor and discontented freedmen or, on the other hand, reducing those freedmen to some new sort of bondage that would shackle their discontent. Bondage was reserved for blacks, who accounted for most of the tobacco and rice produced in the colonies by the middle of the eighteenth century.

Englishmen recognized slavery as the ultimate degradation to which human beings could be subjected, but they showed surprisingly little hesitation in imposing that degradation on peoples of darker complexion than their own. Though slavery had no place in English law, English colonists from the beginning had enslaved Indians who made unsuccessful war on them. The theory was that the lives of captives taken in just wars belonged to the captors; but history records no war acknowledged by the victors to have been unjust, and Englishmen had not been in the habit of enslaving prisoners taken in their European wars. Making slaves of Indians and later of Africans (allegedly purchased from the victors in righteous tribal wars) was somehow different from making slaves of, say, Frenchmen or Germans.

The difference, of course, was race. Although not all blacks were slaves—from the beginning a substantial minority even in the plantation colonies were free—all slaves were either blacks or Indians. Slavery became the dominant form of relationship between whites and other races and was recognized by law in every colony. North of Maryland race relations concerned relatively few people; from Maryland south they concerned most people. Though the plantation had begun with a free or semifree white labor force, it became in the eighteenth century the meeting place of black and white, the primary community in which free and enslaved Americans lived together.

Although the Southern plantation resembled similar establishments in the West Indies and South America, it had distinctive features that were to affect the way Americans of different races lived together after slavery ended. Of first importance was the fact that Southern slave owners, especially in the tobacco colonies, did not make a policy of working their slaves to death. Whether because tobacco required less strenuous labor than sugar, or for other reasons, a slave on a Southern plantation had a longer and less arduous life than a slave on a sugar plantation in the West Indies, where planters counted on replacing a percentage of their worn-out and dying labor force annually by new purchases. The slave women of the West Indies could not or would not raise enough children to match the awful death rate. In the American South, while the planters continued to import slaves throughout the colonial period, the numbers also increased naturally. Though black women, as in the West Indies, worked beside their men in the fields, they were able at the same time to raise children. Southern slaves could thus enjoy some semblance of family life.

The children, like their mothers and fathers, were the property of the master, and he could break up a family by selling any one of them. But so long as they were together slave families could in some measure—at night, on Sundays, and usually on Saturday afternoons—live lives of their own. The planters' policy of doling out the meagerest of rations and obliging the slaves to grow what more they wanted in plots adjoining their cabins even encouraged a close family relationship as father, mother, and children worked together, for themselves, in their own garden.

The planters' success in promoting slave families may be judged by the fact that slaves on Southern plantations raised nearly as many children as free Southerners did. And while the colonies that later formed the United States received only 4½ percent of all the slaves imported into the New World, the descendants of that 4½ percent today constitute over 30 percent of the New World's inhabitants with African ancestry. The slave family was not responsible for all of them: the different shades of color among the children in the slave quarters testified to the fact that black women were not reserved for black men. But miscegenation was probably less than in other slave societies and racial prejudice correspondingly stronger.

On the other hand the estrangement of black and white was in some measure limited by the circumscribed environment in which they coexisted. Since the largest effective unit of tobacco production was a thousand acres (including uncleared and exhausted

*A community in itself: a tidewater plantation*

land), few tobacco plantations had as many as a hundred slaves. A smaller area, with no more than thirty slaves, was the most efficient unit for rice.

The plantation often constituted a small community in itself. At the center lay a great house, normally facing a navigable river, and surrounded by trees and shrubs. Arranged symmetrically around it were attendant buildings: laundry, smokehouse, kitchen, and perhaps a schoolhouse, where a hired tutor taught the planter's children—or at least his free children. At some distance lay the barns and the cabins of the slaves.

In addition to field hands, the community included a small army of household slaves and skilled artisans—carpenter, blacksmith, tailor, cobbler—who might be either indentured white servants (bound by a contract to serve a specific number of years) or slaves educated for the purpose. With its own permanent labor force and with ready access to ocean-going ships, the riverside plantation needed little from its neighbors. What could not be made on the premises was imported directly from London.

And yet the planter and his family were not isolated. The river was a highway to the world by which he kept in touch not only with London but with other planters. His children often went to stay for several weeks at other plantations, and his own home was seldom without guests. Sometimes he gave a ball for friends who came from miles around and stayed for three or four days. Or he might attend the representative assembly in Williamsburg or Charles Town and take the family with him.

In the assembly and in the local county court the planter directed the lives of his lesser neighbors, the small farmers who made up the majority of the population even in the plantation colonies. They worked for themselves, but he dominated the society, buying and selling their surplus crops, sometimes renting them their lands, lending them money, selling them manufactures, and perhaps commanding their votes. His command of their votes was by no means automatic, however. The deference his neighbors paid him was the voluntary tribute that success has generally exacted in a free society. It took the votes of free men to place him in the representative assembly, and votes were withheld often enough to remind him that he represented free men.

By officiating in the assembly, the county court, and the vestry of his church, and by managing his plantation, the planter learned to deal with men both free and unfree. And the ships that arrived at his wharf brought him regular news of the way men were dealing with one another across the water. In their writings he learned that they thought slavery the worst fate that could befall a people. From a closer knowledge than theirs he could agree; and he would, as the years passed, increasingly value and protect his own freedom.

***The New England town.*** Rivers, tobacco, and slavery made the plantation. Puritanism and past experience made the New England town, an institution that also appeared in the parts of New York and New Jersey settled by New Englanders. The past experience of New Englanders (as of other English colonists) included at least three English types of community: the borough, the village, and the parish.

The English borough was a town that normally possessed a charter of incorporation from the king entitling it to send two members to Parliament and to exercise a degree of local governmental independence. The freemen (or burgesses) of the borough, usually a very small proportion of the population, elected the members of Parliament as well as a mayor or a set of aldermen to handle local affairs. In many boroughs the aldermen had become so powerful that they were bypassing the freemen and were filling vacancies in their ranks by themselves.

The English village was not a formal political institution like the borough. It was simply a cluster of houses inhabited by men and women who cultivated the adjoining lands according to customs prescribed by earlier generations. All the village's arable land was laid out in three or four large fields, and every householder had strips of land scattered through all of them. No man's strips were fenced off from those of his neighbors; and everyone worked together at plowing (and subsequently at sowing, tilling, and harvesting) one field before moving on to the next. Thus every man would get part of his crop early, part of it late. By the time the settlers left England, this open-field system was giving way to individual farms, but it still existed in many places.

Every Englishman, whether he lived in a borough or a village, belonged to a parish. Originally the parish was simply the area served by a single church, but it had gradually taken on, outside the boroughs, many of the functions of local government. In most villages a vestry made up of some ten or twenty of the more substantial inhabitants exercised the powers of the parish or chose two or three churchwardens to do so. The churchwardens or vestrymen not only maintained the church and managed its property but provided for the poor, required fathers to support their children, levied taxes, and sometimes acted as a kind of grand jury.

In creating their towns New Englanders drew something from the parish, the village, and the borough; but they also rejected parts of this institutional heritage because of their Puritan ideas about how men ought to live with one another. Puritans generally "gathered" a church before, or about the same time as, they established a town. The two usually covered the same territory, as was true of the English village and parish. But in New England the church and its officers were entirely distinct from the town and its officers. The church owned no property, not even a church building. People worshiped in a meetinghouse, which was owned by the town and used for any community meeting. It was not regarded as sacred. Nor did the church exercise any temporal, political powers. There was no vestry and no churchwarden. The church might elect ruling elders to reprimand erring members or to report them to the church, but neither elders nor church enjoyed coercive authority. The church was a spiritual association; its severest penalty was excommunication, which could be pronounced only by unanimous vote of the members. Excommunication deprived a person of church membership but carried no civil or political disabilities. Once a church assumed temporal powers, Puritans believed, it was on the wicked road to Rome. In New England, therefore, they assigned to the town both the duties of local government, performed in the English borough by the mayor and aldermen, and the secular duties exercised in the English parish by church officers.

New England towns and their governments were created under the authority of the colony's General Court (the legislature). A group of men, perhaps already gathered in a church, approached the court and requested a tract of land, usually adjoining some established town. If the court approved, it had the area surveyed and then renamed the applicants as proprietors of the town of Concord, Sudbury, or whatever name they chose. The proprietors then moved to their new home and laid out the land in a pattern similar to that of an English village. Every man got a house lot in the center of town, where space was also set aside for a meetinghouse, a village green, and perhaps a school. Each man also received one or more parcels of arable land, a parcel of meadow for pasturage, and a parcel of woodland for fuel, all located in different parts of the town. In a few cases there seems to have been an attempt (quickly abandoned) to practice the open-field system. When the land of a town was originally apportioned, most of it was left undivided to meet the anticipated growth in population. The undistributed land, or commons, belonged to the proprietors jointly until they converted it into their private property through subsequent land divisions. A new settler moving into town might buy land from a proprietor's private holdings or might be granted or sold parts of the commons, but he did not necessarily become a proprietor with a share in the ownership of the remaining commons.

The power of the proprietors was limited to control over the commons; government of the town rested in a town meeting, in which they had no greater voice than other inhabitants. The town meeting acted on matters that intimately concerned the inhabitants: repairing roads, building a meetinghouse, hiring a schoolmaster, or deciding whether hogs should be fenced into pens or fenced out of gardens. The meeting also elected representatives to the colonial assembly and town officials of all kinds, including selectmen, who administered the rules made by the meeting. There was some attempt in early Massachusetts to confine voting in town meetings to the freemen, who it will be remembered had to be church members. After 1648, however, and probably before then in many towns, other free adult males, if approved by the freemen, were allowed to vote on all questions except the choice of representatives. Until 1685, representatives continued to be elected only by the freemen.

In the early years of a town's existence there was no conflict of interest between town meeting and proprietors, because all or most of the free adult males were also proprietors. And the inhabitants frequently felt a strong sense of duty to the community, a sense carried over from the religious purposes that guided the settlement. They sought to sustain their brotherhood in the political as well as the spiritual world by talking out any disputes that arose among them and by keeping out any newcomers who appeared likely to disturb their solidarity.

By the opening of the eighteenth century, with the passing of the founders, the waning of the high resolve that had moved them, and the dwindling away of the common lands, the towns began to take on a different character. Fathers could not or would not give their sons the amount of land they needed, and the young began to go west in search of greener pastures. Latecomers quarreled with the proprietors over the remaining common lands. Religious dissent appeared in forms that could not be talked down.

At the same time new towns were being formed by men without the spirit that had moved the first generation. Colonial governments, instead of granting townships gratis to groups of settlers, auctioned them off to groups assembled simply for the purpose of investing in real estate. These proprietors were sometimes not even residents of the towns they founded, and they sold land to settlers with more attention to private profit than to establishing a successful community. The settlers themselves were also less devoted to the community. Instead of living close to the meetinghouse and having their landholdings scattered about the countryside, they scattered their houses and tried to consolidate their land in one piece around the house.

Nevertheless, the New England town remained in the eighteenth century, if not as closely knit as in the

*Patterns of existence*

seventeenth, remarkably homogeneous and neighborly. Men still rubbed elbows often and tried to work out their differences peaceably. On Sunday everyone gathered in the meetinghouse, where the position of a man's pew indicated his place in the community and whether he must be addressed as "Mister," as "Goodman," or by no title at all. In general, the closer he sat to the pulpit, the higher his social rank. But proximity to God's minister was no sign of proximity to God. Though the law required that everyone attend church, only a minority of the town's inhabitants were "members," and membership in itself carried no social prestige. A slave might belong and a gentleman not. During the eighteenth century church membership became increasingly feminine, with women outnumbering men by more than two to one. But members or not, New Englanders went to church, were taxed for the minister's salary, and had a voice in selecting him.

The men of the town met not only at church and town meeting but on training day when the militia exercised. In frontier settlements, under constant threat of Indian attack, this was a serious business; in the older coastal towns it was likely to require more rum than gunpowder. Rum and hard cider lubricated most community activities in New England, whether marrying or burying, raising a meetinghouse or bringing home a harvest. The tavern, originally intended for the convenience of travelers, became another meeting place where men of the neighborhood bent an elbow of an evening and where, according to John Adams, "vicious habits, bastards, and legislators" were frequently begotten.

In tavern, school, and church, at town meeting and militia drill, the New Englander measured out the distance between himself and his fellow man. The distance was small, but it was enough to give him an independence of spirit for which he became famous. For those who needed more room, America offered another way of life.

***The farm.*** In the colonies from New England southward, the average American lived a lonely life. He made his living from the land, as his father had done in Europe. But in the great emptiness of the New World, sheer space separated him from his neighbors in a way that few Europeans knew. His farm might lie miles from any other occupied land, because settlers chose lands, not for neighborliness, but for water supply, for the evenness of the ground, and above all for fertility (frequently indicated by a stand of hardwood).

The sheer size of an American farm also tended to isolate the farmer. Because of the way he used the land, he needed a large tract. It was common practice to clear a plot, crop it for several years until its fertility was exhausted, and then clear another, allowing the first to lie fallow for five, ten, even twenty or thirty years. Clearing often meant no more than girdling the trees at the base to kill them, planting crops between the lifeless trunks, and then disposing of the trunks as they rotted away. By that time, however, the plot might be ready to abandon anyhow. It would gradually recover its fertility (and perhaps its forest) and could be cleared again in the same way.

To European visitors the practice seemed slovenly and shiftless, but it was actually the way to get the maximum in crops for the minimum of labor. It is still common practice wherever land is abundant and people scarce. The first settlers in most colonies probably learned it from the Indians, though a small group of Finnish settlers on the Delaware River may already have been familiar with it (they also introduced the technique of building log cabins, perhaps the easiest way to turn trees into houses). But however effective this kind of farming may have been, it did mean that a farm had to be large, with much of the land under forest or scrub most of the time.

Though most farmers owned the land they lived on, farm tenancy became common in some areas where the soil was fertile enough to support both a landlord and a tenant. In New York's Hudson Valley, for example, landlords exacted high rents and feudal services. In Virginia's tidewater, tenants took farms and even plantations as sharecroppers, paying the owner a proportion of the crop as rent. Even in the uncleared back country it was not always easy for a farmer to obtain title to land in the most fertile areas, because speculators often acquired such lands in ad-

O P M

The Duke of Cumberland

ENTERT AINMENT

1773

*Connecticut tavern sign:*
*to bend an elbow of an evening*

*The mode of common husbandry here [North Carolina] is to break up a piece of woodland, a work very easily done, from the trees standing at good distances from each other; this they sow with Indian corn for several years successively, till it will yield large crops no longer: they get at first fourscore or an hundred bushel an acre, but sixty or seventy are common: when the land is pretty well exhausted they sow it with pease or beans one year, of which they will get thirty or forty bushels per acre; and afterwards sow it with wheat for two or three years.... In this system of crops they change the land as fast as it wears out, clearing fresh pieces of woodland, exhausting them in succession; after which they leave them to the spontaneous growth. It is not here as in the northern colonies that weeds come first and then grass ... but the fallow in a few years becomes a forest, for no climate seems more congenial to the production of quick growing trees. If the planter does not return to cultivate the land again—as may probably be the case, from the plenty of fresh [land]—it presently becomes such a wood as the rest of the country is....*

From ***American Husbandry, 1776.***

vance of actual settlers. By the eighteenth century the headright system (practiced earlier in most of the colonies south of New England) had become a mere form. A speculator could obtain title to as much land as he could afford simply by paying a fee (usually 5 shillings per hundred acres) to the colony's secretary or land office. Later he could rent the land to a bona fide settler or else sell it for a good deal more than he had paid. Not all speculators were rich men. Many farmers, tradesmen, and even parsons invested their small earnings in real estate, for everyone knew that land values would rise as population increased, and everyone could see that population was increasing rapidly.

In New England most of the increase came from natural growth of the old stock who, unlike the early Virginia immigrants, arrived primarily in family groups and began multiplying at once. Also unlike Virginians, New Englanders seem to have lived ten or twenty years longer than their contemporaries in England; and they had far more children. Although women married at a later age than is usually supposed (probably at an average of about twenty-three in the seventeenth century and around twenty-one in the eighteenth), they commonly had five or six children. In spite of the heavy toll taken by smallpox, diphtheria, scarlet fever, and childbirth, the population kept growing at rates unheard of in the Old World. In the Southern colonies a shortage of women and a very heavy death rate held down the natural increase during most of the seventeenth century; but the importation of servants, and later of slaves, kept the population growing rapidly nevertheless. After the sex ratio evened out and the mortality rate diminished, natural increase joined with heavy immigration to send the population soaring in the eighteenth century.

The largest ethnic group of immigrants came involuntarily from Africa to man the plantations of Virginia, Maryland, and South Carolina. But the Middle colonies, especially Pennsylvania, welcomed a flood of voluntary immigrants, mainly from northern Ireland and Germany, most of whom became independent farmers. After landing in the New World, usually at Philadelphia, they traveled west to the Appalachian valleys and spilled down into the hinterland of Maryland, Virginia, and the Carolinas.

At crossroads in the farming areas, storekeepers traded hardware, clothing, and gossip for crops. But there was no real community, no local nucleus of political, social, and religious life. Even the churches responded slowly to the needs of the farmer. In colonies where the Anglican Church was supported by taxation (New York, Maryland, Virginia, and the Carolinas) it organized parishes to keep pace with the westward advance, but they were too large in area to serve the widely scattered farmers, many of whom were not Anglicans anyhow. The parish had been designed for more densely populated areas, where enough people to support a minister lived within Sunday traveling distance of his sermons. By the eighteenth century some denominations, especially Presbyterians and Methodists, were sending itinerant missionaries through the back country. Now the people could hold at least an occasional service, sometimes under a tree, sometimes in a courthouse, sometimes in a church built for the purpose. The circuit-riders, as the missionaries were called, often encountered families whose children had never seen a minister.

In the absence of village or town, colonial farmers relied heavily on a looser and larger community, the county. Every colony was divided into counties, and

*Dancing masters taught the latest steps*

everywhere the county court was an important arm of government. Even in New England the county judges (appointed as elsewhere by the colonial governments) decided administrative as well as judicial questions, questions as important as where to build new roads. Outside New England, the county court took over the duties of the town and sometimes of the parish. Besides trying cases, both civil and criminal, it might record wills and deeds, take charge of orphans and the poor, register births, marriages, and deaths, collect taxes, license taverns, authorize the establishment of ferries, and pay bounties for wolves' heads. On days when the court was in session, usually once a month, farmers from near and far would gather to sue one another for small sums, to exercise in the militia, to elect a representative to the colony's assembly, or simply to watch the proceedings, learn the news, and share talk and a bottle with distant neighbors.

The thinness of community life put a heavy burden on the family. Everywhere during the colonial period the family fulfilled many more functions than it does today, but among farmers it was everything—factory, church, school, hospital, and tavern. Unless a man held especially rich land and had ready access to a market, his crops went to feed his family, with little left over for sale. He and his wife had to make everything they could not buy, which might be most of their clothing and furniture. Without a school, they had to teach their children to read; without a church, to worship at home; without a tavern, to entertain passing strangers; without a doctor, to care for their sick. Children were plentiful and made more hands to do the endless work. Some might take over the farm as their parents grew old, but most of them would eventually leave to carve new farms out of the empty land. The family with three generations under one roof was exceptional everywhere in America, as it was in England.

The farmer, isolated from his neighbors and living a self-sufficient life within his own family, was the typical eighteenth-century American—even the townsman of western New England resembled him. But as farmers spread out through the interior a significant minority of Americans piled up in five cities and several large towns along the coast.

***The city.*** The colonial farmer riding into a city for the first time left a road that was only a ribbon of stumps and mud and came upon streets of gravel or cobblestones, where a bewildering activity surrounded him. Swine roamed everywhere, feeding on the refuse; drovers herded sheep and cattle to the butchers. Elegant carriages rolled impatiently behind lumbering wagons as great packs of barking dogs worried the horses. Sailors reeled out of taverns, and over the roofs of the houses could be seen the swaying masts and spars of their ships. The farmer had been told that the city was a nursery of vice and prodigality. He now saw that it was so. Every shop had wares to catch his eye: exquisite fabrics, delicate chinaware, silver buckles, looking glasses, and other imported luxuries that never reached the crossroads store. Putting up at the tavern, he found himself drinking too much rum. And there were willing girls, he heard, who had lost their virtue and would be glad to help him lose his. Usually he returned to the farm to warn his children as he had been warned. He seldom understood that the vice of the city, if not its prodigality, was mainly for transients like himself. Permanent residents had work to do.

The key men in the community were the merchants, for colonial cities were built on trade. Merchants bought corn, wheat, cattle, and horses from thousands of farms and fish from hundreds of fishermen and shipped them to the West Indies. The planters there could not waste their valuable sugar lands growing corn, but they needed food for their slaves and horses to turn their sugar mills. Colonial merchants supplied them and brought back molasses, a by-product of sugar-making. Distilleries turned it into rum, much of which the merchants shipped off to exchange for slaves on the coast of Africa or to help fishermen fight back the icy winds of the North Atlantic. The merchants also bought beaver and deerskins from Indian traders and huge pine trunks from lumbermen to send to England for masts. From England they brought back woolens and hardware, which the mother country made better and cheaper than the colonists could. Without the merchants there would have been no cities.

Many of the other city-dwellers depended on the merchants for a living. Besides the rum-distillers, there were shipwrights who turned out ships at a lower price than English ones. Workers in ropewalks and sail lofts rigged them. Instrument-makers fitted them with quadrants, telescopes, and clocks. Retail traders helped to distribute the goods imported from abroad. Millers ground wheat and corn into flour, and coopers built barrels to ship it in.

But cities accumulate people by a magic of their own, and many colonists found jobs that had no direct connection with the overseas trade. Schoolmasters were better trained and more plentiful than in the country. Dancing masters taught ladies and gentlemen the newest steps; stay-makers laced them into the newest shapes. Barbers cut their hair; wigmakers put it on again. And dozens of skilled craftsmen offered American-made copies of the latest English fashions in wearing apparel, furniture, and houses.

For all the glamour and excitement of their environment, city-dwellers had problems that other Americans had not yet faced; city opulence bred thieves and vice of all kinds; city filth necessitated sewers and sanitation laws; city traffic required paved streets and lights; and the city's closely packed wooden houses and shops invited fires that might, and repeatedly did, destroy vast areas. To cope with these problems, citizens relied both on voluntary associations, such as fire companies, and on their city governments. Boston and Newport were governed by selectmen and town meetings, New York (after 1731) by a popularly elected city corporation. In all three, city officials, under direct control of the citizens, were responsive to their needs. In Philadelphia and Charles Town, on the other hand, the citizens had no voice in their local government. Philadelphia was badly governed by a self-perpetuating closed corporation, and Charles Town just as badly by the South Carolina assembly.

By contemporary standards these were all substantial cities. Though small compared with London, by the middle of the eighteenth century they were larger than most English cities. Boston, which reached seventeen thousand in 1740, was at that time the largest, but it had already begun a decline that lasted for the rest of the colonial period. In the seventeenth century it had served as the shipping center for most of the mainland colonies, and it continued to serve as New England's major port. But other New England towns were cutting into its business, most notably Newport, which grew to urban dimensions in the eighteenth century.

New York City was the natural outlet and supply point for farmers in the Hudson Valley and adjoining regions of Connecticut and New Jersey; Philadelphia served not only Pennsylvania and the Delaware Valley and Bay but also the Southern back country. From the Carolinas, Virginia, and Maryland, farmers drove their wagons and cattle north along the great Appalachian valleys to the Philadelphia market. Although Baltimore began to drain off some of this trade after about 1750, Philadelphia continued to grow so rapidly that by the 1770s, with thirty-five thousand people, it ranked after London with Bristol and Liverpool as one of the largest cities in the English-speaking world. South of Baltimore the tobacco-planters dealt directly with London and needed no cities; but in South Carolina the rice- and indigo-planters shipped their produce by way of Charles Town, as did the Indian traders who trekked around the southern limit of the Appalachians and brought deerskins from the lower Mississippi Valley.

| ESTIMATED POPULATION OF COLONIAL URBAN CENTERS IN THE 1770s* | | | |
|---|---|---|---|
| Primary Colonial Cities | | Secondary Colonial Cities | |
| Philadelphia | 35,000 | New Haven | 8,000 |
| New York | 25,000 | Norwich | 7,000 |
| Boston | 16,000 | Norfolk | 6,000 |
| Charles Town | 12,000 | Baltimore | 6,000 |
| Newport | 11,000 | New London | 5,000 |
| | | Salem, Mass. | 5,000 |
| | | Lancaster, Pa. | 5,000 |
| | | Hartford | 5,000 |
| | | Middletown | 5,000 |
| | | Portsmouth | 5,000 |
| | | Marblehead | 4,000 |
| | | Providence | 4,000 |
| | | Albany | 4,000 |
| | | Annapolis | 4,000 |
| | | Savannah | 3,000 |

*Figures rounded to the nearest thousand.
Figures found in tables on pages 216–17 of *Cities in Revolt* by Carl Bridenbaugh. Copyright © 1955 by Carl Bridenbaugh. Figure for Philadelphia revised. Used with permission of Alfred A. Knopf, Inc.

*Patterns of existence*

Overseas trade gave city-dwellers and planta-taion-owners communication with the larger world that was denied to most other Americans, and for that matter to most Englishmen and Europeans. Boston and Philadelphia, with hundreds of ships coming and going, were in closer contact with London than many English cities were. The ships carried ideas as well as goods, and colonial cities were as well equipped to distribute one as the other. Every city had at least one newspaper by the middle of the eighteenth century, with every issue devoted largely to news from England and Europe. Through the columns of the newspapers and through the books imported from abroad and sometimes reprinted locally, the city dweller kept up with the times. Although the cities held less than 5 percent of the colonial population, it was the best-informed and most-influential 5 percent.

# The emerging American mind

Before the middle of the eighteenth century, Americans had little occasion to think of themselves as a distinct people. They had no opportunity at all to act as one. There was no American government, no single political organization in which all the colonies joined to manage their common concerns. There was not even a wish for such an organization except among a few eccentric individuals. America, to the people who lived in it, was still a geographical region, not a frame of mind.

Asked for his nationality, the average American in 1750 would have said English or British. In spite of substantial numbers of Dutch, Germans, and Scotch-Irish, Englishmen and English institutions prevailed in every colony, and most colonists spoke of England as home even though they had never been there. Yet none of their institutions was quite like its English counterpart; the heritage of English ideas that went with the institutions was so rich and varied that Americans were able to select and develop those that best suited their situation and forget others that meanwhile were growing prominent in the mother country. Some of the differences were local: the New England town, for example, and the Puritanism that went with it, set New Englanders off not only from Englishmen but from Virginians. But some ideas, in-stitutions, and attitudes became common in all the colonies and remained uncommon in England. Al-though American Englishmen were not yet aware that they shared these "Americanisms" with one another or that Englishmen at home did not share them, many of the characteristic ideas and attitudes that later distinguished American nationalism were already present by mid-century.

***Responsible representative government.*** Eng-lishmen brought with them to the New World the political ideas that still give English and American government a close resemblance. But Americans very early developed conceptions of representative govern-ment that differed from those prevailing in England during the colonial period. Representative govern-ment in England originated in the Middle Ages, when the king called for men to advise him. They were chosen by their neighbors and informed the king of his subjects' wishes. Eventually their advice became so compelling that the king could not reject it, and the representatives of the people, organized as the House of Commons, became the most powerful branch of the English government.

At first the House of Commons consisted of rep-resentatives from each county, or shire, and from selected boroughs. Over the centuries many of these boroughs became ghost towns with only a handful of inhabitants, and great towns sprang up where none had existed before. Yet the old boroughs continued to send members to Parliament, and the new towns sent none. Moreover, only a fraction of the English popu-lation could participate even in the county elections. In order to vote, a man had to own property that would, if rented, yield him at least 40 shillings yearly. Few could meet the test. A number of Englishmen thought the situation absurd and said so. But nothing was done to improve it; in fact, a theory was devised to justify it. A member of the House of Commons, it was said, represented not the people who chose him, but the whole country, and he was not responsible to any particular constituency. Not all Englishmen could vote for representatives, but all were "virtually" repre-sented by every member of the Commons.

Colonial assemblies were far more representative than the House of Commons. Although every colony had property qualifications for voting, probably the great majority of adult white males owned enough land to meet them. In apportioning representation, New England colonies gave every town the right to send delegates to the assembly. Outside New England, the unit of representation was usually the county. The political organization of new counties and the extension of representation seldom kept pace with the rapid advance of settlement westward, but nowhere was representation so uneven or irrational as in Eng-land.

The American colonist knew nothing of "vir-tual" representation; to him, representation was a means of acquainting the government with his needs and demands and with the amount and method of taxation he could most easily bear. A colonial assemblyman was supposed to be the agent of the people who chose him. In the large counties, of course, it was seldom possible, except on election day, for voters to gather in one place and express their opinions. But elections came every two or three years (annually in New England and Pennsylvania), and a representative was unlikely to stray far from his constituents' wishes in so short a time. In New England, where town meetings could be called any time, people often gathered to tell their delegate how to vote on a particular issue. He was supposed to look after their interests first, those of the colony second.

In America, therefore, representative government meant something different from what it did in England. Government existed to do a job, and it had to be kept responsible to its employers. While "virtual" representatives in Parliament created offices whose only purpose was to enrich the men who filled them, colonial assemblymen, watched closely by their constituents, had comparatively little opportunity to dip into the public purse.

**Clergy and laity.** Americans looked on their clergymen as they did on their elected representatives. They wanted the clergy to serve, not rule, them. The attitude had its roots in the English Reformation, and most Englishmen were sufficiently Protestant to share it in some degree; English Dissenters shared it wholeheartedly. But the Anglican Church held great powers in England: it was the only church supported by state taxation; during much of the colonial period only its members could hold public office; and its bishops enjoyed an authority that reached far beyond the realm of the spirit. As ex officio members of the House of Lords they voted on every act of Parliament, and as presiding judges in courts with jurisdiction over probate of wills and breaches of morality they could impose sentence of excommunication on offenders. Since excommunication cut a man off from political rights and from intercourse with his neighbors, it could mean economic ruin as well as social ostracism. An offender could get the sentence lifted only by paying a heavy fee.

In the colonies, churchmen had no such powers. Except in Rhode Island, Delaware, Pennsylvania, and New Jersey, the assemblies did levy taxes in support of churches, favoring the Congregational churches in New England, the Anglican elsewhere. But this was the only connection between church and state that most Americans would tolerate. The Massachusetts rule that only church members could vote had ended with the revocation of the colony's charter in 1684.

In New England, the old Puritan hostility to clerical authority persisted into the eighteenth century. Ministers were influential and highly respected; a few were even elected as representatives to colonial as-

Baptismal in Pennsylvania

semblies. But no minister enjoyed temporal authority by virtue of being a minister.

The Anglicans in America also kept their clergymen on short leash. Because England never sent a bishop to the colonies (and without a bishop there could be no ecclesiastical court), the Anglican Church lost most of its temporal powers when it was transplanted to America. In the Northern colonies, Anglicans, who were a small minority of the population, repeatedly asked for a bishop—much to the annoyance of Congregationalists and Presbyterians. In the Southern colonies, where the Anglican Church was the established church, its members were cool to the proposal. The Southerners, acting through their vestries, ran their churches and hired and fired their ministers almost as independently as any New England Puritan congregation. The minister, unless he had been formally inducted into office (a ceremony performed by the governor at the request of the vestry), could be dismissed at any time. With no bishop at hand to insist on induction, a church could simply omit the ceremony.

Probably one reason for the failure of the Anglican Church to send a bishop was the fear of resistance from non-Anglicans, who multiplied rapidly during the eighteenth century. Besides Congregationalists and Presbyterians, there were Baptists, Quakers, Dutch Reformed, Lutherans, Mennonites, and a host of minor sects. This diversity of religious groups, each growing as population grew, made it increasingly difficult for any one of them to dominate the rest and made the extension of religious authority in America ever more unlikely. Even in New England, where the Congregationalists remained a majority, they ceased after the seventeenth century to persecute Quakers and allowed persons of all denominations to support their own ministers through public taxation.

63

*The emerging American mind*

*Now it pleased God to send Mr. Whitefield into this land ... I longed to see and hear him, and wished he would come this way ... then on a Sudden, in the morning about 8 or 9 of the Clock there came a messenger and said Mr. Whitefield preached at Hartford and Weathersfield yesterday and is to preach at Middletown this morning at ten of the Clock, I was in my field at Work, I ... ran home to my wife telling her to make ready quickly to go and hear Mr. Whitefield preach at Middletown, then run to my pasture for my horse with all my might.... when we came within about half a mile or a mile of the Road that comes down from Hartford Weathersfield and Stepney to Middletown; on high land I saw before me a Cloud or fogg rising; I first thought it came from the great River, but as I came nearer the Road, I heard a noise something like a low rumbling thunder and presently found it was the noise of Horses feet coming down the Road and this Cloud was a Cloud of dust made by the Horses feet; it arose some Rods into the air over the tops of Hills and trees and when I came within about 20 rods of the Road, I could see men and horses Sliping along in the Cloud like shadows and as I drew nearer it seemed like a steady Stream of horses and their riders, scarcely a horse more than his length behind another, all of a Lather and foam with sweat, their breath rolling out of their nostrils every Jump; every horse seemed to go with all his might to carry his rider to hear news from heaven for the saving of Souls, it made me tremble to see the Sight, how the world was in a Struggle ... and when we got to Middletown old meeting house there was a great Multitude it was said to be 3 or 4000 of people Assembled together.... When I saw Mr. Whitefield come upon the Scaffold he lookt almost Angelical; a young, Slim, slender youth before some thousands of people with a bold undaunted Countenance, and my hearing how God was with him every where as he came along it Solemnized my mind; and put me into a trembling fear before he began to preach; for he looked as if he was Cloathed with Authority from the Great God; and a sweet sollome solemnity sat upon his brow And my hearing him preach, gave me a heart wound; By Gods blessing: my old Foundation was broken up, and I saw that my righteousness would not save me.*

**From Nathan Cole, "Spiritual Travels," October 23, 1740.**

***The Great Awakening.*** In the 1740s the number of religious groups was expanded by a rash of schisms that followed a religious revival. The Great Awakening was touched off in 1740 by a traveling English preacher who combined Calvinism and showmanship. George Whitefield, only twenty-seven at the time, was no theologian. But he had perfected a technique of preaching that brought remarkable results: he frightened his audience by depicting in vivid detail the pain awaiting sinners in Hell. He dramatized the scene for them, playing all the parts himself. Now he was an angry God booming out fearful judgments, now a damned soul weeping in anguish. He strained to bring his audience to the point of hysterical despair. He wanted them to writhe in agony, for he had found that thorough "conviction"—of their own sinfulness, helplessness, and utter dependence on Christ for salvation—was usually followed by "conversion," the feeling that they actually had been saved. As Whitefield journeyed from the Carolinas to New England, preaching indoors and out, Sundays and weekdays, he wrought conversions by the hundreds, among old and young, rich and poor, educated and ignorant.

His technique, requiring only a flair for the dramatic, was not hard to imitate. In his wake other self-appointed messengers of Christ traveled about the country, outdoing him in the sound and fury of their preaching. Gilbert Tennent, a Pennsylvania Presbyterian, made a specialty of laughing loud and long at sinners in the throes of conviction. James Davenport, an itinerant Congregationalist, was at his best at night, when smoking torches revealed him half naked, jumping up and down to stamp on the devil.

In spite of these excesses, the Awakening brought religious experiences to thousands of people in every rank of society. One of its staunchest defenders was Jonathan Edwards, minister of Northampton, Massachusetts, who had himself inspired a local revival in 1735. Edwards was the most talented theologian

The Question is, whether it be'nt a plain, stubborn Fact, that the Passions have, generally, in these Times, been apply'd to, as though the main Thing in Religion was to throw them into Disturbance? Can it be denied, that the Preachers, who have been the Instruments of the Commotions in the Land, have endeavoured, by all Manner of Arts, and in all Manner of Ways, to raise the Passions of their Hearers to such a Height, as really to unfit them, for the present, for the Exercise of their reasonable Powers? Nay, in order to alarm Men's Fears, has it not been common, among some Sort of Preachers, to speak and act after such a wild Manner, as is adapted to affrighten People out of their Wits, rather than possess their Minds of such a Conviction of Truth, as is proper to Men, who are endow'd with Reason and Understanding? And under the Notion of speaking to the Affections, were the Things of God and another World ever preached with more Confusion of Thought; with greater Incoherence; with the undue Mixture of more rash, crude, unguarded Expressions; or with Conceit to a higher Degree, appearing in fulsome Self-Applauses, as well as unheard of Contempt of others? These are Things of too publick a Nature to be denied: They have been too often practised, and in Places of too great Concourse, to admit of Debate.

From Charles Chauncy, *Seasonable Thoughts on the State of Religion in New England*, 1743.

**The Great Awakening: Old Light skepticism**

America ever produced. He preached a stricter Calvinism than New England had ever heard, and he recast Calvinist doctrines to give a primary place to the emotions. Although his own manner in the pulpit was an austere contrast to Whitefield's, his doctrines emphasized the emotional impact of an omnipotent God on impotent man. Both conviction and conversion, Edwards insisted, were such overwhelming emotional experiences that the human frame could scarcely contain them. If occasionally someone fell to the ground or cried out in the grip of such powerful experiences, this was no reason to doubt that the spirit of God was the moving cause. Edwards' theology commanded respect in Europe as well as America and furnished the Awakening with an intellectual foundation that Whitefield could not have provided.

But not everyone agreed with Edwards. Many ministers thought that the new method of preaching provoked more hysteria than holiness. They were shocked by the sight of masses of people wallowing in terror or ecstasy on the cue of an ignorant man screaming damnation. They were offended when itinerants entered their churches unbidden and wrung from a hitherto sane congregation a chorus of shrieks and groans and hallelujahs. After listening to an itinerant preacher, people sometimes decided their own minister was worthless, and the most enthusiastic followers of the Awakening deserted their old churches to form new ones with more rigorous doctrines and standards of admission.

Once the shrieking had subsided, it became apparent that the Awakening had seriously undermined the position of the clergy. In every denomination, but especially in the Calvinist ones, ministers had been forced to take sides in favor of the revival (New Light) or against it (Old Light). And those who opposed it were not reconciled by the less exuberant expressions of piety that followed the initial madness. "Nay han't it been common," asked the Boston minister Charles Chauncy, "in some Parts of the Land, and among some Sorts of People, to express their religious Joy, by singing through the Streets, and in Ferry Boats?" The Old Lights, having set themselves against emotional "enthusiasm," prided themselves on a cool rationality. In this mood they reexamined Calvinist dogma and found it wanting. It was absurd, Chauncy decided, that men should suffer eternally by divine predestination: a rational God would allow some merit in human effort. The Old Lights took the road that led ultimately to Unitarianism, Universalism, and deism, to a world in which there was little need either for Christ or for clergymen. Not many Americans went the whole length of that road in the eighteenth century, but many of the best educated traveled it for some distance.

The New Lights undermined the position of the clergy in a more direct manner by teaching congregations to be bold in judging ministers. Itinerant preachers often pronounced local ministers unregenerate and made much of the idea that a minister could not be God's instrument in bringing salvation to others unless he himself was saved. With this principle in mind, the New Lights in a church did not hesitate to interrogate the minister and then declare

*The emerging American mind*

him saved or damned. The minister's learning, which had once won him respect, suddenly became a handicap, for many itinerants, uneducated and uneducable, dismissed religious erudition as an impediment to saving grace.

Ironically, in the decades that followed the Great Awakening, the New Light clergy of New England involved themselves so deeply in learned pursuit of Edwards' Calvinist theology that they in turn alienated their congregations. Edwards was not easily understood at best, but his disciples drew out his doctrines in subtle elaborations that scarcely anyone understood but themselves. The New Divinity it was called, and among many bright young men of the day it became the prevailing intellectual fashion. Entering the ministry, they uttered its complexities in sermons addressed more to one another than to their audience. The passionate preaching of the Awakening was forgotten, and the New Divinity grew into a recondite game for clergymen.

Congregations reacted with the boldness they had been taught by deserting the preachers who seemed to have deserted them. By the third quarter of the eighteenth century the diversity of denominations allowed a man to shop around for a preacher and a religion that suited him. An American minister was expected to serve his people. When they thought he was failing to do so, they dismissed him or left him.

**Education.** If the American colonist stood in no awe of his ministers and government officials, it was because the workings of state and church held no mysteries for him. He understood them better than the average European, not only because he had a large share in operating them but because he was better educated. Europeans were fond of picturing Americans as children of nature who learned wisdom from the trees and flowers but not from books. Actually, in spite of their wilderness life, or perhaps because of it, colonial Americans were a bookish lot.

Most of them were Protestants, and Protestants believed that religious truth was incomprehensible to those who did not read the Scriptures. They wanted to read; they wanted their children to read. And their desire was sharpened by the sight of the real children of nature, the Indians, naked, savage, and ignorant. In Massachusetts the law directed every town of fifty families to maintain a schoolmaster and every town of one hundred families to maintain one who could teach Greek and Latin. Other New England colonies had similar requirements. The laws were not always enforced, but the rate of literacy in New England exceeded that of England from the beginning and rose rapidly in the eighteenth century until nearly all adult males could read and write. Other colonial regions lagged behind but remained ahead of the estimated 50 percent literacy rate among adult males in England.

By the middle of the eighteenth century, nearly every colony had at least one printing press, and the printer usually produced a weekly newspaper, devoted mainly to news from abroad and from other colonies—everybody knew the local news—and to literary and political essays and verse, much of which was culled from English newspapers. The printers also turned out broadsides, almanacs, pamphlets, and books. Though the clergy were the most prolific colonial authors and sermons the most popular reading matter, local political issues were often discussed in print. There were even some efforts at verse. The best of these, the meditative poems of Edward Taylor, minister of Westfield, Massachusetts, were not published until the present century, but colonial readers bought another minister's versified account of the Last Judgment (*The Day of Doom* by Michael Wigglesworth) in such numbers that it went through five editions between 1662 and 1701.

The colonists made early provision for higher education. In 1636, only six years after the Puritans came to Massachusetts, they founded the college that later took the name of its first benefactor, John Harvard. Although the founders' purpose was to furnish the colony with a learned ministry, Harvard was no mere theological seminary. From the beginning, its students followed the traditional curriculum of the liberal arts taught in European universities: they studied grammar (Latin, Greek, and Hebrew), rhetoric, logic, mathematics, astronomy, physics, metaphysics, and moral philosophy. Only once a week, on Saturdays, did they turn to theology. Those who intended to become ministers received their professional training after they graduated, not before. But many Harvard graduates, the majority after the seventeenth century, went into professions other than the ministry.

The same was true of most other colonial colleges: William and Mary, chartered in 1693, remained for some years little more than a grammar school, but Yale (1701) offered a program similar to Harvard's, and so did Princeton (1746), Rutgers (1766), Pennsylvania (1755), Columbia (1754), and Brown (1764). It was not simply the children of the well-to-do who attended these colleges. Tuition rates were low, and every class contained boys fresh from the farm. Education even at the college level was widely diffused by comparison with that of England.

The fact that New Englanders fell victim to hysteria over witchcraft has often been cited as evidence of the shallowness of their education. How could educated people be so superstitious? The answer is that educated people everywhere believed in witchcraft. In 1692 twenty persons were hanged as witches in Massachusetts, and hundreds more had been accused when the ministers' objections to the unfairness of the trials induced the government to stop them. No subsequent execution for witchcraft is recorded in America, but in Europe thousands were executed in the seventeenth century, and the executions continued into the eighteenth.

**The Enlightenment.** The ideas that conquered man's belief in witchcraft were originated, not by Americans, but by a succession of Europeans who had the imagination and daring to take the measure of God's world for themselves. During the sixteenth and seventeenth centuries, Copernicus, Galileo, and Kepler had studied the motions of the planets and accumulated evidence to show that they rotated around the sun. Sir Isaac Newton, building on their work, discovered the laws of motion, the "natural laws" by which God governed the movement of the planets. He also studied light and learned to break it into its different colors and to bend it with mirrors and lenses. Newton's success convinced his contemporaries that human reason was capable of exploring the universe and of ascertaining by observation and experiment the principles by which God governed it. Men who had been taught that reason was a feeble instrument, all but destroyed by Adam's original sin, now turned inquiring eyes on the world around them. They wanted to measure everything, to see how the world worked.

In looking so closely at God's world, men formed a new image of God himself. Where he had formerly been an arbitrary monarch, who glorified himself in the damnation of sinners and the salvation of saints, he now became a divine craftsman whose glory lay in his craftsmanship, a celestial watchmaker whose intricate and orderly handiwork lay everywhere visible to the eyes that reason directed toward it. The new God appeared more reasonable than the old, but also more remote and indifferent, a watchmaker who wound up his universe and then left it to run itself. He seemed, in fact, so reasonable that some men decided he was reason itself, or at least that reason was an adequate substitute for him.

Though few went this far, the eighteenth century earned the title of the Age of Reason. And the English philosopher John Locke furnished the century with a theory about reason that gradually won acceptance and further encouraged the pursuit of experiment and observation. In *An Essay concerning Human Understanding* (1690) Locke concluded that the human mind at birth was not the repository of any innate ideas placed there by the Creator. Rather, it was a complete blank and only gradually accumulated knowledge from the experiences of the five senses attached to it. He who would grow in knowledge, therefore, must devote himself not simply to books,

perhaps not even to the Bible, nor to abstract contemplation, but to seeing, hearing, feeling, tasting—in a word, to observation and experiment.

Man himself was a fair subject for scrutiny, and Locke turned his attention to the relations of men to one another. He decided that God had provided natural laws to make the human world run as smoothly as the physical world; but the enforcement of these natural laws of society God had left to men. In two treatises on civil government (published in 1689 and 1690 but written earlier) Locke explained that men had voluntarily left the free state of nature (in which they were born and originally lived) and had, by mutual agreement, instituted civil government for the purpose of enforcing natural laws. The most important natural law was that no man should take away the life, liberty, or property of another (these were "natural rights" of man). A government that failed to protect life, liberty, and property lost its reason for existence and deserved to be altered or overthrown by the people it governed.

Reason led Locke to condemn absolute government, whether in church or state. It led others to advocate free trade, free speech, free thought. Together, Locke and Newton gave men confidence that all the world's evils as well as its mysteries would yield to the persistent application of human reason.

This confidence in reason, which animated the European philosophers of the eighteenth century, came to be known as the Enlightenment. Although the Enlightenment originated in Europe, its doctrines penetrated society more widely in America. Students in American colleges learned Newton's physics and Locke's psychology. Ministers, whether Old Light or New, adapted their theology to the new ideas and welcomed the discoveries of reason as an aid to revelation, a means to improve their understanding of God's creation. Politicians cited Locke to support their arguments. Gentlemen formed clubs to discuss philosophy. Men awakened to the newness of the New World and turned amateur scientists; they described American plants and animals and made astronomical observations of the American skies to swell the growing body of scientific information that might provide answers to the limitless questions reason could now ask. In Boston the Reverend Cotton Mather and Dr. Zabdiel Boylston demonstrated by experiment the efficacy of inoculation against smallpox. In Philadelphia David Rittenhouse built the first American orrery, a mechanical model that reproduced the motions of the solar system.

Even the common man, who never himself read Locke or Newton, was receptive to their philosophy. To the European peasant, following the footsteps of his ancestors, unable to read or write, with no voice in church or state, the Enlightenment meant little. But

*The emerging American mind*

the ordinary American colonist had constantly to apply his reason to new situations, whether in field or forest, church or state. The Enlightenment made a virtue of his necessity and encouraged him to lift his voice against unreasonableness wherever he met it.

It is perhaps no accident that the man who best exemplified the Enlightenment both to his countrymen and to foreigners was not only an American but an American who came from the ranks of common men and never lost touch with them. Benjamin Franklin (1706–90) was born in Boston, made his fortune in Philadelphia, and then spent much of the remainder of his life in England and France on political missions for the American people. His genius brought him success in everything he tried, whether it was running a Philadelphia newspaper in his youth or wooing the ladies of Paris in his old age. The Enlightenment sang the praises of intellectual freedom; Franklin as a printer defended his right to publish what he pleased. The Enlightenment called for freedom of trade; Franklin worked as a diplomat to achieve that freedom. The Enlightenment encouraged scientific experiment. Franklin made significant observations on a wide variety of scientific subjects (from ocean currents to the theory of heat); he was a prolific inventor (a stove, a clock, a musical instrument); and, as one of the first experimenters with electricity, he made important contributions to both the theory of the subject (positive and negative current) and to its application (lightning rods).

As a son of the Enlightenment, Franklin was at home anywhere in the world, yet everywhere men recognized him as a typical American. Even without the fur cap he wore to emphasize it, no one could miss his American style, his down-to-earth insistence on doing things his own way and finding out for himself. Franklin's insistence on results in everything he undertook accorded with his countrymen's insistence that their governments and churches perform what was expected of them.

**Social structure.** In describing America for Europeans, Franklin advised no one to go there unless he had more to recommend him than high birth, for Americans, he said, "do not inquire concerning a Stranger, *What is he?* but, *What can he do?*" Franklin wrote these words after the period we are considering—probably in 1782. But by mid-century it had already become clear that high birth meant less in America than in Europe.

Europeans learned at an early age that God made men unequal. To some he gave riches beyond measure, to others nothing. Riches brought dignity. It might take more than one generation for a wealthy family to climb to the top of the social ladder, but once there its members enjoyed the security of a title—count, duke, earl, marquis—that passed in perpetuity from father to son. In Europe, men of title generally had a voice in government. In England, even though the House of Commons became the dominant branch of Parliament its members were drawn from the higher ranks of English society, and they could still pass no law without the consent of the highest ranks, assembled in the House of Lords.

Although the eighteenth-century American was taught that God assigned men to different ranks in society, the idea did not have quite the same meaning as in Europe. The American could see plainly that merchants and planters had more wealth and dignity than other men. And in the older settlements, by the middle of the eighteenth century, a larger share of the wealth was concentrated in the hands of a few than had been the case in the seventeenth century. But America was still the land of opportunity; with hard work and luck a humble man could better himself. The top of the social ladder was lower than in Europe and easier to reach but at the same time more difficult to hang on to. Mobility, not nobility, determined the ranks of American aristocrats, who had no titles and no place of their own in the government. They were always having to make room at the top for new arrivals; and, if they wanted to gain and keep the power that came naturally to their European counterparts, they had continually to please other people. American voters commonly recognized the socially and economically successful by electing them to representative assemblies, and governors commonly selected the most successful for seats on the council. But the voters would drop a man who did not suit them as quickly as the governor would. No one could claim a place in the government simply by virtue of his birth or social position.

If the highest born had fewer rights in America than in England, so did the lowest born. No Englishman was born a slave. And though the slave born on a tobacco plantation might have the kind of security enjoyed by a fine horse, though he might live longer than the slave on a sugar plantation in the West Indies, he had virtually none of the rights that Englishmen had attained for themselves over the centuries. By the end of the colonial period 20 percent of the colonial population was in this position. Slaves probably constituted a majority of the labor force, of persons, that is, who worked for another man rather than for themselves. And they had no hope of becoming anything else. Nobody asked either "What are they?" or "What can they do?" Everybody knew.

With so much of the labor force enslaved, the remainder of the American population was far better off than the bulk of the English or European population. A small proportion, perhaps 6 or 7 percent of the total adult males, were artisans or laborers of one sort or another who spent their lives working for other men. Most worked for themselves on land of their own. The average American, neither slave nor slave owner, enjoyed the economic and political independence that everyone in the eighteenth century associated with the ownership of land. If there was not enough land where he was born and raised, a man could find more a little farther west. Standing on his own ground, raising his own food, he could bid defiance to landlords, merchants, and politicians alike. Moreover, he was likely to have in hand an instrument of defiance with which few European peasants were familiar—a gun. It was not safe to push him very hard.

In a number of ways, then, the eighteenth-century American differed from the Englishman or the European. Unless he was a slave, he was better educated and therefore less in awe of his superiors, who were in any case not far above him. He had more control over his government and over his clergymen. He had a greater opportunity to mold his own life. He used whatever tools might serve him to do it, whether ax, plow, musket, or vote; and he got results, from governments as well as from forest and field. He did not yet know it, but he was becoming a new kind of man.

# The contest for the continent

America was the spearhead of European growth. The European population did not begin its own spectacular growth until after the middle of the eighteenth century. Meanwhile, Europe grew in America, where population doubled every twenty-five years.

American ways of living together had been designed for growth: the plantation with its reserve of unused and uncleared land, the New England town with its undivided commons, the farm surrounded by forest. But population rapidly outgrew existing communities, and Americans thrust steadily westward until they came up against other peoples who were uninterested in sharing American ways of living together. Indians, Frenchmen, and Spaniards preferred their own ways, and the contest with these rivals for the continent was one of the persistent facts of life for colonial Americans.

**Indian warfare.** The Indians of eastern North America were slow to perceive that their way of life was incompatible with that of the English. They often

| UNITED STATES POPULATION GROWTH, 1620–1860* | | | |
|---|---|---|---|
| 1620 | 2,000 | 1750 | 1,171,000 |
| 1630 | 5,000 | 1760 | 1,594,000 |
| 1640 | 27,000 | 1770 | 2,148,000 |
| 1650 | 50,000 | 1780 | 2,780,000 |
| 1660 | 75,000 | 1790 | 3,929,000 |
| 1670 | 112,000 | 1800 | 5,297,000 |
| 1680 | 152,000 | 1810 | 7,224,000 |
| 1690 | 210,000 | 1820 | 9,618,000 |
| 1700 | 251,000 | 1830 | 12,901,000 |
| 1710 | 332,000 | 1840 | 17,120,000 |
| 1720 | 466,000 | 1850 | 23,261,000 |
| 1730 | 629,000 | 1860 | 31,513,000 |
| 1740 | 906,000 | | |

*Figures rounded to the nearest thousand.
From *Historical Statistics of the United States: Colonial Times to 1957*, Series A 1–3, Z 1–19.

sold their land or gave it away without realizing that it would no longer be theirs too. They used the land mainly for hunting and were willing to let the English hunt on it with them. But Englishmen taking possession cut the trees, drove out the game, and evicted the Indians. Before the Indians realized what was happening, they were outnumbered.

They could probably have done nothing to stem the English advance anyhow. They were many peoples, not one, and they made war on one another as often as they did on the white invaders. Indeed, they often welcomed the white man for the assistance they hoped he would offer in quarrels with their neighbors. But, except when directed and organized by the French or Spanish, they were not formidable military opponents for the English. Superior woodsmanship gave them some advantage, especially when they were armed with the white man's weapons, and they posed a constant threat to the isolated frontier farmer. But they were too independent, too incorrigibly individualistic, to submit for long to military discipline. They might gather for a surprise assault, but they could not stick together long enough to take advantage of their success.

The colonists, if not more warlike, were better armed, better organized, and more systematic about

The extension of settlement, 1660–1760

| | Settled by 1660 |
| | Settled by 1700 |
| | Settled by 1760 |

killing. Indians of the Powhatan Confederacy in Virginia massacred 347 settlers in a surprise attack in 1622 (Indian victories in American history are generally known as massacres), but from that time on the Virginians pursued a policy of extermination that gradually eliminated the Indian menace in the tidewater area. In 1637 the Puritans, acting in support of a group of tribes, broke the power of the one most dangerous New England tribe, the Pequots. An army led by John Mason surprised their main village at night, set fire to it, and shot men, women, and children as they ran to escape the flames. Thereafter New England suffered no serious Indian attack until 1676, when the Wampanoag chieftain Philip undertook a war that lasted longer than usual but ended with the usual result.

**Rivalry with France and Spain.** After 1676 the surviving Indians east of the Appalachians were too few in number to menace the English settlers. But those farther west, led by the French, stood ready to halt English expansion at the mountains. Frenchmen in Canada, from the time of Champlain's founding of Quebec in 1608, had taken an acquisitive interest in the interior of North America. Missionaries in search of souls and *coureurs de bois* in search of furs traveled up and down the Mississippi and through the wilderness of its eastern tributaries. The *coureurs* were as good woodsmen as the Indians and as casual with their lives as the old English sea dogs. One of them, Louis Jolliet, together with the Jesuit Father Marquette, descended the Mississippi to the Arkansas as early as 1673. Robert Cavelier, Sieur de la Salle, reached the mouth of the Mississippi in 1682, and seventeen years later the French took possession of Louisiana by planting a settlement at Biloxi. In 1702 they started another one at Mobile. They also set up forts and trading posts in the Illinois country at Kaskaskia, Cahokia, and Vincennes, way stations between the St. Lawrence and the Mississippi, the two main arteries into the heart of North America.

In the competition for Indian furs, the French worked under a handicap, because French craftsmen could not supply as cheaply as the English did the textiles and hardware that the Indians demanded in exchange. But, in spite of the better bargains offered by the English, the Frenchman did a better job of winning the Indians' friendship. Instead of evicting them from their land, he lived in their wigwams, married their daughters, and taught them to like Catholicism and hate the English.

The French government during the seventeenth century did not appreciate the exploits of its wandering subjects. In 1663 the king had taken New France from a French trading company, and thereafter the colony was governed by royal decrees (executed

Major Indian tribes in the East

along the St. Lawrence River, and later in Louisiana and in the Illinois country. Immigrants were few, and the total population remained small, no more than fifty or sixty thousand by the middle of the eighteenth century.

Fifty thousand Frenchmen proved formidable to a million and a half Englishmen only because Louis' governors in Canada had not enforced his decrees. Count Frontenac (who governed during most of the period from 1672 to 1698) perceived the strategic importance of what the *coureurs* were doing and disregarded instructions to halt them. Whenever France went to war with England, the *coureurs* led their Indian friends in raids on outlying English settlements in New England and New York. The English protected themselves by an uneasy alliance with the Iroquois. The Iroquois controlled the Mohawk Valley, which, in combination with the Hudson Valley, Lake George, and Lake Champlain, was the only easy invasion route through the mountains that stretched from New England to the Carolinas.

From 1689 to 1713 warfare between England and France was almost continuous, in the War of the League of Augsburg (1689–97) and the War of the Spanish Succession (1702–13), known in the colonies as King William's War and Queen Anne's War. At this time neither France nor England considered America worth the expenditure of royal troops. But the settlers, aware of how much was at stake, carried on their own warfare. The French sent their Indians to raid Schenectady and Deerfield and the thinly populated villages in Maine. The New Englanders in turn captured Port Royal in Nova Scotia in 1690, saw it returned to France at the Peace of Ryswick in 1697, and recaptured it in 1710. The Treaty of Utrecht in 1713, besides recognizing England's claim to Hudson Bay, gave England Nova Scotia with its population of more than a thousand French farmers; it left Cape Breton Island, unpopulated but strategically located at the mouth of the St. Lawrence, to the French.

In the South, where the Appalachian barrier ended, both sides had carried on their warfare largely through Indians. South Carolina fur-traders rivaled the French in their skillful handling of Indian tribes. Ranging as far as the Mississippi in search of deerskins, they gradually gained the allegiance of the Yamasee and of most of the tribes forming the great Creek Confederacy of the Southeast. With Indian assistance they pushed back the Spaniards in Florida and threatened the French in Louisiana. Two years after Queen Anne's War ended, however, the Creeks and Yamasee turned and attacked their English allies. But for the loyalty of the Cherokee, South Carolina might have suffered disaster.

After their assault failed, the Creeks moved westward and the Yamasee southward. Spain had always

through a governor and an intendant, with no representative assembly). The king consistently discouraged the activities of the *coureurs*. He rejected, for example, the scheme of two *coureurs*, Pierre Radisson and Médart Chouart, Sieur de Groseilliers, who proposed a trading company to reach the northern fur supply by sea instead of by land; as a result, in 1672 they formed the Hudson's Bay Company in England instead of France.

Louis XIV was not interested in the wastes of Hudson Bay. Guided by his great minister Colbert, he wanted New France to be populated with hard-working, docile farmers. He sent women to entice the wild *coureurs* into a more settled life; he placed a bounty on large families. He forbade all but a few privileged individuals to engage in the fur trade. He even enlisted the Church in the cause: men who left their farms without permission were liable to excommunication. But all Louis' efforts produced only a meager scattering of agricultural settlements in Nova Scotia,

*The contest for the continent*

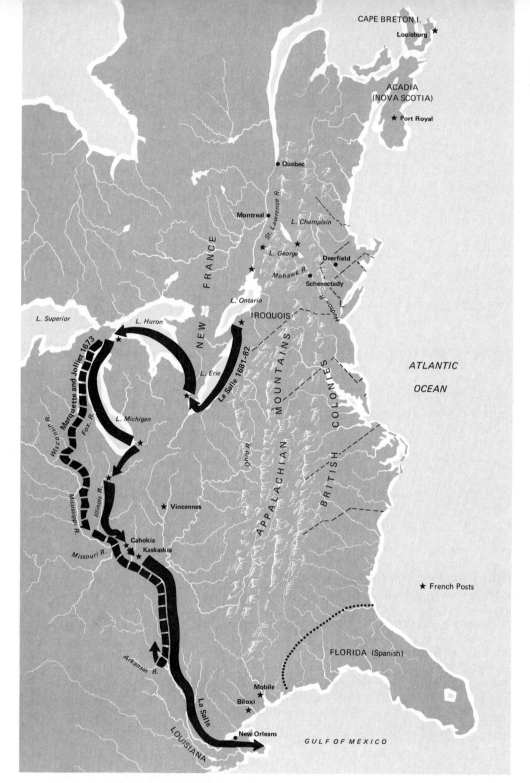

French penetration
of North America

CAPE BRETON I.

★ Louisburg

ACADIA
(NOVA SCOTIA)

★ Port Royal

● Quebec

Montreal ●

St. Lawrence R.

L. Champlain

N E W   F R A N C E

★  L. George

Mohawk R.

Deerfield

Schenectady

L. Ontario

IROQUOIS ★

L. Superior

L. Huron

L. Erie

La Salle 1681-82

Hudson R.

ATLANTIC

OCEAN

Wisconsin R.

Marquette and Joliet 1673

Fox R.

L. Michigan

Ohio R.

A P P A L A C H I A N   M O U N T A I N S

B R I T I S H   C O L O N I E S

Mississippi R.

Illinois R.

★ Vincennes

Cahokia ★

Kaskaskia

Missouri R.

★ French Posts

Arkansas R.

La Salle

FLORIDA (Spanish)

LOUISIANA

Mobile ★

Biloxi ★

New Orleans ★

GULF OF MEXICO

claimed the area they vacated and now threatened to recover it. When England's countermove, the planting of Fort King George on the Altamaha River in 1721, proved ineffective, the English turned to a more familiar method of holding the territory. Forts and missions and Indian diplomacy were a Spanish and French specialty. The English way of occupying America had always been to live in it. English settlers had striven not so much to exploit the Indians as to displace them entirely. And in 1732 Englishmen prepared to move their homes into the area deserted by the Creeks and Yamasee.

*The first American way of life*

**The founding of Georgia.** During the quarter-century of peace following the Treaty of Utrecht, the population of the English colonies passed the million mark. The expansion took place east of the mountains, within the bounds of the old colonies. But one new colony, Georgia, was organized in the exposed region of South Carolina.

Like most of the original colonies, Georgia was founded for two purposes, one worldly and realistic, the other altruistic and hopeful. In order to defend its southern flank in America, England needed settlers. At the same time, an English gentleman with military experience and philanthropic motives wanted to do something for the poor. General James Oglethorpe, while serving on a parliamentary committee, had looked into the appalling condition of English debtors and paupers who frequently wound up in jail through no fault of their own.

General Oglethorpe organized other philanthropic gentlemen to seek a charter for a colony in which the unfortunate but deserving poor might rehabilitate themselves. The English government was glad to get people out of trouble at home and into the firing line on the southern frontier of the Carolinas, but it did not propose to let them get out of hand. In 1732 the government gave Oglethorpe and his friends a charter granting them authority as trustees for twenty-one years, after which the colony would revert to the king.

The trustees collected enough capital to get the enterprise off to a strong start. The area had been pictured in English tracts as a paradise compared to which the Garden of Eden was "at most but equal," and settlers eager to pay their own way appeared from Scotland, Germany, and New England as well as from England. The trustees gave them their blessing and rounded up deserving paupers to go with them. In Georgia, Oglethorpe himself saw that each man got fifty acres of land (those who paid their own way might get up to five hundred acres), tools to work it with, and enough supplies for the first year.

The trustees did their best to bar sin and temptation from the new paradise. To keep the rehabilitated colonist sober they forbade rum. To keep him industrious they forbade slavery. To ensure his livelihood they forbade land sales without their permission. But the zeal was only on the part of the trustees. Georgia proved, after all, to be somewhat less attractive than paradise, and the Georgians thought they deserved at least the compensation of sinning like other men. In 1751 the trustees conceded defeat, allowed slavery and rum, and in 1752, a year before their charter expired, turned their fallen colony over to the king. Thereafter it began to fill up with Americans from other colonies, especially South Carolinians, who were more interested in raising rice than in redeeming paupers.

The trustees had been scarcely more successful in attaining the colony's military objectives. Although Oglethorpe conducted an expedition against Spanish Florida during the War of Jenkins' Ear between England and Spain (1739–42), his troops came mostly from England and South Carolina and accomplished nothing. Georgia never became a military stronghold.

Fortunately, when the European conflict broadened into the War of the Austrian Succession (1740–48), known in the colonies as King George's War, the action shifted to the Northern colonies. There, New Englanders got up an expedition under William Pepperell, a merchant from Maine, to attack the French fortress of Louisburg on Cape Breton Island. The colonists' capture of Louisburg was England's only real success on any front during the war. Although the Treaty of Aix-la-Chapelle (1748) restored the status quo and thus gave Louisburg back to France, its capture had focused the attention of both countries on the increasing strength and importance of England's American subjects.

They were a million and a half now and growing steadily. The advance guard of settlement—speculators, fur-traders, and explorers—were already probing the mountain passes and eyeing the rich bottom lands of the Ohio. France had no settlers to occupy those lands, but it did have men to fight for them. If the English grew any further, France was prepared to make it hurt as never before. The English grew.

**Suggestions for reading**

In many ways the most challenging problem of American history has been to discover in colonial America those institutions, attitudes, and events that found fruition in the later American way of life. George Bancroft first made the attempt on a large scale in his *History of the United States,* 10 vols.* (1834–74), in which he saw divine providence guiding the colonists toward independence. F. J. Turner searched for the answer along the frontier in *The Frontier in American History** (1920), and V. L. Parrington traced a conflict between the common man and the would-be aristocrat in *Main Currents in American Thought,* Vol. 1: *The Colonial Mind** (1927). These men were giants, and their works are too lightly dismissed today. More recent attempts to discern the abiding meaning of the colonial past are

*Available in a paperback edition.

Max Savelle, *Seeds of Liberty** (1948); Clinton Rossiter, *Seedtime of the Republic* (Part I: *The First American Revolution**) (1953); and D. J. Boorstin, *The Americans: The Colonial Experience** (1958). A more controversial but stimulating attempt to discern the early influence of Indian warfare on national character is Richard Slotkin, *Regeneration Through Violence** (1973).

The origins of the plantation system in Virginia are traced in T. J. Wertenbaker, *The Planters of Colonial Virginia* (1922), which argues that the seventeenth century was the heyday of the yeoman farmer. The servants who supplied the colonial labor force, both North and South, before the rise of slavery are the subject of A. E. Smith, *Colonists in Bondage** (1947). The origins of modern slavery are discussed in D. B. Davis, *The Problem of Slavery in Western Culture** (1966), and in W. D. Jordan, *White over Black** (1968). E. S. Morgan, *American Slavery American Freedom** (1975), treats at length some of the developments in Virginia that are described in this chapter; and Peter Wood, *Black Majority** (1974), deals with the beginnings of slavery in South Carolina. G. W. Mullin, *Flight and Rebellion** (1972), discusses slave resistance in Virginia.

The best overall account of plantation agriculture is L. C. Gray, *History of Agriculture in the Southern United States to 1860,* 2 vols. (1933). On the Virginia plantation in the mid-eighteenth century, Louis Morton, *Robert Carter of Nomini Hall** (1941), offers a close-up view. L. B. Wright, *The First Gentlemen of Virginia** (1940), does the same for a number of earlier planters. On domestic life in the South see E. S. Morgan, *Virginians at Home** (1952), and Julia Spruill, *Women's Life and Work in the Southern Colonies** (1938). Carl Bridenbaugh, *Myths and Realities: Societies of the Colonial South** (1952), challenges many conventional ideas about Southern society.

The New England town has been a subject of lively interest among social historians. An important case study of a single town (Sudbury) and its English origins is Sumner Powell, *Puritan Village** (1963). Darrett Rutman has analyzed social changes in *Winthrop's Boston: Portrait of a Puritan Town, 1630– 1649** (1965). K. A. Lockridge, *A New England Town** (1970), traces social and cultural forces in Dedham's first century. Michael Zuckerman, *Peaceable Kingdoms* (1970), stresses the forces making for consensus in eighteenth-century towns, while Paul Boyer and Stephen Nissenbaum, *Salem Possessed* (1974), analyzes the social conflicts in Salem Village that preceded the witchcraft episode there. Charles Grant describes a single eighteenth-century town in *Democracy in the Connecticut Frontier Town of Kent** (1961). Much valuable information about town affairs is contained in Ola Winslow, *Meetinghouse Hill* (1952).

There is no good study of the American farm in the colonial period, but the anonymous *American Husbandry,* H. J. Carman, ed. (1775, reprinted 1939), offers a wealth of information; and a number of works discussing farming and other human ways of exploiting the land have arisen out of a revived interest in historical geography: C. F. Carroll, *The Timber Economy of Puritan New England* (1973); Carl Bridenbaugh, *Fat Mutton and Liberty of Conscience* (1975) (Rhode Island); J. T. Lemon, *The Best Poor Man's Country** (1972) (Pennsylvania); and H. R. Merrens, *Colonial North Carolina in the Eighteenth Century* (1964).

On the colonial cities the works of Carl Bridenbaugh are outstanding: *Cities in the Wilderness, 1625– 1742** (1938); *Cities in Revolt, 1743–1776** (1955); *The Colonial Craftsman** (1950); and, with Jessica Bridenbaugh, *Rebels and Gentlemen** (1942). The last is a study of Philadelphia in the age of Franklin. A valuable history of a colonial merchant firm is J. B. Hedges, *The Browns of Providence Plantation: Vol. I, Colonial Years* (1952). Stuart Bruchey in *The Colonial Merchant** (1966) offers a well-selected collection of source materials. J. F. Shepherd and G. M. Walton, *Shipping, Maritime Trade, and the Economic Development of Colonial North America* (1972), gives a quantitative analysis.

The rise of American representative government is dealt with in L. W. Labaree, *Royal Government in America* (1930), and in J. R. Pole, *Political Representation in England and the Origins of the American Republic** (1966). J. P. Greene, *The Quest for Power** (1963), traces the rising power of the lower houses of assembly in the Southern colonies. Chilton Williamson, *American Suffrage: From Property to*

*Available in a paperback edition.

*The first American way of life*

*Democracy, 1760–1860*\* (1960), shows that the right to vote was enjoyed by the majority of adult males in all the colonies. A sophisticated approach to the distribution of political power is found in Robert Zemsky's analysis of Massachusetts politics, *Merchants, Farmers, and River Gods* (1971), and in Bernard Bailyn, *The Origins of American Politics*\* (1968). A sensitive study of social change is Richard Bushman, *From Puritan to Yankee: Character and Social Order in Connecticut, 1690–1765*\* (1967).

The best general survey of colonial social and intellectual history before the Revolution is L. B. Wright, *The Cultural Life of the American Colonies: 1607–1763*\* (1957). Henry May, *The Enlightenment in America* (1976), is a comprehensive treatment of that subject.

W. W. Sweet, *Religion in Colonial America* (1942), is more concerned with church history than with religion itself. The subject is treated more comprehensively in S. E. Ahlstrom, *A Religious History of the American People*\* (1972). On the Great Awakening, see E. S. Gaustad, *The Great Awakening in New England*\* (1957), and L. J. Trinterud, *The Forming of an American Tradition* (1949). Ola Winslow, *Jonathan Edwards, 1703–1758*\* (1940), is the best biography; Perry Miller, *Jonathan Edwards*\* (1949), is a brilliant interpretation of Edwards' thought. Joseph Haroutunian, *Piety Versus Moralism: The Passing of New England Theology*\* (1932), traces the development of Edwards' theology into the New Divinity, while Conrad Wright, *The Beginnings of Unitarianism in America*\* (1955), shows how a liberal theology developed among the opponents of the Awakening. W. G. McLoughlin, *New England Dissent, 1630–1833,* 2 vols. (1971), is authoritative on the role of the Baptists. Brooke Hindle, *The Pursuit of Science in Revolutionary America, 1735–1798*\* (1956), concentrates on the organization of scientific investigation in this period. R. P. Stearns, *Science in the British Colonies of America* (1970), is a more comprehensive account.

Benjamin Franklin's contributions to science are treated in I. B. Cohen, *Benjamin Franklin's Experiments* (1941) and *Franklin and Newton* (1956). The best biographies of Franklin are Carl Van Doren, *Benjamin Franklin*\* (1941), and V. W. Crane, *Benjamin Franklin and a Rising People*\* (1954). E. S. Morgan, *The Gentle Puritan: A Life of Ezra Stiles, 1727–1795* (1962), shows how the various intellectual forces discussed in this chapter influenced a learned New Englander. Joseph Ellis, *The New England Mind in Transition: Samuel Johnson of Connecticut, 1696–1772* (1973), traces another New Englander's odyssey from Puritanism to Anglicanism.

In *American Education: The Colonial Experience*\* (1970), L. A. Cremin has written a broadly conceived and brilliantly executed treatment of the subject. The history of Harvard College through the seventeenth century has been written by a master in S. E. Morison, *The Founding of Harvard College* (1935) and *Harvard College in the Seventeenth Century,* 2 vols. (1936). Richard Warch has covered the first forty years of Yale College in *School of the Prophets* (1973). Secondary education in New England is ably treated in Robert Middlekauff, *Ancients and Axioms* (1963), and in James Axtell, *The School upon a Hill* (1974).

Francis Parkman made a study of the conflict between England and France in North America his life work, and all his writings are worth careful reading. More recently, George Hunt, *The Wars of the Iroquois*\* (1940), challenges some of Parkman's views; and A. W. Trelease, *Indian Affairs in Colonial New York: The Seventeenth Century* (1960), offers still another interpretation. Wilcomb Washburn, *The Governor and the Rebel*\* (1957), sees Bacon's Rebellion as the result of frontiersmen's desire for Indian lands. Alden Vaughan defends the Puritans' treatment of the Indians in *New England Frontier: Puritans and Indians, 1620–1675*\* (1965). Francis Jennings attacks it in *The Invasion of America* (1975). Later New England relations with the Indians are treated in Douglas Leach, *Flintlock and Tomahawk: New England in King Philip's War*\* (1958) and *The Northern Colonial Frontier, 1607–1763*\* (1966). C. E. Clark, *The Eastern Frontier: The Settlement of Northern New England, 1610–1763* (1970), emphasizes social history. A. F. C. Wallace, *The Death and Rebirth of the Seneca*\* (1970), is an outstanding study of the culture of one Indian group. French institutions in the Mississippi Valley are described in C. E. O'Neill, *Church and State in French Colonial Louisiana* (1966).

\*Available in a paperback edition.

# CHAPTER 4

# The second discovery of America

England had joined the War of the Austrian Succession in order to prevent France from gobbling up the Austrian empire and thus destroying the European balance of power. The Peace of Aix-la-Chapelle, which ended the war in 1748, was recognized everywhere in Europe as more a truce than a treaty. It restored the status quo, returned Louisburg to France, took away French conquests in the Austrian Netherlands, but left French power unbroken. France set about at once to ensure that its position in America would be stronger in the next war. Not only did the French refortify Louisburg, but in a more ominous move they sent their agents along the western slope of the Appalachians to build forts, to cement alliances with the Indians, to claim the region for the king of France.

## Contest for empire

**The Albany Congress.** The English Board of Trade and the Privy Council, in order to bolster the loyalty of their own allies, called on the colonies from Virginia northward to send representatives to a meeting with the Iroquois at Albany. Virginia and New Jersey ignored the summons; but in June 1754 nineteen delegates from New Hampshire, Massachusetts, Connecticut, Rhode Island, Pennsylvania, and Maryland, together with the lieutenant-governor of New York and four gentlemen of his council, rode into Albany to confer with Iroquois chieftains who had slipped down the Mohawk Valley in response to a similar summons. As the Iroquois listened, the white men went through the formalities that Indians demanded in all negotiations: the grandiloquent declarations of esteem, the ceremonial presentation of gifts—scarlet coats, silver buttons, axes, scissors, guns. But the Iroquois had just been watching the French at work on fortifications in the interior, and they found English talk and English gifts less impressive than French action. They departed with the gifts but without offering the hoped-for assurance that they would help when the fighting began.

While in Albany the twenty-four colonial delegates discussed a scheme that had been talked of before: the formation of a permanent intercolonial union to conduct Indian relations. Benjamin Franklin, as he rode north from Philadelphia, had thought out a plan, which he presented at the beginning of the congress. By the time the congress ended, the delegates had agreed to propose to the colonial assemblies a grand council with authority over matters of defense, westward expansion, and Indian relations. The council would handle purchases of land from friendly

*Celebration, July 4, 1776*

*Cartoon by Benjamin Franklin, 1754*

Indians and the planting of new settlements. It would raise armies and build forts and warships. And it would pay its own expenses by levying taxes. Its presiding officer, appointed by the king, would have veto power over all its actions.

When the plan reached the assemblies, their reaction was cool—some rejected it, others ignored it. Experience had shown them that the power to tax was father to every other governmental power. They often used it to get their own way in legislative conflicts with royal governors, and they did not propose to share it with any intercolonial council. Nor did they wish to be deprived of the chance to beat their neighbors in the race for Indian lands.

The assemblies' rejection of the Albany plan spared the English government the embarrassment of having to veto it. England wanted a unified direction of Indian affairs, not a permanent colonial union that might prove more difficult to deal with than the separate assemblies. Failure of the plan suggested that England need not worry about a union: the assemblies were apparently more uncooperative in dealing with one another than with England. No one stopped to think that Indian relations and Western policy had always been the most divisive issues in colonial politics. How to use the unsettled land in the West and how to deal with its Indian inhabitants were questions that divided coast from interior, farmer from fur-trader, merchant from landowner, colony from colony. On other questions the colonists were more united than either they or England knew.

**English defeats.** As the gentlemen at Albany were conducting their elaborate and unsuccessful courtship of the Iroquois, a younger gentleman was already firing on the French in the Ohio country. Virginia, instead of sending delegates to Albany, had sent a twenty-two-year-old colonel of the militia, George Washington, to help construct a fort at the forks of the Ohio (where the Monongahela and Allegheny rivers

*"Defeat and Death of General Braddock"*

The Ohio country

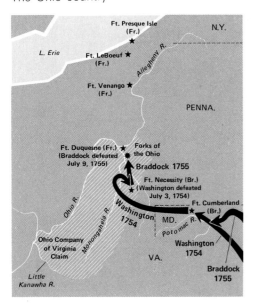

join). When Washington arrived in the Ohio country, the French were already in possession of the forks and hard at work on their own Fort Duquesne. He built a crude stockade, which he called Fort Necessity, at Great Meadows, fifty miles south, but was obliged to surrender it to a superior French force on July 3, 1754. Then the French let Washington march his men home to report that the land over the mountains belonged to France.

Washington's defeat was bad news to his fellow Virginians, for many reasons: as Englishmen they disliked Frenchmen; as Protestants they disliked Catholics; as Virginians they disliked anybody who invaded their empire. On the basis of their 1609 charter, Virginians claimed all land to the west and northwest of their colony, and they were jealous of encroachments on their territory. Reluctance to admit that other colonies should have any voice in dealing with the great Virginian West may have been behind Virginia's absence from the Albany Congress.

One group of Virginians in particular regarded the Ohio country as private property. In 1747 a number of prominent planters, including George Washington's brothers, Lawrence and Augustine, had organized the Ohio Company to trade with the Western Indians and to speculate in Western lands. In 1749, with the approval of the Privy Council, the government of Virginia gave the company 200,000 acres between the Monongahela and the Great Kanawha rivers, and followed this by other grants of Western lands to other speculators. By 1751, when Robert Dinwiddie became governor, many Virginians were looking to the lands of the trans-Appalachian West to make their fortunes, and Dinwiddie himself became a member of the Ohio Company.

Dinwiddie had arranged Washington's expedition in order to hold the Ohio Valley for England, for Virginia, and for the Ohio Company. Upon Washington's return, it was apparent that the job was too big for either the Ohio Company or Virginia, and Dinwiddie signaled for help from England. Although officially England and France remained at peace, the home government recognized that the new war was beginning, and it dispatched General Edward Braddock with two regiments.

Braddock, arriving in Virginia early in 1755, expected to increase his force by a large number of colonists and Indians and then to march on Fort Duquesne and teach the French that the Ohio Valley belonged to England. But Virginia had no wilderness diplomats to furnish the general with Indian braves. South Carolina could have delivered them, but Virginians were wary of letting Carolinians into the affairs of the Ohio country. Some Pennsylvania fur-traders showed up with their own Indian friends, who executed an impressive war dance for the general but disappeared when it came time to march. In the end, Braddock set off with only 8 Indians and about 1,200 colonial militia to supplement his 1,500 regulars. He took them successfully over the mountains, along with enough cannon to pound Fort Duquesne to dust. But as they were approaching the fort on July 9 the French surprised them and turned the march into a disastrous rout. Braddock himself was fatally wounded, and 976 of his men were killed or wounded.

The Indians of the area concluded that the English were finished, and for the next two years it looked as though they were. The colonists, despite their numerical strength, seemed more interested in

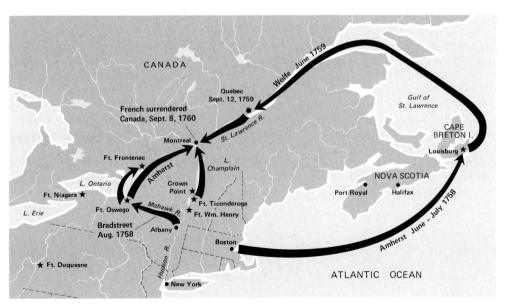

The war in the North, 1758–60

*Contest for empire*

scoring against one another than in defeating the French; and the English government was occupied with its European involvements. England gave Governor William Shirley of Massachusetts the title of commander in chief but left him to collect most of his men and money from the colonists. Shirley was an able man, the most popular of the royal governors, but his abilities were no match for the jealous intrigues of the other governors, the recalcitrance of the colonial assemblies, or the firepower of the French. While the assemblies dallied over raising troops, Shirley's ill-supported expeditions in 1755 against Fort Niagara and Crown Point both failed, but he did manage to build Fort William Henry at the southern end of Lake George.

Fear that France might try to regain Nova Scotia (or Acadia) led the British government in 1755 to deport several thousand French inhabitants from the province. The Acadians had lived under English rule since 1713, but they had never lost their affection for France and conscientiously passed it on to their children. Governor Shirley, recognizing that in case of a French invasion they were likely to side with the enemy, had suggested their deportation as early as 1747. In 1755 the British dispersed them through the other English colonies instead of sending them off to Canada, where they would have augmented the French forces. The circumstances of the deportations and the treatment of the refugees by the English colonists were unnecessarily cruel. But Nova Scotia was made more secure.

In 1756, after gaining the support of Prussia, England finally resolved on a full-scale conflict and declared war. It lasted for seven more years and so earned in Europe the title of the Seven Years' War. In America it was the French and Indian War. The formal declaration of war did nothing to break England's losing streak, for immediately the French defeated the English fleet in the Mediterranean and captured Minorca. In America a new commander in chief, Lord Loudoun, was given military authority over the colonial governors in order to unite the colonies in their own defense. But the colonial assemblies, holding fast the purse strings, regarded Loudoun's authority with suspicion and complied only casually with his requests for men and supplies. Nor did he achieve success with the troops, regular or colonial, that he did get. Shortly after he assumed command, the French captured Fort Oswego; in the following year they took the new Fort William Henry.

**Victory under Pitt.** In 1757 the English at last found a statesman to bring their real strength into play. William Pitt had never doubted England's need for him. "I am sure," he said, "that I can save the country, and that no one else can." Pitt's assurance rested on a view of the war and of England's imperial future unlike that of earlier leaders. Hitherto the war in America had been regarded as an incidental part of a traditional European war. The fighting, it was hoped, would facilitate the continued expansion of colonial population, but English statesmen weighed American victories and defeats on a European scale, for their effect on the balance of power. When Pitt took office, English policy underwent a radical change. Pitt's object was not simply to reduce French power in the European balance or to facilitate colonial expansion. He proposed instead to make England master of all North America and perhaps of the rest of the world too.

In Pitt's vision of empire, Europe loomed less large than America and India. Accordingly, he paid Frederick of Prussia to wage the European war and threw England's weight into a campaign of violent aggression abroad. Territory was his object, and he dipped into the national treasury with a lavish hand to pay the men who would seize it for him. Rather than waste time bickering with colonial assemblies over the cost, he promised them reimbursement for all their expenses in raising troops. The national debt went soaring, but so did colonial enlistments.

To drive France from the New World, Pitt needed not only men and money but military talent. He got it, as statesmen frequently have, by jumping young men over the heads of their elders. His greatest find was a gangly, hollow-chested boy of thirty, with a receding chin and a vile temper. James Wolfe was a prig and a martinet, but Pitt sensed his talent. Pitt also promoted Lieutenant Colonel Jeffry Amherst, who at the age of forty had been in the army twenty-two years without ever holding an independent command, to the rank of major general and put him in charge of a large-scale expedition against Louisburg. With Wolfe supervising the landing operations, Amherst took the fortress on July 26, 1758, giving England its first great victory of the war.

The capture of Louisburg destroyed French power at the mouth of the St. Lawrence and jeopardized communications between New and old France. A month later Lieutenant Colonel John Bradstreet captured Fort Frontenac, which guarded the other end of the St. Lawrence on the shores of Lake Ontario. Now the French in Canada were cut off from the Mississippi Valley and had to give up Fort Duquesne, which the British renamed Fort Pitt (later Pittsburgh).

At last Pitt was ready for his grand strategy, a pincers move on Quebec and Montreal, with troops approaching from the north by the St. Lawrence and from the south by the Hudson River, Lake George, and Lake Champlain. Amherst was to operate from the south, Wolfe from the north. Wolfe sailed up the St. Lawrence with nine thousand men and on Sep-

*The second discovery of America*

tember 12, 1759, made a surprise night attack up one of the steep gullies in the cliffs that protect Quebec. In the battle that then took place on the Plains of Abraham the British were victorious, but both Wolfe and the able French commander, the Marquis de Montcalm, received fatal wounds.

With the capture of Quebec, English victory in North America was only a matter of time. The French immediately laid siege to the city, but, when spring opened the ice-choked river and a British fleet appeared, the French withdrew. During the late summer, the expected troops from the south and a force from Quebec converged on Montreal for the final campaign. On September 8, 1760, the French gave up the city and all Canada with it. The war did not end until 1763, but in its final phases the action shifted from North America to the Caribbean, India, and the Philippines, as England plucked the overseas empires of her European rivals.

***George III.*** Six weeks after the fall of Montreal, King George II died. Between them, George II and his father, George I, had ruled England since 1714, when the latter had been summoned to the throne from the quiet German principality of Hanover. Neither was distinguished in intelligence or character, but George II was the more energetic and enjoyed leading the army, which knew him affectionately as the Little Captain. Though George II took an active part in selecting his ministers, the English government during his reign and his father's fell more and more into the hands of a powerful group of private families. They called themselves Whigs, in memory of the Revolution of 1688, from which they liked to date their ascendancy. Though they made an occasional bow to the principles of liberty, there was nothing revolutionary about them. Comfortable and wealthy, they entered politics to get wealthier and organized small groups or factions to juggle the spoils of office.

George II outlived his eldest son Frederick (who died in 1751 of a blow from a tennis ball); George III, who ascended the throne in 1760, was the old king's grandson. At twenty-two George III had a mind, such as it was, of his own and no intention of letting the great Whig families run *his* government. Under the tutelage of a Scottish peer, the Earl of Bute, he had learned to dislike vice, to distrust talent, and to love patriotism, barley water, and the Earl of Bute. As a Scot, Bute had no seat in the House of Lords, and as a lord he was disqualified from the House of Commons. But the new king gave him at once a place in the inner "Cabinet Council," which was taking the place of the larger Privy Council in conducting the executive branch of government. Together, George and the Earl of Bute set about reforming the wicked ways of English politics.

Quebec, 1759

The politicians shared neither the king's aversion to vice nor his fondness for Bute, and they were not interested in reform. Lacking any party organization, they could not present a united front against the king, but he and they both knew that he could not run the government without their help, and they made him pay dearly for it. For ten years George appointed and dismissed members of the council at a bewildering rate. Ministers responsible for colonial affairs came and went and came again as the king sparred with politicians over issues that usually had nothing to do with the colonies. Consequently, English colonial policy in this crucial decade was inconsistent and incoherent, not to say capricious.

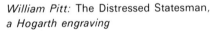
*William Pitt:* The Distressed Statesman, *a Hogarth engraving*

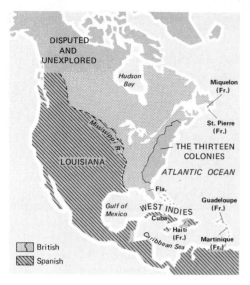

North America in 1763

Legend:
- British
- Spanish

When George took the throne, Pitt was running the war and the government. Trouble broke out almost immediately. Tormented by gout, hobbling about on crutches, Pitt snapped at everyone who disagreed with him and did not gladly suffer the many fools he had to deal with. The politicians liked him as little as they liked Bute. With the fall of Canada and the subsequent British successes in the rest of the world, they were ready to make peace with France and rid themselves of the tyranny of this ailing genius.

Pitt was ready for peace too, provided he could strip France of all its overseas possessions. France, however, though defeated abroad, was still a formidable power in Europe and was courting the support of Spain. Pitt, hearing of the negotiations, stopped talking peace and demanded instead that England declare war at once against Spain—Pitt always preferred to attack. No one had dared oppose Pitt while England was underdog in the war with France. But he had made England strong enough to do without him, and now his colleagues would not agree to take on a new enemy. When he could not have his way, Pitt resigned the ministry.

**The Peace of Paris.** With Pitt's resignation in 1761, the king's "dearest friend" became the leading figure in the council and the most unpopular man in England. Bute did not enjoy either role and retired from politics in 1763, but not until he had presided at Paris over the treaty that ended England's most successful war. The momentum of victory generated under Pitt carried the country through the final year of war without him. As he had foreseen, England ultimately had to add Spain to its list of enemies, but after crushing defeats at Manila and Havana, Spain was ready to call a halt. When Bute made peace in 1763,

he took the whole of North America east of the Mississippi (Florida from Spain, Canada from France), and also took back Minorca, carved up the French possessions in India, and extricated England from its commitments in Germany. But Bute was schooled in the traditional diplomacy of balancing European powers against one another, and he was unmoved by Pitt's imperial ambitions. He gave Cuba and the Philippines back to Spain and let France give Louisiana to Spain. He returned Guadeloupe and Martinique to France and allowed it to keep the two tiny islands of St. Pierre and Miquelon as fishing bases.

Pitt was outraged by Bute's liberality toward France and Spain, and some of the colonists shared his view. But most Englishmen, both in England itself and in the colonies, welcomed the treaty even while they denounced its maker and glorified Pitt. For the colonists it meant the end of a threat that had been hanging over them for as long as anyone could remember. Now, as their children grew up and went looking for new homes, they could trek over the mountains into the lush Ohio Valley, into bluegrass lands they would name Kentucky and Tennessee, into the prairies of the Illinois country. The Indians, without the French to organize and direct them, could offer no serious obstacle to the settlement of the interior by the English.

## A new empire and new ideas

The English looked with pride at their new territories. America was still the spearhead of European growth, and the conquest of New France conjured up the vision of a Mississippi Valley filled with people who spoke English and talked fondly of a small island across the ocean as "home." Englishmen had been the first to think of North America as a place to live. Now their perception was rewarded with an empire that promised to cover the continent.

**The question of imperial authority.** With the coming of peace a few men sensed that the government of the empire again needed overhauling, for it was clearly inadequate for a population of 2 million about to advance into the immense interior of North America. Several colonial governors, who had seen America at first hand, wrote urgently on the subject. From Massachusetts, for example, Francis Bernard warned his superiors in England that this was "the proper and critical time to reform the American governments upon a general, constitutional, firm, and durable plan; and if it is not done now, it will probably every day grow more difficult, till at last it becomes impracticable."

Bernard's sense of urgency was justified. Most of the colonies had been founded before the supremacy of Parliament in England had been firmly established. Even after the question of supremacy was settled Parliament concerned itself little with them. But now that America had grown important to England, Parliament would be giving it more attention. That attention (as Bernard foresaw) might not be welcomed by the colonies; for, since the time of their founding, they had regularly dealt with the mother country through the king, his councils, his governors. Before Parliament began making laws for them or levying taxes on them it needed to establish its own authority over them by reorganizing their governments.

Bernard thought that all the colonial governments should be given identical constitutions by act of Parliament, with governors appointed by the king. He recognized that the colonists, like other Englishmen, expected a share in their government, and he suggested that they be represented in Parliament. He did not think that they had any right to such representation, but he felt that it would be good politics to give them a voice in the decisions that Parliament would doubtless be making about them.

Francis Bernard was an ambitious man, and his superiors probably smiled at his advice. They realized that the empire needed repair, but Bernard's far-reaching plans seemed grandiloquent and prompted as much by a desire for promotion as by the actual needs of the situation. At the moment more immediate and pressing problems demanded their attention. For the next thirteen years a succession of shortsighted politicians and an industriously dull king kept their minds on a succession of immediate and pressing problems. By so doing, they inadvertently and unintentionally taught the colonists that Americans had more in common with one another than with Englishmen.

**Trouble in the West.** After the war England decided to station several thousand troops permanently in America. So much blood and money had been spent winning the continent that it seemed only proper to guard it, and the presence of troops would also help to restrain any possible insubordination on the part of the colonists and discourage France from trying to regain its losses. Almost at once the troops were called into action, not against France but against its former allies, the Indians, for whom the coming of peace presaged another westward surge of English colonists. The Indians of all tribes had been restive ever since the fall of New France, and the contemptuous and shortsighted policies of General Amherst toward them gave them a foretaste of what English

rule of the continent would mean. When the Ottawas, led by their chieftain Pontiac, attacked Detroit in the spring of 1763, other tribes, following his lead, fell upon the English forts and settlements from the Great Lakes to the back country of Pennsylvania, Maryland, and Virginia. Since the British troops were not well located to protect the frontiers, the outlying settlers suffered heavily before the attacks could be stopped.

Pontiac's Rebellion had the divisive effect that Western problems usually produced among Americans. Easterners were reluctant to take it seriously. Westerners blamed the Easterners for the loss of farms and the death of wives, husbands, children, and friends. In western Pennsylvania a group of outraged pioneers known as the Paxton boys fell upon a village of peaceful Indians, massacred them, and marched on Philadelphia to get some action out of the government. They were halted by the Philadelphians, who evidently feared other Pennsylvanians more than Indians.

English statesmen could easily conclude that the Americans were a hopelessly uncooperative and cowardly lot, unwilling to help one another and unable to protect themselves against savages. During the preceding French and Indian War British officers had sent back disparaging reports of colonial troops. General Wolfe himself had characterized his four companies of American rangers at Quebec as "the worst soldiers in the Universe." Now, once again, it seemed, the colonists had demonstrated their weakness—and the British proceeded to demonstrate theirs.

When Bute took the Mississippi Valley from France and returned the islands of Guadeloupe and Martinique, the decision was widely justified on the grounds that the valley was potentially more valuable than the West Indies. But if its potential was to be realized, the area would have to be settled and exploited by Englishmen, not kept as a giant game preserve. British politicians recognized this fact, but most of them saw no need to hurry settlers into the great emptiness beyond the mountains, where they would be less accessible to British control. Moreover, westward expansion would aggravate the most pressing colonial problem—the Indian resistance. While their troops crushed Pontiac's warriors, the politicians drafted a solution to the problem of Indian warfare: keep the colonists out of Indian territory. They had the king issue a proclamation forbidding settlement beyond the crest of the Appalachian Mountains and advising settlers in search of homes to go to Nova Scotia or Florida, for which England now provided governments.

The proclamation had little effect on American westward expansion, for the colonists took little notice of it. But it showed that the British were incapable of grasping the desperate speed of American

*A new empire and new ideas*

growth. They thought they could take their time about developing the West, that they could deflect the expanding population by issuing a proclamation.

**George Grenville's search for revenue.** While the king was erecting his paper fence along the crest of the Appalachians, one of his ministers was occupied with a matter closer to home, the enormous national debt that England had piled up in acquiring Canada and the Mississippi Valley. George Grenville, First Lord of the Treasury, knew his pounds, shillings, and pence. With the end of the French and Indian War and the retirement of Bute, the king turned to him as the man best qualified to put England's finances in order. Grenville was not impressed with a continent full of naked savages, impecunious Frenchmen, and wild beaver; he was impressed with a national debt that had doubled since 1754; and he was still more impressed with the cost of keeping troops under arms to protect England's new possessions. He did not question the need for the troops. That was beyond his concern. But he had to find the money to pay them, as well as the money to pay the interest on the national debt.

Soon after he took office in April 1763 Grenville came upon a remarkable fact: the American customs service was costing the government nearly £8,000 a year in salaries but was collecting less than £2,000 in duties. Everyone knew that the colonists were importing large quantities of molasses from the French West Indies, on which the Molasses Act of 1733 required them to pay a duty of sixpence a gallon. Obviously they were evading the duty. In October 1763 Grenville issued a sharp directive for its collection and ordered the British navy to patrol American waters for smugglers.

Grenville had another grievance against the colonists: they alleviated their perpetual currency shortage (resulting from their unfavorable balance of trade with the mother country) by issuing paper money. Although the money served an essential purpose and showed little depreciation in most colonies, its value was less than that of English sterling coin. English creditors feared that the colonists might manipulate the rate of exchange between their currency and sterling and try to pay their English debts at an artificially low rate. As a result of complaints by creditors, the New England colonies had been forbidden in 1751 to make their paper money legal tender. By the Currency Act of April 1764, Grenville extended the prohibition to all the colonies.

In the same month Grenville directed through Parliament an act (later known as the Sugar Act) revising American customs duties and regulations. With good reason he reduced the duty on foreign molasses from sixpence a gallon to threepence. The purpose of the original levy had been to induce the colonists to buy their molasses from the British West Indies, where they could get it duty free (though higher priced). But colonial rum-distillers balked at paying premium prices for British molasses or the sixpence duty for French. To have done so, they claimed, would have raised the price of their rum to the point where it could not be sold in competition with other spirits. So the colonial importers simply bribed the customs officials (from a halfpenny to a penny and a half per gallon) not to collect the duty. Grenville accepted the fact that the sixpence duty was too high, but he believed that if the merchants could afford to pay bribes, they could afford, instead, a three-pence duty.

The Sugar Act also imposed new duties on colonial imports of sugar, indigo, coffee, pimento, wine, and textiles. To discourage smuggling, it required that elaborate official papers be filed for every ship entering or leaving a colonial port. Finally, it provided that violators of the customs regulations could be tried in admiralty courts, which operated under royally appointed judges acting without juries (in the common-law courts juries made up of local residents were inclined to sympathize with offenders). The colonists had been subject to such an enactment since 1696, but ambiguities in it had often enabled smugglers to avoid admiralty jurisdiction.

The stated purpose of the Sugar Act was to help defray the expenses England would incur in protecting its new American possessions. Grenville did not expect to raise the whole amount from the colonists, but he did expect more than the new duties were likely to yield; and in introducing the bill for the Sugar Act to Parliament he announced that he might levy a stamp tax on the colonies.

There was nothing novel in the idea of stamp taxes. Englishmen at home had been paying them ever since the reign of King William, and there had already been suggestions that Parliament impose such taxes on the colonies. Massachusetts had even tried a stamp tax of its own in 1755. By February 1765 Grenville had

*The Stamp: the Americans would resist*

This is the Place to affix the STAMP.

completed his study of taxable items being used in the colonies and was ready to introduce his Stamp Act to Parliament. It called for taxes on every type of legal document and on newspapers, almanacs, playing cards, and dice (all of which had to bear a stamp, signifying that the tax was paid). As in the case of the Sugar Act, violators would be prosecuted in admiralty courts. A few members of Parliament raised objections to taxing the colonists. Colonel Isaac Barré, who had served under Wolfe in North America, warned that the Americans would resist. But the act passed both houses and was signed by the king on March 22, 1765, to take effect November 1.

In May 1765 Grenville put through a third measure, the Quartering Act, to help support English troops in America. This act provided that any colony in which troops were stationed must furnish them with living quarters and with fire, candles, vinegar, salt, bedding, and beer, cider, or rum.

**Colonial suspicions.** The colonists were stunned by Grenville's actions. In 1763 colonial merchants felt sure that his order calling for the strict collection of molasses duties would ruin the rum trade and the whole New England economy with it. Nor did they welcome the reduction in duties provided by the Sugar Act, for they believed that even a three-pence duty would drive their rum out of the market. Moreover, the act established customs procedures so strict and complicated that all kinds of trade would be hampered. The currency restriction made matters still worse. With silver in short supply and with paper money no longer legal tender, merchants had no medium of exchange and were sometimes reduced to barter. When economic depression followed the acts, Americans blamed Grenville.

But the most shocking aspect of Grenville's measures was that they seemed to embody a new policy—a deliberate aim to disinherit the colonists by denying them the rights of Englishmen. The Americans believed that it was their right as Englishmen not to be taxed except by their own elected representatives; but Parliament had taxed them directly in the Stamp Act, indirectly in the Sugar Act and the Quartering Act. They believed that it was their right as Englishmen to be tried by juries of their peers; but Parliament had made infringement of the Sugar and Stamp acts punishable in admiralty courts. These courts were objectionable not only because they violated the right to trial by jury but because they put the burden of proof on the defendant, assuming that he was guilty until he proved himself innocent. Furthermore, in England admiralty courts tried only cases arising on the high seas. By giving the courts a wider jurisdiction in the colonies, the Sugar and Stamp acts suggested that England thought Americans not enti-

*"Stamp Master Hanged in Effigy"*

tled to rights long recognized in the mother country.

Further evidence of some sinister design seemed apparent in the announced purpose of the acts: to support troops in America. Why, the colonists wondered, did England want to keep armed soldiers in their midst? The troops had helped, to be sure, in crushing Pontiac's Rebellion, which the rash actions of their commander, General Amherst, had actually helped to bring on. But protection against Indians was patently not the purpose of keeping troops in America. Before 1754, while the French were sending their Indian allies to attack the colonists from Maine to Carolina, England had maintained scarcely any military garrison in America. Now, with the danger gone, with the French crushed and the Spaniards pushed beyond the Mississippi, England insisted on keeping several thousand men on hand. Why? Perhaps, it was whispered, England intended to use the army not to protect but to suppress the colonists. There is evidence in British documents that such an intention did in fact exist, but the evidence was not known to the colonists. Grenville's acts, however, were sufficient in themselves to prompt suspicions.

**Colonial convictions.** The British statesmen who started Americans talking of standing armies, taxation without representation, and trials without juries would have done well to consider the origin and history of the colonies. New England and many other parts of America had been founded by Puritans who carried to America the ideas that shortly led to Oliver Cromwell's commonwealth in England. After that

*A new empire and new ideas*

commonwealth ended with the restoration of the monarchy in 1660, many more Dissenters joined the exodus to America, and their descendants could talk of Hampden and Pym and other heroes of the struggle against Charles I with a familiarity that might have struck some Englishmen as quaint. Though loyal to the House of Hanover, the colonists admired much in the writings of James Harrington, the advocate of republican government, of Algernon Sidney, and of John Locke.

Locke no Englishman found quaint. In affirming the natural right of a people to alter their government (see p. 67), he had provided his countrymen with an intellectual justification for their long contest to gain ascendancy over their kings. All Englishmen believed that the course of their history had been a struggle to achieve a government that would protect their lives, liberty, and property. They believed that they had at last achieved such a government with the overthrow of James II in 1688 and the establishment of the House of Hanover in 1714. The colonists shared this belief, and they were proud to be members of the nation whose government stood foremost in the world in protecting the natural rights of its subjects.

Like other Englishmen the colonists regarded the representative nature of English government as the most important guarantee of continued protection. They rejoiced in Parliament's supremacy in England and in the supremacy of their own assemblies in America. In each the elected representatives of the people guarded the rights of Englishmen, and the most precious right they guarded was the right of property, without which neither life nor liberty could be secure. Since the power to tax was a power to take away property, no man could call himself free if he was taxed without his own consent, given either personally or by his representative. The right to be taxed in this way, and in no other, was a hard-won principle of the British constitution. In England only the representative branch of Parliament, the House of Commons, could initiate tax bills; and in the colonies the representative assemblies claimed the same exclusive privilege. It therefore seemed monstrous to Americans that, in the Sugar Act and the Stamp Act, Parliament, a body in which they had no representative, had presumed to tax them. If Parliament could levy these taxes it could levy others. Once the precedent was set, the colonists would be as badly off as England had been before the rise of Parliament. They would, ironically, be oppressed by the very body that had rescued England from the same kind of tyranny.

As the colonists measured acts of Parliament against their own ideas of right, they faced the question that Governor Bernard had wished to settle earlier, the question of Parliament's authority in America. Their decision was different from Bernard's.

Parliament, they believed, had some right to legislate for them; but it had no right to tax them. It was the central legislative body for matters of common concern to the entire empire, and as such it could regulate their commerce, even by imposing duties to discourage certain kinds of trade that it believed prejudicial to the good of the empire as a whole. But it had no right to levy duties to raise money; such duties were taxes, and Parliament had no right to tax the colonies in any manner. Its members could not grant the property of people whom they did not represent.

The American colonists in 1764 and 1765 were remarkably unanimous in adopting this distinction between taxation and legislation. They began to affirm it in pamphlets and newspaper articles as soon as the Sugar Act was passed. New York and Virginia expressed it officially in petitions to Parliament. By the time the Stamp Act was passed, people in every colony were discussing the limits of Parliament's authority, and during the summer and fall of 1765 colonial assemblies passed resolutions setting forth those limits.

**The Stamp Act crisis.** The Stamp Act was to go into effect on November 1. In the May session of the Virginia assembly, Patrick Henry, a young lawyer, presented a series of resolutions declaring that only the House of Burgesses had the right to tax Virginians. The Burgesses adopted the resolutions but rejected some additional ones calling for outright resistance if England should try to collect the stamp tax. The other colonial assemblies rapidly followed Virginia's example, modeling their own resolutions on hers. Although the newspapers had printed Henry's rejected resolutions as though they had actually been passed, thus creating the impression that Virginia had acted more radically than was the case, nevertheless most of the other assemblies stopped where Virginia did, with a simple denial of Parliament's right to tax the colonies.

In addition to the resolutions of their individual assemblies, the colonies prepared a joint statement of their position. In June, before the colonial consensus had become apparent, Massachusetts proposed that all the colonies send delegates to a general meeting for the purpose of concerting their opposition to Parliamentary taxes. Nine assemblies complied: in October 1765 the Stamp Act Congress met at New York. After avowing "all due subordination" to Parliament, the delegates resolved that colonial subordination did not include acceptance of Parliamentary taxation or of admiralty courts operating beyond their traditional limits. They also sent petitions to king and Parliament demanding repeal of the Sugar and Stamp acts.

In objecting to taxation by Parliament, the colonists believed that they had common sense, natural law, and the British constitution all on their side. It was common sense that they already contributed to the wealth of the mother country by submitting to the Navigation Acts. If a more direct contribution was required, it ought to be made by the colonists' own representatives, who alone could know, as the Virginia resolves said, "what Taxes the People are able to bear, or the easiest Method of raising them, and must themselves be affected by every Tax laid on the People." If the members of Parliament could establish their authority to tax the colonies, they would have an all but irresistible motive to shift their own burdens and those of their constituents to America. Every penny collected in the colonies would be a penny less to take from English pockets. It was common sense that such a situation spelled tyranny.

It was also a violation of the British constitution and of the laws of nature by which every free people should be governed. The people's right to be taxed only by their own representatives was "the grand Principle of every free State . . . the natural Right of Mankind," proclaimed the members of the New York assembly. The Massachusetts assembly, in the same vein, announced that "there are certain essential Rights of the British Constitution of Government, which are founded in the Law of God and Nature, and are the common Rights of Mankind." Among those rights was "that no man can justly take the Property of another without his Consent."

Besides informing Parliament and posterity of what was right, the colonists took practical steps to see that right prevailed. Merchants in New York, Philadelphia, and Boston agreed to stop importing British goods, hoping by economic pressure to enlist British merchants and manufacturers against the Stamp Act. Other Americans, too impatient to wait for repeal, were determined to prevent the Stamp Act from taking effect. On the night of August 14, a Boston mob stormed the house of Andrew Oliver, the local stamp-distributor. They broke the doors and windows and roamed through the house calling for the owner's head. Oliver resigned his office the next day. Stamp-distributors in other colonies hastened to follow Oliver's example. Mobs helped those who hesitated to make up their minds. On November 1, when the act was scheduled to go into effect, there was no one to distribute the stamps.

In every colony the violence that forced the resignation of the distributors had been carefully engineered by a group of conspirators. These men now organized under the name of Sons of Liberty and prepared to resist "to the last extremity" any efforts to enforce the Stamp Act. They had learned from John Locke that a people could alter or overthrow a government that exceeded its authority; and they repeated Locke's precepts to their countrymen in resolves, like those adopted at New London on December 10, 1765, declaring that "the People have a Right to reassume the exercise of that Authority which by Nature they had, before they delegated it to Individuals."

The total overthrow of government did not prove necessary. For a few weeks after November 1, people in most colonies simply refrained from doing any business that required stamps. Then newspapers began to appear without them. By threatening mob action, the Sons of Liberty soon persuaded judges to try cases and customs officers to clear ships with unstamped bonds and clearance papers. In less than three months the Stamp Act had been effectively nullified.

English response to colonial defiance was not what it might have been had Grenville remained in power. George III, for reasons that had nothing to do with the colonies, dismissed Grenville in July 1765 and in his place named the Marquis of Rockingham as first minister. Rockingham and the men he brought into the administration with him had opposed the Stamp Act in the first place and wanted nothing more than to escape the embarrassment of trying to enforce it. English merchants, stung by the American boycott, reinforced Rockingham's determination to wipe the act off the books, and he enthusiastically favored a repeal bill in Parliament.

But the spate of resolutions and riots in the colonies made repeal difficult. Most members of Parliament were reluctant to back down, especially after William Pitt, with his usual tactlessness, publicly rejoiced at American resistance and endorsed the colonists' definition of the limits of Parliament's authority. Taxation, he said, was "no part of the governing or legislative power." Other members were baffled by the distinction between taxation and legislation. Grenville declared it absurd. But in March 1766 Parliament repealed the act after first passing a Declaratory Act, which deliberately skirted the distinction and simply affirmed the authority of Parliament to "make laws and statutes of sufficient force and validity to bind the colonies and people of America . . . in all cases whatsoever." Precisely what that meant Americans were to find out later. For the moment they rejoiced in the end of the contest that had led them to the brink of war with the mother country. Repeal of the Stamp Act seemed to signal a return to the Old Colonial System under which England and its colonies had alike enjoyed freedom, prosperity, and harmony. Now they might take up once again the position of leadership in world trade that they had won together.

**Colonial discoveries.** Nevertheless, as the colonists joined their English friends in celebrating repeal, they could reflect on their discoveries of the preceding two years. They had already found out more than England

*A new empire and new ideas*

*The Fact is, that the Inhabitants of the Colonies are represented in Parliament: they do not indeed chuse the Members of that Assembly; neither are Nine Tenths of the People of Britain Electors; for the Right of Election is annexed to certain Species of Property, to peculiar Franchises, and to Inhabitancy in some particular Places; but these Descriptions comprehend only a very small Part of the Land, the Property, and the People of this Island....*

*The Colonies are in exactly the same Situation: All British Subjects are really in the same; none are actually, all are virtually represented in Parliament; for every Member of Parliament sits in the House, not as Representative of his own Constituents, but as one of that august Assembly by which all the Commons of Great Britain are represented. Their Rights and their Interests, however his own Borough may be affected by general Dispositions, ought to be the great Objects of his Attention, and the only Rules for his Conduct; and to sacrifice these to a partial Advantage in favour of the Place where he was chosen, would be a Departure from his Duty; if it were otherwise, Old Sarum would enjoy Privileges essential to Liberty, which are denied to Birmingham and to Manchester; but as it is, they and the Colonies and all British Subjects whatever, have an equal Share in the general Representation of the Commons of Great Britain, and are bound by the Consent of the Majority of that House, whether their own particular Representatives consented to or opposed the Measures there taken, or whether they had or had not particular Representatives there.*

**From Thomas Whately, *The Regulations Lately Made...*, 1765.**

could have wished. A decade earlier, when the Albany Congress proposed a union against a danger in the West, they had unanimously declined. This time, when the danger came from the East, they had spontaneously joined to boycott British goods, to prevent the distribution of stamps, to define the limits of Parliament's authority. Indian tomahawks and French guns had revealed nothing but discord; the threat of tyranny had revealed fundamental agreement. The definition of Parliament's authority that the Stamp Act Congress had formulated was no compromise measure reluctantly agreed to under the pressure of circumstance. The congress merely reiterated principles already familiar in newspapers and pamphlets, principles that the colonial assemblies themselves had embodied in their resolutions. It nevertheless surprised the Americans to find themselves agreeing so readily. "The Colonies until now were ever at variance and foolishly jealous of each other," Joseph Warren of Massachusetts wrote to a friend, "they are now . . . united . . . nor will they soon forget the weight which this close union gives them."

In defending their rights the colonists also discovered that the ideas which united them and which they thought inherent in the British constitution were not shared by most Englishmen. Men in England had denied not only the colonists' distinction between taxation and legislation but their conception of representation. At the outset of the tax controversy Gren-

ville and his backers, admitting that Englishmen had a right to representation in the body that governed them, had claimed that the colonists *were* represented—not actually but virtually. A member of Parliament, Grenville maintained, represented not only the men who elected him, but the whole empire. The concept of virtual representation was widely accepted in England, but it was nonsense to Americans, who thought that a representative should be directly responsible to his constituents. By Grenville's reasoning, they said, Parliament could equally well claim an authority to tax the whole world.

Although a few suggestions had been made, like Governor Bernard's, that England should allow the colonies to send representatives to Parliament, the colonists did not take to the idea. It would be impractical, they thought, because of the great distance. Colonial representatives in London would lose contact with their constituents; it would cost too much to send them back and forth and to pay for their keep; they would be corrupted by the metropolis. But most important, there would be too few of them to have any real effect on the decisions of empire, yet their presence could be used to justify Parliamentary taxation of America.

These objections were serious, but not insuperable had either England or the colonies wanted to resolve them. But the plain fact was that the colonists did not want representation in Parliament. Perhaps

**Representative government: an American view**

they were unconsciously influenced by a new attitude that had been taking shape in the colonial mind but that few yet recognized. England, by treating the colonists differently from Englishmen at home, was teaching them what she should have done her best to conceal: that they actually *were* different, and perhaps even wanted to be.

Though England had no way of knowing it, the men in whom this attitude first took hold included several of extraordinary ability. In Massachusetts three emerged as leaders of the opposition to Parliamentary taxation: James Otis, Samuel Adams, and John Adams. Otis, a lawyer, was volatile, unpredictable, and unbalanced, but powerful in argument and very influential among the people of Boston. Samuel Adams, a failure at everything else he tried, was a brilliant politician, gifted in organizing popular support for any measure. In the years to come, as Otis became more erratic and finally went insane, Adams would become the virtual dictator of Boston, against whom royal governors would write home in helpless

expostulation. John Adams, whose gifts were more those of a statesman than of a politician, was as ardent as his cousin Samuel in hostility to Parliament. He despised everyone who sought political office by royal appointment, and he searched out opportunities to advance the interests of America and Americans.

In Virginia the Stamp Act had alerted another trio of men whose names would likewise become unpleasantly familiar to Englishmen. Patrick Henry, as eloquent and almost as erratic as James Otis, gained instant fame by sponsoring Virginia's resolutions against the Stamp Act. George Washington, known to at least a few outside Virginia for his service in the late war, was more given to actions than to resolutions. He was at the House of Burgesses and may have voted for Henry's resolutions, but his thoughts went more toward home manufactures and new crops as a means of shaking off America's economic dependence on Great Britain. Thomas Jefferson, a twenty-two-year-old law student, was too young for politics in 1765. But he stood at the door of the House of Bur-

*"The Bostonians paying the excise man"*

gesses and listened to Henry's "torrents of sublime eloquence." Later Jefferson would show a certain eloquence himself.

**Townshend's folly.** The repeal of the Stamp Act set the bells ringing in England and America. But the Marquis of Rockingham, who had engineered the happy event, found himself unable to please either king or Parliament. In July 1766 he went the way of Grenville, and George III gave the government once again to William Pitt, now Earl of Chatham. Unfortunately, bad health made Pitt a mere figurehead, and the new government fell under the influence of the headstrong and irresponsible Chancellor of the Exchequer, Charles Townshend.

In taking up the search for revenue, Townshend, like Grenville, looked to the colonies. Fastening on their reviving trade as the likeliest source of new income, he persuaded Parliament in 1767 to pass an ill-considered act levying duties on colonial imports of lead, paint, paper, glass, and tea. Since these items could be legally imported only from England, the new taxes would actually discourage purchases from the mother country and encourage the manufacture of taxable goods in the colonies, thus violating every principle that British economic policy had hitherto supported. The taxes also violated the colonists' expressed views on the limits of Parliament's authority.

The colonial assemblies were at this time registering their unabated disapproval of Parliamentary taxes by resisting Grenville's Quartering Act, which they regarded as a form of taxation. To demonstrate their own superior authority, they voted to supply only part of the provisions that the act specified. Yet Townshend believed, mistakenly, that the colonists were becoming more amenable to taxation, especially to taxes on trade, because they were paying the duty on molasses. In 1766 the duty had been reduced to a penny a gallon, which approximated the cost of a bribe; it had also been extended to include molasses of British production. This new duty was clearly a tax and not a regulation of trade. Encouraged by the colonists' seeming compliance, Townshend decided that, if he but acted boldly, he could now settle the question of Parliament's authority in America for good and all.

To cow the assemblies into obeying the Quartering Act, he made an example of New York, one of the principal offenders: in 1767, at his bidding, Parliament declared all acts of the New York assembly to be void until the colony furnished full supplies for the troops quartered there. To ensure collection of his new taxes on trade and of older regulatory duties as well, Townshend directed a reorganization of the American customs service. Hitherto customs officers throughout the empire had been under the administration of a board of commissioners located in England. From now on a special board of commissioners for America would reside in Boston, the center alike of colonial smuggling and of open resistance to taxation.

Americans did greet the Townshend Acts less violently than they had the Stamp Act, but they made it clear that they were still determined to rid themselves of Parliamentary taxation. In a series of eloquent newspaper letters, John Dickinson, a Philadelphia lawyer who had played a leading role in the Stamp Act Congress, repeated the arguments offered against the Stamp Act and showed that they applied equally to the Townshend acts. Dickinson's "Letters from a Farmer" were printed and reprinted by virtually all the colonial newspapers. And the representative assemblies, stiffened by Dickinson's eloquence and by a circular letter from Massachusetts, again denied the authority of Parliament to tax the colonies. Again merchants joined in nonimportation agreements, and again violators received visits from the Sons of Liberty.

The new customs commissioners were as unpopular as the new duties. They were regarded as superfluous bureaucrats sent by a corrupt ministry to fatten on the toil of Americans. And, it was feared, they were only the first of many to come; soon the colonist would have to support as many functionless officeholders as the taxpayer in England did.

The commissioners lost no time in exceeding

everyone's worst expectations. The procedures prescribed by the Sugar Act were immensely complicated, and it was easy for a merchant to make an unintentional mistake in carrying them out. By insisting on technicalities, an unscrupulous commissioner could usually find a pretext for seizing a ship and its cargo of goods. Rather than take the risk, most merchants were willing to grease the commissioners' palms. Anyone who refused to play the game was likely to have his ship condemned in an admiralty court: unless he could prove that he had fulfilled every provision of the law, the court would order his ship and cargo sold. One-third of the proceeds went to the English Treasury, one-third to the governor of the colony, and one-third to the customs officers prosecuting the case.

The officers had nothing to lose—except perhaps their lives. Even that danger was reduced when the commissioners persuaded the authorities in England to provide special protection against the hazards of their occupation. In September 1768 two regiments of troops were sent to Boston.

England's readiness to send the troops indicated how far its relations with the colonies had deteriorated and what caliber of men had taken over the empire. In 1768 Lord Hillsborough had just been made Secretary of State for the Colonies, a post created to handle the increasingly complex colonial business. His decision to send the troops to Boston may have sprung from ignorance of the situation there, but it was one of a series of blunders that prompted Benjamin Franklin to characterize his conduct in office as "perverse and senseless."

Other Americans had worse things to say. At the time of the Stamp Act the most radical objectors had suspected that it was only the first step in a design of the English ministry to reduce the colonists to absolute subjection, indeed to slavery. Resistance to the Stamp Act had thwarted the plan for the moment, but the measures that followed under Townshend seemed to be proof that the ministry had not given up. The sending of troops argued that they were putting the plan into full operation, for a standing army was the classic method by which would-be tyrants crushed resistance to their illegal and unconstitutional schemes.

When the troops arrived in Boston, therefore, Samuel Adams called for resistance. But few men were as yet ready to believe in a ministerial conspiracy. At the time the troops landed, the Massachusetts assembly was under suspension for refusing to rescind its circular letter against the Townshend Acts, and the extralegal convention that Adams organized in its place was unwilling to act on his radical demand.

The presence of the soldiers in Boston nevertheless spelled tyranny to Americans everywhere and showed again that the English ministry, if not bent on all-out tyranny, regarded Americans as not quite Englishmen. The soldiers themselves contributed to the impression by their arrogance. Even during the French and Indian War, when British and colonial troops were fighting side by side, the regulars had never disguised their contempt for the Americans. Now the feeling was returned with interest.

For a year and a half the soldiers lived in Boston, suffering icy stares, open taunts, and all the subtle harassments the citizens could devise. Hostility was steadily aggravated by the inflammatory speeches and publications of the indefatigable Samuel Adams on the one side and by the rapacity of the customs commissioners on the other. But there was no real violence until March 5, 1770. On that day a crowd looking for trouble found it in front of the Boston customhouse. They jeered the ten soldiers who stood guard before it, pelted them with oyster shells, snowballs, and sticks of wood, dared them to fire. The soldiers did fire, and so, it was later charged, did some of the customs men from the windows of the building. Eleven of the unarmed rioters were hit, five of them fatally. The massacre, as the Bostonians called it, roused such hostility to the troops that Lieutenant-Governor Thomas Hutchinson ordered them to Castle Island in the harbor. There they sat for the next four years.

Meanwhile a movement to repeal Charles Townshend's taxes was growing in England. Townshend died shortly after his acts were passed, and almost at once Englishmen began to realize that the Townshend duties were a mistake. Even without the pressure of colonial nonimportation agreements, English merchants would have protested against taxes that encouraged colonial manufacturing. Many members of the king's council favored outright repeal of the duties, but once again the government was reluctant to back down in the face of colonial defiance. The new Chancellor of the Exchequer, Lord North, who took office January 31, 1770, suggested that all the duties that encouraged colonial manufactures be repealed and that only the duty on tea, which could not be grown in America, be retained. Since Americans were inordinately fond of tea, they were importing substantial quantities of it in spite of the duty. By keeping the duty in force, England would preserve an annual revenue of ten or twelve thousand pounds and would also sustain its authority.

Parliament adopted North's solution, and the king was pleased. North was the kind of politician George had been looking for—a plodding, dogged, industrious man, neither a fool nor a genius, much like the king himself. For the next twelve years, despite the opposition of abler men, he remained at the head of the government.

*A new empire and new ideas*

# Toward independence

North's repeal of all the Townshend duties except the one on tea was well calculated. In England it mollified both the merchants and the Parliamentary critics of the administration. In America it brought a wave of good feeling for the mother country, comparable to that following repeal of the Stamp Act. The Sons of Liberty met defeat when they demanded perseverance in the boycott of British goods until the tax on tea should be repealed. Merchants began importing, and trade boomed. Royal governors reported that only a factious few continued to object to British policies.

**Discord and concord.** As good will toward the mother country rose, the recent harmony among the colonists themselves gave way to new quarrels, from which England concluded, too hastily, that American unity was a fiction. Anglicans in the Northern colonies petitioned for the appointment of an American bishop; most Anglicans in the Southern colonies opposed such an appointment; Congregationalists and Presbyterians everywhere were horrified at the prospect but were unable to cement an effective union amongst themselves to work against it.

The West was also causing trouble again. In both North and South Carolina settlers in the back country complained that the assembly was dominated by Easterners, that its taxes were too high, that its officials were corrupt, that it had failed to extend county organization in the West. In 1771 a large force of Westerners calling themselves Regulators rose against the tax collectors of North Carolina. An army of

Easterners defeated them easily at the Battle of Alamance, but the clash left the back-country men with an enduring hatred of the East.

In other colonies disputes arose over the control of western lands. Connecticut claimed land on the Susquehanna River in northeastern Pennsylvania and even organized a county there. In England Connecticut agents pressed for official recognition of their claim and Pennsylvania agents for its rejection. Meanwhile Pennsylvanians and Virginians were squabbling over lands in the Ohio Valley.

England still adhered to the land policy outlined in the Proclamation of 1763—namely, that a boundary line should be maintained between settlers and Indians. But now, instead of following the crest of the Appalachians, the line was set farther west by treaties with various Indian tribes (with the Iroquois at Fort Stanwix in 1768, with the Cherokee at Hard Labor in 1768 and at Lochaber in 1770). Americans, however, were still competing vigorously for land beyond the line. A group of speculators from the Middle colonies kept agents in England lobbying for the creation of a colony, to be known as Vandalia, south of the Ohio River. The site of the proposed colony was in territory claimed by Virginia, and the speculators of the Ohio Company angrily protested the scheme. The company was also quarreling with other Virginia speculators. Hillsborough refused to authorize the new colony.

To British politicians all these disagreements seemed more serious than they were, and colonial good will toward England seemed stronger than it was. The good will, though real, rested on the hope that Parliament was retreating from its new policies. American hostility to those policies was by no means extinguished, nor was it likely to be, so long as customs commissioners sat in Boston, the British navy patrolled American waters, and admiralty courts condemned American vessels without jury trial. Men like Samuel Adams were able to keep the colonists talking about colonial rights and Parliamentary tyranny by seeing to it that every new affront committed by the British was given wide publicity in the newspapers. And then, in 1772, at Adams' instigation the towns of Massachusetts appointed committees to formulate statements of American rights and grievances and to correspond with one another on the subject. From Massachusetts the idea spread through the rest of New England; and in 1773, as a result of the *Gaspee* affair, it was taken up on an intercolonial basis.

The *Gaspee* was a British naval vessel, which, in 1772, patrolled Narragansett Bay and inflicted daily outrages upon the inhabitants: her commander seized small boats engaged in local traffic; her sailors cut orchards for firewood and helped themselves to livestock. When the *Gaspee* ran aground on one of her missions, the people of Providence came out after

The West: Indian treaties
and speculative claims

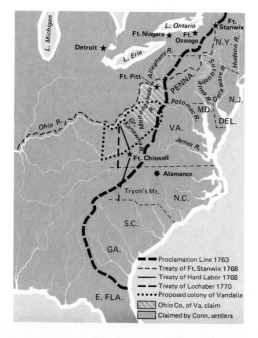

Proclamation Line 1763
Treaty of Ft. Stanwix 1768
Treaty of Hard Labor 1768
Treaty of Lochaber 1770
Proposed colony of Vandalia
Ohio Co. of Va. claim
Claimed by Conn. settlers

dark and burned her. It was a daring action and not the first of its kind. England decided to make an example of the colony. Suspecting that Rhode Island courts would make no serious effort to uncover the culprits, England appointed a special commission to investigate the incident. But Rhode Islanders would give no helpful testimony, and the commissioners never discovered the guilty parties.

The *Gaspee* commission attracted attention throughout America. Because it bypassed the Rhode Island courts, the colonists regarded it as an infringement of common-law procedures and consequently of the rights of Englishmen. In Virginia the assembly felt incited to establish a committee of correspondence for the whole colony (Patrick Henry was a member) and to propose that each of the other colonies appoint a committee of its own. When the proposal was accepted, Americans gained the machinery for coordinating their views and actions on any question affecting their common interests.

***The Intolerable Acts.*** While men like Adams and Henry were laying the foundations of American union, Lord North was worrying over another immediate and pressing problem. England had left the administration of its empire in the East largely in the hands of a giant trading corporation, the East India Company; and the company was in serious financial trouble. After bringing it under more direct supervision of the British government, Lord North secured legislation to increase the company's profits from tea-drinking Americans.

The Tea Act of May 1773 relieved the company of various taxes in England and empowered it to export tea directly from its English warehouses to America, where it would be distributed by company agents. Hitherto the company had been required to sell its tea only by auction to English wholesale merchants, who sold it to American merchants, who in turn sold it to retailers. By eliminating the middlemen's profits and the company's taxes, North hoped to lower tea prices in America so sharply that the colonists would step up their purchases and put the East India Company back on its feet. The Americans would still have to pay the tax imposed by the Townshend Act, but even so they would be able to buy tea cheaper than ever before.

North, it soon became apparent, had misjudged the colonists. By the Tea Act he lost whatever ground he had won in America by repealing the other Townshend duties. Merchants who had been importing tea themselves resented being shut out of the competitive market by a powerful, privileged company. Even the consumers, who would have benefited by the act, were hostile to it. Political leaders warned that the scheme was a trap to make Americans accept

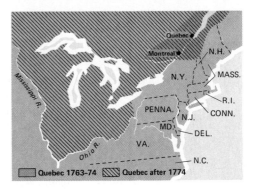

The Quebec Act, 1774

Parliamentary taxation. When the first shipments from London arrived in colonial ports, angry citizens forced the ships to return without unloading or stored the tea in warehouses from which no East India man dared remove it. In Boston, where Governor Hutchinson ruled that the ships could not depart without unloading their cargoes, a well-organized mob boarded the ships and pitched the tea into the harbor.

Lord North, who had had enough trouble with Boston, decided to punish the town with another demonstration of authority. Assisted by a new Secretary of State for the Colonies, Lord Dartmouth (Hillsborough had resigned in August 1772), he drafted the Boston Port Act, which ordered the port closed to shipping until the town made restitution for the tea. Parliament readily passed the act. North and Dartmouth might have been willing to stop there, but their fellow ministers insisted on proving Parliament's authority with three more acts (1774).

The Massachusetts Government Act altered the old constitution established by the charter of 1691 (see p. 47): henceforth the governor's council would be appointed by the king (rather than elected by the assembly) and town meetings would be held only once a year except by express permission of the governor. The Administration of Justice Act provided that any government or customs officer indicted for murder could be tried in England, beyond the control of local juries. A new Quartering Act authorized the quartering of troops within a town (instead of in the barracks provided by a colony) whenever their commanding officer thought it desirable. To underline the meaning of this act the British troops, with heavy reinforcements, were brought back into Boston from the fort in the harbor; and General Thomas Gage, the commander in chief of all the North American troops, was sent to act also as governor of the colony.

The colonists promptly dubbed these new measures the Intolerable Acts. They were followed by the Quebec Act, which had no punitive intention but which the colonists thought as outrageous as the others. Canada, since its acquisition in 1763, had been provisionally in the hands of a military governor; the Quebec Act gave the province a permanent govern-

ment with no representative assembly, established
French civil law, and offered special protection to the
Catholic Church. Although Canada as a French colony had never had a representative assembly, Americans thought it ominous that Parliament had failed to
establish one now that it was an English colony. It
disturbed them even more that the act ignored colonial territorial claims by annexing the whole region
west of the Appalachians and north of the Ohio to the
province of Quebec. Now when settlers moved west
they would have to live under Canada's autocratic
government.

The Quebec Act and the Intolerable Acts were
not the result of hasty or capricious decisions. The
Quebec Act had been drafted only after lengthy discussions with officials who had been in Canada, and
the Intolerable Acts incorporated certain changes that
had often been recommended by royal governors and
customs officers. The redesigning of the Massachusetts government in particular was a long-awaited
assertion of Parliament's authority over colonial governments. It came, however, as Governor Bernard had
feared it would, too late. By subjecting Massachusetts
to direct Parliamentary control and by backing up
that control with an army, Lord North and his colleagues thought they could teach Americans to respect the supremacy of Parliament. But the lesson the
colonists learned was that the supremacy of Parliament meant an end to the power of their own representative assemblies and courts, an end to the right to
trial by jury, an end to every political principle they
held dear.

The committees of correspondence went into
action immediately. Boston had once been known,
and not loved, throughout the colonies for the hard
bargaining of its merchants and the riotous behavior
of its inhabitants. Now the town received universal

admiration and sympathy. It was deluged with gifts of
rice from the Carolinas, flour from Pennsylvania, and
pledges of support from everywhere. To help carry out
the pledges and to coordinate action against the Intolerable Acts, the committees of correspondence arranged for an intercolonial congress to meet in September.

***The First Continental Congress.*** Fifty-five
delegates from twelve colonies (Canada, Florida, and
Georgia sent none) assembled at Philadelphia in September 1774. As soon as the sessions began, it became
apparent that the members were virtually unanimous
in support of Massachusetts and ready to employ
every sanction short of war to secure relief. Samuel
Adams presented a set of resolutions that had just
been passed by a convention in Suffolk County, Massachusetts, recommending outright resistance to the
Intolerable Acts. The Congress unanimously adopted
these Suffolk Resolves and went on to adopt, also
unanimously, a nonimportation, nonexportation, and
nonconsumption agreement, called "The Association," against trade of any kind with Great Britain,
Ireland, and the West Indies.

The members hoped for more than a mere repeal
of the coercive acts. It was time, they agreed, to settle
the limits of Parliament's authority over them. But
when they tried to formulate a statement of those
limits, they found themselves divided. In their disagreement, Joseph Galloway of Pennsylvania, perhaps
the most conservative delegate, saw an opportunity
for accommodation with England. He proposed a plan
for imperial reorganization, which he wanted the
congress to present to the king and Parliament. Galloway's plan called for a grand council of the colonies
along the lines projected at the Albany Congress (see
p. 76). Enactments of the council would be subject to

*Your Excellency adds, "for although there may be but one head, the King, yet the two Legislative bodies will make two governments as distinct as the kingdoms of England and Scotland, before the union." Very true, may it please your Excellency; and if they interfere not with each other, what hinders, but that being united in one head and common Sovereign, they may live happily in that connection, and mutually support and protect each other? Notwithstanding all the terrors which your Excellency has pictured to us as the effects of a total independence, there is more reason to dread the consequences of absolute uncontroled power, whether of a nation or a monarch, than those of a total independence. It would be a misfortune "to know by experience, the difference between the liberties of an English colonist and those of the Spanish, French, and Dutch:" and since the British Parliament has passed an act, which is executed with rigor, though not voluntarily submitted to, for raising a revenue, and appropriating the same, without the consent of the people who pay it, and have claimed a power of making such laws as they please, to order and govern us, your Excellency will excuse us in asking, whether you do not think we already experience too much of such a difference, and have not reason to fear we shall soon be reduced to a worse situation than that of the colonies of France, Spain, or Holland?*

**From the Answer of the Massachusetts House of Representatives
to Governor Hutchinson, 1773.**

Parliamentary review and veto; acts of Parliament affecting the colonies would likewise have to receive the approval of the grand council. But Galloway could not persuade the delegates to subordinate their union to Parliament. In the years since the Stamp Act crisis they had had time and provocation to think further about their relationship to that body.

In 1765 the colonists had categorically denied that Parliament had the authority to tax them; and they had acquiesced in its general legislative authority over the whole empire, mentioning specifically only trade regulation and amendment of the common law as examples of what kind of legislation they thought acceptable. Apart from an unexplained stipulation in some of their resolutions that Parliament should not alter their "internal polity" (as it finally did in the Massachusetts Government Act of 1774), they had not defined the limits of Parliament's legislative authority over them.

Since 1765 many of them had decided that Parliament had no more right to make laws concerning them than it did to tax them. This idea had few adherents until the punishment of the New York assembly, the *Gaspee* commission, and the Intolerable Acts clearly demonstrated that Parliament could destroy men's rights as readily by legislation as by taxation. Thereafter the idea spread rapidly. Benjamin Franklin adopted it privately as early as 1766, and Samuel Adams led the Massachusetts assembly in affirming it to Governor Hutchinson in 1773. In the summer of 1774 prospective members of the coming congress could read powerful demonstrations of it in two pamphlets. In *Considerations on the . . . Authority of the British Parliament*, James Wilson, a Pennsylvania lawyer, pointed out that all the familiar arguments against Parliamentary taxation applied equally well against Parliamentary legislation. Jefferson took the same position in *A Summary View of the Rights of British America.*

Neither Jefferson nor Wilson was present at the First Continental Congress, but enough of the delegates agreed with them to defeat Galloway's plan. The radicals were unable, however, to bring the Congress to repudiate all colonial ties with Parliament. Of those who were no longer willing to admit that Parliament had any authority in the colonies, some still believed that it should be allowed to regulate colonial trade as a just compensation for the British navy's protection of colonial shipping. When the delegates came to framing a statement of colonial rights and grievances, John Adams finally got them to compromise on a resolution, drafted mostly by James Duane, that denied Parliament any authority over the colonies but agreed—as a matter of fairness and expediency—to submit to its acts for regulation of trade.

The Congress was inviting Parliament to return to the same supervisory role it had exercised in the colonies before 1763. Had Parliament been willing to do so, the breach, instead of widening, might have closed. The Earl of Chatham (William Pitt) and Edmund Burke both recognized the opportunity, but neither could muster more than a few votes for pro-

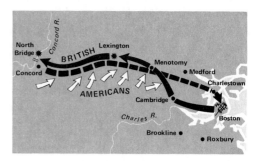

Lexington and Concord, April 19, 1775

"The Battle of Lexington"

posals to repeal the Intolerable Acts and renounce American taxation. Lord North, however, did secure passage in February 1775 of what he regarded as a conciliatory measure proposing to withhold Parliamentary taxation of any colony whose inhabitants taxed themselves "for contributing their proportion to the common defence." The proposal gave no indication of how much each colony's "proportion" might be or how large a total contribution would be required, and it was silent on the other issues raised by the Intolerable Acts and by the declarations of the Continental Congress. To Americans it appeared to be only an insidious attempt by the ministry to draw away individual colonies from the new union.

But English statesmen were in no mood for softer measures. Most of them were convinced that Samuel Adams and his tribe were leading the colonists toward independence and that the march could be halted only by more forceful demonstrations of Parliamentary supremacy. The session that passed Lord North's conciliatory resolve also passed an act excluding New Englanders from the Newfoundland fisheries and prohibiting them from all trade except with the mother country and the British West Indies. At the same time the ministry took steps to prevent exportation of arms and ammunition to the colonies. Even the king expected the worst. "The New England Governments are in a State of Rebellion," he had told Lord North in November 1774. "Blows," he added, "must decide whether they are to be subject to this Country or Independent."

England clearly anticipated war, but its leaders had no conception of the size of the enemy. In spite of the increasingly obvious signs of colonial unity, Lord North and his colleagues persisted in regarding the enemy as Massachusetts alone. General Gage, sitting uneasily in the governor's chair in Massachusetts, did his best to disillusion them. The Americans, he reported, were as ready for blows as the English; to enforce Parliament's authority he would need twenty thousand men. Until England was prepared to send that many, he said, it would be well to suspend the Intolerable Acts.

George III thought Gage's dispatches absurd; Lord North turned from them to ask Parliament for a reduction in the size of Britain's armed forces. Gage was allowed about thirty-five hundred, and by the spring of 1775 he was himself persuaded that it was time to use them.

### From Lexington to Bunker Hill.

The general knew from his informers that the colonial militia were assembling arms and ammunition at strategic points. In Portsmouth, New Hampshire, they carried off a hundred barrels of powder belonging to the crown. Gage did not dare detach any part of his small force to recover the royal gunpowder, but occasionally he marched sizable columns for a few miles into the country around Boston, hoping by this show of strength to overawe incipient rebels. On April 14 he received instructions from Lord Dartmouth to take the offensive against the rebellious colonists, and on April 19 he sent seven hundred men to Concord to seize a supply of arms reportedly stored there.

Although the force got started in the dark of early morning, the tolling of alarm bells and the firing of signal guns showed that its errand was no secret. Anticipating trouble, the commanding officer sent back for reinforcements but ordered six companies under Major John Pitcairn to proceed. At Lexington,

*The second discovery of America*

Pitcairn found colonial militia drawn up on the village green. At his command, they began to disperse. Then suddenly a shot rang out. Whether British or American, musket or pistol, accidental or deliberate, was not apparent; but when they heard the shot, the British soldiers fired a volley into the departing militiamen, killing eight of them and wounding ten.

This episode delayed the troops for only fifteen minutes, and by eight o'clock they were entering Concord. The Americans had already removed most of the military stores they had assembled there, but the British burned a few gun carriages and repulsed a group of militiamen who tried to drive them off. Two colonials and three British were killed in the skirmish. By noon the "battles" of Lexington and Concord were over and the British troops started back to Boston.

Now a real battle began, a battle unlike any the troops had ever seen. Colonial militiamen for miles around had been alerted by a system of riders organized for just such an emergency, and the seven hundred British regulars were obliged to run a gauntlet of fire from three or four thousand Americans. At Lexington the returning troops were joined by nine hundred reinforcements, but still the Americans fired from rock and tree at the massed target of moving redcoats.

The total casualties on both sides were not large: the British lost 73 killed, 192 wounded, and 22 captured, the Americans, 49 killed, 39 wounded. But Gage's earlier fears had been justified: his offensive had turned into a rout. That night, as haggard British soldiers dragged themselves into Boston, watch fires dotted the landscape around the city: militia were beginning to move in from all over New England. Boston was already under siege by a people who had no proper army, no system of command, no regular government.

On June 17, less than two months later, Gage found how tightly he was held. Reinforced by sea with 1,100 troops and 3 major generals (William Howe, John Burgoyne, and Henry Clinton), he decided to roll back the siege. On the night of June 16, the Americans, forewarned of his plans, marched 1,200 men to Breed's Hill (just south of Bunker Hill, from which the ensuing action, for no good reason, received its name), overlooking Boston from the north. By morning, when 400 more joined them, they had dug a formidable redoubt.

That afternoon General Howe set out with 2,200 men to displace the rebels from their position. Since Breed's Hill was on a peninsula, Howe could have cut the Americans off by landing a force at their rear. Instead, he bombarded nearby Charlestown at the end of the peninsula and launched a frontal assault. The Americans inside the redoubt held their fire as the

enemy, firing regularly and harmlessly, marched coolly up the hill. When the Americans returned the fire, the British went down in rows.

Howe regrouped his forces and tried again, with the same result. But now the Americans were low on ammunition, and the British regulars, reinforced by 600 men, finally forced the redoubt with bayonets. The Americans, clubbing their muskets, retreated slowly, leaving 140 of their men dead, 271 wounded, and 30 captured. Howe's victory had cost him 226 killed and 828 wounded. Another such victory, wrote Clinton ruefully, "would have ruined us." It had now been demonstrated beyond dispute that Americans with guns were dangerous. The British never again underestimated the men they were fighting.

Boston and Charlestown,
June 17, 1775

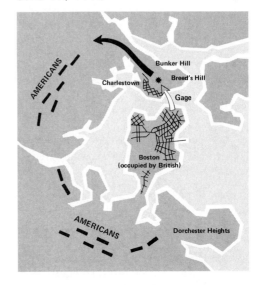

97

**One people.** While sixteen thousand colonial militia pinned down the British forces in Boston, other Americans were taking the necessary steps to support the war. Royal governors everywhere watched their authority collapse, as surely as Gage's had collapsed outside Boston. A few tried to organize loyalist support to combat the rebellion, but sooner or later they all gave up and fled to the safety of British warships. The colonial assemblies, which had hitherto met under royal authorization, now gathered as extralegal provincial congresses and began to act as independent governments, raising troops and issuing forbidden paper money to pay them. The transition in government presented no serious difficulty, because the representatives to the provincial congresses were for the most part former assemblymen and they simply carried on with their usual business.

A more extraordinary task faced the delegates who, in May 1775, assembled at Philadelphia for the Second Continental Congress (which had been arranged by the First Congress). Previous intercolonial meetings, the Albany Congress, the Stamp Act Congress, and the First Continental Congress, had devoted themselves to hammering out agreements of principle. But by the time the Second Congress met, the colonists were already deeply committed to common principles and a common cause. Fighting had just begun, and the delegates, instead of conducting another debating council, found themselves conducting America's first central government: they assumed responsibility for the provincial militia besieging Boston, ordered their transformation into a Continental Army, named George Washington as commander, issued paper money to support the troops, and appointed a committee to negotiate with foreign countries.

Although in taking these actions the Congress assumed many of the powers of an independent government, the members still did not intend to establish an independent nation. Delegates from the middle colonies, led by John Dickinson, were especially reluctant to take any steps in that direction. Repudiation of Parliament was not repudiation of England, and the Congress did not see why Englishmen in America and in England should not retain their brotherhood in loyalty to a common king. In July they laid their cause at the feet of the king with a petition asking him personally to promote repeal of the oppressive measures. Significantly they placed the blame for those measures on the ministry—"those artful and cruel enemies who abuse your royal confidence and authority for the purpose of effecting our destruction." They issued at the same time a "Declaration of the causes and necessity for taking up arms," in which they explained that they were "reduced to the alternative of choosing an unconditional submission to the tyranny of irritated ministers, or resistance by force." In choosing resistance, they said, they had no "ambitious designs of separating from Great Britain, and establishing independent states." As soon as England acknowledged their rights, they would lay down their arms.

Although some Americans had already begun to think of independence, the declarations of the Congress were made in good faith. Even at this date the repeal of the Intolerable Acts and the restriction of Parliamentary legislation to the regulation of trade might have kept the colonists in the empire. They still thought of their rights as the rights of Englishmen and of their union as a means of protecting those rights. But George III and Lord North were bent on subjecting the colonists to a Parliament in which they elected no representative. The king did not answer their petition; Parliament did, however, answer their "declaration"—by voting to send twenty-five thousand more troops against them. The addition would bring British military strength in America to forty thousand. In August the king issued a proclamation declaring the colonies in a state of rebellion, and in December Parliament passed an act outlawing all their trade and subjecting their ships and goods to confiscation.

Each British action weakened the colonists' emotional attachment to England. The principal ingredient in their national feeling had been admiration for the British form of government, which better than any other guaranteed the human rights of its subjects. When their admiration for Parliament crumbled, they had fastened the last shreds of their loyalty on the king alone. But he had enthusiastically supported Parliament against them. If the whole English government was determined to destroy the rights of its subjects, then it was a dubious privilege to be an Englishman.

In January 1776 the new image of George III as a tyrant was presented to the colonists with biting eloquence in a publication called simply *Common Sense*. The author, Thomas Paine, an Englishman who had arrived in America only in 1774, argued that it was foolish for Americans to stake their lives and fortunes simply to obtain a repeal of Parliamentary laws. "The object contended for," he said, "ought always to bear some just proportion to the expence. . . . Dearly, dearly, do we pay for the repeal of the acts, if that is all we fight for." Common sense forbade that Americans should remain loyal to a king who sanctioned the spilling of their blood. In fact monarchy itself was an absurdity, a form of government that had laid the world in blood and ashes. "Of more worth," declared Paine, "is one honest man to society and in the sight of God, than all the crowned ruffians that ever lived." Here Paine struck a responsive chord. Since the days of Cromwell republican government had never ceased

*The second discovery of America*

to have its devotees both in Great Britain and in America, and the old distrust of kings had never entirely died out. The colonists' very devotion to the House of Hanover was in part an expression of this distrust, an oblique way of denouncing the House of Stuart (which the Hanovers had replaced) and of affirming the right of a people to change kings. By calling on Americans to cast off kings altogether, Thomas Paine kindled a latent enthusiasm for republican government.

In the six months that followed the publication of *Common Sense*, sentiment in favor of independence and republicanism grew rapidly. Many who hoped that George III would save American liberty had been convinced by Paine that no king could help them. Many who had considered independence impossible to attain now began to change their minds. Ever since Lexington, American forces throughout the colonies had been fighting the British with heartening success in one engagement after another. And, as men thought beyond the mere repeal of Parliamentary laws, they began to cut their ties with England and England's king. The provincial congress of South Carolina established a republican constitution in March, and in May the Rhode Island congress repealed the law requiring allegiance to the king. North Carolina in April and Virginia in May instructed their delegates in the Continental Congress to vote for independence.

The Continental Congress, with representatives from thirteen colonies (delegates from Georgia had arrived in September 1775), was itself behaving more and more like an independent national government. In March it authorized privateering against British ships. In April it forbade the further importation of slaves and declared other trade open to all the world except Great Britain. In May, urged by John Adams, it even recommended that any member colonies who had not already done so should suppress all vestiges of royal authority within their borders and establish governments resting on popular consent.

By this time Adams and many other delegates from New England and the Southern colonies were prepared to make an outright declaration of independence. They were restrained only by the reluctant rebels of the Middle colonies. Although virtually the whole Congress had by now concluded that Parliament had no constitutional authority at all in America, some Americans still felt bound to England by a lingering loyalty to the king and a sentimental attachment to the English people. By the end of June the continuing war had worn both feelings thin. Independence was becoming more and more attractive and a

*Signing the Declaration of Independence*

declaration of it perhaps necessary to show foreign countries that Americans were playing for keeps. To sustain the war, the colonists needed help—arms and ammunition and maybe men—from England's European enemies. But England was powerful, and no one wished to be exposed to her wrath by subsidizing a rebellion that might collapse into a reconciliation. When rumors mounted that England was engaged in a Machiavellian maneuver to forestall foreign assistance to the colonies and was proposing to France and Spain that they partition the North American continent among the three of them, it seemed high time for Americans to come to a decision. On July 2, the Congress finally agreed to a motion that had been introduced by Richard Henry Lee of Virginia nearly a month before: "That these United Colonies are, and of right ought to be free and independent states." Thomas Jefferson, assisted by Franklin and John Adams, expanded the resolution into the famous declaration that was adopted on July 4.

Jefferson's declaration was an eloquent application of the ideas made familiar by John Locke and by a century and a half of American experience. It affirmed the origin of government in the consent of the governed, its obligation to protect natural rights, and the duty of a people to alter or abolish a government that failed to fulfill its obligation. That the British government had failed was demonstrated by a long list of misdeeds. These were attributed not to Parliament, whose authority the colonists had already denied, but to the king, the only remaining link between the colonies and England. Every grievance suffered by Americans since 1763 was laid at his door. The indictment was not altogether realistic, but it effectively expressed the American rejection not only of George III but of monarchy itself. Embedded in the preamble was evidence that the colonists had learned the lesson England had taught: "When in the course of human events, it becomes necessary for one people to dissolve the political bands which have connected them with another. . . ." Englishmen were "another" people; and the colonists, who twenty-two years before had rejected the union proposed at Albany, now spoke of themselves as "one people."

*Suggestions for reading*

The period covered by this chapter was first treated in the grand manner by George Bancroft in Vols. IV–VII of his *History of the United States,* 10 vols. (1834–74); Bancroft is still grand reading. Although subsequent historians have been able to correct him on many points, few if any have matched him in literary gifts or in comprehensive knowledge of the sources. Where Bancroft saw events with the future of the United States always in mind, G. L. Beer, in *British Colonial Policy, 1754–1765* (1907), viewed the French and Indian War from a British point of view. L. H. Gipson sees events in America in relation to Britain's imperial problems throughout the world in *The British Empire Before the American Revolution,* 15 vols. (1936–70). Vols. V–VIII deal with the French and Indian War, which Professor Gipson has renamed "The Great War for the Empire." Vols. IX–XII cover the years from 1763 to 1776. The first two volumes of Douglas Freeman, *George Washington,* 7 vols. (1948–57), cover Washington's role in the war.

The understanding of British politics in the 1760s and 1770s has been considerably altered since Bancroft's time. The older views were well expressed in G. O. Trevelyan's magnificently written *The American Revolution,* 4 vols. (1898–1907, reprinted 1964). L. B. Namier, in *The Structure of Politics at the Accession of George III,* 2 vols.\* (1929), and *England in the Age of the American Revolution*\* (1930), has since shown that the party system assumed by Trevelyan did not yet exist and that George III was a better monarch than anyone had supposed. Bernard Donoughue, *British Politics and the American Revolution: The Path to War, 1773–75* (1965), spells out the implications of Namier's views, as does John Brooke, *King George III* (1972), a sympathetic and well informed biography of the king. On the other hand, Herbert Butterfield, *George III and the Historians* (1959), argues that the older views were not quite so mistaken as Namier and his followers thought them to be. A valuable study of the radical political tradition in England is Caroline Robbins, *The Eighteenth-Century Commonwealthman*\* (1959).

Clarence Alvord, *The Mississippi Valley in British Politics,* 2 vols. (1916), is a classic study of British policy toward the American West. This should be supplemented by T. P. Abernethy, *Western Lands and the American Revolution* (1937), and J. M. Sosin, *Whitehall and the Wilderness: The Middle West in British Colonial Policy, 1760–1775* (1961).

\*Available in a paperback edition.

Perhaps the best introduction to the multitude of books on the origins of the Revolution is C. M. Andrews, *The Colonial Background of the American Revolution*\* (1924, rev. ed., 1931). A good one-volume account of the events from 1763 to 1783 is J. R. Alden, *A History of the American Revolution* (1969). A fuller account of the years 1763–76, stressing political history, is Merrill Jensen, *The Founding of a Nation* (1968). E. S. Morgan, *The Birth of the Republic*\* (1956), is a brief account of the period 1763–89. There are numerous specialized studies of particular developments that contributed to the Revolution. J. A. Ernst, *Money and Politics in America, 1755–1775* (1973), deals with British fiscal policy, especially the Currency Act of 1764. O. M. Dickerson, *The Navigation Acts and the American Revolution*\* (1951), argues that the Navigation Acts were not a cause of the Revolution. A. M. Schlesinger, *The Colonial Merchants and the American Revolution, 1763–1776*\* (1917), shows how the merchants initially took the lead in opposition to England but became wary as popular feeling seemed to threaten their own position. John Shy, *Toward Lexington*\* (1965), traces the role of the British troops in bringing on the Revolution. B. W. Labaree, *The Boston Tea Party*\* (1964), shows how this event precipitated the crisis. H. B. Zobel, *The Boston Massacre*\* (1970), emphasizes the provocations that led the British to fire. A contemporary Tory view of the coming of the Revolution, pungently expressed, is Peter Oliver, *Origin and Progress of the American Rebellion*\*, Douglas Adair and John Schutz, eds. (1961). David Ammerman, *In the Common Cause*\* (1974), is a fresh analysis of American response to the Coercive Acts.

Several books discuss the political and constitutional principles developed by the colonists before 1776. E. S. and H. M. Morgan, *The Stamp Act Crisis: Prologue to Revolution*\* (1953), describes the events and ideas of the years 1764–66; and E. S. Morgan, *Prologue to Revolution: Sources and Documents on The Stamp Act Crisis, 1764–1766*\* (1959), reprints many of the resolutions, petitions, newspaper articles, and pamphlets in which the colonists expressed their views. Later development of colonial opinion is treated in Carl Becker, *The Declaration of Independence*\* (1922), and R. G. Adams, *The Political Ideas of the American Revolution*\* (1922). Bernard Bailyn, ed., *The Pamphlets of the American Revolution, 1750–1776* (1965), reprints the most important tracts on the American side, with an important introduction analyzing the arguments, printed separately as *The Ideological Origins of the American Revolution*\* (1967). Richard Merritt employs techniques of modern political science to trace the rise of American nationalism in *Symbols of American Community, 1735–1775* (1966). Pauline Maier, *From Resistance to Revolution: Colonial Radicals and the Development of American Opposition to Britain, 1765–1766* (1972), traces the evolution of popular hostility to England.

A number of able books describe the internal developments within different colonies in the years preceding independence. R. E. Brown, *Middle-Class Democracy and the Revolution in Massachusetts, 1691–1780*\* (1955), stresses the absence of internal class conflict, but R. J. Taylor finds more evidence of such conflict in the West in *Western Massachusetts in the Revolution* (1954), as does S. E. Patterson, *Political Parties in Revolutionary Massachusetts* (1973). A good close-up of Boston is found in G. B. Warden, *Boston, 1689–1776* (1970). David Lovejoy, *Rhode Island Politics and the American Revolution, 1760–1776* (1958), traces political divisions and shows that all sides in Rhode Island were united against the British. Carl Becker, *The History of Political Parties in the Province of New York, 1760–1776*\* (1909), shows that in New York the Revolution was a contest not only about home rule but also about "who should rule at home." Becker's views are modified in P. U. Bonomi, *A Factious People*\* (1971). Similar studies for other states are Theodore Thayer, *Pennsylvania Politics and the Growth of Democracy, 1740–1776* (1953); J. H. Hutson, *Pennsylvania Politics, 1746–1770* (1972); C. A. Barker, *The Background of the Revolution in Maryland* (1940); Ronald Hoffman, *A Spirit of Dissension: Economics, Politics, and the Revolution in Maryland* (1973); D. C. Skaggs, *Roots of Maryland Democracy, 1753–1776* (1973); R. E. and B. K. Brown, *Virginia 1705–1786: Democracy or Aristocracy* (1964); C. S. Sydnor, *Gentlemen Freeholders* (1952); Carl Bridenbaugh, *Seat of Empire: The Political Role of Eighteenth Century Williamsburg*\* (1950); and Oscar Zeichner, *Connecticut's Years of Controversy, 1750–1776* (1950). An important volume of essays discussing internal class conflicts in several different states is Alfred Young, ed., *The American Revolution: Explorations in the History of American Radicalism* (1976).

\*Available in a paperback edition.

CHAPTER **5**

# *An American people*

*Continental currency:*
*one-sixth of a dollar*

Although the colonists had moved slowly and reluctantly toward declaring independence, once the deed was done most of them had no regrets. There were, of course, loyalists, whose sympathies remained with England. They varied in number from place to place, but the best modern estimates put the total at no more than a fifth of the colonial population. Many of the most ardent left for Canada or England. Of those who remained, some were ready to fight their countrymen for their king—some, but never enough to win. There were also men indifferent to who ruled them and willing to sell supplies to either side, depending on the price offered. But in every colony that joined in the Declaration of Independence, the patriots were sufficiently numerous, vociferous, and aggressive to outweigh the loyalists and the indifferent. Once the royal governments collapsed, it proved impossible to revive British authority except in the immediate vicinity of British guns.

## The winning of independence

**The rebel army.** Perhaps because they could overawe the loyalists, the patriots counted too easily on doing the same to the British armies. After the rout on April 19 and the slaughter on June 17 (see pp. 96 and 97), they were inclined to believe that their militia could handle any force the British sent against them. George Washington knew better; the men encamped around Boston did have spirit, courage, and marksmanship, but they were not an army. To make them

into one was Washington's first concern after taking command at Cambridge on July 3, 1775.

It was not simply a matter of instruction and training in the art of war. Militia units had to be reorganized under a corps of officers appointed from above. In the process, many of the old officers lost rank and stalked off in a huff. Furthermore, many of the militia who had come to besiege Boston had elected their own officers and were touchy about taking orders from higher up. They were also used to short terms of service (for a local emergency or a particular campaign) and eager to get home to their crops. Wherever the enemy appeared, Americans from miles around would turn out to fight him; but they did not want to join the army. To join the army was to desert one's family for danger, discomfort, and disease hundreds of miles from home. The pay was low, and no pension system existed to compensate a man or his family for the loss of life or limb. It therefore took all of Washington's diplomacy and tact to persuade ten thousand militiamen to enlist until the end of 1776 as regular soldiers in the Continental Army. In addition the provincial governments supplied him with about seven thousand short-term militiamen.

The total was much smaller than Washington had hoped for. Throughout the war Congress was able to provide him with an ample army of men on paper. But men with arms, legs, heads, and guns remained in short supply. Since Congress had no power either to raise money or to draft men, it was dependent on requisitions to the states for both; and when the states lagged in supplying their assigned quotas, Congress could do nothing to coerce them. Supplies were as hard to come by as men; Washington had to spend much of his time pleading for both, and he had to

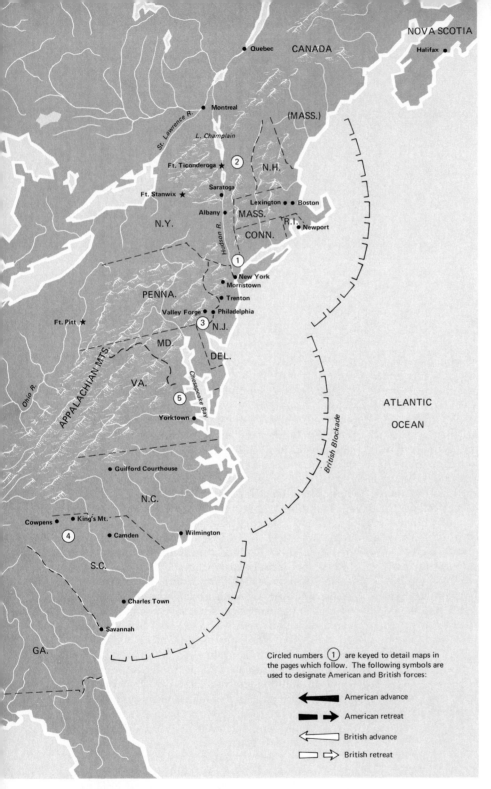

Major campaigns
of the Revolutionary War

NOVA SCOTIA

Quebec • CANADA
Halifax •

• Montreal
(MASS.)
L. Champlain
Ft. Ticonderoga ★ ②  N.H.
Saratoga •
Ft. Stanwix ★          Lexington • • Boston
Albany •  MASS.
N.Y.        CONN.  R.I.
                            • Newport
①
• New York
Morristown •
PENNA.     • Trenton
Valley Forge • • Philadelphia
Ft. Pitt ★  ③ N.J.
MD.
DEL.
VA.
⑤
Yorktown •

• Guilford Courthouse

N.C.

Cowpens •  • King's Mt.
④  • Camden  • Wilmington

S.C.

• Charles Town

• Savannah

GA.

ATLANTIC

OCEAN

British Blockade

Circled numbers ① are keyed to detail maps in
the pages which follow. The following symbols are
used to designate American and British forces:

◄━━  American advance

◄▪▪▪▪▶  American retreat

◁═══  British advance

▭ ⇨  British retreat

fight the war with an army that was constantly in danger of dissolution.

The new army's first venture away from Boston began while Boston was still under siege, before independence was declared. Congress had invited the people of Canada to join their union, and, though the Canadians had failed to respond, some reports suggested that they would welcome an invading army. In any case, it was desirable to strike at the British in Quebec and Montreal in order to forestall an attack from that direction. After a grueling winter march, the effective forces that converged on Quebec amounted to only a thousand men, and the Canadians showed no disposition to help them. Colonel Benedict Arnold and General Richard Montgomery, who had already taken Montreal on his way north, besieged the city through the winter; but smallpox, hunger, cold, and an unsuccessful assault so thinned their ranks that in the spring they retreated to Ticonderoga. The colonists made no further military effort to draw Canada into their union.

In the South the Americans fared better. In June 1776, when Generals Henry Clinton and Charles, Lord Cornwallis, and Admiral Sir Peter Parker arrived at Charles Town, South Carolina, with fifty ships and an army of three thousand men, they made every mistake possible and were turned back by fire from a single fort constructed of palmetto logs and dirt. After a ten-hour duel the British withdrew and left Charles Town alone for the next four years.

In Massachusetts, Washington had meanwhile built a force strong enough to close in on Boston. He began by occupying and fortifying Dorchester Heights, which overlooked the city on the south as Breed's Hill did on the north. This time the British did not try to storm the hills. Instead, on March 17, 1776, they departed by sea for Halifax, Nova Scotia, taking over a thousand loyalists with them.

A few months after the British evacuation of Boston, when Americans declared their indepen-

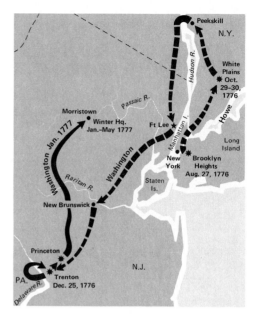

① Washington's moves in New York and New Jersey, 1776–77

*"The American Rifle Men"*

dence, they appeared to be in a strong position. Although they were challenging the world's greatest military and naval power and had failed to win Canada to their cause, they had overpowered the British army in the march from Concord, withstood its assaults at Breed's Hill, forced its withdrawal from Boston, and fought off the British navy at Charles Town. But the British war machine, always a slow starter, was now grinding into action. Parliament had authorized an army of fifty-five thousand, and, when recruitment lagged in England, the government hired thirty thousand German mercenaries, seventeen thousand of them from Hesse-Cassel (hence the name Hessians). General William Howe and his brother, Admiral Richard Howe, were given command.

The Howes were authorized to end the war as soon as the colonists submitted. Hoping to end it before they began, they addressed a conciliatory letter to "George Washington, Esq." (thus ignoring his military status). But General Washington was not receiving letters for George Washington, Esq., letters that denied American independence even in the address. The Howes therefore proceeded according to plan. On August 12, 1776, they arrived in New York harbor with thirty-two thousand troops and ten thousand seamen (the city's normal population was twenty-five thousand) aboard four hundred transports and thirty warships. Ten days later twenty thousand of the troops landed on Long Island near Brooklyn.

Washington had twenty-three thousand men in the New York area, but most of them were inexperi-

*The winning of independence*

*British fleet in New York harbor*

enced local militia. When Howe, with plenty of men to spare, launched both frontal and flank attacks, Washington was forced to withdraw to Manhattan with heavy losses. Thinking that this taste of British power might have chastened the Americans, Howe offered to confer about a settlement before any more blows were struck. Congress sent Franklin, John

*The Surrender of General Burgoyne, by John Trumbull*

Adams, and Edward Rutledge to deal with him, but the resulting conference broke off when it turned out, as Washington had suspected, that Howe was empowered to negotiate only with submissive colonists, not with the proud representatives of an independent nation. In September the British drove Washington off Manhattan Island; and by November the Continental Army, depleted by captures and desertions, was in full retreat across New Jersey.

Washington crossed the Delaware River into Pennsylvania on December 7. Now, with the river between him and the enemy, he planned his next move. The outlook was bleak. While pursuing him across New Jersey, the British had been able simultaneously to send a large force to Rhode Island, where on December 8 they occupied Newport. Washington's force was down to fewer than eight thousand effective fighting men, all of them dispirited, exhausted, ready to quit. By the end of the month all but fifteen hundred would have completed their term of enlistment, and with winter coming on they would sling their packs, head for home, and let someone else fight the war. While he still had them, Washington attacked. On the night of December 25, 1776, in high, freezing winds, he shuttled his men back across the river, marched them nine miles to Trenton, and caught the enemy asleep and befuddled. With a loss of only four men he took nine hundred prisoners. The brilliant reversal so cheered the troops that Washington was able to persuade many of them to reenlist. A few days later at Princeton he dealt the British another smashing blow, and they pulled back to New Brunswick for the winter. With spirits high again, the Continental Army moved into winter quarters at Morristown.

General Howe, contemplating the reverses that Washington had dealt him, had difficulty making up his mind about what to do when spring should come. After changing plans several times he finally decided to storm the rebel capital of Philadelphia, which, like New York, contained a large loyalist population. In July he took fifteen thousand men by sea from New York to the head of Chesapeake Bay. From there they marched north toward Philadelphia, the Hessians helping themselves to food, furniture, and women along the way. Washington intercepted them at Brandywine Creek; but, as on Long Island, Howe won the pitched battle and entered Philadelphia on September 26, 1777. When Washington challenged him a week later at Germantown, where most of the British troops were quartered, foggy weather broke up a powerful American attack, and Howe again was victorious.

These defeats discouraged the colonists, but actually Howe's success was hollow. Though he had captured America's largest cities and repeatedly defeated her generals, he had captured no armies and controlled only a small portion of American territory. And to the north of him disaster was brewing. General John Burgoyne had been authorized by the high command in England to mount an expedition for a march south from Canada by the Lake Champlain route. He set out from Fort St. John's in June with four

thousand British, three thousand Germans, fourteen hundred Indians, and a pleasing mistress to cheer him along. Everything went swimmingly for a time. But American forces, under Horatio Gates and Benedict Arnold, gathered ever stronger before him, and each time they clashed Burgoyne lost several hundred men. On October 17, 1777, he finally surrendered at Saratoga.

***The French alliance.*** Saratoga was one of the turning points of history, but not because it turned back any threat to the American armies. Burgoyne's march, if successful, would have signified little in a military sense; his surrender did not seriously reduce the British margin of superiority in troops and equipment. Saratoga had its great effect, not in New York or Philadelphia, but in London and Paris.

In London a complacent Parliament began to sense the possibility that England might lose the war. Better make peace, the ministry decided, and it authorized a commission headed by Lord Carlisle to offer the Americans virtually everything they had previously demanded: renunciation of Parliamentary taxation, repeal of the Intolerable Acts, and suspension of every other objectionable act passed since 1763. Two years earlier such concessions would probably have kept the colonies within the empire. But by now the rebels found independence exhilarating. Eng-

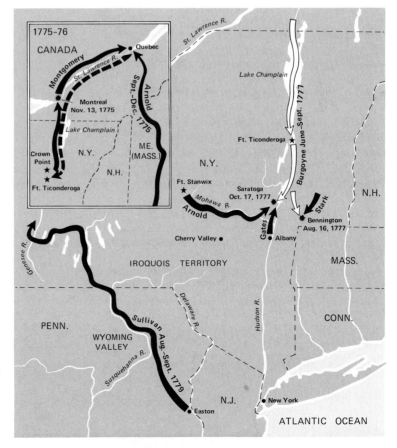

② The war in the North, 1775–79

land's eagerness to have them back merely furnished them with the final weapon they needed to make their independence last: the recognition and assistance of France.

From the outset the Americans had been hoping for help from England's traditional enemy, and on November 29, 1775, Congress had appointed a secret committee to seek foreign aid. Louis XVI, delighted by the rebellion of England's colonies, had sent Achard de Bonvouloir to observe the situation in America. With Bonvouloir's encouragement the committee dispatched Silas Deane, a shrewd and sophisticated Yankee, to negotiate with France. Deane arrived in Paris on July 7, 1776, to find that the French foreign minister, the Comte de Vergennes, had already persuaded the king to help the American rebellion with a million livres' worth of munitions and supplies. Furthermore, Spain had matched the amount. The goods were to be dispensed secretly through a fake trading company run by Pierre Beaumarchais (author of *The Barber of Seville*). They were Deane's for the asking, though whether as a gift or as a loan remained uncertain.

Deane's negotiations took place before news of the Declaration of Independence reached France, when secret assistance was all the Americans dared ask for. Once the declaration had been announced, they hoped that France would recognize their independence and offer open assistance. To help Deane push these more ambitious requests, Congress sent Arthur Lee, a Virginian who had been serving the American cause in London, and Benjamin Franklin, who arrived from Philadelphia in December 1776. The three men constituted a commission with power to make treaties of amity and commerce.

The French at this time envisaged America as an Arcadia peopled by noble savages and almost equally noble farmers, rich in nature's wisdom; Franklin, seeing what was expected, donned his fur cap and played the role to the hilt. Completely enchanted, the Parisians showered the arch-American with favors, but Vergennes and his royal master remained cautious. Besides furnishing supplies to the colonists, they sometimes allowed American privateers the use of French harbors. They hesitated, however, to join in open war on England when the British armies, with the capture of New York, appeared to be winning.

As American military fortunes declined, Congress instructed the commissioners to go beyond their request for French assistance and to seek the deeper commitment of an alliance. All Franklin's charm was insufficient to win it. Vergennes wanted Spain by his side before he took on the British lion, and Spain was unwilling. Spain feared even to give open assistance to the Americans lest she encourage her own colonies to revolt.

When news of Saratoga reached Paris on December 3, 1777, Vergennes perceived at once that the American victory might produce a conciliatory temper in England, and the last thing he wanted was to see the rebellious colonies reconciled to the mother country. Franklin played on his fears, and Vergennes sent frantic messages to Spain. When Spain remained immovable, he finally told the commissioners that France was ready to enter into a treaty of commerce and amity and a treaty of alliance with the Americans. He indeed required an alliance before entering the war, in order to prevent the United States from making peace before England was humbled.

The terms of the alliance, signed on February 6, 1778, were all that the United States could have wished for. The stated purpose of both parties was to maintain the independence of the United States. In case of war between France and England (which the signing of the treaty made inevitable), neither France nor the United States was to make peace without the consent of the other. France renounced all future claims to English territory on the continent of North America and agreed that any such territory captured in the war would go to the United States. These generous terms were less the result of American diplomatic skill than of French determination to weaken England and French distaste for further colonizing in the New World.

Even before the alliance the Americans had depended heavily on aid from France. The victory at Saratoga, for example, would have been impossible without French supplies. And French financial support helped to bolster American credit at a time when Congress, with no authority to tax, was financing the war with money begged from the states or manufactured by the printing presses. With the signing of the alliance the hopes of the Americans soared, for France was the first nation to recognize them as "one people," and France had the military and naval power to make that recognition meaningful.

***From Saratoga to Yorktown.*** After the battle of Saratoga the British fought a cautious war, their dreams of easy victory gone. Howe, snug in Philadelphia during the winter of 1777–78, did not even try to attack Washington's wretched forces, who were starving and freezing in their winter quarters at nearby Valley Forge. In the spring Howe was replaced by Sir Henry Clinton, who was to prove somewhat less languid though no bolder. The spring of 1778 also brought France's entry into the war and American refusal of the Carlisle Commission's peace overtures (see p. 107). Uncertain of where France would throw her weight, the British high command decided to play safe and ordered Clinton to withdraw from Philadelphia to New York. There he should plan a major campaign in the South, where—according to the strategists—loyalists would lend a decisive hand.

At Valley Forge, as mild weather came on, Washington's forces thawed out and were drilled with Prussian precision by Baron Friedrich von Steuben, an idealist from the Old World who had come to help usher in the independence of the New. By June he and a good supply of provisions had turned the haggard men into a hard and maneuverable army. When Clinton pulled out of Philadelphia to march across New Jersey to New York, Washington kept pace with him on a parallel route and watched for a chance to strike. But the only opportunity that came (the Battle of Monmouth Courthouse on June 28) was badly bungled by General Charles Lee, and the main body of Clinton's troops arrived safely in New York.

While the British and American armies were marching across New Jersey, the first French forces arrived in America—Vice Admiral the Comte d'Estaing with seventeen ships and four thousand troops. Washington proposed to use them in recovering Newport. But in August, just before the American-French assault was to begin, a storm scattered and damaged the French fleet, and the unsupported land forces withdrew when British reinforcements arrived. D'Estaing took his ships to Boston to refit and, in November 1778, sailed south to protect the French West Indies.

The departure of D'Estaing was a serious disappointment to Washington, for the Americans had no

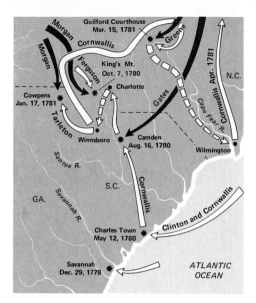

④ Southern campaigns, 1778–81

means of their own to combat the British navy. It offered deadly support to British land troops along the coast, and it regularly sent raiding parties to devastate towns far from any army. Though the Americans commissioned hundreds of privateers (probably over two thousand in all), which rendered invaluable service in disrupting the merchant shipping, communications, and supply lines of the enemy, the privateers were no more a navy than the militia were an army; they were simply not up to engaging British warships in a sustained action.

The Congress had tried to create a navy, but it could scrape together the money for only a few ships, which were no match for the Royal Navy. Nevertheless, one of them, commanded by the unpopular but unsinkable John Paul Jones, carried the war to the British Isles, raiding coastal towns and seizing British ships. Unfortunately there were not enough Joneses to divert the British navy from North America, and Clinton kept most of his troops near the coast within reach of naval assistance. Without naval assistance of his own Washington dared not risk an all-out assault on the British army, and after following it from New Jersey to New York he had camped outside the city at White Plains and waited for the French fleet to return or to draw the British ships to other waters. For a year and a half he waited while the fighting was carried on mostly by small forces remote from New York, the strategic center. In the fall of 1779 all prospect of French naval support disappeared when D'Estaing took his fleet from the West Indies back to France.

Meanwhile a British expeditionary force had occupied Georgia, and Clinton prepared to go ahead with the Southern campaign he had been ordered to conduct. Leaving an army equal to Washington's to hold New York, he pulled his troops out of Newport

③ Central campaigns, 1777–79

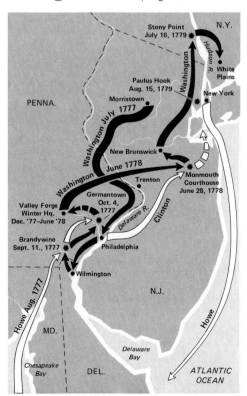

109

*The winning of independence*

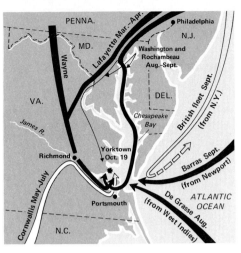

(5) The convergence of troops
on Yorktown, 1781

*Yorktown: "The World Turned Upside Down"*

(thus freeing New England of all British troops) and, in December 1779, sailed with an expeditionary force of over eight thousand for Charles Town, South Carolina. He took it on May 12, 1780, along with its defending general, Benjamin Lincoln, and his entire force of fifty-five hundred men. The Carolinas now lay open to a British sweep. On June 8 Clinton sailed for New York, leaving Cornwallis in command with instructions to secure the British hold on South Carolina and then to recover North Carolina. Cornwallis was at first successful. On August 16, 1780, near Camden, he intercepted and routed over three thousand men under General Horatio Gates who were coming to the defense of South Carolina. Washington sent General Nathanael Greene, his ablest commander, to pick up the pieces.

With the assistance of Daniel Morgan, a Virginia rifleman, Greene built a mobile fighting unit, which

*British camp*

owed much to the Southern militiamen who appeared whenever a fight was in the offing. A group of these tough campaigners had already demonstrated their worth before Greene arrived by capturing a British force atop King's Mountain in North Carolina (October 7, 1780). Greene and Morgan lured Cornwallis into trap after trap, chewing off a bit of his force here and a bit there (notably at Hannah's Cowpens on the Broad River, January 17, 1781, and at Guilford Courthouse, March 15).

In April 1781 the two generals turned their backs on each other: Greene headed south to pick off more British outposts in South Carolina and Georgia, while Cornwallis, having failed in the Carolinas, set out to conquer Virginia. By July, after a few inconclusive engagements, he had settled at Portsmouth, from which he later moved to Yorktown. Portsmouth and Yorktown both lay on the seacoast, the only safe place for a British army in America; but the coast would remain safe only so long as the British navy commanded the sea. And Yorktown, at the end of the peninsula between the York and the James rivers, was particularly vulnerable (earlier in the war Washington had warned one of his own generals not to encamp there for fear of being cut off). Without naval support Cornwallis could be isolated from his own forces in Charles Town and Savannah and from Clinton's forces in the North.

In New York Clinton still looked out at Washington's waiting army, and Washington still waited for the French navy. The French had sent five thousand land troops under the Comte de Rochambeau to occupy Newport in July 1780, but the eleven warships that accompanied them under the Comte de Barras had been promptly bottled up inside the harbor by a superior British fleet.

In August 1781 Washington's patience was finally rewarded by news that Admiral de Grasse with twenty warships was heading for the Chesapeake but would be able to stay only a short time. Washington immediately decided to dash south for a try at Cornwallis. Leaving behind a part of his New York troops to fool Clinton, he marched the rest to the head of Chesapeake Bay and placed them aboard transports for the last leg of the journey. Additional forces under Anthony Wayne and the French volunteer, Lafayette, were already within marching distance of the target. Barras meanwhile had managed to slip out of Newport and was sailing south loaded with siege guns. When the British naval squadrons discovered what was going on, they hurried to the Chesapeake to drive off Barras and de Grasse but found themselves hopelessly outnumbered and outgunned. French naval power was at last decisive. Back went the British fleet to New York for repairs and reinforcements, and Washington with fifty-seven hundred Continentals, thirty-one hundred militia, and seven thousand French began to close in on Yorktown. On October 19, when a relief expedition was already under way from New York, Cornwallis gave up. With the bands playing "The World Turned Upside Down," seven thousand British troops marched out of Yorktown and stacked their arms in surrender.

**Peace.** Yorktown was as much a French as an American victory. And because the war, too, was a French war, it could not end at Yorktown. France was ready for peace but encumbered by a commitment to Spain.

*The winning of independence*

Vergennes, upon concluding the treaty of alliance with the United States on February 6, 1778, had continued his efforts to bring Spain into the war; he finally succeeded after agreeing not to stop fighting until Spain had won Gibraltar from England. Since the United States had agreed not to make peace without French consent, Americans were indirectly bound to await the capture of Gibraltar also. Spain, on the other hand, refused to recognize the independence of the United States, and after entering the war on June 21, 1779, accorded only a devious and frosty tolerance to the American cause. Once Spain had seized the thinly held territory of West Florida (a former Spanish possession) from the British, she confined herself mainly to blockading Gibraltar.

After the defeat at Yorktown, most Englishmen were ready to give up the struggle for the colonies even though George III was bent on continuing it. On March 20, 1782, Lord North was forced from office, and the king was obliged to accept a ministry favorable to peace, which immediately sent agents to get in touch with the American commissioners in France.

Congress had first formulated American war aims in August 1779, when it optimistically sent John Adams to France as minister plenipotentiary. Adams was then forbidden to enter into any peace negotiations with Great Britain unless she first recognized the United States as a sovereign, free, and independent state. After that recognition had been granted, he was to insist on certain boundaries for the new nation: the Mississippi on the west, the thirty-first parallel and the Flint and St. Mary's rivers on the south, and roughly the present boundary on the north.

In June 1781 the French ambassador to the United States, the Chevalier de la Luzerne, persuaded Congress to revise its arrangements for making peace. John Adams was replaced as sole negotiator by a five-man commission consisting of himself, John Jay (minister to Spain), Franklin (minister to France), Henry Laurens (designated as minister to the Netherlands but captured by the British en route and held in the Tower of London), and Thomas Jefferson (who was unable to go and was dropped from the commission). The commissioners' instructions were weak: they were still to insist on British recognition of American independence before undertaking peace negotiations, but they were free to accept any settlement "as circumstances may direct and as the state of the belligerent and the disposition of the mediating powers may direct." What was worse, they must do nothing without the knowledge and concurrence of the French and, indeed, must be governed by their advice and opinion.

These instructions put the commissioners under the direction of Vergennes, a position none of them relished. When secret information reached them that he would not support the American demand for prior recognition of independence, and that his secretary, Rayneval, had secretly encouraged the British to think of a boundary well to the east of the Mississippi, with Spain and England dividing up the territory between, they decided they would do better to negotiate with the British separately rather than to sit down at the peace table under French direction. Violating their instructions, they negotiated with British representatives without insisting on advance recognition of independence, and they did not keep Vergennes informed of what they were doing.

By playing on British desires to destroy the American alliance with France, the commissioners were able to secure both recognition of independence and the boundaries prescribed in John Adams' original instructions. In preliminary articles signed on November 30, 1782, they presented this diplomatic triumph to Vergennes as an accomplished fact. Actually there had been no violation of the alliance, for the treaty based on the articles was not to go into effect until France and England had concluded a treaty of their own. The commissioners' coup enabled Vergennes to exert pressure on Spain to give up the fight for Gibraltar, and in the end Spain settled for East and West Florida and Minorca. The final treaties were signed at Paris on September 3, 1783, and the last British troops left New York on November 25. The Declaration of Independence was at last a statement of fact, not a wish.

# The Experimental Period

At Lexington, Concord, and Bunker Hill Americans had fought against Parliamentary taxation. After July 2, 1776, they had fought for independence, though in the beginning probably·few of them had any clear idea of what independence would mean besides the end of British tyranny. Between 1776 and 1789 they explored the possibilities of their new freedom. These thirteen years may be considered the Experimental Period in American history, the time when Americans were trying their wings, discovering their nationality. They formulated ideas and ideals that had been only half articulate before, and they found ways and means to put their ideas and ideals into practice. During this period the Americanisms discussed earlier (see Chapter 3) underwent further development, and some of them were transformed from characteristic attitudes into national principles.

**The fruition of Americanisms.** American ideas about the separation of church and state and about education advanced less rapidly during the Experimental Period than did political and social concepts. But the assumption that widespread education was desirable did show itself in a revival of schooling, which had lapsed during the war, and in the proliferation of new educational institutions, most of them private. Many academies were founded (especially in New England) to furnish instruction at the secondary level, and sometimes beyond, to both boys and girls. And the number of colleges in the United States doubled: in 1776 there were nine; by 1789 as many more had been opened or chartered; and every state but Delaware had at least one in operation or being organized. Writers in newspapers and pamphlets argued about what kind of education was best suited to Americans. Many demanded that it be made more practical, and new textbooks reoriented traditional subjects like arithmetic and grammar in this direction.

The colonists' wariness of allowing their clergy a hand in government gave rise to a greater separation of church and state. Though most states continued to levy taxes in support of the Protestant religion, the Anglican Church lost the exclusive claims to that support which it had enjoyed in the Southern colonies. Under all the state constitutions a man could at least specify which Protestant church his taxes should support. And in Virginia the principle of complete separation of church and state received its finest expression in an act drafted by Thomas Jefferson and adopted by the Virginia legislature in 1786. Beginning with the assertion that "Almighty God hath created the mind free," the act provided that "no man shall be compelled to frequent or support any religious worship, place, or ministry whatsoever."

Jefferson was also author of the phrase that translated social mobility into an American principle. By declaring on July 4, 1776, that "all men are created equal," the United States committed itself to a doctrine that was to prove the world's most powerful lever for social and political change. The declaration was intended simply to justify the colonists' withdrawal from the mother country, which had refused to treat them as the equals of Englishmen. But no great imagination was needed to see wider implications in Jefferson's axiomatic statement of human equality.

Its relevance to black slavery was inescapable. As soon as Americans complained that British taxation would reduce them to slavery, they began to feel uneasy about their own enslavement of Africans; they even forswore the slave trade in their nonimportation agreements. In the Experimental Period most of the states, Southern as well as Northern, forbade the further importation of slaves, and the Northern states passed laws for the eventual liberation of those already within their borders. Massachusetts seems to

Negroes for Sale.

A Cargo of very fine stout Men and Women, in good order and fit for immediate service, just imported from the Windward Coast of Africa, in the Ship Two Brothers.— Conditions are one half Cash or Produce, the other half payable the first of January next, giving Bond and Security if required. The Sale to be opened at 10 o'Clock each Day, in Mr. Bourdeaux's Yard, at No. 48, on the Bay. May 19, 1784. JOHN MITCHELL.

have rid herself of the institution by judicial decision: her constitution, echoing the Declaration of Independence, stated that "all men are born free and equal," and her courts interpreted the phrase literally. Many Southerners also freed their slaves voluntarily at this time. But Americans were not yet ready to face up to the racial meaning of their egalitarian creed. Black slavery was not abolished in any Southern state; Jefferson himself continued to hold slaves throughout his lifetime; and slaves continued to do the work that accounted for the major exports of the United States. Eventually Americans would have to pay for their failure. Meanwhile the contradiction between the creed of equality and the practice of slavery was heightened as white Americans gradually turned their written commitment into an active force to better their own lives.

The principle of equality was as hostile to aristocracy as to slavery. Having got along without a titled nobility for a century and a half, Americans were determined to continue without one and looked suspiciously at anything that smacked of special privilege. States forbade their citizens to accept titles from foreign nations. And when officers of the Continental Army formed the Society of the Cincinnati in 1783, they met with a storm of protest from critics who feared that the association might become the nucleus of an aristocracy. In Connecticut even a medical society, seeking to raise the standards of the profession by licensing practitioners, was at first denied a charter because its members were to be chosen for life and might thus become a privileged order.

The Revolutionary War itself had an equalizing effect on property: wealthy merchants had lost heavily from the British blockade of commerce, while many a poor farmer had prospered in selling his produce to the armies. Wartime finance, with its reliance on steadily inflating paper currency, favored debtors (who were most often farmers) at the expense of creditors. The confiscation and sale of loyalists' lands and the abolition of primogeniture (the inheritance of a man's entire estate by his eldest son) by the state governments likewise contributed to a more equal distribution of property by breaking up some of the larger concentrations of wealth. Although in many cases the initial purchasers of loyalist lands were large-scale speculators, the overall effect of the confiscations was probably to increase the number of landowners, because speculators sold the confiscated lands in small lots. By the time the war ended many Americans regarded equality of property as a goal in itself. When economic depression struck in the 1780s, legislators in some states sponsored bills favoring debtors, on the grounds that republican government required a general equality of property.

The emerging doctrine of equality can also be detected in the reform of voting laws. Property qualifications had disfranchised only a small minority of adult males in most colonies (because most owned property) and there had been few complaints. But every state except Massachusetts reduced the amount of property required for voting. There remained, nevertheless, a strong belief that political rights should be confined to property-holders. Only two states, Georgia and Pennsylvania, opened the franchise to all taxpayers. And in most states there were higher property qualifications for holding office than for voting. In the eighteenth century it was assumed that a man without property had no reason to participate in government either by voting or by holding office. The major purpose of government was to protect property, so a man without any was thought to have little stake in society. Moreover, only property could free a man from the control of employers or landlords. Without property that would support him, a man was not a free agent and could not be trusted with authority or even with a voice in the selection of those who were to wield it. Hence the concern already noted for the maintenance of a wide distribution of property. If America were to become like Europe, with a mass of propertyless workers and peasants, liberty would fall with equality; and authority, concentrated in the hands of a few, would turn into tyranny.

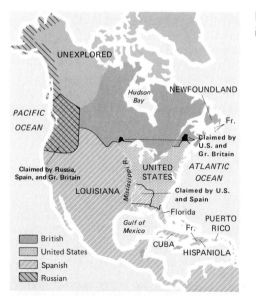

North America
in 1783

Authority in the hands of the many, of the people, was the essential characteristic of a republic; and with independence colonial insistence on responsible representative government turned into a conscious pursuit of republicanism. Although nothing in the Declaration of Independence had precluded the possibility of monarchy, Americans took it for granted that the new states would be republics. After severing their ties with England, Connecticut and Rhode Island, which in effect were republics already, simply continued the governments defined by their old charters. In other colonies the provincial congress, which replaced the representative assembly (often with the same membership), acted without formal authority until independence was declared. Then, sooner or later, it drafted a written constitution establishing and defining a new government, usually similar in structure to the old one but more responsible to the people.

Since the colonial representative assembly (or lower house) had always been the branch of government most directly dependent on the people, the state constitutions gave the greatest powers to the lower houses of the new legislatures. In some states the lower house chose both the upper house and the governor. Only Pennsylvania, which had had a unicameral legislature since 1701, actually did without an upper house. In other states there was a marked change in the composition of this body: the members were not as "upper" in wealth or social position as their colonial counterparts. Many were former members of a colonial lower house. They sat, not as the favorites of a governor, but as representatives of the whole people, indistinguishable in this respect from the lower house.

Determination that the government should be the servant of the people and not their master also prompted the inclusion of bills of rights in most of the state constitutions. The Virginia Bill of Rights began by asserting that "all men are by nature equally free and independent, and have certain inherent rights, of which, when they enter into a state of society, they cannot by any compact deprive or divest their posterity." It then enumerated the rights that lay beyond the reach of government, such as freedom of religion and of the press and the right to trial by jury.

In most states, after the provincial congress had drafted and approved a constitution, it went into effect without being submitted to a popular vote. But Massachusetts (the last state to adopt a constitution) elected a special convention to draft one and submitted its work to direct vote by the people. Once it had been ratified in 1780, it could be changed only by another popularly elected convention called for that specific purpose. This was a step that other states had groped for but never quite reached. The purpose of writing out a constitution was to set limits to govern-

ment by a fundamental law embodying the will of the people. British jurists had often maintained that the unwritten British constitution, consisting of traditions and customs, was superior to government, but custom and tradition had failed to protect the colonists from what they regarded as tyranny by the British government. They wanted something in black and white by which to measure any departure by their own governments from the proper limits of authority. They began to get what they wanted when their provincial congresses wrote and adopted state constitutions. But keen minds soon noted a flaw in this procedure: as the town of Concord pointed out in 1776, a constitution adopted by a legislative body could be altered or abolished by the same body and thus would constitute no protection against legislative tyranny. The device of a special convention and popular ratification elevated the constitution above the legislature and made it easier for the other branches of government to nullify unconstitutional legislation. The courts, for example, could and would refuse to enforce any law that violated the constitution. The Massachusetts invention of the constitutional convention was so widely admired by other Americans that subsequent constitution-making in America followed the Massachusetts method.

**Building a national government.** The same passion for responsible government that resulted in written constitutions and constitutional conventions prevented for a long time the creation of an effective national government. Americans, like other people of the eighteenth century, believed that republican government was not adaptable to large areas. In a large republic the central legislature must inevitably sit so remote from most of its constituents that it would eventually escape their control and thus cease to be republican. On the other hand, a small republic could never survive in a world of aggressive large nations. There was only one way, it was thought, to overcome these difficulties: a number of small republics might join in a federation and exert their united power for specific purposes.

Americans had formed such a federation in 1774 in the Continental Congress, and after independence the Congress had continued to exercise governmental powers for the whole nation. It was composed of delegates (usually several from each state) appointed annually by the state legislatures. Each state had one vote, determined by the majority of its delegates (if they were evenly divided the state's vote was lost).

In the absence of a more effective central organization, Congress served a useful purpose. But it existed only by common consent, and from the beginning the members felt the need for a more binding union. As Americans joined against a common enemy and became aware of their shared principles and beliefs, their feeling of nationality grew stronger. Something more than an unstable succession of congresses was necessary to embody this sentiment and to demonstrate to other nations that the United States too was a nation and not merely a diplomatic alliance of thirteen small republics. Congress accordingly, in the intervals between dealing with the everyday problems of the war, often discussed the formation of a permanent national government. As early as July 12, 1776, a committee had brought in the draft of a constitution, but acceptance had foundered on how expenses and voting power should be apportioned among the states and on the old question of Western policy.

On November 17, 1777, Congress finally agreed on a constitution to be presented to the state legislatures for approval or rejection. The Articles of Confederation provided for a congress like the existing one. Each state, whatever its size, was still to have only one vote, to be cast, as before, by delegates appointed by the state legislatures; each state (by taxing itself) was to contribute to the common expenses according to the value of its lands; none was to be deprived of its Western lands for the benefit of the United States; and each was to retain its "sovereignty, freedom and independence, and every power, jurisdiction, and right" not expressly delegated to Congress. Congress was permitted to decide on war or peace, appoint military and naval officers, requisition the states for men and money, send and receive ambassadors, enter into treaties and alliances, establish a post office, coin money, borrow money or issue paper money on the credit of the United States, fix weights and measures, regulate Indian affairs, and settle disputes between states.

Although the states found much to object to in the Articles of Confederation, the need to give permanent form to the union moved all but Maryland to accept it by 1779. Maryland's refusal, though probably prompted by narrow, partisan, and pecuniary motives, forced the settlement of a problem that might have wrecked the union—the problem of Western lands.

The West had always been a divisive force, as Bacon's Rebellion, the failure of the Albany Congress, and the Regulator movement all testified. Even more serious trouble lay ahead. Colonial assemblies from Pennsylvania southward had failed to extend full representation to their Western regions as population increased there. Pennsylvania remedied the inequality in her state constitution, but Virginia and the Carolinas did not, and the result was Western resentment against the Eastern-dominated state governments.

Concurrent with these internal disputes, the state governments quarreled with one another about the West. The Revolution had dissolved their ties to England but not their territorial boundaries, which had been fixed by royal charters. By their charters, Georgia, the Carolinas, Virginia, Connecticut, and Massachusetts extended to the Pacific Ocean, while Maryland, Delaware, Pennsylvania, New Jersey, and Rhode Island were limited to a few hundred miles on the seacoast. The "landless" states wanted Congress to take control of unoccupied Western lands and restrict the western boundaries of the "landed" states. The landed states resisted any such proposal and squabbled with one another over their conflicting charters. Virginia, whose charter was the oldest, could claim most of the West all to itself. The people of every state, when they looked west, found reason for jealousy or distrust of their neighbors.

The problem was aggravated by land speculation. Before the war, speculators from Pennsylvania, Maryland, and New Jersey (all landless states) had purchased land from the Indians and sought authorization from the king to establish a new colony (Vandalia) in the Ohio Valley. Though bitterly opposed by Virginia's Ohio Company, they had been on the verge of success when the Revolution upset their plans. Now they argued that Congress had inherited the king's authority over all unoccupied lands; and, supported by their state governments, they pressed Congress to recognize their claims. The landed states had fought them off by including in the Articles of Confederation a guarantee that no state should be deprived of territory for the benefit of the United States. But Maryland stubbornly refused to approve the Articles as long as the proposed union lacked control over Western lands. Without her the union was stalled, for it was not to go into effect until unanimously approved.

Maryland could produce better arguments than the mere greed of her land-speculators. The landed states, she pointed out, would be able to command such an abundant source of revenue by selling their Western lands that their citizens would pay few or no taxes. People from the landless states would consequently move to the landed ones. Maryland, next door to the leviathan Virginia, would be depopulated.

In Virginia the sentiment for union was strong, and some patriots wanted to give up the state's Western territory, which they thought was too large for a single republican government anyhow. Rather than jeopardize republicanism in Virginia, they preferred to see new states formed in the West and joined to the old ones by the Articles of Confederation. Thomas Jefferson accordingly led Virginia (on January 2, 1781) to offer Congress her claims to all lands north of the Ohio. The transfer was contingent on a number of conditions that in effect canceled speculative claims to the region and required that the land be divided into "distinct republican States," which should ultimately be admitted to the union on equal terms with the old ones. When Virginia's cession was made known, Maryland capitulated (though the speculators still tried to block her) and approved the Articles of Confederation in February 1781. New York had already ceded her shadowy Western claims, and the other landed states eventually followed suit (Georgia held out until 1802).

***Congress under the Confederation.*** In the Articles of Confederation the American people got what most of them at that time wanted. Having just suffered from the power of a distant British government, they were wary of allowing much authority to their own central government. They charged Congress with

*An American people*

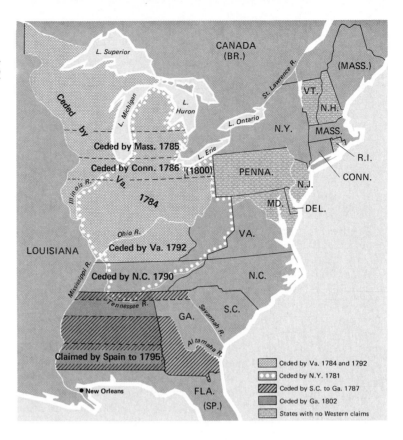

Western lands ceded by the states, 1781–1802

CANADA (BR.)

L. Superior

L. Michigan

L. Huron

St. Lawrence R.

L. Ontario

L. Erie

Ceded by Mass. 1785

Ceded by Conn. 1786

Illinois R.

Va.

1784

(1800)

PENNA.

N.Y.

MASS.

(MASS.)

VT.

N.H.

R.I.

CONN.

N.J.

MD.

DEL.

Ohio R.

Ceded by Va. 1792

VA.

Ceded by N.C. 1790

LOUISIANA

Mississippi R.

Tennessee R.

N.C.

S.C.

GA.

Savannah R.

Altamaha R.

Claimed by Spain to 1795

New Orleans

FLA. (SP.)

Ceded by Va. 1784 and 1792
Ceded by N.Y. 1781
Ceded by S.C. to Ga. 1787
Ceded by Ga. 1802
States with no Western claims

the responsibility for making decisions about a multitude of their common concerns, but they neglected to give it the powers to carry its decisions into effect. It could pass resolutions, make recommendations, enact ordinances; but it had no courts, no way of enforcing its orders either on individuals or on states. It could not even levy taxes to pay its own expenses but had to rely on the several states to furnish its funds. In fact, Congress was allowed less authority than the colonists had once acknowledged in Parliament: Congress did not even have the right to regulate trade. The disadvantages of such a powerless central government soon became apparent.

After the coming of peace diminished the urgency of united action, the states became increasingly enamored of their own power and increasingly casual, even contemptuous, in their relations with Congress, ignoring its resolutions, refusing to fill its requisitions for funds, sending inferior men to represent them or sometimes none at all. Congress was unable to cope with the situation because the Articles of Confederation had provided it with no means to enforce obedience. The weakness of the national government made the years from 1783 to 1789, in the phrase of one historian, the "Critical Period" of American history.

A man elected to Congress during these years might arrive at the meeting place on the appointed day and find a dozen or more delegates like himself eager to proceed to business. But the Articles of Con-

federation required that each state be represented by at least two delegates and that the representatives of at least seven states be present to make a quorum. Unless more than seven states were represented, every decision had to be unanimous; and the assent of nine states was necessary in most matters having to do with war and peace (including treaties) and with appropriating money. Because the states were often slow about appointing delegates and the delegates themselves slow in taking up their duties, the first arrivals at a session sometimes had to wait several weeks before enough members were present to transact business. Even after a session was organized, it led a precarious existence; for if one or two delegates fell sick, the rest might have to twiddle their thumbs until more arrived or the sick got well.

Each delegate was elected for a one-year term and was prohibited from serving for more than three years in six. As a result, the membership of Congress was constantly shifting. The government was further handicapped by the failure of the Articles of Confederation to provide a regular executive department. Congress exercised executive powers through special commissions and committees and won some continuity by appointing three secretaries to manage crucial executive matters (Benjamin Lincoln, followed by Henry Knox, as Secretary of War; Robert Morris as Superintendent of Finance; and Robert Livingston, followed by John Jay, as Secretary for Foreign Affairs).

These officers struggled to give the United States the appearance of a government. But Congress, pursuing its intermittent existence, belied the appearance. Even when it could scrape together a quorum it had no permanent headquarters or capitol. A mutiny in the Philadelphia barracks frightened it out of that city in 1783, and thereafter the delegates wandered from Princeton to Annapolis to Trenton to New York—talking endlessly about where they should settle permanently. Shortly after they began their travels, Oliver Ellsworth, a congressman from Connecticut, observed dryly, "It will soon be of very little consequence where Congress go, if they are not made respectable as well as responsible, which can never be done without giving them a power to perform engagements as well as make them." Congress, in short, had responsibility without power. It could recommend endlessly but no one inside or outside the country paid much attention to what it recommended.

The impotence of Congress made the United States a beggar in the eyes of the world. During the Revolution, Congress had boldly capitalized on popular enthusiasm for the cause of independence by printing paper money, but the money had become worthless before the war's end. Congress had also begged money and supplies from France, but after the peace France preferred to keep her ally poor and humble. Dutch bankers, with more vision than many Americans, did continue to lend. But when Congress turned to the states for funds or for the power to levy a 5 percent tariff on imports, the states turned the beggar down. The power to levy tariffs needed the unanimous approval of the states, and each time it was pro-

posed (in 1781 and again in 1783) at least one state refused; and the others insisted on conditions that would have made the power meaningless anyhow.

The one area in which the United States enjoyed at least the appearance of power was the wilderness north of the Ohio River, a region thinly populated by squatters, Indians, and French. When Virginia offered to cede the area in 1781, Congress had been prevented from taking any formal action to accept it because of pressure from speculators who objected to the terms attached to the cession. Early in 1784, when Virginia renewed the offer, Congress was stalled for lack of a quorum. But by March 1 enough members were present to act favorably, and the United States gained formal authority over the Northwest.

Now Congress might begin to raise the funds it needed by selling land in the newly acquired territory. On April 23 the delegates passed an ordinance, drafted by Thomas Jefferson, that embodied the results of much previous discussion in Congress. It divided the territory into states, each of which was to be admitted into the Union on equal terms with the existing states as soon as its free population equaled any of theirs. Until then the inhabitants could govern themselves according to the constitution and laws of any of the existing states.

To prepare for the sale of lands to individuals, Congress passed an ordinance in 1785 providing that the Northwest be surveyed into townships six miles square along lines running east-west and north-south. Each township was divided into thirty-six lots one mile square (640 acres). A lot (later called a section) was the smallest unit that could be purchased, and

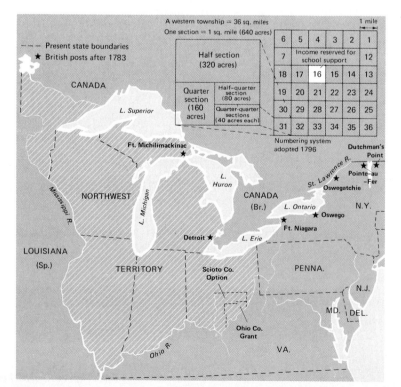

The Old Northwest

neither a township nor a lot was to be sold for less than a dollar an acre in specie. To speed up the transformation of the national domain into hard cash, land offices were to be established in all the states.

Surveying and the settlement of Indian claims proceeded slowly. Before the lands were ready for public sale, a group of ambitious and not very scrupulous speculators from New England came to Congress with a proposition. Calling themselves, like an earlier group, the Ohio Company, they offered to buy a million and a half acres, for which they would pay in currency so badly depreciated that the price amounted to less than 10 cents an acre in specie. Presumptuous as the offer was, the United States needed the money desperately, and Congress decided to accept it. The Ohio Company also agreed to take an option on 5 million additional acres, to be turned over to a subsidiary company known as the Scioto Company. By no coincidence, this company included several congressmen.

To oblige the Ohio Company, Congress passed a new ordinance for governing the Northwest. Jefferson's ordinance of 1784 had never gone into operation, because the area as yet contained no authorized settlers. It did, however, contain many squatters who had helped themselves to public lands and stoutly resisted eviction. Because of the difficulty anticipated in establishing property rights against squatters, and because of the frontier's reputation for violence and disorder, many Easterners believed that congressional rule would be more appropriate than self-government during the initial years of settlement. Accordingly, the Northwest Ordinance of 1787 provided for a period during which a governor, a secretary, and a court of three judges, all appointed by Congress, would hold full powers. Once the population had reached five thousand free adult males, a representative legislature would be established, but none of its actions would be valid without the approval of the governor, who would still be appointed by Congress. The legislature could send a representative to Congress, but he would have no vote. The whole area was to be divided into not fewer than three or more than five territories, each of which would be admitted to the Union on equal terms with the existing states when it attained a population of sixty thousand. Slavery was forbidden throughout the area; no person was to be "molested" for his religious beliefs or mode of worship; and "schools and the means of education" were to be encouraged. Though the ordinance did not say how the encouragement was to be effected, the Land Ordinance of 1785 had already reserved one lot in each township "for the maintenance of public schools."

The Northwest Ordinance established for the United States a Western policy that embodied the most cherished American principles. Though the ordinance applied to only a part of the West, it set a precedent that guided the territorial expansion of the nation until the end of the nineteenth century.

***National humiliation.*** One serious obstacle stood in the way of Congress' noble aspirations for the American West: the United States held only a tenuous grip on the area. England had never completely evacuated the Northwest, nor had Spain recognized American possession of any territory south of the Ohio. As the weakness and poverty of the new nation grew more apparent, European statesmen intrigued to push its western boundary back to the Appalachians.

When England made peace in 1783, she was not fully persuaded—nor was the rest of Europe—that the United States would last. While the king officially proclaimed the treaty and commanded his subjects to comply with it, his ministers sent secret orders to the governor-general of Canada to retain Britain's trading posts and military garrisons in the Northwest. The United States, with its own armies disbanded and the French forces gone, was in no position to compel the British to withdraw. To excuse their continued occupation of the posts, the British charged that the Americans had violated the treaty.

Again the weakness of the national government was to blame. The treaty required that neither side make laws impeding the collection of private debts contracted before the war, and it required that Congress "earnestly recommend" to the states the restoration of confiscated loyalist property. Congress did recommend the restitution, and the fact that the states did not follow the recommendation was not technically a violation of the treaty. But when some states passed laws impeding the collection of British debts, they violated the treaty as surely as England did in keeping troops on American territory. Congress was as helpless to prevent one violation as the other. It sent John Adams to England as American minister; and he protested the British garrisons with characteristic Adams vigor, but in vain, for England knew that no American troops stood behind him.

England showed its contempt for the government of its former colonies by failing to establish a legation in the United States to match the American legation in London. More ominously it dickered with the influential Allen brothers, Ethan and Levi, for help in acquiring Vermont. Claimed by both New Hampshire and New York, Vermont had asserted its independence of both and applied for statehood. Congress was reluctant to antagonize either claimant by admitting Vermont into the Union, and there was danger that the Vermonters might attach themselves to Canada (Vermont was not admitted until 1791).

In the Southwest, Spain was grasping for the area that later became the states of Kentucky and Tennessee. Americans were moving into it at such a rate that by 1790 it contained more than a hundred thousand of them, but their presence was hardly a guarantee of permanent American possession. Barred by the mountains from trade with the East, the settlers relied on the Mississippi River to float their produce to market at New Orleans. New Orleans belonged to Spain, and so did the lower Mississippi. The Spaniards had gained Louisiana in 1763, the Floridas in 1783; and they maintained forts on the west bank of the Mississippi as far north as St. Louis, on the east bank as far as the present site of Memphis. Anyone who wanted to use the river had to do business with Spain.

Although commercial exports from the Southwest were still meager, everyone in the region was expecting future prosperity through the Mississippi trade. Spain was well aware of that expectation. In 1784 it closed the river to navigation by Americans and waited for the settlers to abandon their feeble Congress for the solid commercial advantage of Spanish citizenship. For a time it seemed that the settlers might do just that, for they were far from pleased with the way Eastern Americans were treating them. In 1772, by the Watauga Compact, pioneers in the Tennessee area had formed a government of their own, which lasted until 1776, when North Carolina organized them into Washington County. In 1784, after her land-speculators had established claims to the most valuable land, North Carolina ceded the region to Congress in order to avoid the expense of protecting it from the Indians. When she changed her mind the next year and tried to regain possession, many settlers grew disgusted and began to look favorably toward Spain. In Kentucky, the Western region of Virginia, a similar secessionist movement and a similar flirtation with Spain threatened to disrupt the Union.

As the Southwest began to draw away from the United States, Spain in 1785 sent Don Diego de Gardoqui to wring from Congress a formal recognition of her exclusive control over the Mississippi. Congress instructed its Secretary of Foreign Affairs, John Jay, to insist in his negotiations with Gardoqui on the right of Americans to navigate the Mississippi through Spanish territory to its mouth. This was a subject about which the two men had tilted inconclusively once before, during the Revolution, when Jay had gone to Spain in search of assistance in the war against England. Jay now found Gardoqui as adamant as ever about refusing to recognize an American right of navigation but willing to make other concessions. The Spaniards would agree to recognize American territorial rights as far south as the old border of British West Florida and as far west as the Mississippi and to give American merchants new trading privileges in Spain. In return, he asked only that the United States agree to give up navigation of the Mis-

sissippi for twenty-five years. The offer was attractive to New Englanders and to the Middle states, whose merchants badly needed new markets. But it offered nothing to Southerners that they did not, in their own view at least, already have. And it was anathema to the settlers on the Ohio River, most of whom had come from the South. In Congress the Northern delegates now pushed through a vote that allowed Jay to accept the offer. Thus, even before he presented his treaty for ratification, his negotiations had polarized Congress on North-South lines.

But the Northern majority consisted of only seven states, and nine were required for ratification. As Northerners began talking of a separate confederation, and Westerners talked of betrayal, Gardoqui's shrewdness became apparent. Though he did not get his treaty, he had brought on a sectional confrontation that threatened the union's very existence.

While Gardoqui led Jay into alienating the Westerners, the Spanish governor of Louisiana, Esteban Rodriguez Miro, was wooing them with bribes and privileges. General James Wilkinson, a veteran of the Revolutionary War and a consummate double-dealer, took a trip to New Orleans in 1787. While there, he took a secret oath of allegiance to Spain in return for trading concessions. The following year he accepted a Spanish pension, with the understanding that he would lead his neighbors in the Tennessee region to repudiate the United States. Wilkinson was not the only Southwestern traitor. Daniel Boone, James Robertson, and John Sevier all accepted Spanish gold. Instead of doing what they were paid to do, however, they cheerfully deceived both sides while they waited to see what was going to happen. If, as seemed likely, the United States should break up, they were ready to learn Spanish.

The United States had troubles even in the Mediterranean. For years European countries had been protecting their Mediterranean shipping from pirates by paying an annual tribute to the rulers of Morocco, Algiers, Tripoli, and Tunis. As long as American ships carried the British flag, they were safe; but after 1776, when they began to fly the Stars and Stripes, pirates swarmed out upon them. The captured American captains and crews were put on the auction block and sold as slaves. Congress bought protection from Morocco in 1787 but had neither money nor guns to stop the other African pirates.

Nor were pirates the only difficulty to beset American trade. The whole American economy was in a precarious position. With the coming of peace, American merchants had sensed a huge demand for the British dry goods and hardware to which American consumers had been accustomed before the war. The merchants placed their orders, and warehouses and stores were soon bulging, with the British extend-

*An American people*

ing liberal credits. The American merchants in turn extended credit to retailers and consumers, and the country indulged itself in a buying spree. Only when it came time to pay the bills did the Americans discover their situation.

The colonial economy had been a complex one, in which Americans paid for British imports by carrying their own and other people's goods to market in various ports throughout the world, but mostly within the empire. Now they were no longer a part of the empire, and Britain closed her West Indian ports to American vessels. Prices of American produce dropped, merchants found themselves cut off from usual channels of trade, and depression settled over the land—while British merchants called for payment.

Americans blamed themselves and their merchants. Having won their political independence, they had promptly mortgaged it by extravagant purchases from their old masters. It seemed that the British, by craftily extending liberal credits and closing their ports to Americans, had rewon economically the position of dominance that they had lost politically. Congress instructed John Adams to ask England for a commercial treaty, but he was no more successful in this than in pressing for the evacuation of British garrisons in the Northwest.

There were loud demands for retaliation against the British restrictions on American trade, and some states passed laws to discourage imports. But such partial legislation by single states, each imposing different restrictions, only added to the difficulties by injuring the economies of sister states. As John Sullivan confessed concerning the New Hampshire law, "It was a blow aimed at Britain but wounds us and our friends." What was needed was an overall national regulation of commerce, not simply to discourage unnecessary imports, but to create a balanced economy in which manufacturing, agriculture, and commerce would all find their place. Only in this way could the United States become economically as well as politically independent and insure herself against domination by Britain or any other nation. But the American Congress, with no power to regulate commerce, could not even begin to direct the economy toward such a goal.

# The crisis of American nationality

Many Americans found the impotence of the national government intolerable. The Revolution had widened their vision beyond the affairs of town or county or colony and had taught them to think, as Alexander Hamilton put it, "continentally." They knew that the only way to solve the difficulties of the United States was to strengthen the national government—they had known it before the ink was dry on the Articles of Confederation. Now, as the weakness of the government became more and more embarrassing, they spoke out ever more loudly.

***Thinking continentally.*** The Americans had had plenty of practice in making and breaking governments. Their usual method had been to call an extralegal convention—like the Stamp Act Congress or the Continental Congress or the provincial congresses that replaced the royal governments. Conventions were also summoned whenever the people of a state or region wanted to achieve a public purpose for which their regular government had proved inadequate. Several interstate conventions had met during the war in an effort to regulate prices. Connecticut held a convention in 1783 to protest the founding of the Society of the Cincinnati and the granting of extra pay to army officers. And, as we have seen, Massachusetts called a convention to draft a state constitution.

It was only natural, then, for men who had begun to think "continentally" to turn to a convention for the purpose of strengthening the continental government. As early as 1784 they had talked of it, but at that time public sentiment was overwhelmingly against it. The opposition did not arise from a deficiency of national patriotism or from too much local patriotism. Nationalism, which has proved the most lively—and deadly—force in the modern world, attached itself in America to the Union rather than to the states. Thomas Paine, in his first publication after the peace, wrote: "I ever feel myself hurt when I hear the Union, the great palladium of our liberty and safety, the least irreverently spoken of. . . . Our citizenship in the United States is our national character. Our citizenship in any particular state is only our local distinction."

This sentiment was echoed by statesmen, poets, painters, and schoolmasters. George Washington, the nation's hero, was a great Virginian but a greater American. "We are known by no other character among nations," he declared in 1783, "than as the United States." Connecticut during the 1780s produced a host of brilliant young men who celebrated in literature and art not their own state but America. John Trumbull depicted the great events of the American Revolution in a series of historical paintings. Joel Barlow attempted an American epic in *The Vision of Columbus.* Noah Webster wrote schoolbooks designed to teach American English. Jedidiah Morse published an *American Geography.* And Ezra Stiles, the president of Yale, preached of *The United States Elevated to Glory and Honor.* Some authors, to be sure, wrote

**Thinking locally**

*It is the opinion of the ablest writers on the subject, that no extensive empire can be governed upon republican principles, and that such a government will degenerate to a despotism, unless it be made up of a confederacy of smaller states, each having the full powers of internal regulation. This is precisely the principle which has hitherto preserved our freedom. No instance can be found of any free government of considerable extent which has been supported upon any other plan. Large and consolidated empires may indeed dazzle the eyes of a distant spectator with their splendour, but if examined more nearly are always found to be full of misery. The reason is obvious. In large states the same principles of legislation will not apply to all the parts. The inhabitants of warmer climates are more dissolute in their manners, and less industrious, than in colder countries. A degree of severity is, therefore, necessary with one which would cramp the spirit of the other. We accordingly find that the very great empires have always been despotick.... It is under such tyranny that the Spanish provinces languish, and such would be our misfortune and degradation, if we should submit to have the concerns of the whole empire managed by one legislature.... The attempt made by Great Britain to introduce such a system, struck us with horrour, and when it was proposed by some theorist that we should be represented in parliament, we uniformly declared that one legislature could not represent so many different purposes of legislation and taxation. This was the leading principle of the revolution, and makes an essential article in our creed.*

**From *The Letters of Agrippa*, 1787, attributed to James Winthrop.**

the history of their own states (Jefferson, for example, published his *Notes on the State of Virginia* in 1785), but the local pride they exhibited was different in kind from the national pride that was evident throughout the Union.

Yet, however proud of their country's past and confident of its future, Americans needed leadership and a government capable of elevating the United States to the glory and honor they wanted for it. National policy was drifting, and continental-minded men warned that the nation faced collapse or conquest if its government was not strengthened. But their appeals met resistance from people who feared that a stronger government might become aristocratic or tyrannical; it might threaten the principles that had brought the Union into being—the principles of equality and of responsible, republican government. In 1785, for example, when the legislature of Massachusetts proposed a general convention to strengthen the national government, its delegates in Congress objected. Would-be aristocrats, they argued, would use such a convention to establish a government based on special privilege, loaded with lucrative positions for themselves, and bolstered by a standing army.

Because of such sentiments on the part of honest and patriotic men, a national constitutional convention, though often talked of, had failed to materialize.

By 1786, however, Americans had become so impatient with British trade restrictions, conflicting state commercial laws, and national economic helplessness that they arranged for an interstate meeting at Annapolis, Maryland, to consider the extension of national authority to the regulation of commerce. Probably from the beginning, one of the delegates, James Madison, had hoped for something more than an increase in congressional power. It was Madison who had originated Virginia's call for the meeting. By September 1786, when the delegates began to assemble, he and other continental-minded men were alarmed by the sectional antagonisms that Jay's proposed treaty had aroused. The accumulating threats to the Union were too great to be dealt with by a convention called to consider regulation of trade. When representatives from five states had convened, though more were on the way, they drew up a proposal to Congress and the several states and dissolved the convention. What they proposed was another convention the next year at Philadelphia for the larger purpose of making "the constitution of the Federal Government adequate to the exigencies of the Union."

The message reached the states along with some disturbing news from Massachusetts. In the summer of 1786 the citizens in the economically depressed western part of the state, laboring under a heavy burden of debt, had called a number of local conven-

*I rejoice most exceedingly that there is an end to our warfare, and that such a field is opening to our view as will, with wisdom to direct the cultivation of it, make us a great, a respectable, and happy People; but it must be improved by other means than State politics, and unreasonable jealousies and prejudices; or (it requires not the second sight to see that) we shall be instruments in the hands of our Enemies, and those European powers who may be jealous of our greatness in Union.... No man in the United States is, or can be more deeply impressed with the necessity of a reform in our present Confederation than myself. No man perhaps has felt the bad efects of it more sensibly, for to the defects thereof, and want of Powers in Congress may justly be ascribed the prolongation of the War, and consequently the Expences occasioned by it. More than half the perplexities I have experienced in the course of my command, and almost the whole of the difficulties and distress of the Army, have there origin here....*

**From George Washington, Letter to Alexander Hamilton, March 31, 1783.**

***Thinking continentally: George Washington***

---

*I find also the pride of independance taking deep and dangerous hold on the hearts of individual states. I know no danger so dreadful and so probable as that of internal contests. And I know no remedy so likely to prevent it as the strengthening the band that connects us. We have substituted a Congress of deputies from every state to perform this task: but we have done nothing which would enable them to enforce their decisions. What will be the case? They will not be enforced. The states will go to war with each other in defiance of Congress; one will call in France to her assistance; another Great Britain, and so we shall have all the wars of Europe brought to our own doors.... I feel great comfort on the prospect of getting yourself and two or three others into the legislature. My humble and earnest prayer to Almighty god will be that you may bring into fashion principles suited to the form of government we have adopted, and not of that we have rejected, that you will first lay your shoulders to strengthening the band of our confederacy and averting those cruel evils to which it's present weakness will expose us, and that you will see the necessity of doing this instantly before we forget the advantages of union, or acquire a degree of ill-temper against each other which will daily increase the obstacles to that good work.*

**From Thomas Jefferson, Letter to Edmund Randolph, February 15, 1783.**

***Thinking continentally: Thomas Jefferson***

---

*We have now happily concluded the great work of independence, but much remains to be done to reach the fruits of it. Our prospects are not flattering. Every day proves the inefficacy of the present confederation, yet the common danger being removed, we are receding instead of advancing in a disposition to amend its defects. The road to popularity in each state is to inspire jealousies of the power of Congress, though nothing can be more apparent than that they have no power; and that for the want of it, the resources of the country during the war could not be drawn out, and we at this moment experience all the mischiefs of a bankrupt and ruined credit. It is to be hoped that when prejudice and folly have run themselves out of breath we may return to reason and correct our errors.*

**From Alexander Hamilton, Letter to John Jay, July 25, 1783.**

***Thinking continentally: Alexander Hamilton***

tions to demand changes in the state government: they objected to the state senate (the upper house of the legislature) as a needless expense and an aristocratic influence; they objected to the heavy taxation of land; and they objected to the high fees charged by lawyers and county courts. After the conventions had voiced their protests and adjourned, mobs prevented the county courts from sitting and thus put an end to the collection of debts. Then, during the winter of 1786–87, some two thousand Western farmers rose in armed rebellion under the leadership of Daniel Shays, a veteran of the Revolutionary War.

Though Shays' Rebellion was easily quelled by the loyal militia of Massachusetts, it alarmed Americans in every part of the United States. By threatening law and order, the rebellion threatened property: the closing of the courts in western Massachusetts had halted mortgage foreclosures and deprived creditors of property owed to them. Others states, too, had depressed areas and discontented debtors who, it was feared, might imitate the Shaysites. Property was also endangered from other directions. In several states, the coming of peace had brought no end to the flood of paper money that inflated values and defrauded creditors. Rhode Island made it illegal to refuse the state's worthless paper money as payment for debts.

Even before Shays' Rebellion, people had realized that something must be done about this undermining of property rights. It would be a mockery of the national purpose if Americans who had undertaken a revolution to defend property, should themselves destroy property through irresponsible government. After the shock of Shays' Rebellion, every state but Rhode Island agreed to send delegates to Philadelphia to revise the Articles of Confederation.

**The great convention.** The United States in the Revolutionary period produced six men of indisputable greatness: Franklin, Washington, Jefferson, Madison, Hamilton, and John Adams. Four of them— Franklin, Washington, Madison, and Hamilton—were among the fifty-five delegates sent by the state governments to the convention that met in Philadelphia from May 25 to September 17, 1787. Jefferson and Adams would doubtless have been there too if they had not been representing the United States in Europe, for the convention was an extraordinary assemblage of talent. The delegates had a wealth of experience and tradition to draw upon: the heritage of British political and constitutional ideas stretching back to Magna Carta and beyond; the experience of five generations of colonists in representative assemblies, town meetings, and county courts; the searching debates about authority that preceded the Declaration of Independence; the drafting of state constitutions; the running of state governments and

of a rudimentary national government. In no period of American history could a group have been gathered with more sophistication in political thought or with more practical experience in the construction and reconstruction of governments.

Almost without exception the delegates were men who thought continentally; and they were eager for a central government that would preserve and embody the national feeling that had grown out of the Revolution, a government that would be respected at home and abroad. The only way to achieve that end, they believed, was to give the central government more authority than Congress had been allowed. It had to be able to levy taxes so that it could support itself and not be starved into impotence, so that it could raise the armies and build the navy that might one day be needed to defend the independence so dearly won. It had to be able to regulate commerce so as to bargain effectively with foreign nations. It had to offer better protection to private property than the existing national or state governments did. And it had to have coercive powers to enforce its decrees.

The delegates, while agreeing on these objectives, realized that two obstacles stood in the way of attaining them. The first was the fear of the American people that a national government, if given enough power to do its job, would quickly seize more than enough, that it would fall into the hands of a select group of wealthy and clever men who would use it to their own advantage and to the disadvantage of ordinary men. The American people would not accept an effective central government unless they could be sure of controlling it.

The second obstacle was rivalry among the states. Each state feared that a strong national government might give unfair advantage to the others. For example, it might levy taxes that would injure one state and benefit another. Fortunately, quarrels over the West were momentarily at a minimum because of Virginia's renunciation of claims to the Northwest and because the status of future states in the territory was determined by Congress (in the Northwest Ordinance) while the convention was sitting. The convention itself, after preliminary debates, skirted the knotty question of whether new states should be equal to old and decided simply that "New States may be admitted by the Congress into this Union."

But another form of state rivalry could not be bypassed and threatened to deadlock the convention: in a national government composed of states, how was representation to be apportioned? Under the Articles of Confederation, each state, no matter what its size, had one vote in Congress (this manner of voting was also followed in the convention). Such an arrangement gave undue advantage to the citizens of small states: 68,000 Rhode Islanders had the same influence

*An American people*

*Constitutional Convention:
a new kind of republic*

on decisions as 747,000 Virginians. The large states would not be satisfied with any national government in which their influence was not at least approximately commensurate with their size. But the small states believed that unless they retained an equal vote the large states would be able to advance their own interests at the expense of the small states.

The rivalry between small and large states masked a more serious rivalry between North and South, which had already appeared in voting alignments in the Continental Congress. The Southern states, where slave labor produced crops for export, were wary of subjecting their labor or its produce to a government dominated by the more numerous Northern states, where free labor, diversified farming, and large commercial interests prevailed.

When the convention opened, Edmund Randolph of Virginia presented a plan, drafted by his colleague James Madison, that was designed to overcome both the fears of the people and the fears of the states. Madison, who at thirty-six was the most astute political thinker of his day, proposed to rest the government of the United States on the people rather than on the state governments and to apportion representation not by states but by population. The population of the Southern states (including slaves) equaled that of the Northern states and was expected to grow more rapidly in the future. In a government where representation was proportioned according to population, the South would be safe.

Nor would small states be endangered by large ones. Their fears, Madison perceived, were partly an illusion: the people of a small state did not necessarily have different interests from the people of a large state. The people of Delaware, for example, probably had more in common with their neighbors in Pennsylvania than with distant Rhode Islanders.

To keep the government from seizing more power than it was assigned, Madison proposed to divide it into different branches that would check and balance one another: a two-house legislature, an independent executive, and an independent judiciary. Each would have specific functions and would see to it that the others did not overstep their bounds. Thus the most distant constituent in America would have guardians within the government itself watching to make sure that it did not get out of hand. The Americans had already endorsed the principle of separation of powers in their state governments, but their discussions of national government had usually revolved around the granting of further powers to the existing unicameral Congress. Only a few, like Jefferson and John Jay, had seen the need for separation of powers in the national government itself; but as soon as Madison made the proposal, its advantages were obvious, and many of the fears about the government's escaping control were dispelled. Pierce Butler, a delegate for South Carolina, said that "he had opposed the grant of powers to Congress heretofore, because the whole power was vested in one body. The proposed distribution of the powers into different bodies changed the case, and would induce him to go great lengths."

The delegates spent two weeks revising Madison's plan and working out its details, without altering its basic structure. Then on June 15 William Paterson of New Jersey suddenly came up with a new plan calling for a continuation of the existing unicameral Congress with increased powers, but with each state retaining its equal vote. Paterson and his supporters would allow Congress the power to tax, to regulate

*The crisis of American nationality*

trade, and to enforce its own decrees, but they wanted the national government to remain what it had been, an assembly of the states, not of the people, its members chosen by the state governments, not by popular election. Paterson's plan was rejected, but the small-state delegations had rallied to it and finally threatened to bolt the convention unless each state was given an equal vote in at least one house of the national legislature. To pacify them, the other members of the convention agreed on July 16 that all the states would have equal representation in the upper house; but to this concession they attached several provisions, designed mainly to protect the interests of the South: representation in the lower house and direct taxation would be apportioned according to population, with five slaves to be considered the equivalent of three free men; all bills for raising or spending money would originate in the lower house; a census would be taken every ten years.

These conditions in effect gave the voters of slaveholding states a larger representation in the lower house than the voters of nonslaveholding states. And if Southern population grew as rapidly as expected, the representation would be increased. On the other hand, the voters of small states (mostly Northern) would have a far larger share of power in the upper house than their numbers would entitle them to.

Once they had made this Great Compromise there was no longer any serious danger that the delegates would fail in their attempt to strengthen the national government. They had started out in substantial agreement about what needed to be done, and they had overcome, in large measure at least, both the rivalry of the states and the fear of tyranny. They still argued about details; but within three and a half months of assembling, they had finished their job.

Their proposed Constitution provided for a national government with authority to collect taxes, make treaties with foreign countries, maintain an army and a navy, coin and borrow money, regulate commerce among the states and with foreign nations, and make any laws necessary to carry its powers into execution. The United States Constitution and all the treaties and laws made under it were to be the supreme law of the land, superior to state laws and binding on state courts. Moreover, the federal government would have its own executive and its own courts to enforce its treaties, Constitution, and laws, and to settle disputes between states. As a last resort it could call on the militia for help.

The national legislature, or Congress, was to consist of an upper house, or Senate, and a House of Representatives. Each state was to have two senators, both appointed by the state legislature for six-year terms, and one representative for every thirty thousand persons, to be popularly elected for a two-year term by the same persons who were qualified to vote for members of "the most numerous Branch of the State Legislature." The executive, known as the President, was to be elected every four years by an electoral "college" to which each state might appoint (in any way its legislature prescribed) as many members as the total of its representatives and senators in Congress. It was intended, of course, that the members of this body should exercise their own discretion in selecting the best man in the country. The man with the second largest number of votes became the Vice President, who was to preside over the Senate.

The Constitution hedged both the federal and the state governments with specific prohibitions. To protect private property, it forbade the state governments to pass laws impairing the obligation of contracts, or to coin money, issue paper money, or make anything but gold and silver legal tender in payment of debts. To prevent the states from encroaching on the sphere of the federal government, it forbade them to make treaties, levy import or export duties, or engage in war unless actually invaded. Conversely the states were protected by clauses prohibiting the federal government from levying direct taxes except in proportion to population, from levying export taxes at all (a protection for the tobacco- and rice-exporters of the South), and from restricting immigration "or Importation of such Persons as any of the States now existing shall think proper to admit" before the year 1808 (a protection for the slave trade until that time). Republicanism and individual rights were protected by clauses forbidding either the states or the federal government to grant titles of nobility, or to pass bills of attainder or ex post facto laws. And the federal government could not make any religious test a qualification for public office or suspend the writ of habeas corpus "unless when in Cases of Rebellion or Invasion the public Safety may require it."

Apart from these prohibitions, the Constitution did not contain any guarantee of individual rights such as freedom of speech or religion or trial by jury. In the last days of the convention, Elbridge Gerry of Massachusetts and George Mason of Virginia proposed that this omission be corrected, but their colleagues rejected the suggestion as unnecessary on the grounds that the Constitution defined and limited the powers of the national government to specified actions and that the state constitutions already contained bills of rights. But in case experience should prove this or any other of their decisions to be unwise, the convention provided a means of correction: the Constitution could be amended if two-thirds of both houses of Congress and three-fourths of the state legislatures agreed. The convention adjourned on September 17, after sending a copy of its work to Congress for transmission to the states.

**Ratification.** The constitution drafted at Philadelphia was the greatest creative triumph of the Experimental Period, and it showed how much its authors had learned during those experimental years. After the war the initial reaction against monarchy and aristocracy had led Americans to create state governments with feeble executives and ineffective upper houses; the new Constitution proposed a powerful executive and a Senate equal in power to the House of Representatives. The Articles of Confederation had created a national government controlled by the state governments and having no direct relation to the individual citizen; the new Constitution proposed a national government independent of the state governments, with a House of Representatives elected directly by the people of the United States and with federal courts acting directly on them. The Articles of Confederation had placed the national government in the hands of a single congress of delegates and had provided it with little authority; the new Constitution split up the national government to prevent abuses and gave it real authority.

The members of the Philadelphia Convention had been empowered only to revise the Articles of Confederation. Actually, they had drawn up a completely new government to take the place of the debating society that Congress had become. Knowing that their ambitious plan would meet opposition, and unwilling to have it defeated by the stubbornness of a few states, the delegates boldly proposed that as soon as nine states had accepted the new Constitution it should go into effect among those nine (revisions of the Articles of Confederation required unanimous approval). The convention also proposed the revolutionary technique of bypassing the state legislatures, where power-hungry state politicians and pressure groups might exert an influence as pernicious as the speculators had exerted against ratification of the Articles of Confederation. In each state the people would elect a special convention to judge the new constitution. The state government would issue the call for the ratifying convention but would have no part in accepting or rejecting the Constitution. The new national government, if adopted, would thus be authorized directly by the people; its power would derive from them.

The prestige of its authors, especially Washington and Franklin, as well as its intrinsic merits assured the Constitution a hearing. But its adoption was not at all certain. Several members of the convention, including the influential Edmund Randolph, had refused to sign the completed document. When it reached Congress, Richard Henry Lee took an immediate dislike to it. Why, he asked, should Congress approve its own dissolution? Why should nine states be allowed to withdraw from the Confederation to form a new and dangerously powerful government? Before transmitting the document to the states, Lee proposed at least the insertion of a bill of rights.

Lee's proposal was defeated by what he termed "a coalition of monarchy men, military men, aristocrats and drones whose noise, impudence and zeal exceeds all belief." When the Constitution reached the American people, many reacted as Lee had. But in every state the legislature eventually, if sometimes reluctantly, issued the necessary call for a popular ratifying convention.

The opponents of the Constitution were moved less by a desire to perpetuate the superiority of the state governments than by the old fear that a strong national government would escape from popular control and become oppressive. The system of checks and balances, they felt, was not adequate insurance against tyranny. The House of Representatives was too small to represent so many people and would be filled with the rich and well-born. The failure to include a bill of rights seemed an ominous indication of the direction the national government would take. Madison had argued at the convention, and now wrote in the newspapers, to persuade people that there were no grounds for the long-accepted notion that a large republic would fall into tyranny. In a large republic there would be so many different groups with such varied and opposing interests that they would be unable to submerge their differences and combine into a tyrannical majority. The danger of a tyrannical coalition was far greater in a small republic, Madison pointed out, because of the fewer divergent interests and the greater ease of communication.

The supporters of the Constitution were generally more aggressive than their opponents, and sometimes their tactics were unworthy of their cause. In Pennsylvania they pushed through the call for a convention after the legislature had voted to adjourn; they rounded up a quorum only by forcibly detaining two members. Everywhere they campaigned with a vigor and invective born of urgency. This, they felt, was the crisis of American nationality. If the Constitution failed to be adopted, the Union might be doomed.

Opposition to the Constitution was generally weakest in the small states, which would have more than their share of power in the new government. But the Federalists, as the supporters of the Constitution called themselves, knew that it was imperative to win over the four largest states: Massachusetts, Pennsylvania, New York, and Virginia. For any one of them to abstain would imperil the success of the new government. Pennsylvania, in spite of determined opposition, fell in line first, on December 12, 1787. Massachusetts ratified on February 6, 1788, by a narrow majority, which included several anti-Federalist dele-

127

gates. They had been persuaded after John Hancock proposed that a recommendation for a bill of rights accompany ratification.

In Virginia the opposition, led by Patrick Henry, was weakened when Edmund Randolph swung back in favor of adoption. The state accepted the Constitution by a vote of eight-nine to seventy-nine on June 26. Meanwhile every other state but New York, North Carolina, and Rhode Island had voted for ratification. Several had, like Massachusetts, included recommendations for amendments. In New York Alexander Hamilton, John Jay, and James Madison had campaigned for the Constitution in an impressive series of newspaper articles, known as *The Federalist*. Though these were perhaps the most searching discussion of the Constitution ever written, they did not prevent the election of a hostile ratifying convention. Only after news of Virginia's decision reached New York did the state fall into line, on July 26. North Carolina did not ratify until November 21, 1789; and Rhode Island withheld its approval until May 29, 1790. But the rest of the country did not wait for them. As soon as the four big states had given their assent, Congress arranged for its own demise by ordering national elections to be held in January 1789.

The United States was at last to have a government that would embody on a national scale the American principle of responsible representative government. The world had said that republican government was impossible for a country the size of the United States, that only a federation of republics or a powerful monarchy or aristocracy could extend so wide. But here was a new kind of republic, a federation that would be more than a federation, a government that would remain responsible to the people though its territory and population expanded tenfold, a union in which the people would be joined not as citizens of rival states but as a nation of equals.

***Suggestions for reading***

A good brief survey of the military history of the Revolution is Howard Peckham, *The War for Independence** (1958). Christopher Ward, *The War of the Revolution,* 2 vols. (1952), is more comprehensive. Don Higginbotham, *The War of American Independence* (1971), emphasizes the political and social aspects of military policies. Piers Mackesy, *The War for America* (1964), views the conflict from the British perspective. The standard account of naval operations is G. W. Allen, *Naval History of the American Revolution,* 2 vols. (1913), but for the exploits of John Paul Jones see S. E. Morison, *John Paul Jones: A Sailor's Biography** (1959). T. G. Frothingham, *Washington, Commander in Chief* (1930), is still a good assessment of the general's military genius, but more thorough accounts will be found in the two major biographies of Washington: D. S. Freeman, *George Washington,* 7 vols. (1948–57), and J. T. Flexner, *George Washington in the American Revolution* (1968).

The classic account of the diplomacy of the Revolution is S. F. Bemis, *The Diplomacy of the American Revolution** (1935). R. B. Morris gives a lively and detailed narrative of the peace negotiations in *The Peacemakers** (1965). Clarence Ver Steeg, *Robert Morris* (1954), deals largely with financing of the Revolution. A more extensive study is E. J. Ferguson, *The Power of the Purse: A History of American Public Finance, 1776–1790** (1961).

Since 1909, when Carl Becker offered his opinion that the Revolution, in New York at least, was a contest about who should rule at home, many historians have addressed themselves to the effect of the Revolution on social conflicts within the participating states. J. F. Jameson, *The American Revolution Considered as a Social Movement** (1926), argued that the Revolution acted as a leveling movement in the direction of greater democracy and accelerated social change. Not all of the studies of individual states in the period from 1776 to 1789 bear out this contention. For example, Richard McCormick, *Experiment in Independence: New Jersey in the Critical Period, 1781–1789* (1950), finds little evidence of class conflict, but E. W. Spaulding, *New York in the Critical Period, 1783–1789* (1932), finds a good deal, as do Staughton Lynd, *Class Conflict, Slavery and the United States Constitution* (1968), and Merrill Jensen, *The American Revolution within America* (1974). Robert Brown, *Middle-Class Democracy and the Revolution in Massachusetts, 1691–1780** (1955), argues that there was little democratizing of Massachusetts during the Revolution, because Massachusetts already had democratic government, with the vast majority of adult males enjoying the right to vote. Chilton Williamson, *American Suffrage from Property to Democracy, 1760–1860* (1960), finds that the majority of males in most colonies had the right to vote but that the majority became larger during the

*Available in a paperback edition.

Revolution as a result of reductions in property qualifications. E. S. Morgan, *The Birth of the Republic** (1956), emphasizes the growth of common principles rather than conflicts among Americans of the period 1763–89. J. T. Main, *The Social Structure of Revolutionary America** (1965), contains valuable statistical information about the distribution of property, and his *Upper House in Revolutionary America, 1763–1788* (1967) shows the democratizing effect of the Revolution on this legislative branch. J. K. Martin, *Men in Rebellion: Higher Governmental Leaders and the Coming of the American Revolution* (1973), similarly shows how the Revolution opened up opportunities for political leadership to a wider spectrum of the population. And see again, on internal social conflicts, Alfred Young, ed., *The American Revolution** (1976).

The first general study of the loyalists, C. H. Van Tyne, *The Loyalists in the American Revolution* (1902), saw them as exemplars of the colonial upper class. More recent studies, particularly Wallace Brown, *The King's Friends* (1965), show that they came from all classes. The most comprehensive account of them is R. M. Calhoon, *The Loyalists in Revolutionary America, 1760–1781* (1973). Their point of view is analysed in L. W. Labaree, *Conservatism in Early American History** (1948); W. H. Nelson, *The American Tory** (1962); and M. B. Norton, *The British Americans: The Loyalist Exiles in England, 1774–1789* (1972). Two good biographies of prominent loyalists are L. H. Gipson, *Jared Ingersoll* (1920), and Bernard Bailyn, *The Ordeal of Thomas Hutchinson* (1974).

John Fiske, *The Critical Period of American History, 1783–1789* (1883), painted a black picture of the United States under the Articles of Confederation and told of the nation's rescue by the Constitution of 1787. Merrill Jensen, *The Articles of Confederation** (1940, 2nd ed., 1959), and *The New Nation** (1950), sought to redeem the reputation of the Articles, which he saw as a true embodiment of the principles of the Declaration of Independence. Irving Brant, *James Madison the Nationalist, 1780–1787* (1948), gives a view of the period through the eyes of one of America's most perceptive statesmen. Gordon Wood, *The Creation of the American Republic, 1776–1787** (1969), traces the development of popular influences in government during the period. Two studies analyze political factionalism and voting blocs: J. T. Main, *Political Parties before the Constitution** (1973) on the state level, and H. J. Henderson, *Party Politics in the Continental Congress* (1974), on the national level.

Most modern accounts of the Constitutional Convention take their point of departure from Charles Beard, whose *Economic Interpretation of the Constitution of the United States** (1913) exercised a powerful influence. Beard maintained that the authors of the Constitution had invested heavily in public securities and sought to bolster the national government in order to gain protection for the economic interests of their own class. Beard's thesis has been attacked and all but demolished by Robert Brown, *Charles Beard and the Constitution** (1956), and Forrest McDonald, *We the People: The Economic Origins of the Constitution** (1958). In *E Pluribus Unum* (1965), McDonald gives his own view of the economic and political maneuvering that brought about the Philadelphia convention, while J. T. Main, in *The Antifederalists** (1961), examines the forces of opposition. Max Farrand, *The Framing of the Constitution of the United States** (1913), is still a good account of the convention itself, but there is no substitute for the records of the convention and the debates in it, which are published in Max Farrand, ed., *Records of the Federal Convention of 1787*, 4 vols.* (1911–37), and C. C. Tansill, ed., *Documents Illustrative of the Formation of the Union of the United States* (1927). J. E. Cooke, ed., *The Federalist* (1961), is the definitive edition of these papers, which are also available in a reliable paperback edition by Clinton Rossiter (1961).

For the reader who wishes to approach this period through the original sources, a wealth of material, besides *The Federalist* and the *Records* of the convention, is readily available in complete modern editions, now in process of publication, of the *Papers* of the period's great men. These editions, besides printing everything that a man wrote, include letters and communications written to him. Among the men whose *Papers* are thus being published are Thomas Jefferson (J. P. Boyd, ed.), John Adams (Lyman Butterfield and R. J. Taylor, eds.), Benjamin Franklin (L. W. Labaree and W. B. Willcox, eds.), Alexander Hamilton (H. C. Syrett and J. E. Cooke, eds.), and James Madison (W. T. Hutchinson, W. M. E. Rachal, and R. A. Rutland, eds.).

*Available in a paperback edition.

# CHAPTER 6

# *Establishing national*

# institutions

New York salutes President Washington

In adopting the Constitution, Americans gave the United States a permanent and effective government with powers that would enable it to shape the future of the nation. But the men who drafted the Constitution were well aware that they had left many details undecided and that the first officers of the new government would have a greater opportunity than their successors to determine what the United States should be and become.

## Launching the new government

Fortunately many of the leaders of the Philadelphia convention were eager to finish the job they had begun. Franklin was too old now to do more than give his blessing, but most of the nation's other great men repaired to New York in 1789 to launch the new government and help shape its institutions. There had never been any question about the candidate for President: Washington's election was unanimous and unopposed. His progress from Mount Vernon to New York was marked by a succession of triumphal arches, cheering spectators, and pretty girls strewing his path with flowers and offering him crowns of laurel. He bore it all with his usual dignity. Though he would rather have stayed at home, he was excited by the opportunity to give stature to the nation he had done so much to create.

The Vice President, John Adams, who had just returned from England, was a more complicated man, vain enough to invite laughter, but so quick, so keen, so talented in every way that hardly anyone dared laugh. Benjamin Franklin had once said of him that he was "always an honest man, often a wise one, but sometimes, and in some things, absolutely out of his senses." Adams soon found that the Vice Presidency carried little prestige or power, and an Adams could not be comfortable without a good deal of both. During Washington's Administration the Vice President set the pattern for future holders of the office by keeping himself in the background.

More influential in the first years of the new government was James Madison, the young Virginian who had played so large a role at Philadelphia. Madison's old political opponent, Patrick Henry—a powerful figure in the Virginia legislature—had succeeded in preventing Madison's election to the Senate, but his neighbors had elected him to the House of Representatives. There, in spite of his lack of humor, his small frame and unimposing appearance, Madison quickly became the dominant figure. In the early months he was also Washington's principal adviser.

Madison, like many Americans who had lived through the Revolution, was passionately interested in the art of government. So were his two friends, Thomas Jefferson and Alexander Hamilton, both of whom Washington also called on for advice and assistance. Hamilton, the younger of the two, had a brilliant analytical mind and great talents as an administrator. He also had large ambitions, both for the United States and for himself. Thomas Jefferson was as intensely devoted to the new nation as Hamilton but had a greater range of interests and loyalties. Jefferson was interested in government because he was interested in human beings, of whom he thought well. The new government, he believed, was going to be a good thing for them, but he remained less committed to it than to them.

*A strong executive.* In this galaxy of leaders, Washington was the most limited and at the same time the strongest. His strength came, not only from the fact that he had earned the unbounded confidence of the people, but from his simplicity of mind. As commanding general of the Revolutionary armies, he had devoted himself wholly to winning the war. As President of the United States he devoted himself with equal singleness of purpose, equal detachment, and equal success to making the new government respected at home and abroad.

The biggest part of the job, Washington felt, was to establish respect for his own office. In the first flush of republican revulsion from England, Americans had identified executive power with hereditary, irresponsible monarchy, and they had accordingly neglected or suppressed it in their new governments. Most of the state constitutions, while affirming the need for a separation of powers, had actually made the executive the creature of the legislature; the Articles of Confederation had provided for no real executive. The Constitutional Convention had rectified that error by creating the office of President and assigning extensive

powers to it: command of the army and navy, responsibility for foreign negotiations, and authority to appoint other governmental officers. Some of the powers were to be shared with the Senate, but the line of demarcation between the executive and legislative branches was not clear. It was up to him, Washington believed, to establish the extent of executive power and to organize the office so that future Presidents would be able to keep it strong.

Simply by taking office Washington went a long way toward achieving that end, for his own immense prestige could not fail to lend weight to any position he accepted. But he took pains to surround himself with more of the trappings of honor than he allowed himself at Mount Vernon. When he rode abroad it was on a white horse, with a leopard-skin saddlecloth edged in gold, or in an elegant coach pulled by six cream-colored horses. He rented one of the most sumptuous mansions in New York and stationed powdered lackeys at the door. He held "levees" in the manner of European monarchs, passing among the dignitaries to give each a moment of the presidential presence.

Some of Washington's associates thought this was going too far; others could not get enough of it. After the President's inauguration on April 30, 1789, his admirers in Congress had brought on a heated debate by proposing to address a formal congratulatory message to "His Highness the President of the United States and Protector of their Liberties." John Adams and Richard Henry Lee argued strenuously that some such title was needed to testify to the President's eminence, especially for the edification of the foreigners for whom he would personify the United States. The idea horrified ardent republicans, and James Madison carried the majority with him by proposing that the message be addressed simply to "George Washington, President of the United States."

By eliminating ostentatious titles Madison had no intention of minimizing the executive office. He had written most of the President's inaugural address as well as the congressional reply to it. In the first crucial months of the new government his was the hand that guided President and Congress alike in the legislation that organized the executive office and gave it the strength the President sought.

Though the Constitutional Convention had not directly provided for any executive departments except the Treasury, it clearly envisaged them in stating that the President should have power to call for the opinions of the principal officer in each such department. One of the first acts of the new government was to pass laws establishing the departments of the Treasury, State, and War, which, together with the offices of Attorney General and Postmaster General, were the only executive departments under Washington.

132

Had Washington and Madison been less insistent on executive independence, these departments might have formed the nucleus of a "cabinet" responsible to the legislative branch, as in the emerging British system. Such a development was prevented when Madison persuaded the House of Representatives, against considerable opposition, that the heads of departments, though appointed by the President with the consent of the Senate, should be subject to removal by the President alone.

Washington's first appointments to the new offices included Jefferson at State and Hamilton at the Treasury. His other choices were less distinguished: Henry Knox as Secretary of War and Edmund Randolph as Attorney General. Washington did not regard his secretaries as a team or cabinet that must act collectively. Rather, he thought of them as assistants, and in the first years they held no regular meetings. The President might refer decisions to them when he was absent from the seat of government, and he expected them to take the initiative in developing plans within their own fields of responsibility. But he kept the reins in his own hands. Executive decisions were his decisions.

Legislative decisions were not. Washington made only very general suggestions for legislation and scrupulously refrained from disclosing his views on specific measures being considered by Congress. He was extremely reluctant to use his veto power and did so only twice during his Presidency. It was his business, he believed, to administer the laws, not to make them. Consequently, while he established the authority and independence of executive action within the range allowed by the Constitution, he took no active part in the formation of public policy by legislation.

In the absence of presidential initiative three men guided Congress: Madison, Hamilton, and Jefferson. For the first five months Madison had the job to himself, for no other member of Congress combined the requisite political talents with the imagination that the new situation demanded. Hamilton acquired a position of leadership by his appointment to the Treasury on September 11, 1789, because in creating that department Congress had provided for a close connection between the Secretary and the legislature. At Madison's insistence, Congress had authorized the Secretary to prepare plans for collecting revenue and sustaining public credit and to present them to the House of Representatives, which under the Constitution had the sole right to initiate money bills. Washington approved Hamilton's active participation in the affairs of the House for, though he refrained from legislative matters himself, he did not think it necessary or desirable that his department heads should do so.

Jefferson did not accept the Secretaryship of State until January 1790 and did not arrive in New York

The first cabinet:
Knox, Jefferson, Hamilton, Washington

until two months later. His office was less closely connected with legislative affairs than Hamilton's. Moreover, while Hamilton ran the Treasury pretty much by himself, Washington took an active part in the management of foreign affairs and frequently overruled his Secretary of State. Nevertheless, Jefferson's close friendship and alliance with Madison gave him considerable influence in Congress.

**The Bill of Rights.** In ratifying the Constitution, six states had suggested amendments to specify the popular rights that the government must never invade. Many of the legislators who had been elected to the first Congress under the new Constitution arrived in New York prepared to carry out the suggestions. Although Madison had opposed a bill of rights both before and during ratification, when it became clear to him that the people of the United States were determined to have one he decided to draft it himself.

Madison had initially opposed a bill of rights, for two reasons. First, he thought that declarations of popular rights, while useful against a monarch, would be ineffective against a republican government, in which the people themselves were ultimately the lawgivers. Second, he feared that any explicit statement of rights would prove too narrow and might be used to limit freedom instead of limiting authority: a

*Launching the new government*

wayward government might construe the specified rights as the only rights of the people. The debates over ratification had introduced another ground for fear: many advocates of amendment, including some members of Congress, wanted to reduce the authority of the federal government in relation to that of the state governments. In order to forestall amendments that might weaken the new government or ones that might undermine American freedom, Madison wanted to frame the bill of rights himself.

From the proposals he first presented to Congress in June 1789 there emerged the first ten amendments to the Constitution, which were ratified by the necessary number of states in December 1791. Known as the Bill of Rights, the amendments protected freedom of religion, of speech, and of the press, and the rights to assemble, to petition the government, to bear arms, to be tried by a jury, and to enjoy other procedural safeguards of the law (see Appendix). They forbade general warrants, excessive bail, cruel or unusual punishments, and the quartering of troops in private houses.

To prevent the government from ever claiming that the people had no rights except those specifically listed, the Ninth Amendment provided that "The enumeration in the Constitution of certain rights shall not be construed to deny or disparage others retained by the people." The Tenth Amendment reassured the state governments about their relationship to the federal government by affirming, "The powers not delegated to the United States by the Constitution, nor prohibited by it to the States, are reserved to the States respectively, or to the people."

Madison fought hard for his amendments, because in preparing them he had convinced himself that a bill of rights might be more effective than he had originally supposed. If a republican legislature proved hard to control, specific prohibitions would at least form a rallying point around which popular resistance could gather. The amendments would also assist the executive and judiciary branches in checking the legislature, for the amendments would be part of the Constitution, which every officer of government must swear to uphold. Even the state governments might be brought into action to resist encroachments, a thought that recurred some years later to Madison and Jefferson alike (see p. 150).

While Madison guided the Bill of Rights through Congress, the Senate passed a judiciary bill establishing the Supreme Court and thirteen inferior district courts. When the bill came to the House of Representatives, some members wanted to eliminate the provision for district courts and leave the everyday enforcement of federal laws to the state courts. But Madison persuaded the majority that the states could not be trusted in the matter. The Judiciary Act of 1789, as finally passed, established thirteen district courts and three circuit courts with both concurrent and appellate jurisdiction. It also explicitly provided that the Supreme Court should review decisions of state courts and nullify state laws that violated the United States Constitution or the laws and treaties made under it.

# The shaping of domestic policy

By adopting the Bill of Rights and by establishing federal courts to uphold the Constitution, Americans completed the work of the Constitutional Convention and made the legacy of the Revolution secure. The next pressing problem was to recover the nation's economic credit.

**National credit and national debt.** At the Constitutional Convention it had been understood that the new government would levy taxes to pay not only its own expenses but the debts of the old government. The debts were the debts of the nation, regardless of which government contracted them. On July 4, 1789, Congress established customs duties on all imports and two weeks later placed a tonnage duty on all shipping, with high rates for foreign vessels, low ones for American. When Alexander Hamilton took office at the Treasury, it became his task to apply the income from these duties to the national debt.

Hamilton found that the United States owed $54,124,464.56, including interest. It was widely assumed that the amount would be scaled down, at least the amount owed to creditors who were themselves citizens of the United States. Much of the domestic debt was in the form of certificates that had been either issued as pay to soldiers during the Revolution or bought by patriotic citizens to further the war effort. But by now most of the certificates were held by speculators or merchants who had bought them at much less than face value when the credit of the government fell and hard times forced the owners to sell. The restoration of national credit, it seemed to many Americans, did not require payment at face value to men who had themselves discounted that value. Hamilton thought otherwise. In his Report on Public Credit, presented to Congress on January 14, 1790, he proposed to fund—that is, to pay—the entire national debt, both foreign and domestic, at its face value. Existing certificates of indebtedness would be redeemed by interest-bearing government bonds worth the original value plus the unpaid interest, calculated at 4 percent.

The very boldness of the proposal won acclaim, and there was no real opposition to the full payment of the nation's obligations. The only question—and a large one—was who should be paid. On this question Madison and Hamilton came to a parting of the ways.

Hamilton insisted that payments be made to whoever held the certificates. Many of his associates had known that his report would contain such a recommendation and had begun buying up certificates wherever they could be found. Madison, shocked by the scramble, rose in the House of Representatives to offer an alternative to Hamilton's scheme. Madison proposed to pay the face value of the certificates only to original holders who still possessed them. To subsequent purchasers he would have paid the highest market value that the certificates had formerly commanded (fifty cents on the dollar). He would have paid the difference between this amount and the face value to the soldiers and citizens who had supported the Revolution and who had then been obliged to part with their certificates at less than face value because of the government's inability to maintain its credit.

Madison's plan would not have reduced the amount paid by the government. It would simply have prevented speculators from making large profits at the expense of the government's original creditors. Unhappily for Madison, and not by accident, the speculators included many members of Congress, who did not hesitate to wrap their own shady transactions in the national honor. Men who had agents combing the country for certificates stood on the floors of Congress and denounced Madison's proposal as an attempt to make the government evade its just obligations. Madison, hitherto the master of Congress, now saw his motion defeated in the House of Representatives by a vote of thirteen to thirty-six.

Madison's proposal was defeated not by greed alone. If accepted, it would have jeopardized the basic purpose of funding the debt: to restore national credit. The credit of the government had to be sustained without regard to the motives or merits of its creditors, because when the government had need for more money than it could obtain by current taxation (and every government has such a need in national emergencies), it would have to rely on bankers and speculators, men with money to lend. Their confidence had to be purchased in advance.

Before bringing Hamilton's funding scheme to a vote, Congress took up an even more controversial matter, which Hamilton had also recommended in his report—the assumption by the national government of debts owed by the state governments. Such a move was not necessary to sustain national credit, and many supporters of the funding measure failed to see the point of it. Gouverneur Morris, a staunch

conservative, was in London when he heard of the scheme and wrote back in puzzlement: "To assume the payment of what the States owe, merely because they owe it, seems to my capacity not more rational, than to assume the debts of corporations, or of individuals." Senator Robert Morris of Pennsylvania, to whom the letter was written, had other views. "By God," he said, "it must be done."

The crucial difference between Gouverneur Morris and Robert Morris was that one was in England and the other in America. Robert, like other speculators in America, had an opportunity to take advantage of assumption before it became a fact. During the Revolutionary War the states, like the national government, had borrowed money by issuing securities. Many of these state securities had since depreciated even more than national ones. Speculators, including congressmen, now rushed to buy them. And with the prospect of making fortunes they lined up behind the assumption of state debts as they did behind the funding of the national debt.

But there was more opposition to assumption than to funding because Hamilton's proposition contained no allowance for states that had already paid a large proportion of their debt. These states included Virginia, Maryland, North Carolina, and Georgia. The largest debts were owed by Massachusetts and South Carolina. As a result, Virginians, for instance, having been taxed by the state government to pay its debt, would be taxed again by the federal government to help pay the debts of Massachusetts and South Carolina.

The inequity of the scheme enabled Madison to muster a small majority against it on a test vote in the House. But he did not dare to push his advantage, because the speculative interests threatened to vote against funding unless they got assumption as well. Much as he disliked Hamilton's funding plan, Madison knew that the rejection of funding altogether would mean the total destruction of national credit and possibly of the national government itself.

In July 1790, after Hamilton and his friends agreed to a partial allowance for states that had already paid a large part of their debts, Madison and his friends agreed to a bill providing for both funding and assumption. The fact that the two sides had been able to reach a compromise was heartening, but the line of division was ominous: Hamilton spoke for the merchants and creditors of the North, who would benefit enormously from funding and assumption, because they had accumulated most of the government's certificates of indebtedness; Madison and Jefferson spoke for the planters and farmers of the South, whose taxes would flow steadily north to pay the debt. The same division was evident in a simultaneous dispute about the location of the national capital, settled by a thir-

*The shaping of domestic policy*

It is now proper ... to enumerate the principal circumstances from which it may be inferred that manufacturing establishments not only occasion a positive augmentation of the produce and revenue of the society, but that they contribute essentially to rendering them greater than they could possibly be without such establishments. These circumstances are:

1. The division of labor.
2. An extension of the use of machinery.
3. Additional employment to classes of the community not ordinarily engaged in the business.
4. The promoting of emigration from foreign countries.
5. The furnishing greater scope for the diversity of talents and dispositions, which discriminate men from each other.
6. The affording a more ample and various field for enterprise.
7. The creating, in some instances, a new, and securing, in all, a more certain and steady demand for the surplus produce of the soil.

Each of these circumstances has a considerable influence upon the total mass of industrious effort in a community; together, they add to it a degree of energy and effect which are not easily conceived.

**From Alexander Hamilton, Report on Manufactures, 1791.**

teen-to-twelve vote in the Senate for a site on the Potomac River. The differing interests of North and South, which Madison had already perceived in 1787, were beginning to affect national politics.

**The Hamiltonian program.** Hamilton's victory, for it amounted to that, was not simply a successful swindle. The speculative frenzy set off by his measures was a calculated part of one of the boldest programs ever envisaged for the development of the nation and the nation's economy. Hamilton believed that the future of the United States depended on a large-scale expansion of industry and commerce. The suspension of imports from England during the war had forced the growth of manufacturing in America, and the production of hardware and textiles had continued in some measure afterward. To effect the kind of growth that Hamilton wanted the primary need was capital, capital in large quantities concentrated in the hands of men willing to risk investing it. By means of funding and assumption Hamilton created just such a group of wealthy investors, or, to use a less attractive word, profiteers. Hamilton was no profiteer himself—he was too interested in power to give much attention to his own finances. But he was well satisfied with the huge speculative profits that others reaped from his measures, for those profits meant capital for business investment. Moreover, funding and assumption, by restoring national credit, would make investment in American enterprises more attractive to foreign capital.

Hamilton's measures were prompted not merely by economic considerations but by his consistent determination to strengthen the national government and to overcome the centrifugal force of the state governments. He anticipated that all the capitalists created by funding and assumption would be eager to maintain the national credit and the national government, if only to protect their investments. By the same token, the assumption of state debts would deprive the state governments of such support. The national government, working hand in glove with powerful investors, would grow strong as industry and commerce grew.

Hamilton's scheme generated its own support. The opportunity to get rich easily and by methods not strictly illegal was more than congressmen could resist. Washington was disturbed by the rumor that "the funding of the debt has furnished effectual means of corrupting such a portion of the Legislature as turns the balance between the honest voters whichever way it is directed." Hamilton, who was doing the directing, assured the President that "there is not a member of the Legislature who can properly be called a stock-jobber or a paper-dealer. . . . As to improper speculations on measures depending before Congress, I believe never was any body of men freer from them." Washington believed him.

Hamilton's next objective was a national bank with capital supplied partly by the government and partly by private investors. But since the investors would be permitted to pay in government bonds for

*Those who labour in the earth are the chosen people of God, if ever he had a chosen people, whose breasts he has made his peculiar deposit for substantial and genuine virtue. It is the focus in which he keeps alive that sacred fire, which otherwise might escape from the face of the earth. Corruption of morals in the mass of cultivators is a phenomenon of which no age nor nation has furnished an example. It is the mark set on those, who not looking up to heaven, to their own soil and industry, as does the husbandman, for their subsistance, depend for it on the casualties and caprice of customers. Dependance begets subservience and venality, suffocates the germ of virtue, and prepares fit tools for the designs of ambition. This, the natural progress and consequence of the arts, has sometimes perhaps been retarded by accidental circumstances: but, generally speaking, the proportion which the aggregate of the other classes of citizens bears in any state to that of its husbandmen, is the proportion of its unsound to its healthy parts.... While we have land to labour then, let us never wish to see our citizens occupied at a workbench, or twirling a distaff ... for the general operations of manufacture, let our workshops remain in Europe.*

**From Thomas Jefferson,** *Notes on the State of Virginia,* **1787.**

three-fourths of the bank stock they purchased, the bank's notes would rest very largely on the national debt. With the government furnishing most of the capital and assuming most of the risk, the bank could offer an irresistible invitation to wealthy men to invest their money. Furthermore, the national debt, if utilized for a bank, could be a national advantage. In arguing for funding and assumption, Hamilton had emphasized the fact that where a national debt "is properly funded, and an object of established confidence, it answers most of the purposes of money." He intended to make it serve this purpose through the bank: notes issued by the bank would serve as a much needed medium of exchange (specie being scarce) and would greatly facilitate business and the financing of new commercial and industrial enterprise. Besides acting as a central exchange, the bank would handle government finances; and it would expedite borrowing both by the government and by individuals. Through this government-sponsored expansion of credit, the bond between private capital and the national government would be tightened.

When the bill to charter the bank came before the House early in February 1791, Madison attacked it with arguments he would not have used two years earlier. Before the adoption of the Constitution, he had argued strenuously that Congress should assume all the powers it needed to do its job. Under the new government he had hitherto taken a generous view of the extent of congressional authority. By now, however, he was thoroughly worried over the emerging shape of Hamilton's program and intent on stopping it. He argued that because the Constitution did not specifically empower Congress to issue charters of

incorporation it had no right to do so. Hamilton answered that the Constitution empowered the government to do anything "necessary and proper" to carry out its assigned functions.

This was the first great debate over strict, as opposed to loose, interpretation of the Constitution. Congress readily accepted Hamilton's loose construction and passed the bill. Washington weighed the question more seriously, listening carefully to Madison and Jefferson as well as to Hamilton. Though he remained doubtful to the end, at the last minute, on February 25, 1791, he signed the bill. Hamilton's program moved ahead another step.

Having provided capital and credit, Hamilton was now ready to direct the expansion of manufacturing. In December he presented to Congress his Report on Manufactures, a scheme to make investment in industry attractive by means of protective tariffs and bounties. It was Hamilton's aim to direct the nation toward a balanced economy that would include manufacturing as well as agriculture and commerce. Only through such a balance could the United States make the most of its resources, reduce its foreign debt and its reliance on foreign nations, and attain true independence. But Hamilton was not allowed to add this capstone to his economic edifice. Farmers and merchants, fearing that protective tariffs would prompt retaliatory action by other countries against American agricultural exports, preferred free competition to keep down the price of manufactures. And almost everyone wondered whether the United States could afford a measure that would discourage importation, since the government's principal income came from import duties. To raise them to protective

137

levels might reduce the volume of imports so drastically as to endanger the national credit. Moved by these considerations, Congress dealt Hamilton his first defeat by shelving his report.

Madison and Jefferson, who engineered the defeat, were both alarmed by the apparent intent of Hamilton's program. No one had done more than Madison to resuscitate and strengthen the central government a few years earlier at the Constitutional Convention, but in the Hamiltonian system he saw the beginnings of a national government so strong that it would endanger the individual liberties he had been trying to protect in the Bill of Rights. Jefferson, even more than Madison, was wary of governmental power.

To this distrust of government, Jefferson joined a dislike of cities and of the merchants and manufacturers who thrived in them. Farmers, he believed, enjoyed a greater virtue and a closer contact with their Maker than did the inhabitants of cities. From Paris he had written to Madison in 1787, "I think our governments will remain virtuous for many centuries; as long as they are chiefly agricultural. . . . When they get piled upon one another in large cities, as in Europe, they shall become corrupt as in Europe." Jefferson and Madison were both convinced that the federal government would have all the strength it needed and would be less likely to exceed its authority if it depended not on an alliance with powerful creditors but on the support of the producing classes, especially the farmers, who formed the bulk of the population. Opponents of the Constitution had feared that a strong central government would be manipulated to bring power and wealth to a few. Hamilton seemed bent on justifying their fears, which he and Madison had earlier joined to combat in *The Federalist*. Moreover, Hamilton's program was driving a wedge between the North, where capital and credit were accumulating, and the South, whose farmers and planters feared that the accumulation was at their expense. Almost all the stock in Hamilton's United States Bank was purchased by Northern and European creditors; and Hamilton made it plain that the bank was intended to assist the expansion of commerce and industry, not agriculture, which in his view needed no encouragement. He dismissed out of hand a proposal that the bank lend money to Southern planters on the security of tobacco warehouse receipts.

Thus, within three years of the inauguration of the national government, its leaders had reached a fundamental disagreement over its scope and policy. The disagreement was perhaps less dangerous than it seemed at the time, because both sides were still determined to make the new government work and because slavery, the issue in which Southerners most feared interference, had gone unchallenged. In 1793 when they introduced a bill in Congress requiring all courts, state and federal, to assist slave owners in recovering fugitive slaves, Northern congressmen readily supplied the votes to pass it, in spite of the fact that its terms were so vague as to imperil the rights of every free black.

Nevertheless, the gap between the views of Hamilton on the one hand and of Jefferson and Madison on the other was about as wide as constitutional government could stand. Each now aimed more at defeating and suppressing the other than at bargaining. Fortunately, Washington stood above the quarrel, and both sides could still join in persuading him to accept another term when the national elections were held in 1792. But during his second term the dissension spread from domestic to foreign affairs, increasingly open, increasingly bitter, and accompanied by a public rhetoric that grew increasingly violent, as each side became convinced that the other was betraying the republican ideals of the Revolution.

# Foreign affairs under Washington

The Constitution assigned to the President the conduct of relations with Europeans and Indians, and Washington undertook the task himself. While he gave Hamilton a free hand in developing financial policy and refused to meddle in congressional enactments of that policy, he gave Jefferson no such freedom as Secretary of State. He turned to Jefferson for advice, but he sought advice from other department heads as well. As foreign affairs assumed greater and greater complexity, he began the practice of calling together the Attorney General and the Secretaries of State, War, and the Treasury to discuss policy. During these meetings, from which grew the Cabinet as an institution, Jefferson and Hamilton again revealed their differing conceptions of the national welfare.

*Jeffersonian neutrality.* The discord in foreign affairs first showed itself in 1790, when a threatened war between Spain and England offered the United States an opportunity to press American claims against both countries. Spain had seized three British vessels trading in Nootka Sound, Vancouver Island, which had been Spanish territory ever since its discovery. England demanded the return of the ships, reparation for damages, and recognition of British trading rights in the area. It seemed likely that Spain would fight rather than submit.

Washington's advisers all agreed that the United States should remain neutral in case of war, but they did not agree on what the United States should do if England decided to march troops through American territory in the Mississippi Valley in order to attack the Spaniards in Florida and Louisiana. Since Hamilton had just tied his funding program to duties on British trade, he was reluctant to do anything that might offend England and was ready to declare American neutrality at once. Jefferson, on the other hand, had just come from five years as the United States Ambassador to France, where he had seized every opportunity to bargain for national advantages. He wanted to bargain now, to keep both Spain and England guessing about America's intentions and to make them bid high for assurance of American neutrality. In particular, he hoped to make England open its West Indian ports to American ships.

As it happened, Spain gave in to the British ultimatum. No war occurred, and the ports remained closed, with Hamilton giving the British secret assurances against retaliatory regulations by the United States. But another European war was clearly in the making, and mounting tensions in Europe generated a notable increase in the cordiality of European countries toward the United States. In 1791 England sent a minister plenipotentiary, George Hammond, to reside in Philadelphia; the United States in turn sent Thomas Pinckney to London. Full diplomatic relations had thus been established between England and the United States when war finally did break out in 1793 between England and France—and something close to war between Hamilton and Jefferson.

Thomas Jefferson, as American minister to France during the 1780s, had learned to admire French civilization and French people. Just before returning to the United States late in 1789, he had witnessed the beginnings of their revolution. He was skeptical that a people who had lived so long under absolute monarchy could successfully undertake republican government. But he heartily approved their efforts to curb their king. When he took up his post as Washington's Secretary of State, he brought with him a warm sympathy for the French and their cause, a sympathy that was not destroyed by the execution of Louis XVI in 1793 or by the reign of terror that followed.

Hamilton, by contrast, watched with horror as the French Revolution overturned the foundations of society, destroying monarchy and aristocracy, exalting democracy and demagogues. His horror mounted when the French Revolutionists launched the "war of all peoples against all kings," with England and Spain as primary targets. England, even under King George III, seemed to Hamilton a safer friend for Americans than mob-wracked republican France. Hamilton was moved not simply by his repugnance for the French Revolution but by the belief that, if the United States had to choose sides, England was more to be feared than France, because England had the stronger navy. American commerce was more vulnerable to English sailors than to French soldiers.

Hamilton agreed with Washington's other advisers that the United States should stay out of the war, but he wanted to use the crisis as an opportunity to scrap the French alliance. The treaties of 1778, he argued, had been made with the French monarchy and were no longer binding now that the monarchy had been overthrown. The United States should therefore declare its neutrality and refuse to receive the minister, Edmond Genêt, sent by the new French republic early in 1793.

Jefferson argued that the treaties had been made with the French nation and were still binding. He was as certain as Hamilton that the United States should stay out of the war but wanted the country to do so without publicly announcing its intention. A declaration of neutrality would affront the French and would destroy the possibility of bargaining with the British, who still had troops stationed in the American Northwest and still withheld trading privileges in the empire. Washington decided the matter on April 22, 1793, by issuing a proclamation of neutrality addressed to American citizens only and not actually mentioning the word "neutrality." The treaties with France were not repudiated, and Citizen Genêt was accorded formal recognition. But the bargaining power that Jefferson valued was gone. Shortly afterward he announced that he would retire at the end of the year.

Genêt was a fool. From the moment of his arrival he assumed powers that no independent country could permit a foreign envoy: he commissioned American ships to sail as privateers under the French flag; he set up courts to condemn the ships they captured; he arranged an expedition of Western frontiersmen to attack Spanish New Orleans. Jefferson tried hard to like him but gave up in disgust. Finally Washington demanded Genêt's recall.

While Genêt was losing friends for France, the British government was losing them for England. Under the slogan "free ships make free goods," Americans claimed the right as neutrals to carry noncontraband goods (including naval stores) to and from the ports of belligerents. France had lifted some of its mercantilist restrictions regulating trade with its West Indian islands, and American ships were swarming there to take advantage of the new opportunity. But England adhered to its rule of 1756 that trade closed in peacetime could not be opened to neutrals in wartime. In December 1793, without warning, British naval vessels began seizing American ships trading with the French West Indies.

The seizures combined with an Indian episode in

*Foreign affairs under Washington*

the Northwest to bring the United States, in spite of Hamilton, to the brink of war with England. The record of Washington's government in dealing with hostile Indians had not been good. He had arranged a treaty with Alexander McGillivray, the half-breed chieftain of the Creeks, but the Creeks had broken it as soon as it was made. He had sent General Josiah Harmar to crush the Miamis in Ohio, but they had crushed him. He had sent Arthur St. Clair with a much larger force in 1791, but St. Clair, like Braddock in 1755, had been surprised just short of his objective and completely routed. In February 1794, as General Anthony Wayne gathered a force to try again, the governor-general of Canada, Lord Dorchester, made a speech to the Indians in which he in effect exhorted them to do their worst. Reports of the speech reached Congress along with news of the Caribbean seizures.

The House of Representatives was then debating whether restrictions against British commerce (suggested by Jefferson shortly before his resignation) might lead England to reduce its own restrictions against American commerce. News of the seizures precipitated an overwhelming demand for much stronger anti-British measures, to which Hamilton felt sure England would react by declaring war on the United States—if indeed the United States did not declare war first. The country was swept by war hysteria; volunteer defense companies sprang up. Mobs mistreated English seamen and tarred and feathered pro-British Americans. To prevent a plunge into actual warfare, Hamilton urged Washington to send a special mission to England. Hamilton seems to have thought of heading it himself, but Washington gave the job to Hamilton's alter ego, John Jay.

*A Hamiltonian treaty.* Although Jay had had abundant experience as a diplomat, in the eyes of most Americans it had been unsuccessful experience. As envoy to Spain during the Revolution, he had failed to gain either alliance or recognition of American independence. As Secretary for Foreign Affairs under the Articles of Confederation, he had conducted the nearly disastrous negotiations with Gardoqui. In both cases failure arose less from lack of skill on his part than from the fact that the other side held all the cards. This time, with England engaged in a major European war, Jay was in a strong position to play the game that Jefferson had recommended all along: namely, to convince England that unless it made concessions it could not count on continued American neutrality. Edmund Randolph, the new Secretary of State, agreed with the Jeffersonian strategy. He instructed Jay to consult with Russia, Sweden, and Denmark about the possibility of an armed-neutrality agreement in order to bring pressure on England to stop seizures of neutral shipping.

Once again, however, Jay found himself on the losing side through no fault of his own. Denmark and Sweden, which shared the American view of the rights of neutral ships, took the initiative, and just after Jay's departure for Europe the United States received an invitation from them to join in forming an alliance of neutrals. Randolph wanted to accept, for he felt that such backing would strengthen Jay's hand. But Hamilton persuaded Washington to decline, on the grounds that the alliance would jeopardize Jay's mission by antagonizing the British. Not content with rejecting the assistance of other neutrals, and eager to create a friendly climate of opinion in England, Hamilton weakened Jay's position still further by informing George Hammond, the British minister in America, of Washington's decision.

With this information to guide him, Lord Grenville, the British foreign minister, felt safe in conceding little. He promised again to surrender the Northwest posts—provided the United States permitted the continuation of the English fur trade with the Indians in the area; he promised recompense for the American ships that had been seized without warning in December 1793 in the Caribbean—provided the United States compensated British creditors for prerevolutionary debts whose collection had been impeded by state governments. He refused to compensate American slave owners for slaves kidnaped or liberated by the British during the Revolution, and he refused to give any guarantee against the British navy's practice of stopping American vessels to impress alleged British subjects as seamen. Instead of stopping the seizure of neutral ships, he required the United States to give up its own view of neutral shipping rights for the duration of England's war with France and for two years thereafter. He consented to reciprocal trading rights between England and America but restricted American trade with the British West Indies to vessels of no more than seventy tons, and even these he allowed only in return for an American promise to ship no molasses, sugar, coffee, cocoa, or cotton from the islands or from the United States to any other part of the world. The only generosity he showed was at the expense of the Spanish: it was agreed that both British subjects and Americans should have the right to navigate the Mississippi through Spanish territory to the sea.

When the treaty containing these terms reached Washington on March 7, 1795, Hamilton was no longer at the Treasury. He had resigned at the end of January, a little more than a year after Jefferson, but he retained as much influence over the President out of office as in. His replacement, Oliver Wolcott, Jr., had been his assistant and continued to consult him on every important matter. Hamilton thought that the treaty was satisfactory and that failure to ratify it

*Negotiating the Treaty of Greenville*

would mean war. Washington reluctantly agreed, but he could see that other Americans might not. To avoid a premature hardening of opposition, he tried to keep the terms secret until he could present the treaty for ratification at a special session of the Senate called for June 8. It was impossible. By the time the Senate met, rumors of the contents had produced wide public hostility, which increased as the details became known. Nevertheless, the senators, after striking out the clause regarding trade with the West Indies, accepted the treaty by the exact two-thirds majority required.

As the treaty came before Washington for his signature, the press was denouncing Jay, the treaty, the Senate, and even the President. Popular meetings in Boston, Philadelphia, New York, and other cities urged Washington to reject it. In the Cabinet everyone but Randolph urged him to sign. Dismayed by the public antagonism, Washington hesitated. In the meantime, the British minister handed to Oliver Wolcott some intercepted dispatches written by the French minister, Jean Fauchet. In them Fauchet, referring to some transactions with Randolph, seemed to imply that Randolph had turned over state secrets to him for money. Although the dispatches had nothing to do with the treaty, they discredited the only Cabinet member who opposed it. Washington signed the treaty, and, after confronting Randolph with the dispatches, refused his explanations and accepted his resignation.

**The winning of the West.** Jay's Treaty was the low-water mark of foreign affairs under Washington. General Wayne had defeated the Indians of the Northwest at the Battle of Fallen Timbers (August 20, 1794) and had gone on to devastate their settlements.

At the Treaty of Greenville (August 3, 1795) they gave up most of the territory that was to become the state of Ohio. In the next year the British at last honored their agreement to evacuate their posts in the Northwest.

Meanwhile, Spain had become fearful that the United States would throw its small weight on the British side in the precarious European balance. The clause about the Mississippi in Jay's Treaty suggested that England and the United States might be contemplating joint action against Louisiana. Taking advantage of this fear, Thomas Pinckney, who was sent to negotiate a treaty, won for the United States everything it had been seeking from Spain: free navigation of the Mississippi, permission for American traders to deposit goods for shipment at the mouth of the river, acknowledgment of the American southern boundary at the thirty-first parallel and the western boundary at the Mississippi, and an agreement by each country to prevent Indians within its territory from making incursions into the territory of the other.

The Treaty of Greenville, 1795

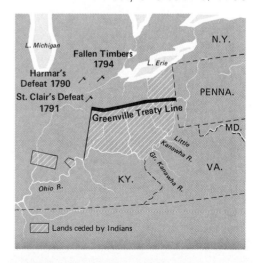

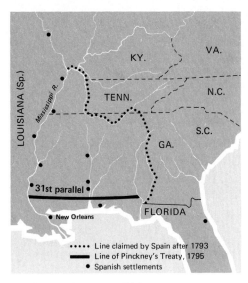

Pinckney's Treaty, 1795

The Senate accepted Pinckney's Treaty unanimously on March 3, 1796. With it the danger of secession in Kentucky and Tennessee (admitted to the Union in 1792 and 1796) disappeared; with the Mississippi open to trade, any attachment to Spain lost its charm for the Americans of the Southwest. Although Washington's foreign policy had produced some vastly unpopular concessions to Britain, it must be credited with the restoration of reciprocal trading rights and with achieving, at last, recognition by both Spain and Britain of United States sovereignty over the area first won from Britain in 1783.

New states, 1791–96

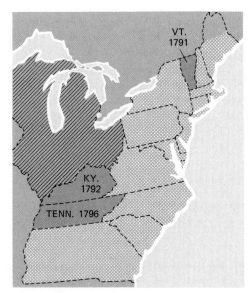

# Federalists versus Republicans

Alexander Hamilton, by dictating domestic policy to Congress and foreign policy to the President, gave the national government its initial direction. Although Madison and Jefferson managed to modify some of his measures, in all essentials Hamilton prevailed. But in their efforts to defeat him, Madison and Jefferson set a pattern of political action that in ten years' time gave them control of the government and thereafter became the only way of gaining or keeping control. They started a political party.

***The Republican challenge.*** The framers of the Constitution, Madison included, had not thought well of parties. "Faction" was the word generally used for party in the eighteenth century, and a faction meant, by Madison's own definition, a group of men organized to procure selfish advantages at the expense of the community. Denunciation of factions or parties was a standard ingredient in every discussion of politics in the eighteenth century, as safe and as platitudinous as denunciation of corruption and praise of honesty.

The parties of the time deserved denunciation. In the British House of Commons, and to some degree in the colonial assemblies, politicians had joined forces from time to time in order to make legal raids on the public purse. Because neither Madison nor Jefferson had any such end in view, they did not at first think of their opposition to Hamilton as constituting a party. Madison, to be sure, had a following in the House of Representatives and was an old hand at collecting votes in support of his measures. But in lining up opposition to indiscriminate funding and wholesale assumption, neither Jefferson nor Madison anticipated a continuing, organized opposition.

It was only as the full dimensions of Hamilton's program revealed themselves that the two men deliberately set out to gather and consolidate their strength against him inside the government and out. Jefferson was aware that Washington consulted Hamilton on every kind of measure, including matters that seemed to belong properly in the Department of State; in response, he tried to extend his own influence within the executive departments. Washington liked Jefferson, as did most of the other members of the presidential entourage. And yet Jefferson made little headway in his campaign. Though he succeeded in having the Mint established under the State Department instead of the Treasury, his attempts to get the Post Office transferred to the State Department failed, and so did his efforts to get his friend Tench Coxe appointed as Comptroller and Thomas Paine as Postmaster General.

*Establishing national institutions*

Madison was more successful. In the House of Representatives he was often defeated, but every defeat strengthened the loyalty of his followers. Though he lacked Jefferson's personal charm and was not eloquent in debate, he knew how to work in the corridors; and on the floor his colleague from Virginia, William Branch Giles, was an able spokesman of his views. John Beckley, the perennial Clerk of the House, who seemed to know everybody's secrets, turned over valuable information to him. As the Madison forces hardened around a nucleus of Southern congressmen, they began to call themselves the "republican interest," and by 1792 they even dared to say the "republican party"—a phrase that gradually acquired capital letters.

Their opponents, not considering themselves a party, appropriated the name of Federalists, which had been used earlier by the advocates of the Constitution of 1787. This maneuver identified the Republicans with the anti-Federalists of that period. Actually there was no connection. The leaders of the Republican party had supported the Constitution in 1787 and still did; the Federalists of the early 1790s were distinguished, not by any special reverence for that document, but by a conception of the national welfare that included a permanent national debt, a national bank, and dependence on England.

Madison and Jefferson believed that that source of Federalist strength, apart from Washington's support of Hamilton, was typical of faction or party in the traditional sense: it lay in the corruption of congressmen through the speculative opportunities that accompanied funding and assumption. Their own strength, they believed, lay with the people at large. Perhaps because they assumed that the people were on their side, they did not at first organize their party except within the government itself; they did, however, take steps to let the people know, through the press, what their side was.

Before 1791 the *Gazette of the United States* was the only newspaper that gave full coverage to national politics, and its editor, John Fenno, was an ardent Hamiltonian. Madison and Jefferson persuaded the poet Philip Freneau, whom they knew to be Republican in sentiment, to establish a newspaper that would report national issues from their point of view. On October 31, 1791, the first issue of the *National Gazette* was published, and the Republicans gained a medium for spreading attacks on the Hamiltonian program (some of them written by Madison) throughout the country.

At the same time spontaneous popular societies that might have furnished the basis for Republican party organization at the local level began to form. Admiration for the French Revolution and discontent with the government's evident bias in favor of England prompted the formation of these "Democratic Clubs," first in Pennsylvania and then all over the country. The clubs, which were imitations of the Jacobin societies in France, felt that they were continuing the tradition of the Sons of Liberty of the 1760s and 1770s. They sympathized with the French Revolution and passed resolutions against the government's pro-British foreign policy; they supported the Republicans in Congress and in elections for Congress. But before Madison and his friends could capitalize on their support, the Federalists found an opportunity to discredit the clubs and capture a wide popular following for themselves.

***The Federalist response.*** The Federalist opportunity arose from a tax on whiskey passed by Congress in 1791 to help pay the expenses of funding and assumption. Excise taxes, especially on alcoholic beverages, were unpopular in the eighteenth century. A cider tax nearly caused rebellion in England in 1763, and so did a rum tax in Massachusetts in 1754. By 1794 the federal excise tax on liquor did cause rebellion, or what looked like it, in Pennsylvania. Farmers in the western part of the state generally turned their surplus grain into whiskey. This could be transported over the mountains more easily than wheat or corn, and it brought a better price in the Eastern markets. But the profit was small even without the excise, and hence there was much evasion of the tax. In July 1794 the United States marshal, summoning offenders to court, met with mass resistance.

The governor of the state, Thomas Mifflin, thought that the courts could handle the situation, but Hamilton wanted an immediate show of force. Washington weighed the situation, delayed until the rebels' rejection of every overture had turned public opinion against them, and then marched fifteen thousand militiamen to western Pennsylvania. No rebel fired a shot against him, and Washington returned to Philadelphia, leaving Hamilton to complete the arrest of the ringleaders.

When Congress assembled shortly after his return, Washington delivered an address that made clear how he felt about all organized opposition to the policies of the national government, whether from whiskey rebels, Democratic Clubs, or Republicans. Although there is no evidence that the clubs had anything to do with the rebellion, Washington had somehow got the notion that they had. In spite of the fact that the Constitution guaranteed the right to assemble, he rebuked the clubs as "self-created societies." Dismayed by his disapproval, many of them dissolved at once, and the rest expired within a year or two.

Washington's personal popularity was thus revealed as the strongest weapon in the Federalist arse-

*Washington: President and General*

nal. The Republicans were not fully aware of how strong it was or of how it could be used against them. Nor was Washington aware. He continued to regard himself as standing above party and seems never to have realized that as he came more and more to rely on Hamilton he was choosing sides in a party conflict. Hamilton did realize it and used Washington's prestige to turn popular opinion against the Republicans.

When the President signed Jay's Treaty, in spite of popular meetings that urged him not to, the Republicans, instead of conceding defeat, carried the battle to the House of Representatives. Although the Constitution gave only the Senate the authority to approve or reject treaties, the House, under Madison's leadership, asserted its right to examine treaties before appropriating funds to implement them. On this basis, the House demanded copies of the papers that had passed to and from Jay during the negotiations. Washington, defending the integrity of the executive department, indignantly refused; Hamilton, by decrying the demand of the House as an insult to the President and a step toward war, soon had Congress flooded with petitions supporting the President. Republican efforts to secure counterpetitions were less successful, and Madison saw his majority dwindle to a minority. The House in the end supported the treaty.

**The election of 1796.** When the Republicans attacked the treaty in the House of Representatives, they had an eye on the presidential election that was to take place later in the year. In the elections of 1788 and 1792 there had been no serious contest for the Presidency. In 1796 it was probable, though not certain, that Washington would retire. If he did, the

Republicans would have a chance to challenge Hamilton at the polls. But the Republican hope of unseating the Federalists received a strong setback when Madison's attack on the treaty foundered against Washington's popularity.

As the election approached, Washington gave the Federalists another advantage by delaying his decision to withdraw. The Republicans were wary of advancing any candidate of their own unless the still insuperable national hero was out of the race. It was understood that if Washington chose not to run, Adams would be the Federalist candidate; for Hamilton, though influential among politicians, did not have a wide enough popular following to assure election. For the same reason the Republicans had settled on Jefferson rather than Madison. In September Washington finally announced his retirement and delivered a farewell address written by Hamilton. The address contained a strong warning against partiality for foreign countries (meaning France) and against political parties (meaning Republicans). Washington still refused to think of the Federalists as a party.

Having secured Washington's support for a Federalist successor, Hamilton set about substituting a more pliable candidate for the prickly, independent Adams. Because of Adams' popular following, Hamilton could not renounce him publicly, but he hoped to achieve his purpose by manipulating the electoral vote.

The maneuver was made possible by the peculiar constitutional provisions for electing the President. Each state could select its members for the Electoral College in any manner it saw fit. Six did it by popular vote, nine by vote of the state legislature, and one, Massachusetts, by a combination of the two. Most candidates for the college announced beforehand for whom they would vote; but this practice was not universal, and the college as an institution retained some small measure of choice. Each elector cast two ballots, without specifying which man he preferred for President; the candidate who received the largest vote became President, and the candidate with the second largest vote became Vice President. Since this was a system designed for a partyless government, complications arose when political parties appeared. If all the electors who favored the strongest party voted for both its candidates, a tie vote would result. In order to elect the party's preferred presidential candidate some electors had to divert their second vote from the party's vice-presidential candidate to some other candidate. This could be dangerous: if too many votes were diverted from the party's vice-presidential candidate he might be left with fewer than the presidential candidate of the opposing party, who would then become Vice President instead. There was also the possibility that if both parties wanted the same man for Vice President, he might receive more votes than either presidential candidate and thus become President.

It was this latter possibility that led Hamilton to arrange for Adams' running mate on the Federalist ticket to be Thomas Pinckney of South Carolina. Pinckney, who had just returned in triumph from his Spanish mission, enjoyed great popularity in the South, where the Republicans were strongest. Southerners would certainly give most of their votes to Jefferson, but they might be persuaded to designate Pinckney as second choice. If a substantial number of electors did so, the combined Federalist-Republican vote might be large enough to put Pinckney into the Presidency.

But Hamilton was not the only one who knew the deficiencies of the electoral system. When the votes of the Electoral College were cast, it appeared that his advocacy of Pinckney had failed. Adams' friends in Connecticut and New Hampshire, refusing to endanger his success, had all scattered their second votes, and the Southern Republicans had actually given Pinckney nothing. Even so, he had fifty-nine votes; but Adams with seventy-one became President and Jefferson with sixty-eight became Vice President. Jefferson's running mate, Aaron Burr of New York, had only thirty.

Had the Federalist electors of Connecticut and New Hampshire given Pinckney their second votes, Hamilton's strategy could have succeeded. Pinckney would have tied Adams' vote, and tied presidential elections, according to the Constitution, were to be decided in the House of Representatives. There, with Jefferson out of the contest, Southern Republicans might have joined with Hamilton's forces to make Pinckney President. For Adams it was a bitter thing to have come so close to losing and to know that Hamilton was to blame.

# The Presidency of John Adams

The new President was a man of conflicting emotions, ideas, and loyalties. Round of face and frame, he looked like an English country squire and often behaved like one, lashing out at those who crossed him as though he were lord of the manor. Yet he was sometimes remarkably patient when there was real cause for anger. Like Washington and Jefferson and George III, he loved the land and found high office uncongenial and inconvenient. Yet no man wanted the Presidency more or would have found defeat more humiliating.

Adams had had a distinguished career during the Revolution, both in the Continental Congress and in negotiating the peace treaty. His political experience and his study of history had given him strong ideas about the proper form of government: liberty, he believed, could be preserved only where a strong executive presided over a legislature divided into two houses, the upper representing the wealthy and well-born, the lower representing the people at large. This idea, expounded at length in his *Defence of the Constitutions of the United States* (1787), had influenced the Philadelphia convention and had helped produce the strong executive office that Adams inherited from Washington. As President, Adams continued to think that the executive must stand above the other branches of government and mitigate differences between them.

**The President and the politicians.** Adams, like his contemporaries, spoke of political parties only to condemn them. Though he had been elected in a contest between parties, the circumstances were not such as to endear either side to him. The Republicans had branded him a monarchist because of his openly avowed advocacy of a strong executive, while the Federalists had almost betrayed him for Thomas Pinckney.

In his inaugural address Adams did his best to minimize party differences. Answering for the first time the accusations that had been made against him during the campaign, he assured the Republicans that he did not want a monarchical or aristocratic or, indeed, any but a republican government. Lest anyone think him an enemy of the French alliance, so dear to Jefferson, he affirmed his personal esteem for the French nation, "formed in a residence of seven years, chiefly among them"; and his "sincere desire to preserve the friendship which has been so much for the honor and interest of both nations."

The Republicans were delighted. Newspaper editors who had been warning of the approach of tyranny suddenly discovered the President's "incorruptible integrity," his intelligence, his patriotism. Jefferson had always liked Adams. The two had become estranged in 1791 when one of Jefferson's friends published a private letter from him criticizing Adams' political writings. Before the inauguration they made it up and took rooms in the same Philadelphia boardinghouse. In assuming office as Vice President, Jefferson hailed the man "whose talents and integrity have been known and revered by me through a long course of years."

The political backers of both men were suspicious of the new harmony and uneasy about the effect it might have on the party organizations they had been building. Before coming to Philadelphia,

145

**Benjamin Franklin on John Adams**

*I am persuaded that he means well for his Country, is always an honest Man, often a wise one, but sometimes, and in some things, absolutely out of his senses.*

**From Benjamin Franklin, Letter to Robert R. Livingston, July 22, 1783.**

**Thomas Jefferson on John Adams**

*I suppose the newspapers must be wrong when they say that Mr. Adams has taken up his abode [in Paris] with Dr. Franklin. I am nearly at a loss to judge how he will act in the negotiation [of the peace treaty with England]. He hates Franklin, he hates Jay, he hates the French, he hates the English. To whom will he adhere?... Notwithstanding all this he has a sound head on substantial points, and I think he has integrity. I am glad therefore that he is of the commission and expect he will be useful in it. His dislike of all parties, and all men, by balancing his prejudices, may give the same fair play to his reason as would a general benevolence of temper.*

**From Thomas Jefferson, Letter to James Madison, February 14, 1783.**

**John Adams on John Adams**

*There is a Feebleness and a Languor in my Nature. My mind and Body both partake of this Weakness. By my Physical Constitution, I am but an ordinary Man. The Times alone have destined me to Fame—and even these have not been able to give me much. When I look in the Glass, my Eye, my Forehead, my Brow, my Cheeks, my Lips, all betray this Relaxation. Yet some great Events, some cutting Expressions, some mean Hypocrisies, have at Times, thrown this Assemblage of Sloth, Sleep, and littleness into Rage a little like a Lion.*

**From John Adams, *Diary*, April 26, 1779.**

Jefferson had drafted an open and generous letter to Adams, declaring his pleasure in the outcome of the election. He had always served as a junior to Adams and would be glad to continue doing so. He sent the letter to Madison to deliver at his discretion. Madison thought it best not to: if made public, it might alienate Jefferson's supporters and embarrass him in a future contest. Jefferson himself avoided getting too close to the Administration: the separation of powers, he decided, should prevent his sitting in the President's Cabinet.

Federalist leaders, equally cautious, were worried about Adams' charity toward the Republicans and blocked him when he proposed appointing Madison as special envoy to France. Adams, who had already told Jefferson of his intention, with some embarrassment withdrew the nomination when Oliver Wolcott, Jr., the Secretary of the Treasury, threatened to resign in protest. Thereafter relations between the President and the Vice President deteriorated, for Adams' behavior seemed to indicate that in spite of his good beginning he would not stand very far above party.

It might, in the end, have been better for Adams if he had used his famous temper on Wolcott. Since there was as yet no tradition requiring Cabinet officers to submit their resignations when a new President took office, Adams inherited the Cabinet that Washington left behind. And a sorry lot they were. Besides Wolcott at the Treasury, there was James McHenry in the War Department and Timothy Pickering at State. Hamilton, in suggesting McHenry's appointment to Washington, had said that "he would give no strength to the administration, but he would not disgrace the office." Three years later, Hamilton had to admit that "my friend McHenry is wholly insufficient for his place." Timothy Pickering had originally served as Postmaster, a position that strained his talents to their limits. When Randolph resigned, Washington gave Pickering the State Department temporarily but was unable to persuade a more competent man to take the job.

146

Apart from their palpable mediocrity, the only thing that Wolcott, McHenry, and Pickering had in common was that they all took orders from Hamilton. Adams was too keen a man not to perceive the quality of their minds, but he did not realize that the advice they gave him came by mail from New York. Even had he known, he might have hesitated to drop them. They had been appointed by the great Washington, and it would have been brash for a President who had barely won the office to cashier the advisers whom the national hero had thought adequate. Even if Adams had let them go, he might have had difficulty replacing them. Cabinet officers received a salary of only $3,000 a year, and a man of talent who could earn much more in private business might be reluctant or unable to make the financial sacrifice, especially since there was as yet little prestige in any appointive office. Washington had kept second-rate men simply because he could not get first-rate ones.

Surrounded by incompetent advisers who remained loyal to a politician who had betrayed him, Adams could have preserved the strength of the executive department only by showing a resolute determination to make his own decisions. Instead, he spent much of his time at home in Quincy, Massachusetts, leaving the members of his Cabinet to deliberate by themselves. Consequently his Administration drifted into policies with which he did not fully agree and from which he finally extricated it only at the expense of his political career.

**The end of the French alliance.** In the opening months of his Administration Adams' cordiality for France, and for Jefferson, cooled rapidly. During Washington's Presidency the French government had become increasingly angered by the apparent partiality of its American ally for England. Although the commercial treaty of 1778 stated that the United States would give no nation greater trading privileges than it gave to France, Congress had never given France anything more than equality with other nations—and that only on paper. In operation, the laws that Congress passed consistently favored England. Jay's Treaty had outraged France, and the French minister to America, Pierre Adet, had warned that his country would henceforth treat American ships "in the same manner as they suffer the English to treat them." Actually the French had already intercepted several American vessels bound for England and had impounded them in French harbors. Now France announced that it would no longer recognize the treaty principle that free ships made free goods and that it would treat American sailors serving on British ships as pirates. France went even further: it refused to have anything to do with the American minister, Charles Cotesworth Pinckney (brother of Thomas).

*John Adams:*
*no man wanted the Presidency more*

President Adams proposed to meet the crisis diplomatically by sending a three-man mission to France, the mission for which he had considered Madison. The members of his Cabinet were at first opposed not only to Madison but to any mission. Only after Hamilton cautioned them not to get too far ahead of public opinion did they fall in with Adams' plan. The commissioners appointed were the Virginia Federalist lawyer, John Marshall; the rejected minister to France, C. C. Pinckney; and an astute but unpredictable Massachusetts politican, Elbridge Gerry. To announce the mission the President called a special session of Congress in May and delivered a message that he and the cabinet alike had thought the proper accompaniment to negotiations. It called for strengthening coastal defenses, arming merchant vessels, completing three frigates begun in 1794, and establishing a provisional army.

Jefferson, the former advocate of bargaining from strength, now thought that the recommended belligerence would be offensive to France and would make the mission's task impossible. As it turned out, neither American nor French belligerence but French corruption prevented the mission's success. The French minister of foreign affairs, Talleyrand, after keeping the envoys waiting for several weeks, informed them through three unaccredited go-betweens, known only as X, Y, and Z, that the price of negotiating would be $250,000 for himself. The price of a treaty would be several million dollars for France. "Not a sixpence," said Pinckney, as he and Marshall departed, leaving Gerry to continue the futile conversations until he was ordered home.

When Adams reported the XYZ Affair, incredulous Republicans in Congress demanded to see the commission's papers. Adams did not follow Washington's example in the case of the Jay's Treaty papers, probably because he knew that the record would fully sustain him. He turned the papers over, and Congress supported the President in retaliating against France by actions just short of war. The treaties of 1778 were repudiated. Commercial intercourse was suspended. American ships were authorized to seize French armed vessels, and for the next two years French and American ships fought an undeclared war on the seas.

It would have been foolhardy to go to such lengths without preparing for full-scale war. But the President and his advisers could not agree on the kind of preparation to make. The most ardent Federalists saw in the crisis an opportunity to strengthen themselves as well as the government at the expense of the Republicans. They wanted a large standing army, not merely to repel a French invasion but to overawe and if necessary to suppress their political opponents. Hamilton also dreamed of leading an army of conquest into Florida and Louisiana. Adams, while denouncing the French and their American friends, had a more realistic and more comprehensive view of the national interest. He thought it wise to keep a small army in readiness, but he discounted the possibility of a French invasion, and he had no ambition to rule by military force or to conquer territories peopled by Frenchmen and Spaniards. What the country really needed, he believed, was a navy to defend its commercial interests in the shifting tides of European conflict. To concentrate on an army would leave the United States no choice but to side always with the country whose navy dominated the seas, in other words, with England. Though Adams' own sympathies lay with England, he thought it was bad policy to let the safety of American commerce depend on the good will of any foreign country. Accordingly, in May 1798 he persuaded Congress to establish a Department of the Navy, with Benjamin Stoddert, a Maryland merchant, as Secretary. In Stoddert, Adams gained his first loyal adviser in the Cabinet.

While Adams and Stoddert proceeded with the construction and commissioning of warships, the High Federalists, as the more extreme branch of the party came to be called, continued their buildup of the army, dragging the reluctant President with them, and levying heavy taxes to pay for it. Washington was persuaded to accept command again, and Hamilton was eager to join him. Adams agreed to make Hamilton a general but refused at first to rank him above Henry Knox, Daniel Morgan, and Benjamin Lincoln, Hamilton's seniors in the Revolutionary army. Hamilton, perhaps with more than military ends in view, declined to play second fiddle to anyone but Washington and made his refusal a test of strength. When Washington, still willing to play Hamilton's game, joined with the Cabinet in demanding that Hamilton be his second in command, Adams was forced to back down.

After this victory, the High Federalists pressed hard for a declaration of war against France. The harder they pressed, the more apparent it became that their aims were domestic rather than foreign. England's depredations against American shipping had continued unabated, while France, according to reports from Elbridge Gerry, had become far more conciliatory in response to the violent American reaction to the XYZ Affair. Gerry was denounced by the Federalists upon his return in 1798, but he was courted by the Republicans and heeded by the President. George Logan, an ex-Quaker from Philadelphia who had conducted an unauthorized peace mission of his own, confirmed Gerry's view of the shift in France's attitude. Adams objected to private citizens meddling in the country's foreign relations and got the Logan Act passed to prevent it in the future, but he was impressed by what Logan told him. Similar reports were arriving from the President's son, John Quincy Adams, also in Europe, and from Rufus King, the American minister in London, and from William Vans Murray at The Hague. In January the President received from Murray a letter sent by Talleyrand to the French chargé at The Hague, specifically stating that an American envoy to France would "undoubtedly be received with the respect due to the representative of a free, independent and powerful nation."

Adams did not assume that Talleyrand's character had improved, but he suspected that American firmness had worked a change in French policy. To declare war now would be to lose all the advantages of neutrality, to sacrifice the national interest to party politics. To make a gesture toward peace, on the other hand, would still leave the United States a free hand and would reduce party tensions at home. Such a reduction would not please the High Federalists, who had visions of a Republican rebellion that the new army commanded by old heroes would crush. That way, Adams believed, lay disaster for the Union, and he decided for once to be President. In February 1799, without consulting his Cabinet further, he sent to the Senate the nomination of William Vans Murray as minister to negotiate a new agreement with France.

Having done so, Adams went off to Quincy, leaving the High Federalists furious and frustrated and the Republicans delighted. With party tensions eased, Adams was not in any hurry to get his mission under way. He was by no means sure that it would succeed, and he wanted to have his new naval vessels ready in case it should fail. By October, three squadrons were fit for duty, and Adams gave orders for Murray's departure. Murray was accompanied now by Oliver Ellsworth (Chief Justice of the United States) and William R. Davie (former governor of North Carolina). When the three-man commission arrived in France, they found Bonaparte in control. He was eager to line up a coalition of neutral nations against England and ready to renew Franco-American relations on friendly terms. Although the American commissioners were unable to secure compensation for former French seizures, they did obtain a "convention" that recognized the principle of "free-ships-free-goods" and thereby put an end to French spoliation of American commerce. The President's declaration of independence from party pressures had thus saved his country from a needless war and gained it greater freedom on the seas.

**The Alien and Sedition laws.** In sending the mission to France, John Adams had risen above party, as he believed a President should. But he never fully admitted, even to himself, how much he had been and still remained a member of the Federalist party. After his initial *rapprochement* with Jefferson had faded, his very devotion to the national interest and to the dignity of his office betrayed him, as it had Washington, into regarding himself and his supporters as impartial patriots and the Republican opposition as a criminal conspiracy.

After the disclosure of the XYZ Affair, Adams had been deluged by addresses from groups of patriotic citizens declaring their readiness to fight the French. In his public replies he commended his correspondents and deplored the "few degraded or . . . deluded characters" who viewed the crisis differently. "These lovers of themselves," he announced, "who withdraw their confidence from their own Legislative Government, and place it on a foreign nation, or Domestic Faction, or both in alliance, deserve all our contempt and abhorrence." The references to Republicans were oblique but unmistakable. Even Hamilton thought the President might be pushing anti-Republican sentiment a little too far. But other Federalist leaders (without specific encouragement from either Adams or Hamilton) persuaded Congress to pass legislation designed to harass, if not destroy, the Republican opposition.

The Alien Acts, three in number, were passed in June and July 1798. One, the Alien Enemies Act, was a

*Lyon and Griswold:*
*"congressional pugilists"*

nonpartisan measure that simply provided for the restraint of enemy aliens in time of war. Since war was never declared against France, the act did not operate during Adams' Presidency. The other two were partisan measures aimed against immigrants, who were widely suspected of being Republican in politics. The Naturalization Act required that an alien seeking citizenship must have resided for fourteen years in the United States, five of them in the state where naturalization was sought. The Alien Friends Act, which was to run for two years only, gave the President power to deport any alien whom he considered dangerous to the welfare of the country.

The Sedition Act, which was passed in July 1798, was one of the most repressive measures ever directed against political activity in the United States. It provided fines and imprisonment for persons unlawfully combining or conspiring "with intent to oppose any measure or measures of the government of the United States," or counseling or advising such opposition, or writing, printing, uttering, or publishing "any false, scandalous, and malicious writing or writings against the government of the United States, or the President of the United States, with intent to defame . . . or to bring them or either of them, into contempt or disrepute." The blatant political purpose of the act was admitted in the date it was to expire: March 3, 1801, when the next President would be inaugurated. The act would last long enough to gag Republican criticism of the Administration until the next election was safely over; it would expire soon enough to permit Federalist criticism in case the election brought in a Republican administration.

The first victim of the Sedition Act was Matthew Lyon, Republican representative from Vermont. On the floor of the House, Lyon and the Connecticut Federalist Roger Griswold had already engaged each other

149

**Federalist rhetoric, 1800**

The fate of Frenchmen will be the fate of Americans. The French boasted that they were the most civilized and humane people in the world. We can say no more of ourselves. Their Jacobins were wicked, cruel, profligate, atheistical—ours are the same. Their pretence ever was, to consult the good of the people—ours make the same. The people in that country have been robbed, enslaved, and butchered—we shall be served in the same manner, unless we arouse instantly, and rescue our government from the fangs of those who are tearing it in pieces. The struggle will be great, but, if successful on our part, it will also be glorious. Look at your houses, your parents, your wives, and your children. Are you pre-pared to see your dwellings in flames, hoary hairs bathed in blood, female chastity violated, or children writhing on the pike and the halberd? If not, prepare for the task of protecting your Government. Look at every leading Jacobin as at a raven-ing wolf, preparing to enter your peaceful fold, and glut his deadly appetite on the vitals of your country. Already do their hearts leap at the prospect. Having long brooded over these scenes of death and despair, they now wake as from a Trance, and in imagination seizing the dagger and the musket, prepare for the work of slaughter. GREAT GOD OF COMPASSION AND JUSTICE, SHEILD MY COUNTRY FROM DESTRUCTION.

From *The Connecticut Courant*, September 29, 1800. Signed "Burleigh."

with canes, fire tongs, and spit. In the autumn follow-ing the passage of the Sedition Act, Lyon, who was up for reelection, directed his campaign against the Fed-eralist party's conduct of the government. Although his attacks were returned measure for measure by his opponent, Lyon was indicted, convicted, and sen-tenced (by a Federalist judge) to four months in jail and a $1,000 fine. He was reelected while serving his jail sentence.

The Republicans were alarmed—and rightly so. The Alien and Sedition Acts demonstrated that the Federalists were prepared to abandon the principles of the Enlightenment, of the Revolution, and of the Constitution. When Madison sponsored the first amendments to the Constitution, he had recognized that they might one day have to be defended against an ambitious executive or legislature. He had sug-gested that the federal courts might protect them, but thus far the courts had shown a disposition to restrain the states more than the national government. They had declared a few state laws unconstitutional, and in the case of *Chisholm* v. *Georgia* (1793) the Supreme Court had awarded judgment against the state of Georgia in a suit brought by citizens of South Caro-lina. This affront to state sovereignty caused so many protests that an eleventh amendment to the Constitu-tion was adopted to deny federal jurisdiction in suits brought against a state by foreigners or by citizens of another state.

The Eleventh Amendment, which was ratified in January 1798, was a direct blow at the federal courts, whose prestige was already at a low ebb. Men of high talents refused to serve on them. John Jay had re-signed as Chief Justice of the United States in 1795 in order to run for the governorship of New York. The judges who remained and who presided at sedition trials had no more scruples about the constitutionality of the Alien and Sedition Acts than John Adams had had when he signed them.

Since there seemed to be no other way of pro-tecting the Constitution from the Federalists, Madison and Jefferson turned to the state governments. With the election of Adams, Madison had retired tempo-rarily from Congress and returned to Virginia. In the Virginia legislature, he now secured passage (Decem-ber 24, 1798) of a series of resolutions affirming the authority of the states to judge the constitutionality of federal legislation and declaring the Alien and Sedi-tion Acts unconstitutional.

Madison's resolutions did not go beyond the statement of unconstitutionality. But Vice President Jefferson had framed another set, for the state of Kentucky (November 16, 1798), which declared the acts to be "void and of no force." When the other states declined to support Virginia and Kentucky, Kentucky reaffirmed in another set of resolutions (November 22, 1799) that "nullification" by the states was the proper remedy for unconstitutional actions by the federal government. But the other states still refused to follow suit and allowed the Alien and Sedition Acts to expire under their own terms. Though the resolutions of Kentucky and Virginia failed in their immediate object, they posed a ques-tion that would trouble the nation for many years to

It is not so well known, as it should be, that this federal gem [John Adams], this apostle of the parsons of Connecticut, is not only a repulsive pedant, a gross hypocrite, and an unprincipled oppressor, but that he is, in private life, one of the most egregious fools upon the continent. When some future Clarendon shall illustrate and dignify the annals of the present age, he will assuredly express his surprise at the abrupt and absurd elevation of this despicable attorney. He will enquire by what species of madness, America submitted to accept, as her president, a person without abilities, and without virtues; a being alike incapable of attracting either tenderness, or esteem. The historian will search for those occult causes that induced her to exalt an individual, who has neither that innocence of sensibility, which incites us to love, nor that omnipotence of intellect which commands us to admire. He will ask why the United States degraded themselves to the choice of a wretch, whose soul came blasted from the hand of nature; of a wretch, that has neither the science of a magistrate, the politeness of a courtier, nor the courage of a man.

From James T. Callender, *The Prospect before Us,* 1800.

**Republican rhetoric, 1800**

come. The Philadelphia convention had not decided which was sovereign, state governments or national government, and the resolutions were a reminder that the question was still open.

***The election of 1800.*** The steadily declining fortunes of the Republicans convinced them that in order to survive they would have to build a national organization. As a result of the XYZ Affair they had lost congressional seats in the elections of 1798; even Virginia, the Republican stronghold, had returned five "certain Federalists" and three moderates who leaned toward Federalism. With Jefferson directing party strategy, the Republicans resolved to do better in the next election. Following regional patterns of local government, they appointed county committees in the South and township committees in the North to instruct the voters about the vices of Federalists and the virtues of Republicans. The local committees were supervised by state committees, which in turn took their direction from a caucus of Republican congressmen in Philadelphia. By now there were Republican newspapers scattered throughout the country, the most prominent of which was Philadelphia's *Aurora.* The editors, defying the Sedition Act, charged the government with aristocratic and monarchical pretensions and with levying heavy taxes to support an expensive navy, a standing army, and a corrupt funding system.

The charges struck home, for they were substantially correct. Armies and navies are always expensive, and in 1798 the Adams Administration had levied an extremely unpopular direct tax on houses, lands, and slaves to pay the rising costs. What was worse, in 1799 the army had been ordered into action to enforce collection of the tax, after a mob led by one John Fries released two tax-evaders from prison in Northampton County, Pennsylvania. Although the army, as in the case of the Whiskey Rebellion, could find no one to fight, the use of it lent support to Republican accusations of tyranny.

Federalist newspapers replied by calling Republicans the tools of the godless French. Federalist attorneys and judges made full use of the Sedition Act to silence Republican editors, but the wheels of the law did not turn rapidly enough to make more than a few martyrs. The Federalists also caucused at Philadelphia and tried to organize support at the local level. But their efforts were hampered by their own divisions. The rank and file of the party approved John Adams' peace mission to France and would have been outraged by a proposal to support any other candidate for the Presidency. The High Federalists, however, considered Adams a traitor. Pickering thought that the mission to France would "subvert the present administration and with them the government itself." Hamilton declared he would never again support Adams and even wrote a pamphlet attacking him.

In spite of the defection in his own camp, Adams made a strong bid for reelection. By the spring of 1800 it had become probable that he would take New England and New Jersey,that Jefferson (the natural Republican candidate) would win most of the South, and that a deadlock would neutralize Pennsylvania. New York and South Carolina, both uncertain, held the balance. In New York the legislature chose the presidential electors, and the state was so divided that the thirteen representatives from New York City held the balance of power in the legislature. In 1800 Aaron Burr, perhaps the Republican's best working politician

## The election of 1800

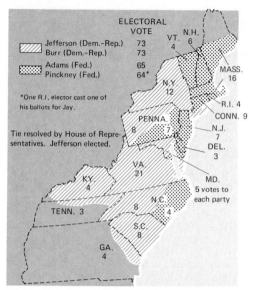

ELECTORAL VOTE

| | |
|---|---|
| Jefferson (Dem.-Rep.) | 73 |
| Burr (Dem.-Rep.) | 73 |
| Adams (Fed.) | 65 |
| Pinckney (Fed.) | 64* |

*One R.I. elector cast one of his ballots for Jay.

Tie resolved by House of Representatives. Jefferson elected.

N.H. 6
VT. 4
MASS. 16
N.Y. 12
R.I. 4
CONN. 9
PENNA. 8 7
N.J. 7
DEL. 3
VA. 21
KY. 4
MD. 5 votes to each party
N.C. 8 4
TENN. 3
S.C. 8
GA. 4

**Note:** For all election maps in this book, the electoral vote will be given within each state. When a state's electoral vote is split, as were the votes of Pennsylvania, Maryland, and North Carolina in this election, the split will be shown with the number of electoral votes going to each candidate. The graphic presentation in such cases is not intended to indicate the geographic distribution of votes within the state.

on the local level, was able to offer the city a slate of thirteen extremely influential and popular candidates for representative. They took the city by five hundred votes, thus assuring Republican control of the state legislature and of New York's electoral votes in the coming national contest.

New York City had hitherto been the private preserve of Alexander Hamilton, and the significance of his defeat was not lost on John Adams. The President knew that he had been right about the peace mission, regardless of party considerations; but he knew now that he was also right politically and that the High Federalists were wrong. After putting up with their insolence for three years, he had had enough. On May 6 he asked for and received McHenry's resignation from the War Department. On May 10 he asked for Pickering's; when Pickering refused, Adams simply discharged him.

While Adams was cutting loose from the High Federalists, the Republicans had decided that Aaron Burr would again make the best running mate for Jefferson. The Federalists' vice-presidential candidate was Charles Cotesworth Pinckney. Hamilton, who had been responsible for the choice, used the same strategy as in 1796: to throw support to a vice-presidential candidate in the hope that he would overtake both presidential candidates.

The outcome of the election was in doubt for some time, for electors were still chosen at different times and in different ways; but when the ballots

were finally counted, Adams had sixty-five electoral votes, and Pinckney sixty-four. The Republican machine, working a little too well, had given Jefferson and Burr each seventy-three. It had been understood that Burr was the vice-presidential candidate, but no Republican elector had diverted one of his two ballots to preclude a tie. To prevent this situation from recurring, the Twelfth Amendment to the Constitution, adopted in 1804, required the Electoral College to vote separately for President and for Vice President. But in February 1801, as directed by the Constitution, the choice between Jefferson and Burr was thrown into the House of Representatives, with each state allowed only one vote. Voting went on for a week through thirty-five ballots without the necessary nine-state majority being reached. Finally Hamilton, who considered Jefferson a lesser evil than Burr, persuaded some of the latter's supporters to cast blank ballots. Jefferson was declared elected.

Since Republican candidates for Congress were also victorious, the election of 1800 brought to an end Federalist control of the national government. Nevertheless, the Federalists could look forward to a continuing influence: the United States judiciary, manned by Federalist appointees, enjoyed a lifetime tenure. The last acts of the Adams Administration made the most of this fact. A new judiciary act of February 27, 1801, created sixteen circuit courts; and Adams, instead of leaving the appointment of the new circuit judges to his successor, filled the offices with loyal Federalists. Even more significantly, Adams in January 1801 appointed as Chief Justice of the United States John Marshall of Virginia, an ardent Federalist. Under Marshall the Court was to rise to new heights of prestige and power, to the considerable annoyance of Marshall's fellow Virginian in the White House.

Jefferson liked to think of his election as the "Revolution of 1800." But the election had been no landslide. John Adams had only eight votes fewer than the winners. If he had taken either New York or South Carolina, he would have won; and he might have taken them had he parted sooner from the High Federalists. Actually John Adams' capture of the Federalist party marked as great a political change as Jefferson's triumph at the polls, a change possibly more crucial to the preservation of national unity. Hamiltonian policies, tied to urban business interests at home and to Great Britain abroad, had repeatedly threatened to divide the nation. By sending the mission to France and by repudiating Hamilton, Adams reduced the gap between Federalist and Republican views of the national interest. His action came too late to win an electoral majority for himself or his party, but it did ensure peace, not only between the United States and France, but between two groups of Americans who had drifted dangerously far apart.

*Establishing national institutions*

**Suggestions for reading**

The period covered by this chapter is surveyed by J. C. Miller, *The Federalist Era*\* (1960). L. D. White, *The Federalists*\* (1948), assesses the achievements of the Washington and Adams Administrations in establishing the bureaucratic machinery of national government. The political foundations of Federalist power are analyzed in Manning Dauer, *The Adams Federalists*\* (1953). In *The Economic Origins of Jeffersonian Democracy*\* (1915), Charles Beard saw the rise of the Republican Party as a continuation of the small-farmer hostility to the Constitution, which he had described in his *Economic Interpretation of the Constitution of the United States*\* (1913). Joseph Charles, *The Origins of the American Party System*\* (1956), denies that there was any such continuity.

A. F. Young, *The Democratic Republicans of New York: The Origins, 1763–1797* (1967), finds some elements of continuity in that state. But Paul Goodman finds none in *The Democratic-Republicans of Massachusetts* (1964). In *The Partisan Spirit* (1972), Patricia Watlington discloses a complex relationship between state and national politics in Kentucky. Noble Cunningham, *The Jeffersonian Republicans*\* (1957), describes the political organizing activities of the Republicans and is particularly good on the election of 1800. A good general account of the first parties is W. N. Chambers, *Political Parties in a New Nation*\* (1963). Richard Hofstadter, *The Idea of a Party System*\* (1969), stresses the absence of such a system in the 1790s. Richard Buel, *Securing the Revolution: Ideology in American Politics, 1789–1815*\* (1972), emphasizes the role of public opinion.

Two aspects of political discontent during the 1790s are treated in E. P. Link, *Democratic-Republican Societies, 1790–1800* (1942), and L. D. Baldwin, *The Whiskey Rebels*\* (1939). R. A. Rutland, *The Birth of the Bill of Rights, 1776–1791*\* (1955), discusses the origins of the first ten amendments. Irving Brant, *The Bill of Rights*\* (1965), is more comprehensive and deals with the later interpretations of the amendments. L. W. Levy, *Legacy of Suppression*\* (1960), shows that the First Amendment offered less firm protection for freedom of speech and the press than has generally been supposed. J. M. Smith, *Freedom's Fetters*\* (1956), is the most complete account of the Alien and Sedition Acts. J. M. Banner, *To the Hartford Convention* (1970), emphasizes the Federalists' adherence to republican principles of government.

S. F. Bemis, *Jay's Treaty*\* (1923, rev. ed., 1962) and *Pinckney's Treaty*\* (1926, rev. ed., 1960), definitively treats two important episodes in foreign relations in the Federalist decade. Felix Gilbert, *To the Farewell Address*\* (1961), discusses the origins of attitudes classically expressed in Washington's warning against alliances. Alexander De Conde, *Entangling Alliance* (1958) and *The Quasi-War*\* (1966); L. M. Sears, *George Washington and the French Revolution* (1960); Charles Hazen, *Contemporary American Opinion of the French Revolution* (1897, reprinted 1964); L. S. Kaplan, *Jefferson and France* (1967); and A. H. Bowman, *The Struggle for Neutrality* (1974), discuss relations with France. In *Number 7* (1964), Julian Boyd gives evidence of Hamilton's efforts in the Nootka Sound crisis to turn American policy in favor of the British. Harry Ammon, *The Genet Mission*\* (1973), is a good account of that episode.

So many men of large stature shared in the making of public policy during the 1790s that much of the history of the period has been written in the form of biography. D. S. Freeman, *George Washington,* 7 vols. (1948–57), is the most complete account; Vol. VII was written after Freeman's death by J. A. Carroll and M. W. Ashworth. J. T. Flexner, *George Washington and the New Nation* (1970) and *George Washington: Anguish and Farewell* (1972), conclude a perceptive four-volume study. J. C. Miller, *Alexander Hamilton: Portrait in Paradox*\* (1959), is the best biography of Hamilton. Hamilton's great reports are conveniently gathered in J. E. Cooke, ed., *The Reports of Alexander Hamilton*\* (1964). Irving Brant, *James Madison: Father of the Constitution, 1787–1800* (1950), the third volume of a six-volume study of Madison, contains a wealth of information about the formation of the Republican party. Gilbert Chinard, *Honest John Adams*\* (1933), is good, but C. P. Smith, *John Adams* (1962), is more thorough. J. R. Howe, *The Changing Political Thought of John Adams*\* (1966), is a sensitive interpretation. Stephen Kurtz, *The Presidency of John Adams*\* (1957), is very good on the election of 1796; Zoltan Haraszti, *John Adams and the Prophets of Progress*\* (1952), is a charming account of Adams' notes in the margins of his books. Dumas Malone, *Jefferson and His Time,* 5 vols. (1948–74), is authoritative. A stimulating interpretation of Jefferson's thought is D. J. Boorstin, *The Lost World of Thomas Jefferson*\* (1948). Merrill Peterson, *Thomas Jefferson and the New Nation*\* (1970), is an excellent one-volume biography.

\*Available in a paperback edition.

# CHAPTER 7

# Jeffersonian Republicanism

*Victory banner, 1801*

The peaceful inauguration of Thomas Jefferson as President, on March 4, 1801, was an event of uncommon significance, for it marked the first occasion under the new Constitution when executive power passed quietly from one political party to another. Only a short time before, Federalist partisans had attacked "mad Tom" Jefferson as a "Jacobin" and an atheist, and many of them had regarded the Republican party as a treasonable organization against whose activities the Sedition Act was a justifiable defense. The Jeffersonians, in turn, had denounced the Federalists as a "faction" with "aristocratical tendencies," ready even to conspire "with the enemies of their country."

Moreover, as we have seen, few Republican or Federalist leaders viewed political parties as legitimate organizations essential to a republican electoral process. In the view of most, parties were intrinsically evil and corrupt; they promoted selfish interests, appealed to the passions of men, and prevented public leaders from deliberating rationally in search of the common good. Republicans had suspected that Federalists planned to subvert the Constitution and establish a monarchy. An organization with such designs could never be legitimate; and Jefferson, neither before nor after his election, ever really acknowledged Federalist legitimacy. He viewed his own party as a temporary expedient aimed at uniting the people against a threat to republican institutions. The Federalists, on their side, had questioned Republican legitimacy by accusing the Jeffersonian "faction" of seeking to usurp functions that belonged to the government itself.

Yet, in spite of deep anxieties, Federalists accepted their loss of control of both Congress and the executive department. Actually, the election gave them little choice, unless they were prepared to set it aside and rule by military force; and for this, fortunately, they had no taste. Since the Federalists still controlled the New England states, which formed a powerful base for future political activity, and since they believed that the Republicans were incompetent, they could comfort themselves with hopes of an early return to power. Besides, Jefferson may have reassured certain Federalist leaders privately on various matters—especially that no Jacobin reign of terror would follow the "Revolution of 1800." Hamilton found solace in his view of Jefferson as a man inclined "to temporize; to calculate what will be likely to promote his own reputation and advantage." This trait, he thought, would cause Jefferson to accept financial policies "which being once established, could not be overturned without danger to the person who did it." Hence the heated rhetoric of the campaign had no violent aftermath; and the two-party system, whatever theoretical objections to it Americans may have had, won a more secure footing and a kind of practical legitimacy that it had never enjoyed before.

After a decade of protest against Federalist policies, Jefferson was now obliged to spell out policies of his own. This, in broad outline, he did in a brilliant inaugural address (the first to be delivered in the new capital on the banks of the Potomac) that affirmed his liberal democratic philosophy and his faith in the wisdom of the people. Once again he soothed the Federalists by inviting them to join Republicans "in common efforts for the common good." He cautioned Republicans that though the will of the majority must prevail, "the minority possess their equal rights, which equal law must protect." He reminded members of both parties that in spite of the acrimonious campaign just past

> every difference of opinion is not a difference of principle. We have called by different names brethren of the same principle. We are all Republicans, we are all Federalists. If there be any among us who would wish to dissolve this Union or to change its Republican form, let them stand undisturbed as monuments of the safety with which error of opinion may be tolerated where reason is left free to combat it.

These conciliatory words reveal Jefferson's basic strategy in dealing with the Federalists. Though still opposed to parties and convinced that good citizens would spurn them, his method was not harsh repression but gentle absorption. He would destroy the party system by winning the support of all reasonable Federalists ("the honest part"), leaving the irreconcilables not a party but a small and harmless faction. "Nothing shall be spared on my part," he wrote pri-

**Thomas Jefferson on the American political experiment**

*I know, indeed, that some honest men fear that a Republican government can not be strong, that this Government is not strong enough; but would the honest patriot, in the full tide of successful experiment, abandon a government which has so far kept us free and firm on the theoretic and visionary fear that this Government, the world's best hope, may by possibility want energy to preserve itself? I trust not. I believe this, on the contrary, the strongest Government on earth. I believe it the only one where every man, at the call of the law, would fly to the standard of the law, and would meet invasions of the public order as his own personal concern. Sometimes it is said that man can not be trusted with the government of himself. Can he, then, be trusted with the government of others? Or have we found angels in the forms of kings to govern him? Let history answer this question.*

**From Thomas Jefferson, First Inaugural Address, 1801.**

vately, "to obliterate the traces of party and consolidate the nation, if it can be done without the abandonment of principle." It is ironic that a party leader as skilled as Jefferson never understood how indispensable and inevitable the party system was and that he failed to esteem the role he played so well.

## Economy and simplicity

**The new regime.** The rustic simplicity and democratic manners that Jefferson thought proper for the leaders of an agrarian republic seemed appropriate in the crude, half-built capital city. Though the President was a learned and cultivated gentleman to the manner born, his informality was uncontrived. Unlike his predecessors, he sent his annual messages to Congress to be read by a clerk, lest reading them in person should suggest that he was imitating the British monarch speaking from the throne. Jefferson abandoned the elegant weekly presidential levees that had so delighted the capital's aristocracy. At his infrequent state dinners and receptions and in his dealings with the diplomatic corps he avoided anything that smacked of the pomp and pretentiousness of European courts. In the White House he lived simply and made himself accessible to citizens who claimed to have business with him.

Although Jefferson believed in the sovereignty of the people and tended to romanticize the independent farmer, he did not assume that untrained men could handle the responsibilities of important administrative posts. He rejected the notion that society should be governed by a political élite based on wealth or birth, believing instead that it should be governed by the "natural aristocracy" of virtue and

talent. The men in the key posts of his Administration were able, educated, and experienced upper-class Republicans of as high a caliber as their Federalist predecessors. James Madison, Jefferson's close friend and political collaborator, a Virginia aristocrat who had led the fight against the Federalists, joined the new Administration as Secretary of State. Albert Gallatin of Pennsylvania, a gifted and devoted Jeffersonian, accepted the crucial office of Secretary of the Treasury and served with such distinction that he won the respect of even the Federalists.

In spite of his doubts about the value of political parties, Jefferson, far more than his predecessors, played the dual role of President and party-leader. As party-leader he was concerned about the weakness of the Republicans in the Northern states, where Federalists had identified them with the interests of the South. In order to strengthen his party in the bastion of Federalism, Jefferson appointed three New Englanders to major offices: Levi Lincoln of Massachusetts as Attorney General, Henry Dearborn of Massachusetts as Secretary of War, and Gideon Granger of Connecticut as Postmaster General. He also made skillful use of the patronage. Though permitting many Federalists to remain in non-policy-making offices, he was determined that Republicans should have their fair share—two-thirds or three-fourths, he once suggested. Jefferson removed Federalists whom Adams had appointed after the election of the preceding year, those who were guilty of "malversation" (misconduct in public office), and those who had shown "open, active and virulent" partisanship. As a wise politician he showed some restraint, but party advantage—his desire to destroy the Federalists—clearly governed his policy; nearly all his appointees were Republicans.

**Republican policies.** Jefferson repudiated most of Hamilton's mercantilist theories in favor of a general

*I agree with you that there is a natural aristocracy among men. The grounds of this are virtue and talents.... There is also an artificial aristocracy founded on wealth and birth, without either virtue or talents; for with these it would belong to the first class. The natural aristocracy I consider as the most precious gift of nature for the instruction, the trusts, and government of society. And indeed it would have been inconsistent in creation to have formed man for the social state, and not to have provided virtue and wisdom enough to manage the concerns of the society. May we not even say that that form of government is the best which provides the most effectually for a pure selection of these natural aristoi into the offices of government? The artificial aristocracy is a mischievous ingredient in government, and provision should be made to prevent its ascendancy....*

*I think the best remedy is ... to leave to the citizens the free election and separation of the aristoi from the pseudo-aristoi, of the wheat from the chaff. In general they will elect the real good and wise. In some instances, wealth may corrupt, and birth blind them; but not in sufficient degree to endanger the society.*

**From Thomas Jefferson, Letter to John Adams, October 28, 1813.**

policy of laissez faire. The success of his Administration, therefore, cannot be measured in terms of positive legislation or innovative action. His ideal was "a wise and frugal Government, which shall restrain men from injuring one another . . . [and] leave them otherwise free to regulate their own pursuits of industry and improvement." The principal responsibilities of such a government, Jefferson explained, would be to honor the Bill of Rights, seek equal justice for all men, respect the rights of the states ("the surest bulwarks against antirepublican tendencies"), and practice strict economy, "that labor may be lightly burthened."

But the Jefferson Administration soon discovered—as would future administrations when power passed from one party to another—that it could reverse the actions and repudiate the commitments of its predecessor only at the risk of serious confusion. "Some things," wrote the essentially cautious Jefferson, "may perhaps be left undone from motives of compromise for a time, and not to alarm by too sudden a reformation." He and his fellow Republicans, therefore, thought it best not to tamper with some of Hamilton's economic measures. The Bank of the United States, for example, continued its operations undisturbed until 1811, when its charter expired. By then many Republicans, including Madison and Gallatin, favored granting the Bank a new charter, a proposal that failed in each house of Congress by a single vote. Nor did the Republicans reverse Federalist measures for refunding the national debt, or for federal assumption of the Revolutionary debts of the states, or for encouraging American shipping. "What is practicable," Jefferson confessed, "must often control what is pure theory."

Indeed, in his quest for national unity Jefferson even sought to win the political support of at least a portion of the banking, commercial, and manufacturing interests, and in this he had much success. In Providence, Rhode Island, he saw to it that federal funds were transferred from a Federalist-controlled to a Republican-controlled state bank. "I am decidedly in favor of making all the banks Republican," he wrote, "by sharing deposits among them in proportion to the disposition they show." To justify this sort of fiscal politics, he explained that it was important "to detach the mercantile interest" from the enemies of republicanism "and incorporate them into the body of its friends."

Without changing his opinion about the primacy of agriculture, Jefferson as President developed a greater respect for other economic pursuits. In his first message to Congress he referred to manufacturing, commerce, and navigation, along with agriculture, as "the four pillars of our prosperity"; and he even suggested, though somewhat vaguely, that "within the limits of our constitutional powers" measures to protect them from "casual embarrassments" might be "seasonably interposed."

The "Revolution of 1800" did not, however, lack substance, for the Republicans lost no time in disposing of some of the Federalists' pet measures. They refused, of course, to renew the Alien Act when it expired in 1801. They reduced the residence requirement for naturalization from fourteen years to five; once again, Jefferson hoped, America would become an "asylum" for "oppressed humanity." The Sedition Act also expired in 1801, and Jefferson saw to it that those who had been imprisoned for violating it were freed and that all fines were refunded. The Republi-

The Old Plantation, ca. 1800:
they were still slaves

can Congress repealed the Judiciary Act of 1801 and abolished, as a needless extravagance, the sixteen new circuit judgeships that act had created. Thus, defeated ("lame duck") Federalists to whom Adams had given "midnight appointments" in the judicial branch lost their jobs; and the courts, as one Republican explained, ceased to be a "hospital for decayed politicians." The House of Representatives then turned on the Supreme Court and, in 1804, impeached Associate Justice Samuel Chase, an arch-Federalist who had used the bench as a political stump. But the Senate did not interpret Chase's offense as a misdemeanor within the meaning of the Constitution and refused to convict him. Henceforth, the Republicans relied on new appointments in their effort to reduce Federalist influence in the courts.

The Jeffersonian revolution also wrought a significant change in fiscal policy. According to the new President, government tends "to multiply offices . . . and to increase expense"—to leave to labor only a small portion of its earnings and to "consume the whole residue of what [government] was instituted to guard." Unlike Hamilton, Jefferson believed that a public debt and the accompanying interest charges benefited only a small class of investors while acting as a "mortal canker" on the rest of the community. With the able support of Secretary of the Treasury Gallatin, he strove to retire the whole public debt, which had grown to $83 million, at the earliest possible date—in sixteen years, according to the original plan. Since the excise tax had been repealed, the only way to retire the debt was through revenues from import duties and the sale of public lands and through the most rigid government economy. To cut costs in the executive department Jefferson reduced the number of officers in the diplomatic corps and revenue service. He urged Congress to abolish other public

offices, to replace wasteful general appropriations with grants of "specific sums to every specific purpose," and to hold the Treasury Department responsible for all funds spent.

Jefferson was convinced, too, that military and naval expenditures could be cut without jeopardizing national defense. America, he said, was fortunately "separated by nature and a wide ocean from the exterminating havoc" of the Old World and consequently needed no large standing army. For defense against invasion, the country should rely on "the body of neighboring citizens as formed into a militia." Accordingly, the regular army was reduced from four thousand to twenty-five hundred officers and men. Jefferson realized, however, that the state militia systems needed to be improved, and in 1808 the federal government began to take a hand in reorganizing them and in defraying part of the cost of arms and equipment. Moreover, in 1802 Jefferson was instrumental in establishing the U.S. Military Academy at West Point.

Turning to the navy, the new Administration proceeded to sell some ocean-going vessels, lay up others, and halt construction on still others; it discharged many Navy Department employees, reduced the number of officers and enlisted men, and abandoned the improvement of navy yards and dry docks. Shore defense was to be maintained by coastal fortifications and by a fleet of small, inexpensive gunboats serving as a kind of naval militia. This policy was designed, Jefferson explained, "merely for defensive operations," not to protect commerce or to establish the United States as a sea power. The quarreling European states would thus be kept "at a distance" and at little cost.

Here, in short, was Jefferson's formula for an agrarian utopia: simplicity, frugality, and "a government founded not on the fears and follies of man, but on his reason"—a government whose authority the ordinary citizen would scarcely feel. For a time all worked according to plan, and in his second annual message Jefferson congratulated Congress for the "pleasing circumstances . . . under which we meet." The United States had become a nation of peaceful, prosperous citizens "managing their own affairs in their own way and for their own use, unembarrassed by too much regulation, unoppressed by fiscal exactions."

Jefferson's cheerful view of the state of the Union was valid enough for most white Americans, but not for those Americans (approximately 19 percent of the population) who were Negroes or of mixed white and Negro ancestry. In 1800 nearly 90 percent of those people (894,000) were still slaves, and the rest were everywhere more or less the victims of a deep and pervasive racial prejudice. Though the federal government had no constitutional power to interfere with slavery in the states, slavery had already provoked several sharp congressional debates during the decade of Federalist ascendancy. In earlier years Jefferson, though himself a large slaveholder, had professed, usually privately, antislavery sentiments; but during the eight years of his Presidency, like every other chief executive before the Civil War, he carefully avoided the subject. The "Revolution of 1800" brought no change in the condition of black Americans, and Jefferson seems always to have assessed the state of the Union without giving them a thought.

However, in his annual message of December 2, 1806, Jefferson did remind Congress that the time was approaching when it could constitutionally stop citizens of the United States from participating in the African slave trade—a trade that every state except South Carolina had already made illegal. Congress responded with a law prohibiting the trade after January 1, 1808, and punishing violators with fines and imprisonment. But it was a poor law with no machinery for enforcement, and many thousands of African slaves were imported after it was passed. In 1820 Congress passed another law defining participation in the African slave trade as piracy; but, significantly, not until 1862 was anyone convicted under its terms.

# Ferment in the West

**The westward movement.** In his vision of America as the ideal republic, Jefferson projected upon the nation at large an image of the stable, mellow society of Virginia's rural gentry. However, this image did not fit much of the rest of the country—not even the trans-Appalachian West in whose future Jefferson placed such confident hopes. In 1800 nearly a million settlers were living in the vast area between the Appalachians and the Mississippi River. A new land act that year encouraged others to come by offering land for sale in individual tracts of 320 acres and by permitting four-year credits with a down payment of 25 percent. A revision of this law in 1804 reduced the minimum tract to 160 acres; thus, with public land selling at a minimum price of $2 an acre, a buyer could obtain a farm for an initial payment of $80. This generous federal policy brought a steady tide of immigrants into the West, whose rich lands Jefferson thought would afford "room enough for our descendants to the thousandth and thousandth generation." As the forests were cleared and farms and villages began to dot the land, new states were created from time to time—Kentucky in 1792, Tennessee in 1796, and Ohio in 1803.

Most Westerners liked Jefferson's politics and found much in his philosophy that pleased them, but they had mixed feelings about his economics and scarcely understood his agrarian dream—in fact, they did much to destroy it. Jefferson's ideal of a stable, self-sufficient yeomanry free of the corrupting influences of commercialism was hardly the ideal of the traders and speculators who infested the West—or, for that matter, of many of the farmers. Soon after they arrived, most Westerners began to dream not of self-sufficiency but of cash crops, of outlets to markets, and of the comforts and luxuries of the East.

**The problem of transportation.** Between the Western settlers and their ambitions stood two major obstacles: the mountains, which cut them off from the East, and the French, who were preparing to take over from Spain possession of New Orleans and the mouth of the Mississippi. Before Jefferson left office, he was to find solutions to both these problems—solutions that in the long run helped to undermine his original goal of a simple agrarian society. In 1806 Congress authorized the building of a road from Cumberland, Maryland, across the mountains to Wheeling, Virginia, as a government-financed "internal improvement." Jefferson approved the measure, even though, without the constitutional amendment he had urged, it required a stretching of federal power to do so. Construction on the National Road, as it was called, began in 1811 and was completed in 1818. In subsequent years the road was extended westward to Vandalia, Illinois.

The second problem—navigation of the Mississippi River—forced Jefferson to take vigorous action

Population 1800

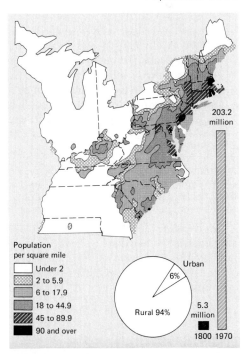

Population per square mile

☐ Under 2
▦ 2 to 5.9
▨ 6 to 17.9
▩ 18 to 44.9
▧ 45 to 89.9
■ 90 and over

203.2 million

Urban 6%

Rural 94%

5.3 million

1800  1970

that compromised not only his constitutional scruples but his fiscal policy, his foreign policy, and perhaps even his principles of public ethics. Since 1763 the mouth of the Mississippi and the immense territory of Louisiana, stretching westward to the Rockies, had been held by a declining and enfeebled Spain; and Spain, in Pinckney's Treaty of 1795, had opened the Mississippi to American navigation and granted Western flatboatmen the right to deposit their cargoes at New Orleans for shipment abroad. This arrangement satisfied the Westerners, who saw in Spain no serious threat. But they were bound to react violently if Louisiana were to fall into the hands of a stronger power or if their river outlet were cut off. As Madison explained: "The Mississippi is to them every thing. It is the Hudson, the Delaware, the Potomac, and all the navigable rivers of the Atlantic states, formed into one stream."

***The Louisiana Purchase.*** Soon after Jefferson became President two events shocked and angered the Western settlers. The first was the revelation that Bonaparte, in the secret Treaty of San Ildefonso (1800), had negotiated the transfer of Louisiana from Spain to France (though formal possession by France was long delayed). The second was a proclamation by the Spanish intendant at New Orleans, on October 16, 1802, that the right of deposit was to be suspended. Taking this as a foretaste of Bonaparte's future policy, indignant Westerners looked to Jefferson for support.

Alarmed, Jefferson feared for a time that Bonaparte might force him to reconsider his basic foreign policy, perhaps even to abandon temporarily his opposition to "entangling alliances." The United States, he told Robert R. Livingston, the American minister in Paris, has always looked upon France as her "natural friend"; but there was

> on the globe one single spot, the possessor of which is our natural and habitual enemy. It is New Orleans, through which the produce of three-eighths of our territory must pass to market. . . . France placing herself in that door, assumes to us the attitude of defiance. The day that France takes possession of New Orleans . . . [we will be forced to] marry ourselves to the British fleet and nation.

To Congress he spoke of "the danger to which our peace would be perpetually exposed whilst so important a key to the commerce of the Western country remained under foreign power."

But before considering more vigorous action, Jefferson tried to negotiate peacefully with France. He instructed Livingston to offer to purchase New Orleans and West Florida; he obtained from Congress an appropriation of $2 million for vaguely defined ex-

penses; and he sent James Monroe, who had the confidence of Westerners, as a special envoy to assist Livingston. Monroe arrived in Paris on April 12, 1803, two days after Talleyrand, negotiating for France, had startled Livingston by asking whether the United States would like to buy the whole of Louisiana! The two American diplomats, whose instructions were essentially to buy a city, hesitated, though only momentarily, before agreeing to buy an empire that would double the size of their country.

There were several reasons for Bonaparte's sudden decision to abandon his imperial ambitions in America and to concentrate on Europe. First, he had suffered a major disaster when his troops failed to crush a slave insurrection, led by Toussaint L'Ouverture, in the French colony of San Domingo. Second, the Peace of Amiens of 1802 had really settled nothing, and a renewal of war between France and Great Britain seemed all but inevitable. Third, Bonaparte needed money, and it was obviously wise to sell a province that the British navy could prevent France from occupying in any case. Finally, selling Louisiana to the United States would remove a source of friction and avoid an Anglo-American *rapprochement.* Accordingly, on April 11 Bonaparte told one of his ministers: "I renounce Louisiana. It is not only New Orleans that I will cede, it is the whole colony without any reservation."

Livingston and Monroe soon decided that this was a poor time to quibble over the letter of their instructions. On April 30, 1803, after some higgling over price, they made the purchase for $15 million and a promise (written into the purchase treaty) to give citizenship and religious freedom to the Catholics residing in Louisiana. The boundaries of Louisiana were then only vaguely defined, and the treaty merely stated that they were to be the same as they had been when Spain possessed it. "You have made a noble bargain for yourselves," said the realistic Talleyrand, "and I suppose you will make the most of it." In later years the United States did precisely that.

Westerners were delighted with the terms of the treaty, and their devotion to Jefferson and confidence in the federal government grew correspondingly stronger. But New England Federalists, viewing the West as enemy territory, criticized Jefferson severely for accepting a treaty that was tainted with duplicity. In making the sale, they pointed out, Bonaparte had violated the French constitution and a promise to Spain not to cede Louisiana to another power. Yet Jefferson approved the transaction knowing this to be the case—knowing, too, that the Constitution did not explicitly authorize the acquisition of new territory. Federalists also complained that the purchase of these worthless lands was a wasteful expenditure and meant a staggering addition to the public debt.

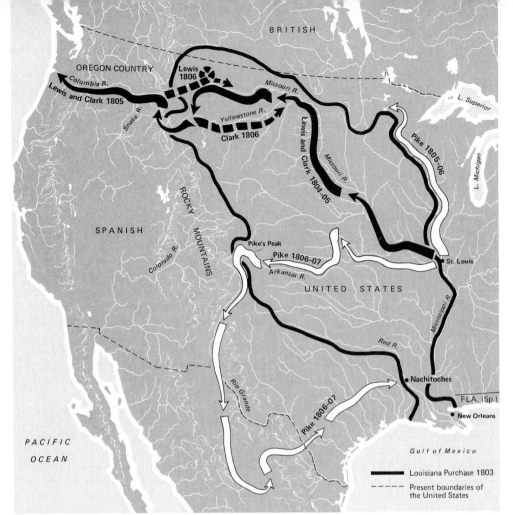

The Louisiana Purchase
and explorations
of the Far West

Jefferson was sensitive to such criticism, especially to the charge that he was exceeding the limits of the Constitution strictly construed. His first impulse was to urge an amendment to the Constitution expressly granting the power to acquire territory; but the amending process was painfully slow, and Livingston warned that Bonaparte might have a change of heart. Moreover, some Republicans argued that the power to acquire territory might be *implied* from the power to make treaties. Such an argument could hardly have satisfied Jefferson, but he concluded that Congress would be wise to cast aside "metaphysical subtleties." Trusting that "the good sense of our country will correct the evil of [constitutional] construction when it shall produce evil effects," Jefferson submitted the treaty to the Senate.

During the debate Federalists and Republicans reversed their former positions on questions of constitutional interpretation—a few extreme Federalists even spoke of dissolving the Union. But the treaty was ratified by a vote of twenty-four to seven, and the House appropriated the money required to fulfill its terms. Thus the United States acquired the whole of

the Mississippi River and its tributaries, some 828,000 square miles of territory, millions of acres of rich farmland, and a vast store of natural resources. Moreover, the purchase of Louisiana removed a major source of American concern about the internal politics of Europe; and, in the long run, it produced a basic shift in the national balance of political power. After the treaty was ratified, Jefferson seemed to forget quickly his anxieties about it—except to regret that Spanish West Florida had not been part of the bargain. Though for the present neither threats nor money—he tried both—could pry the Floridas loose from Spain, Jefferson was confident that it was America's destiny to obtain them, too, "and all in good time."

**Western exploration.** On December 20, 1803, just a few weeks after France had taken formal possession of Louisiana from Spain, the French prefect at New Orleans turned the lower part of the territory over to the United States. The transfer of the upper part was delayed until the spring of 1804, when, at St. Louis, Meriwether Lewis, Jefferson's private secretary, ac-

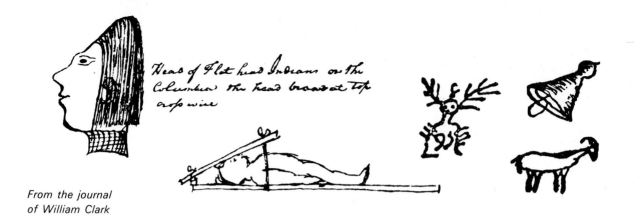

From the journal
of William Clark

cepted it in behalf of the United States. But Lewis was not there for that specific purpose; in fact, his presence was the result of presidential plans that antedated the Louisiana Purchase.

In January 1803 Congress had secretly appropriated money for an expedition to explore the upper reaches of the Missouri River and from there westward to the Pacific—though none of this territory at the time belonged to the United States. The expedition, which Jefferson had been trying to promote for many years, had several purposes. The President assured the Spanish minister that it would "have no other view than the advancement of geography"; and, to be sure, his scientific curiosity about the great unexplored interior was genuine. Lewis and his fellow explorer, William Clark (a brother of George Rogers Clark), were instructed to make astronomical observations, to study the flora and fauna, and to compile the fullest possible records. But they were to be alert to more practical matters, too, especially trading opportunities and mineral deposits. Moreover, Jefferson was fully aware that explorations had diplomatic value when nations laid claim to unsettled lands.

The Lewis and Clark expedition, which took more than two years to complete, was a remarkable success. The party of forty-five men ascended the Missouri River to the Great Falls, crossed the Rockies, and descended the Snake and Columbia rivers to the Pacific. The explorers brought back with them an enormously expanded factual knowledge of Western North America (first made available to the public when their journals were published in 1814), a large botanical collection, information of value to American fur-traders, and a strengthened foundation for an American claim to the Oregon country. This was only one of several Western explorations that Jefferson promoted. Two others were led by Zebulon Pike: one in 1805 up the Mississippi River in search of its source, and a second in 1806 up the Arkansas River to the Rockies in what is now Colorado. All of them combined the scientific and practical interests that Jefferson himself personified.

## Political complications

Even though Jefferson accommodated his political and economic principles to some of the realities of American life, and though he converted many rank-and-file Federalists to Republicanism, he never managed to appease his more ardent opponents or to bring party politics to an end. Groups of disgruntled old Federalists, such as the Essex Junto around Boston, deplored the growth of democratic "licentiousness" and the decline of public virtue. The new Administration, said Hamilton, seems "to imagine that to govern well, is to amuse the wondering multitude with sagacious aphorisms and oracular sayings." Senator Timothy Pickering of Massachusetts described Jefferson as a "cowardly wretch," a "Parisian revolutionary monster," who debased the public morals by his "corrupt and corrupting system. . . . Men are tempted to become apostates, not to Federalism merely, but to virtue and to religion, and to good government." Seeing the Republicans growing stronger even in New England, Pickering and a handful of Northern Federalists in Congress privately urged that the Union be dissolved before it was too late; but their radical schemes won little support.

Not this old guard, however, but a younger generation of Federalists, more flexible and less embittered, kept the party alive and a significant force in national politics. Aware of the failures that had caused their defeat, they worked to build party organizations, to imitate Republican electioneering techniques, to alter their pro-British, antidemocratic image, and to find popular issues that would broaden their appeal. "We must court popular favor," advised Fisher Ames of Massachusetts. "We must study popular opinion and accommodate measures to what it is." The young Federalists never won a national election, for the intransigence of the old guard and the élitist image that the Jeffersonians had fixed on them were more than they could overcome. Yet they made an important contribution to the development of two-party politics, were partly responsible for a dramatic increase in voting, and helped to reconcile to the politics of a new age men who had once scorned popular electioneering.

In addition to the Federalist threat, Jefferson was troubled with factionalism in his own party. Personal rivalries and patronage disputes in New York and Pennsylvania produced for a time local third-party movements, some of whose leaders assumed the label of "Tertium Quids." More distressing to Jefferson was the criticism he received from the uncompromising state righters of Virginia, who felt that he had moved too far toward Federalism. His good friend, John Taylor, observed with dismay that "Federalism . . . has gained a new footing, by being taken into partnership with republicanism." Jefferson's most persistent Virginia critic was the brilliant but erratic Congressman John Randolph of Roanoke, who would tolerate not the slightest deviation from the principles of the Kentucky Resolutions of 1798 (see p. 150). "Asking one of the states to surrender part of her sovereignty," he said, "is like asking a lady to surrender part of her chastity."

Randolph grumbled about several Administration-sponsored measures, even more about Jefferson's repeated and highly successful efforts to intervene in the affairs of Congress. He bitterly opposed a proposal to use federal funds to settle the claims of certain land-speculators organized into the so-called Yazoo Land Companies. These speculators had corruptly obtained a large grant from the Georgia legislature before the state, in 1802, ceded its Western lands to the federal government. Jefferson's desire to facilitate the transfer by compensating the Yazoo claimants, even though many of them were Northern speculators and their claims were tainted with fraud, drove Randolph and a small faction of Republicans into open rebellion. Randolph completed his break with Jefferson in 1806, when he announced his willingness to support *"quidism,"* that is, a third-party movement. He and his Virginia friends blocked the settlement of the Yazoo claims for many years and tormented Jefferson with accusations of apostasy. However, neither the Quid movements in New York and Pennsylvania nor the Randolph defection in Virginia ever reached the proportions of a national third party; eventually Randolph himself simply lost his influence in Congress.

Meanwhile, Vice President Aaron Burr, whom Jefferson had deprived of patronage and excluded from party councils after the disputed election of 1800 (see p. 152), seemed ready for almost any reckless maneuver that might improve his political fortunes. By 1804 he was willing to accept support from Federalists and dissident Republicans in a campaign for the governorship of New York. A handful of Federalists who had been toying with a scheme to unite New York and New England in an independent Northern Confederacy now hoped to enlist the services of Burr. But Hamilton exposed and denounced the plot and played a major role in Burr's defeat. The enraged Burr then challenged his old New York rival to a duel, in which Hamilton, on July 11, 1804, was mortally wounded. In the presidential election of that year, Jefferson replaced Burr with George Clinton of New York as his running mate; together they crushed the discredited Federalists. Charles Cotesworth Pinckney, the Federalist candidate, carried only Connecticut and Delaware.

The talented Burr had wrecked a promising political career by overreaching himself; having been indicted for murder in both New York and New Jersey, he now courted final disaster by entering into a quixotic intrigue whose exact nature was obscured in a maze of conflicting reports. The British minister had heard that for a half-million dollars Burr would separate the Western part of the United States from the East; the Spanish minister had heard that Burr planned to establish a buffer state between Louisiana and Mexico; others had heard that he planned to conquer Mexico and establish an empire. Whatever his scheme was, Burr won the support of two confederates: General James Wilkinson, who commanded the American troops in Louisiana and had as great a taste for conspiracy as Burr; and Harman Blennerhassett, a wealthy Irish exile who lived on an island in the upper Ohio River. In the summer of 1806 Burr and some sixty men on thirteen flatboats departed from Blennerhassett's Island and floated down the Ohio and Mississippi for some unknown purpose to some nameless glory.

The enterprise collapsed when General Wilkinson shifted sides and sent Jefferson a report that Burr was plotting treason. On Jefferson's orders the fleeing Burr was caught and taken to Richmond, where, in 1807, he was indicted for treason and conspiracy. In the curious trial that followed, Jefferson seemed determined to get a conviction whether or not the evidence warranted it; and the presiding judge, John Marshall, a Federalist, seemed as interested in discrediting Jefferson as in giving Burr justice. In the end Burr was acquitted, for the case against him did not fulfill the terms of the Constitution's definition of treason. According to the Constitution, treason consists in "levying war" against the United States or in "adhering to their enemies, giving them aid and comfort." A conviction for treason requires "the testimony of two witnesses to the same overt act." In his charge to the jury, Marshall insisted that the witnesses must have directly implicated Burr in a specific "overt act" of treason, not merely in planning treason or just loosely in organizing "a military assemblage." Since

*The attack on Tripoli*

the witnesses had failed to fulfill this constitutional requirement, Marshall's charge prepared the way for Burr's acquittal. It also set an important precedent that made convictions for treason extremely difficult and indictments rare.

## Trouble on the high seas

**War and American trade.** When Jefferson became President in 1801, he was determined that the United States pursue its destiny free from "entangling alliances" and from the wars and diplomatic duplicity of the Old World. Yet he found himself entangled in world affairs throughout most of his second Administration, and he left office with the country fast approaching total involvement. The abrogation of the French alliance in 1800, it appeared, did not mean that America had closed the door on Europe. Since the United States exported foodstuffs and raw materials, imported foreign manufactured goods, and sent merchant ships to distant ports, it was bound to be affected by the course of international politics and by the state of the world economy.

Even during Jefferson's first Administration pirates, operating from bases on the Barbary coast of North Africa, had provoked the pacifistic President into surprisingly vigorous action. For many years these corsairs had been harrying American vessels and forcing the federal government, like the governments of Europe, to buy immunity by paying tribute to the rulers of Morocco, Algiers, Tunis, and Tripoli. Jefferson found this costly and humiliating practice intolerable, and in 1801 he dispatched a naval squadron to

the Mediterranean. For several years the United States was engaged in virtual war with Tripoli, until the Pasha, in 1805, was obliged to make a satisfactory peace. However, tribute payments to other Barbary states did not cease altogether until 1816.

The Tripolitan War, though a minor affair, had forced Jefferson to modify his naval policy. But the resumption of hostilities between Great Britain and France in 1803—a conflict that raged without interruption for the next eleven years—provided a far more strenuous test of the President's pacifism. In a larger sense, it was a test of how much the American people were ready to endure and sacrifice to remain at peace, for peace has its price as well as war. As Jefferson warned Congress, with "the flames of war lighted up again in Europe . . . the nations pursuing peace will not be exempt from all evil." To him the price was not too great, and he thanked "that kind Providence which . . . guarded us from hastily entering into the sanguinary contest and left us only to look on and to pity its ravages." America's sole interest and desire, he said, would be "to cultivate the friendship of the belligerent nations by every act of justice and of innocent kindness." Of them he would ask only respect for the rights to which American vessels and citizens were entitled as neutrals under international law. Since American friendship and trade were useful to them, Jefferson was certain that "it can not be the interest of any to assail us, nor ours to disturb them."

While Jefferson professed confidence in his country's capacity to bring "collisions of interest to the umpirage of reason rather than force," the European belligerents were locked in a conflict whose stakes seemed to justify any means that promised ultimate victory. In 1805 Napoleon's smashing victory over the armies of Austria and Russia at Austerlitz made him for the time master of much of the European continent, while Lord Nelson's decisive defeat of the French and Spanish fleets at the Battle of Trafalgar gave Britain control of the high seas. Thereafter, in a savage war of attrition, neither antagonist showed much concern for the rights of neutrals or the punctilios of international law. Both rained blows on American shipping interests and insults on sensitive patriots.

Trouble began in 1805, when a British court ruled that goods from the French West Indies bound for Europe on American vessels, even though shipped by way of the United States, were subject to seizure. When the commercial provisions of Jay's Treaty of 1794 expired in 1807 and American diplomats were unable to negotiate a new agreement satisfactory to Jefferson, British interference with American shipping increased. Meanwhile Napoleon had developed a program of economic warfare; his so-called Continental System, elaborated in his Berlin Decree of 1806 and Milan Decree of 1807, closed the European ports under his control to British goods and stated that neutral ships complying with British trade regulations would be confiscated. The British government retaliated with a series of Orders in Council, the most important of which proclaimed a blockade of the ports of France and of the nations under its control. Thereafter American ships bound for western Europe risked seizure by one or the other of the belligerents, depending on whose rules they flouted. In the three years prior to 1807 the British seized at least a thousand American merchantmen and the French half that many.

To Americans the most grievous British wrong was the revival and vigorous application of the centuries-old system of impressment, by which the Royal Navy procured its manpower. In times of crisis British law permitted the commander of a warship, when he needed men, to draft able-bodied subjects of the king wherever they could be found. In enforcing the system British warships stopped American merchantmen on the high seas to search for deserters; they took off British-born sailors who had become Americans by naturalization; and in the process they heedlessly impressed an unknown number of native-born Americans as well. The issue reached a crisis in June 1807, when the British frigate *Leopard* overhauled the United States frigate *Chesapeake* within sight of the Virginia coast and demanded the right to search her for deserters. When the commander of the unprepared *Chesapeake* refused, the *Leopard* fired three broadsides that killed three Americans and wounded eighteen others. The crippled *Chesapeake* submitted to the seizure of four deserters and then returned to Norfolk. This humiliation of an American frigate infuriated both Federalists and Republicans. "Never,

*Building the frigate* Philadelphia

since the battle of Lexington," wrote Jefferson, "have I seen this country in such a state of exasperation as at present." Judging from the tone of the press and the speeches of politicians, the country seemed ready to unite behind a war policy. But Jefferson asked for less: he ordered British warships out of American waters and demanded reparations and an apology.

***The embargo.*** Jefferson asked something of Americans, too. He called for a supreme effort, not to win a war, but to achieve what he considered the nobler goal of keeping the country at peace. To avoid further provocative incidents, Jefferson proposed a policy that he had long cherished as an alternative to war, a policy he described as "peaceable coercion." On December 22, 1807, in response to his urgent plea, Congress passed an Embargo Act that stopped the export of American goods and prohibited all United States ships from clearing American ports for foreign ports. This act, in effect, required shipowners to abandon their risky but extremely profitable wartime trade and obliged planters and farmers to give up their rich European export market.

Jefferson asked for a greater sacrifice than most Americans seemed ready to make. Angry New England merchants, preferring risks and insults to commercial stagnation, denounced the embargo as a ruthless attempt to enlarge the federal government's constitutional power to regulate foreign commerce into an unconstitutional power to prohibit it altogether. Many of them defiantly engaged in an illicit trade that severe enforcement measures, some of dubious legality, could not entirely suppress. The Feder-

*Trouble on the high seas*

alists, having at last found a popular issue, enjoyed a modest revival. Some again hinted at secession. Timothy Pickering described Jefferson as capable of almost any "nefarious act" and called on the states to resist "the usurpations of the general government." The agricultural interest was equally distressed when farm commodities began to accumulate at the ports and prices declined. John Randolph's assaults on the Administration matched those of the Federalists. The embargo, he complained, had furnished "rogues with an opportunity of getting rich at the expense of honest men." Eventually Congress yielded to overwhelming pressure and passed an act repealing the embargo. On March 1, 1809, a disappointed Jefferson, his prestige somewhat diminished, signed it.

"Nature intended me for the more tranquil pursuits of science by rendering them my supreme delight," wrote the weary Jefferson at the close of his second Administration. Retirement was a welcome relief not only from the vicissitudes of domestic politics, in which he counted more successes than failures, but from the trials of international affairs, in which he suffered his greatest defeat.

# The decision for war

By declining to run for reelection in 1808, Jefferson helped to establish the two-term tradition. His favorite, Secretary of State James Madison, easily won the nomination of the Republican caucus over James Monroe, the candidate of the Randolph faction. Though the Federalists, who again nominated Charles Cotesworth Pinckney, regained control of New England and increased their strength in the new Congress, Madison won the Presidency by a decisive majority of 122 to 47 in the Electoral College. His inaugural address reflected the changing conditions of the preceding eight years, especially in its concern for the promotion of commerce and industry; but in spirit it was still a thoroughly Jeffersonian document that endorsed the domestic and foreign policies of his predecessor. Few Presidents have brought to the White House such rich experience in public life as did Madison; none, save John Adams, was so profound a student of political philosophy. Yet, though Madison had contributed much to the formulation of Republican doctrine and had never been Jefferson's mere pliant tool, he lacked Jefferson's political acumen and administrative skill.

**The failure of diplomacy.** The overshadowing problem confronting the new President and Congress was the continuing European holocaust, which still created difficult situations for neutrals. Although the embargo had been repealed, the policy of "peaceable coercion" persisted in less drastic forms. However, the Madison Administration blundered badly in applying it. The first substitute for the embargo was a Nonintercourse Act, passed in 1809, which reestablished trade with all nations except Great Britain and France so long as the latter continued to enforce their obnoxious orders and decrees. This act encouraged the British government to try negotiation. David Erskine, the friendly and sympathetic British minister, concluded an agreement that was highly satisfactory to the United States, though he violated his instructions in doing so. On June 10, 1809, the delighted President renewed trade with Great Britain without waiting for the agreement to be approved in London, and hundreds of American ships cleared their home ports for the first time in many months. Unfortunately the British government repudiated the Erskine "treaty" as soon as it arrived and recalled its too-generous minister. Madison, embarrassed and humiliated, then proclaimed the restoration of nonintercourse, and Anglo-American relations worsened.

On May 1, 1810, nonintercourse gave way to a new policy incorporated in a curious measure called Macon's Bill Number 2. This bill restored trade with both Great Britain and France but threatened to resume nonintercourse with either of them whenever the other agreed to respect America's neutral rights. Now it was Napoleon's turn to try some shifty diplomacy. Proclaiming his love for Americans and his concern for their prosperity, he announced that on November 1, 1810, the French commercial restrictions would be repealed—but he attached conditions that made his promise almost meaningless. Madison fell into Napoleon's trap and on February 2, 1811, reestablished nonintercourse with Britain, though, in fact, the French continued to seize American ships. Unable to get Britain to repeal her Orders in Council, Madison recalled the American minister, William Pinkney, and thus virtually severed diplomatic relations.

Ironically, a few months later the policy of "peaceable coercion" won a striking victory. On June 23, 1812, beset by an economic crisis at home, the British foreign secretary announced the immediate suspension of the Orders in Council (but not impressment). The announcement came too late. On June 1, Madison had asked for a declaration of war against Great Britain, and Congress soon complied: the House on June 4 by a vote of seventy-nine to forty-nine, the Senate on June 18 by a vote of nineteen to thirteen. The division in both houses was largely political, for all Federalists voted against war, while the Republicans voted for it ninety-eight to twenty-two. Geographically, the representatives from Pennsylvania and the Southern and frontier states, including Ver-

*James Madison:*
*a greater man than President*

mont, voted sixty-five to fifteen for war; those from New York, New Jersey, and the New England maritime states voted fourteen to thirty-four against.

Though the Federalist commercial interests were directly affected by British impressment and interference with American shipping on the high seas, they considered war with Great Britain the ultimate folly. War would be more devastating to their trade than the Orders in Council had been—and the blow would be dealt by their own government. Moreover, to them, Britain was not only a profitable market but the defender of conservatism, stability, and order against the obscenities of Napoleonic France. Sharing these views with the Federalists were a handful of Republican Congressmen representing Southern coastal districts and about a third of the Republicans representing the Northeast. John Randolph, a severe critic of the war policy, urged Republicans to live up to their principles of economy and retrenchment and not to become "infatuated with standing armies, loans, taxes, navies, and war."

**The aims of the prowar Republicans.** An able and highly articulate group opposed the declaration of war, but the majority seemed to support it. Although this majority did not include the New England commercial interests, neutral rights and impressment were issues of major importance in the decision to go to war. The grievances Madison stressed in his war message were "the injuries and indignities which have been heaped upon our country"—the British actions "hostile to the United States as an independent and neutral nation." Most Americans felt those insults keenly and resented the implicit unwillingness of the British to concede the reality of American independence. According to one Kentuckian, "we must now oppose the farther encroachments of Great Britain by war, or formally annul the Declaration of Independence, and acknowledge ourselves her devoted colonies." The vindication of national honor, many Republicans believed, would also be a vindication of republican institutions against their foreign and domestic enemies. This notion of an American mission to defend republicanism was widespread; according to Jefferson, "The last hope of human liberty in this world rests on us."

Neutral rights involved economic interests, too; as Madison explained, British policy struck not only at commerce but at agriculture as well. By closing European markets to American staples, the British threatened the prosperity of farmers and planters, many of whom lived hundreds of miles from the sea and might never have seen an ocean-going vessel. "The interests of agriculture and commerce are inseparable," said Representative Langdon Cheves of South Carolina.

The Congress that voted for war contained a remarkable little band of youthful Republicans from the Southern and Western states. Some of them had taken their seats for the first time in November 1811 and had at once begun to badger the President and harangue their colleagues with truculent anti-British speeches. They managed to elect the thirty-four-year-old Henry Clay of Kentucky Speaker of the House; Clay in turn gave important committee assignments to aggressive young Republicans such as Richard M. Johnson of Kentucky, Felix Grundy of Tennessee, and John C. Calhoun of South Carolina. These second-generation Republicans—the Federalists called them "War Hawks"—were critical of the pacifistic measures of Jefferson and Madison, indifferent to the state-rights political tradition embodied in the Resolutions of 1798, more nationalistic than the Federalists in their prime, and eager for geographic expansion and economic growth, with none of the anxieties that Jefferson sometimes seemed to feel. To them, after diplomacy had failed, only war could demonstrate America's power and redress intolerable wrongs too long endured: impressment, violations of America's neutral rights, disregard for its dignity as a sovereign power.

Eventually these so-called War Hawks tried to use the war as justification for the acquisition of additional territory. The insatiable Southern and Western demand for land was an indirect and perhaps secondary source of the crisis that culminated in war. The American frontier was not advancing in a slow, orderly manner, with contiguous tracts of the public domain successively opened for sale and then compactly settled. Rather, farmers and speculators rushed into new areas, often before Indian claims were cleared and surveys completed, and sought out the most fertile parcels. With such an abundance of good land, few buyers were interested in land of second- and third-rate quality. Hence, the government was under constant pressure to open additional tracts even before those already open had been fully settled.

The government seldom raised a restraining hand. Even Jefferson, in spite of a professed concern for the welfare of the Indians and a promise that "not a foot of land" would ever be taken from them "without their own consent," as President had been more often a party to the land grabs than a protector of Indian rights. "Our system," he told William Henry Harrison, governor of Indiana Territory, "is to live in perpetual peace with the Indians," to protect them from injustice, to introduce among them "the implements and the practice of husbandry and of the household arts," and to persuade them to "incorporate with us as citizens of the U.S." When they became farmers they would no longer need their extensive forests and would trade land "for necessaries for their farms and families." But Jefferson also suggested means of speeding the process of land acquisition. At the government trading houses "the good and influential" Indians might be encouraged to run into debt, thus forcing them eventually to make a settlement

Tecumseh:
Shawnee chief

"by a cession of land." If any tribe should be "foolhardy enough to take up the hatchet . . . the seizing [of] the whole country of that tribe and driving them across the Mississippi" would be justified. Finally, Jefferson advised Governor Harrison on ways to cajole the various tribes into making land cessions.

An unfortunate consequence of both the planless expansion and the cajolery was that Western Indians were repeatedly induced to make treaties whose terms they rarely comprehended, treaties by which they surrendered more and more of their hunting grounds. In the Ohio Valley alone, during the first decade of the nineteenth century, the Indians had been obliged to cede more than a hundred million acres of land. In 1809, in Indiana Territory, Governor Harrison negotiated the last of a series of cessions under particularly dubious circumstances, bargaining with the demoralized remnants of several tribes for nearly three million acres in the lower Wabash Valley. The Indians realized that if they were ever to make a stand east of the Mississippi, it would have to be now.

At this crucial time two Shawnees of uncommon ability, Tecumseh and his brother Tenskwatawa ("the Prophet"), managed to unite the tribes east of the Mississippi for resistance against further white encroachments. Tecumseh supplied political leadership, while the Prophet provided spiritual inspiration and a call for moral regeneration. Together they organized an efficient Indian confederation supported by braves determined to preserve their lands and uncorrupted by the white man's proffered gifts of liquor. Terror spread along the frontier. In the summer of 1811, when Tecumseh went south to bid for the support of the Creeks, Governor Harrison decided to take advantage of his absence. He advanced with a force of a thousand men to the outskirts of Prophetstown, the chief Indian settlement, on the Wabash River near the mouth of Tippecanoe Creek. There, on November 7, after repelling an Indian attack, his men destroyed the town. The Battle of Tippecanoe marked the beginning of a long and savage Indian war.

In asking for a declaration of war against Great Britain Madison expressed an opinion held by the majority of Westerners: that the Indians had been receiving arms and encouragement from the British in Canada. Some of the young militants, though lacking evidence, were certain of it. "I can have no doubt of the influence of British agents in keeping up Indian hostility" and of encouraging them "to murder our citizens," cried Richard M. Johnson of Kentucky. Felix Grundy of Tennessee agreed, adding that there would be no peace on the frontier until the British were driven out of Canada. "We shall drive the British from our continent," Grundy affirmed; "they will no longer have an opportunity of intriguing with our Indian neighbors. . . . That nation will lose her Cana-

**Why the war must be fought**

THE IMPRESSMENT OF AN
**American Sailor Boy.**

dian trade, and, by having no resting place in this country, her means of annoying us will be diminished." To Westerners, once war was declared, the conquest of the rich lands of Upper Canada was one of the anticipated fruits of victory. To Southerners the conquest of East and West Florida, still in the possession of Spain, Great Britain's ally, might well be another. As early as 1810 Madison, in collusion with American settlers, had seized a portion of West Florida; but nothing short of the whole of the Floridas would now satisfy the expansionists. This "agrarian cupidity," as John Randolph called it, was not a cause of the war with Great Britain, but it characterized many of those who voted for that war.

In a letter summarizing the causes of the war, Andrew Jackson of Tennessee mentioned neutral rights, impressment, national vindication, Indian pacification, and the desire for territorial conquest. He then condensed all these motives into two phrases: "to seek some indemnity for past injuries, some security against future aggression." Jackson seems to have reflected the sentiment of the majority in the Southern and Western states, and in the presidential election of 1812 they, along with Pennsylvania and Vermont, endorsed the war policy by giving their electoral votes to Madison. De Witt Clinton of New York, the candidate of the Federalists and Peace Republicans, carried the rest of the New England and Middle Atlantic states.

Madison's rather narrow margin in the Electoral College (128 to 89—the shift of one state, Pennsylvania, could have changed the result), together with the bitter resentment of the commercial centers, meant that the country went to war dangerously divided. No patriot, wrote a Boston editor, "conceives it his duty to shed his blood for Bonaparte, for Madison or Jefferson, and that Host of Ruffians in Congress." The revitalized New England Federalists wanted no part of "Mr. Madison's war."

## The War of 1812

**National unpreparedness.** The prowar Republicans were convinced that the war could be won with little effort and a minimum of sacrifice. Henry Clay announced that "the militia of Kentucky alone are competent to place Montreal and Upper Canada at your feet." His friends in Congress must have believed him, for they led into war a country that was not only internally divided but hopelessly unprepared. As war approached, the Madison Administration loyally adhered to Jefferson's policy of relying on small gunboats and continued to neglect the regular navy; even in his message to Congress of November 1811 Madison made no recommendation for naval expansion. The following January two-thirds of the representatives who were to vote for war five months later helped to defeat a modest proposal to add ten frigates to the navy. During the debate on this measure, Richard M. Johnson of Kentucky, one of the young militants, vowed that he would not vote a penny for a naval force "destined to entail upon this happy Government perpetual taxes and a perpetually increasing public debt."

Congress made no effort to increase American naval power until months after the outbreak of war, and the new forty-four-gun frigates and seventy-four-

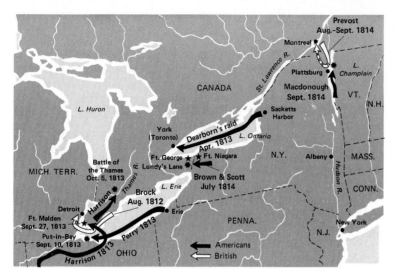

The War of 1812:
Northern campaigns,
1812–14

gun ships of the line then provided for were not ready for action until the war had ended. Indeed the United States had an ocean-going navy of only sixteen vessels fit for service with which to challenge the world's foremost sea power, whose warships numbered in the hundreds. The American navy had the advantage of a talented, well-trained group of officers but suffered from a serious shortage of experienced seamen. It had no real fleet organization, each ship operating more or less as an independent unit. Moreover, since most of the ships were expected to function as commerce-raiders, the question of naval strategy seemed superfluous.

But the Republican majority, after all, was thinking primarily of a land war, not of challenging Britain's naval supremacy. With Florida weakly defended, with fewer than five thousand British troops in Canada, and with war raging in Europe, the odds seemed to favor the Americans. Had the United States trained, equipped, and put in the field an army of only fifty thousand men—no serious strain on the country's resources—it might have conquered Canada and Florida with relative ease. Congress seemed to act boldly enough: it authorized an expansion of the small regular army by the recruitment of twenty-five thousand five-year volunteers; provided for the raising of an additional fifty thousand one-year volunteers; and made repeated calls on the state militias, which numbered, on paper, some seven-hundred thousand men.

However, even in the regions most enthusiastic for war, Americans were reluctant to abandon their civilian pursuits; neither coercion nor persuasion, such as offers of cash bounties and land grants, had much effect. Never during the war did the army number more than thirty-five thousand men, and even this small force was poorly trained and unimaginatively commanded by over-age veterans of the Revolution and incompetent militia officers. Moreover,

militiamen, especially in the Federalist states, generally felt that their duty was limited to state defense, and some refused to leave their states for operations across the frontier.

The members of Congress, including those who had voted for war, hesitated to adopt the fiscal measures demanded by a war policy. Eventually Congress doubled tariff rates and levied a new excise tax, a stamp tax, and a direct tax on the states, but those unpopular measures brought the government little revenue until near the end of the war. It authorized loans, but the Treasury Department managed to market the bulk of about $80 million in securities only at a discount and at high interest rates. Since most New England capitalists opposed the war, and since the Bank of the United States had been abolished in 1811, Secretary of the Treasury Gallatin had to rely on state banks, which were poorly equipped to handle business of this sort. In short, Republican policy over the past decade had been designed for a simple agricultural nation at peace with the world; now Republicans, in effect, attempted to apply Jeffersonian means to a non-Jeffersonian end. In so doing, they barely escaped national disaster.

***The military campaigns.*** Plans for the conquest of Canada (which Southern Republicans, incidentally, had never viewed with much enthusiasm) ended in a fiasco. Effective strategy called for a concentration of forces in an attack on Montreal, whose fall would have cut British communications along the St. Lawrence and the Great Lakes and made the British position in Upper Canada untenable. But, in response to the Western demand for protection from Tecumseh's Indian confederation, the nation's forces were diffused. As a result, the military campaign of 1812 was a feeble, poorly planned, uncoordinated attempt to invade Canada at three separate points. General William Hull marched an army from Detroit toward the British garrison at Malden. But, doubting the wisdom of an invasion before winning control of Lake Erie, and hearing that Tecumseh and his warriors had joined the British, Hull soon lost his nerve and returned to Detroit. There, on August 6, a brilliant British commander, General Isaac Brock, surrounded Hull's army and forced him to surrender without firing a shot. A second invasion across the Niagara River culminated in defeat and surrender when New York militiamen refused to enter Canada to reinforce their countrymen. Finally, General Henry Dearborn led an advance along Lake Champlain toward Montreal. When he reached the Canadian border he found that his militiamen would not cross it and was obliged to march back to Plattsburg. So ended the land campaigns of 1812. If they had made no conquests and won no glory, at least they had cost few lives.

Things went little better the next year. Canadians astonished their would-be "liberators" by vigorously supporting British efforts to drive the invaders out. Two events, however, enabled the Americans to recover lost ground on the Northwest frontier and all but eliminate the danger of another British offensive there. The first was Captain Oliver Hazard Perry's notable victory at Put-in-Bay on Lake Erie, September 10, 1813. When Perry reported, "We have met the enemy and they are ours," he gave the Americans control of the Great Lakes and made the British position at Detroit hopeless. The second event was General Harrison's victory over the retreating British at the Battle of the Thames, October 5, 1813. Here the

great Indian leader Tecumseh was killed; with his death the Indian confederacy collapsed, and the Northwest frontier was secure. But the conquest of Canada was as remote as ever.

By 1814 the Americans were striving desperately to prevent the British from invading their land and, perhaps, taking a slice of it. With the defeat of Napoleon and his exile to Elba, the British were able for the first time to give their undivided attention to the American war and to send some of their best troops across the Atlantic. Their plan was to harass the cities on the Atlantic coast with amphibious operations while launching invasions at three points: Niagara, Lake Champlain, and New Orleans.

The most ambitious coastal attack was a thrust up Chesapeake Bay culminating in the capture of Washington on August 24. As the President and other Administration officials fled, the British burned the Capitol, the White House, and other public buildings. Having avenged an earlier American raid on York (Toronto) with this crowning humiliation, and failing in an attempt to capture Baltimore, the British withdrew. The military significance of the raid was negligible, but it underscored the utter failure of the Administration's war policy.

The British invasion plans, however, seriously miscarried, for by 1814 the Americans had found some vigorous young officers and no longer had to rely on untrained, undisciplined militia units. The projected British offensive at Niagara was thwarted by the aggressive operations of General Jacob Brown and his able young subordinate, Winfield Scott. The Battle

*"We have met the enemy":
battle on Lake Erie, 1813*

of Lundy's Lane, near Niagara Falls, on July 25, was itself indecisive, but it ended the British invasion threat from that position. In August a powerful force of British veterans commanded by Sir George Prevost advanced toward Lake Champlain with the apparent purpose of cutting off the New England states from the rest of the Union. Early in September Prevost paused before the strong American fortifications at Plattsburg to await the outcome of a bitter duel between British and American flotillas on Lake Champlain. On September 11 Captain Thomas Macdonough's American fleet won a decisive victory, forcing Prevost to abandon his campaign and retire to Canada. Clearly, the war on the Canadian frontier had reached a stalemate.

The final campaign took place in the Southwest. Here Andrew Jackson of Tennessee, an authentic self-trained military genius, somehow managed to make soldiers out of militiamen and to furnish them with supplies. Jackson had already smashed the military power of the Southwestern Indians by defeating the Creeks at the Battle of Horseshoe Bend, on March 27, 1814, and had also forced them to cede some of their richest lands in Mississippi Territory. Next he captured and destroyed Pensacola in Spanish Florida to prevent the British from using it as a base and then marched his army to New Orleans to meet the invaders. Placing his men behind earthworks and bales of cotton, he awaited the attack of eight thousand seasoned British troops commanded by Sir Edward Pakenham. Contemptuous of Jackson's motley army of militiamen, sailors, and pirates, Pakenham, on January 8, 1815, led his men in tight formation in a rash frontal assault. American rifles and artillery raked the British columns with a deadly fire. Before the British withdrew, the Americans had killed the British commander and inflicted more than two thousand casualties, while suffering little more than a dozen of their own. The Battle of New Orleans was the last engagement of the war—in fact, it was fought two weeks after a treaty of peace had been signed. But it helped sweeten the bitter taste of the defeats and disappointments of the previous two and a half years, and it launched Andrew Jackson, the Hero of New Orleans, on his dazzling career.

On the high seas in the early months of the war the tiny American navy won a series of stunning victories in single-ship engagements, bolstering public morale during the disasters on the Canadian frontier. The most spectacular of these victories were those of the American frigate *Constitution* (Old Ironsides) over the British frigates *Guerrière* and *Java*, and of the *United States* over the *Macedonian*. These successes shocked the British public, which had heard the American navy described as a "few fir-built frigates, manned by a handful of bastards and outlaws"; but they constituted no real challenge to British naval supremacy, nor did they have any great strategic significance.

By 1813 most of the American men-of-war were bottled up in their home ports by a British blockade, and by the end of the war only the *Constitution* and a few smaller vessels were still at sea. American cruisers and privateers continued to prey on British commerce and altogether captured more than a thousand merchantmen. These commerce-raiders were a costly annoyance to the British but fell far short of seriously crippling her overseas trade or disrupting her economy. The decisive fact of the naval war was the British blockade of the American coast, which dealt an almost mortal blow to the American carrying trade. In 1814 exports and imports fell to less than 10 percent of what they had been in the peak year of 1807. Flour exports declined from 1,443,000 barrels in 1812 to 193,000 barrels in 1814. The blockade was equally disastrous to American interstate commerce, most of which still moved along coastal waterways. Francis Wayland described the devastating impact of the blockade on the whole economy: "Our harbors were blockaded; communications coastwise between our ports were cut off; our ships were rotting in every creek and cove where they could find a place of security; our immense annual products were mouldering in our warehouses; the sources of profitable labor were dried up." If the land war was a stalemate, the war on the high seas culminated in a British victory that was well-nigh complete. Floating in the wreckage was Jefferson's gunboat policy.

**Disaffection in New England.** These disasters were what antiwar Federalists in the Northeast had anticipated—what Josiah Quincy of Massachusetts

The War of 1812:
Southwestern campaigns, 1813–15

had in mind when he said, "This war, the measures which preceded it, and the mode of carrying it on, are all undeniably southern and western policy, not the policy of the commercial states." Feeling betrayed by their own government, convinced that the Madison Administration had deliberately set about to destroy their political and economic power, New England Federalists throughout the war regarded the Republican politicians in Washington, not the British, as their mortal enemies. And, having regained political control of all the New England states, they were in a position to translate their angry polemics into defiant deeds.

Federalist governors contested federal calls on the state militias, insisting that their proper function was to repel invasion, not to invade foreign territory. Federalists discouraged voluntary enlistments; and when Congress debated a militia draft they defended state sovereignty against national tyranny. "Where is it written in the Constitution," asked Daniel Webster, a young Federalist congressman from New Hampshire, "that you may take children from their parents, and parents from their children, and compel them to fight the battles of any war in which the folly or the wickedness of government may engage it?" Federalists resisted tax measures and boycotted government loans. According to a Boston editor, "any man who lends money to the government at the present time will forfeit all claim to common honesty." Meanwhile, defiant New Englanders continued to trade with Canada and even furnished supplies to the British fleet. The more extreme dissenters, especially the

ardent Federalists of the Connecticut River Valley, favored either a separate peace and the withdrawal of New England from the war or else secession from the Union.

In 1814 British depredations along the New England coast and the belief that the federal government would do nothing to check them precipitated a serious political crisis. In October the Massachusetts legislature called for a convention of the New England states to prepare an adequate defense against invasion and to consider amendments to the federal Constitution. The call asserted that in the existing Union the "Eastern sections" had not obtained "those equal rights and benefits which are the greatest objects of its formation." Twenty-six delegates—twelve from Massachusetts, seven from Connecticut, four from Rhode Island, and three from Vermont—assembled in Hartford on December 15 and deliberated secretly for nearly three weeks. Federalist extremists, such as Timothy Pickering, were not among the delegates; the moderates, led by Harrison Gray Otis of Massachusetts, gained control and adopted a final report that was relatively mild.

The report, much of which dealt with the problem of defending the New England coast, began with a gloomy account of the evils the country had endured under the "withering influence" of the Republicans. The Jeffersonians, it claimed, had debauched the civil service; destroyed "the balance of power which existed among the original states" by creating new Western states; and entertained a "visionary and superficial theory in regard to commerce, accompanied by a real hatred but a feigned regard to its interests." As a remedy for these grievances the Hartford report demanded a series of constitutional amendments that would abolish the three-fifths compromise, require a two-thirds vote of both houses of Congress to declare war and to admit new states, prohibit embargoes lasting for more than sixty days, exclude the foreign-born from federal offices, limit the President to one term, and prohibit the election of two successive Presidents from the same state. If these demands were ignored and the war continued, the report recommended that another convention be called and given "such powers and instructions as the exigency of a crisis so momentous may require."

When representatives from the Hartford Convention arrived in Washington with their ultimatum, they found the capital rejoicing over Jackson's victory at New Orleans and over the signing of a treaty of peace. Now their complaints seemed pointless, and their demands were ignored. But the Hartford Convention was remembered; to nationalists it symbolized the disloyalty, the narrow, selfish provincialism, of the Federalists. Consequently, the Federalist party, though for a time it remained strong in several New England states, was itself one of the casualties of the War of 1812.

Oddly enough, New England, in spite of its political disaffection, was the only region that profited materially from the war. Since the British blockade was not enforced along its coast until 1814, it received the bulk of foreign imports. Gold from the rest of the country flowed to its banks, which were thus able to maintain specie payments while other banks were forced to suspend payments. Above all, the war gave a strong impetus to New England manufacturing; between 1810 and 1814 the number of cotton spindles in the area increased sixfold. A war that many had hoped would result in the acquisition of more land for the farmers and planters of the Northwest and South ended without an acre of new territory but with many thousands of spindles whirling in New England factories.

## Peace negotiations

**The Treaty of Ghent.** Almost from the start of this curious conflict there had been talk of peace. As early as September 1812 the czar of Russia, anxious that the British give their full attention to Napoleon, offered to act as mediator. President Madison responded favorably and, early in 1813, sent Albert Gallatin and James A. Bayard to work with John Quincy Adams, the American minister in St. Petersburg. The British de-

clined the Russian offer—Russia could not be trusted to support the British position on neutral rights—but soon indicated a willingness to negotiate directly with the Americans. This, too, was acceptable to Madison, though he did not hear of the suggestion until January 1814. He then appointed Henry Clay and Jonathan Russell to join the three commissioners already in Europe, and in August negotiations began in the city of Ghent.

The British diplomats, an unimpressive group, were under the strict control of the Foreign Office in London. The Americans, superior in talent, had received from their government broader powers and greater freedom to negotiate. But they sometimes disagreed among themselves on matters of policy, and during the tedious months of negotiation their personal relations occasionally became tense. Adams' colleagues found him an irritating companion, and Adams, in turn, took a dim view of them, especially of Clay with his taste for cards and late hours. "They sit after dinner and drink bad wine and smoke cigars, which neither suits my habits nor my health, and absorbs time which I cannot spare," wrote the austere new Englander. Gallatin turned out to be the chief peacemaker in dealings not only with the British but with his own colleagues.

Had the two delegations adhered to their initial instructions, the negotiations would have been brief and the result complete failure. The Americans were to insist that the British abandon impressment, agree to respect international law in setting up blockades, and pay indemnity for their illegal seizure of American ships. The British, anticipating decisive military victories in the campaigns of 1814, presented a list of terms that would have jeopardized the sovereignty and future growth of the United States. They demanded territorial cessions in northern New York and Maine, the surrender of American control of the Great Lakes, the creation of an autonomous Indian buffer state south of the Great Lakes, the right to navigate the Mississippi River, and the relinquishment of American fishing rights off the coasts of Newfoundland and Labrador. The Americans made it clear that if the British insisted on these terms the war would continue. "Our negotiations may be considered at an end," wrote Gallatin to his government.

But the British did not insist. News of Macdonough's victory on Lake Champlain and Prevost's retreat from Plattsburg drastically changed the military picture, and the Duke of Wellington, when consulted by the British ministry, argued that failure to gain control of the Great Lakes made the British demands unreasonable. "I confess," he said, "that I think you have no right, from the state of the war, to demand any concession of territory from America." British merchants and manufacturers, eager to resume

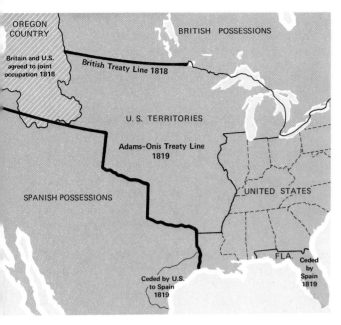

OREGON COUNTRY

BRITISH POSSESSIONS

Britain and U.S. agreed to joint occupation 1818

British Treaty Line 1818

U.S. TERRITORIES

Adams-Onis Treaty Line 1819

SPANISH POSSESSIONS

UNITED STATES

FLA. Ceded by Spain 1819

Ceded by U.S. to Spain 1819

Boundary treaties, 1818–19

trade with the United States, favored an end to hostilities. The tax-burdened British public, too, had had enough of war.

As negotiations proceeded, the diplomats dropped one demand after another and eventually agreed to a peace treaty that settled nothing but simply restored the status quo antebellum. The Treaty of Ghent, signed on December 24, 1814, was silent on impressment and neutral rights, boundaries and fisheries, trade and indemnities—although it referred some of those questions to joint commissions for future settlement. In submitting the treaty to the Senate for ratification, Madison claimed no victory. "The late war," he said with more than a little ambiguity, "has been waged with a success which is the natural result of the wisdom of the legislative councils, of the patriotism of the people, of the public spirit of the militia, and of the valor of the military and naval forces of the country." As Adams described the document, "Nothing was adjusted, nothing was settled—nothing in substance but an indefinite suspension of hostilities was agreed to." Clay, though he signed it, described it as a "damned bad treaty."

Nevertheless, Americans looked back on the war with pride and satisfaction. They ignored the fact that the British had yielded nothing on neutral rights or impressment, because these issues lost their significance when the war ended in Europe. In the selective memories of patriots the military defeats, the bungling of the Canadian campaigns, and British supremacy on the high seas faded into insignificance; the early exploits of American frigates and privateers, Perry's victory on Lake Erie, and, best of all, Jackson's victory at New Orleans were remembered vividly as

the crucial events of the war. The very fact that no territory had been lost—that the British had abandoned their extreme demands—contributed to this myth of military success. Moreover, the death of Tecumseh, the collapse of the Indian confederation, and the destruction of Indian military power east of the Mississippi meant that at least one purpose of the war had been fully achieved. Finally, the rise of manufacturing made the country more self-sufficient, and the preservation of their threatened independence gave Americans a greater feeling of national identity than ever before. As Gallatin observed: "The war has renewed and reinstated the national feelings and character which the Revolution had given. . . . The people now have more general objects of attachment. . . . They are more Americans; they feel and act more as a nation."

***Postwar settlements.*** Though memories of the war were to keep alive an undercurrent of Anglo-American hostility for many years, several specific issues that might have caused trouble were resolved soon after the stalemate at Ghent. In 1815 a commercial treaty removed most of the restrictions on Anglo-American trade (except with the British West Indies). An agreement of 1817, signed by Richard Rush, the acting Secretary of State, and Charles Bagot, the British minister, provided for naval disarmament on the Great Lakes. Though either side could terminate it on six months' notice, the Rush-Bagot Agreement became a permanent policy. Another agreement the following year reopened the coasts of Newfoundland and Labrador to American fishermen, established the forty-ninth parallel as the northern boundary of the Louisiana Purchase from the Lake of the Woods to the Rocky Mountains, and provided for a joint occupation of Oregon for the next ten years. Neither the British nor the Americans could have guessed it then, but these postwar negotiations, rather than the War of 1812, were to set the pattern for subsequent Anglo-American relations.

Another long-standing source of diplomatic friction was removed when Spain finally agreed to give up the Floridas. Internally weak and rapidly losing her once great empire in South and Central America, Spain maintained only a tenuous hold on the Floridas. Her feeble garrison was unable to control the Seminole Indians or to prevent white outlaws and runaway slaves from using the region as a sanctuary. In 1818 Andrew Jackson, giving the broadest possible interpretation to vague instructions from his government, led a military force into the Floridas to punish the Seminoles for depredations along the American frontier. In the process he seized St. Marks and Pensacola, deposed the Spanish governor, and raised the American flag; he also arrested two British subjects for inciting the Indians, tried them by court-martial, and executed them. At home Jackson's highhanded conduct added to his popularity, but it immensely complicated matters for Secretary of State John Quincy Adams, who had been negotiating with the Spanish minister, Luis de Onís.

Making the best of a bad situation, Adams brazened his way through. He not only refused to apologize for Jackson's behavior but threw responsibility on the Spanish for failing to preserve order in the Floridas. Spain, he insisted, must either govern the provinces efficiently or cede them to the United States, for they had become "a derelict, open to the occupancy of every enemy, civilized or savage, of the United States, and serving no other earthly purpose than as a post of annoyance to them." This was a challenge that the Spanish were in no position to accept, and in 1819 the Adams-Onís Treaty arranged for the transfer of the Floridas to the United States. In exchange, the American government agreed to assume payment of $5 million worth of claims that American citizens held against the Spanish government. The treaty also drew a boundary between the Louisiana Territory and Spanish possessions in the Southwest. The line followed the Sabine, Red, and Arkansas rivers to the Rocky Mountains, then the forty-second parallel west to the Pacific. Thus the United States gave up her claim to Texas (as part of the Louisiana Purchase) and Spain her claim to territory in the Pacific Northwest. Ratification of the treaty was delayed for two years, but in 1821 Jackson triumphantly reentered the Florida Territory as the first American governor.

Those who had moral sensibilities about the rough tactics of Jackson and Adams soothed their consciences with the argument that since the Floridas were contiguous to American territory, Providence intended that America should have them. A later generation would call this argument "Manifest Destiny." Even so, the age of the Jeffersonians, who believed in man's reason and disliked the cynicism of the Old World, was closing on a slightly sour note.

## Suggestions for reading

### JEFFERSON IN POWER

Jefferson's political philosophy has had an enduring influence on American thought; it is analyzed sympathetically in Adrienne Koch, *The Philosophy of Thomas Jefferson** (1943). How it has been interpreted and used by subsequent generations is explained in Merrill Peterson, *The Jefferson Image in the American Mind** (1960). The best completed biographies of Jefferson are Nathan Schachner, *Thomas Jefferson: A Biography*, 2 vols. (1951), and Merrill Peterson, *Thomas Jefferson and the New Nation: A Biography** (1970). Dumas Malone, *Jefferson the President: First Term, 1801–1805** (1970), and *Jefferson the President: Second Term, 1805–1809** (1974), are parts of a masterful multivolume biography not yet completed. F. M. Brodie, *Thomas Jefferson: An Intimate History** (1974), attempts a psychoanalytic approach, with mixed results, to reveal Jefferson's personal life. The contributions of Jefferson's two ablest lieutenants can be studied in four excellent works: Adrienne Koch, *Jefferson and Madison: The Great Collaboration** (1950), Irving Brant, *James Madison: Secretary of State, 1800–1809* (1953), Ralph Ketcham, *James Madison* (1971), and Raymond Walters, Jr., *Albert Gallatin: Jeffersonian Financier and Diplomat** (1957).

The best and most comprehensive survey of the Republican era is Marshall Smelser, *The Democratic Republic, 1801–1815** (1968). Three brief, well-written surveys are also useful: Marcus Cunliffe, *The Nation Takes Shape, 1789–1837** (1959), C. M. Wiltse, *The New Nation, 1800–1845** (1961), and Morton Borden, *Parties and Politics in the Early Republic, 1789–1815** (1967). An older analysis that is a classic, in spite of its hostility to Jefferson and Madison, is Henry Adams, *History of the United States of America During the Administrations of Jefferson and Madison*, 9 vols.* (1889–91). Two excellent accounts of the party battles and Republican party organization are W. N. Chambers, *Political Parties in a New Nation, 1776–1809** (1963), and Noble Cunningham, *The Jeffersonian Republicans in Power: Party Operations, 1801–1809* (1963). Richard Hofstadter, *The Idea of a Party System** (1969), is a lucid essay on the beginnings of two-party politics in America. Richard Buel, Jr., *Securing the Revolution: Ideology in American Politics, 1789–1815* (1972), focuses on both issues and ideology. The role of the Federalist opposition is traced in D. H. Fischer, *The Revolution of American Conservatism: The Federalist Party in the Era of Jeffersonian Democracy** (1965). L. K. Kerber, *Federalists in Dissent: Imagery and Ideology in Jeffersonian America* (1970), is a study of Federalist

*Available in a paperback edition.

political and social thought. L. D. White, *The Jeffersonians: A Study in Administrative History, 1801–1829* * (1951), is an expert analysis of Republican administrative organization. J. S. Young, *The Washington Community, 1800–1828* * (1966), stresses the failure of the Jeffersonians, because of certain negative attitudes, to develop an effective federal government. Alexander Balinky, *Albert Gallatin: Fiscal Theories and Policy* (1958), is a sharply critical evaluation of Jeffersonian finance.

John Randolph and other conservative Republicans are studied in N. K. Risjord, *The Old Republicans: Southern Conservatism in the Age of Jefferson* (1965). The case for Aaron Burr is presented in Nathan Schachner, *Aaron Burr: A Biography* * (1937); the case against him, in T. P. Abernethy, *The Burr Conspiracy* (1954).

### FOREIGN POLICY AND THE WAR OF 1812

Two useful works on the Louisiana Purchase are E. W. Lyon, *Louisiana in French Diplomacy, 1759–1804* * (1934), and A. P. Whitaker, *The Mississippi Question* (1934). The best account of the conflict with the Barbary pirates is R. W. Irwin, *Diplomatic Relations of the United States and the Barbary Powers* (1931).

Several excellent works are available on the problems of American neutrality. A good place to begin is with Irving Brant's study of Madison as Secretary of State, mentioned above, and with the same author's *James Madison: The President, 1809–1812* (1956). Brant's multivolume biography of Madison is available in a one-volume abridged edition, *The Fourth President: A Life of James Madison* (1970). Outstanding monographs include W. W. Jennings, *The American Embargo* (1921); J. F. Zimmerman, *Impressment of American Seamen* (1925); L. M. Sears, *Jefferson and the Embargo* (1927); Harry Bernstein, *Origins of Inter-American Interest, 1700–1812* (1945); and Bradford Perkins, *First Rapprochement: England and the United States, 1795–1805* (1955).

B. W. Sheehan, *Seeds of Extinction: Jeffersonian Philanthropy and the American Indians* * (1973), stresses the assault on Indian culture by even the best intentioned whites. Reginald Horsman, *Expansion and American Indian Policy, 1783–1812* (1967), is a fair account of a sordid chapter of American history. The same author's *The Frontier in the Formative Years, 1783–1815* * (1970), an excellent work of synthesis, is especially valuable for conditions on the frontier in the years before the War of 1812.

The view that the War of 1812 was caused by Western and Southern expansionism and fear of the Indians is developed in J. W. Pratt, *Expansionists of 1812* (1925). A stronger case for impressment and neutral rights as the fundamental causes is presented, with varying emphases, in A. L. Burt, *The United States, Great Britain, and British North America from the Revolution to the Peace after the War of 1812* (1940); Bradford Perkins, *Prologue to War: England and the United States, 1805–1812* * (1961); and Reginald Horsman, *The Causes of the War of 1812* * (1962). R. H. Brown, *The Republic in Peril: 1812* (1964), stresses the desire of Jeffersonians to defend Republican institutions as a force leading to war. The careers of two militant young Republicans can be studied in Bernard Mayo, *Henry Clay, Spokesman of the New West* (1937), and C. M. Wiltse, *John C. Calhoun: Nationalist, 1782–1828* (1944).

Irving Brant, *James Madison: Commander in Chief, 1812–1836* (1961), strongly defends Madison's wartime leadership. The best general account of the war is F. F. Beirne, *The War of 1812* (1949). Two good brief surveys are H. L. Coles, *The War of 1812* * (1965), and Reginald Horsman, *The War of 1812* (1969). Military history is treated at length in J. K. Mahon, *The War of 1812* (1972), and briefly in Alan Lloyd, *The Scorching of Washington: The War of 1812* (1975). Marquis James, *Andrew Jackson,* Vol. I: *The Border Captain* * (1933), gives an absorbing account of the campaigns in the Southwest. Federalist disaffection is treated perceptively in George Dangerfield, *The Era of Good Feelings* * (1952); J. M. Banner, *To the Hartford Convention* (1970); and S. E. Morison, *Harrison Gray Otis, 1765–1848: The Urbane Federalist* (1969). Excellent analyses of the peace negotiations and postwar diplomacy are in S. F. Bemis, *John Quincy Adams and the Foundations of American Foreign Policy* * (1949), and Bradford Perkins, *Castlereagh and Adams* (1964).

*Available in a paperback edition.

Cincinnati, 1835

CHAPTER **8**

# Nationalism and economic expansion

the South, the Northeast, and overseas. Farm-commodity prices were good, and land values were rising. Settlers were swarming into the West, and within a few years after the Treaty of Ghent five new states—Indiana (1816), Mississippi (1817), Illinois (1818), Alabama (1819), and Missouri (1821)—entered the Union. A new economic interest, manufacturing, was growing in importance and striving to expand at the rate it had achieved during the wartime dearth of British goods. Shipping, though it would never regain the prominence it once had in the Northeastern maritime states, was recovering from blows the embargo and the war had dealt.

This vast land, with its burgeoning economy and its optimistic, nationalistic people (9½ million of them by 1820), was no longer the plain, uncomplicated republic that Jefferson had once so admired. Jefferson's party was changing with the country and now counted manufacturers, factory workers, and other urban groups, as well as farmers and planters, among those it had to serve. Henry Clay, John C. Calhoun, and John Quincy Adams were impatient with the old-fashioned Virginia Republicans' emphasis on constitutionalism, state rights, and agrarianism. They had a vision of national growth, economic expansion, and social progress that required a more dynamic federal government pursuing more positive and imaginative policies. In fighting their political battles, postwar Republicans still used Jeffersonian rhetoric, but the old creed had lost much of its substance. In 1801 Jefferson's remark that "We are all Republicans, we are all Federalists" was only a loose figure of speech; in 1816 it was almost a fact.

## The triumph of neo-Federalism

**The American System.** Circumstances had forced Madison, like Jefferson, time after time to compromise traditional Republicanism. In his seventh annual message to Congress, December 5, 1815, Madison's surrender to the nationalists was well-nigh complete; Hamilton himself could hardly have composed a message that embraced orthodox Federalist doctrine more fully. In the name of national defense, Madison urged an expansion of the navy, a reorganization of the militia, and an enlargement of the Military Academy at West Point. Without a blush he recommended federal assumption of certain state debts incurred for militia expenses during the recent war. To establish a stable money and credit supply, he suggested that "a national bank will merit consideration." Because of the resumed flow of cheaper British manufactures, a

O ne might have expected the prowar Republicans to be discredited by their failure to capture Canada and their general mishandling of military affairs. But when peace came the Republican party was still firmly in power. Though the record of Madison's wartime Administration was less than brilliant, the country was still intact, and for several years the economy flourished. Southern cotton-planters were regaining their European markets, and a growing number of Western farmers were taking advantage of cheaper transportation to send their agricultural surpluses to markets in

New states, 1812–21

MAINE 1820

ILL. 1818

IND. 1816

MO. 1821

MISS. 1817

ALA. 1819

LA. 1812

federal tariff should provide industry with the protection that "is due to the enterprising citizens whose interests are now at stake." Finally, Madison urged Congress to finance such internal improvements as required "a national jurisdiction and national means," thus "binding more closely together the various parts of our extended confederacy."

Congressional leaders had few qualms about this program of neo-Federalism, and Henry Clay soon labeled it the "American System." The prewar economy, Clay and his supporters thought, had depended too much on the exchange of American raw materials for European manufactured goods, a dependence that exposed it to the whims of other powers and made it the victim of every international crisis. "Dame Commerce," said Clay, "is a flirting, flippant, noisy Jade and if we are governed by her fantasies, we shall never put off the muslins of India and the cloths of Europe." Hence the foundation of Clay's American System was a protective tariff to stimulate domestic manufacturing and to create an enlarged domestic market for the surplus agricultural products of the South and West. Internal improvements, financed with tariff revenues, would encourage interstate commerce; and a national bank would provide banknote currency of uniform value to facilitate an expanding volume of business transactions, as well as the short-term credits required for economic growth. This nationalistic program, Clay believed, would bring to all interests and sections of the country both prosperity and independence from the outside world.

**The Tariff of 1816.** The first postwar Congress, one of the most fruitful of the nineteenth century, took long strides toward Clay's goal of an American System. By 1816 the Republican party numbered in its ranks a large cluster of interest groups, both urban and rural, clamoring for protective duties on certain for-

eign goods entering the American market. Leading the protectionists were those who had invested in New England textile mills and Pennsylvania iron-smelters when the embargo and war had choked off European supplies. Seconding them were the hemp-growers of Kentucky, the wool-growers of Ohio and Vermont, and an assortment of Southerners and Westerners who hoped either to promote industry or to expand their domestic market behind a tariff wall.

The cries of the protectionists grew louder when British exporters, seeking to dispose of surpluses accumulated during the war and to drive competing American manufacturers out of business, flooded the American market with relatively low-priced goods. A member of Parliament suggested that British goods might even be sold at a loss for a time, in order "to stifle in the cradle, those rising manufactures in the United States, which war has forced into existence, contrary to the natural course of things." In the critical years immediately following the war, British competition forced many small, less efficient American manufacturers to close their doors. Protectionists claimed that the British were plotting to wreck the American economy and asserted that a higher tariff was essential for national economic survival. America's "infant industries" were fragile things, they said, requiring the tender care of the federal government while they matured.

Congress responded with the Tariff of 1816, an act that raised duties to an average of 20 percent to meet the need for increased revenues and the demand for greater protection. In the House the Western and Middle Atlantic states gave the bill overwhelming support; New England divided seventeen to ten for it, the South twenty-three to thirty-four against. Webster and other Federalists, speaking for the shipping interests, opposed higher duties as an obstacle to foreign trade; John Randolph, like most Southerners, vowed that he would not "agree to lay a duty on the cultivator of the soil to encourage exotic manufactures." On the other hand, Calhoun, the South Carolina nationalist, hoped that the manufacturing interest would "at all times, and under every policy . . . be protected with due care." In 1816 a substantial minority in the South shared Calhoun's point of view; within a few years, as conditions and expectations changed, Southern support for the tariff—and for the American System in general—diminished considerably.

**The second Bank of the United States.** Republican leaders, chastened by their fiscal experiences during the war, made their most dramatic surrender to Federalism when they revived both Hamilton's plan and his arguments for a national bank. When the first Bank of the United States perished in 1811, its busi-

180

ness had fallen to the state-chartered banks; within five years the number of those banks had increased from 88 to 246, their issues of bank notes from $28 million to $68 million. Since many state-chartered banks did not maintain adequate specie reserves (gold and silver), their notes often circulated at a discount. The bewildering variety of notes, their fluctuating values, and a rash of counterfeiting brought the country to the edge of fiscal chaos. The final blow came when the state banks, except those in New England, suspended specie payments altogether during the war—and showed no disposition to resume specie payments with the restoration of peace.

Meanwhile, the federal government lacked a safe depository for its funds, a reliable agency to transfer them from place to place, and adequate machinery to market securities when it needed to borrow. The absence of a uniform paper currency was a handicap to businessmen engaged in interstate commerce. Even some of the old Republican agrarians, though they opposed all banks that issued paper currency, favored chartering a new national bank as the lesser of two evils. Madison discarded his constitutional doubts and decided that the question had been settled "by repeated recognitions . . . of the validity of such an institution, in acts of the legislative, executive, and judicial branches of the government, accompanied by . . . a concurrence of the general will of the nation." Changed circumstances, he concluded, required measures "which may be as proper now as they were premature and suspicious when urged by the champions of federalism." Calhoun, taking a thoroughly nationalistic position, attacked the state banks for usurping the federal government's exclusive power to issue and regulate the country's currency. Clay, who had opposed rechartering the first Bank, confessed that he had not anticipated the evils its demise had caused.

In 1816 a bill to grant a twenty-year charter to a second Bank of the United States, with headquarters in Philadelphia, passed both houses of Congress over the opposition of state banking interests, Federalist partisans, and Virginia agrarians. The functions and structure of the second Bank were essentially the same as those of the first, except that its capital was increased from $10 million to $35 million; and, under the power given it to disperse its facilities over the nation as needed, the number of its branches eventually increased from eight to twenty-five. The federal government again held one-fifth of the stock, and the President appointed five of the twenty-five directors. Its liabilities were not to exceed its capital, one-fifth of which had to be in specie; and it was to report annually to the Treasury Department and open its books to that department for periodic inspection.

This powerful banking corporation served a number of useful purposes: it assisted the government in its fiscal business by helping to market federal securities and by providing a depository for federal funds; it regulated the banknote currency (and thus the credit policies) of the state banks; and it encouraged business enterprise by providing a sound paper currency in national-bank notes and by making available short-term credits, principally to merchants. But as the largest capitalistic institution in the country, exercising immense power over the supply of money and credit, depending as it did upon the government for special favors, it was essential that the Bank be responsibly directed and that its operations be subjected to adequate federal control. In the absence of such control, it was bound to find itself in political trouble, for it would then loom as a threat to democracy and an instrument of economic tyranny. Indeed, even under the best of circumstances, the Bank, because of its size and strength, was always a tempting political target.

***Internal improvements.*** The War of 1812, by disrupting coastal shipping, had demonstrated the inadequacy of the country's internal transportation system for both interstate commerce and national defense. The Northwest, where high transportation costs still deprived many farmers of outside markets and tied them to an economy of pioneer self-sufficiency, was the most persistent solicitor of federal funds for internal improvements. New England, suffering a loss of population and a decline of political strength, was the center of opposition. President Madison, stretching his constitutional scruples to support projects that were national in scope, approved appropriations for the continued building of the National Road, which had been started during Jefferson's Administration. But he doubted that Congress had the power to subsidize local roads and canals without an appropriate amendment to the Constitution. In 1817 Congress ignored his doubts and passed a bill to distribute among the states for local internal improvements a $1,500,000 bonus that the Bank of the United States had paid the government for its charter. For Madison this was going too far, and in one of his last presidential acts he vetoed the so-called Bonus Bill. Calhoun, disgusted with this narrow view of federal power, grumbled that the Constitution "was not intended as a thesis for the logician to exercise his ingenuity on . . . it ought to be construed with plain good sense." But Madison's veto stalled this crucial phase of the American System. Local internal improvements remained, for the time being, the responsibility of the individual states, communities, and private enterprise.

*Along the National Road*

**The Era of Good Feelings.** Nearing the end of his second term, Madison supported another Virginian, his Secretary of State, James Monroe, to succeed him to the Presidency. The Randolph Republicans preferred William H. Crawford of Georgia, and some Northern Republicans fretted about the long domination of their party by the "Virginia Dynasty." But Madison had his way, and Monroe won an easy victory over his Federalist opponent, Rufus King of New York. Four years later, with the Federalists too feeble even to run a candidate, Monroe was reelected without opposition.* After a few more years of activity in scattered localities, the Federalist party ceased to exist. The party's war record, the failure of its older leaders to adjust to new conditions, its narrow particularism, and the Republican pirating of its program all contributed to its death. Thus the eighteenth-century ideal of a republic without political "factions" seemed to have been achieved at last. "Surely our government may go on and prosper without the existence of parties," wrote Monroe, who shared Jefferson's views of both the Federalists and the party system. "I have always considered their existence the curse of the country." In his first inaugural address, Monroe told his countrymen that they could rejoice when they reflected "how close our Government has approached to perfection; that in respect to it we have no essential improvement to make."

*One elector from New Hampshire voted for John Quincy Adams.

James Monroe, a representative of the small-planter class of the Virginia piedmont, reached the Presidency at the age of sixty-one after many years of devoted, though not brilliant, public service. Once the favorite of John Randolph and other Virginia state righters, Monroe continued to interpret the Constitution more narrowly than the nationalists in his party. He accepted the tariff and the banking legislation passed during Madison's last year in office as well as the use of federal funds for internal improvements national in scope, but while he was President the American System made only limited progress. Though Monroe was less talented than his distinguished predecessors, his contemporaries found something solid and reassuring in this member of the Revolutionary generation. In Monroe, with his wig, his cocked hat, and his knee-length pantaloons, the postwar generation had a last nostalgic look at the eighteenth century.

The year of Monroe's inauguration, 1817, found the country in a complaisant mood. On a good-will tour that ultimately carried him into once-hostile New England, the new President saw everywhere abundant signs of national unity. His warm reception in Boston caused the *Columbian Centinel*, a Federalist paper, to speak of an "Era of Good Feelings," thus giving a popular label to Monroe's Administrations. Political factionalism was at a low ebb, and there was relative harmony among the sections. Above all, as Monroe observed in his first message to Congress, the country was in a "prosperous and happy condition. . . . The abundant fruits of the earth have filled it with plenty." However, the "Era of Good Feelings" lasted only about two years—until the middle of Monroe's first Administration—when political strife and sectional bitterness suddenly revived, and the national prosperity came to an abrupt and shocking end.

# John Marshall and the Supreme Court

**Marshall's role.** In these postwar years still another Virginian played a key role in the shaping of public policy and in the molding of the American political structure. This was John Marshall, Chief Justice of the United States from 1801 to 1835, who gave the judicial branch of the government the prestige it had previously lacked and who, unlike most of his fellow Virginians, supported a relatively broad interpretation of federal power. Born in 1755, Marshall saw military service during the Revolution and then went home to become one of the most successful lawyers before the Richmond bar. In 1792 Jefferson, already suspicious of Marshall's politics, suggested to Madison that Marshall ought to be appointed a judge to keep him out of mischief. As it turned out, Jefferson understood his man—Marshall became a Federalist—but he could scarcely have been more mistaken about how to render him harmless. After a term in Congress and brief service as John Adams' Secretary of State, Marshall received his appointment as Chief Justice shortly before the last Federalist President left office. The Supreme Court, at least, would remain in Federalist hands!

In personal appearance and social intercourse Marshall impressed one as a plain, homespun democrat, for he was the most unpretentious of men, an amiable lover of sports and other simple pleasures. But underneath he was a resolute Federalist, suspicious of popular government and contemptuous of what he considered Jefferson's sentimental trust in the people. Marshall was in no sense a scholar or philosopher of the law; he lacked the patience for intensive study and the imagination for metaphysical speculation. But he had a keen intelligence and a tough mind that readily discovered the logic of a case and swiftly drove to its core. According to Joseph Story, whom Madison made an Associate Justice in 1811, Marshall "examines the intricacies of a subject with calm and persevering circumspection and unravels its mysteries with irresistible acuteness." His personal magnetism and intellectual powers gave him enormous influence over his colleagues on the bench, including those appointed by Republicans. Marshall's domination of the Court is evident from the fact that during his thirty-four years as Chief Justice he wrote almost half the decisions and dissented from the majority opinion only eight times. Caring little for precedents, avoiding legal jargon, using crisp prose and careful reasoning, Marshall delivered a series of the most momentous decisions in American judicial history.

**Judicial review.** Soon after assuming his new office, Marshall found an opportunity to pronounce a vigorous and, in the long run, decisive opinion on a matter of prime importance to a federal system based on a written constitution. While the Federalists were in power there had been a persistent but inconclusive debate over who was to decide when Congress had exceeded its delegated powers or encroached upon the rights of the states. Since the Constitution is not explicit on this point, the answer had to be found by inference rather than from the plain language of the document. Probably the majority of delegates to the Constitutional Convention had expected the Supreme Court to pass on the constitutionality of the acts of Congress, and Hamilton, in one of the articles in *The Federalist*, had upheld the principle of judicial review. Jeffersonian Republicans, however, were later to argue that the federal government was the agent of the sovereign states and that those who had created it must define its powers. The individual states, said Jefferson in the Kentucky Resolutions of 1798, would decide when the Constitution had been violated, as well as "the mode and measure of redress."

That is where things stood when, in 1803, Marshall wrote the Court's decision in the case of *Marbury* v. *Madison*. Intrinsically of minor importance, this case related to a section of the Judiciary Act of 1789, which, according to Marshall, expanded the Court's original jurisdiction beyond what the Constitution intended it to be. "The question whether an act repugnant to the constitution can become the law of the land, is a question deeply interesting to the United States," Marshall asserted. His answer to the question was clear: The wording of the Constitution establishes the principle "that a law repugnant to the constitution is void; and that courts, as well as other departments, are bound by that instrument." Moreover, "It is emphatically the province and duty of the judicial department to say what the law is. Those who apply the rule to particular cases must of necessity expound and interpret that rule."

*Marbury* v. *Madison* thus established a precedent for the Supreme Court to determine the constitutionality of congressional legislation and to act as the final authority on the meaning of the Constitution. This doctrine of judicial review has been challenged many

### John Marshall's liberal construction of the Constitution

*[The Constitution] contains an enumeration of powers expressly granted by the people to their government. It has been said that these powers ought to be construed strictly. But why ought they to be so construed? Is there one sentence in the constitution which gives countenance to this rule? In the last of the enumerated powers, that which grants, expressly, the means for carrying all others into execution, congress is authorized "to make all laws which shall be necessary and proper" for the purpose.... What do gentlemen mean by a strict construction? If they contend only against that enlarged construction which would extend words beyond their natural and obvious import, we ... should not controvert the principle. If they contend for that narrow construction which, in support of some theory not to be found in the constitution, would deny to the government those powers which the words of the grant, as usually understood, import, and which are consistent with the general views and objects of the instrument; for that narrow construction, which would cripple the government, and render it unequal to the objects for which it is declared to be instituted, and to which the powers given, as fairly understood, render it competent; then we cannot perceive the propriety of this strict construction, nor adopt it as the rule by which the constitution is to be expounded.*

**From Gibbons v. Ogden, 9 Wheat. 1, 1824.**

times, but it has weathered all the storms and survives to this day. Having established the precedent, Marshall and his colleagues never again disallowed an act of Congress—more than a half-century passed before the Supreme Court exercised this power again. But the Marshall Court sometimes applied the positive side of judicial review—that is, it reviewed and *approved* congressional legislation as constitutional.

**National supremacy.** As a nationalist Marshall was inclined to give the powers of Congress a broad interpretation and to assert the federal government's supremacy in the exercise of its constitutional authority. For example, in two important cases, *Martin v. Hunter's Lessee* (1816) and *Cohens v. Virginia* (1821), the Marshall Court affirmed its right to review and reverse decisions of state courts when they concerned issues arising under the federal Constitution. On thirteen occasions it voided state laws as violations of "the supreme law of the land." One of the most significant of these cases, *Gibbons v. Ogden* (1824), involved a New York law giving a steamboat company a monopoly of the business of carrying passengers on the Hudson River to New York City. In rejecting the law Marshall gave the term "commerce" an extremely broad definition and came close to saying that the power of Congress over interstate commerce is absolute. This power, he ruled, "is complete in itself, may be exercised to its utmost extent, and acknowledges no limitations other than are prescribed in the constitution."

The Chief Justice expounded the nationalist doc-

trine most fully in the case of *McCulloch v. Maryland* (1819), which tested the constitutionality of the second Bank of the United States. Conceding that the Constitution does not explicitly grant Congress authority to charter a bank, Marshall insisted that Congress must have some discretion in exercising the powers it does possess. Surely the authority could be implied from the "necessary and proper" clause. Then Marshall made a classic statement of the doctrine of "loose construction": "Let the end be legitimate, let it be within the scope of the Constitution, and all means which are appropriate, which are plainly adapted to that end, which are not prohibited, but consist with the letter and spirit of the constitution, are constitutional." After this decision the nationalist advocates of the American System had no reason to anticipate any judicial obstacles to the development of their program.

**Sanctity of contracts.** As a conservative defender of property rights and a believer in laissez faire, Marshall also sought to make the federal courts a sanctuary of the propertied classes whenever they were harassed by unfriendly state legislatures. He sympathized with creditors and entrepreneurs who considered contracts sacred and inviolable, and he admired the clause in the Constitution that prohibited states from "impairing the obligation of contracts." In the case of *Fletcher v. Peck* (1810), Marshall gave evidence of the extremes to which he would go to defend this principle. As we have seen (p. 163), the Georgia legislature, in 1795, had granted a large tract of Western land to the Yazoo Land Companies. The following year a new legislature, discovering bribery and fraud, repudiated the grant and thus provoked litigation that ultimately reached the Supreme Court. To Marshall the case was perfectly clear: the grant of land was a binding contract, and the circumstances under which it was negotiated did not concern the Court. The withdrawal of the grant, therefore, was an unconstitutional violation of the obligation of contract.

Another case, *Dartmouth College* v. *Woodward* (1819), enabled the Marshall Court to make an equally extreme application of the contract clause. The case originated in an attempt of the New Hampshire legislature to revise Dartmouth's charter, which dated back to colonial days, and to transform the college into a state institution. The trustees went to court and employed Daniel Webster, a Dartmouth alumnus, to represent them. Webster's sentimental plea in behalf of his alma mater brought tears to the eyes of the unsentimental Chief Justice, who ruled that a charter was a contract and could not be violated. Thereafter, to escape this restriction, the states usually wrote reserve clauses into corporation charters permitting subsequent amendment of the charters' terms.

Some old-line Republicans believed that Marshall's decisions had dealt "a deadly blow to the sovereignty of the states." Judge Spencer Roane of Virginia sent angry dissenting opinions to the newspapers, and John Taylor waged a pamphlet war against the Supreme Court. To Jefferson the federal justices were a "corps of sappers and miners" steadily undercutting the powers of the states. "The Constitution," he wrote, "is a mere thing of wax in the hands

of the judiciary, which they may twist and shape into any form they please." Yet, except for Marshall's interpretation of the contract clause (which later courts have modified), there was little in these decisions that the dominant element in the postwar Republican party really cared to criticize. Giving his blessing to the nationalistic trend of Republican legislation, Marshall used the Constitution as a flexible instrument adaptable to conditions that the Founding Fathers could never have anticipated. If judicial review was a usurpation, no majority in Congress ever agreed on any alternative to it. As for Marshall's defense of property rights, the Republicans could hardly have been called enemies of property.

## The Monroe Doctrine

***Revolutions in Latin America.*** One of the most striking expressions of postwar American nationalism was in the field of foreign policy. While Spain was preoccupied with France during the Napoleonic wars, her South and Central American colonies had had a pleasant taste of freedom from her strict political and commercial control. Their appetite whetted, the colonies revolted and soon expelled the Portuguese from Brazil and the Spanish from all their American possessions save Cuba and Puerto Rico. When, in 1820, revolutions broke out in Spain and Portugal, all hope of recovering the lost colonies perished—unless other European powers could be induced to intervene.

185

To the people of the United States this was 1776 all over again. Henry Clay, a warm admirer of the Latin American patriots, rejoiced at "the glorious spectacle of eighteen millions of people, struggling to burst their chains and to be free." When a modest commerce developed with South America, Clay, optimistic about its further expansion, incorporated Pan-American trade into his American System. Both justice and self-interest, thought Clay, required quick recognition of the revolutionary governments.

After 1815 the State Department had pursued a policy of neutrality that recognized the revolutionists as belligerents and permitted them to purchase supplies in the United States; but a Neutrality Act of 1818 prohibited American citizens from serving in the rebel armies. Impatient with Secretary of State Adams' coolness toward the rebel cause, Clay introduced a resolution in the House giving the *de facto* governments of Latin America immediate recognition. The resolution alarmed Monroe and Adams, who feared that it would end the negotiations then in progress for the purchase of Florida or even lead to war. After the President and Secretary of State exerted their influence against the Clay resolution, the House finally voted it down. Recognition came in 1822, after the Florida negotiations had been completed and after the new governments in South America had shown themselves capable of maintaining their independence. To Clay this recognition was disgracefully late, but the United States was still the first nation to grant it.

**The fear of foreign intervention.** Granting recognition at that time was in fact a bold step. Thus far the British had refrained from establishing diplomatic relations with Latin America and had even indicated a willingness to see Spain reestablish its authority there. Moreover, the reactionary governments of Russia, Prussia, Austria, and France had formed an alliance pledged not only to preserve the status quo and to suppress liberalism but to intervene in the internal affairs of any country that threatened the peace and security of Europe. Under this mandate Austria had invaded Italy and France had invaded Spain to liquidate revolutionary movements for which many Americans felt a deep sympathy. Perhaps the alliance would now apply its policy to the New World and assist Spain in the reconquest of its colonies. France, it was rumored, had an eye on Cuba as a reward for intervening in Spain; and Russia seemed intent on spreading its influence southward from Alaska along the Pacific coast. Actually there was not much danger that any European power would intervene in Latin America without British support, and, when Adams warned Russia that the Western Hemisphere was closed to further colonization, the two countries soon negotiated a satisfactory agreement. Nevertheless, the time seemed appropriate for formulating some kind of policy that would cover all contingencies.

By 1823 Great Britain, too, was ready to take a stronger stand. Its liberals resented the reactionary schemes of the continental alliance, and its merchants and manufacturers were determined to maintain the profitable markets they had established in Latin America. Accordingly, the British foreign minister, George Canning, approached the American minister in London, Richard Rush, with a proposal that their governments make a joint statement of policy. Canning told Rush that his government was now convinced that Spain could not recover its colonies and that recognition of their independence was only a matter of time. Great Britain had no designs on any of them, nor would it permit any portion of them to be transferred to another power. If the American government shared these feelings, Canning asked, "why should we hesitate mutually to confide them to each other; and to declare them in the face of the world?"

In October 1823 President Monroe had the British proposal before him and turned to the Republican elder statesmen for advice. Jefferson and Madison both supported his own inclination to accept it. An exception to the policy of nonentanglement in European politics was justified in order, as Jefferson explained, to bring British power into the scale of free government and to "emancipate a continent at one stroke." Oddly enough, it was a statesman from New England, the traditional center of pro-British sentiment, who objected most strenuously to accepting British leadership in the Western Hemisphere. Secretary of State Adams opposed any agreement by which the United States would, in effect, commit itself not to annex additional territory. With an eye on Texas and Cuba, Adams argued that "we should at least keep ourselves free to act as emergencies may arise." Moreover, he disliked a joint statement that would make the United States appear "to come in as a cockboat in the wake of the British man-of-war." After long discussion in the Cabinet, Adams noted with satisfaction that his position "was acquiesced in on all sides." The President, it was agreed, would make a statement of *American* policy emphasizing the separateness of the Old World and the New.

**The American response.** Monroe incorporated his famous doctrine rather unsystematically in his annual message to Congress on December 2, 1823, a message that dealt with many other topics as well. With some rearranging, the relevant passages run substantially as follows: First, wherever American sympathies may lie, it does not comport with American policy to intervene in the "internal concerns" of European powers, or in their wars when they involve matters only "relating to themselves." Second, the United States will

*Nationalism and economic expansion*

not interfere with "existing colonies or dependencies" in the Western Hemisphere. Third, with the Latin American governments "whose independence we have . . . acknowledged, we could not view any interposition for the purpose of oppressing them, or controlling in any other manner their destiny, by any European power in any other light than as the manifestation of an unfriendly disposition toward the United States." Fourth, "the American continents, by the free and independent condition which they have assumed and maintain, are henceforth not to be considered as subjects for future colonization by any European powers." Finally, Monroe warned the autocrats of Europe that "we should consider any attempt on their part to extend their [political] system to any portion of this hemisphere as dangerous to our peace and safety." In brief, the essence of this nationalistic pronouncement was the concept of two worlds, each of which was to refrain from intervening in the internal affairs of the other.

Monroe and Adams, of course, were responsible for the precise phrasing of these principles, but they owed much to earlier Presidents and Secretaries of State. They had brought together the elements of an American foreign policy that had been gradually evolving since the Revolution. To European diplomats, the promulgation of a policy that the young republic lacked the power to enforce was a piece of presumptuous impertinence. Canning, who knew that British diplomacy and the British navy had been decisive in preventing continental powers from meddling in America, was particularly annoyed. He was aware that Monroe's unilateral statement could be invoked against Great Britain as well as against other nations. Yet, though the response of the American people was overwhelmingly favorable, within a few years the President's dramatic message had been nearly forgotten. A generation later it would be rediscovered and identified as the Monroe Doctrine; and for many years thereafter it would be accepted as the authoritative and almost definitive statement of American foreign policy.

# The westward movement

These displays of nationalism in domestic politics and foreign policy reflected the underlying optimism of the American people—their confidence in the destiny a kind Providence had planned for them. To be sure, their nationalistic creed also embraced an awareness of their past: they had their nostalgic and sentimental side; they gloried in their traditions each Fourth of July; and they were deeply stirred when a Webster waxed eloquent upon the Constitution and the Founding Fathers. But most Americans would have agreed with Jefferson's affirmation that he liked "the dreams of the future better than the history of the past," for there existed among them a widespread feeling of emancipation from history. According to one editor, "Our national birth was the beginning of a new history . . . which separates us from the past and connects us with the future only." America was still primarily a promise: as Ralph Waldo Emerson rejoiced, it was "a country of beginnings, of projects, of designs, of expectations."

The general confidence and optimism of the American people were rooted both in a popular belief that the potentialities of men and women are unlimited when they are free to develop them and in the practical social and economic realities of nineteenth-century America. One of the most important of these realities was the virgin land—the seemingly unlimited space and inexhaustible resources that promised a life of greater dignity and abundance than Europe's common people had ever dreamed of. The West—the untapped wealth of the great interior stretching from the Appalachians to the Rockies—helped to give the future its rosy hue; and the West became one of the central interests of the American people in the decades after the Treaty of Ghent.

***Advance of the agricultural frontier.*** The story of the westward movement of population is, in the main, the story of the expansion of American agriculture—of the development of new areas for the raising of livestock and the cultivation of wheat, corn, tobacco, and cotton. After 1815 improved transportation enabled more and more Western farmers to escape a self-sufficient way of life and enter a national market economy. Farmers involved in this kind of commercial agriculture specialized in a "money crop"—one produced chiefly for sale in nearby and distant markets—and used the proceeds to buy consumer goods manufactured in the Northeast or in Europe. During periods when commodity prices were high, the rate of westward migration, the sale of public lands, and eventually the supply of Western staples increased spectacularly.

"Old America seems to be breaking up and moving westward," observed an English visitor in 1817, during the first great wave of postwar migration. After falling off for a few years during the depression following the Panic of 1819 (see p. 201), the number of emigrants increased again and reached a peak in the 1830s. Whereas in 1810 only a seventh of the American people lived west of the Appalachians, by 1840 more than a third lived there. On the next page is a table showing population growth in the new Western states between 1810 and 1840:

|          | 1810    | 1840      |
|----------|---------|-----------|
| Ohio (1803) | 230,760 | 1,519,467 |
| Louisiana (1812) | 76,556 | 352,411 |
| Indiana (1816) | 24,520 | 685,866 |
| Mississippi (1817) | 40,352 | 375,651 |
| Illinois (1818) | 12,282 | 476,183 |
| Alabama (1819) |  | 590,756 |
| Missouri (1821) | 20,845 | 383,702 |
| Arkansas (1836) | 1,062 | 97,574 |
| Michigan (1837) | 4,762 | 212,267 |

Some of the people who settled the great Mississippi Valley were recent immigrants from Europe, but most of them came from the older states, whose agricultural populations were also growing rapidly. Kentuckians and Tennesseeans moved to the new cotton lands of the Southwest or crossed the Ohio River into the Northwest; migrants from New England and the Middle Atlantic states generally settled in the Great Lakes region; and people from the South Atlantic states (the largest group of all) invaded not only the Southwest but southern Ohio, Indiana, and Illinois as well. By and large those who moved west came from the lower middle classes and traveled with their few worldly possessions loaded on wagons or flatboats—or even on pack horses or pushcarts.

**Factors encouraging migration.** Why were these hundreds of thousands of settlers—most of them farmers, some of them artisans—drawn away from the cleared fields and established cities and villages of the East? Apart from the fact that the West happened to be an inviting land of opportunity, certain characteristics of American society help to explain this remarkable migration. The European ancestors of the American people had lived century after century rooted to the same village or the same piece of land until some religious or political or economic crisis uprooted them and drove them across the Atlantic. Many of those who experienced this sharp and devastating break thereafter lacked the ties that had bound them and their ancestors to a single place. Moreover, in the relatively stratified European society men usually inherited the occupations and social status of their fathers, but in American society there was a less rigid class structure. Men changed occupations easily and believed that it was not only possible but almost a moral duty to improve their social and economic position. As a result, Americans were, as many European visitors observed, an inveterately restless, rootless, and ambitious people.

The Frenchman Alexis de Tocqueville, who published a remarkably penetrating study of American society after a tour in the early 1830s, observed these traits:

> In the United States, a man builds a house in which to spend his old age, and he sells it before the roof is on . . . he brings a field into tillage and leaves other men to gather the crops . . . he settles in a place, which he soon afterwards leaves to carry his changeable longings elsewhere . . . the tie that unites one generation to another is relaxed or broken . . . every man there loses all trace of the ideas of his forefathers or takes no heed of them.

The reasons for this "strange unrest," Tocqueville believed, were, first, the American "taste for physical gratifications"; second, a social condition "in which neither laws nor customs retain any person in his place"; and, third, a pervasive belief that "all professions are open to all, and a man's own energies may place him at the top of any one of them." These social traits helped to produce the nomadic and daring frontiersmen who kept pushing westward beyond the

*Westering on a flatboat*

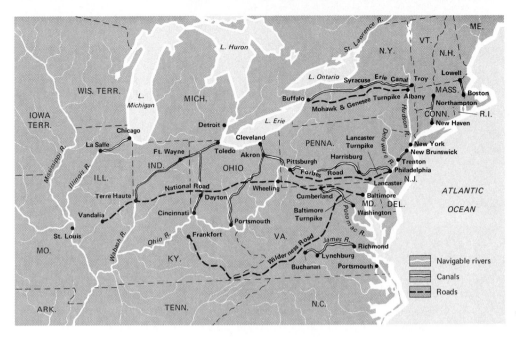

Transportation to the West, about 1840

Navigable rivers
Canals
Roads

fringes of settlement, as well as the less adventurous immigrants who followed them across the mountains in search of new homes, material success, and a better life for themselves and their children.

The West had plenty of attractions for a people conditioned to appreciate them. The alluvial river bottoms, the fecund soils of the rolling forest lands, and the black loams of the prairies were tempting to New England farmers working their rocky, sterile acres and to Southeastern farmers plagued with soil depletion and erosion. The Indian menace east of the Mississippi was now substantially reduced; after 1815 the helpless tribes made a succession of treaties ceding lands, which the government surveyed and put up for sale. In 1820 a new land law ended the credit system but reduced the minimum tract for individual sales to eighty acres and the minimum price to $1.25.* Now it was possible for a man to buy a farm for $100, and the continued proliferation of state banks made it easier for those without cash to negotiate loans in paper money. Western farmers borrowed with the confident expectation that the expanding economy would keep farm prices high, thus making it easy to repay loans when they fell due.

Transportation was becoming less of a problem for those who wished to move west and for those who had farm surpluses to send to market. Prior to 1815 Western farmers who did not live on navigable waterways were connected to them only by dirt roads and mountain trails. Livestock could be driven across the mountains, and high-value products, such as whiskey and furs, might be carried profitably on pack horses or

by wagon, but the cost of transporting bulky grains in this fashion was several times greater than their value in Eastern markets. Goods could be shipped across the Atlantic for less than the cost of transportation from western New York or western Pennsylvania to cities along the seaboard.

The first step toward an improvement of Western transportation was the construction of graded and planked or macadamized turnpikes. Built by private corporations that charged tolls, most of the turnpikes were designed to connect Eastern cities, but a few served the tramontane West. By the 1820s migrants could follow the Baltimore Turnpike to Cumberland, Maryland, and then the National Road to Wheeling (ultimately, to Vandalia, Illinois); the Lancaster Turnpike and Forbes Road to Pittsburgh; or the Mohawk and Genesee Turnpike to Lake Erie. These roads made possible a reduction in transportation costs and thus stimulated the commercialization of agriculture along their routes.

Two other developments, however, presaged the end of the era of turnpikes and started a transportation revolution that resulted in increased regional specialization and the growth of a national market economy. First came the steamboat. In 1811, four years after Robert Fulton's *Clermont* made its celebrated voyage up the Hudson River, Nicholas J. Roosevelt launched the steam-powered *New Orleans* at Pittsburgh and sent it on a successful voyage down the Ohio and Mississippi. A witness found it an awesome spectacle: "a boat moving without appearance of sail, oar, pole, or any manual labor—moving within the secrets of her own mechanism and propelled by power undiscoverable." Within twenty years some two hundred shallow-draft sternwheelers were plying the

*New lands, however, were first put up at auction, and the best often sold for a good deal more than the minimum price.

*The westward movement*

*Lockport on the Erie Canal, 1836*

construction began in 1817 and was completed in 1825. After the Erie Canal went into operation, the cost per mile of transporting a ton of freight between Buffalo and New York City declined from nearly 20 cents to less than 1 cent. Until the 1840s the canal was used primarily by the shippers of farm products and lumber from western New York, but eventually the Western states diverted much of their produce from the rivers to this shorter route to Eastern markets.

The Erie Canal's immediate success (tolls enabled the state to recover the cost within seven years) launched the country into the Canal Age. New York's rivals, such as Philadelphia and Baltimore, strove to tap the West with their own canal systems, but with less success. Ohio and Indiana built canals to connect the Ohio River with the Great Lakes. Between 1815 and 1840 (after which construction declined), various states invested about $125 million in three thousand miles of canals. By the 1830s the country had a complete water route from New York City to New Orleans. By then, however, many were looking to a new marvel, the railroad, for an even more dazzling answer to the West's transportation needs (see p. 291).

In all phases of this transportation revolution government provided a large proportion of the needed funds. State and local governments sometimes helped finance the turnpike companies with land grants or by subscribing to their stocks; the states built most of the important canals; federal and state governments paid for all river and harbor improvements; and in later years federal, state, and local governments aided the Western railroads with various forms of subsidies. Thus even in the years of alleged laissez faire the states had begun to play a more important role in the nation's economic life. In transportation until the 1850s state and local governments were more active than the federal government.

**Life on the frontier.** Only the hope of a better future could make bearable the hardships of a farmer getting his start on the Western frontier. The propaganda literature of the land-speculators abounds in descriptions of the salubrious climate, the health-giving waters, the ease with which one could make the land bloom, and the increasing comforts of civilization. The realities, for some years at least, were quite different. Clearing a piece of land for cultivation—girdling the trees to kill them, cutting the branches and rolling the logs into great piles to burn, grubbing out the stumps, and breaking the root-clogged ground with primitive plows—meant backbreaking labor for pioneer families. Disease and death hung over the Western settlements; trained doctors were scarce, and the only resort was to home remedies or the patent-medicine panaceas of itinerant quacks. Malaria, dysentery, pneumonia, smallpox, yellow fever, cholera,

Western waters, and, although flatboats and keelboats continued to be important until the 1850s, steamboats eventually superseded all other craft in the carrying of passengers and freight. Steamboats were not only faster but transported upriver freight for about one-tenth of what it previously had cost on hand-propelled keelboats.

Next came the Erie Canal, an enormous project in its day, spanning the three hundred fifty miles between Buffalo on Lake Erie and Albany on the Hudson River. With the support of Governor De Witt Clinton and funds from the New York legislature,

*Nationalism and economic expansion*

and dietary deficiencies took a heavy toll; travelers often commented on the pale and sickly appearance of Westerners. Living in primitive lean-tos or floorless cabins, surviving on a diet mainly of corn and salt pork, making their own clothing from homespun and deerskin, enduring the almost unmitigated bleakness of frontier life, these pioneers would have been hard put to discover the Arcadian quality that some romanticists see in their isolated, self-sufficient agrarian society. A prospective migrant to Illinois warned his family: "What awaits you in this region, which, as of now, is not much better than a wilderness, is a life full of hardships, want and toil. By this choice we shall close ourselves off from the rest of the world for many years."

But the settlers looked beyond the ordeal of these early years, and eventually better times did come. Life softened for them as schools and churches were built, as neighbors became less remote, as transportation improved and Eastern manufactured goods became cheaper and more plentiful, and as the growing villages and county seats acquired printing presses and newspapers, developed small local industries, and offered social diversions to the surrounding countryfolk. These cultural amenities, the modest comforts earned from operating a family-size farm, and the feeling of independence derived from landownership, were the ultimate rewards of many who made their homes in the Western wilderness.

For many others, however, this was not enough. The more ambitious Westerners, if they came to farm, thought of agriculture as a business enterprise and of themselves as small capitalists producing for the market. Moreover, to those who invaded the West in search of wealth, farming was only one way—and perhaps the slowest—to gain their end. Along with the yeomen came the frontier boomers, the speculators in real estate to whom land was simply a commodity to be bought and sold for a profit. Indeed, many of the yeomen themselves were as much interested in land speculation as in agriculture. The largest profits in the West were not always earned by industrious and thrifty farmers; they were often won by shrewd operators who knew how to exploit the vagaries of federal land policy or to buy favors at the local land offices. A long chapter in the history of the West belongs to the land companies—one of the earliest forms of large-scale American business enterprise—whose agents spied out the best tracts, bought them at public auction, and then sold them at higher prices to authentic settlers.

Other Westerners engaged in the fascinating business of promoting towns at strategic trading sites. Many of these wilderness metropolises never materialized, and often the giddy purchasers of unseen town plots wound up with a "business block" knee-deep in swamp water. But important urban centers, such as Cincinnati, Cleveland, Detroit, Indianapolis, St. Louis, and Chicago, did grow with amazing speed. To them came not only promoters and speculators but men with capital to invest in banking, commerce, and manufacturing. Surprisingly early these cities became the centers of Western political and economic power, and of Western culture when it pushed out its first tender shoots.

**The significance of the frontier.**  What impact did the New West make on American society? Not much in the way of political innovation, for state and local government in the West was for the most part modeled after the East. Apparently the forces generating the trend toward increased political democracy in these years were as much Eastern as they were Western. Socially and culturally the West was dependent on the East and again showed a greater tendency to copy than to innovate. This was natural enough, for those who moved west were less often critical of the fundamental structure of Eastern society than dissatisfied with their position in it.

But the impact of the New West was not insignificant. Because of its lack of local traditions, its interior position, and its need for military protection and improved transportation, the West was usually the most nationalistic section of the country. Certainly the problems that settlers faced on a raw frontier encouraged them to develop to a high degree such qualities as individualism and resourcefulness. By stripping Eastern and European civilization down to its fundamentals, Westerners exposed some of its shams and discarded some of its superficialities. Though the West did not produce a society of social and economic equals, it did give emphasis to the notion that all artificial barriers to advancement must be removed—that all must have an equal chance to make their way in the world. Moreover, Westerners showed great respect for the man who, starting with little, achieved success in the competitive struggle.

Above all, the New West was America's treasure house of unused land and untapped resources. It was a major, though not exclusive, factor in producing the economic expansion and rising standard of living from which most white Americans profited more or less. When the historian Frederick Jackson Turner, near the end of the nineteenth century, called his colleagues' attention to the significance of the frontier in American history, he doubtless claimed too much, as recent critics have shown. But there is some truth in his assertion that "this expansion westward with its new opportunities" accounted for the "fluidity of American life." These Western wilds, Turner wrote, "constituted the richest free gift that was ever spread out before civilized man."

*The westward movement*

*Turner's Rebellion*

Nat has survived all his followers, and the gallows will speedily close his career. His own account of the conspiracy ... reads an awful, and it is hoped, a useful lesson, as to the operations of a mind like his, endeavoring to grapple with things beyond his reach.... [The conspiracy] was not instigated by motives of revenge or sudden anger, but the result of long deliberation, and a settled purpose of mind....

... It has been said he was ignorant and cowardly ... [but] for natural intelligence and quickness of apprehension, [he] is surpassed by few men I have ever seen.... He is a complete fanatic, or plays his part most admirably. On other subjects he possesses an uncommon share of intelligence, with a mind capable of attaining any thing; but warped and perverted by the influence of early impressions.... I shall not attempt to describe the effect of his narrative, as told and commented on by himself, in the condemned hole of the prison. The calm, deliberate composure with which he spoke of his late deeds and intentions, the expression of his fiend-like face when excited by enthusiasm, still bearing the blood of helpless innocence about him; clothed with rags and covered with chains; yet daring to raise his manacled hands to heaven, with a spirit soaring above the attributes of man; I looked on him and my blood curdled in my veins.

**From Thomas R. Gray, *The Confessions of Nat Turner*, 1831.**

## Slavery and the Cotton Kingdom

***Southern expansion.*** The migration into Alabama, Mississippi, and Louisiana was, as we have seen, a part of the westward movement; and the great majority of the early settlers were pioneer farmers, mostly from Virginia and the Carolinas, who endured the same hardships and cherished the same ambitions as those who settled north of the Ohio River. They engaged in subsistence farming or grazing to begin with, and many of them never managed to produce more than occasional small surpluses for the market. But enterprising farmers in the Southwest knew that cotton-planters in the South Carolina and Georgia piedmonts had been making fortunes ever since Eli Whitney, in 1793, invented a gin that efficiently separated seeds from the lint of "upland," or short-staple, cotton. Before Whitney solved this technological problem, most of the cotton used in European textile mills had come from Brazil, Egypt, and Asia. Southerners had grown small amounts of high-quality "sea-island" cotton on the coast of South Carolina and Georgia, but this variety could not be grown inland. In 1793 the

South produced only about ten thousand bales of cotton; but by the 1820s, with the Cotton Kingdom spreading westward and responding to a rapidly growing demand in Europe, the South's annual production rose to a half-million bales.

Since cotton prices before 1825 seldom fell below 15 cents a pound and sometimes rose much higher, those who obtained suitable land soon devoted at least part of their time to cotton cultivation, usually with the labor of Negro slaves. A fortunate few—some beginning as small farmers, others bringing slaves with them from the Southeast—established large plantations on the rich, silt-loamed prairies of the Alabama-Mississippi Black Belt, or on the alluvial bottom lands of the Mississippi and Yazoo delta. These great cotton-planters, together with the rice-planters of coastal South Carolina and Georgia and the sugar-planters of Louisiana, developed agriculture to the highest levels of efficiency, complexity, and commercialization to be found anywhere in America before the Civil War.

After 1815 the economy of the South was tied to the cultivation of cotton, for investments in new cotton lands and slaves brought higher returns than any of the possible alternatives. Indeed, during the next few decades cotton was a crucial factor in the whole developing national market economy and in the economic growth of all regions. It accounted for more than half the country's exports and thus paid for a large part of its imports. The cotton plantations provided a substantial market for manufactured goods from the Northeast, and the marketing of Southern cotton gave the Northeastern commercial interests a highly profitable trade.

Soon after the War of 1812 the booming Gulf states were ceasing to be part of the New West and were becoming increasingly identified with the Old South, even though they differed socially from Virginia and the Carolinas in many significant ways. Their identification with the South Atlantic states came at a time when Southerners were becoming more, rather than less, conscious of their special sectional problems and interests.

***The survival of slavery.*** What was it that gave the Old South its special identity? Not physical isolation, for it lacked natural barriers separating it from the rest of the country; nor geographic and climatic uniformity, for it had great diversity of soils, topography, mean temperatures, growing seasons, and average rainfalls. Not a difference in population origins, for the South, like the North, was originally settled by middle- and lower-class people; nor contrasts in religion or political philosophy, for here, too, the similarities outweighed the differences. Not even the economies of North and South were altogether dissimilar, for, although there were important differences, the majority of the white people of both sections were independent yeomen farmers who worked their own lands. In contrast to the Western farmers, however, few Southern farmers benefited from improved transportation and became part of the national market economy. Wealth was less evenly distributed in the South than in the West; less money was invested in education; and the rate of illiteracy was higher. Fewer towns and less local industry developed. In short, the Old South remained more rural and economically less diversified than the North, and a larger proportion of its small farmers lived a life of pioneer self-sufficiency and isolation.

But these differences between North and South were of secondary importance. By far the most significant difference was the presence and survival in the South of Negro slavery, which Southerners themselves called their "peculiar institution." More than anything else, it was slavery, with all its ramifications, that eventually gave the Old South its identity and white Southerners their feeling of separateness from the rest of the Union.

In the eighteenth century, of course, Southern slavery had not been a peculiar institution, for it existed in the Northern colonies and throughout the Western Hemisphere. During or soon after the Revolution, however, the Northern states abolished it, and in the first half of the nineteenth century slaves gained their freedom in most of Central and South America. Some Southerners of Washington's and Jefferson's generation, moved by anxieties about social dangers as well as by the ideals of the American Revolution, were cautiously and rather abstractly critical of slavery. As late as the 1820s a scattering of emancipation societies in the Upper South, supported mostly by Quakers, carried on a discreet campaign for gradual emancipation and the colonization of free blacks outside the boundaries of the United States.

In Virginia, in the late eighteenth and early nineteenth centuries, a prolonged agricultural depression resulting from low tobacco prices and soil depletion led some to believe, or hope, that slavery would soon die. In August 1831, Southampton County, Virginia, was the scene of the South's bloodiest slave insurrection, led by a bondsman named Nat Turner, in which sixty whites and scores of blacks lost their lives. (Turner himself was captured, brought to trial, and executed.) The Turner rebellion, which caused profound alarm throughout the South, precipitated an earnest debate in the Virginia legislature the following January, during which various legislators denounced slavery as a social canker and an economic blight. The antislavery legislators, showing clearly that their concern was not for blacks but for the safety and welfare of whites, demanded a program of gradual emancipation and colonization. But the Virginia emancipationists, like those in other states of the Upper South, were defeated; and soon after 1832 Southern critics were either silenced or driven into exile.

Southern slavery, then, did not die of natural causes; it did not even decline. Instead, with the rise of the Cotton Kingdom and the eventual improvement of agriculture in the seaboard states, it flourished and seemed to have the vitality to survive indefinitely. Since the federal Constitution recognized slavery as a local institution within the jurisdiction of individual states, Southerners saw nothing to prevent them from introducing it into the Southwest. Some moved there with their slaves, while others stayed behind and operated new plantations as absentee owners. Still others took advantage of high slave prices resulting from the labor shortage in the Southwest and sold a portion of their slaves to professional traders who took them to the busy markets in New Orleans and Natchez. There at the slave auctions the self-made men of the Cotton Kingdom, some of whom had started with no slaves at all, purchased "prime field hands" to work their growing estates.

Negro slaves thus became an important element in the migration to the Southwest and played a major role in clearing the land for cultivation. By 1840 almost half the population of Alabama and Louisiana and more than half the population of Mississippi (by then the leading cotton-producing state) consisted of Negro slaves. Yet at all times nearly three-fourths of the white families in the South as a whole held no slaves and depended on their own labor alone. Moreover, the great majority of slaveholders owned just a few slaves; as late as 1860 only ten thousand Southern families belonged to the planter aristocracy operating large estates with slave gangs numbering more than fifty.

Why did Southern slavery survive far into the nineteenth century? Not because Negroes were innately suited to be slaves; nor because white labor could not adjust to the Southern climate and successfully cultivate the Southern crops; nor because the Negroes' health was not adversely affected by living in the malarial swamps, where the sugar and rice plantations and many of the cotton plantations were located. The reasons the South clung so tenaciously to slavery are to be found in the fears, ambitions, and aspirations of white Southerners.

By the nineteenth century the South's peculiar institution was two hundred years old, and to abolish it would have brought painful changes in long-established habits and attitudes. Those who would destroy slavery, warned a Georgian, "would have to wade knee-deep in blood"; indeed, slavery is "so intimately . . . mingled with our social conditions that it would be impossible to eradicate it." Most white Southerners—indeed, most white Americans—believed that blacks were by nature shiftless, untrustworthy, and sexually promiscuous. Slavery, therefore, was a means of controlling an inferior race, of preventing it from becoming a burden on society, and of maintaining the purity and supremacy of the white race. To nonslaveholders slavery symbolized their link with the privileged caste of free whites and the blacks' social and legal subordination. "Now suppose they was free," explained a poor Southern farmer to a Northern visitor, "you see they'd all think themselves as good as we." To the master class the possession of slaves brought great prestige, for in the South the ownership of a plantation worked by slave labor was the sign of success and high social position.

But, above all, slavery survived because it was a viable and profitable labor system representing an enormous investment of Southern capital. Slavery, of course, did not make every master a rich man, nor did every master strive to wring the last ounce of profit from his toiling bondsmen. Nevertheless, in the long run most slaveholders earned good returns on their investments—and this accounts for the generally heavy demand for slaves and for their high price in the market. The system, moreover, was highly adaptable. Slaves were employed not only in agriculture and as domestics but as skilled artisans, as laborers in construction gangs, and as workers in mines, iron foundries, textile mills, and tobacco factories. In short, the master class had no compelling economic reason for wanting to abolish slavery; as late as 1860 it was still a vigorous and remunerative economic institution.

***The nature of slavery.*** In governing their bondsmen most masters were neither inordinately cruel nor remarkably indulgent; they simply dealt with their human property in the manner they deemed necessary to make the system work. They bought and sold slaves, used them as security for loans, and divided them among heirs. In these transactions husbands were often separated from their wives and children from their mothers, for state laws gave slave marriages no legal protection. Except for the deliberate killing or maiming of a slave, the master's power to administer physical punishment was virtually unlimited, and planters could delegate this power to white overseers employed to manage their estates. Most slaveholders used the whip for "moderate correction" only when they believed it essential to maintain discipline; but an element of cruelty was inseparable from slavery, as even many of its defenders recognized. Some slaves fell into the hands of brutal masters, or of men who were corrupted by the power the institution conferred upon them. Since blacks were unable to give testimony against whites, the justice they received in court was, at best, very eccentric.

The standard of living of most slaves was near the subsistence level. They lived on a diet mainly of corn and pork (seasonally supplemented with other foods), adequate in bulk but often unbalanced and monotonous; they wore coarse, skimpy clothing made from some variety of cheap "Negro cloth"; and they lived in cabins that were too often drafty, cramped, and scantily furnished. Their labor routine kept them at work from dawn to dusk. By nineteenth-century standards, they were not often worked excessively, but a long day of hard toil was usually exacted from them. The slaves were most in danger of being overworked to the detriment of their health on the large cotton and sugar plantations of absentee owners managed by overseers, and on the estates of ambitious new planters "on the make."

One cannot pretend to know all that being a slave meant to the Negroes, for slaves were seldom able to express their feelings and most of the evidence comes from white sources. There is no reason to assume that they accepted slavery as their natural lot and cheerfully submitted to their white masters. No doubt they made certain psychological adaptations to their condition; no doubt they enjoyed the occasional holidays

*Nationalism and economic expansion*

**An escaped slave's observations on slave music**

and simple pleasures that most masters permitted them; no doubt their untrained intellects seldom dwelt on freedom as a philosophical abstraction. But to conclude from this that they had no idea of the meaning of freedom, no comprehension of its practical advantages, no desire to obtain it, would be quite unwarranted. The evidence of their submission and obeisance suggests not so much contentment as the superior power of the white caste and the effectiveness of its elaborate techniques of control. Moreover, there is some direct and much circumstantial evidence indicating that most plantation slaves consciously played the role of a docile, cheerful Sambo as a protective device in their relationships with whites. Consequently, slaveholders often knew less about the true character of their slaves than they thought. "The most general defect in the character of the Negro," complained one planter, "is hypocrisy . . . and if the master treats him as a fool, he will be sure to act the fool's part." The swift and ruthless suppression of Nat Turner's followers drove home to the slaves the futility of organized rebellion. But it did not deter some of the bolder ones from less spectacular forms of protest. Of these protests, running away was one of the most common—and certainly the most irksome to the master class.

White Southerners paid a high price for slavery: artisans and yeoman farmers suffered from the competition of cheap slave labor; most slaveholders were more or less distressed by the obvious paradox of slavery in a republic whose moral commitment was to individual freedom and natural rights; and all were bedeviled by a nagging fear of slave rebellions, a fear that occasionally reached the proportions of mass hysteria. But the blacks, not the whites, were the chief victims of the system. Slavery exposed them not only to its cruelties and meager rewards but to its strong dehumanizing tendencies and its powerful pressures toward emasculated personalities. It destroyed most of the rich and varied cultural tradition that Negroes had brought with them from Africa and for long left them, in many respects, a culturally rootless people; it made the slave family unstable and exposed black women to the lust of white men; and it encouraged irresponsible behavior and put a premium on docility. Above all, slavery deprived its victims of the opportunity to develop their potentialities and of the freedom that white Americans treasured so much.

Yet, in spite of the damage done to them, South-

**$150 REWARD**

RANAWAY from the subscriber, on the night of the 2d instant, a negro man, who calls himself *Henry May*, about 22 years old, 5 feet 6 or 8 inches high, ordinary color, rather chunky built, bushy head, and has it divided mostly on one side, and keeps it very nicely combed; has been raised in the house, and is a first rate dining-room servant, and was in a tavern in Louisville for 18 months. I expect he is now in Louisville trying to make his escape to a free state, (in all probability to Cincinnati, Ohio.) Perhaps he may try to get employment on a steamboat. He is a good cook, and is handy in any capacity as a house servant. Had on when he left, a dark cassinett coatee, and dark striped cassinett pantaloons, new—he had other clothing. I will give $50 reward if taken in Louisvill; 100 dollars if taken one hundred miles from Louisville in this State, and 150 dollars if taken out of this State, and delivered to me, or secured in any jail so that I can get him again. WILLIAM BURKE.

*Bardstown, Ky., September 3d, 1838.*

ern slaves found ways to maintain a degree of psychic balance and to avoid total dehumanization and infantilization. Though slave marriages had no legal support and slave fathers could not be the authority figures traditional in nineteenth-century families, slaves nevertheless customarily lived in family groups. In the plantation slave quarters they were not under the constant scrutiny of their masters; and there, in their relationships with each other, they could play roles other than Sambo and develop a community life of their own. They found opportunities for self-expression in their religious services, in their music and folklore, and in other social activities. In later years these experiences of slave community life, which blended a modified white culture with fragments of African cultural survivals, would provide the ingredients from which a semiautonomous Afro-American subculture would grow.

### Missouri and the issue of slavery expansion.

Eventually the South's peculiar institution was to have a tragic impact upon the whole nation—indeed, a few intimations of the ultimate tragedy were evident even in the early years. Slavery was a topic of debate at the Constitutional Convention of 1787, and its future under the new Constitution was a subject of inquiry at Southern ratifying conventions. The compromise by which Southerners obtained congressional representation for three-fifths of their slaves (see p. 126) provoked repeated complaints, especially from New England. Antislavery Northerners frequently resisted enforcement of the Fugitive Slave Act of 1793, which enabled Southern masters to recover runaways in the free states. In the Deep South some doubted the wisdom of the federal law closing the African slave trade, and, as we have seen, the law was not very effectively enforced.

But these were minor irritants compared to the succession of national political crises generated by the steady march of slavery into the Southwest. Before 1820 five additional slave states (Kentucky, Tennessee, Louisiana, Mississippi, and Alabama) had been admitted to the Union; these increased the total number to eleven, which, as it happened, were balanced by eleven free states. The resulting political equilibrium in the Senate was threatened, however, when the territory of Missouri, settled mostly by proslavery Kentuckians and Tennesseeans, petitioned for admission as a slave state. In February 1819, a House committee reported an act authorizing Missouri to frame a state constitution; but Representative James Tallmadge, Jr., a Republican from New York, proposed an amendment to prohibit the introduction of additional slaves into Missouri and to provide gradual emancipation for those already there. The Tallmadge Amendment passed the House on a sectional vote but was defeated in the Senate. When neither chamber would yield, slavery's critics and defenders plunged into an ill-tempered debate that revealed a deep sectional cleavage.

Much of the Missouri debate revolved around constitutional issues. Southerners, especially Virginians, insisting that new states had the same sovereign rights as the old, denied that Congress could make the abolition of slavery a condition of admission. Northerners claimed that the Founding Fathers had thought of slavery as a temporary institution and had not intended that it should spread into the Western territories. In the heat of the debate angry Southerners accused Federalists of deliberately fomenting a crisis in order to win popular support in the North and revive their dying party. Jefferson, who strongly opposed the Tallmadge Amendment, was convinced that the Federalist leader Rufus King was "ready to risk the Union for any chance of restoring his party to power and wriggling himself to the head of it." Northern opposition to slavery expansion, wrote Charles Pinckney of South Carolina, "sprang from the love of power, and the never ceasing wish to regain the honors and offices of the government."

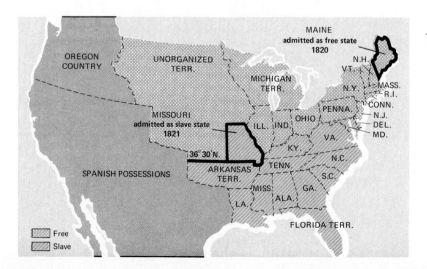

The Missouri Compromise, 1820

No doubt political advantage and sectional power—the North already had a substantial majority in the House—were basic ingredients of the Missouri controversy. But the crisis might have looked less portentous had this been all there was to it. Tallmadge himself appeared to have no crass political motive; rather, he seems to have acted from a conviction that slavery was a moral evil that should not be permitted to spread. So did many others whose humanitarian impulses were aroused by the obvious vitality of Southern slavery. In urging his colleagues to prevent its further spread, Representative Arthur Livermore, of New Hampshire, stressed the importance of the decision they were about to make:

> An opportunity is now presented, if not to diminish, at least to prevent the growth of a sin which sits heavy on the soul of every one of us. By embracing this opportunity, we may retrieve the national character and, in some degree, our own. But if we suffer it to pass unimproved, let us at least be consistent, and declare that our Constitution was made to impose slavery, and not to establish liberty.

Never before had the peculiar institution been so severely attacked—and so vigorously defended—on moral grounds as it was during the Missouri debate.

The basic issue was not resolved on this occasion; it was simply postponed by a compromise that passed largely through Henry Clay's efforts. In 1820 Congress finally agreed to admit Missouri as a slave state, but it preserved the balance by admitting Maine as a free state. It divided the remaining territory acquired in the Louisiana Purchase along the line 36°30′ north latitude. North of that line, except for Missouri, slavery was "forever prohibited."

The Missouri crisis made some Americans apprehensive about the future of the federal Union. John Quincy Adams foresaw the possibility of a realignment of political parties along sectional lines, hastening the "emancipation of all . . . [Southern] slaves, threatening in its immediate effect that Southern domination which has swayed the Union for the last twenty years." Tallmadge, said a Georgia congressman, had "kindled a fire which all the waters of the ocean can not put out, which seas of blood can only extinguish." And Jefferson, showing hardly a glimmer of his earlier antislavery sentiments, poured his indignation on Northerners for opening this sensitive issue. "All, I fear, do not see the speck on our horizon which is to burst on us as a tornado, sooner or later. The line of division lately marked out between different portions of our confederacy is such as will never, I fear, be obliterated." Writing thus in 1821, Jefferson had, in effect, formulated the doctrine of an "irrepressible conflict" between North and South.

Even in an era of nationalism and expansion, then, slavery disturbed the politics and threatened the survival of the young republic. And in the South the conflict between slavery, which Southerners would not abolish, and the American liberal tradition, which they claimed as their birthright, created tensions that were ultimately to become unbearable.

# Another frontier: industry and technology

**Beginnings of the factory system.** The western edge of settlement was not the only frontier that attracted Americans and promised a future of increased abundance. Since the War of 1812 growing numbers had been drawn to the thriving towns and cities of the New England and Middle Atlantic states. Here lived the pioneers of the American Industrial Revolution—the men who devoted their lives to the promotion of business enterprises and to the application of science and technology to the goals of increasing productivity and profits, lightening the burdens of labor, and multiplying the comforts of human life. Their efforts gradually rendered obsolete the system of household manufacturing that had been almost universal in colonial days. Under this system farm families outside the market economy had made their own clothes and household necessities, while village artisans had produced items such as cloth, shoes, hats, and tools for sale to consumers in local markets. The independent artisan survived longer in some crafts than in others, and household manufacturing was always a part of life on the isolated agricultural frontier; but after 1830 both were clearly doomed by the factory and the spreading market economy.

In a sense the Industrial Revolution, in America as in Europe, was merely an acceleration of technological changes that had no clear beginning and as yet have no foreseeable end. It involved the development and increasing use of power-driven machines in industrial production; the location of those machines in factories that tended to grow in size and complexity; and, with the decline of transportation costs, the distribution of their products in ever widening mass markets. As the domestic market expanded, manufacturing enterprises became increasingly specialized. The early textile mills, for example, marketed their own products and constructed their own machinery; but eventually they concentrated on spinning and weaving, selling their products to wholesalers, and buying their machinery from independent machine shops. The essential features of the Industrial Revolu-

197

tion, then, were mechanization, specialization, and a trend from local to regional and national distribution.

American industrial technology was in part copied from Europe, especially England, and was in part an outgrowth of the genius of American inventors, skilled mechanics, and entrepreneurs. Manufacturers found an impelling incentive for mechanization in the relative scarcity and high cost of domestic labor. The dearness of labor was the direct result of the high productivity of American agriculture, which forced industry to pay wages comparable to what could be earned on the land. Another incentive was the presence of cheap waterpower to which machinery could easily be harnessed. Moreover, the optimistic American entrepreneurs, anticipating continued technological advances, usually built cheaper machines that wore out quickly, thus making it relatively inexpensive to retool. Nowhere in Europe did environmental conditions provide so many inducements for mechanical innovation; nowhere was there a society so free from the sort of hampering traditions that impede technological change. "Everything new is quickly introduced here," wrote a European visitor in the 1820s. "There is no clinging to old ways; the moment an American hears the word 'invention' he pricks up his ears."

The Northeastern states, for a variety of reasons, were the first to industrialize to a significant degree. In the years before the embargo and War of 1812, their profitable foreign trade had enabled them to accumulate the necessary capital and to build the banks and other commercial facilities that were now useful to industry. Their substantial urban centers provided large local markets, coastal waterways opened regional markets, and turnpikes gave them early access to the hinterland. In addition, the Northeast had superior entrepreneurial talent, a relatively abundant and well-educated labor supply, easy access to Southern cotton, and rich resources in the waterpower of New England and the iron and coal of Pennsylvania. In the years after 1815 manufacturing gradually superseded commerce as this region's primary economic concern.

What the pioneers in technology accomplished lacks the romance and drama of the Western frontiersman's elemental struggle for survival. Yet their work was equally vital to national growth and expansion, and its long-run social and economic consequences were much greater. In the field of transportation, for example, the builders of turnpikes experimented with various kinds of road-surfacing and with truss-type and suspension bridges; engineers on the Erie Canal designed new excavating equipment and developed a special cement for use in its eighty-eight locks; and Henry M. Shreve, among others, built flat-hulled steamboats of shallow draft especially adapted to service on the Western rivers. Meanwhile,

a patent act adopted by Congress in 1790 (revised in 1793) encouraged numerous men to pursue fame and fortune through the improvement or invention of devices useful to humanity. As Hamilton claimed in his Report on Manufactures, there did seem to exist "in the genius of the people of this country, a peculiar aptitude for mechanical improvements."

The factory system in the United States had its beginnings during the Presidency of Washington. In 1790 Samuel Slater, an English immigrant who knew the secrets of English textile machinery, built a cotton-spinning mill at Pawtucket, Rhode Island, for the merchant Moses Brown. This first successful American factory contained seventy-two spindles tended by nine children, and its machinery was soon harnessed to waterpower. After years of slow and faltering growth, Jefferson's embargo and the War of 1812 gave the American cotton-textile industry a chance to become a significant part of the national economy. By the end of the war cotton factories were counted in the hundreds, most of them in New England, and the number of spindles in operation approximated 130,000. Immediately after the war many of these mills failed because of renewed British competition; but others survived, and by 1840 the number of spindles in operation exceeded 2 million.

In the years of expansion constant improvements were made in the machinery for carding the raw cotton and for spinning it into yarn and thread. But the weaving long continued to be done in the homes of small craftsmen, who sold the cloth in their own shops or who worked for wages for merchant capitalists. After 1814, however, the introduction of the power loom soon brought weaving as well as spinning into the factory. Many American mills specialized in the manufacture of a coarse white cloth called "sheeting," which was in wide demand and could be mass produced. American manufacturers of sheeting could compete successfully with the British in the domestic market, and by the 1830s they were even selling in foreign markets.

From cotton textiles the factory spread to other industries. In 1793, at Byfield, Massachusetts, John and Arthur Schofield, who came to the United States from Yorkshire, England, built the first factory to manufacture woolens. War in Europe, a series of improvements in carding, napping, and shearing machines, and the introduction of waterpower soon placed the American woolens industry on a secure foundation. Meanwhile, merchant capitalists were taking the manufacture of shoes out of the cobblers' shops and into the homes of semiskilled workers who specialized in making a single part of the finished product. By mid-century, when the shoe industry was being mechanized, the workers were brought into factories where their role changed from that of crafts-

*Nationalism and economic expansion*

men to that of tenders of machines. Similarly, in the iron industry Pennsylvania's furnaces and rolling mills were fast supplanting small local forges.

In 1804 Oliver Evans of Philadelphia, one of the most remarkable pioneers of American technology, developed a high-pressure steam engine that was adaptable to a great variety of industrial purposes. Within a few years it was being used not only in steam navigation but to run sawmills, flour mills, and printing presses—and, in 1828, steam power replaced waterpower at the Slater cotton mills. Earlier, Evans had experimented with the techniques of mass production and built the first completely mechanized flour mill. Eli Whitney and Simeon North, a Connecticut clockmaker, applied those techniques to the manufacture of guns and developed the system of interchangeable parts. Whitney taught his workers to make identical parts from metal molds, or "gigs"; after the perfection of this system, guns could be assembled in a fraction of the time required by a skilled gunsmith. North then introduced his system in the clock industry, and Connecticut manufacturers were soon mass-producing inexpensive clocks for a national market.

To build a factory equipped with expensive machinery run by steam or waterpower required more capital than the average individual entrepreneur or even partnership could obtain. While these older forms of business organization predominated as late as the 1850s, the ultimate answer to this financial problem was the corporation. Chartered under state laws, corporations could accumulate capital from numerous small investors; and the stockholders enjoyed "limited liability"—that is, they were financially responsible for the corporation's debts only in proportion to their share of ownership. Used first by bankers and the builders of turnpikes, bridges, and other internal improvements, the corporate form slowly spread to manufacturing, especially textiles, after the War of 1812. In 1813 a group of wealthy merchants known as the Boston Associates, including Francis Cabot Lowell, Nathan Appleton, and Patrick Tracy Jackson, formed the Boston Manufacturing Company in Waltham, Massachusetts. With capital exceeding a half-million dollars and with an efficient managerial staff, these men built the first integrated textile factory that performed every operation from the carding of raw cotton to the weaving of cloth with power looms. A decade later the Boston Associates shifted the center of their activies to Lowell, "the Manchester of America," where they chartered the Merrimack Manufacturing Company. During the 1820s and 1830s they chartered additional companies in Massachusetts and New Hampshire, until, by the 1850s, they and their imitators had made the manufacturing corporation an entrenched economic institution.

Power loom weaving

In other areas, too, the American economy began to show the effects of advancing technology. Eastern merchants used improved transportation and marketing techniques to compete for the trade of the hinterland, with New York merchants rapidly outstripping their rivals. The New York group siphoned much of the Western trade through the Great Lakes and the Erie Canal and captured a large share of the cotton trade between the South and Europe. The skill of Yankee shipbuilders and the initiative of New York merchants combined to improve transatlantic service for passengers and cargo. The New York packet lines, beginning with the Black Ball Line in 1818, were the first to post sailing dates and observe them, whether or not a full cargo was on board. The sleek vessels in this service were built for speed and maximum cargo; they were, said an English reporter, "probably the finest and fastest sailing vessels in the world . . . beautifully modeled and of the best workmanship." The whaling industry, concentrated at New Bedford and Nantucket Island, Massachusetts, was also more highly organized after the War of 1812 than before, because the depletion of the Atlantic supply necessitated long, expensive voyages to the Pacific. Still another sign of the new era was John Jacob Astor's American Fur Company, a million-dollar corporation chartered in New York in 1808. Until the 1830s, when the fur supply of the Northwest began to near exhaustion, Astor used efficient organization and ruthless methods to destroy his weaker competitors and lay the foundation for the first great American fortune. Eventually he transferred his capital from the fur trade to real estate operations in New York City.

As mechanical devices played an increasingly important part in the lives of the American people, the study of applied science began to invade the precincts of American education. A network of mechan-

199

ics' institutes, beginning with one in Boston in 1795, spread through American cities to train men in the mechanical arts. When President Madison, like his predecessors, urged the founding of a national university, he stressed its potential value as a "temple of science" to diffuse "useful knowledge." Nothing came of this, but several private colleges soon added applied science to their curricula. At Harvard, in 1814, Dr. Jacob Bigelow began to lecture on "The Elements of Technology" and tried to awaken his students to the possibilities of this exciting frontier. At Yale, Benjamin Silliman brought a similar message not only to his students but to a wider audience through his *American Journal of Science*, founded in 1818, and through his enormously popular public lectures. In 1825 Rensselaer Polytechnic Institute, the first of its genre, opened its doors at Troy, New York, "for the purpose of instructing persons who may choose to apply themselves in the application of science to the common purposes of life."

If newspapers and periodicals accurately reflected public opinion, the American people were proud of their technological achievements and fascinated by the many useful products of applied science. The promise of a rising standard of living encouraged them to rationalize agriculture, to build great internal improvements, to mechanize industry, and to widen commercial horizons. Looking back at the half-century of economic growth following independence, Tocqueville concluded that "no people in the world had made such rapid progress in trade and manufactures as the Americans; they constitute at the present day the second maritime nation in the world"; their manufacturing makes "great and daily advances"; "the greatest undertakings and speculations are executed without difficulty. . . . The Americans arrived but as yesterday on the territory which they inhabit, and they have already changed the whole order of nature for their own advantage."

***Capital and labor.*** Yet, while they found the promises of the Industrial Revolution irresistible, many Americans were at the same time a little uneasy about what had been happening to their society since industry got a foothold. Carrying with them into the new age the assumptions of a simple agrarian society, they watched apprehensively the growth of cities, the "paper-money speculations" of urban businessmen, and the movement of young people from the land to the factory. They wondered whether the American tradition was somehow being betrayed, whether the craving for material success was undermining their morals and compromising their virtue. To be sure, those fears were still rather vague and sporadic, for in the 1820s and 1830s the cities and the factories were not very large, and the urban industrial population

was a small fraction of the whole. But the trend was clear.

One consequence of the factories and machines was the gradual emergence of two new social classes. The first were the industrial capitalists, whom the agrarian gentry regarded as vulgarly ambitious and dangerously powerful. With their wealth they gained considerable political power and, as James Fenimore Cooper complained, substituted their "fluctuating expedients for the high principles of natural justice." Industrialists operated in mysterious ways, some through corporations, those cold, impersonal institutions "having neither a body to be kicked nor a soul to be damned." The second new social class were the factory workers, the hirelings who tended machines for a weekly wage and, in the larger establishments, had no personal contact with either owners or ultimate consumers. They were recruited from the farms and, increasingly by the 1830s, from among newly arrived immigrants.

Thanks to a chronic labor shortage, workingmen's living conditions were, on the average, better in America than in Europe. Visitors to Lowell often commented on the attention that the Boston Associates gave to the welfare of the young women who worked in their mills. The "Lowell girls" lived in comfortable boardinghouses built by the company; their morals were strictly supervised; and they were provided with recreational facilities, educational opportunities, and religious instruction. They published their own monthly magazine, the *Lowell Offering*, "as a repository of original articles, written by females employed in the mills." After a visit to Lowell, Charles Dickens reported that he had seen "no face that bore an unhealthy or an unhappy look." According to Anthony Trollope, Lowell was "the realization of a commercial utopia," where the women were "taken in, as it were, to a philanthropical manufacturing college."

But industrial paternalism soon declined in the Lowell mills as professional managers fought competitors by cutting costs and making increased use of immigrant labor. Even in the 1830s the working day at Lowell was thirteen hours in summer and from sunrise to sunset in winter. Another visitor had a less happy report about conditions among the women employees: "The great mass wear out their health, spirits, and morals without becoming one whit better off than when they commenced labor." Children under sixteen, who constituted two-fifths of the labor force in New England textile mills, worked twelve or more hours a day. Real wages declined; in 1830 it was estimated that some twenty thousand of the lowest-paid women in Eastern cities worked sixteen hours a day for $1.25 a week. The callousness of the factory system in a laissez-faire economy began to be reflected, too, in the crowded dwellings of drab factory towns.

Such conditions ultimately produced disturbing social fissures and a greater awareness of class interests and class identity than had been the case before the rise of industry. When workingmen tried to improve their status through united action, severe tensions developed in the relations between labor and capital. In the 1790s carpenters, printers, and cordwainers had begun to organize in several cities; in the early nineteenth century other skilled trades followed their example. The next step was the formation of city federations of craft unions, six of which united, in 1834, to form the short-lived National Trades' Union. Strikes for higher wages usually failed, first, because labor organizations were still weak and inexperienced and, second, because state courts usually treated them as criminal conspiracies under common law.* Turning briefly to political action in the 1820s, workingmen's parties, especially in New York and Philadelphia, agitated for free public education, shorter working hours, and other social reforms to aid the laboring class. Distressed by such novel phenomena as trade unions and workingmen's parties, some conservatives might well have recalled Jefferson's pessimistic predictions about the evil consequences of industrialization.

**Economic crisis.** The Panic of 1819 introduced the United States to still another hazard of a commercial-industrial economy: the depression phase of the modern business cycle. When Americans first began to experience the rhythmic rotation of booms, panics, and depressions, they were so mystified that many of them turned to the supernatural for an explanation. An angry deity, they said, periodically brought hard times to punish men and women for their moral delinquencies—extravagance, speculation, and greed. This first modern panic followed several years of postwar prosperity. In the boom years, when cotton sold for more than 30 cents a pound and wheat for $2 a bushel, land speculation financed by the state banks became a national disease. Soon the Bank of the United States caught the spirit of the times; rather than acting as a stabilizing force, it extended credit generously to speculators and business-promoters in both the East and the West. Public land sales rose sharply; and between 1814 and 1819, under the impetus of high prices, cotton production doubled.

*The common law, introduced to America from England in colonial days, consists of a body of judicial decisions based on custom and precedent. It became the basis of the legal system in all the states except Louisiana. In the early nineteenth century, state courts repeatedly used common-law precedents to find guilty of criminal conspiracies the combinations of workmen attempting to force employers to bargain with them over wages and working conditions.

At length an accumulation of adverse economic forces brought these flush times to a sudden end. First came a decline in the European demand for American agricultural products, especially wheat, flour, and cotton, then a shrinking of the market for textiles. Early in 1819 the Bank of the United States, now under new and more conservative management, began to call in its loans and to exert pressure on the state banks to redeem their notes with specie. The Bank's attempt to save itself from its own recent follies was the immediate cause of a financial panic that forced many state banks to close their doors. In the subsequent depression prices fell disastrously—in 1823, because of the decline in foreign demand, cotton sold for less than 10 cents a pound—and public land sales nearly ceased. Thousands of farmers and planters saw their lands sold at public auction to satisfy the claims of creditors; numerous speculators and business-promoters forfeited property to the Bank of the United States for failing to repay their loans. In the Eastern cities a half-million workers lost their jobs when factories, offices, and shops closed down or curtailed their operations.

Those suffering from economic distress turned to government for relief. Manufacturers demanded higher tariff protection, and after a long battle Congress came to their aid with the Tariff of 1824. To help Western farmers who had bought public land on credit, Congress permitted them to delay payments or to keep as much of the land as they had paid for. Several Southern and Western states passed "stay laws" postponing the time when creditors could foreclose on the property of debtors. The demand for "stay laws" and other measures of debtor relief became bitter issues in the politics of various states, especially Kentucky and Tennessee.

By the mid-twenties prosperity had returned, but not before the panic and depression had created angry feelings that were reflected in national politics. Many accused the Bank of the United States of coldly sacrificing thousands of innocent victims to protect the interests of its stockholders. Thereafter much of the anxiety about the new economic order was focused on the monopolistic Bank, the most powerful of the "soulless" corporations. Senator Thomas Hart Benton of Missouri pictured the Bank as a ruthless "money power" to which the Western cities were enslaved: "They may be devoured by it at any moment. They are in the jaws of the monster! A lump of butter in the mouth of a dog! One gulp, one swallow, and all is gone!"

The ground had been prepared for the growth of the Jacksonian movement, which, in a strange way, benefited from both the acquisitive impulses that the new order had aroused in the American people and the lingering doubts they felt about its results.

## Suggestions for reading

### POSTWAR NATIONALISM

George Dangerfield has written two superb books on the period from the War of 1812 to the election of Andrew Jackson as President: *The Era of Good Feelings** (1952) and *The Awakening of American Nationalism, 1815–1828** (1965). P. C. Nagel, *One Nation Indivisible: The Union in American Thought, 1776–1861* (1964), is a study of the intellectual roots of American nationalism. An excellent study of the postwar decline of the Federalists is Shaw Livermore, Jr., *The Twilight of Federalism* (1962). The period may also be studied through several good biographies of Republican leaders: Harry Ammon, *James Monroe: The Quest for National Identity* (1971); C. M. Wiltse, *John C. Calhoun: Nationalist, 1782–1828* (1944); G. G. Van Deusen, *The Life of Henry Clay** (1937); and Clement Eaton, *Henry Clay and the Art of American Politics** (1957). Bray Hammond, *Banks and Politics in America from the Revolution to the Civil War** (1957), provides a sympathetic account of the chartering of the second Bank of the United States and its role in the American economy.

The role of the Supreme Court in the Marshall era is treated fully in A. J. Beveridge's distinguished biography of the great Chief Justice, *The Life of John Marshall*, 4 vols. (1916–19). Leonard Baker, *John Marshall: A Life in Law* (1974), is a warmly sympathetic modern biography. Valuable special studies include C. G. Haines, *The Role of the Supreme Court in American Government and Politics, 1789–1835* (1944); D. O. Dewey, *Marshall Versus Jefferson: The Political Background of Marbury v. Madison** (1970); and R. E. Ellis, *The Jeffersonian Crisis: Courts and Politics in the Young Republic** (1971). R. K. Faulkner, *The Jurisprudence of John Marshall* (1968), provides a comprehensive analysis of Marshall's thought. A. M. Bickel, *Justice Joseph Story and the Rise of the Supreme Court* (1971), is a satisfactory biography of one of Marshall's most brilliant contemporaries. Story's thought is analyzed in James McClellan, *Joseph Story and the American Constitution: A Study in Political and Legal Thought* (1971).

Several excellent monographs on the Monroe Doctrine are available: Dexter Perkins, *The Monroe Doctrine*, Vol. 1; *1823–1826* (1927); E. H. Tatum, Jr., *The United States and Europe, 1815–1823* (1936); C. C. Griffin, *The United States and the Disruption of the Spanish Empire* (1937); and A. P. Whitaker, *The United States and the Independence of Latin America, 1800–1830** (1941). Two fine biographies should also be consulted: J. H. Powell, *Richard Rush: Republican Diplomat, 1780–1859* (1942), and S. F. Bemis, *John Quincy Adams and the Foundations of American Foreign Policy** (1949). Frank Thistlethwaite, *The Anglo-American Connection in the Early Nineteenth Century** (1959), describes the economic and intellectual ties of the United States and Great Britain.

### THE WESTWARD MOVEMENT

Two good syntheses of the westward movement in this period are Dale Van Every, *The Final Challenge: The American Frontier, 1804–1845* (1964), and F. S. Philbrick, *The Rise of the West, 1754–1830** (1965). The classic statement of the importance of the West to the whole of American society is F. J. Turner, *The Frontier in American History** (1920). R. A. Billington, *America's Frontier Heritage** (1967), is a sympathetic appraisal of the Turner thesis in the light of modern scholarship. The best studies of public land policy in the West are R. M. Robbins, *Our Landed Heritage: The Public Domain** (1942), and M. J. Rohrbough, *The Land Office Business: The Settlement and Administration of American Public Lands, 1789–1837** (1968). P. W. Gates, *The Farmer's Age: Agriculture, 1815–1860** (1960), is a comprehensive study of Southern and Western agricultural development. The importance of urban development in the West, long neglected, is stressed in R. C. Wade, *The Urban Frontier** (1959). R. C. Buley, *The Old Northwest: Pioneer Period, 1815–1840*, 2 vols. (1950), provides an exhaustive study of social conditions in the West.

G. R. Taylor, *The Transportation Revolution, 1815–1860** (1951), a general study, has much detail on efforts to deal with this problem in the West. L. C. Hunter, *Steamboats on the Western Rivers* (1949), is a classic. Other valuable studies are P. D. Jordan, *The National Road* (1948); L. D. Baldwin, *The Keelboat Age on Western Waters* (1941); Carter Goodrich, *Government Promotion of American Canals and Railroads, 1800–1890* (1960); Carter Goodrich, *et al.*, *Canals and American Economic Develop-*

---

*Available in a paperback edition.

# CHAPTER 9

# Politics for the Common Man

ment (1961); R. E. Shaw, *Erie Water West: A History of the Erie Canal, 1792–1854* (1966); a
Scheiber, *Ohio Canal Era: A Case Study of Government and the Economy, 1820–1861* (19

## THE OLD SOUTH AND SLAVERY

The best surveys of the Old South are Clement Eaton, *A History of the Old South* (3rd ed., 197
Monroe Billington, *The American South** (1971). Clement Eaton, *The Growth of Southern Civil
(1961), is a perceptive study of the social and cultural life of the Old South. W. R. Taylor, *Cava*
*Yankee: The Old South and American National Character** (1961), is a study of the evolution
Southern legend. U. B. Phillips. *Life and Labor in the Old South** (1929), is a somewhat sentir
description of life on the plantations. F. L. Owsley, *Plain Folk of the Old South** (1949), deals, alm
sentimentally, with the life of the nonslaveholders, whom Phillips almost ignored. E. D. Genovese
*World the Slaveholders Made* (1969), attempts to apply a Marxian class interpretation to the s
structure of the Old South. An indispensable book, based on extensive travels in the South ir
1850s, is F. L. Olmsted, *The Cotton Kingdom* (1861). A new edition of Olmsted, edited by A
Schlesinger, was published in 1953.

Slavery may be studied from several perspectives in U. B. Phillips, *American Negro Slavery** (191
K. M. Stampp, *The Peculiar Institution** (1956); Stanley Elkins, *Slavery** (2nd ed., 1968); J.
Blassingame, *The Slave Community** (1972); E. D. Genovese, *Roll Jordan, Roll** (1974); and L.
Owens, *This Species of Property* (1976). The economics of slavery are sharply debated in R. W. Fog
and S. L. Engerman, *Time on the Cross*, 2 vols. (1974), and P. A. David, *et al, Reckoning with Slaver*
(1976). Among the best books on special aspects of slavery are Frederic Bancroft, *Slave Trading in th
Old South** (1931); R. C. Wade, *Slavery in the Cities** (1964); W. K. Scarborough, *The Oversee*
*Plantation Management in the Old South* (1966); and R. S. Starobin, *Industrial Slavery in the Old
South** (1970). C. N. Degler, *Neither Black Nor White: Slavery and Race Relations in Brazil and th*
*United States** (1971), is an excellent comparative study. D. L. Robinson, *Slavery in the Structure of
American Politics, 1765–1820* (1971), traces the issue through a series of national crises. The best
study of the Missouri Compromise is Glover Moore, *The Missouri Controversy** (1953).

## INDUSTRY AND TECHNOLOGY

V. S. Clark, *History of Manufactures in the United States,* 3 vols. (1928), is a good survey. E. P.
Douglass, *The Coming of Age of American Business* (1971), covers all fields of economic enterprise.
Nathan Rosenberg, *Technology and American Economic Growth** (1972), is an excellent brief synthesis.
Books especially valuable for their interpretations are Roger Burlingame, *The March of the Iron Men*
(1938); T. C. Cochran and William Miller, *The Age of Enterprise** (1942); D. C. North, *The Economi*
*Growth of the United States, 1790–1860** (1961); D. C. North, *Growth and Welfare in the America*
*Past** (1966); Stuart Bruchey, *The Roots of American Economic Growth** (1965); T. C. Cochra
*Business in American Life: A History** (1972); and P. A. David, *Technical Choice, Innovation a*
*Economic Growth** (1975). H. J. Habakkuk, *American and British Technology in the Ninetee*
*Century** (1962), is a penetrating analysis of the relationship between high labor costs and mechar
tion.

Three outstanding studies of the early textile industry are A. H. Cole, *The American Wool Manufa*
2 vols. (1926); C. F. Ware, *The Early New England Cotton Manufacture* (1931); and P. F. McGou
*New England Textiles in the Nineteenth Century: Profits and Investment* (1968). C. W. Pursell, Jr
*Stationary Steam Engines in America: A Study in the Migration of Technology* (1969), stres
importance of steam power in American industry before the Civil War. The beginnings of the
tion can be studied in E. M. Dodd, *American Business Corporations until 1860* (1954). 1
treatments of the early labor movement are in J. R. Commons, *et al.*, Vol. 1 of *History of Lab*
*United States,* 4 vols. (1918–35), and Edward Pessen, *Most Uncommon Jacksonians: Th*
*Leaders of the Early Labor Movement** (1967). The best work available on the Panic of 181
Rothbard, *The Panic of 1819: Reactions and Policies* (1962).

*Available in a paperback edition.

The rapid economic growth and social change that followed the War of 1812 had a profound effect on the nation's political life. During the 1820s the death of the Federalists (see p. 182) and the subsequent fragmentation of the Republicans brought the first American party system to an end. But in the sixteen years between the presidential elections of 1824 and 1840 a new party system took shape—one that differed from the first in many crucial ways, most notably in the willingness of its leaders to abandon the eighteenth-century ideal of social harmony and to accept parties and political conflict as both inevitable and constructive. As vigorous two-party politics developed in all sections of the country—it had never before existed in the South and West—a growing number of voters turned out in national elections, and control of public affairs became less exclusively the business of prudent gentlemen from old and distinguished families. The Democratic party, under the leadership of Andrew Jackson and Martin Van Buren, made skillful and dramatic appeals to the fears and aspirations of the common man; but the National Republicans (replaced by the Whigs in the 1830s), under the leadership of Clay and Webster, also made an effective bid for mass support and became equally adept in the use of the new political tactics. The politics of the Jacksonian era was enlivened by bitterly fought presidential contests—they were the lifeblood of the second American party system—by disputes over who were the friends and who were the enemies of the people, by ill-tempered conflicts between nationalists and state righters, and by a heightened sectionalism. Party battles were waged with intense fervor and with an unprecedented amount of demagoguery and political flimflam, each party predicting that the victory of its rival would bring disaster to the nation. Yet, though the heated rhetoric of political partisans should not be taken at face value, though party leaders were far more pragmatic and less ideological than they sometimes sounded, and though the parties tried to mute divisive national issues, these political wars often did involve important questions of public policy.

## The new democracy

**The celebration of the Common Man.** The Jacksonian era, it was once claimed, marked the "rise of the common man," a concept whose meaning is vague and whose validity is doubtful. It is true that in the 1820s and 1830s some ambitious and energetic young white men (most black men, of course, remained in slavery) found opportunities in their thriving and still relatively fluid society to achieve material success. With economic affluence they or their children would, more than likely, soon gain both political influence and social prestige. This was the road followed by a limited number of men who began with modest means—in effect, they emerged from the ranks of common men and pushed their way into the ranks of the élite, as Jackson himself did.

However, if this is what was meant by the rise of the common man, there was nothing remarkable about the Jacksonian era. For in this sense some common men had been rising ever since the colonial period. We have seen that the people who came to the English colonies seldom carried much in the way of worldly possessions or social prestige; hence, the fact that America, by the end of the eighteenth century, had an upper class of wealthy merchants and landowners indicates that success had already rewarded the enterprise of at least a few. In the years of prosperity and expansion after the War of 1812, other common men flourished and rose by engaging in manufacturing in New England and the Middle Atlantic States, or by speculating in Western lands, or by growing cotton with slave labor in Alabama and Mississippi. And long after the Jackson era had closed a portion of the American élite continued to be recruited from the ranks of common men.

But the great majority of common men, in this era as in those that preceded and followed it, neither grew rich nor rose to high social position. Instead they managed only to make a more or less comfortable living and continued to be common men—small farmers, village mechanics, city laborers. The social mobility of Jackson's America was neither new nor remarkably great—it may even have been less than in earlier years—and the existence of social classes was as evident at the end of the era as at the start. To be sure, a major goal stated by the Jacksonians was to remove obstacles to success and to provide equal opportunities for all to prosper materially. Nevertheless, the striking feature of the period was not social fluidity; it was the emergence of a new party system combined with certain changes in political procedures that broadened the base of American democracy and increased the influence of the common man while he *remained* a common man. More than ever before politicians were obliged to square their goals with the desires and adapt their tactics to the tastes of a mass of ordinary voters. In consequence, the Jacksonian era was notable less for the rise than for the celebration of

Village mechanic: little social mobility

the Common Man—for its rhetorical equalitarianism, which honored the average voter's moral virtue and common-sense wisdom. "Never for a moment believe," said Jackson, "that the great body of the citizens . . . can deliberately intend to do wrong."

**Democratic reforms.** This was not the beginning of American democracy, only its expansion; nor was the expansion initiated by President Jackson, for the trend had been evident long before. The impulse came in part from the newly settled West, where conditions of life encouraged a spirit of equalitarianism; but it also came from the cities of the East, where middle-class reformers, small businessmen, and spokesmen for urban artisans demanded that government be not only *for* the people but *of* and *by* the people as well. Armed with the Declaration of Independence and the doctrine of natural rights, they argued that they were seeking no radical innovations but merely harmonizing political practices with the principles on which the nation was founded. Restrictions on the popular will, insisted one reformer,

"arose from British precedents." Moreover, America was safe for political democracy, because there were no sharp class lines, no mass poverty, and no need for ambitious men to remake society before they could advance in it. Indeed, conservative property-holders could yield, if sometimes grudgingly, to the democratic upsurge and to the new form of mass politics without fearing that they were paving the way to their own destruction.

When, for example, political reformers urged the removal of property restrictions on the suffrage, they invariably stressed the argument that no one would be hurt. A delegate to the New York constitutional convention of 1821 agreed that if manhood suffrage would in fact impair the rights of property "this would be a fatal objection." But this was not the case: "Will not our laws continue the same? Will not the administration of justice continue the same? And if so, how is private property to suffer?" Unlike Europeans, said another delegate, "We have no different estates, having different interests, necessary to be guarded from encroachments. . . . We are all of the same estate—all commoners."

The best-remembered protest against manhood suffrage was that of Chancellor James Kent, a New York Federalist. Though Kent warned of the "tendency in the poor to covet and to share the plunder of the rich," he did not advocate the rule of a small aristocracy of large property-holders. Rather, he accepted the election of the governor and the lower house of the state legislature by manhood suffrage and asked only that the upper house be chosen by owners of freehold estates worth at least $250. In defending his position he sounded more like a Jeffersonian than a champion of a capitalist plutocracy, for he spoke of the "freeholders of moderate possessions" as the "safest guardians of property and the laws." Like Jefferson, Kent feared "the crowds of dependents connected with great manufacturing and commercial establishments, and the motley and undefinable population of crowded ports." In large cities like New York, "one master capitalist with his one hundred apprentices, and journeymen, and agents, and dependents will bear down at the polls an equal number of farmers of small estates who cannot safely unite for their common defense." Another New York conservative professed "great veneration for the opinions of Mr. Jefferson," quoted his view that cities are "ulcers on the body politic," and expressed fear that manhood suffrage "would occasion political demoralization, and ultimately overthrow our government." But these conservatives frightened few and went down to overwhelming defeat.

Indeed, it is remarkable how easily the reformers carried the day—how feeble the resistance of the conservatives proved to be. The constitutions of the

*Politics for the Common Man*

new Western states provided for white manhood suffrage—or at least enfranchised all taxpayers, which was almost the same thing. The Eastern states had originally restricted the suffrage to property-holders, but one by one they gave way, until, in the 1850s, the last of them, Virginia and North Carolina, adopted manhood suffrage. Only in Rhode Island did the movement for reform result in violence—in the so-called Dorr Rebellion—but even there, by 1843, the conservatives had surrendered.

Manhood suffrage alone, however, had only a minor impact on American politics until the mass of qualified voters began to take a personal interest in it. Since the Revolution, a large proportion of the voters had been apathetic; save for an occasional state election, they turned out in limited numbers and seemed willing to accept the leadership of a small political élite. To the mass of village artisans and self-sufficient farmers, both federal and state governments seemed remote, and in an age of laissez faire neither visibly affected their daily lives. Politics was the business of wealthy men who had things at stake and had the experience necessary for the management of public affairs. State governments, therefore, were often controlled by a few great families, who ruled through factional alliances and only occasionally faced the challenge of an aroused electorate.

But when ordinary voters became involved in the money economy as small entrepreneurs, industrial wage-earners, or farmers producing for the market, they developed a greater personal interest in questions of public policy such as the tariff, internal improvements, and banking. The shock of the Panic of 1819 and the depression that followed intensified their political concerns and shook their confidence in the old political leadership. The Virginia Dynasty came to an end in 1825; and the subsequent growth of a second American party system, which began at the state level, soon gave politics an unprecedented vitality. Eventually the new system brought two-party politics to every state, and the close political contests that occurred in most of them caused public interest to increase dramatically. Inexpensive party newspapers appeared in every town to arouse and educate the people; and the new breed of politician, skilled in the art of popular appeal, developed the business of electioneering into a unique cultural phenomenon, second only to religious revivalism in its emotional charge. These new, pragmatic political leaders came less often from the well-established American élite; they viewed politics as a profession and loyalty to party as a supreme virtue. Focusing as they did on efficient organization for the presidential campaigns, the parties were like corporations that made bids every four years for the job of administering the federal government.

It was in this new political environment that attendance at the polls began to rise. When Jackson was elected President in 1828, 56 percent of the adult white males voted, which was more than double the percentage of 1824; and in 1840, 78 percent of them voted. Since no state yet had the secret ballot, ordinary voters were still subject to the influence of powerful neighbors. Nevertheless, an increasing number paid less deference to the gentry and became more independent in exercising their political rights. To be sure, voting behavior in the new party system was significantly affected by religious and ethnic affiliations and by irrational influences such as local traditions, appeals to party loyalty, spectacular electioneering tactics, and pure demagoguery, but local and national issues were seldom irrelevant to the decisions voters made.

Another democratic reform supposedly gave the common man a more direct role in the selection of presidential candidates. From the time of Jefferson, Federalists and Republicans had named their candidates in secret congressional caucuses. This system was used for the last time in 1824; by 1832 "King Caucus" had given way to the national nominating convention, which in theory gave the party rank and file a voice in the nominations. Meanwhile, one state after another transferred the election of presidential electors from the legislature to the voters, and by 1832 only South Carolina adhered to the old system. The states also made an increasing number of state offices elective rather than appointive.

Finally, the idea of a trained—and therefore, presumably, aristocratic—civil service was repudiated so that common men could aspire to state and federal offices as a reward for faithful party service. Party leaders "claim as a matter of right, the advantages of success," said William L. Marcy, a leader of the New York Jacksonians. "They see nothing wrong in the rule, that to the victor belong the spoils of the enemy." In its day the "spoils system" appeared to be another step toward the democratization of American politics. The anti-Jacksonians were critical of this debasing of the civil service, but when they came to power they found the system irresistible and used it with equal enthusiasm.

# John Quincy Adams and National Republicanism

**The election of 1824.** As the end of his second term approached, President Monroe hoped that his successor would be William H. Crawford, his Secretary of the Treasury, a Virginian by birth though a resident of

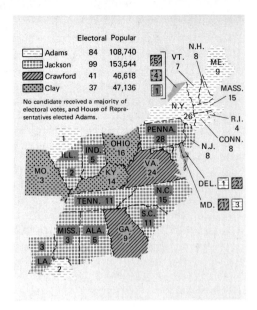

| | Electoral | Popular |
|---|---|---|
| Adams | 84 | 108,740 |
| Jackson | 99 | 153,544 |
| Crawford | 41 | 46,618 |
| Clay | 37 | 47,136 |

No candidate received a majority of electoral votes, and House of Representatives elected Adams.

The election of 1824

Georgia, and a state-rights representative of the planter class. A sparsely attended congressional caucus nominated Crawford as the official Republican candidate. But this time there were other ambitious politicians in the field—all professed Republicans—whose supporters repudiated the caucus system as undemocratic and won endorsements for their candidates from state legislatures and mass meetings. Crawford's competitors included John Quincy Adams, the talented Secretary of State, a nationalist, and the favorite of New England; Henry Clay, Speaker of the House, champion of the American System, and a man of captivating charm; and Andrew Jackson, a military hero with wide popular appeal but, at the time, rather vague political views. With four competing candidates, each attracting somewhat different sections and interests, the Republican party quickly disintegrated as a national political organization.

In the election Jackson won a plurality of the popular vote and ninety-nine electoral votes; he had substantial support everywhere except in New England. Adams' eighty-four electoral votes came chiefly from New York and New England, Crawford's forty-one from the Southeast, and Clay's thirty-seven from the Northwest.* Since none of the four polled a majority in the Electoral College, the choice had to be made by the House of Representatives from among the three leading candidates, with the congressional delegation from each state casting one vote. Clay, who had come in fourth, was thus eliminated from the competition, and a serious illness had put Crawford out of the running. The choice was between Adams and Jackson.

*Calhoun easily won election as Vice President.

Clay, because of his power in the House and his control over the three states he had carried, could swing the election either way. Jackson's friends approached Clay and argued that their man had the stronger claim, because he had polled the largest popular vote; and the Kentucky legislature instructed Clay to support the Hero of New Orleans. But Clay not only feared Jackson as a formidable competitor in Western politics but doubted that he was qualified to be President—doubted, too, that he would support the American System. Adams, meanwhile, was tortured by a conflict between his ambition to be President and his distaste for the political higgling that was required to win the prize. Eventually his ambition triumphed: he made the necessary promises and had an interview with Clay that seemed to satisfy the President-maker and win his support. Adams and Clay were as different as two men could be, and their personal relations had been far from cordial; but Adams was still the logical man for Clay to favor, because he shared Clay's views on public policy. Accordingly, when the House voted on February 9, 1825, Adams, with Clay's backing, won a clear majority on the first ballot (Adams thirteen, Jackson seven, Crawford four).

When President Adams appointed Clay Secretary of State, the disappointed Jacksonians immediately detected a shocking case of political jobbery. Adams, they claimed, had purchased Clay's support by giving him the post from which he could best hope to succeed to the Presidency. It was, said John Randolph, an alliance "of the puritan and the black-leg." The nation's political virtue, wrote an angry Jacksonian editor, had died "of poison administered by the assassin hands of John Quincy Adams, the usurper, and Henry Clay." For the next three years the enemies of the Adams Administration charged that "bargain and corruption" had betrayed the plain will of the people. Though Adams doubtless had reached a political understanding with Clay, he had in fact made no corrupt bargain. But neither man ever successfully refuted the accusation. Jackson resigned his seat in the Senate, the Tennessee legislature again nominated him for the presidency, and the political campaign of 1828 was under way almost as soon as Adams was settled in the White House.

**The Adams Administration.** Adams' term as President was a tragic episode in an otherwise brilliant public career, which included service as a diplomat, as Secretary of State, and in later years as a congressman from Massachusetts. Unfortunately the superb talents of this son of John Adams did not include a sensitivity to trends in public opinion or the adroitness, tact, and personal warmth essential to presidential leadership. As a result he met with a series of political disasters. This was all the more unfortunate because Adams represented a point of view on the federal government's role in the national economy, and on its responsibilities to the states and the people, that deserved to be considered on its own merits.

The new President was an enthusiastic champion of national economic growth, especially of commercial and manufacturing expansion, and he looked benevolently upon the new capitalistic enterprises that were spawned by the Industrial Revolution. He was, moreover, as he made clear in his first annual message, a nationalist who believed that the Constitution gave the federal government ample power to direct and encourage this growth and to undertake numerous projects "for the common good." Adams spoke in support of the American System with as much fervor as Clay, especially when he urged the use of federal funds for internal improvements. Citing the National Road as a precedent, he asked: "To how many thousands of our countrymen has it proved a benefit? To what single individual has it ever proved an injury?" After the retirement of the public debt he would use the proceeds from the sale of public lands for roads and canals to facilitate communication "between distant regions and multitudes of men." More, he would build a great national university at Washington for "moral, political, and intellectual improvement," finance explorations of the interior and of the Northwest coast, and establish an astronomical observatory. Adams believed that Congress might even pass laws designed to promote "the elegant arts, the advancement of literature, and the progress of the sciences." Congress would, in fact, betray a sacred trust by not doing so; nor should it use as an excuse for inaction "that we are palsied by the will of our constituents." The time was ripe for action, said Adams confidently, for "the spirit of improvement is abroad upon this earth."

But these very sentiments prompted his critics to assail him as a tyrant and an aristocrat. Crawford found them "replete with doctrines which I hold to be unconstitutional." Jefferson accused Adams of seeking to establish "a single and splendid government of an aristocracy . . . riding and ruling over the plundered ploughman and beggared yeomanry." Congress responded to the President's proposals with little enthusiasm—even his friends thought he had gone too far—and after the congressional election of 1826 his enemies had full control of the Senate and the House. Appropriations for internal improvements far surpassed those provided during previous administrations but fell short by a great deal of Adams' grand design. A new tariff, enacted in 1828, sponsored by both Administration and anti-Administration congressmen from the Middle and Western states, was not the judicious measure he had called for. The bill was poorly drawn, and because of its concessions to

*John Quincy Adams: scrupulous nationalist*

the extreme protectionists the Southern cotton interest called it the "tariff of abominations." Yet Adams signed it.

Somehow his good intentions always seemed to lead him to personal disaster. He conscientiously repudiated a fraudulent Indian treaty by which the Creeks were to be shorn of all their lands in Georgia and ordered the negotiation of a new one. But his scrupulous concern for the rights of Indians irritated both Southerners and Westerners. Worse, when the governor of Georgia defied the federal government and threatened to take jurisdiction over the disputed lands, Adams flouted the principle of state rights: he warned that it was the president's duty to vindicate federal authority "by all the force committed for that purpose to his charge." Even in foreign affairs, in spite of Adams' rich experience, the Administration failed to achieve its goals. In 1826, chiefly for partisan reasons, Congress obstructed Clay's attempt to strengthen ties with Latin America by sending delegates to a conference at Panama. Adams also failed to persuade the British to open their West Indian islands to American trade.

*John Quincy Adams and National Republicanism*

## Jackson Forever!
### The Hero of Two Wars and of Orleans!
## The Man of the People!
#### HE WHO COULD NOT BARTER NOR BARGAIN FOR THE
## PRESIDENCY!

Who, although "*A Military Chieftain*," valued the purity of Elections and of the Electors, MORE than the Office of PRESIDENT itself! Although the greatest in the gift of his countrymen, and the highest in point of dignity of any in the world,

## BECAUSE
### It should be derived from the
## PEOPLE!

No Gag Laws! No Black Cockades! No Reign of Terror! No Standing Army or Navy Officers, when under the pay of Government, to browbeat, or

## KNOCK DOWN

Old Revolutionary Characters, or our Representatives while in the discharge of their duty. To the Polls then, and vote for those who will support

## OLD HICKORY
#### AND THE ELECTORAL LAW.

At home, while his foes continued their savage attack, Adams further weakened his position by spurning the role of party leader and refusing to use the patronage weapon in his own defense. Many hostile politicians continued to hold office in his Administration—among them Postmaster General John McLean, whose appointment policy seemed to be to reward the President's enemies and punish his friends. Adams was, in fact, the last of the Presidents to look upon parites as an evil and to cling to the eighteenth-century ideal of a national consensus with himself as its spokesman.

**The triumph of the Jacksonians.**  Adams realized that his chances for reelection in 1828 were slim; "the base and profligate combination" of his critics, he wrote bitterly, would probably succeed in defeating him. During the preceding three years the anti-Administration forces had rallied around the charismatic figure of Andrew Jackson. Joining the original Jacksonians was a heterogeneous group that included most of the previous supporters of Crawford and Calhoun and others who disliked the nationalistic American System or had been alienated by the President's inept handling of public affairs and public relations. Though political divisions did not follow class or occupational lines, the Jacksonians seemed to win a majority of the planters and farmers in the South and West, many small entrepreneurs in all parts

of the country, and a substantial number of artisans and factory workers in the towns and cities. What strength remained to Adams and the National Republicans was concentrated in the Northeast, mostly in New England.

Thinking it proper to remain aloof from electioneering, the President gave little help to those who ran his campaign. He would not "exhibit himself" to the public or in any other way actively seek a second presidential term. "If my country wants my services, she must ask for them," was his naive but altogether sincere response to those who urged more vigorous action. But his lieutenants were no match, in any case, for the Jackson organization and its able, hard-hitting leaders, among whom were three senators: Martin Van Buren of New York, Thomas Hart Benton of Missouri, and John H. Eaton of Tennessee; and three newspapermen: Amos Kendall and Francis Preston Blair of Kentucky and Isaac Hill of New Hampshire. These men and their associates skillfully exploited the fears and prejudices as well as the ideals of the mass electorate.

In the background of the campaign were a number of specific public-policy issues: the tariff, internal improvements, banking, land policy, and at the local level the question of bankruptcy laws and debtor-relief laws. But the politicians and party editors were usually vague on these issues, first, because they feared to divide their friends and hoped to win over the doubtful and, second, because they found other appeals that seemed better calculated to win votes. In a campaign that revolved largely around personalities, few political leaders showed much respect for the intelligence of the American electorate.

Jacksonians described the election as a contest between democracy and aristocracy. Their candidate, Old Hickory, they said, was a man of the people who had their interests at heart. Adams was a monarchist, an enemy of the people, a parasite who had lived off the taxpayers all his life, the head of a band of rascally officeholders, an extravagant waster of public funds for his own pleasure, and the darling of the old Federalists. (Actually, many one-time Federalists supported Jackson.) Voters were also reminded of the "corrupt bargain" of 1825 and of the need to vindicate the will of the people. Friends of Adams retaliated by describing Jackson as an inexperienced, hot-tempered incompetent—a demagogue having no program and totally unfitted for the responsibilities of the Presidency. At a still lower level, campaign leaders, resorting to mud-slinging and character assassination, exchanged charges of pandering, adultery, and murder.

The outcome of such a campaign cannot be explained apart from its substantial element of irrationality. Moreover, sectional feelings doubtless accounted for much of Jackson's Southern and Western

*Politics for the Common Man*

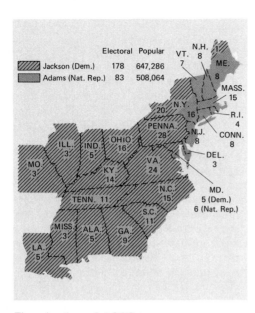

The election of 1828

election represented a victory for the nationalistic West, to others a victory for the state-rights South, and to still others a victory for those everywhere who would dislodge entrenched privilege from positions of power.

Above all, Jackson's victory was interpreted as a vindication of the common man. Born in poverty to Scotch-Irish immigrant parents in the Carolina back country, lacking formal schooling, he had moved to Tennessee and made his own way as a lawyer, land-speculator, soldier, politician, and planter. He was the first President who did not come from a well-established American family in comfortable circumstances. Jackson was, in fact, the first President to embody the American success story in its most romantic form: from a log cabin to the White House. This does not mean, however, that he was at the time of his election still a crude and simple frontiersman, as his political enemies described him. For he had already held several public offices; he had accumulated lands and more than a hundred slaves and lived in a mansion, "The Hermitage," near Nashville; and he had been allied with affluent speculators and creditors in Tennessee politics. In fact, Jackson had entered the ranks of the gentry of the Southwest and with advancing years had become increasingly mellow and perhaps a little pompous. A visitor who met him after his inauguration reported that he had seen dukes and princes and kings, "but none of such elegance and courtliness of manners, and of so commanding presence, as were possessed by General Jackson."

Nevertheless, Jackson was closer to the people than any of his predecessors had been, and his view of himself as their special defender was not a mere demagogic pose. As the one officer of the federal govern-

support. Even so, many of those who voted for Jackson evidently had come to the conclusion that he would better protect the interests of the people against special privilege. Though scarcely more than half the adult males went to the polls, they gave Jackson a substantial popular majority: 647,286 to 508,064. The electoral vote was 178 to 83, with Adams carrying only New England, New Jersey, Maryland, and Delaware. Observing the boisterous celebration in Washington on the day of Jackson's inauguration, men with different perspectives came to different conclusions. Some saw the start of the reign of King Mob, others the triumph of the common man. Webster observed dryly, "People have come five hundred miles to see General Jackson, and they really seem to think that the country has been rescued from some dreadful danger."

## Jacksonian democracy

**The new President.** Andrew Jackson was a controversial figure in his own day and has been one ever since. This may be explained in part by the complexity of the man, in part by the divergent expectations of those who supported him, and in part by the fact that he soon became not only a man but an abstraction—a symbol and a myth. Jackson's original appeal was not as an experienced statesman with a clear-cut program but as a nationally popular figure who embodied numerous American virtues and towered above the ranks of "mere" politicians. To some his

*Andrew Jackson: commanding Democrat*

To the
VICTORS
BELONG
THE
SPOILS.
A. JACKSON.

ing; a rotation of civil servants every four years would force them to "go back to making a living as other people do." Jackson saw little to be gained from long incumbency, for in general the duties were "so plain and simple that men of intelligence may readily qualify themselves for their performance; and I can not but believe that more is lost by the long continuance of men in office than is generally to be gained by their experience."

Jackson thus elevated the spoils system to a democratic principle, though its practical purpose was to reward loyal party workers with public offices. His rejection of an experienced civil service was not a major disaster in an age when the functions of government were relatively few and uncomplicated; but it did nothing to encourage efficiency or to increase the devotion of officeholders to the public interest. One Democrat observed with dismay that "office-seeking and office-getting was becoming a regular business, where impudence triumphed over worth." Clay indignantly described the "lank, lean, famished" Jacksonians who descended on Washington in 1829 with the cry: "Give us bread! Give us treasury pap! Give us our reward!" But Clay and other critics exaggerated the thoroughness with which Jackson applied his principle. In practice he left 80 percent of the officeholders undisturbed during his eight years as President, and at least a few of the removals were not for political reasons but for dereliction of duty. Though Jackson used the spoils system more freely than his predecessors, subsequent administrations, as the new party system developed, used it with far less restraint than he.

In selecting heads of departments Jackson recognized the various regions and factions that had elected him. But save for Van Buren, who became Secretary of State, the men he appointed were an undistinguished lot, and he never consulted them as an organized group of Cabinet advisers. Instead he counseled informally with a shifting group of men in whom he had confidence, among them the shrewd, talented, ambitious Van Buren; the Second Auditor of the Treasury, Major William B. Lewis of Tennessee, who lived with Jackson in the White house; Francis Preston Blair of Kentucky, who came to Washington to edit the Washington *Globe* as an Administration organ; Isaac Hill, editor of the New Hampshire *Patriot*; Roger B. Taney of Maryland, who later became Attorney General, Secretary of the Treasury, and Chief Justice of the United States; and the Fourth Auditor of the Treasury, Amos Kendall, a man of great influence, who helped Jackson prepare many of his state papers. This so-called Kitchen Cabinet, which was not a Cabinet in any formal sense, played an important role in the development of Administration policies and ideas.

ment chosen in a truly national election, he felt that he was in a position of peculiar responsibility. He was not intimidated by congressmen, whose acts, he felt, were too often controlled by small, selfish groups of powerful constituents, and he used his veto power more freely than had all previous Presidents combined. Nor would Jackson agree that the Supreme Court had the final word on matters of constitutional interpretation, for he believed that the President's oath bound him to support the Constitution "as he understands it, and not as it is understood by others." The decisions of the Court were entitled "to have only such influence as the force of their reasoning may deserve." Beyond being governed by the dictates of his own judgment, Jackson professed to know of no tribunal to which a public man "can appeal with greater advantage or more propriety than the judgment of the people."

In his dual role as party leader and guardian of the people's interests, Jackson promised to use his appointive power to "reform" the civil service and to make it more responsive to the public will. He would discharge all "unfaithful or incompetent" officeholders who had acquired a "habit of looking with indifference upon the public interest" or who had come to regard their offices "as a species of property" and "a means of promoting individual interests." Long tenure in the civil service, he said, was corrupt-

212

**The Jacksonian philosophy.** To speak of a Jacksonian philosophy may be to dignify too much the ideas of its pragmatic leaders. The Jacksonians, of course, were never of one mind; nor were their differences with the Whigs always sharp and clear, for the two parties were not ideological opposites. In fact, they were often divided more over means than ends. Nevertheless, there was a Jacksonian way of looking at things, and much of its ideology can be found scattered unsystematically in the President's inaugural addresses, annual messages to Congress, and veto messages.

The Jacksonians lived in a more complex society than had Jefferson, and they generally favored the advances in political democracy that individual states had recently achieved. Yet they were strikingly traditional and conservative on most questions of public policy at the federal level. In a sense, John Quincy Adams had endorsed a more radical program for national economic growth and social progress with the aid of a vigorous federal government. Adams' call for government action was in sharp contrast to Jackson's warning: "To suppose that because our government has been instituted for the benefit of the people it must therefore have the power to do whatever may seem to conduce to the public good is an error into which even honest minds are too apt to fall." Jackson repeatedly emphasized that the federal government was one of limited powers and cautioned against "overstrained constructions" of the Constitution. He would guard against "all encroachments upon the legitimate sphere of State sovereignty."

Federal intervention in the affairs of the people, Jackson believed, usually came in the form of special favors to influential minorities or of encouragement to monopolistic corporations. There would always be distinctions in society, he conceded, as a result of "superior industry, economy, and virtue . . . but when the laws undertake to add to these natural and just advantages artificial distinctions, to grant titles, gratuities, and exclusive privileges, to make the rich richer and the potent more powerful, the humble members of society—the farmers, mechanics, the laborers—who have neither the time nor the means of securing like favors to themselves, have a right to complain of the injustice of their Government."

As an exponent of federal laissez faire, Jackson promised to reduce the government "to that simple machine which the Constitution created." Experience had vindicated the Founding Fathers in their decision to withhold "the power to regulate the great mass of the business and concerns of the people" and to leave them to "free enterprise . . . aided by the State sovereignties." The people would find happiness not in a "splendid government . . . but in a plain system, void of pomp, protecting all and granting favors to none,

dispensing its blessings, like the dews of Heaven, unseen and unfelt save in the freshness and beauty they contribute to produce."

Some Jacksonians favored this formula of state sovereignty, strict construction, and federal laissez faire because they hoped for a return to old-fashioned, agrarian-oriented Jeffersonianism. On numerous occasions Jackson, unlike Adams with his enthusiasm for economic and social progress, looked back wistfully to the simpler, and presumably purer, young republic of Jefferson's day. He praised "the examples of public virtue left by my illustrious predecessors"; he suggested that it was "time to pause in our career to review our principles"; and, disillusioned by his own earlier speculations and resulting bankruptcy, he expressed a desire "to revive and perpetuate those habits of economy and simplicity which are so congenial to the character of republicans." Like Jefferson, Jackson idealized an agrarian society. He described the agricultural interest as "superior in importance" to all others and the cultivators of the soil as the "best part" of the population. "Independent farmers are everywhere the basis of society and true friends of liberty."

But the agrarian ideal was already hopelessly out of date. Reducing the government's role in the economy made it harder for favored groups to win special privileges, but it also gave free rein to irresponsible entrepreneurs in a period of frantic economic activity. At best, Jackson's followers had mixed feelings about his conception of the ideal society. Many of them doubtless shared his nostalgia, but few could resist the temptations of their age. Indeed, more often than not they liked Jackson because, in one way or another, they expected him to help them get ahead in the world—and it was not Jefferson's world that interested them.

# Internal improvements and public lands

After his inauguration in 1829, Jackson faced a problem that every American President has faced: that of holding together the disparate groups that had elected him. Typical of the second American party system, the national Democratic party of Jackson's day was essentially a federation of state parties—an unstable coalition of men from many regions with differing needs and interests. Insofar as voters had favored Jackson over Adams for rational reasons, they preferred what they believed would be his stand on most, but seldom all, of the issues that concerned them. Moreover, since the Democrats were loosely organized at the national level, party discipline tended to be lax. Not even the Democratic majority in Congress shared Jackson's view on every issue, and it seldom voted as a unit. Those who differed with the President on questions of secondary importance might rebel momentarily but still remain in the party and continue their general support of the Administration. But those who differed with him on a crucial issue might break away entirely and join the opposition party. This is what actually happened to many of the men who had supported Jackson in 1828, while some of his original opponents turned to him because of his stand on one or another major issue.

***The Maysville veto.*** On one issue, internal improvements, Jackson was bound to antagonize either his friends in the West who favored federal support or his friends in the South and in New York and Pennsylvania who opposed it. He gave a full statement of his position in 1830 when he vetoed a bill to subsidize the construction of a sixty-mile road from Maysville on the Ohio River to Lexington, Kentucky. In this veto message as well as in other state papers, apparently in part because of Van Buren's influence, he opposed in principle federal spending for internal improvements of any kind. But, like Madison and Monroe, Jackson insisted that if such appropriations were to be made without a constitutional amendment, they must be for projects that were national and not local in character. The Maysville Road, he protested, had "no connection with any established system of improvements; is exclusively within the limits of a State . . . and even as far as the State is interested . . . [it gives] partial instead of general advantage."

Federal appropriations for such purposes, Jackson feared, would bring logrolling, wasteful spending, and corruption; they would lead to a consolidated government with powers so vast as to endanger the liberties of the people. It would be far better for the government, after the public debt was retired, to distribute its surplus revenues among the states and permit them to manage their own internal improvements. (At the state level the Jacksonians were anything but consistent proponents of laissez faire.) Yet, in spite of these views, Jackson did not veto all the internal-improvement bills that Congress passed, not even all that were for local projects. At most it can be said that his Maysville veto checked the acceleration of such appropriations and diminished the role of the federal government relative to that of the states. Jackson even saw to it that the completed portions of the National Road were turned over to the four states that contained them, thus enabling the federal government to escape the burden of maintenance costs. This general policy gave the National Republicans an issue which they exploited in those parts of the West where the need for improved transportation influenced the political affiliations of many voters.

***Land policy.*** On the question of public land policy Jackson redeemed himself somewhat in the West. In general, Westerners wanted the government to encourage the rapid settlement of unoccupied lands by offering generous terms rather than to seek maximum revenue for the federal treasury. With this in mind, Senator Thomas Hart Benton of Missouri advocated a gradual reduction of the minimum price of public lands of inferior quality from $1.25 (the starting price when land was put up for auction) to 50 cents an acre, after which any lands still unsold might be given free to actual settlers. Another favorite scheme of Westerners was to permit "squatters"—that is, men who had settled on the public domain before the land was surveyed and offered for sale—to purchase at the minimum price the land they had improved. Neither the first of these schemes (called "graduation") nor the second (called "preemption") was enacted into law during Jackson's Administration, but the President clearly shared the Western point of view. In his message to Congress in 1832 he urged that "the public lands shall cease as soon as practicable to be a source of revenue." To give everyone a chance to obtain a freehold, land should be sold to settlers in small tracts at a price barely sufficient to cover the cost of surveys and clearing Indian titles. More, Jackson recommended that each new state be given that portion of the public domain that lay within its boundaries.

Easterners, especially manufacturers, hoped to slow down the westward movement and the resulting depletion of the labor supply. They strongly opposed both graduation and preemption and even looked with favor on a proposal to stop temporarily the survey and sale of new Western lands. Henry Clay, seeking a plan that would satisfy all sections, suggested that rather than giving public lands to individual Western states the proceeds from the sale of the lands should be distributed among all the states, to be used as each saw fit. In 1833 Congress passed such a bill, but the President vetoed it. Land policy thus remained an unsettled issue when Jackson left office.

# Religious and ethnic minorities

Although President Jackson repeatedly professed his devotion to and trust in "the people" and claimed to speak for them, he never really had in mind all the people who lived within the boundaries of the United States. The idea of equality or of political rights for women interested neither him nor his political opponents. Of the country's three largest racial and religious minorities—Negroes, Indians, and Irish Catholics (the last of whom came in increasing numbers during the 1830s and 1840s)—most Jacksonian leaders showed concern only for the Irish. Because antiforeign, especially anti-Catholic, sentiment was centered in the Whig party, recent immigrants in general and Irish Catholics in particular voted overwhelmingly Democratic. Their votes were vital to the Jacksonian organizations in the cities of the Northeast.

In the case of the American Negroes, however, Democratic leaders were at best indifferent to their condition. Jackson was not only one of the largest slaveholders in the Southwest; he was a good deal less troubled about the morality of the institution than Jefferson had been. (On one occasion he advertised for a runaway slave and offered the captor a double reward if he would punish the runaway with one hundred lashes.) The Jackson Administration tried to keep the divisive issue of slavery out of national politics, but the President and Postmaster General Amos Kendall showed their hostility to antislavery organizations by refusing to protect their right to use the mails to distribute their literature in the Southern states. Though race prejudice was rampant in all sections and among members of both political parties, it is still true that in the Northern states the Democrats were more aggressively anti-Negro and more prone to make demagogic, racist appeals than the Whigs. In New York State the small Negro vote was almost solidly anti-Democratic.

**Indian removals.** Since Indians could not vote, neither party cared very much about them, and Indian policy caused President Jackson relatively little political trouble. Criticism of his policy was limited to a handful of humanitarians concentrated in the Northeast, most of them already affiliated with the anti-Jackson party. Jackson, to the delight of land-hungry Southerners and Westerners, vigorously enforced a plan, favored by both Monroe and Adams and approved by Congress, to remove all the Indian tribes to lands west of the Mississippi. Lewis Cass, a Jacksonian politician from Michigan, was certain "that the Creator intended the earth should be reclaimed from a state of nature and cultivated; . . . a wandering tribe of hunters . . . have a very imperfect possession of the country over which they roam." Removal would be better for the Indians themselves, said Jackson, because they were not only unhappy living among the whites but threatened with extinction. "Doubtless it will be painful to leave the graves of their fathers," he conceded, but we need only "open the eyes of those children of the forest to their true condition" to make them appreciate the "hu-

manity and justice" of removal. "Rightly considered," Jackson concluded, "the policy of the General Government toward the red man is not only liberal, but generous." Federal Indian policy, President Van Buren told Congress a few years later, had been "just and friendly throughout . . . its watchfulness in protecting them from individual frauds unremitting."

These unctuous words covered a policy that was callous in its conception and often brutal in its execution. Most of the tribes were more or less coerced into signing removal treaties; usually the lands they received in the West were inferior to those they gave up; the migrations themselves were poorly planned and caused much suffering; and in some cases the Indians were literally driven from their old homes by military force. Only a few tribes put up organized resistance. In 1832 about a thousand Sac and Fox Indians, led by Chief Black Hawk, defiantly returned to Illinois, but militiamen and army regulars easily drove them back across the Mississippi. This so-called Black Hawk War was hardly more than a skirmish, but the resistance of the Seminoles in Florida was a good deal more formidable. In 1835 many of them, led by Chief Osceola and supported by scores of runaway slaves, rose in rebellion and thus began a costly war that dragged on into the 1840s. The highly civilized Cherokees of Georgia, on the other hand, tried resistance through legal action. When the government of Georgia refused to recognize their autonomy and threatened to seize their lands, the Cherokees took their case to the Supreme Court and won a favorable decision. Marshall's opinion for the Court majority was that Georgia had no jurisdiction over the Cherokees and no claim to their lands. But Georgia officials simply ignored the decision, and the President refused to enforce it. At length the Cherokees had to leave, too, and when Jackson retired from office he counted the near-completion of Indian removals as one of his major achievements. Indeed, he had always been prepared to accept Indian extinction as a likely consequence of the white man's conquest of the continent. In his second annual message to Congress, he solemnly declared:

Humanity has often wept over the fate of the aborigines of this country, and Philanthropy has been busily employed in devising means to avert it, but its progress has never for a moment been arrested, and one by one have many powerful tribes disappeared from the earth. To follow to the tomb the last of his race and to tread on the graves of extinct nations excites melancholy reflections. But true philanthropy reconciles the mind to these vicissitudes as it does to the extinction of one generation to make room for another.

215

*Religious and ethnic minorities*

# The tariff and nullification

**Disaffection in South Carolina.** Jackson favored a fiscal policy that, in its broad outlines, was consistent with old-fashioned Republican principles: he promised rigid economy and a swift reduction of the public debt in order to "counteract that tendency to public and private profligacy" encouraged by large federal expenditures. But on one critical issue, the tariff, he wavered. Some of his early statements gave aid and comfort to the protectionists—for example, in his first inaugural address he endorsed protective duties on all products "that may be found essential to our national independence." As Southern opposition increased, however, Jackson's position began to change. By 1832 he advocated a tariff designed primarily to provide the government with revenue, one that would give only "temporary and, generally, incidental protection"; and he warned manufacturers not to expect the people to "continue permanently to pay high taxes for their benefit." This shift in favor of tariff reduction antagonized the Northern protectionists. Subsequently, however, when South Carolina resorted to direct action to force a reduction of duties, Jackson firmly denounced the state and thereby alienated many Southerners who believed in free trade and extreme state rights.

Though the tariff was never a clear-cut sectional issue, protectionist sentiment was concentrated in the North and free-trade sentiment in the South. By the 1820s the majority of Southerners, especially the cotton-growers, were convinced that the protective tariff was a discriminatory tax—designed, according to a public meeting in Charleston, to elevate the manufacturing interest "to an undue influence and importance" and thus to benefit "one class of citizens at the expense of every other class." Clay's American System, most Southerners believed, gave no advantage to the South, because the South had built few factories and because it exported two-thirds of its cotton crop to European markets. Southern exports, they reasoned, paid for most of the country's imports, and the federal government supported itself chiefly by taxing this exchange. Hence Southerners complained that they were paying more than their share of federal taxes; and, to make matters worse, much of the income from the tariff was spent on internal improvements, mostly in the North. In short, the tariff was a peculiar tax on Southern farmers and planters, one that raised the price of everything they consumed and the cost of everything they produced. Such an arrangement, many Southerners soon concluded, was unconstitutional. They agreed that the Constitution had empowered Congress to levy moderate duties on imports, but the purpose was to provide the government with revenue, not to protect industry.

These were the opinions of cotton-growers everywhere, but nowhere were they so strongly held as in South Carolina. Here a combination of economic adversity and social anxiety caused a reaction not only against the tariff but against nationalism generally. Looming large in the background was the fear—widespread in this state, whose black population outnumbered the white by a considerable margin—that federal power might somehow be used to weaken or destroy slavery. The Missouri debate had increased the concern of white South Carolinians; and in 1822 rumors (which had some basis in fact) of a formidable slave conspiracy, led by Denmark Vesey, a Charleston free Negro, created a veritable frenzy. Throughout the 1820s white South Carolinians were inordinately sensitive to the slightest criticism of their peculiar institution from any source. The tariff, many said, was only the first dangerous manifestation of federal usurpation; the same arguments that justified protection might subsequently justify congressional emancipation.

More immediately, however, South Carolina was in the midst of a severe economic crisis. Prior to 1819 the state had flourished, and its proud and aristocratic planters had made fortunes from the cultivation of rice and cotton. But the Panic of 1819 and the subsequent depression were cruel blows, for they brought a sharp decline in cotton prices—a decline that hit South Carolina planters with exceptional force. Facing the competition of the new cotton states in the Southwest, South Carolinians found production costs on their long-used lands relatively high and their crop yield per acre and profit margin correspondingly low. Charleston's commercial interest was languishing, and the state's population had almost stopped growing as farmers moved west in search of better land. Economic troubles, along with worries about slavery, caused political unrest and a swing to extreme state rights.

The majority of white South Carolinians had a simple explanation for their plight. Not soil exhaustion, not the competition of the Southwest, but the high tariff and other federal encroachments on the rights of the states, they said, were to blame. They looked suspiciously at their leading politician, John C. Calhoun, who had supported the Tariff of 1816 (see p. 180) and still in the early 1820s appeared to be a nationalist and protectionist. To have a political future in his state Calhoun had no choice but to revise his views; to advance his ambitions in national politics he had to find some remedy that would satisfy the South without alienating all his friends in the North and West. He faced this challenge while he was still Vice President under Adams, and he faced it even more after the passage of the high Tariff of 1828 while he was seeking reelection with Jackson.

*Politics for the Common Man*

**Calhoun and state interposition.** By then Calhoun had changed his mind and adopted his state's position that the protective tariff was not only discriminatory but unconstitutional. Now, in 1828, he proposed a remedy in an essay entitled *The South Carolina Exposition and Protest*, which the state legislature published without revealing the name of its author. This document indicated that Calhoun had abandoned much of his earlier nationalism and that he had become a conservative spokesman for the Southern planter class. From his new state-rights position he found a way for a numerical minority, such as the South, to protect itself from obnoxious legislation adopted by the majority. His solution was the doctrine of nullification, or state "interposition," which he offered as a procedure less drastic than secession from the Union. He hoped that this remedy would find approval in other sections and thus enable him to protect the interests of the South while continuing his pursuit of the Presidency.

Calhoun was an able student of political theory and a skillful logician. The premises on which he based his doctrine of nullification, however, were not altogether original, for he borrowed much from Madison's and Jefferson's Virginia and Kentucky Resolutions of 1798 (see p. 150). As they had, Calhoun argued that before 1787 the states had been completely sovereign and that in framing and ratifying the new Constitution they had not given up their sovereignty. Rather, they had merely formed a "compact" and created the federal government as their "agent" to execute it. This agent had only limited powers, and the sovereign states, not the Supreme Court, were the judges of what powers had been delegated to it.

From these premises Calhoun concluded that if Congress exceeded its delegated powers by enacting, say, a protective tariff, any one of the states might interpose state authority to block enforcement of the law. To accomplish this, the people of a state would elect delegates to a state convention; if the convention decided that the act in question was unconstitutional, it would declare the act null and void within the state's boundaries. Congress might then choose between acquiescing in nullification or proposing a constitutional amendment specifically granting to the government the desired power. Thus whenever a single state challenged the constitutionality of an act of Congress, the cumbersome amending process, requiring ratification by three-fourths of the states, would be the government's only recourse. This system, thought Calhoun, would provide a sufficient safeguard for the interests of the minority South. True democracy, he said, was not the rule of an absolute, or numerical, majority, for such a majority could ride roughshod over the rights of minorities. Instead, he proposed rule by the "concurrent" majority, with the people of each

*Plantation on the Mississippi: competition for South Carolina*

state having a veto over federal legislation. Minority rights would thereby be protected, and only legislation beneficial to all sections would be enacted.

Calhoun's ingenious system had a full review in the United States Senate early in 1830 during a debate that began over public land policy but soon centered on the nature of the federal Union. Robert Y. Hayne of South Carolina and Daniel Webster of Massachusetts, both brilliant orators, were the chief contestants, while Vice President Calhoun listened carefully as presiding officer of the Senate. Hayne explained and defended the doctrine of nullification, enumerated his section's grievances, appealed to the West to join the South in resisting the avarice of the Northeast, and reminded New Englanders that they themselves had toyed with both nullification and secession during the War of 1812. Webster, now an intense nationalist, denied that the Constitution was a mere compact to be interpreted as individual states might please. The people, not the states, had created it, and the Supreme Court was the proper authority to settle disputes over its meaning. Nor was the federal government simply an agent of the states; in exercising its powers it was sovereign and acted directly on the people. "It is," he said, "the people's Constitution, the people's government, made for the people, made by the people, and answerable to the people." The Union was not a voluntary federation of sovereign states; it was intended to be perpetual, and any attempt to dismember it would be treasonable and would lead to civil war. There may have been flaws in Webster's logic and in his history, but he understood better than Hayne the direction of events and the views of the

217

*The great and leading principle is, that the General Government emanated from the people of the United States, forming distinct political communities, and acting in their separate and sovereign capacity, and not from all of the people forming one aggregate political community; that the Constitution of the United States is, in fact, a compact, to which each State is a party, in the character already described; and that the several States, or parties, have a right to judge of its infractions; and in case of a deliberate, palpable, and dangerous exercise of power not delegated, they have the right, in the last resort, to use the language of the Virginia Resolutions, ''to interpose for arresting the progress of the evil, and for maintaining, within their respective limits, the authorities, rights, and liberties appertaining to them.'' This right of interposition ... be it called what it may—State-right, veto, nullification, or by any other name—I conceive to be the fundamental principle of our system, resting on facts historically as certain as our revolution itself, and deductions as simple and demonstrative as that of any political or moral truth whatever; and I firmly believe that on its recognition depend that stability and safety of our political institutions.*

From John C. Calhoun, Fort Hill Address, July 26, 1831.

majority. The South sympathized with Hayne's expression of its grievances, but outside South Carolina few Southerners showed much sympathy for his remedy.

The cold response of Congress to the doctrine of nullification disappointed Calhoun, but the response of President Jackson produced a major crisis in Calhoun's political career. Jackson had a deep respect for the rights of the states, and he was now convinced that Southerners had reason to complain about the existing tariff; but to talk of nullification or secession, as South Carolinians did, was another matter. Soon after the Webster-Hayne debate, at a public banquet, Jackson rose, looked squarely at Calhoun, and proposed his famous toast: "Our *Federal* Union—*It must be preserved.*" This incident was only one of numerous signs of a growing rift between the President and the Vice President, a rift that Secretary of State Van Buren encouraged in his effort to supersede Calhoun as Jackson's successor to the Presidency. Even a petty social tiff among Administration wives contributed to Calhoun's downfall. Mrs. Calhoun, a South Carolina aristocrat, snubbed the wife of the Secretary of War, Peggy Eaton, the attractive daughter of a Washington tavernkeeper. Jackson had no patience for this kind of snobbery, and Van Buren, a widower, made it clear that he shared the irritated President's admiration for Mrs. Eaton. Meanwhile, Calhoun's enemies let Jackson know that back in 1818, Calhoun, as Secretary of War, had denounced Jackson for his high-handed invasion of Florida. Explanations were offered and rejected. In 1831 there was a Cabinet reorganization,

and Calhoun's friends were forced out of the Administration. Van Buren was now Jackson's candidate to succeed him, and Calhoun found himself pushed more and more out of his role of national leadership into the position of chief defender of the South.

***The nullification crisis.*** The doctrine of nullification was put to the test in 1832, when Congress passed a new tariff bill that conceded little to the Southern demand for lower duties. After Jackson signed the bill, South Carolina's congressmen sent an address to their constituents stating that "all hope for relief from Congress is irrecoverably gone," and Calhoun now openly announced his support of nullification. The nullifiers won control of the South Carolina legislature, and when it met in October it ordered the election of delegates to a state convention. On November 24, 1832, the convention, by an overwhelming majority, adopted an ordinance that pronounced the tariffs of 1828 and 1832 "unauthorized by the Constitution" and therefore "null, void, and no law, nor binding upon this State, its officers or citizens." The ordinance prohibited state or federal officers from enforcing the tariff laws after February 1, 1833, forbade appeals to federal courts, and warned that any federal attempt to coerce the state would force South Carolina to secede from the Union. At this juncture Hayne resigned from the Senate to become governor of South Carolina, and Calhoun resigned as Vice President to take Hayne's place and lead the fight on the Senate floor. The tariff issue had precipitated a serious national crisis.

*The ordinance is founded ... on the strange position that any one State may not only declare an act of Congress void, but prohibit its execution; that the true construction of that instrument permits a State to retain its place in the Union and yet be bound by no other of its laws than those it may choose to consider as constitutional.... But reasoning on this subject is superfluous when our social compact, in express terms, declares that the laws of the United States, its Constitution, and treaties made under it are the supreme law of the land, and, for greater caution, adds "that the judges in every State shall be bound thereby, anything in the constitution or laws of any State to the contrary notwithstanding." And it may be asserted without fear of refutation that no federative government could exist without a similar provision....*

*If the doctrine of a State veto upon the laws of the Union carries with it internal evidence of its impractical absurdity, our constitutional history will also afford abundant proof that it would have been repudiated with indignation had it been proposed to form a feature in our Government....*

*I consider, then, the power to annul a law of the United States, assumed by one State, incompatible with the existence of the Union, contradicted expressly by the letter of the Constitution, unauthorized by its spirit, inconsistent with every principle on which it was founded, and destructive of the great object for which it was formed.*

**From Andrew Jackson, Proclamation to the People of South Carolina,
December 10, 1832.**

But South Carolina's position was an uncomfortable one, for no other Southern state was prepared at that time to approve of its radical action. And the angry President reacted vigorously: he threatened to hang Calhoun, he sent a warship and revenue cutters to Charleston harbor, and he announced his readiness to take the field personally in case of a clash of arms. In a proclamation to the people of South Carolina, Jackson endorsed Webster's position on the nature of the Union and warned them of the serious consequences of their action. As President he had no choice but to see that the laws of the United States were executed.

Tension increased when the legislature of South Carolina defiantly replied that Jackson's views were "erroneous and dangerous" and that the state would "repel force by force . . . and maintain its liberty at all hazards." It increased further when Congress considered a "force bill" authorizing the President, if necessary, to use the army and navy to enforce the laws. Yet Jackson hoped to avoid violence except as a last resort, and South Carolina politicians, feeling their isolation, were eager to find a way to escape from their predicament without losing face. At length Henry Clay came forward with a compromise tariff, the details of which he worked out in consultation with Calhoun. It provided that tariff schedules would be gradually reduced over a period of nine years, until by 1842 no

duty would exceed 20 percent. On March 1, 1833, Congress passed both the compromise tariff and the force bill, and Jackson signed them. On March 15, the South Carolina convention accepted the compromise and withdrew its nullification of the tariff; but, yielding nothing in principle, it solemnly declared the force bill null and void. Since the crisis had passed, Jackson had the good sense to overlook this final petulant gesture.

Though Jackson irritated both the uncompromising protectionists and the state-rights followers of Calhoun, nationalists in subsequent sectional crises remembered him fondly for his bold action against the nullifiers. At the same time, even though most Southerners rejected nullification, the fight over the tariff made them more conscious than ever before of their minority position. Looking back at the tariff crisis, Chancellor Harper of South Carolina was pessimistic about the future:

> It is useless and impracticable to disguise the fact that the South is a permanent minority, and that there is a *sectional* majority against it—a majority of different views and interests and little common sympathy. . . . We are divided into slave-holding and non-slave-holding states; and . . . this is the broad and marked distinction that must separate us at last.

# The Bank war

***Criticism of the Bank.*** Before the controversy over the tariff and nullification had been resolved, Congress and the Administration were engaged in an equally bitter dispute over whether the charter of the Bank of the United States should be renewed when it expired in 1836. Jackson had been hostile to the Bank long before he became President, criticized it repeatedly during his first term in office, made it a basic issue in his campaign for a second term, and gave it so much attention after his reelection that he seemed almost obsessed with a desire to destroy it. To many agrarian-oriented Jacksonians the Bank was by far the most crucial problem, for opposition to it went to the very heart of their philosophy; and Jackson himself doubtless counted his ultimate victory over "the Monster" his greatest single accomplishment. To his critics, however, the destruction of the Bank was a major blunder in public policy, a singularly irresponsible exercise of presidential power that did incalculable harm to the country. The merits of the two positions remain a subject of historical debate.

After a shaky start this powerful financial institution had settled down to become, in the decade after the Panic of 1819, a conservative, prosperous, and reasonably responsible business enterprise. Since 1823, the president of the Bank had been Nicholas Biddle, an aristocratic, cultivated, and talented Philadelphian, whose acumen as a banker was unfortunately matched by his ineptitude in dealing with politicians. Many of his admiring contemporaries credited him with developing the Bank and its twenty-nine branches into an effective regulator of the expanding American economy. The Bank marketed government bonds and served as a reliable depository for government funds; it was an important source of credit for the business community; its bank notes provided the country with a sound paper currency; it exerted a restraining influence on the state banks by forcing them to back their notes with adequate specie reserves; and it thus helped to create confidence in the entire banking system of the United States. The source of its power was its control of one-fifth of the bank notes and one-third of the bank deposits and specie of the country.

But it was in part the Bank's possession of this vast economic power that made it so vulnerable politically. Many Jacksonians had not forgotten its seemingly selfish behavior during the Panic of 1819 (see p. 201), and they believed that democracy was in peril when so much power was concentrated in a single corporation. During the 1820s Biddle ran the Bank with considerable restraint, but he tactlessly admitted to a congressional committee that most state banks might have been "destroyed by an exertion of the powers of the [United States] Bank." Moreover, its control over the supply of short-term credit was not subjected to sufficient government regulation. Its charter did not assign to it the public responsibilities of a central bank, as did the legislation creating the Federal Reserve System a century later. This Bank was responsible primarily to its own investors, and its chief function was to earn dividends for them. Many state bankers resented it not only because it forced them to maintain adequate specie reserves but be-

**Death of the Bank**

cause its federal charter gave it a considerable competitive advantage.

Senator Benton complained that it was to this privileged monopoly that "the Federal Government, the State Governments, and great cities, must, of necessity, apply, for every loan which their exigencies may demand." Biddle's enemies also accused him of corrupting the nation's political life, because many influential politicians and editors were indebted to the Bank for loans. Webster was not only a heavy borrower but was on the Bank's payroll as a legal counsel. "I believe my retainer has not been renewed or *refreshed* as usual," he once wrote to Biddle. "If it be wished that my relation to the Bank should be continued, it may be well to send me the usual retainer."

Thus, by the time Jackson became President the Bank had incurred the hatred of numerous groups for either practical or ideological reasons. Curiously, it antagonized both those who favored "soft money" (more state-bank notes) and those who favored "hard money" (only gold and silver coins). The former included some state banking interests, land-speculators, and small entrepreneurs who felt that their needs were best served by an abundant paper currency. The latter included Eastern workingmen who resented receiving their wages in paper of uncertain value, and agrarian-oriented Southerners and Westerners, such as Senator Benton, who considered any currency other than gold and silver dishonest. The hard-money men were hostile to banks of any kind, state or national,

that issued bank notes; they tended to look upon banking as a parasitic enterprise. Among them was Jackson, who once told Biddle, "I do not dislike your Bank any more than all banks." By using gold and silver in ordinary business transactions, he told Congress, the country would avoid "those fluctuations in the standard of value which render uncertain the reward of labor."

**Veto of the Bank bill.** Jackson's first two messages to Congress left little doubt that he would veto any bill to recharter the Bank. In his first message, in December 1829, he affirmed that "both the constitutionality and the expediency of the law creating this bank are well questioned by a large portion of our fellow-citizens." A year later he again pointed to the dangers posed by the Bank as it was then organized. If a national bank was needed, he suggested that it be established as a branch of the Treasury Department, to act simply as a bank of deposit without power to issue notes, make loans, or acquire property. Such a bank, "having no stockholders, debtors, or property," would raise no constitutional objections. To be sure, the Supreme Court had already affirmed the constitutionality of the present Bank, but to Jackson this was irrelevant. "I have read the opinion of John Marshall," he said, "and could not agree with him."

Biddle, in his campaign to save the Bank, could not avoid getting deeply involved in national politics. He had started as a Jeffersonian Republican and had tried to appease Jackson by appointing some of his supporters to directorships of the branch banks. But Jackson's hostility drove Biddle into the camp of the opposition, and Biddle's loans to congressmen and newspaper editors became increasingly motivated by politics. At length, in 1832, he took the advice of Clay and Webster and applied for a new charter, though the old one would not expire for four more years. Clay assured Biddle that Congress would pass the bill, and he was ready to make a presidential veto an issue in the coming campaign. The bill to recharter the Bank, amended to meet some of Jackson's objections, easily passed both houses of Congress with the support of a substantial minority of the Democrats. Jackson accepted the challenge. "The Bank," he told Van Buren, "is trying to kill me, but I will kill it."

Jackson's veto message, a powerful political document, maintained that the Bank was unconstitutional in spite of the changes in its charter and described the dangers of "such a concentration of power in the hands of a few men irresponsible to the people." Much of the stock was held by foreigners, "and the residue is held by a few hundred of our own citizens, chiefly of the richest class." Their demands for "grants of monopolies and special privileges" had "arrayed section against section, interest against interest, and man against man, in a fearful commotion which threatens to shake the foundations of the Union." Webster bitterly denounced the President for executive usurpation and for seeking "to inflame the poor against the rich," but the veto stood and became a central issue in the presidential election of 1832. Indeed, Clay, Biddle, and the National Republicans helped to make it so by giving the veto message wide circulation, mistakenly thinking that it would serve to discredit Jackson. Whatever the weaknesses of its reasoning, however it may have exposed Jackson's limitations as a student of money and banking, the election showed that Jackson knew how to reach the ordinary voter better than they.

*Jackson vindicated.* The campaign of 1832 was notable not only for its vindication of Jackson but for two political innovations: the appearance of the first national third party, the Anti-Masonic party, and the holding of the first national nominating conventions. The new party, like so many third parties, at first focused on a single issue: opposition to secret societies, especially the Society of Freemasons. The party's strength was concentrated in the rural districts of New England and the Middle Atlantic states, where its supporters objected to the secrecy, exclusiveness, and allegedly undemocratic character of these societies. In 1826 William Morgan of Batavia, New York, a former Mason who was about to publish an exposure of the secrets of Freemasonry, suddenly vanished, and rumors spread that members of the society had murdered him. The resulting popular indignation eventually took the form of a political movement designed to drive the "grand kings" of Freemasonry out of public office. In September 1831 the Anti-Masonic party held a national convention at Baltimore and nominated William Wirt of Maryland for President, the first candidate to be selected in this fashion. The new party, in spite of its democratic assaults on a presumably privileged group, was essentially anti-Jacksonian —Jackson was himself a Mason—and in a short time most of its leaders joined the National Republicans.

Wirt hoped to win the nomination of the National Republicans, too, but in December 1831 this party held its own convention in Baltimore and nominated Henry Clay for President and John Sargeant of Pennsylvania for Vice President. The Democrats also met in Baltimore, in May 1832, but Jackson had already been renominated by numerous local conventions, and a party platform seemed superfluous. All that remained was to nominate a candidate for Vice President, and Jackson saw to it that his choice, Van Buren, was selected.

National Republicans attacked Jackson for abusing the patronage and the veto power, endorsed Clay's American System, and boldly demanded the rechartering of the Bank, but to no avail. Jackson was then at the peak of his popularity, and with Wirt taking votes away from Clay the outcome of the campaign was never in doubt. Jackson won by a comfortable majority in the popular vote, and in the Electoral College he polled 219 votes to Clay's 49. Wirt carried only Vermont, while the disaffected leaders of South Carolina gave their state to John Floyd of Virginia. To Jackson the significance of the election was clear: he had been given a mandate to press his war against the Bank of the United States until this "Hydra of corruption" had been destroyed.

*The Bank destroyed.* Nicholas Biddle was not yet ready to surrender. "This worthy President," he said, "thinks that because he has scalped Indians and imprisoned judges, he is to have his way with the Bank. He is mistaken." So the battle went on, and in its final phase the friends and enemies of the Bank fought so recklessly that they impaired the stability of the entire American economy.

Jackson refused to wait for the Bank's charter to expire, for he feared that Biddle might still use its political and economic power to buy a new charter from Congress. Soon after the election Jackson decided to deprive the Bank of federal support for its financial operations by ceasing to use it as a depository for government funds. He justified his decision by accusing the Bank of "misconduct," charging that it had attempted to influence the outcome of the election by playing on "the distress of some and the

"The Downfall
of Mother Bank"

fear of others"—a charge that a special congressional committee failed to sustain. Jackson had to remove two uncooperative Secretaries of the Treasury before he found a man in complete sympathy with his scheme: Roger B. Taney, the former Attorney General. Taney accomplished the gradual removal of federal funds from the Bank simply by paying government expenses from existing deposits and by refusing to place current revenues in its vaults. Those revenues were now distributed among numerous state banks—eventually, eighty-nine of them—which critics called "pet banks." The use of state banks of varying degrees of soundness was, as Jackson himself admitted, an unsatisfactory expedient subject to strong political pressures.

Jackson's enemies struck back hard. In the Senate Clay mustered a majority in 1834 to pass a resolution censuring the President for (among other things) removing the deposits and thus assuming power "not conferred by the constitution and the laws." Not until 1837 were indignant Jacksonian partisans able to get this resolution expunged from the Senate record. Meanwhile, as federal deposits diminished, Biddle began calling in the Bank's loans and contracting credit, in part to protect himself and in part as a form of economic coercion to force the government to return the deposits and renew the charter. The resulting credit shortage brought delegations of businessmen to Washington to petition for relief. But the angry President told them to "go to Biddle." "I never will restore the deposits," he vowed, "I never will

recharter the United States Bank, or sign a charter for any other bank, so long as my name is Andrew Jackson." At length the businessmen turned against Biddle and forced him to relax his credit policy, but not before he had managed to increase his unpopularity and thus to destroy even the faint hope that a drastically revised federal charter could be obtained. In 1836 Biddle received a charter from the state of Pennsylvania, which enabled the Bank to continue in business until 1841, when, because of economic depression and unwise speculations, it was finally forced to close its doors.

The Bank war was over, and Jackson's victory was complete. The anti-Jacksonians fumed at his highhanded tactics; they spoke indignantly of the "reign of King Andrew I"; they renamed themselves the "Whigs" in imitation of the British party that, in the eighteenth century, had sought to reduce the power of the monarch; and they formed a loose coalition of those who opposed the Administration. In 1836, in their extremity, they held no national convention and drew up no platform; still lacking effective national party leadership, they ran not one but three presidential candidates: Webster to appeal to New England, Hugh Lawson White of Tennessee to appeal to the South, and General William Henry Harrison of Ohio to appeal to the West. The Whigs hoped thus to throw the election into the House of Representatives, where they might unite behind a single candidate. The Democrats held a convention at Baltimore, dutifully nominated Van Buren, and presented

BORN TO COMMAND.

OF VETO MEMORY.

HAD I BEEN CONSULTED.

CONSTITUTION of the UNITED STATES of America.

Internal Improvements U.S. Bank.

KING ANDREW THE FIRST.

him on Jackson's record without a formal platform. In the election Van Buren won by a slim majority in the popular vote and by 170 electoral votes to 124 for his several opponents.

## Panic and depression

***Economic crisis.*** Jackson remained in Washington to witness Van Buren's inauguration, and Benton observed that "the rising was eclipsed by the setting sun." It was not easy to follow the dynamic Jackson into the Presidency, not even for Van Buren, whose political adoitness had earned him the title of "the Little Magician." Like Jackson, this New Yorker of Dutch descent was a self-made man from a rural family of modest means. After a successful law career that gave him financial independence, Van Buren turned to state politics and soon became the leader of an efficient Republican machine called the Albany Regency. A career politician who relished the give-and-take of political life, he was a founder of the

second American party system and a defender of parties as "inseparable from free governments" and "highly useful to the country." Following the presidential campaign of 1824, he linked his political fortunes with Jackson's and rose with him as a faithful advocate of his principles. But Van Buren was a pale copy of his chief: he lacked Jackson's forcefulness and popular appeal and had to rely on his tact and his skill in the management of men. Unfortunately neither these talents nor the Jacksonian philosophy enabled him to cope with the serious economic problems that beset the nation while he was President. Jackson was fortunate to have left office when he did, for within two months the country plunged into a panic and depression. Van Buren thus had the misfortune of being remembered as a "depression President."

During Jackson's two Administrations, except for the brief "Biddle panic" of 1833–34, the country enjoyed a period of glorious prosperity and unprecedented economic expansion. Southerners found seemingly limitless markets for their cotton at good prices, and planters and slaves poured into the states of the Southwest to open up vast new cotton lands. Between 1831 and 1836, because of rising prices and expanded production, the value of cotton exports trebled. In the West farmers, also finding ample markets and enjoying high prices, continued to be drawn into the spreading money economy. Western cities experienced a phenomenal growth as they developed commercial facilities and manufacturing enterprises to serve local needs. In the Northeast merchants prospered from the flourishing cotton trade, and manufacturers expanded to supply their growing Southern and Western markets. Land prices shot up as speculation once again became a national mania; between 1834 and 1836 the speculators were responsible for a fivefold increase in government land sales. Meanwhile, the states and private entrepreneurs undertook ambitious canal and railroad projects. In the years between 1830 and 1838 state debts increased by nearly $150 million, two-thirds of which were spent for internal improvements.

Funds for all this economic activity came from British capitalists, who assumed that investments in state bonds were as safe as investments in federal bonds, and from the multiplying state banks and other domestic investors. Between 1829 and 1837 the number of state banks more than doubled, their note issues trebled, and their loans quadrupled. In an economically "underdeveloped" country with a rapidly growing population, much of this business activity was healthy. But some of it was reckless and speculative—and the economy now lacked even the modest control that the Bank of the United States had once exercised.

Before Van Buren took office, the Jackson Administration, besides trying to divorce the government from business, had adopted fiscal policies that probably intensified the crisis when it came. First, as Jackson himself observed, the deposit of federal funds in numerous "pet banks" tended to multiply state-chartered banks and "had a great agency in producing a spirit of wild speculation." Though most state banks maintained adequate specie reserves, some indulged in "wildcat financiering" by recklessly expanding their note issues and by making loans without demanding adequate collateral. Speculators borrowed paper of dubious value from these institutions and gave it to the government land offices for new lands; the government in turn deposited the paper in the "pet banks," which made the money available again for further speculation. This was a happy situation for those who favored soft money, but it distressed the hard-money men who, as Benton said, had not joined "in putting down the paper currency of a national bank in order to put up a paper currency of a thousand local banks." Jackson shared this point of view and, in July 1836, suddenly intervened with his so-called Specie Circular. In the future, he ordered, federal land offices would accept only gold and silver in payment for public lands. This was a severe blow to the speculators, and for a time land sales almost ceased and inflated land prices dropped precipitously.

Next, the Congress, with Jackson's approval, gave an enormous stimulus to costly internal-improvement projects launched by the states. In 1836, with the federal government out of debt and with a surplus of almost $40 million, an act provided that beginning on January 1, 1837, the surplus above $5 million was to be distributed among the states in proportion to population in four quarterly installments. Many states, assuming that they would receive a similar subsidy each year and ignoring the fact that the federal funds were intended to be only a loan, immediately designed ambitious projects that exceeded the limits of their own resources. At the same time, the act deprived the "pet banks" of the bulk of their federal deposits and, in consequence, obliged them to call in their loans from private borrowers.

But the economic crisis had causes more fundamental than federal fiscal policy. For example, most of the inflation that preceded it was caused not by the expansion of state bank notes but by a substantial increase in specie imports, some of it from Great Britain and France but most of it from Mexico; by a decline of specie exports to the Far East; and by British credits that permitted the purchase of British goods at high prices without the loss of specie. Under these circumstances, in a period of prosperity and free spending, the country sustained a considerable international balance-of-payments deficit. When, eventually, Great Britain suffered from hard times, British investors began to withdraw their support of American economic expansion; and the British demand for American cotton began to decline just as the opening of new Western lands caused a sharp increase in the supply. Business conditions in the United States had been deteriorating for some months, but the real panic began in May 1837, when New York banks, soon followed by banks in the rest of the country, suspended specie payments. It was at this point that the Bank of the United States was missed, for its destruction reduced confidence in the whole banking system, thus stimulating runs on state banks. The state banks in turn were forced to curtail loans in an effort to increase their specie reserves.

The Panic of 1837 was followed by a brief period of economic recovery, but in 1839 the collapse of cotton and other agricultural prices and the decline of foreign investments brought on one of the most severe depressions in American history. Banks and business houses failed by the hundreds, factories closed and unemployment mounted, cotton sold for as low as 6 cents a pound (more than a 50 percent drop from the early 1830s), internal-improvement projects were abandoned, and some states, their credit exhausted, either stopped payments on their debts or repudiated them outright. The most feverish economic activity was among lawyers and auctioneers who arranged the foreclosure sales of farms, plantations, and urban business properties. Recovery did not come until the middle of the 1840s.

***The Independent Treasury.*** Understanding of the causes of business cycles had advanced very little since the depression following the Panic of 1819— President Van Buren attributed the present crisis to "overbanking" and "overtrading." The idea that government might give assistance to distressed farmers, workers, and businessmen was not yet seriously considered. In so far as the government did react to the crisis, it adopted fiscal policies that served to deepen the depression and heighten economic distress. Distribution of funds to the states for internal improvements was stopped, federal spending was curtailed, and the president concentrated on getting the government out of debt. Van Buren also rejected pleas for the withdrawal of the Specie Circular and continued the hard-money policy of his predecessor; he scorned the argument that the crisis justified the chartering of a new national bank. He thus identified himself with the radical, or Locofoco,* wing of his party—the ex-

*"Locofoco" was a popular name for the newly invented friction matches. Radical New York Democrats once carried candles and "locofocos" to a party meeting, because they feared that the conservatives would try to break it up by turning off the gaslights. This incident explains how the Locofocos got the name.

treme hard-money, antibank, antimonopoly faction that was especially strong among workingmen and reformers in his own state of New York.

One aim of the Locofocos was to divorce the federal government from banking altogether by denying all private banks the use of federal deposits. Van Buren urged such a step repeatedly, and finally, in 1840, Congress passed the Independent Treasury Act. This act authorized the establishment of subtreasuries in various cities where government funds could be placed in vaults for safekeeping. Although this system insured the government from loss, it made economic recovery more difficult, because it deprived the banks of funds that otherwise could have been used for private loans.

Banking was now entirely in the hands of the states. A few, notably New York and the New England states, managed to establish reasonably satisfactory and responsible state banking systems; a couple of Western states adopted the Locofoco philosophy and for a time abolished banking altogether. In many states the Jacksonians established "free banking" systems, which enabled promoters to secure a bank charter without a special act of the legislature. Free banking and so-called general incorporation laws were important aspects of Jacksonian Democracy at the state level. By eliminating the need for small entrepreneurs to have political influence in order to obtain state charters, these laws were expected to provide equal opportunities for all.

**The election of 1840.** As the presidential campaign of 1840 approached, the country was still deep in economic depression; the Democrats were bound to lose the support of many voters who would express their discontent by turning against the party in power. The Democratic national convention at Baltimore was a gloomy affair. The delegates renominated Van Buren unanimously, but with restrained enthusiasm, and adopted a platform reaffirming the party position on state rights, banking, internal improvements, and the Independent Treasury. The Democrats were on the defensive throughout the campaign.

The Whigs, however, were in an optimistic mood when their convention assembled at Harrisburg, Pennsylvania. Having been branded the enemies of the common man, a party of aristocrats and monopolists, having endured a succession of humiliating defeats, they now looked forward to giving the Democrats some of their own medicine. They had already attributed the depression to Democratic fiscal measures, charged that the Independent Treasury scheme was a callous attempt of the government to protect itself without regard for the welfare of the country, and accused Van Buren of indifference to the suffering of the people. Now, with a far more efficient party

organization, having learned much from the tactics of their enemies and from their own mistakes, they prepared to out-Jackson the Jacksonians in a bid for popular support. The Whigs passed over Clay in favor of a military hero: William Henry Harrison of Ohio, who had defeated the Indians at the Battle of Tippecanoe and the British at the Battle of the Thames. With an eye on the South, they nominated John Tyler of Virginia, a conservative state-rights Whig, for the Vice Presidency. They adopted no platform, for the campaign they planned was to have little relevance to concrete issues.

The Democrats were guilty of much low-level electioneering, but their campaign seemed almost dignified compared to the antics of the Whigs. Though Harrison was descended from an aristocratic Virginia family and lived as an Ohio country gentleman in a sixteen-room mansion, the Whigs transformed "Old Tippecanoe" into a simple frontier farmer and man of the people. When a blundering Democratic editor sneered that Harrison would be satisfied to retire to a log cabin with a barrel of hard cider, the Whigs happily accepted the statement as true. They praised his simple tastes, made log cabins and cider barrels their party symbols, and boasted of their own log-cabin backgrounds. (Webster apologized for not having been born in one.) The Whigs described Van Buren as a squanderer of public funds on lavish entertainment, a man of expensive aristocratic tastes who fancied fine wines, ate from gold plates, and effeminately scented his whiskers with cologne. They dazzled the voters with boisterous mass meet-

The election of 1840

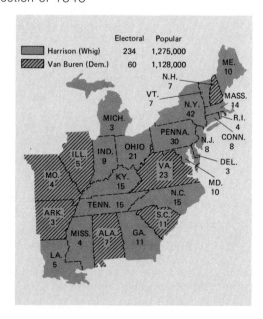

*Politics for the Common Man*

**TIPPECANOE LOG CABIN**
corner of Main & Eagle Streets. Erected on the 18th March, by the
**WHIGS OF BUFFALO;**
and dedicated to the cause
**HARRISON** and **TYLER**
Pub. & Lith. by Hall & Mooney        on the 20th March 1840.        Size. 20 feet by 30.

ings, barbecues, and torchlight processions; they nicknamed Van Buren "Martin Van Ruin" and "Sweet Sandy Whiskers"; they promised to cleanse the civil service of corruption and to restore prosperity; and they chanted their campaign slogans: "Tippecanoe and Tyler too" and "Van, Van is a used-up man." If this was the way to win democratic elections, the Whigs proved that they had mastered the technique as well as their opponents.

The voters responded by turning out in larger numbers than in any previous presidential election—even Jackson had not attracted so large a proportion to the polls. Harrison's popular majority was small, but he won overwhelmingly in the Electoral College: 234 votes to 60 for Van Buren. After twelve years of Democratic supremacy, the Whigs were to have their turn. Equally important, the presidential election of 1840 marked the final emergence of a fully developed second American party system, with vigorous two-party politics in every section and in all the states.

**The Supreme Court under Taney.** But the Democrats, like the Federalists in 1801, retained a firm hold on the third branch of the federal government: the judiciary. While he was President, Jackson had appointed six new Associate Justices to the Supreme Court, all of them staunch Democrats; and when Chief Justice Marshall died in 1835, Jackson had se-

lected Roger B. Taney, a one-time Federalist but now a state-rights agrarian, to replace him. Jacksonians thus controlled seven of the nine positions on the Court, and conservatives such as Webster feared an irresponsible and radical new departure from the constitutional doctrines laid down by Marshall. Actually, though the Taney Court modified Marshall's opinions on the rights of corporations and the sanctity of contracts, the main corpus of Marshall's decisions remained almost intact. Even the doctrine of judicial review went unchallenged; in several important cases the Court threw out state and (on one occasion) federal legislation that it found to be unconstitutional.

The chief departure from the extreme nationalism of Marshall was the new Court's tendency to give the states greater power to regulate corporations. This change is best illustrated in the case of *Charles River Bridge* v. *Warren Bridge* (1837). The issue was whether the state of Massachusetts, having earlier given a charter to the Charles River Bridge Company to build and operate a toll bridge, could now grant a charter to a second company to build and operate another and competing bridge. The first company contended that this would constitute a breach of contract, but the Court disagreed and held that the rights of corporations are subordinate to the interests of the community—"that the community also have rights, and that the happiness and well-being of every citizen depends on their faithful preservation." The Court thus provided an admirable statement of two of the basic goals of Jacksonian Democracy: encouragement to new entrepreneurs, and an attack on special privilege and entrenched "monopoly."

# Tyler and paralysis

**The Whig disaster.** As the Whigs organized their first administration, they looked forward to a period of progress along the lines of Whig principles. Harrison, who appeared to favor the goals of the American System, seemed ready to accept guidance from Webster and Clay, for he made Webster Secretary of State and gave most of the other Cabinet posts to followers of Clay. Then disaster struck. Only a month after his inauguration the sixty-eight-year-old President died of pneumonia, and for the first time the Vice President rose to the Presidency. Unfortunately for the Whigs, their new President, John Tyler, a Virginia aristocrat, sympathized with those Southern planters who opposed nearly everything the Whig majority hoped to accomplish. As a result, within less than a year, the Whig party was so torn by factionalism that it accomplished little, and the country had to suffer through a period of almost complete political stalemate.

Tyler had once been a Democrat but had broken with Jackson over nullification and the removal of federal deposits from Biddle's Bank. He drifted over to the Whigs because in his state they were dominated by affluent men of high social status and because he opposed the radical, Locofoco tendencies of the Democrats under Jackson and Van Buren. Tyler was thought to be a political friend of Clay, but he made it clear that the imperious Kentuckian was not going to run his Administration; none of his messages showed any sympathy for Clay's views on banking, tariffs, or internal improvements.

Clay, however, confidently planned a legislative program that would at last put his American System into full operation. In 1841 he introduced a bill to distribute the proceeds from the sale of public lands among the states to finance internal improvements. In a bid for Western support, this bill also contained a provision for preemption by which squatters on the public domain could purchase 160 acres of land they had improved at the minimum price of $1.25 an acre when the land was put up for sale. To get his bill adopted, Clay had to agree that the distribution of proceeds from land sales would cease if tariff schedules were increased. A year later, in 1842, the Whigs tried to raise the tariff without repealing distribution. But a presidential veto forced them to give up distribution in order to get the increase in duties for which manufacturers were clamoring. Tyler then reluctantly approved the Tariff of 1842 to solve the government's need for more revenue, though it restored the level of duties provided in the Tariff of 1832. The new tariff was virtually the only Whig achievement—Tyler not only forced the abandonment of distribution but vetoed internal-improvement bills with essentially the same arguments Jackson had used.

The final disappointment came when Clay and the majority of Whigs attempted to establish a third Bank of the United States. Tyler approved the repeal of the Independent Treasury Act, but it was well known that he would not accept a new system of national banking in its place. Hence the Whigs tried to disguise their purpose by using other names. First they provided for the creation of a "Fiscal Bank," but Tyler was not deceived and vetoed the bill; then they proposed the chartering of a "Fiscal Corporation," only to be thwarted by another presidential veto. With that, national banking ceased to be a serious issue in national politics for two decades. The angry Whigs in Congress formally read Tyler out of the party, the Cabinet resigned (except Webster, who was involved in diplomatic negotiations with the British), and Clay gave up his seat in the Senate to try again for the Presidency. After making a fiasco of the Whig victory, Tyler and his Southern allies began to drift back to the Democratic party, where in subsequent years they would challenge the Jacksonians for control.

**Foreign affairs under Tyler.** The political paralysis at home did not prevent the Tyler Administration from solving several problems in the country's foreign relations. Jackson, in spite of his blunt tactics, had already disposed of two issues that had survived the negotiations following the War of 1812: he managed to persuade the British to permit American merchants to trade with their West Indian islands; and, after a rather unnecessary crisis in American-French relations, he made a satisfactory settlement of claims against France for damages inflicted on American shipping during the Napoleonic wars. But new sources of friction in Anglo-American relations had begun to appear during the 1830s and had reached serious proportions by the time Tyler became President. The traditional undercurrent of hostility, heightened by British travelers who made disparaging comments on American culture and by local politicians bidding for the Irish vote, made it dangerous to permit disagreements to go unsettled.

Trouble began in 1837, when an insurrection broke out in the eastern provinces of Canada. Though many Americans hoped the uprising might ultimately lead to annexation, the British suppressed it with relative ease. But while it was in progress Americans along the frontier aided the rebels and afterward gave the defeated rebel leaders refuge. When raids across the border continued from American bases on the Niagara River, Canadian officials one night impetuously crossed the river, killed one American, and burned an American steamer, the *Caroline*, which had been carrying supplies to the rebels. In spite of growing tension, the British government ignored the American demand for reparations and an apology. Then, in 1840, a Canadian named Alexander McLeod was arrested in New York on suspicion of being a member of the party that had attacked the *Caroline;* he was brought to trial for murder and arson. The British government responded with a vigorous protest: it assumed responsibility for the attack on the *Caroline* and warned that McLeod's conviction would have serious consequences. Fortunately McLeod established an alibi and was acquitted, much to the relief of the State Department.

Meanwhile, a long-standing controversy over the Maine boundary flared up when, in 1838, American and Canadian lumberjacks battled for possession of part of a disputed area along the Aroostook River. Another dispute grew out of a British request that its naval patrols along the west coast of Africa be permitted to stop and search ships flying the American flag to determine whether they were engaging in the slave trade. This request revived memories of British practices during the Napoleonic wars, and the American government would not agree to it. Finally, in 1841, a group of slaves being transported from Virginia to New Orleans on the American brig *Creole* mutinied and sailed to Nassau, where British officials freed them. Prodded by angry Southerners, Secretary of State Webster demanded that the slaves be returned, but the British refused.

At this point a new British government decided that the time had come for negotiations and sent Lord Ashburton to Washington as a special envoy. Ashburton was a happy choice, for he was friendly to the United States and a man of infinite tact; moreover, he had met Webster in England, and the two men liked each other. Neither was an experienced professional diplomat, but both were in a conciliatory mood, and their patient and highly informal negotiations culminated in the important Webster-Ashburton Treaty of 1842.

Except for Oregon, which remained under joint occupation, the treaty settled all border controversies by awarding seven-twelfths of the disputed territory along the Maine boundary to the United States and by making minor adjustments around Lake Champlain and between Lake Superior and the Lake of the Woods. The treaty also included an agreement for the mutual extradition of fugitives accused of any of

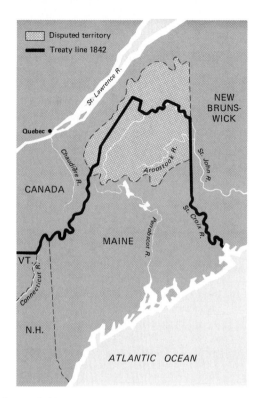

The Webster-Ashburton Treaty, 1842

seven major crimes. As for the slave trade, the United States did not agree to British search of her vessels but did agree to maintain a squadron off the African coast to apprehend slavers flying the American flag. Neither the *Caroline* nor the *Creole* affair was dealt with in the treaty, but Ashburton disposed of them through an exchange of notes that Webster chose to accept as satisfactory. With regard to the *Caroline* affair, Ashburton simply expressed regret "that some explanation and apology for this occurrence was not immediately made." In the case of the *Creole*, the slaves were not to be returned, but he promised that in the future there would be no "officious interference" with American vessels forced to enter British ports by "violence or accident."

Webster, after concluding these negotiations and seeing the treaty ratified by both governments, followed the example of the other Whigs and resigned from Tyler's Cabinet. Thereafter the Tyler Administration, disrupted and lacking congressional support, looked rather futile in the face of increasing sectional conflict. The resulting tensions would have a shattering effect on both national parties and, eventually, on the federal Union itself. In the critical years ahead, disheartened patriots would remember the strength and firmness of Andrew Jackson with growing admiration. As the country moved from crisis to crisis, the cry that would be heard more and more frequently was "Oh, for an hour of Old Hickory."

*THE ADVANCE OF DEMOCRACY*

The most perceptive contemporary analysis of the workings of American democracy in the Jacksonian era, in spite of some factual errors, is Alexis de Tocqueville, *Democracy in America,* 2 vols.* (1945). Moisie Ostrogorski, *Democracy and the Organization of Political Parties,* 2 vols.* (1902), though dated, is still a useful general work on the democratization of American politics. Chilton Williamson, *American Suffrage from Property to Democracy, 1760–1860*\* (1960), supersedes all other works on the extension of the suffrage. M. E. Gettleman, *The Dorr Rebellion: A Study in American Radicalism, 1833– 1849* (1973), examines the Rhode Island crisis from a radical perspective. J. S. Chase, *Emergence of the Presidential Nominating Convention, 1789–1832* (1973), is an able study. Two important revisionist studies that stress social stratification and a decline in class mobility are D. T. Miller, *Jacksonian Aristocracy: Class and Democracy in New York, 1830–1860* (1967), and Edward Pessen, *Riches, Class, and Power before the Civil War* (1973), the latter a quantitative study of men of wealth in Boston, New York, Brooklyn, and Philadelphia.

The disputed election of 1824, as well as the goals and misfortunes of the Adams Administration, are described with rich detail in George Dangerfield's two books: *The Era of Good Feelings*\* (1952), and *The Awakening of American Nationalism, 1815–1828*\* (1965). Three biographies are useful for an understanding of those years: G. G. Van Deusen, *The Life of Henry Clay*\* (1937), S. F. Bemis, *John Quincy Adams and the Union* (1956), and C. C. Mooney, *William H. Crawford, 1772–1834* (1974). A fascinating personal record of Adams' presidency can be found in C. F. Adams, ed., *The Memoirs of John Quincy Adams,* 12 vols. (1874–77). R. V. Remini, *The Election of Andrew Jackson*\* (1963), is the best study of the election of 1828.

*THE AGE OF JACKSON*

Three recent surveys, based on modern scholarship, deal critically with Jacksonian Democracy: G. G. Van Deusen, *The Jacksonian Era*\* (1959), C. M. Wiltse, *The New Nation, 1800–1845*\* (1961), and Edward Pessen, *Jacksonian America*\* (1969). The latter is the most interesting and the most decidedly anti-Jackson. Marquis James, *Andrew Jackson,* Vol. 2: *Portrait of a President*\* (1937), is a sympathetic and lucid biography of the presidential years. R. V. Remini, *Andrew Jackson*\* (1966), brief and breezy, portrays Jackson sympathetically as a skilled politican. Two of Jackson's strongest supporters in Congress are the subjects of distinguished biographies: C. G. Sellers, Jr., *James K. Polk: Jacksonian, 1795–1843* (1957), and W. N. Chambers, *Old Bullion Benton: Senator from the New West* (1956). There are also excellent biographies of two key figures in the Jackson Administration: C. B. Swisher, *Roger B. Taney* (1936), and W. B. Hatcher, *Edward Livingston: Jeffersonian Republican and Jacksonian Democrat* (1940). An authoritative study of administrative organization is L. D. White, *The Jacksonians: A Study in Administrative History, 1829–1861*\* (1954). R. P. McCormick, *The Second American Party System: Party Formation in the Jacksonian Era*\* (1966), is a revisionist study of major importance.

The meaning of Jacksonian Democracy is still the subject of animated controversy. In addition to the study by Edward Pessen, cited above, the following books, each notable for its distinctive interpretation, provide a sample of the various ways in which Jacksonian Democracy can be viewed: A. M. Schlesinger, Jr., *The Age of Jackson*\* (1945); Richard Hofstadter, *The American Political Tradition*\* (1948); J. W. Ward, *Andrew Jackson: Symbol for an Age*\* (1955); Joseph Dorfman, *The Economic Mind in American Civilization,* 5 vols. (1946–49); Marvin Meyers, *The Jacksonian Persuasion*\* (1957); Lee Benson, *The Concept of Jacksonian Democracy: New York as a Test Case*\* (1961); and R. P. Formisano, *The Birth of Mass Political Parties: Michigan, 1827–1861* (1971).

All the above books deal with Jackson's views on banking and are important to a study of the controversy over the second Bank of the United States. But the key work on this topic is Bray Hammond, *Banks and Politics in America from the Revolution to the Civil War*\* (1957). R. V. Remini, *Andrew Jackson and the Bank War*\* (1967), is a brief, balanced study stressing the political side of the controversy. Two other works merit consultation: W. B. Smith, *Economic Aspects of the Second Bank of the United States* (1953), and J. M. McFaul, *The Politics of Jacksonian Finance* (1972). The best

*Available in a paperback edition.

possible case for Nicholas Biddle is presented in T. P. Govan, *Nicholas Biddle: Nationalist and Public Banker* (1959). J. A. Wilburn, *Biddle's Bank: The Crucial Years* (1967), is a study of sources of public support for the Bank before the election of 1832. J. R. Sharp, *The Jacksonians versus the Banks* (1970), is a study of banking policy at the state level after the Panic of 1837. W. G. Shade, *Banks or No Banks: The Money Issue in Western Politics, 1832–1865* (1972), finds banking to be a durable cause of political divisions.

Angie Debo, *A History of the Indians of the United States* (1970), is an excellent survey. W. E. Washburn, *The Indian in America** (1975), is a cultural study. William Brandon, *The Last Americans: The Indians in American Culture* (1974), emphasizes Indian-white relations. The tragedy of Indian removals is the subject of Angie Debo, *The Road to Disappearance: A History of the Creek Indians* (1941); A. H. DeRosier, Jr., *The Removal of the Choctaw Indians** (1970); and Grant Foreman, *Indian Removal: The Emigration of the Five Civilized Tribes of Indians** (1932). J. K. Mahon, *History of the Second Seminole War, 1835–1842* (1967), is a vivid account of Seminole resistance. F. P. Prucha, *American Indian Policy in the Formative Years** (1962), is a history of federal legislation. M. P. Rogin, *Fathers and Children: Andrew Jackson and the Destruction of American Indians* (1975), is a less than successful attempt at psychohistory. Land policy in the Jacksonian era is treated fully in R. G. Wellington, *The Political and Sectional Influence of the Public Lands, 1828–1842* (1942), and R. M. Robbins, *Our Landed Heritage: The Public Domain** (1942).

### THE NULLIFICATION CONTROVERSY

C. S. Sydnor, *The Development of Southern Sectionalism, 1819–1848** (1948), analyzes the nullification crisis in the broad setting of Southern history. The best study of nullification is W. W. Freehling, *Prelude to Civil War** (1966). Calhoun's ideas can be studied in a collection of his writings edited by R. K. Crallé: *Works of J. C. Calhoun,* 6 vols. (1851–55). Sympathetic analyses are provided in A. O. Spain, *The Political Theory of John C. Calhoun* (1951); C. M. Wiltse, *John C. Calhoun, Nullifier, 1829–1839* (1949); and M. L. Coit, *John C. Calhoun: American Portrait** (1950). More critical appraisals appear in Richard Hofstadter, *The American Political Tradition** (1948); G. M. Capers, *John C. Calhoun, Opportunist** (1960); and R. N. Current, *John C. Calhoun** (1966).

### DEPRESSION AND THE WHIG INTERLUDE

The best available biographical studies of Van Buren are Holmes Alexander, *The American Talleyrand* (1935), and R. V. Remini, *Martin Van Buren and the Making of the Democratic Party** (1959). These should be supplemented by Van Buren's relatively candid account of his own life: *The Autobiography of Martin Van Buren,* edited by J. C. Fitzpatrick (1920). The Van Buren Administration is analyzed in J. C. Curtis, *The Fox at Bay: Martin Van Buren and the Presidency, 1837–1841* (1970). In a challenging new interpretation of the panic and depression, Peter Temin, *The Jacksonian Economy** (1969), absolves the Jacksonians from major responsibility for the inflation and subsequent collapse. Earlier studies of the economic crisis are R. C. McGrane, *The Panic of 1837** (1924), and W. B. Smith and A. H. Cole, *Fluctuations in American Business, 1790–1860* (1935).

R. P. McCormick, *The Second American Party System**, and G. G. Van Deusen, *The Jacksonian Era**, both cited above, are the best introductions to a study of the origin and growth of the Whig party. Three biographies of Whig leaders also need to be consulted: the biography of Clay by Van Deusen, cited above; C. M. Fuess, *Daniel Webster,* 2 vols. (1930, 2nd ed., 1968); and R. N. Current, *Daniel Webster and the Rise of National Conservatism** (1955). R. G. Gunderson, *The Log-Cabin Campaign* (1957), is a brisk account of the election of 1840. The Tyler Administration is treated competently in O. D. Lambert, *Presidential Politics in the United States, 1841–1844* (1936), and O. P. Chitwood, *John Tyler: Champion of the Old South* (1939). A. B. Corey, *The Crisis of 1830–1842 in Canadian-American Relations** (1941), and J. B. Brebner, *North Atlantic Triangle* (1945), are good monographs on foreign policy under Tyler.

*Available in a paperback edition.

# CHAPTER 10

# *An era of reform*

New-Harmony 1832.

K. Bodmer

Many nineteenth-century Americans believed that the destiny of their country concerned not only themselves but all humanity. In America's congenial environment men and women would reveal their capacity to govern themselves, to live in harmony with the laws of God's universe, and to eradicate social injustice; they would build an ideal society of righteous men and women whose leaders would be motivated by disinterested benevolence. In achieving these noble goals America would serve as a model for the rest of the world. To fail would be to betray a sacred trust.

This belief in a divine mission, together with a nagging awareness of their shortcomings, made Americans inordinately sensitive to criticism from European visitors. Tocqueville noted that their "irritable patriotism" caused them to take offense at any comment that was even mildly unfavorable. Outsiders could not speak freely, without risking resentment, "of anything at all except, perhaps, the climate and the soil; and even then Americans will be found ready to defend both as if they had cooperated in producing them."

But if Americans regarded criticism by outsiders as impertinent, many of them periodically displayed an ample capacity for self-criticism. For they knew that neither they as individuals nor their society had yet achieved that state of near-perfection toward which they hopefully aimed. Though they cherished an optimistic belief that a benign providence made progress inevitable, improvements did not always come fast enough to satisfy them, and they sometimes tried to give providence a helping hand. "We could not retard the great forward movement of Humanity if we would," wrote Horace Greeley, editor of the New York *Tribune*, "but each of us may decide for himself whether to share in the glory of promoting it or incur the shame of having looked coldly and indifferently on."

In the 1820s movements for moral uplift and social reform began to attract people who were unwilling to compromise with evil and were impatient with the slow pace of progress. The causes they championed were by no means peculiarly American—British and American reformers had considerable influence on each other—but there was a millennial quality about the American crusades that was unique. Theodore Parker, a distinguished Boston clergyman, described the aims of the reformers who kept the country in a turmoil for a whole generation: They hoped to create a society

> full of industry and abundance, full of wisdom, virtue, and the poetry of life; a state with unity among all, with freedom for each; a church without tyranny, a society without ignorance, want, or crime, a state without oppression; yes, a world with no war among the nations to consume the work of their hands, and no restrictive policy to hinder the welfare of mankind.

233

The goals of this perfectionist program, the reformers believed, not only were attainable but could be achieved with relative speed and without violent upheaval. There existed in America, one of them explained, "abundant elements for progress, and a field of action comparatively free from those obstacles which so impede reform elsewhere." Other countries might have to resort to violence in order to overthrow injustice, but here "the better course of effecting reform by moral and intellectual means is more trustingly expected." The proper agencies of reform were the churches and benevolent societies, rather than revolutionary movements or even political parties. To be sure, some clergymen frowned on the crusaders and refused to become involved in secular affairs, but many of them thought it their proper function to help realize the promise of American life by advancing the cause of reform.

# The religious background

**The decline of orthodox Calvinism.** Tocqueville believed that there was "no country in the world where the Christian religion retains a greater influence over the souls of men than in America." Certainly the Americans of the first half of the nineteenth century were still deeply religious, and the church was still a powerful force in their lives. But the various Protestant sects, especially those that had been based on Calvinist theology, had gone through some critical times during the century since the Great Awakening and Jonathan Edwards' stout defense of orthodoxy. By the start of the nineteenth century many of the Puritan dogmas—predestination, infant damnation, and the total depravity of man—had already been rejected, or at least qualified, by a more liberal theology that replaced Calvin's God of wrath with a benevolent God of love. The conservatives fought back: they admonished the faithful to "guard against the insidious encroachments of innovation—that evil and beguiling spirit which is now stalking to and fro in the earth, seeking whom it may devour." But this was no more than a rear-guard action.

Even in the eighteenth century a number of heresies, some of them actually quite old, had begun to trouble the minds of a few New England clergymen—heresies that raised doubts about doctrines such as predestination, the Trinity, and the divinity of Christ. These early challenges were fortified by the rationalism of the Enlightenment and the more optimistic view of human nature expressed by the philosophers of the American and French revolutions. Respect for the dignity of the individual, confidence in the individual's capacity for self-improvement, and belief in the idea of progress led to a decline in otherworldliness and a growing interest in temporal affairs. Life on earth, according to this new view, was not a mere preparation for the hereafter, at best a kind of winnowing of the saved from the damned; rather, it had its own beauty and value.

These intellectual trends caused orthodox Calvinism to give way to a theology that was at once more rational and more humanistic. Many leaders of the Revolutionary generation, such as Jefferson and Franklin, withdrew from the established churches and became deists. Deism, which originated in Europe in the early eighteenth century, emphasized the ethics of Christianity but rejected the Trinity, the divinity of Christ, the idea of original sin, and the Bible as divine revelation. It held that God had created the universe and set it in motion to run by natural laws. He did not perform miracles or intervene in the everyday affairs of the world. The humanistic implications of deism were evident in Thomas Paine's *The Age of Reason*: "I believe in the equality of man, and I believe that religious duties consist in doing justice, loving mercy, and endeavoring to make our fellow creatures happy." Paine accepted the creed of no church; indeed, he described the established churches as "human inventions set up to terrify and enslave mankind and monopolize power and profit." But few intellectuals were prepared to carry rationalism this far, and most church leaders saw no significant difference between deism and atheism.

*Unitarianism.* In the long run those who worked for a liberalized theology within the churches had a broader influence than the freethinkers who deserted organized Christianity entirely. These liberalizers rebelled especially against the deterministic Calvinist doctrine of salvation only for the elect in favor of the more hopeful doctrine of free will and salvation open to all. The revolt against traditional Calvinism produced several new sects, such as the Universalists, and a division of the Presbyterians into Old and New schools. But the largest and most influential of the organized religious groups produced by eighteenth-century rationalism and humanism was the Unitarian Church. An offshoot of Congregationalism, it appealed chiefly to the better-educated and more affluent descendants of the New England Puritans. It showed its greatest vitality and grew most vigorously in the early decades of the nineteenth century. Unitarians, as their name indicates, did not believe in the Trinity—Jesus was mortal, the founder of a great religion but not the son of God. They denied that men and women were conceived in sin or that they were totally depraved; rather, they were capable of goodness and virtue through the development of a

Christian character. Moreover, according to this comfortable theology, good Christians received their reward on earth as well as in the hereafter, for they "enjoy the world more than other men [and] find more satisfaction in it." God was a merciful and loving Father, not a vindictive and arbitrary deity who predestined the mass of mankind to damnation. Unitarians were skeptical of fine-spun theological systems and urged each individual to search the Scriptures for truth. And once found, it must not be perverted into dogma to be imposed on others. Instead, Unitarians preached tolerance of differences among sincerely devout men and women.

William Ellery Channing (1780–1842), pastor of the Federal Street Church in Boston, was the most eminent Unitarian clergyman of the early nineteenth century. Channing stressed the primary responsibility of individuals to their own consciences and helped to link the liberal Unitarian creed with humanitarianism. To him "God is infinitely good, kind, benevolent," and the essence of religion is "the adoration of goodness." Belief in predestination and the God of Calvinism tends "to form a gloomy, forbidding, and servile religion, and to lead men to substitute censoriousness, bitterness, and persecution, for a tender and impartial charity." Since Channing believed in a human capacity for virtue and denied original sin, he found the doctrine of atonement preposterous—it was as if "the Creator, in order to pardon his own children, had erected a gallows in the centre of the universe, and had publicly executed upon it . . . an Infinite Being, the partaker of his own Supreme Divinity." Channing supported humanitarian reform, "because I have learned the essential equality of men before the common Father . . . because I see in him a great nature, the divine image, and vast capacities." In Channing, Unitarianism found its ideal leader, for he balanced its rationalism and tolerance with a humanistic warmth and with an active concern for the welfare of humanity.

**The transcendentalists.** In the course of time, however, Unitarianism began to crystallize into a new orthodoxy. The Church's well-fed members, though more reasonable and tolerant than their Puritan ancestors, became at least as smug; though given to philanthropy, they were free to pursue individual gain with far less restraint. Unitarianism struck a growing number of New England intellectuals as distressingly cold, formal, and passionless and its communicants as more concerned with material than with spiritual well-being. "Nothing quieted doubt so completely as the mental calm of the Unitarian clergy," wrote Henry Adams. "For them, difficulties might be ignored; doubts were waste of thought; nothing exacted solution. Boston had solved the universe."

Moreover, eighteenth-century rationalism, the foundation of Unitarianism, was succumbing to a romantic movement that was associated with the German writers Friedrich von Schiller and Johann Wolfgang von Goethe, and with the British men of letters Samuel Coleridge, Thomas Carlyle, and William Wordsworth. The romanticists rejected experience and pure reason as the keys to truth and substituted for them intuition, or spiritual insight, which they believed produced knowledge that could not be derived through the senses. They idealized natural, spontaneous individuals rather than the educated and sophisticated. In a sense, Jacksonian Democracy, with its faith in the intuitive good judgment of common people, was the political manifestation of romanticism in America.

In 1836, a small group of intellectuals living in and around Boston and Concord, Massachusetts, began to meet informally to exchange ideas about philosophy and theology. Though the group had no formal organization or membership list, it was known as the Transcendental Club. The former Unitarian minister Ralph Waldo Emerson was always its moving spirit. In addition to Emerson, this distinguished group included, at one time or another, Unitarian clergymen such as Theodore Parker, George Ripley, and James Freeman Clark; literary figures such as Henry Thoreau, Amos Bronson Alcott, Nathaniel Hawthorne, and Orestes Brownson; and talented women such as Sophia and Elizabeth Peabody, and Margaret Fuller.

The transcendentalists were appalled by the crass materialism of a country preoccupied with economic

*Margaret Fuller*

*The religious background*

## Ralph Waldo Emerson: the goodness in man

*The intuition of the moral sentiment is an insight of the perfection of the laws of the soul. These laws execute themselves. They are out of time, out of space, and not subject to circumstance. Thus in the soul of man there is a justice whose retributions are instant and entire. He who does a noble deed is instantly ennobled. He who does a mean deed is by the action itself contracted. He who puts off impurity, thereby puts on purity. If a man is at heart just, then in so far is he God; the safety of God, the immortality of God, the majesty of God do enter into that man with justice.... Good is positive. Evil is merely privative, not absolute: it is like cold, which is the privation of heat. All evil is so much death or nonentity. Benevolence is absolute and real. So much benevolence as a man hath, so much life hath he. For all things proceed out of this same spirit, which is differently named love, justice, temperance, in its different applications.... Whilst a man seeks good ends, he is strong by the whole strength of nature. In so far as he roves from these ends, he bereaves himself of power, or auxiliaries; his being shrinks out of all remote channels, he becomes less and less, a mote, a point, until absolute badness is absolute death.*

**From Ralph Waldo Emerson, "Divinity School Address," 1838.**

development and were concerned that spiritual progress was not keeping pace. They were too individualistic and too hostile to institutional restraints to start a church of their own, but the philosophy of transcendentalism was shot through with theological implications. It was clearly an outgrowth of Puritanism and Unitarianism (with a touch of Quakerism and mysticism) as well as romanticism.

The transcendentalists, like the Unitarians, rejected Calvinist dogma and hopefully believed in the essential goodness of humanity and in a God of love. But their idealism was warm and affirmative, not the bland concoction of "pale negations" that Emerson found so unsatisfying in Unitarianism. As Theodore Parker explained, transcendentalists held that man has "faculties which give him ideas and intuitions which transcend sensational experience; ideas whose origin is not from sensation, nor their proof from sensation." The mind of man "is not a smooth tablet on which sensation writes its experience, but is a living principle which of itself originates ideas." Moreover, God dwells in every person, and human nature, therefore, is not simply excellent but divine. Since the transcendentalists discovered no evil in the human mind and had faith in the individual's intuitive knowledge of right and justice, they urged everyone to follow the dictates of conscience even when it led to the defiance of church or state. "To know what is right," said Parker, "I need not ask what is the current practice, what say the Revised Statutes, what said holy men of old, but what says conscience? what, God?" So far as the laws are just they deserve to be obeyed. "But so far as they are unjust they have no

claim to be obeyed; it is a sin to obey them. Who gave us the right to do wrong?" Thoreau, in his famous *Essay on Civil Disobedience,* asked: "Must the citizen ever for a moment, or in the least degree, resign his conscience to the legislator? Why has every man a conscience, then?" Carrying an old Jeffersonian slogan to what he thought was its logical conclusion, he argued: "That government is best which governs not at all."

The transcendental belief that God, or the Oversoul, permeated both matter and spirit, and that humanity, blessed with a spark of divinity, enjoyed limitless potentialities, had several consequences. It led to a celebration of individualism and self-reliance and to an admiration of those who had the strength and confidence to strike out on their own—sentiments that abounded in many of Emerson's essays. In this spirit Thoreau, in 1845, built a cabin on Walden Pond near Concord, where he lived for two years to illustrate that individuals can rely on themselves and live a full life without the baubles and trivia of civilized society. Transcendentalism also produced a rather naive faith that in the long run everything would turn out well. Emerson wrote: "An eternal beneficent necessity is always bringing things right. . . . The league between virtue and nature engages all things to assume a hostile front to vice."

But although the transcendentalists were optimists, they did not ignore the shortcomings of American society or wait complacently for an inevitable progress to produce the remedies. Instead, they were severe critics of governments, laws, social institutions, and debasing commercialism—whatever prevented humanity from realizing its full potential. "Their quarrel with every man they meet," said Emerson, "is not with his kind, but with his degree." Hence the transcendentalists, though they were not given to organizing or joining reform societies, nonetheless contributed to the country's intellectual climate of reform. Emerson asked,

> What is man born for but to be a Re-former, a Re-maker of what man has made; a renouncer of lies; a restorer of truth and good, imitating that great Nature which embosoms us all, and which sleeps no moment on an old past, but every hour repairs herself, yielding to us every morning a new day, and with every pulsation a new life?

**The Protestant sects and revivalism.** If Unitarianism was too cold, transcendentalism was too intellectual (and perhaps too cheerful) to attract a large following. Most Americans remained in the Congregational, Presbyterian, Baptist, and Methodist churches or joined one of the numerous evangelical sects that proliferated in the nineteenth century. Even at the popular level, however, the hard tenets of orthodox Calvinism began to soften. Devout Protestants continued to believe in man's sinful condition, but they accepted the doctrine of a benevolent God who offered everyone the chance of salvation through the experience of spiritual conversion and through faith. Moreover, the material opportunities that lay before Americans in a growing and flourishing society discouraged otherworldliness and tempted them to expect virtue to be rewarded on earth as well as in heaven.

Even so, much of orthodoxy still survived in the religion of the common people. In their cosmology, the Copernican revolution in astronomy notwithstanding, the earth was still the center of the universe; and God continued to be actively and intimately involved in human affairs. Ordinary churchgoers still believed in the Trinity, in the Bible as divine revelation, and in a literal heaven and hell. They might doubt man's total depravity, but they could never accept the transcendentalist's extreme optimism about human nature. For the reality of evil in the world was too manifest, human frailty in the face of temptation too obvious. The continued prevalence of endemic and epidemic diseases, and the resulting short life expectancy and high infant mortality, made most Americans acutely conscious, sometimes almost obsessed, with the imminence of death. This awareness helps explain the persistence of a measure of gloom and pessimism in their outlook on life; it intensified their religious fervor and turned them to the church for strength and solace.

With few exceptions, notably the Quakers, the various Protestant denominations actively proselytized those who were seeking comfort and salvation. Some had greater success than others. After the Revolution the Protestant Episcopal Church, formerly the Anglican Church, was discredited by the fact that much of its clergy had been Loyalist; it grew only slowly, appealing mostly to well-to-do Eastern conservatives. The Congregationalists of New England lost members to the Unitarians. In the newly settled regions of the West they joined with the Presbyterians in 1801 to adopt a Plan of Union, by which they agreed to establish united churches that might select either Congregational or Presbyterian ministers. In the long run the Plan of Union benefited the Presbyterians, because most of the united churches entered their fold. Although the Presbyterians thus experienced a considerable growth, they were far surpassed by two other Protestant denominations. One of these, the Baptists, had phenomenal success with their system of autonomous congregations and with an untrained, uneducated clergy that spoke the language of the common people. Their ministers brought a primitive but passionate message of hellfire for sinners and redemption for those who experienced conversion and admitted God into their souls. The second, and most successful of all, were the Methodists, each of whose itinerant ministers rode a circuit of several congregations in the scattered settlements of the West and preached an equally simple Christianity.

After the Great Awakening of the mid-eighteenth century, revivalism became a periodic phenomenon. During these interludes of religious enthusiasm Presbyterians, Baptists, and Methodists won new converts by the thousands. In the course of the Second Awakening, which began around 1800, the religious frenzy spread with increasing intensity from east to west. An innovation of this revival was the camp meeting, which brought crowds together for several days of uninterrupted preaching and prayers. Under the emotional influence of exhorters who called for repentance, many experienced conversion. Since the battle with Satan was often violent, a familiar spectacle was the jumping, shouting, and moaning of tortured souls. When the battle had been won and Satan put to rout, as one witness observed, "hundreds were prostrate upon the earth before the Lord."

The intensity of religious feeling and the relative autonomy of many individual congregations often led to disputes over questions of doctrine, church organization, and ritual, and these in turn caused schisms and the formation of numerous small fundamentalist denominations. For example, the quest of a group of Methodists in western New York for holiness and perfect love led them ultimately to separate from the Methodist Episcopal Church and to form the Free

*The religious background*

*Methodist camp meeting: new converts by the thousands*

Methodist Church. The divisions among Baptists produced the Hard-Shells, Soft-Shells, Primitives, and Free Willers, as well as new denominations such as the Campbellites (Disciples of Christ). Among the new sects, one of the most important was the Mormon Church, founded in 1830 by Joseph Smith. The Church of Jesus Christ of Latter-Day Saints, as it was officially called, was based on miraculous revelations that Smith claimed to have received from God and that he incorporated in the Book of Mormon. Still another sect, the Adventists, believed in the imminence of the Bible's prophesied second coming of Christ. Early in the 1840s, William Miller, a Vermont Baptist preacher, after a series of elaborate calculations, predicted the start of the millennium, first in 1843, then in 1844. The disappointment that Miller's Adventist followers eventually experienced led most of them to desert him, but for a few years they numbered hundreds of thousands.

During another period of revivalism in the 1820s many of its leaders, for the first time, combined a desire to save souls with an active interest in social reform. The greatest preacher of this revival was the Reverend Charles G. Finney, who gathered his first harvest of converts from the fertile soil of upstate New York, a land of transplanted New Englanders. Finney preached not only salvation through repentance and faith but the importance of good works and the obligation of the churches to take "right ground . . . on all the subjects of practical morality which come up for decision from time to time." To him original sin was a "deep-seated but voluntary . . . self-interest. . . . All sin consists in selfishness; and all holiness or virtue, in disinterested benevolence." Salvation was not the end but the beginning of life—a life of useful work and benevolent activity. Since Finney's doctrine, as one contemporary observed, encouraged mankind "to *work* as well as to *believe*," Finney became a powerful influence for social reform. In addition to winning the support of many established preachers, he sent out a remarkable group of young converts to advance his work, notably Theodore Dwight Weld, who went into the West to preach and to advance the cause of moral reform.

In 1830 Finney brought his revival to New York City, which he regarded as carrying the Gospel into the precincts of hell itself. Here he met two remarkable brothers, Arthur and Lewis Tappan, wealthy merchants and pious men who were already devoting most of their energy and fortunes to philanthropy.

The Tappans welcomed Finney and organized an Association of Gentlemen to give financial support to both his religious and his reform work. Lewis Tappan, once a Unitarian, had become dissatisfied with that faith and had moved not toward transcendentalism but back to evangelical Protestantism. He had concluded, he explained, that the Unitarians "did not, in an equal degree, consider themselves as stewards, and their property as consecrated to the cause of Christianity; and that they were deficient in a devotional frame of mind."

Religion thus encouraged reform in two different but parallel trends. First, the transcendentalists celebrated the divinity of man and called on everyone to trust their consciences in their quest for right and justice. Thoreau wrote: "It is not desirable to cultivate a respect for the law, so much as for the right. The only obligation which I have a right to assume is to do at any time what I think right." Second, the evangelical Protestantism of the revivalists made good works a manifestation of holiness and of the experience of conversion, and reform a vital function of the churches. "And what is to reform mankind but the truth?" asked Finney. "And who shall present the truth if not the church and the ministry? Away with the idea that Christians can remain neutral and keep still, and yet enjoy the approbation and blessing of God."

## The movement for reform

***The nature of the movement.*** William Ellery Channing observed that one of the remarkable circumstances of his age was "the energy with which the principle of combination, or of action by joint forces, by associated numbers, is manifesting itself. It may be said, without much exaggeration, that everything is done now by Societies. . . . You can scarcely name an object for which some institution has not been formed." Though the benevolent societies were numerous, there was a considerable overlapping of both leaders and members. Active reformers tended to be attracted to several causes, and the same names appeared repeatedly among the directors of the various reform organizations. In its early phase the movement was an inherently conservative effort of clergymen and wealthy philanthropists to fight infidelity and preserve the country's Christian character. Organizations such as the American Sunday School Union, American Home Missionary Society, and American Bible Society all had as their goal a general moral regeneration. But under the influence of various perfectionist groups the movement soon transcended its cramped moralism and grew into a multifaceted crusade for social betterment.

The reformers, for a variety of reasons, were severely criticized by their conservative contemporaries and have been treated unsympathetically by some historians as well. In the first place, as a leading reformer himself noted, there is a "tendency of every reform to surround itself with a fringe of the unreasonable and half-cracked"; and the reformers had within their ranks a full quota of cranks whose bizarre crusades exposed the whole movement to ridicule. Some devoted their energies to stopping the wearing of corsets; others to food fads, such as the eating of whole-wheat bread; and still others to the "science" of phrenology. A surprising number of them developed an interest in Spiritualism, especially in the ideas of the Swedish philosopher Emanuel Swedenborg, who described a spirit world where all were received and were able to strive for perfection. Reformers were accused, too, of being more concerned with denouncing evil than with advancing constructive remedies. Their movement, it has been said, was a vehicle for righteous men and women to assert their righteous-

*William Ellery Channing*

ness—for teetotalers to deplore the use of alcohol, and for the virtuous to denounce immorality. Moreover, as Emerson complained, many of them were "narrow, self-pleasing, conceited men" given to petty bickering and "personal and party heats." They often exhibited an uncompromising inflexibility that made them unattractive as human beings and ineffective in striving toward their own goals.

From the perspective of the twentieth century, these reformers have also been criticized for their naive optimism about human nature, for their belief that social evils result from the selfish acts of individuals, and for their confidence that social problems can be solved simply by the regeneration of individuals and by appealing to the innate goodness in humanity. In addition, many of them were not very well informed about the social problems of the growing class of urban factory workers. Reform leaders usually came from the old middle-class families of rural and small-town New England; their social backgrounds and economic assumptions caused them to be rather insensitive to conditions in the industrial centers—or prone to blame the plight of the working man on his use of liquor and tobacco.

Though the shortcomings of the reformers were real enough, the movements they launched were not merely the enterprises of impractical, shortsighted cranks and neurotics. The ranks of reform contained many dedicated men and women who demonstrated a keen understanding of, and sensitivity to, at least some of the social problems of their day. The severe dislocations of a period of rapid economic growth and unsettling social change, which produced both a widespread feeling that traditional values were being lost and a cluster of new or sharply intensified social problems, undoubtedly contributed to the reform impulse. But the dislocations of growth and change were not new phenomena in America, nor were the social problems all of recent vintage. The crucial ingredient that acted as the catalyst in producing a reform movement seems to have been the changes in secular and religious thought noted above. These changes best explain why the reformers were sensitive to certain social problems, why certain organizational methods appealed to them, and why they resorted to the tactics they used in fighting their foes.

The accomplishments of the reformers were far from negligible. If they were a trial to their friends, it was in part because their work, by its very nature, forced them to "disregard the peace and proprieties of the social world." Each reformer seemed to bear a burden of personal guilt for the evils in society and felt driven to do something to eliminate them. This sense of individual responsibility, which can easily be lost in a mass society, was in itself a thing of inestimable value.

**Treatment of criminals and the insane.** Humane and sensitive men and women who investigated the care of paupers, criminals, and the insane in their own communities found an ample field for reform. These social derelicts, the victims of public ignorance or indifference, were treated almost as they had been in the Middle Ages. In atrocious jails and dungeons young offenders were thrown together with hardened criminals and the violently insane; in neglected almshouses idiots and the destitute were left to the mercy of low-paid, untrained attendants. Humanitarians managed at least to start the painfully slow process of providing prisons with better physical accommodations. With their more enlightened approach to penology, they urged, with some success, that the community concentrate on reforming, rather than punishing, criminals. Meanwhile, the states, one by one, responded to the new spirit by abolishing several vestiges of primitive justice: the imprisonment of debtors, public floggings, and public executions.

Since little was known about the causes of insanity, or about therapy, society provided almost no mental hospitals; the insane were either cared for by relatives or committed to jails and almshouses. Among those who took an interest in the treatment of the insane, Dorothea Dix, a Boston schoolmistress, was the most active advocate of state-supported mental hospitals and of experiments in therapy. In 1841 she launched her crusade by investigating the condition of the insane in her own state. Two years later, she presented the legislature with an eloquent but factual memorial that described "the present state of insane persons confined in this Commonwealth, in cages, closets, cellars, stalls, pens! Chained, naked, beaten with rods, and lashed into obedience." Until her death in 1887 she worked with tireless patience to arouse public officials throughout the country, and her sincerity and command of the facts won her considerable success.

**Temperance.** Concern for criminals, paupers, and the insane was intimately related to another goal of the reform movement: temperance. It was commonly believed that excessive drinking was a basic cause of the condition of these unfortunates, as well as of the poverty that plagued city workers. Temperance, therefore, would not merely redeem the individual sinner but would advance the whole program of social reform. There can be no doubt that drunkenness was a genuine problem, for this was an age of heavy drinking in which the per capita consumption of whiskey, hard cider, and rum was staggering. The temperance movement began with the formation of numerous local societies, which, in 1826, combined to form a national organization, the American Society for the Promotion of Temperance. Some leaders

*Dorothea Dix: sincerity and sensitivity*

merely preached moderation in the use of liquor, but others sought converts who would pledge total abstinence. Some relied on the voluntary decisions of individuals; others urged the use of the coercive power of state governments. In 1846 Maine passed the first prohibition law; within the next decade a dozen other Northern and Western states followed Maine's example, but most of these laws remained in force for only a few years. At its height the temperance movement resembled a religious revival; its flavor is suggested by a stanza from one of its popular songs, "One Glass More":

> Stay, mortal, stay! nor heedless thus
>   Thy sure destruction seal;
> Within that cup there lurks a curse,
>   Which all who drink shall feel.
> Disease and death forever nigh,
>   Stand ready at the door,
> And eager wait to hear the cry—
>   "O give me one glass more!"

**Women's rights.** Women took a special interest in temperance, but when they tried to participate actively in this or other reform movements they confronted a wall of prejudice and the rebuff that a woman's place was in the home. American men characteristically treated women with deference but would not accept them as equals. Women, according

to their male protectors, were physically, intellectually, and emotionally unsuited for participation in public affairs or for the pursuit of professional careers. In the growing cities, where men spent most of their time away from home working in factories or offices, women were expected to devote themselves to child-rearing and homemaking. Accordingly, their lives were almost totally defined by their domestic responsibilities as mothers and wives.

Except for female seminaries where the daughters of the well-to-do could learn the social graces, schools were closed to girls. Women were excluded from the professions and from nearly all other rewarding economic activities that might afford attractive alternatives to marriage and homemaking. Their inferior position was reinforced by laws that denied them the right to vote or hold public office, treated unmarried women as minors and made them wards of their nearest male relatives, and recognized the husband as the dominant figure in the family. The husband was even given control over the property his wife brought to the marriage or subsequently inherited. Divorce was rare, but when it occurred the father received custody of the children no matter what the circumstances causing the divorce may have been.

Not only were the boundaries of a women's life severely confined, she also had to endure a humiliating double standard of morality. Premarital and extramarital sexual activity, though absolutely taboo for respectable women, was at least tolerated, if not condoned, for men. The difference in standards, according to the prevailing wisdom, resulted from differences in the natures of men and women. Women were not expected to find pleasure in sex; submitting to their husbands' desires was simply another domestic duty. Indeed, in an age when abstinence from intercourse was almost the only way to avoid repeated pregnancies, women had reasons other than social pressures for suppressing their sexuality. The double standard was reinforced by the availability of lower-class prostitutes—ten thousand of them plied their trade in New York City during the 1830s—who enabled upper- and middle-class women to remain chastely on their pedestals for men to admire. Men idealized the pure, submissive wife and mother who devoted her life to domestic chores; and, according to one European visitor, they guarded her with "a seven-fold shield of insignificance."

So strict was the prevailing code of respectable female behavior that it was considered unfeminine for women even to speak in public places or to offer prayers in church. When Sarah and Angelina Grimké, members of a South Carolina slaveholding family, came north to join the crusade against slavery, they were denounced for addressing "promiscuous" audiences—that is, audiences of both men and women. In

241

### The grievances of American women

*The history of mankind is a history of repeated injuries and usurpations on the part of man toward woman, having in direct object the establishment of an absolute tyranny over her. To prove this, let facts be submitted to a candid world.*

*He has never permitted her to exercise her inalienable right to the elective franchise.*

*He has compelled her to submit to laws, in the formation of which she had no voice....*

*He has made her, if married, in the eyes of the law civilly dead.*

*He has taken from her all right in property, even to the wages she earns....*

*He has monopolized nearly all the profitable employments, and from those she is permitted to follow, she receives but a scanty remuneration.*

*He closes against her all the avenues to wealth and distinction, which he considers most honorable to himself....*

*He has denied her the facilities for obtaining a thorough education—all colleges being closed against her....*

*He has created a false public sentiment, by giving to the world a different code of morals for men and women, by which moral delinquencies which exclude women from society, are not only tolerated but deemed of little account in man....*

*He has endeavored, in every way that he could, to destroy her confidence in her own powers, to lessen her self-respect, and to make her willing to lead a dependent and abject life.*

**From the Seneca Falls, New York, "Declaration of Sentiments and Resolutions," 1848.**

1838, Sarah wrote bitterly that men had "endeavored to . . . drive women from almost every sphere of moral action." She called on women to think for themselves, "to rise from that degradation and bondage to which we have been consigned by men, and by which the faculties of our minds . . . have been prevented from expanding to their full growth, and are sometimes wholly crushed." In 1840, a group of American women, including Elizabeth Cady Stanton and Lucretia Mott, went as delegates to a World Anti-slavery Convention in London, but they were denied the right to participate.

This and similar experiences provoked a women's rights movement that became at once an integral part of the general reform crusade and a divisive issue among male reformers, some of whom favored but most of whom opposed permitting women to join their organizations. In 1844, Margaret Fuller published a book, *Women in the Nineteenth Century*, which passionately protested against the inferior position assigned to women, and against their inability to obtain any identity except through their husbands. In 1848, the first Women's Rights Convention was held at Seneca Falls, New York. Here the delegates adopted a statement that paraphrased the Declaration of Independence and proclaimed that "all men and women are created equal." After listing women's specific grievances, the statement demanded that women

"have immediate admission to all the rights and privileges which belong to them as citizens of the United States." They had, it concluded, "too long rested satisfied in the circumscribed limits which corrupt customs and a perverted application of the Scriptures" had marked out for them. The Seneca Falls convention was the first of a series that met during the following decade.

In the years before the Civil War, the women of the United States did make some limited gains. A few states gave married women control over their own property, and everywhere one profession, elementary education, was opened to them. They secured admission to a few high schools and normal schools, and in 1837 Oberlin College became the first coeducational college. Also in 1837 the first women's college, Mount Holyoke, opened its doors. But most important was the example set by a courageous group of women who defied prejudice and played an active and constructive role in public affairs. Dorothea Dix, as we have seen, contributed to improved treatment of the insane; Dr. Elizabeth Blackwell won distinction as a physician; Margaret Fuller for a time edited the transcendentalist journal, *The Dial*, and then served as literary editor of the New York *Tribune*; Emma Willard campaigned for educational reform; Lucy Stone was a popular lecturer as well as a crusader for equal suffrage; and a small host of women, notably Frances

Wright, Elizabeth Cady Stanton, Susan B. Anthony, Lucretia Mott, and Sarah and Angelina Grimké, worked to abolish slavery. Indeed, women abolitionists often united antislavery with women's rights to form a double crusade. Most men (and more than a few women) sneered at these "unsexed" women, citing Mrs. Amelia Bloomer's wearing of pantalettes as evidence of where it would all end. But the feminists had effectively challenged the myth that women were physically and intellectually unfitted for any useful activity outside the home.

**Education.** Some reformers revealed their debt to Jacksonian Democracy as well as their concern for the welfare of the common people in the crusade for free, tax-supported public education. In the early nineteenth century, except in Massachusetts, the children of the poor obtained their elementary education at home or in church or charity schools, and the children of the rich in private schools or from tutors. The lack of public support, together with the fact that most teaching was done by low-paid, untrained young men who regarded it as a temporary occupation, left a mass of people, both urban and rural, in a state of semiliteracy. In the two decades after 1830 the crucial battle to establish public responsibility for elementary education was fought and won, though in many states it took much longer for the idea to be translated into reality.

Opposition came from those who considered education a private concern, from taxpayers who objected to paying for the education of other people's children, and from religious groups that maintained their own schools. Support came from practical men in an increasingly commercial society, where more and more occupations required the ability to read, write, and cipher. It came, too, from those who believed that mass education was essential to a political system based on manhood suffrage. Further support came from those who viewed public education as a means of providing the common man with better opportunities to advance. They hoped thus to achieve a more general diffusion of property ownership and a softening of class lines. In 1848, Horace Mann, in one of his celebrated reports as secretary of the Massachusetts Board of Education, noted the alarming contrasts of wealth and poverty in his state; he maintained that "nothing but Universal Education can counterwork this tendency to the domination of capital and the servility of labor." Educate the workingman, and he will improve his position and acquire property, for "such a thing never did happen, and never can happen, as that an intelligent and practical body of men should be permanently poor." Education, Mann concluded, "is the great equalizer of the conditions of men—the balance wheel of the social machinery. . . .

It does better than to disarm the poor of their hostility toward the rich; it prevents being poor." The city workers themselves made state-supported education one of their prime demands. A resolution adopted by the mechanics of Philadelphia in 1830 declared "that there can be no real liberty without a wide diffusion of real intelligence . . . [and] that until means of equal instruction shall be equally secured to all, liberty is but an unmeaning word, and equality an empty shadow."

By the 1850s the states were committed to making tax-supported public education available to all without the stigma of charity. Some of the states had already passed laws requiring local communities to establish elementary schools, and most of the others had at least required that when schools were established they must admit all children, not just those able to pay tuition. One of the decisive battles was fought in Pennsylvania, where in 1834 a state school law was passed. But opposition to the law was so formidable that the legislature seemed ready to repeal it in favor of one providing free education only for the poor. After a bitter struggle, the law was saved largely through the efforts of a young Whig legislator, Thaddeus Stevens, whose brilliant defense of free education carried the day. Similar battles were fought and won in other states. As a result, outside the South, where the movement was impeded by rural conditions and the indifference of the planter class, a steadily growing number of children found free public schools available to them.

But this was only the beginning, for compulsory-attendance laws had not yet been passed, school terms were short, the curriculum was thin, and teaching methods were still based on rote memorization and corporal punishment. Massachusetts led the way in remedying these conditions in 1837 by establishing a

*Mount Holyoke Seminary*

state Board of Education, with Horace Mann as secretary. Mann had devoted many years to teaching and the study of education, and during his eleven years as secretary his annual reports made him the most influential man in the public-school movement. In Massachusetts he did much to improve the curriculum and teaching methods, lengthen the school year, raise teachers' salaries, establish the first state-supported normal school for teacher-training, and organize a state association of teachers. Other states appointed their own boards or superintendents of education, who tried, with varying degrees of success, to achieve similar reforms.

For most American children formal education ceased after a few years in an elementary school. Secondary education was limited to those who could afford to pay the tuition to a private academy, where, in preparation for college, they took courses in mathematics, rhetoric, and the classics. In 1827 Massachusetts passed a law requiring every town of five hundred or more families to set up a public high school, and the other New England states soon followed suit. But as late as 1860 there were only slightly more than three hundred public high schools in the United States, with almost a third of them in Massachusetts and only a scattering in the South and West.

In higher education, which was less influenced by reform, the most notable development was the proliferation of private denominational colleges throughout the country. In the two decades between 1830 and 1850 about eighty of these colleges were founded. Most of them had meager endowments, small student bodies, and incompetent faculties; but every village seemed determined to have a college, and every religious sect wanted a network of colleges to train its clergy and indoctrinate its youth. The idea of state-supported institutions of higher learning was an old one, and four states (Vermont, North Carolina, Georgia, and Tennessee) chartered them in the late eighteenth century. The first one actually to win academic distinction, however, was the University of Virginia, founded in 1819. By the 1850s numerous state universities, most of them in the South and West, had been founded, but few were in reality more than small colleges limping along on slender budgets.

Both state and private colleges offered a traditional liberal-arts curriculum, which stressed Latin, Greek, science, mathematics, moral philosophy, and political economy. True universities in the modern sense, with professional schools, graduate teaching, and emphasis on scholarly research, did not emerge until after the Civil War. Too many colleges were founded during these years, and few of them had the libraries and scholars they needed to become centers of creative intellectual life. The idea of academic freedom, moreover, had few defenders, and countless instructors fell victim to the political and sectarian controversies of the age.

Since the colleges served only a tiny fraction of the population, the mass of adults with a thirst for learning searched for other and more accessible avenues to cultural advancement. The "penny press," which began in 1833 when the New York *Sun* went on sale at a penny a copy, put newspapers within the reach of everyone and served up a mixed fare of sensationalism, news, and essays on practical and scientific subjects. Hundreds of magazines catered to all tastes, but the best of them offered essays, poetry, and fiction by the most distinguished European and American writers. This was an era of organized efforts for self-improvement, and most communities had their debating societies, literary societies, and library associations. The lyceum movement, a nationally organized program of adult education initiated in 1826 by a New Englander, Josiah Holbrook, was the most ambitious of these enterprises. The original plan was to encourage local lyceums to assemble libraries, study scientific subjects, and form discussion groups, but most of them soon concentrated on lecture courses. Though many a fraud and charlatan managed to get on the lyceum lecture circuit, men of letters such as Emerson and Charles Dickens, scientists such as Harvard's Louis Agassiz, and a host of reformers made the program a useful instrument of mass education.

***The peace movement.*** Reformers not content with the piecemeal alleviation of domestic social ills turned to more ambitious projects, such as the cause of world peace. Remembering the dreadful suffering and waste of the Napoleonic wars, some reformers were attracted to the pacifist principles of the Quakers or at least hoped to find nonviolent ways of settling international disputes. Local peace societies, which had begun to appear soon after the War of 1812, united in 1828 to form the American Peace Society. William Ladd, the Maine merchant who founded the national organization, proposed the formation of a Congress of Nations to interpret international law and a Court of Nations to apply it. Most peace men, however, distinguished between the use of force for aggressive and for defensive purposes and condemned only the former. In 1838 the peace movement split when the "ultraists," headed by Henry Clark Wright and William Lloyd Garrison, formed a Non-Resistance Society committed to oppose violence even in self-defense. Their constitution denounced military service, forceful resistance to tyranny, capital punishment, and actions at law for civil damages. This millennial program was designed to put Christian precepts into immediate action—to prepare the way "for the full

lish a national organization, the American Anti-Slavery Society. During the next few years abolitionist agents were busy establishing local societies, until by 1840 a network of some two thousand of them with nearly two hundred thousand members stretched across the North. To many, Garrison was the embodiment of abolitionism, and the angry response of the South to his harsh words kept him in the public eye. But he was more an editor and publicist than an effective leader and tactician, and the movement soon grew too large for him to control. Other abolitionists also played significant roles: Wendell Phillips in New England, Gerrit Smith and the Tappans in New York, and Theodore Dwight Weld in the West. Weld, a product of the Finney revival in upstate New York, was perhaps the most successful of the abolitionist organizers. In 1834, at the Lane Theological Seminary in Cincinnati, Weld persuaded the students to engage in a prolonged debate on the subject of slavery. In the course of the debate many students became converts to abolitionism; and when the conservative trustees ordered them to cease discussing slavery, Weld's converts withdrew from Lane in a body and moved to Oberlin College. In subsequent years the Lane rebels joined Weld as agents and organizers for the American Anti-Slavery Society. Using the techniques of the revivalists, these men had notable success in New York, Pennsylvania, and the Old Northwest; they won thousands of converts and sometimes managed to abolitionize entire communities.

At length, in 1840, resentment against Garrison, disagreement over his effort to admit women to full participation, and differences over tactics caused a split in abolitionist ranks and led to the withdrawal of the anti-Garrisonians from the American Anti-Slavery Society to form a society of their own. Thereafter abolitionism was only loosely organized at the national level, and the real force of the crusade came from the state and local groups.

By the end of the 1830s, for several reasons, abolitionism had become the most popular cause of the whole reform movement. Most of the reformers had come to agree that slavery was the greatest social evil in the way of the nation's moral regeneration. In this romantic age they found particularly obnoxious a system that denied individuals control over their own destiny. To prove its wickedness, the abolitionists dwelt on the cruelties of slavery, for they were always less interested in presenting a balanced picture than in winning converts. Slavery provided them with plenty of illustrations of cruelty. In 1839 Weld published a powerful abolitionist tract, *Slavery As It Is*, which was simply a documented compilation of incidents reported in Southern newspapers and court records. The Southern states made themselves especially vulnerable to criticism by refusing to eliminate the system's worst abuses: its physical cruelty, its failure to give legal recognition to slave marriages, the separation of children from their parents, the callous practices of the interstate slave-traders, and the denial to Negroes of opportunities for self-improvement.

Abolitionism also attracted Northern reformers because the Southern manumission societies had failed to accomplish their purpose; slavery, it appeared, would never be destroyed without intervention by the North. It no longer seemed to be a weak and declining institution that could be left to die a natural death; instead it was flourishing and spreading westward into new territories and states. The reformers were shocked by the Southerners' growing tendency to regard slavery as a desirable and permanent institution and by their increasingly harsh treatment of even native Southern critics. One reformer expressed his dismay at "the sentiments openly expressed by the southern newspapers, that slavery is not an evil . . . [and] that it is criminal toward the South . . . to indulge even a hope that the chains of the captive may some day or other, no matter how remote the time, be broken." Moreover, the reformers were acutely conscious of the hypocrisy of America's posing as a model of liberal institutions while remaining one of the last countries in the Western world to tolerate human bondage. Finally, the success of British abolitionists in securing emancipation in the British West Indies (1833) stimulated the reformers to undertake a similar crusade in America.

One small group of Americans, the free blacks, needed no prodding from white reformers to support abolitionism, and in the North they made a significant contribution to the movement. Northern free Negroes always constituted the majority of subscribers to Garrison's *Liberator*, and after the organization of the American Anti-Slavery Society three Negroes always served on its executive committee. Among the most prominent Negro abolitionist agents and orators were Samuel Ringgold Ward, who escaped from slavery in Maryland; Lunsford Lane, who was born a slave in North Carolina and bought his own freedom; Sojourner Truth, who was born a slave in New York and was freed by the state emancipation act; Charles Lenox Remond, a well-educated Massachusetts Negro who lectured in Great Britain as well as in the United States; and Frederick Douglass, who escaped from slavery in Maryland to become editor of an antislavery newspaper, one of the greatest of all antislavery orators, and the preeminent American Negro leader of the nineteenth century. Though most black abolitionists accepted the peaceful tactics of their white comrades, a few helped to build a tradition of militant activism. In Boston, in 1829, David Walker, a free Negro born in North Carolina, published an angry *Appeal to the Colored Citizens of the World*, justify-

manifestation of the reign of Christ on earth." It would secure "the reconciliation and salvation of a warring and lost world."

**Communitarianism.**  Other perfectionists worked for the complete regeneration of society by building model communities that they hoped would form the nuclei of a better social order. Early communitarian projects had been undertaken by several small religious sects, such as the Rappites and the Shakers, with the goal of achieving holiness through a form of Christian communism. In 1825 Robert Owen, a Scottish textile-manufacturer and philanthropist, established the first significant nonreligious communitarian enterprise at New Harmony, Indiana. Owen hoped to abolish poverty and crime through cooperative labor and the collective ownership of property, but within two years New Harmony proved an economic failure. In 1836 the perfectionist John Humphrey Noyes organized a far more successful association of Bible Communists at his home in Putney, Vermont. In 1847, after outraging his neighbors by introducing a system of "complex marriage," involving both polygamy and polyandry, he and his followers moved to central New York, where they formed the Oneida Community. Here, in spite of persistent outside hostility to its sexual practices, the community grew to about three hundred members, established a model educational system, and prospered economically, operating a large farm and several manufacturing enterprises. The Oneida Community survived until 1879, when both internal and external troubles caused Noyes to dissolve it.

Communitarianism reached its peak during the 1840s, when the ideas of the French reformer Charles Fourier were embraced by many transcendentalists and other perfectionists and popularized by his chief American champion, Albert Brisbane. The perfectionists were attracted by Fourier's optimistic view of human nature, his goal of social harmony, and his plan of voluntary associations, or "phalanxes," free of governmental intervention. Association, explained the idealistic Brisbane, offered "the means of effecting peaceably and in the interest of all classes, a complete transformation in the social condition of the world." The successful establishment of only one association, he believed, would inspire men and women to form others. At last the movement would become universal, and there would emerge "a true Social and Political Order in the place of the old and false one." Of the many phalanxes that briefly put Fourier's ideas into practice, the best remembered was Brook Farm near Boston, founded in 1841 by George Ripley. Until its abandonment in 1847 a number of transcendentalists repaired to it, as Ripley explained, "to prepare a society of liberal, intelligent, and cultivated persons" who

could lead "a more simple and wholesome life, than can be led amidst the pressures of our competitive institutions."

Young Nathaniel Hawthorne was one of the transcendentalists who went to Brook Farm, but he left with doubts about the divinity of man and a conviction that the perfectionist reformers did not understand the true source of evil in the world. "The heart, the heart," he wrote, "there was the little yet boundless sphere wherein existed the original wrong of which the crime and misery of this outward world were merely types." His caution to the perfectionists is perhaps more understandable to our generation than it was to his: "The progress of the world, at every step, leaves some evil or wrong on the path behind it, which the unrest of mankind, or their own set purpose, could never have found the way to rectify."

# The crusade against slavery

**The beginnings of abolitionism.**  In Boston on January 1, 1831, William Lloyd Garrison began publishing a weekly newspaper, *The Liberator*, dedicated to the immediate abolition of Southern slavery without compensation to the masters. This event, though an important turning point, did not mark the beginning of the crusade against slavery, for organized activity, especially among the Quakers, dated back to the eighteenth century. Pressure from antislavery groups had already achieved the abolition of slavery in the Northern states, and in the 1820s a small manumission movement in the Upper South, supported mostly by Quakers, had called for gradual, compensated emancipation with colonization of the free Negroes in Africa. Benjamin Lundy, a New Jersey Quaker, helped to organize local societies in Tennessee, North Carolina, and Virginia and at the same time edited an antislavery newspaper, *The Genius of Universal Emancipation*, in Baltimore. Garrison got his start writing for Lundy's paper, but he was a man of different temperament who brought a new stridency and militancy to the attack. He set the tone for his crusade in the prospectus printed in the first issue of *The Liberator*:

> I *will* be as harsh as truth, and as uncompromising as justice. On this subject, I do not wish to think, or speak, or write with moderation. . . . I am in earnest—I will not equivocate—I will not excuse—I will not retreat a single inch—AND I WILL BE HEARD.

In 1832 Garrison organized the New England Anti-Slavery Society and a year later helped to estab-

Sojourner Truth

therefore, relied on "moral suasion." Their first goal was to persuade slaveholders that slavery was a sin requiring repentance, as well as a denial of the "unalienable rights" with which, according to the Declaration of Independence, all men are endowed. Though abolitionists believed in immediate emancipation—slaveholding being a sin, a moral person could not advocate abandoning it gradually—they were practical enough to understand that the actual implementation of emancipation might take a little time. In an era of revivalism they might hope for mass conversions of slaveholders, but they could hardly hope that all slaveholders would give up the institution in a single year. Moreover, they understood that there would probably have to be a period of transition while the Negroes were prepared for their new status as freedmen. Hence they usually qualified their "immediatism" by defining it, in one way or another, as a program of emancipation "promptly commenced" but "gradually accomplished." Thus Garrison, while demanding immediate abolition, agreed privately that "it will, alas, be gradual abolition in the end. We have never said that slavery would be overthrown by a single blow: that it ought to be, we shall always contend." But the theoretical immediatism to which abolitionists were committed strengthened the conviction of indignant Southerners that abolitionists were reckless incendiaries seeking to bring ruin upon the South.

When the abolitionists failed to move the slaveholders to action, when they found it nearly impossible to carry their message into the South, they turned to building up antislavery opinion in the North. Their propaganda hammered relentlessly at their central argument: every person of full age and sane mind has a right to freedom unless convicted of a crime; "mere difference of complexion is no reason why any man should be deprived of any of his natural rights"; "man cannot, consistently with reason, religion, and the eternal and immutable principles of justice, be the property of man"; "whoever retains his fellow-man in bondage is guilty of a grievous wrong." Abolitionists sometimes spoke of the alleged economic waste of slavery, but their indictment was chiefly moral and religious.

Whether moral suasion might be supplemented by some form of political action was a question on which abolitionists differed. Garrison's nonresistance principles turned him against government as an instrument of force and therefore against involvement in politics. Moreover, he viewed the political parties as tools of the slaveholders, the Union as their protector, and the Constitution as a proslavery document (in his words, "a covenant with death and an agreement with hell"). Most abolitionists, however, though recognizing that Congress could not touch slavery in

ing violence to destroy slavery and warning white masters of the consequences of holding blacks in bondage. In 1843, Henry H. Garnet, in an address before a Negro convention in Buffalo, urged slaves to strike for their liberties: "Let your motto be resistance! . . . No oppressed people have ever secured their liberty without resistance." Many free Negroes guided fugitives to freedom over the so-called underground railroad. Among them was Harriet Tubman, who escaped from slavery in Maryland but returned nineteen times to help several hundred slaves flee from their bondage.

***Abolitionist tactics.*** The tactics of the abolitionists were determined by their optimistic assumptions about human nature, by their belief in the power of truth, by their belief that slavery was essentially a moral issue, and by the restrictive political structure within which they had to operate. They were confronted with the problem that Congress, unlike the British Parliament, had no constitutional power to abolish slavery. At the same time, the pacifism of most abolitionists discouraged the use of force. In its statement of principles, the New England Anti-Slavery society affirmed that "we will not operate on the existing relations of society by other than peaceful and lawful means, and that we will give no countenance to violence or insurrection." Abolitionists,

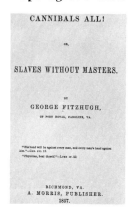
*The negro slaves of the South are the happiest, and, in some sense, the freest people in the world. The children and the aged and infirm work not at all, and yet have all the comforts and necessaries of life provided for them. They enjoy liberty, because they are oppressed neither by care nor labor. The women do little hard work, and are protected from the despotism of their husbands by their masters. The negro men and stout boys work, on the average, in good weather, not more than nine hours a day.... Besides, they have their Sabbaths and holidays. White men, with so much of license and liberty, would die of ennui; but negroes luxuriate in corporeal and mental repose. With their faces upturned to the sun, they can sleep at any hour; and quiet sleep is the greatest of human enjoyments.... The free laborer must work or starve. He is more of a slave than the negro, because he works longer and harder for less allowance than the slave, and has no holiday, because the cares of life with him begin when its labors end. He has no liberty, and not a single right.*

**From George Fitzhugh, *Cannibals All!*, 1857.**

the states, believed that some things might be accomplished through political action—for example, the abolition of slavery in the District of Columbia, the outlawing of the interstate slave trade, and the exclusion of slavery from federal territories. Hence they took an active part in politics and put pressure on congressional candidates to take antislavery positions. In 1840 a group of political abolitionists organized the Liberty party and nominated James G. Birney for the Presidency, but the small vote the party attracted in this and subsequent elections indicated that most abolitionists preferred to operate through existing parties. With the growth of political abolitionism there was a notable decline in pacifist sentiment, and the sectional conflict of the 1850s prepared many abolitionists to turn from moral suasion to force as the ultimate remedy.

In the early years of the movement most Northerners shared the opinion of Southerners that abolitionists were irresponsible fanatics, and antislavery meetings were frequently broken up by violence. In 1834 a mob invaded Lewis Tappan's house and destroyed the furnishings; in 1835 a Boston mob treated Garrison so roughly that authorities took him to jail for his own protection; and in 1837 a mob in Alton, Illinois, murdered Elijah Lovejoy, an abolitionist editor. After being mobbed on several occasions, Weld warned fellow abolitionists that each would have to decide "whether he can lie upon the rack," or "if cloven down, fall and die a martyr."

Northern businessmen, viewing antislavery agitation as a threat to their profitable trade with the South, more than once joined or encouraged the mobs. Nationalists opposed the abolitionists, because their crusade endangered the federal Union; conserv-

ative churchmen feared that attacks on slavery might divide the churches along sectional lines. However, race prejudice, which was nearly as intense in the North as in the South, was always the fundamental cause of the hostility to abolitionism. The prevailing prejudice exposed Northern free Negroes to many forms of discrimination. They were prohibited from entering most trades and professions and forced into menial occupations; they were excluded from the public schools or sent to segregated schools; they were assigned segregated seats in white churches and on public transportation; they were barred from office-holding and jury duty; they were denied the ballot except in five New England states and in New York (where they had to meet a property qualification not required of whites); and they were prohibited from settling in several Western states. Indeed, it is safe to say that if Southern slaves had been white rather than black, Northerners would have been far less prone to advance practical arguments against antislavery agitation. Even some of the abolitionists were unable to free themselves entirely from the prevailing prejudice and shrank from personal contacts with Negroes, but as a group their racial attitudes were so liberal that their contemporaries often denounced them as "nigger-lovers." There is much evidence that the efforts of abolitionists to eliminate discrimination and segregation in the North, which was a second goal of many of them, greatly intensified Northern hostility toward them.

***A broadening appeal.*** Though abolitionists had only limited success in reducing Northern prejudice against Negroes, the growing sectional tension of the 1840s and 1850s caused Northerners to listen more

The slave is held simply for the use of his master, *to whose behests his life, liberty, and happiness are devoted, and by whom he may be bartered, leased, mortgaged, bequeathed, invoiced, shipped as cargo, stored as goods, sold on execution,* [and] *knocked off at public auction ... all according to law. Nor is there anything, within the limit of life, inflicted on a beast, which may not be inflicted on the slave. He may be marked like a hog, branded like a mule, yoked like an ox, hobbled like a horse, driven like an ass, sheared like a sheep, maimed like a cur, and constantly beaten like a brute,—all according to law. And should life itself be taken, what is the remedy? The Law of Slavery ... openly pronounces the incompetency of the whole African race, whether bond or free, to testify against a white man in any case, and thus, after surrendering the slave to all possible outrage, crowns its tyranny by excluding the very testimony through which the bloody cruelty of the Slave-Master might be exposed....*

*... Unhappily, there is Barbarism elsewhere in the world; but American Slavery, as defined by existing law, stands forth as the greatest organized Barbarism on which the sun now looks.*

**From Charles Sumner, Speech in the United States Senate, June 4, 1860.**

---

sympathetically to what they had to say about the evils of slavery. Eventually abolitionist agitation helped to persuade large numbers of Northerners that even black slavery was morally wrong and therefore could not be accepted as a permanent institution. This agitation also produced an image of slaveholders as undemocratic, arrogant, immoral, and cruel. The slaveholders and their political henchmen, said the abolitionists, formed a sinister "Slave Power" that ruled the South and conspired to rule the entire Union in order to destroy freedom. Theodore Parker described the Slave Power as

> the blight of this nation, the curse of the North and the curse of the South. . . . It confounds your politics. It has silenced your ablest men. It has muzzled the pulpit, and stifled the press. It has robbed three million men of what is dearer than life; it has kept back the welfare of seventeen million more.

Meanwhile, as the abolitionists braved mobs to defend freedom of assembly and of the press, they began to win admiration as champions of civil liberties not only for blacks but for whites. They aroused sympathy when Southern mobs broke into post offices to seize and destroy packages of antislavery pamphlets, for now the right of minority groups to disseminate their ideas through the mails seemed to be at stake. In 1836, when the abolitionists deluged Congress with petitions urging the abolition of slavery in the District of Columbia, Southerners forced through the House a so-called gag rule, which provided that petitions relating to slavery were to be laid on the table without being printed, referred to committee, or

debated. Until the repeal of the gag rule in 1844, abolitionists stood as defenders of another sacred liberty: the right of petition.

Most Northerners also sympathized with the more or less systematic efforts of abolitionists to assist fugitive slaves to freedom along the routes of the underground railroad. Few could help feeling compassion for pathetic fugitives seeking their own liberty, and even a Negrophobe might resent the activities of the professional slave-catchers who roamed the free states. In 1842 an important case (*Prigg v. Pennsylvania*) involving the constitutionality of the Fugitive Slave Act of 1793 came before the Supreme Court. Though the Court ruled that the act was constitutional, it conceded that a state might prohibit its own officers from helping to enforce it. Thereafter a number of states, under pressure from the abolitionists, adopted "personal-liberty laws" that withheld assistance in the capture of fugitives.

On one issue—whether slavery should be introduced into new territories and states—the abolitionists eventually gained overwhelming Northern support. Northerners continued to agree that the Constitution prevented federal interference with slavery in the Southern states, but by the 1850s they felt strongly that slavery ought to be confined to its present limits. Often this sentiment sprang less from sympathy for the black than from a determination of free white farmers to keep slaveholders out of the territories they coveted. But the abolitionist indictment of slavery proved a handy weapon for them to use against Southern expansionists.

In one fundamental respect the abolitionist crusade was a failure. Since it did not convert the slaveholders, it never achieved its original goal: peaceful abolition through the triumph of Truth over Evil. Abolitionists who hoped to eliminate prejudice and discrimination in the Northern states, of course, suffered a second defeat. But in another and unexpected way the crusade was a success. Though it was launched by pacifists, by 1861 abolitionism, which had itself grown increasingly militant, had helped to arm the Northern population morally for the terrible struggle that lay ahead.

# The proslavery argument

*Slavery a positive good.* In January 1837 Senator John C. Calhoun boldly took a position toward which many Southerners had been drifting:

> I hold that in the present state of civilization, where two races of different origin, and distinguished by color and other physical differences, as well as intellectual, are brought together, the relation now existing in the slaveholding states between the two is, instead of an evil, a good—a positive good.

There would be no more apologies—no concessions that slavery was at best a necessary evil—as Southern dialecticians spun out the arguments affirming the benign qualities of their peculiar institution. Never before had the justification of human bondage been presented with so much moral fervor and in such elaborate detail as in the antebellum South. Indeed the proslavery argument was one of the most impressive products of its intellectual life. Southern poets, theologians, moral philosophers, social theorists, jurists, and scientists combined their talents to uphold slavery and denounce heresy and radicalism.

This body of proslavery literature is significant not only because it was one of the principal contributions of Southern men of letters but because it was a rare expression in nineteenth-century America of deep pessimism about human nature, of doubt about the liberal tradition, and of skepticism about progress. One Southerner wrote with sarcasm:

> No word in the English language is so much used as the dissyllable *progress.* In America we use it so much, that we have made a verb of it. This is an age of progress—a country of progress—a people of progress. Progress is synonymous with enlightenment, and he who falls into the rear rank, is considered recreant to the cause of civilization.

And yet, insisted another Southerner, "it cannot be denied that we must still look to antiquity for the

"Sun of intellectual light & liberty, stand ye still, in masterly inactivity, that the Nation of Carolina may continue to hold Negroes & plant Cotton till the day of Judgment!"

*Calhoun on slavery*

noblest deeds and grandest thoughts that illustrate the race of men." Romanticism, which found expression in the North in the reform movement and in a remarkable burst of literary productivity, found expression in the South in a cult of chivalry and in the identification of the planter class with traditional aristocratic values.

*The nature of the defense.* Since the average slaveholder was highly religious, a theological defense of slavery was fully developed and almost invariably incorporated in the numerous treatises on the subject. Out of the mass of Scriptural arguments, three were of crucial importance. The first identified the Negroes as the descendants of Canaan, the son of Ham, of whom Noah said, "Cursed be Canaan; a servant of servants shall he be unto his brethren." The second pointed to

Mosaic law, which authorized the Jews to make bondsmen "of the heathen that are round about you." The third noted that neither the prophets of the Old Testament nor Christ and his apostles ever condemned slavery. Rather, they repeatedly admonished servants to obey their masters and to submit to their earthly lot. The proper role of the church, therefore, was not to attack slavery but to bring spiritual salvation to the slaves and to urge benevolence on their masters.

Turning to history, the defenders argued that slavery had always existed in some form and that it had been the foundation of all the great civilizations of antiquity. Aristotle, whose thought permeates the proslavery argument, taught that in every organized society the men of superior talents would become masters over those of inferior talents. Slavery thus enabled a class to emerge that could devote its genius to art, literature, and other intellectual pursuits. "It is a common remark," wrote George Fitzhugh of Virginia, "that the grand and lasting architectural structures of antiquity were the results of slavery."

Yet, in spite of such generalizations, few Southerners were prepared to defend their own slave system on a class basis—that is, as a desirable condition for certain classes of men of all races. Rather, their defense was essentially a defense of *black* slavery—of the subordination of the black race to the white. Since all Southern slaves had at least some African ancestors, evidence that Africans were innately inferior to whites was crucial to the Southern justification of the peculiar institution. By a curious combination of comparative anatomy and the pseudoscience of phrenology, Southern ethnologists attributed to blacks certain distinct physical and psychic traits that suggested their inferiority to the whites. In the Negro, claimed a Georgia doctor, "the animal parts of the brain preponderate over the moral and intellectual," which explains why he is "deficient in reason, judgment and forecast . . . thoughtless of the future, and contented and happy in the enjoyment of the mere animal pleasures of the present moment." The inevitable conclusion was that "nothing but arbitrary power can restrain the excesses of his animal nature: for he has not the power within himself." These and other alleged racial diversities established the master-slave relationship between whites and blacks as a natural condition, its abolition a profound disaster to both.

Belief in the Negro's inferiority led also to the conclusion that the affirmations of the Declaration of Independence, the provisions of state bills of rights, and the benefits of citizenship did not and were not intended to apply to him. Society must have a class "to perform the drudgery of life," affirmed James H. Hammond of South Carolina, a class "requiring but a low order of intellect," a class that "constitutes the very mud-sill of society." Black slavery provided this class and, by freeing the whites from menial tasks, elevated all members of the privileged caste to a condition of perfect equality.

The South had found in slavery, argued its defenders, a way to avoid the dangers to order and property posed by the laboring classes in free society. Slavery served as a conservative bulwark against all the radical "isms" that threatened the North with revolution. "There are two kinds of labor, hireling labor and slave labor," explained a writer in the Charleston *Courier*. "The task of each is the same—continued hard work. The promised reward of each is the same also—subsistence." In the North and in Europe the hirelings were discontented; they clamored for change, for "communism, socialism, the organization of labor." In the South the slaves were "orderly and efficient," and society had within it no element of disharmony. "It is the only condition of society in which labor and capital are associated on a large scale in which their interests are combined and not in conflict. Every plantation is an organized community . . . where *all work*, where *each member gets subsistence and a home.*" Slavery, in short, was a practical form of socialism.

In every respect, said Southern apologists, the slaves were better off than so-called free laborers. They were happy and contented, because they were well treated, well fed, well housed, and well clothed; they were cared for in childhood, in old age, and in times of sickness. The free-labor system, which left the worker to shift for himself, was far more cruel and heartless. "I may say with truth," said Calhoun, "that in few countries so much is left to the share of the laborer, and so little exacted from him." Indeed, wrote a Virginian, "a merrier being does not exist on the face of the globe, than the Negro slave of the United States."

The endorsement of such ideas in the South at a time when a great reform movement was agitating the North produced an ideological conflict between the sections that threatened the survival of the Union. Slavery was no longer open to discussion in the South, and slaveholders intensely resented its denunciation on moral grounds in the North. Not even the two largest Protestant churches were able to bear the strain, and the slavery issue led to sectional splits—the Methodists in 1844, the Baptists in 1845. Eventually the national political parties would also disintegrate, and thus another major institutional tie would be broken. Abolitionists and proslavery polemicists had raised a moral issue—the right and wrong of slavery—that stubbornly resisted resolution by the best efforts of a generation of able politicians and statesmen.

*The proslavery argument*

**RELIGION**

All the surveys of American cultural and intellectual history devote much space to religion in the first half of the nineteenth century. The best on this subject are R. H. Gabriel, *The Course of American Democratic Thought* (rev. ed., 1956); Perry Miller, *The Life of the Mind in America: From the Revolution to the Civil War*\*, Vol. I (1966); and R. B. Nye, *Society and Culture in America, 1830–1860*\* (1974). I. H. Bartlett, *The American Mind in the Mid-Nineteenth Century*\* (1967), is brief and readable. S. E. Ahlstrom, *A Religious History of the American People*\* (1972), is an outstanding survey that stresses the importance of religious ideas in American culture. Several useful general studies of American religion should also be consulted: W. W. Sweet, *The Story of Religion in America*\* (rev. ed., 1950); W. L. Sperry, *Religion in America*\* (1946); E. S. Gaustad, *A Religious History of America*\* (1966); M. E. Marty, *Righteous Empire: The Protestant Experience in America*\* (1970); and J. W. Smith and A. L. Jamison, eds., *Religion in American Life*\*, 4 vols. (1961). H. F. May, *The Enlightenment in America* (1976), is a major study of religious thought in the early years of the Republic.

The revolt against orthodox Calvinism can be traced in H. M. Morais, *Deism in Eighteenth Century America* (1934); Albert Post, *Popular Free Thought in America* (1943); Conrad Wright, *The Beginnings of Unitarianism in America*\* (1955); R. L. Patterson, *The Philosophy of William Ellery Channing* (1952); D. P. Edgell, *William Ellery Channing* (1955); and M. H. Rice, *Federal Street Pastor: The Life of William Ellery Channing* (1961). D. W. Howe, *The Unitarian Conscience: Harvard Moral Philosophy, 1805–1861* (1970), is a lucid, comprehensive analysis of Unitarian thought. Transcendentalism is examined in all the surveys of American intellectual history and in two distinguished works on American literature covering the period: V. W. Brooks, *The Flowering of New England, 1815–1865*\* (1936), and F. O. Matthiessen, *American Renaissance*\* (1941). P. F. Boller, Jr., *American Transcendentalism, 1830–1860: An Intellectual Inquiry* (1974), is an excellent brief study. There are good biographies of several transcendentalist leaders: H. S. Commager, *Theodore Parker: Yankee Crusader*\* (1936); A. M. Schlesinger, Jr., *Orestes A. Brownson: A Pilgrim's Progress*\* (1939); J. W. Krutch, *Henry David Thoreau*\* (1948); and R. L. Lusk, *The Life of Ralph Waldo Emerson* (1949). Perry Miller, ed., *The Transcendentalists*\* (1950), is an excellent collection of transcendentalist writings.

A good survey of Protestant revivalism is W. W. Sweet, *Revivalism in America*\* (1944). Much valuable detail is added in W. R. Cross, *The Burned-Over District*\* (1950); C. A. Johnson, *The Frontier Camp Meeting* (1955); B. A. Weisberger, *They Gathered at the River*\* (1958); and W. G. McLoughlin, Jr., *Modern Revivalism: Charles Grandison Finney to Billy Graham* (1959). Two important books tie revivalism to the reform movement: C. C. Cole, Jr., *The Social Ideas of the Northern Evangelists, 1826–1860* (1954), and T. L. Smith, *Revivalism and Social Reform in Mid-Nineteenth Century America*\* (1957). F. M. Brodie, *No Man Knows My History: The Life of Joseph Smith* (1945), is an outstanding biography of the founder of Mormonism. K. J. Hansen, *Quest for Empire: The Political Kingdom of God and the Council of Fifty in Mormon History*\* (1967), is a study of Mormon theology and church government.

**REFORM**

A. A. Ekirch, *The Idea of Progress in America, 1815–1860* (1944), is a critical analysis of one of the reformers' basic assumptions. A. M. Schlesinger, *The American as Reformer*\* (1950), is a perceptive introduction to the reform movement. The most comprehensive general treatment is A. F. Tyler, *Freedom's Ferment: Phases of American Social History to 1860*\* (1944). C. S. Griffin, *The Ferment of Reform, 1830–1860*\* (1967), is an excellent brief, interpretive, and historiographical essay. Other useful books are E. D. Branch, *The Sentimental Years, 1836–1860*\* (1934); R. E. Riegel, *Young America, 1830–1840* (1949); and C. S. Griffin, *Their Brothers' Keepers: Moral Stewardship in the United States, 1800–1865* (1960).

In the vast literature on specific reforms, the following are among the best: Blake McKelvey, *American Prisons: A Study in American Social History Prior to 1915*\* (1936); H. E. Marshall, *Dorothea Dix: Forgotten Samaritan* (1937); F. L. Byrne, *Prophet of Prohibition: Neal Dow and His Crusade* (1961);

\*Available in a paperback edition.

R. E. Riegel, *American Feminists** (1963); A. S. Kraditor, ed., *Up from the Pedestal: Selected Writings in the History of American Feminism** (1968); W. L. O'Neill, *Everyone Was Brave: The Rise and Fall of Feminism in America** (1970); Page Smith, *Daughters of the Promised Land** (1970); Gerda Lerner, *The Woman in American History** (1971); Eleanor Flexnor, *Century of Struggle: The Woman's Rights Movement in the United States** (rev. ed., 1975); Paul Monroe, *The Founding of the American Public School System* (1940); L. H. Tharp, *Until Victory: Horace Mann and Mary Peabody* (1953); Jonathan Messerli, *Horace Mann: A Biography* (1972); Carl Bode, *The American Lyceum** (1956); Peter Brock, *Pacifism in the United States: From the Colonial Era to the First World War* (1968); A. E. Bestor, Jr., *Blackwoods Utopias: The Sectarian and Owenite Phases of Communitarian Socialism in America, 1663–1829** (1950); and Charles Crowe, *George Ripley: Transcendentalist and Utopian Socialist* (1967).

## ABOLITION AND PROSLAVERY

The best available surveys of the abolitionist movement are Louis Filler, *The Crusade Against Slavery** (1960), and Gerald Sorin, *Abolitionism: A New Perspective** (1972). G. H. Barnes, *The Antislavery Impulse, 1830–1844** (1933), now dated but a pioneer work, stresses the role of Theodore Dwight Weld at the expense of Garrison. It should be compared with A. S. Kraditor, *Means and Ends in American Abolitionism: Garrison and His Critics on Strategy and Tactics, 1834–1850** (1967). D. G. Mathews, *Slavery and Methodism* (1965), traces the conflict in one of the largest Protestant denominations. Three important facets of abolitionism are examined in R. B. Nye, *Fettered Freedom: Civil Liberties and the Slavery Controversy, 1830–1860** (rev. ed., 1963); Carleton Mabee, *Black Freedom: The Nonviolent Abolitionists from 1830 through the Civil War* (1970); and Lewis Perry, *Radical Abolitionism: Anarchy and the Government of God in Antislavery Thought* (1973). Benjamin Quarles, *Black Abolitionists** (1969), and J. H. and W. H. Pease, *They Who Would Be Free: Blacks' Search for Freedom, 1830–1861** (1974), describe the role of the Negro in the antislavery movement. Arthur Zilversmit, *The First Emancipation** (1967), traces the abolition of slavery in the Northern states. D. B. Davis, *The Problem of Slavery in the Age of the Revolution, 1770–1823* (1974), is an excellent study of the intellectual origins of the American antislavery movement.

Among the best biographies of abolitionist leaders are B. P. Thomas, *Theodore Weld: Crusader for Freedom* (1950); Betty Fladeland, *James Gillespie Birney: Slaveholder to Abolitionist* (1955); I. H. Bartlett, *Wendell Phillips: Brahmin Radical* (1962); J. L. Thomas, *The Liberator: William Lloyd Garrison* (1963); M. L. Dillon, *Benjamin Lundy and the Struggle for Negro Freedom* (1966); Gerda Lerner, *The Grimké sisters from South Carolina: Rebels Against Slavery* (1967); T. G. Edelstein, *Strange Enthusiasm: A Life of Thomas Wentworth Higginson** (1968); and Bertram Wyatt-Brown, *Lewis Tappan and the Evangelical War Against Slavery** (1969). J. H. and W. H. Pease, *Bound with Them in Chains: A Biographical History of the Antislavery Movement* (1972), illustrates the varieties of antislavery thought through the lives of ten abolitionists.

Racism, one of the chief obstacles the abolitionists confronted, is analyzed in William Stanton, *The Leopard's Spots: Scientific Attitudes Toward Race in America, 1815–1859** (1960); Lorman Ratner, *Powder Keg: Northern Opposition to the Antislavery Movement, 1831–1840* (1968); and G. M. Fredrickson, *The Black Image in the White Mind: The Debate on Afro-American Character and Destiny, 1817–1914** (1971). L. F. Litwack, *North of Slavery: The Negro in the Free States, 1790–1860** (1961), is an excellent empirical study of race prejudice in the North. Violence against abolitionists is analyzed in L. L. Richards, *Gentlemen of Property and Standing: Anti-Abolition Mobs in Jacksonian America** (1970).

W. S. Jenkins, *Pro-Slavery Thought in the Old South* (1935), is a comprehensive analysis of the proslavery argument. Harvey Wish, *George Fitzhugh: Propagandist of the Old South* (1943), is an excellent biography of a leading defender of slavery. A special aspect of proslavery thought is analyzed by Richard Hofstadter in his essay on Calhoun in *The American Political Tradition** (1948).

*Available in a paperback edition.

CHAPTER **11**     # Expansion

The acquisition of Louisiana and Florida in the early nineteenth century quieted for a time the American urge for expansion. Feeling secure from foreign intervention, and satisfied that there was ample space for a growing population, most Americans who moved west in the 1820s and 1830s were content to take up the vacant lands in their already immense country. They occupied the unsettled regions of Mississippi, Missouri, and Illinois and poured into new territories that soon would become states: Arkansas (1836), Michigan (1837), Florida (1845), Iowa (1846), and Wisconsin (1848). Except for the Mexican province of Texas, the vast area beyond Missouri and Arkansas, stretching out to the Rocky Mountains, was then of no interest to the westward-moving settlers. Because explorers reported that the land was too arid for farming, cartographers labeled it the "Great American Desert," and white Americans presented it as a "permanent" gift to the Indians. The donors felt there was room enough and plenty for white men to the east of this "Indian Country."

Or so it seemed until the 1840s, when the impulse to expand suddenly stirred anew. Actually, few Americans had ever assumed that the boundaries of the United States would stand forever unchanged, though it is surprising that the desire for more territory revived so soon. Some Americans pressed expansion more aggressively than others, but not many challenged the idea that providence had destined their country to continued growth. Expansion in itself was not an issue that seriously divided the electorate. But it had a vexatious consequence: it raised the touchy question of whether slavery should be permitted to spread into the territories that were acquired.

*Along the Oregon Trail*

# and sectional crisis

Much of the controversy recently generated by pro-slavery and antislavery propagandists began to center on that problem, and by the end of the 1840s it had precipitated a national crisis. In 1850, after months of bitter debate, a compromise was painfully constructed—a makeshift arrangement that settled nothing yet somehow served to hold the Union together for another decade.

## Westward to the Pacific

**Manifest Destiny.** The reasons for the revived interest in territorial expansion were several. The first and most obvious was that the American people, with their sense of mission, were sorely tempted by the boundless tracts of unsettled or sparsely settled land lying just beyond the borders of their country. During the 1820s and 1830s American fur-trappers, in their search for beaver streams, had been blazing trails, searching out passes through the mountains, and ranging over the fertile valleys of the Far West. The publicity they gave to the region beyond the Great American Desert at once strengthened the myth of the West as a land of romance and adventure and aroused interest in its agricultural possibilities.

A second reason was a growing desire to develop trade with the Far East and the belief, as one expansionist politician expressed it, that along the valley of the Columbia River "lies the North American road to India." Many Eastern businessmen began to look covetously at the three best natural harbors on the Pacific coast, at San Diego, San Francisco, and Puget Sound.

A third reason—and the one that probably explains the rebirth of expansionism at this precise time—was renewed fear that the security of the United States might be impaired by foreign intervention in areas along its borders, especially by British activity in Texas, California, and Oregon. Once again freedom and republican institutions in North America seemed threatened by the aggressive meddling of Europeans.

The expansionist drive was further strengthened by a mystical and romantic concept that, though hardly new, now received an attractive label. In 1845 a New York editor wrote exuberantly that it was America's "manifest destiny to overspread and to possess the whole of the continent which Providence has given us for the development of the great experiment of liberty and federated self-government entrusted to us." This doctrine of Manifest Destiny, quickly taken up by the press and politicians, was in part the kind of rationalization that expansionists everywhere have used to justify territorial aggrandizement. They invar-

iably celebrate the superiority of their own culture and insist that their conquests are merely the fulfillment of a divine mission impelled by forces beyond human control. So did Americans when they spoke of their Manifest Destiny, and editors and stump-speakers often advocated expansion in terms so extravagant as to make the United States sound like a nation of swashbucklers. "Make way, I say, for the young American Buffalo," shouted a New Jersey politician, "he has not yet got land enough."

But running through the boasts and the threats was a thread of idealism that tied expansion to America's supposed mission to serve as a model of political democracy. Expansion in these terms was simply a means of "extending the area of freedom," to quote a popular phrase of the day. America's destiny was not merely to teach by precept but to bring more land and more people under the nation's jurisdiction—in short, to spread its democratic institutions over the entire North American continent. Thus, as one politician explained, America would become "a vast theatre on which to work out the grand experiment of Republican government."

Unfortunately, along with the thread of democratic idealism, there was also a thread of racism in the arguments used to justify the conquest of Indians and Latin Americans and their subordination to the authority of the North American republic. The "grand experiment," politicians and publicists often noted, was to be carried out "under the auspices of the Anglo-Saxon race." American expansionists, when they spoke of "extending the area of freedom," commonly assumed a racial explanation for the political instability and the weakness of democracy in the countries south of the United States. Thus the same racial attitudes that justified the enslavement of blacks in the South and discrimination against them in the North helped to make manifest America's "destiny" to expand.

**Texas.** The first area outside the United States to which settlers moved in substantial numbers was Texas. Many Westerners had been disappointed when the national government, in the Florida-purchase treaty of 1819, accepted the Sabine River as a southwestern boundary, thereby surrendering whatever vague claim the government might have had to Texas, as part of the Louisiana Purchase. Mexico, after winning her independence from Spain in 1822, twice rejected American offers to buy this sparsely settled province; but during the 1820s she welcomed Americans who would submit to her jurisdiction and abide by her laws. Among the promoters of settlement, the first and most successful was Stephen F. Austin, who obtained a huge land grant from Mexico and planted a flourishing colony on the banks of the Brazos River.

256

**Manifest Destiny**

Most of the immigrants were Southern yeoman farmers and small slaveholders who were attracted by the rich lands suitable for cotton culture and available for a few cents an acre. By 1830 eastern Texas had been occupied by nearly twenty thousand whites and a thousand Negro slaves from the United States.

The Mexican government soon had cause to regret its hospitality, for the American settlers had no intention of giving their allegiance to a nation whose culture was so different from their own. Among numerous sources of friction, one of the most irritating was the fact that Texas did not have its own state government but remained a part of the state of Coahuila, whose legislature the Mexicans controlled. Moreover, the Americans were suspicious of Mexican land titles, which were unlike those they had been used to in the United States. In 1830 the mounting tension had prompted the Mexican government to make a drastic switch in policy: it prohibited further immigration from the United States, stopped the importation of slaves, placed heavy duties on American goods, and dispatched troops to the frontier to see that these laws were enforced. The final blow came when General Santa Anna, who had seized political power in Mexico, not only repudiated his promise to give Texas separate statehood but nearly abolished Mexico's federal system altogether.

To Texans, the parallel between British oppression under George III and Mexican oppression under Santa Anna was clear, and revolution was the obvious and justifiable remedy. For a short time they claimed to be fighting in defense of the old Mexican constitution, but on March 2, 1836, they declared their independence. The struggle was brief. Santa Anna moved into Texas with a large army and won a few minor skirmishes, the most notable being the extermination of a small garrison of Texans at the Alamo mission in San Antonio. But on April 21, 1836, at the Battle of San Jacinto, an army commanded by General Sam Houston decisively defeated the Mexicans and took Santa Anna prisoner. Santa Anna was forced to sign a treaty recognizing Texan independence; and though Mexico later denounced the treaty as having been signed under duress, it made no further attempt to reestablish its authority. The new Republic of Texas then framed a constitution, but in September 1836, when the voters ratified it, they also indicated overwhelming support for annexation to the United States. President Houston forthwith began negotiations with the government at Washington, first for recognition and then for annexation.

American volunteers and supplies had contributed to the Texans' victory over Santa Anna, and proannexation sentiment was strong, especially in the South and West. But opposition to the admission of another slave state began to grow among Whigs and abolitionists in the Northeast. Some practical Whig politicians feared that annexation would lead to war with Mexico and objected that it would increase the South's power to block legislation favorable to Northern economic interests. Abolitionists charged that the settlement of Texas, the revolution, and the movement for annexation were all parts of a slaveholders' plot to enlarge their empire and open new markets for the vendors of human flesh. Texas thus became an issue between the critics and the defenders of slavery.

*San Jacinto: Houston wounded, Santa Anna captured*

President Jackson was an ardent annexationist, but he acted cautiously lest he impair Van Buren's chances of winning the presidential election of 1836. Jackson even delayed recognition of Texan independence until the eve of his retirement from office, and Van Buren refused to recommend annexation during his term as President. Rebuffed by the United States, Texas in 1838 turned to Europe for recognition and aid; its leaders began to talk boldly of creating a nation that would expand to the Pacific and rival the United States in size and strength. This was a pleasing prospect to the British, who saw in Texas a buffer to American expansion, a threat to the American cotton monopoly, and a promising new market. Moreover, British abolitionists hoped to persuade the Texans to abolish slavery and prove that cotton could be produced with free labor. As Texan leaders doubtless expected, British interest in their affairs alarmed the United States government, and the talk of abolition angered the slaveholders of the South.

These developments spurred President Tyler to reopen negotiations with Texas, and he worked vigorously to get a treaty of annexation before his term expired. By April 1844 Tyler's new Secretary of State, John C. Calhoun, had secured the desired treaty, and it was submitted to the Senate for approval. Unfortunately Calhoun also sent a note to the British govern-

ment concerning its interest in Texas, in which he defended slavery as a positive good and thus strengthened the abolitionist claim that annexation would be the culmination of a proslavery plot. This, along with the continued anxiety about war with Mexico, doomed the treaty; only sixteen senators voted for it, while thirty-five voted against. Annexation was again delayed, and Texas became an issue in the approaching presidential election.

**The Santa Fe trade.** Meanwhile, a resourceful group of small entrepreneurs had aroused American interest in another of Mexico's remote provinces: New Mexico. Santa Fe and other smaller Spanish outposts on the upper Rio Grande, planted in the seventeenth century, were hundreds of miles from the nearest Mexican settlements, and Spain's rigid trade restrictions had long deprived them of supplies from the United States. In the 1820s, however, the independent Mexican government had opened the Santa Fe trade to Americans. Every spring for the next two decades petty merchants assembled their wagons at Independence, Missouri, for the long journey along the Santa Fe Trail. Only a few merchants engaged in the trade—usually not many more than a hundred—but they always found a highly profitable market for their goods. In 1844, to the dismay of the traders, bad feeling generated by the Texas question caused Santa Anna again to exclude Americans from Santa Fe. By then, however, the trade had enlarged the American vision of Manifest Destiny to encompass New Mexico. Though few of the traders had actually settled in Santa Fe, they had opened a route into the Far West, demonstrated that heavily laden wagons could cross the plains, and developed a system of organized caravans for protection against the Indians. Another sparsely settled territory seemed ripe for American plucking.

**Oregon.** Far to the northwest, in the Oregon country, during the 1830s and early 1840s, merchants, fur-trappers, and missionaries were awakening Americans to the potentialities of still another area, one to which the United States had a solid, though not exclusive, claim. That claim was based on the voyages of Boston merchants to the Oregon coast to buy furs from the Indians in the late eighteenth century; on Captain Robert Gray's discovery of the mouth of the Columbia River in 1792; on the explorations of the Lewis and Clark expedition between 1804 and 1806; and on the founding of Astoria on the Columbia River in 1811 by John Jacob Astor's Pacific Fur Company. In addition, the United States had acquired the French claim to Oregon in the Louisiana Purchase treaty of 1803 and the Spanish claim in the Florida-purchase treaty of 1819. But the British claim was at least as good as the American. Sir Francis Drake, the British insisted, had discovered the Oregon coast in 1579; Captain James Cook and Captain George Van-

*Spanish church at the Santa Fe mission*

couver had visited it again in the eighteenth century; and Alexander Mackenzie had made the first overland trip to Oregon in 1793 as an agent of British furtrading interests. In short, both the Americans and the British could make strong claims to a huge territory bounded on the south by the forty-second parallel, on the north by the line of 54° 40′ (the southern boundary of Russian Alaska), on the east by the Rocky Mountains, and on the west by the Pacific Ocean.

In the early nineteenth century, though neither the British nor the Americans claimed the whole of Oregon, they were unable to agree on a line of division. On several occasions the United States proposed an extension of the forty-ninth parallel to the Pacific, while the British suggested that the line follow the Columbia River from the forty-ninth parallel to its mouth. In 1818 the two countries postponed the settlement of this question and agreed to leave Oregon "free and open" to the citizens of both for a period of ten years. In 1827 they extended the agreement indefinitely, with the proviso that either country could terminate it on a year's notice. There the matter rested until the 1840s.

For many years Americans showed little interest in Oregon, and British fur-traders had the area largely to themselves. After 1821 the Hudson's Bay Company monopolized the fur trade, establishing its headquarters at Fort Vancouver on the north bank of the Columbia and sending Dr. John McLoughlin there to serve as its chief factor. For more than twenty years McLoughlin gave Oregon the only government it had; he was scrupulously fair in dealing with the Indians, and under his efficient direction the company flourished. In the 1830s, however, agents of the Hudson's Bay Company operating in the Rockies began to encounter fierce and ruthless competitors: the intrepid Mountain Men, who hunted beaver skins for the Rocky Mountain Fur Company, directed by Thomas Fitzpatrick, James Bridger, and Milton Sublette. The Mountain Men, along with the agents of Astor's American Fur Company, were the advance guard of American overland penetration of Oregon. One of the most famous of them, Jedediah Smith, a major figure in Western exploration, led expeditions along the Colorado and Gila rivers and through California's interior valleys as well as over much of the Oregon country.

Efforts by several Eastern promoters to stimulate American migration to Oregon in the 1820s and 1830s ended in failure. But the impulse for settlement soon came from another source. In 1833 an Eastern religious periodical published a report that the Indians of the Oregon country were eager for instruction in the Christian faith. In response to this report (which had little substance to it) the Methodists sent the Reverend Jason Lee, who established a mission in the fertile Willamette Valley; the Presbyterians and Congregationalists sent Dr. Marcus Whitman, who was active farther east, near Fort Walla Walla; and the Catholics sent Father Pierre Jean de Smet, a Jesuit priest from St. Louis, who worked among the Indians in the Rockies. Dr. McLoughlin gave the missionaries a cordial welcome and much assistance, but the Indians showed little interest in the Gospel. Indeed, the religious work of the missions proved to be less important than the publicity they gave to Oregon. Scores of missionary letters and reports filled with reference to Oregon's fecund soil and salubrious climate found their way into the Eastern press.

As word spread that the Willamette Valley was a new Garden of Eden, the people of the Mississippi Valley began to catch the "Oregon fever." In the late 1830s and early 1840s a trickle of emigrants began to follow the Oregon Trail in quest of free virgin land; in 1843 the first substantial caravans of covered wagons made the two-thousand-mile journey; and soon after the movement to Oregon was taking on the dimensions of a mass migration. The Oregon Trail began at Independence, Missouri, ran northwest to the Platte River, followed the Platte and its north fork into southern Wyoming, made an easy crossing of the Rockies at South Pass, followed the Snake River to a cutoff that led to the Columbia River, and then fol-lowed the Columbia to the Willamette Valley. By 1845 at least five thousand Americans had reached Oregon along this route; they had already formed a provisional government and were now demanding that the United States establish exclusive jurisdiction over them. Joint occupation with the British was no longer a satisfactory formula, and a final settlement could not be delayed much longer.

*California.* South of Oregon lay California, another of Mexico's remote provinces and the fourth area in the Far West where Manifest Destiny seemed to beckon Americans. In the eighteenth century the Spanish, in order to strengthen their control over California and to convert the Indians to Christianity, had encouraged Franciscan friars to build a chain of missions along the coast from San Diego to San Francisco. The missions, at best a mixed blessing to the Indians, were highly successful as large-scale agricultural enterprises; but in 1834 the Mexican government began to deprive them of their lands, and the mission system soon fell apart. Under a succession of weak, inefficient, and often corrupt secular administrators, California sank into political chaos. But the sparse Mexican population, which in 1846 numbered approximately seven thousand settlers, still managed to live in easygoing comfort, most of them on cattle ranches.

**Expansion and sectional crisis**

The first American contacts with California were made by whaleboats stopping for supplies. By the 1820s New England merchant ships were putting in along the coast to trade manufactured goods for hides and tallow—a trade vividly depicted in Richard Henry Dana's classic account, *Two Years before the Mast* (1840). Now and then an American sailor deserted his ship and settled down; an occasional party of Mountain Men found its way to California on a trapping expedition; and by the 1830s a few merchants had come to trade with the Indians and Mexicans. Among the merchants was Thomas O. Larkin, who arrived at Monterey in 1832, built a flourishing trade, and worked tirelessly to promote American immigration to California. In the 1840s a few emigrants began to leave the Oregon Trail near the Snake River to follow the California Trail across the Nevada desert and the Sierra Nevada to the Sacramento River Valley. Invariably their goal was Sutter's Fort, the center of a private empire ruled by John A. Sutter, a Swiss immigrant who had acquired Mexican citizenship and was a law unto himself. Sutter welcomed the Americans, furnished them with supplies, and helped them find land. By 1845 California was the home of about seven hundred Americans, almost none of whom expected to give up their American citizenship or to remain beyond the jurisdiction of their government very long.

The "California fever" had become almost as virulent as the "Oregon fever." Emigrants were attracted by the abundance of fertile, unoccupied land and by extravagant descriptions of California as "the richest, the most beautiful, and the healthiest country in the world." Eastern businessmen became increasingly interested in the commercial opportunities, and the American government coveted the harbors at San Diego and San Francisco—the latter was described as "capacious enough to receive the navies of all the world." Reports of British designs on California, though inaccurate, gave the matter a special urgency. In 1842 Commodore Thomas ap Catesby Jones, commander of the United States Pacific squadron, somehow got the impression that his country had gone to war with Mexico and that British warships were moving toward California. Accordingly, he sailed into Monterey Bay, seized the city, ran up the American flag, and proclaimed the annexation of California to the United States. The embarrassed State Department disavowed Jones' act and made apologies to the Mexican government, but the incident was a clear sign of what the expansionists had in mind.

***The Mormon migration.*** One group of emigrants to the Far West had no interest in Manifest Destiny—indeed, they sought to escape the jurisdiction of the United States. These were the Mormons (see p. 238), who in 1847, after many years of persecution, crossed into Mexican territory and established a settlement in the isolated Great Salt Lake basin. From the beginning the Mormon Saints had annoyed the "gentiles" about them with their close-knit communitarian social pattern, their thriving economic life, and their contempt for other religious sects. In their search for a Zion where they could escape this hostility and live in peace, they first moved from New York to Kirtland, Ohio, then to Missouri, then (in 1839) to Nauvoo, Illinois, where their numbers soon grew to fifteen thousand. In 1843, after five prosperous years, a new crisis developed when Joseph Smith claimed to have received another revelation, this one justifying polygamy. The result was a schism in the Church, a rash of violence, and Smith's arrest and imprisonment. On June 27, 1844, an anti-Mormon mob took him from jail and murdered him. Once more the Mormons were obliged to abandon their homes and renew their wanderings.

*Salt Lake City, 1853*

Leadership now passed to Brigham Young, a brilliant, strong-willed man, who organized the most remarkable migration and settlement in the annals of the American West. In 1846 Young led almost the whole Mormon community across Iowa to the Council Bluffs on the Missouri River; the next year he sent the first band to the Salt Lake basin, which he had selected for the new Zion. No place could have appeared less promising; the first to arrive saw only "a broad and barren plain . . . a seemingly interminable waste of sagebrush . . . the paradise of the lizard, the cricket and the rattlesnake." But within a decade the Mormons, under the stern leadership of Young and the theocratic control of the Church, had transformed the landscape. Substituting cooperative labor for the individual effort of the typical pioneer, they built a thriving city and an efficient irrigation system with which they made the desert bloom. In the critical early years their economy benefited from the sale of supplies to emigrants passing through on their way to California. When their lands were annexed to the United States soon after they arrived, the Mormons tried first to organize their own state of "Deseret." Failing, they acquiesced when Congress created the Territory of Utah. Even then, however, the Mormon Church continued to be the dominant political as well as religious force in the land of the Saints.

## Polk and the triumph of Manifest Destiny

**The election of Polk.**   The presidential election of 1844 exposed a variety of tensions that had been growing in American society in recent years. First, the long depression following the Panic of 1837 had kept alive issues of national policy concerning money, banking, and public lands, issues that sometimes divided labor and capital, sometimes farm and city. Second, the entrance of the abolitionist crusade into politics had given sectional differences a moral dimension that made compromise increasingly difficult to achieve. Third, the doctrine of Manifest Destiny was reaching the height of its influence, and the drive for expansion to the Pacific was becoming an irresistible force. The complexity of these issues, all of which were more or less interrelated, sorely tried the national party system and led ultimately to a fragmentation of the Whig and Democratic organizations.

In 1844 Henry Clay and Martin Van Buren expected to receive the presidential nominations of their respective parties. They found the unsettled Texas question a source of embarrassment, because it had become involved in the slavery controversy.

Hence they tried to eliminate it as a campaign issue by making separate but very similar statements (apparently after private consultation) opposing the annexation of Texas at that time without the consent of Mexico. The Whig convention unanimously nominated Clay and adopted a platform that avoided taking a stand either on Texas or on most other national issues. But the Democratic convention, where expansionist sentiment was stronger, denied Van Buren the nomination he coveted. Instead, on the ninth ballot, after a bitter conflict on the convention floor, the delegates chose James K. Polk of Tennessee, whose commitment to territorial expansion (including the immediate annexation of Texas) was clear and unqualified. To avoid the accusation of sectional favoritism, the Democratic platform cleverly united a demand for the admission of Texas with the dubious assertion that "our title to the whole of the Territory of Oregon is clear and unquestionable; that no portion of the same ought to be ceded to England or any other power." It followed, therefore, "that the re-occupation of Oregon and the re-annexation of Texas at the earliest practicable period are great American measures, which this convention recommends to the cordial support of the Democracy of the Union."

By combining the expansionist desires of South and West, the Democrats had found a winning formula. Throughout the campaign Manifest Destiny transcended all other issues, so much so that Clay began to shift his position on Texas. He would favor annexation after all if it could be accomplished without war and upon "just and fair terms." But this commitment still sounded halfhearted when compared with the spread-eagle oratory and aggressive slogans of the Democrats. Clay converted few of the expansionists but lost some antislavery votes to the Liberty party (see p. 248), especially in New York. In the election Polk won by a small plurality of 38,000 in the popular vote and by a margin of 170 to 105 in the Electoral College.

Though Polk is remembered as the first "dark-horse" presidential candidate, the term is valid only in the sense that he had not been considered for the nomination before the Democratic convention. He was far from a political unknown in 1844. Born in North Carolina, he had moved to Tennessee as a young man and soon became a successful lawyer and planter. He entered politics as a Jacksonian Democrat and served seven terms in the House of Representatives (two as Speaker) and one term as governor of Tennessee. As President, Polk displayed neither extraordinary talent nor a striking personality, but by hard work and stubborn determination he had remarkable success in redeeming the pledges his party had made during the campaign. His inaugural address was unimaginative—a mere reiteration of the old-fashioned republican principles with which Jefferson and Jackson had been identified. Polk, showing little understanding of the new problems of his age, promised a passive domestic role for government "by abstaining from the exercise of doubtful or unauthorized implied powers."

Polk's Administration reflected both the continuing influence of Jacksonian principles on the Democratic party and the growing power of the South within the party. As a planter and slaveholder Polk shared the Southern hostility toward abolitionists; if they achieved their goal, he warned, "the dissolution of the Union . . . must speedily follow." He favored a low revenue tariff, and in 1846 his Secretary of the Treasury, Robert J. Walker of Mississippi, helped to frame such a measure, which Congress passed. The Walker Tariff delighted the South, but it angered Northern protectionists and increased their hostility to further strengthening the antiprotectionists by the admission of any more slave states. Polk shared Jackson's views on national banking and persuaded Congress to reestablish the Independent Treasury system, which it had abolished during the Tyler Administration. On two occasions, to the intense annoyance of Westerners in the Great Lakes region, he vetoed internal-improvements bills. In short, Polk blocked every effort to revive the American System of Henry Clay and John Quincy Adams, and in his last message to Congress he devoted much space to attacking that system and celebrating its demise.

***The acquisition of Texas and Oregon.*** Important as these domestic policies were, the Polk Administration's primary concern was with geographic expansion. The Texas question was the first to be disposed of, for Congress had virtually settled the matter shortly before Polk's inauguration. After the presidential election Tyler assured Congress that the verdict of the voters had been in favor of annexation, and he proposed now that the two houses accomplish it by a joint resolution. Annexation would thus require only a simple majority, rather than the two-thirds majority needed in the Senate to approve a treaty. The introduction of a resolution for this purpose provoked a heated debate between proslavery and antislavery congressmen, but it finally passed the House by a vote of 120 to 98 and the Senate by a vote of 27 to 25. President Tyler signed the joint resolution on March 1, 1845. Polk approved of this action, and within a few months Texas had accepted the terms of annexation. In December 1845 Texas was admitted to statehood.

The problem of Oregon was not so easily resolved, for the Americans and British still had not agreed on a line of division. Indeed, the restless settlers in Oregon and the expansionists in the East were

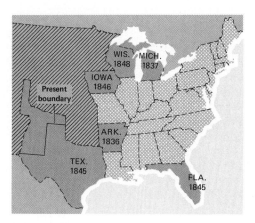

New states, 1836–48

growing increasingly belligerent in their demand that the government make no division at all but, as the Democratic platform of 1844 had insisted, take the whole territory to its northern limits. "Where shall we find room for all our people, unless we have Oregon?" asked Representative Andrew Kennedy of Indiana. "What shall we do with all those little white-headed boys and girls—God bless them!—that cover the Mississippi valley, as the flowers cover the western prairies?" America claimed Oregon for a noble purpose, explained John Quincy Adams: "To make the wilderness blossom as the rose, to establish laws, to increase, multiply, and subdue the earth, which we are commanded to do by the first behest of God Almighty." In January 1845 the British government, realizing that continued joint occupation was impossible, proposed arbitration, but the State Department rejected the offer.

In referring to the Oregon question in his inaugural address, Polk seemed to stand firmly on his party's platform; it would be his duty, he said, "to assert and maintain by all constitutional means the right of the United States to that portion of our territory which lies beyond the Rocky Mountains. Our title to the country of the Oregon is 'clear and unquestionable,' and . . . those rights we are fully prepared to maintain." Meanwhile, there was a good deal of irresponsible saber-rattling on both sides of the Atlantic, and the situation threatened to get out of hand. "We want thirty thousand rifles in the valley of the Oregon," cried Senator Benton of Missouri. "They will make all quiet there . . . and protect the American interests."

But Polk did not want war with England at a time when there was danger of war with Mexico; accordingly, he soon decided to abandon the Democratic platform and try for a compromise. In July 1845 he notified the British minister in Washington, Richard Pakenham, that the United States was willing to

*Polk and the triumph of Manifest Destiny*

renew its offer to divide Oregon along the forty-ninth parallel. Pakenham, without even consulting his government, rejected the offer and held firm to the earlier British demand for a division at the Columbia River. The indignant President then withdrew his offer, concluded that "the only way to treat John Bull was to look him straight in the eye," and decided to pursue "a bold and firm course." In his message to Congress that December, Polk recommended that the British government be given the year's notice required to end joint occupation. He also invoked the almost forgotten Monroe Doctrine to fortify his case: "it should be distinctly announced to the world as our settled policy that no future European colony or dominion shall with our consent be planted or established on any part of the North American continent." Meanwhile, truculent American expansionists, apparently ready for another war with the British, repeated the slogans "All of Oregon or none," and "Fifty-four forty or fight." Once Congress had approved the termination of joint occupation of Oregon, the only remaining hope for a peaceful settlement seemed to be an offer of concessions by the British.

Fortunately the British Foreign Office disapproved of Pakenham's blunt rejection of Polk's offer to compromise, for it did not believe that the disputed segment of Oregon between the Columbia River and the forty-ninth parallel was worth a war. Indeed, the flood of American settlers and the depletion of the fur resources had already prompted the Hudson's Bay Company to transfer its headquarters from Fort Vancouver on the Columbia northward to Fort Victoria on Vancouver Island. In June 1846 Secretary of State James Buchanan received from Pakenham the draft of a proposal to divide Oregon at the forty-ninth parallel but to retain for the British all of Vancouver Island and the right to navigate the Columbia River. Polk was at first inclined to reject the proposal, but he decided to submit it to the Senate and let that body assume responsibility for the decision.

After an angry debate the Senate advised acceptance; the treaty was signed on June 15, and the Senate approved it by a vote of forty-one to fourteen. Most of the opposition came from Western Democrats who bitterly criticized Polk for backing down on the demand for the whole of Oregon. But most of the country was satisfied with the settlement, for the British, rather than the Americans, had given up their original claim. Eastern business interests had no taste for a war to secure the area north of the forty-ninth parallel; nor did Southerners, whose interest in Oregon waned once Texas had been safely annexed. Besides, the United States was already at war with Mexico and had a richer prize in view.

## War with Mexico

**The background.** Among the causes of the war with Mexico were the inability of United States citizens to obtain compensation for claims against the Mexican government, the anger of Mexican patriots over American annexation of Texas, a dispute over the southern and western boundaries of Texas, and the instability of the Mexican government, which made negotiation with it difficult and irritating. But even more important was the determination of Polk (and of the expansionists generally) to obtain the provinces of New Mexico and California—with money if possible, by force if necessary. Though Mexico was far from blameless for the war that came— indeed, welcomed it—the central cause was nevertheless the readiness of the Polk Administration to resort to arms to achieve its expansionist goals.

As soon as the United States annexed Texas, Mexico broke off diplomatic relations, thus closing the normal channels of negotiation. Yet there was need for negotiation, because Texas was not satisfied with its traditional southern boundary, which in Spanish days had been the Nueces River, but claimed instead the Rio Grande. Polk, convinced that the Texas claim was justified, ordered General Zachary Taylor to take fifteen hundred troops into the disputed area. By the summer of 1845, Taylor's small army was encamped at Corpus Christi on the Nueces River; in March of the following year it obeyed Polk's command and advanced to the Rio Grande. To Mexican patriots this act, following soon after what they

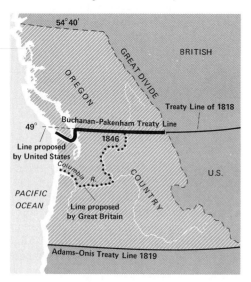

The Oregon controversy, 1818–46

*Expansion and sectional crisis*

**Mr. Polk's war**

*The responsibility of the President and his administration in permitting the country to become involved in a war which could and should have been avoided, is fearfully great. Among a virtuous and wise people, this condemnation alone should be enough to overwhelm those who have been guilty of so great a crime....*

*... The Constitution constitutes Congress the war-making power of this government; but in this case ... the President made the war. The Constitution contemplates that before deliberate hostilities shall be undertaken in any case, a declaration of war shall be made; but in this case, a hostile aggressive movement was made under the personal orders of the President....*

*... The President thought to glorify his reign by pushing the limits of the Progressive Republic in one direction or another, far beyond any serious dream of any Anglo-American land-robber of preceding times. He first tried his hand with England, by protesting that he would have the whole of Oregon, every minute of it, up to "fifty-four forty".... Disappointed in not being able to carry the nominal line of our national jurisdiction quite as far ... as his unmeaning ambition had prompted him to desire, he turned his regards to the opposite quarter of North America, and there ... he saw New Mexico and the Californias.... It is to the influence of this motive on his mind, that we attribute the daring resolution which he took originally to precipitate this war. He counted on a weak enemy, an easy conquest, and a speedy accomplishment of his purpose.*

**From *The American Review*, October 1847.**

considered the illegal seizure of Texas, was a further aggressive invasion of their territory, and the war spirit grew among them.

There was now little hope that Polk could persuade Mexico to give up California and New Mexico peacefully, but he decided to try nonetheless. In the fall of 1845 he explored the possibility of resuming diplomatic relations. When he learned that Mexico would receive an American commissioner to settle the Texas dispute, he appointed John Slidell of Louisiana as envoy extraordinary and minister plenipotentiary with authority to discuss not only Texas but California and New Mexico as well. Slidell was instructed to offer (1) the assumption by the United States of all claims of its citizens against Mexico if Mexico would accept the Rio Grande boundary; (2) $5 million for the rest of New Mexico west of the Rio Grande; and (3) as much as $25 million for California. Since the Mexican government needed money and since its hold on these distant territories was weak, to Polk it seemed the course of wisdom for Mexico to sell.

When Slidell reached Mexico City on December 6, 1845, news about his purpose had already leaked out, and Mexican nationalists were furious at this brazen attempt to dismember their country. The existing government was collapsing, in part because of its alleged lack of firmness in dealing with the United States, and a new revolutionary government came to

power pledged to uphold the national dignity. Neither the old nor the new government would receive Slidell. Mexico, he was reminded, had agreed only to receive a commissioner to negotiate on Texas, and until that question was settled there could be no regular diplomatic relations. The Slidell mission had failed. "Be assured," the angry diplomat wrote Polk, "that nothing is to be done with these people until they shall have been chastised."

Polk apparently agreed. On May 9, 1846, he told his Cabinet that the unpaid claims and the snubbing of Slidell would justify a declaration of war, and he began at once to prepare a war message to Congress. That evening news arrived that on April 25 Mexican troops had crossed the Rio Grande and engaged in a skirmish in which sixteen American soldiers were killed or wounded. Polk hastily revised his war message and sent it to Congress on May 11. After reviewing recent relations between Mexico and the United States, his message concluded: "The cup of forbearance had been exhausted even before the recent information from the frontier. . . . But now, after reiterated menaces, Mexico has passed the boundary of the United States, has invaded our territory and shed American blood on the American soil." Therefore, "war exists, and, notwithstanding all our efforts to avoid it, exists by the act of Mexico herself." Two days later Congress passed a resolution declaring that "by the act of the Republic of Mexico, a state of war exists between that government and the United States," the Senate by a vote of 40 to 2, the House by a vote of 174 to 14. It then appropriated $10 million for war purposes and authorized the recruitment of an army of fifty thousand volunteers.

The country went to war somewhat less united than these votes in Congress indicated. Though most Whig politicians felt they had no choice but to support the military measures, they showed less enthusiasm for the conflict than the Democrats. War sentiment was strong in the Southwest, but it diminished to the east and north. Abolitionists and antislavery Whigs (who called themselves Conscience Whigs) denied that Polk had tried to avoid war and insisted that American blood had been shed not on American soil but on disputed soil that American troops should never have occupied. Senator Tom Corwin of Ohio accused Polk of involving the country in a war of aggression, and added bitterly: "If I were a Mexican, I would tell you, 'Have you not room in your own country to bury your dead men? If you come into mine, we will greet you with bloody hands and welcome you to hospitable graves.'" Another Whig, though seeing no alternative to supporting the war, was distressed to think "that when we pray 'God defend the right' our prayers are not for our own country." Abolitionists viewed the war as another attempt of the Slave Power to enhance its strength. In 1847 the Massachusetts legislature resolved that the war was "unconstitutionally commenced by the order of the President" and that it was being waged for the "dismemberment of Mexico" with "the triple object of extending slavery, of strengthening the slave power, and of obtaining the control of the free states." A new sectional crisis thus began to take shape almost as soon as the war commenced.

***The military campaigns.*** In all probability the Mexicans entered the war with greater unity and enthusiasm than the Americans. They had concluded that war was the only way to check Yankee aggression, and they were confident that their regular army, vastly superior in numbers to the American, could easily defeat the invaders. But the Mexicans were sadly deluded, for they did not take into account their outdated weapons, their limited supplies and inferior resources, and their oversupply of incompetent generals. The United States War Department was inefficient enough, but the Mexican was even less efficient. Though the United States had a regular army of fewer than eight thousand officers and men, it was able quickly to raise a force of sixty thousand volunteers. With this manpower, with superior equipment, and with at least one gifted military commander, General Winfield Scott, the Americans won the war with relative ease.

Polk, who planned the military operations himself, hoped that a few quick victories would persuade Mexico to make the desired territorial cessions. According to Senator Benton, Polk "wanted a small war, just large enough to require a treaty of peace." In the first of three major campaigns, General Taylor crossed the Rio Grande, captured Matamoros, and pushed on to Monterrey. There, in a severe battle (September 21–23, 1846), Taylor defeated the Mexican garrison but permitted it to withdraw rather than surrender. Because of these early victories, Old Rough and Ready, as Taylor's men affectionately called him, became a national hero, but he had betrayed limitations as a tactician and a tendency to be overcautious— serious flaws in a commanding officer. As a result, Polk lost confidence in him, took away half his army for a new offensive at Vera Cruz, and would have been content to let him remain idle for the rest of the war. But Santa Anna, who had regained power in Mexico, moved north to attack Taylor's weakened forces. At the Battle of Buena Vista (February 22–23, 1847) Taylor added to his national popularity by defeating Santa Anna and forcing him to return to Mexico City. This action ended the war in northern Mexico, but the decisive victories were still to be won elsewhere.

The second offensive was designed to bring the coveted Mexican provinces under American occupation before a peace treaty was negotiated. In the summer of 1846 a force of seventeen hundred men, commanded by Colonel Stephen W. Kearny, marched from Fort Leavenworth to Santa Fe and, on August 18, captured it without firing a shot. After proclaiming the annexation of New Mexico to the United States, Kearny sent part of his troops to join Taylor, left a small garrison at Santa Fe, and took the rest to California. There some of the American settlers, in the "Bear Flag Revolt," had already declared the independence of California; and Captain John C. Frémont, who had arrived earlier at the head of an exploring expedition, was in command of the rebels. Meanwhile, naval forces had landed at Monterey and raised the American flag. Hence, when Kearny arrived late in 1846 the only remaining task was to subdue scattered resistance to American authority in southern California. By January 1847 the United States had virtually undisputed possession of both New Mexico and California.

It took a third American campaign to force Mexico to accept these realities. In March 1847 an army commanded by General Scott landed near Vera Cruz, forced that city to surrender after an eighteen-day siege, and then began a slow and difficult advance toward Mexico City. Scott won a decisive victory over Santa Anna at Cerro Gordo (April 17–18, 1847), and by August he was on the high plateau before the Mexican capital. On September 14 American troops

*Expansion and sectional crisis*

*Scott entering Mexico City*

forced their way into the city, and soon after Mexico surrendered.

**The Treaty of Guadalupe Hidalgo.** A new Mexican government was now ready to sign a treaty of peace. In anticipation of this outcome, Polk had sent Nicholas P. Trist, chief clerk in the State Department, along with Scott's army "to take advantage of circumstances, as they might arise to negotiate a peace." Trist was instructed to offer essentially the same terms that Slidell had offered. In November 1847, after a long and irritating delay, negotiations were about to begin when Trist received orders from the impatient President to return to Washington. But Trist, convinced that he was on the verge of getting all he had been sent for, decided to ignore his orders and enter into negotiations. On February 2, 1848, he signed the Treaty of Guadalupe Hidalgo, by which the United States obtained California, New Mexico, and the Rio Grande boundary for $15 million and the assumption of the claims of United States citizens against Mexico. Trist then hurried back to Washington, but he got no thanks from the President. Instead, Polk denounced

him as an "impudent and unqualified scoundrel" for disobeying orders and dismissed him from his job.

But Polk could find no fault with the treaty and, notwithstanding "the exceptional conduct of Mr. Trist," decided to submit it to the Senate. By then some of the more rabid expansionists were asking why the United States should settle for only California and New Mexico. Why not take the whole of Mexico? As one partisan of Manifest Destiny asked, why "resign this beautiful country to the custody of the ignorant cowards and profligate ruffians who have ruled it for the last twenty-five years?" But after a volley of bombastic oratory, the Senate, on March 10, 1848, approved the treaty by a vote of thirty-eight to fourteen. Thus, as one disgruntled Whig observed, the Mexican War ended with a peace "negotiated by an unauthorized agent, with an unacknowledged government, submitted by an accidental President to a dissatisfied Senate." Through it the United States gained possession of more than a half-million square miles of territory as well as jurisdiction over additional Indian populations and another ethnic minority, the Mexican-Americans. As a power on the Pacific, it also

*Polk and the triumph of Manifest Destiny*

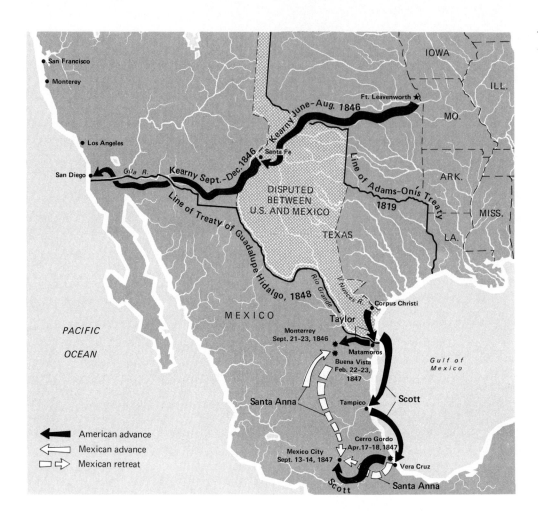

acquired substantial new defense problems and enlarged diplomatic interests. But the most immediate legacy of expansion was a dangerous sectional crisis.

## Crisis and compromise

**The issue of slavery expansion.** On August 8, 1846, shortly after the outbreak of the Mexican War, the House of Representatives had under consideration a request from the President for passage of a bill appropriating $2 million to facilitate the purchase of territory from Mexico when a peace treaty was negotiated. The bill immediately provoked several Northern congressmen to announce their opposition to the spread of slavery into whatever territory might be acquired. One of them, David Wilmot, a Pennsylvania Democrat with close ties to the Van Buren wing of the party, finally rose and moved an amendment making it "an express and fundamental condition to the ac-

quisition of any territory" that "neither slavery nor involuntary servitude shall ever exist in any part of said territory." The Wilmot Proviso, as the amendment was called, twice passed the House but each time failed in the Senate, and on several other occasions it was reintroduced and bitterly debated. During the next fifteen years the issue of slavery expansion, which had been a latent source of trouble ever since the Missouri controversy, was to drive a wedge ever deeper between North and South.

Support for the proviso came from resentful Northern Whigs who felt that Polk had been less than candid with Congress in explaining the background of the Mexican War. It also came from Northern Democrats who were discontented with the Walker Tariff, with Polk's veto of internal-improvements bills, with the Oregon compromise, with the rejection of Van Buren in 1844, or, more generally, with what they regarded as the unduly pro-Southern stance of the Administration. What personal motives Wilmot may have had for introducing his proviso are of no great historical importance, because other Northern congressmen were prepared to offer similar proposals had Wilmot not acted first.

More important is the question whether the subsequent long and angry controversy over slavery expansion involved a genuine problem or was simply a flight from reality. Polk was the first of many contemporaries to denounce the Wilmot Proviso as "mischievous and foolish" and to accuse "Southern agitators and Northern fanatics" of raising a false issue merely for political advancement. He and other conservatives held that, since none of the territory acquired from Mexico was suitable for plantation agriculture with slave labor, legislation to exclude slavery from it would be unnecessarily provocative. Such a law would needlessly reenact a "law of nature." From this, presumably, it followed that irresponsible demagogues were creating a great national crisis and endangering the Union over a mere abstraction.

By the end of the 1840s the Southern plantation system may well have reached its natural geographic limits within the existing boundaries of the United States, but it does not necessarily follow that the debate over slavery expansion was therefore meaningless. Though the politicians who had to deal with the problem may not have handled it well, many of them were convinced that the problem had substance to it. In the first place, not all Northerners and Southerners were sure that geography alone would keep slavery out of California and New Mexico. Some believed that even if the familiar plantation system could not be developed in these areas, slavery might still be introduced in other forms of agriculture, as well as in industry and mining. Slaves, after all, were employed in many occupations in the South. In the second place, few Americans thought that their country's growth would stop with the territory acquired in the Treaty of Guadalupe Hidalgo. There was a widespread conviction that at least Cuba would one day become part of the United States, and perhaps other Caribbean islands and Central America as well. In these tropical lands slavery would certainly not be merely an academic question. Indeed, much of the controversy over slavery expansion was waged with an eye on prospective future annexations and with the understanding that laws excluding slavery from existing territories would provide significant precedents.

Finally, and perhaps most important, the issue was decidedly relevant to the moral positions of proslavery and antislavery interests in the two sections. The debate over slavery expansion was in part an extension of the debate over slavery where slavery already existed. When Northerners with antislavery sentiments argued that it would be morally wrong to legalize slavery in New Mexico, they were by implication arguing that it was also morally wrong to tolerate it in Virginia. Constitutional limitations on federal power prevented them from doing anything about slavery in the Southern states; hence their efforts to prohibit it in the territories, where they believed Congress had authority to act, had symbolic as well as practical significance. Southerners understood this perfectly well, which explains in part why they so vigorously opposed all exclusion proposals, such as the Wilmot Proviso, even when applied to territories where they might have doubted that slavery would ever be introduced. For example, Southern congressmen delayed for two years (until 1848) the passage of a bill creating Oregon Territory, because the bill contained a clause excluding slavery. Representative James R. Seddon of Virginia protested that territorial exclusion was a "direct attack on the institutions" of the Southern states, an "insult and injury, outrage and wrong, on them and theirs."

Support for the Wilmot Proviso, however, did not arise exclusively from hostility toward slavery or concern for the Negro. Many opponents of slavery expansion, because of sectional tensions over other questions of public policy, seemed to be more anti-Southern than antislavery. Many more betrayed essentially racist motives—that is, a determination to keep Negroes, whether slave or free, out of the Western territories. Wilmot himself assured his colleagues that he felt no "squeamish sensitiveness upon the subject of slavery, nor morbid sympathy for the slave. I plead the cause of the rights of white freemen. I would preserve for free white labor a fair country, a rich inheritance, where the sons of toil, of my own race and own color, can live without the disgrace which association with negro slavery brings upon free labor." An Ohio congressman confessed that he was selfish enough "greatly to prefer the welfare of my own race to that of any other," and vindictive enough "to wish . . . to keep [in] the South the burden which they themselves created." In short, Northern support for the Wilmot Proviso arose from three sources: from ideological antislavery feelings, from sectional anti-Southern feelings, and from racist anti-Negro feelings.

Much of the debate over the Wilmot Proviso centered on the question of how much power the Constitution had given Congress to govern the territories. Supporters of Wilmot cited the clause authorizing Congress to "make all needful rules and regulations respecting the Territory or other Property belonging to the United States." Until the 1840s, as Henry Clay observed, this clause had been accepted as giving Congress power over slavery in the territories "by the uniform interpretation and action of every department of our government, legislative, executive, and judicial." Moreover, the power had repeatedly been used. The First Congress had reenacted the Ordinance of 1787, which prohibited slavery in the Northwest Territory; a later Congress had applied the same restriction to the Illinois and Michigan territories when they were created; and overwhelming majorities in the House and Senate had voted in 1820 to prohibit slavery in that portion of the Louisiana Purchase north of the line 36° 30'. After the Mexican War, when President Polk and many other Southern moderates suggested extending the Missouri compromise line to the Pacific, they were again, in effect, agreeing that Congress did have the authority to regulate slavery in the territories.

Calhoun, however, led proslavery Southerners toward an extreme state-rights position similar to the stand that some Virginians had taken during the Missouri debates. In 1847 he introduced a series of resolutions in the Senate asserting that the territories were the common property of all the states; that Congress had no power to deprive the citizens of any state of their right to migrate to the territories with their property, including slaves; and that only when a territory was ready for statehood could it constitutionally prohibit slavery. Calhoun's position, therefore, was that *all* the territories must be open to slavery—which made even the Missouri Compromise unconstitutional. Some of his supporters went a step further and insisted that it was the duty of Congress to *protect* slavery in the territories if necessary. This being the case, the Wilmot Proviso was, in the words of one Southern congressman, "treason to the Constitution," and its adoption would justify the secession of the South.

Between these uncompromising antislavery and proslavery doctrines, a third doctrine, called "popular sovereignty," began to win the support of moderates in all sections, but especially in the Old Northwest. With two Democratic senators, Lewis Cass of Michigan and Stephen A. Douglas of Illinois, its chief advocates, popular sovereignty was designed in part to remove the explosive territorial question from the halls of Congress. Why not respect the American tradition of local self-government, these moderates asked, and permit the people who actually settled in a territory to decide the question of slavery for themselves? Congress could then organize new territories without reference to slavery. Southerners would escape the humiliation of congressional prohibition, while Northwestern farmers might hope that their numerical superiority over Southern slaveholders would enable them to win the territories for freedom.

**The election of 1848.** Meanwhile, as the debate over the territorial question dragged on, California and New Mexico were left without government, and the issue was injected into the presidential campaign of 1848. President Polk had failed to unite the Democrats behind his Administration, and as the election approached the party was torn by factionalism. Calhoun

led a group of Southern-rights men unwilling to accept anything less than his extreme position on slavery expansion. Martin Van Buren commanded a faction of disaffected New York Democrats, called the "Barnburners" (presumably because they would burn the barn to get rid of the rats), who had thirsted for revenge ever since Polk defeated Van Buren for the presidential nomination in 1844. Throughout the North, especially in the Northeast, groups of free-soil Democrats endorsed the Wilmot Proviso. When the Democratic convention met in Baltimore, the party leaders, having decided that a Northern candidate was essential, threw the nomination to Lewis Cass of Michigan, a colorless old party wheel horse whose opposition to the Wilmot Proviso and support of popular sovereignty would appease the Southern moderates. The platform praised Polk for his territorial acquisitions and domestic policies but was silent on the slavery question. As a result, the Barnburners and pro-Wilmot delegates left the convention prepared for revolt.

The Whigs, meeting in Philadelphia, again staked their chances on a military hero, General Zachary Taylor. Born in Virginia and now a Louisiana slaveholder, Taylor was expected to reassure Southern Whigs who had grown uneasy about the antislavery sentiments of Northern Whigs. Old Rough and Ready had spent his whole career in the regular army; he had neither political principles nor political experience—and, indeed, had discovered only recently that

*Taylor: "Old Rough and Ready"*

he was a Whig ("but not an ultra Whig"). After nominating Taylor on the fourth ballot, the convention tried to avoid controversy by writing no platform at all. But this surrender to expediency was more than the Northern Conscience Whigs could bear. Many of them decided that rather than support a slaveholder whose views were unknown and who was uncommitted to a platform they would bolt their party.

Antislavery leaders saw in the disgruntled Van Buren Barnburners, free-soil Democrats, Conscience Whigs, and political abolitionists the elements of a powerful third party, one that would take a firm stand on the territorial question and make a broader appeal than the Liberty party had made in the two preceding elections. In August 1848 delegates representing all these groups met in Buffalo, organized the Free-Soil party, and nominated Van Buren for President and Charles Francis Adams (a Conscience Whig, the son of John Quincy Adams) for Vice President. The platform bluntly demanded that slavery be excluded from the territories and opposed any additional concessions to the Slave Power. It supported federal appropriations for internal improvements and the passage of a homestead act giving actual settlers free farms from the public domain. In a concluding statement the platform summarized the principles of the new party as "Free Soil, Free Speech, Free Labor, and Free Men." Among the Free-Soilers were numerous self-seeking politicians and an abundance of Negrophobes, but the organization also reflected much of the idealism of the antislavery crusade.

In spite of the intensity of feeling about the territorial question, the campaign itself was unexciting, the voters apathetic. Taylor defeated Cass by a small plurality in the popular vote (1,360,967 to 1,222,342) and by a majority of 36 in the Electoral College (163 to 127). The Free-Soil party failed to carry a single state, but its popular vote of 291,263 was impressive for a party organized less than three months before the election. A dozen Free-Soilers were elected to Congress, among them Ohio's new senator, Salmon P. Chase.

**Taylor and the crisis.** President Taylor was a man of honesty, integrity, and determination; he was capable of quick action, and he had a store of plain common sense. But these virtues were not sufficient to offset his limitations as chief executive in a time of crisis: his lack of training in politics and civil administration, his ignorance of public affairs—above all, his tendency to oversimplify complex problems. In a brief and vacuous inaugural address, he promised to devote his Administration "to the welfare of the whole country, and not to the support of any particular section or merely local interest." This pledge he tried conscientiously to fulfill; though he was a

Southerner, he was a nationalist with no strong sectional loyalties.

When Taylor came into office, California and New Mexico, still lacking civil government, were being ruled by army officers directly responsible to the President. The settlers found this situation annoying under the best of circumstances, but it became intolerable soon after the discovery of gold in California. James Marshall had made the discovery in January 1848, along the American River about forty miles from Sutter's Fort; within six months San Francisco and other coastal towns were all but deserted as men rushed headlong into the "diggings" in the Sierra. By the end of 1848 the news had spread to the East, and during the next year some eighty thousand "forty-niners" came to California from the Mississippi Valley, from the Atlantic coast, and from Europe, Asia, and Australia. Most of them followed the overland trails across the continent, others took the easier but more expensive route by ship aound Cape Horn, and still others risked death by taking a shortcut through the jungles of Panama. The miners dreamed of fortunes in gold as they worked the beds of streams with picks, shovels, and wash-pans; a few struck it rich, but most of them gained only modest returns from their backbreaking labor and their months of discomfort in primitive mining camps. Much of the gold ultimately found its way into the pockets of merchants in San Francisco and Sacramento, who in effect mined the miners by selling them supplies at exorbitant prices.

*A few struck it rich*

By the end of 1849 California's population had grown to one hundred thousand, and in the absence of civil government crime and violence were rampant in the cities and mining camps. With military authorities unable to restore law and order, with Congress seemingly paralyzed by the slavery issue, President Taylor decided to take matters into his own hands. As he saw it, there was a simple solution to the problem that had bedeviled Congress ever since the introduction of the Wilmot Proviso. He proposed to avoid the territorial issue by encouraging the people of California and New Mexico to frame constitutions and apply for immediate admission to the Union as states. Californians wasted no time in taking Taylor's advice; by October 1849 a convention had drafted a constitution prohibiting slavery, and in November the voters ratified it and elected state officers to whom the military gladly yielded its political authority. The people of New Mexico took more time, but by May 1850 they too had adopted a free-state constitution. Hence, when Congress met in December 1849, Taylor congratulated the country on the fact that the problem had been solved. All that remained was for Congress to admit California as a free state at once, and New Mexico as soon as it was ready.

**The Compromise of 1850.** Taylor had miscalculated. Rather than settling the matter, he helped precipitate one of the most bitter sectional debates in American history, one that carried the country dangerously close to disunion and civil war. Southerners denounced Taylor as an apostate and a tool of the abolitionists, while the followers of Calhoun vowed that they would break up the Union rather than see slavery excluded from California and New Mexico. Several other issues intensified the crisis: Texans and New Mexicans were on the verge of a private war over their common boundary; abolitionists were gaining Northern support for their demand that slavery be abolished in the District of Columbia; and Southerners were clamoring for a more effective fugitive-slave law. Legislatures and mass meetings in both the North and the South adopted fiery resolutions, and violence threatened to break out in the halls of Congress. A Massachusetts convention of Democrats and Free-Soilers resolved that "we are opposed to slavery in every form and color, and in favor of freedom and free soil wherever man lives." Mississippi contributed to the atmosphere of crisis by issuing a call for a convention of the Southern states to meet at Nashville in June 1850. Many feared that the friends of Calhoun would use the convention to expedite Southern secession.

Moderates in both sections were convinced that nothing short of a comprehensive settlement of all outstanding issues could save the Union. And it was

*I wish to speak to-day, not as a Massachusetts man, nor as a northern man, but as an American, and a member of the Senate of the United States.... I speak to-day for the preservation of the Union. ''Hear me for my cause''....*

*In the excited times in which we live, there is found to exist a state of crimi-nation and recrimination between the North and South. There are lists of griev-ances produced by each....*

*I should much prefer to have heard, from every member of this floor, declara-tions of opinion that this Union could never be dissolved, than the declaration of opinion that in any case, under the pressure of circumstances, such a dissolution was possible. I hear with pain, and anguish, and distress, the word secession....*

*Instead of speaking of the possibility or utility of secession, instead of dwell-ing in these caverns of darkness ... let us come out into the light of day.... Let us cherish those hopes which belong to us.... Let us make our generation one of the strongest, and brightest links in that golden chain which is destined, I fully be-lieve, to grapple the people of all the States to this Constitution, for ages to come.*

**From Daniel Webster, Seventh of March Speech, 1850.**

to Henry Clay, then in his seventy-third year and near the end of his long career, that lovers of the Union looked almost instinctively for a just and durable compromise. On January 29, 1850, Clay offered the Senate a series of resolutions proposing (1) that Cali-fornia be admitted as a free state; (2) that territorial governments be provided for the rest of the Mexican cession without any restriction on slavery; (3) that Texas abandon its claim to the eastern portion of New Mexico; (4) that the federal government compensate Texas by assuming the public debt Texas had con-tracted before annexation; (5) that the use of the District of Columbia as a depot in the interstate slave trade be prohibited; (6) that slavery in the District of Columbia be abolished only with the consent of its residents and of the state of Maryland and with com-pensation to the slaveholders; (7) that a new and more rigorous fugitive-slave act be adopted; and (8) that Congress declare that it had no power to interfere with the interstate slave trade. Among the many moderates who labored long and hard to secure the adoption of these compromise proposals, Stephen A. Douglas of Illinois was second only to Clay.

Congress debated the proposals for more than seven months, with the moderates under constant attack from both proslavery and antislavery oppo-nents of compromise. Clay opened the memorable debate in February. For two days he spoke in defense of his measures and urged mutual concessions for the sake of the Union. He asked Northerners why they insisted on the Wilmot Proviso when they had a stronger force working for them: "You have got nature itself on your side." He warned Southerners that they

would gain nothing and lose a great deal by seces-sion—that secession was certain to lead to civil war, "furious, bloody, implacable, exterminating." On March 4, John C. Calhoun, ill and close to death, listened to a colleague read his last address to the Senate. The present crisis, Calhoun insisted, was due to a breakdown of the old sectional equilibrium, to Northern aggression against the South, and to the destruction of the rights of the states and the creation of a consolidated government. Nothing could save the Union but an end of antislavery agitation, a faithful enforcement of the Fugitive Slave Law, equal rights for the South in the territories, and a constitutional amendment restoring the balance between the two sections. If these points were not conceded, if the South were forced to choose between "submission or resistance," it would know how to act.

On March 7, three days after Calhoun had sounded his grim protest against Clay's compromise, Daniel Webster delivered the last great oration of his career. To the dismay of his antislavery constituents, he repudiated his free-soil sentiments and announced that he would speak "not as a Massachusetts man, nor as a northern man, but as an American." Though Webster refuted Calhoun's charges against the North, his speech was clearly an attempt to make the com-promise palatable to his own section. He denounced antislavery agitation, urged Northerners not to insist on the Wilmot Proviso when slavery would not ex-pand into the new territories in any case, called for an end to resistance to the Fugitive Slave Act, and con-cluded with a tearful plea for the Union. Webster's speech immensely strengthened the forces of compro-

*Henry Clay: advocate of mutual concessions*

mise, but for the remaining two years of his life anti-slavery men vilified him for his apostasy.

Most of the Northern Conscience Whigs stood firm. Senator William H. Seward of New York spoke for them when he denounced compromise as "radically wrong and essentially vicious." There was only one way to end antislavery agitation, he said, and that was by "yielding to the progress of emancipation." In reply to Calhoun's constitutional defense of the right to carry slaves into the territories, Seward appealed to "a higher law than the Constitution," a divine law that intended these rich lands to be enjoyed by free men.

As the debate wore on and the House and Senate considered numerous variations of Clay's proposals, it became increasingly evident that opinion in favor of a compromise of some kind was steadily building up in both North and South. Northern businessmen, frightened by the talk of secession, favored a compromise in order to protect their Southern trade and investments. The country had recovered from the depression of the 1840s, and practical men longed for political peace so that they could make the most of a new era of prosperity and economic growth. Those who were indifferent to the moral issue of slavery saw no point in permitting continued antislavery agitation to endanger the Union. The compromisers were further strengthened when the moderates won control of the Southern convention at Nashville and indicated that they were ready to accept a fair settlement. Now the most formidable obstacle to compromise was President Taylor, who bitterly resented Clay's rejection of the Administration's recommendations on New Mexico and California in favor of proposals of his own. The possibility of a presidential veto loomed until Taylor's sudden death on July 9 after an attack of gastroenteritis. His successor, Vice President Millard Fillmore, though a New York Whig of free-soil proclivities, immediately allied himself with Webster and Clay and used his influence in favor of compromise.

Even then, the adoption of a compromise was not easy. When Clay's major proposals had been combined in an "omnibus bill," they were threatened with defeat by a combination of Free-Soilers, antislavery Whigs, and Southern-rights men. But the moderates discovered that each of the measures might be enacted separately, for the moderates could then combine with those who opposed the compromise as a whole but favored individual parts of it. In the final weeks of the battle, Senator Douglas replaced the exhausted Clay as leader of the compromisers, and by September 1850 all the measures had been passed and signed by President Fillmore.

The Compromise of 1850 as it was finally adopted was essentially like the one Clay had proposed the January before: California was admitted as a free state; the territories of New Mexico and Utah were created from the rest of the Mexican cession, with no

*Millard Fillmore: influence for compromise*

The Compromise of 1850

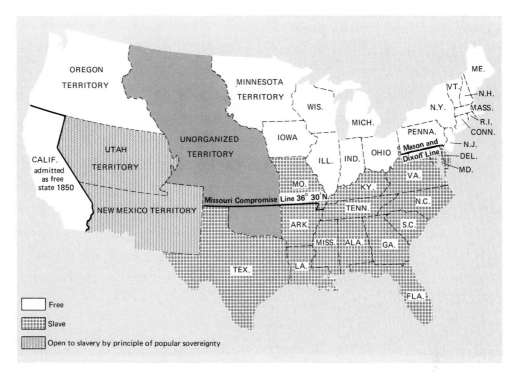

OREGON TERRITORY

MINNESOTA TERRITORY

WIS.

MICH.

ME.

VT.

N.H.

N.Y.

MASS.

R.I.

CONN.

PENNA.

N.J.

CALIF. admitted as free state 1850

UTAH TERRITORY

UNORGANIZED TERRITORY

IOWA

OHIO

Mason and Dixon Line

DEL.

MD.

ILL. IND.

VA.

MO.

KY.

NEW MEXICO TERRITORY

Missouri Compromise Line 36° 30' N.

TENN.

N.C.

ARK

S.C

MISS. ALA. GA.

TEX.

LA.

FLA.

Free

Slave

Open to slavery by principle of popular sovereignty

restriction on slavery; the Texas boundary was fixed as it exists today; Texas was paid $10 million from the federal treasury as compensation for yielding to New Mexico in their boundary dispute; slave-trading was prohibited in the District of Columbia; and what was expected to be a more effective fugitive-slave act replaced the old one of 1793.

## The aftermath

***Public reaction to the compromise.*** Few Northerners or Southerners were altogether satisfied with the Compromise of 1850, and some in each section spurned it as an unclean thing. Abolitionists and Free-Soilers refused to be bound by its terms and denounced as unprincipled tools of the Slave Power the Northern congressmen who had voted for it. Emerson publicly declared that no man could obey the new Fugitive Slave Law "without loss of self-respect and forfeiture of the name of a gentleman." In 1851 the Massachusetts legislature delivered a stern rebuke to Webster (who had joined Fillmore's Cabinet as Secretary of State) by electing Charles Sumner, a radical Free-Soiler and enemy of the compromise, to the United States Senate.

In the South, "fire-eaters" like Robert Barnwell Rhett of South Carolina and William L. Yancey of

Alabama termed the compromise a fatal defeat for their section and called for drastic action. The position of the South in the Union was now hopeless, they said, and the proper remedy was immediate secession. In South Carolina the secessionists were defeated with the greatest difficulty, and then only because the "moderates" insisted that action be delayed until other Southern states were ready for independence. A state convention in Georgia adopted a series of resolutions, known as the Georgia Platform, that were probably an accurate expression of public opinion in the Deep South. These resolutions accepted the Compromise of 1850 but warned that Georgia would resist, "even (as a last resort) to a disruption of every tie which binds her to the Union," any congressional act abolishing slavery in the District of Columbia, refusing to admit a slave state, excluding slavery from the territories, or repealing the Fugitive Slave Law.

But most Americans in both sections, though doubting the wisdom of some provisions of the compromise, accepted it with great relief and hoped for a respite from sectional agitation. Mass meetings throughout the country celebrated its passage, and the merchants of New York City formed a Union Safety Committee to mobilize public opinion in its defense. Stephen A. Douglas announced that he had resolved "never to make another speech on the slavery question. . . . Let us cease agitating, stop the debate, and drop the subject." In his annual message of December

275

*The aftermath*

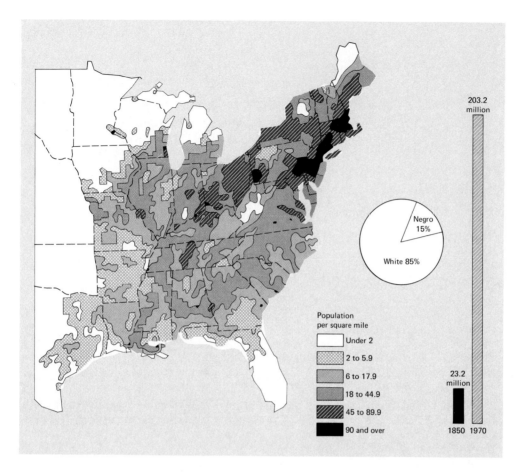

Population
per square mile

- ☐ Under 2
- ▨ 2 to 5.9
- ▦ 6 to 17.9
- ▩ 18 to 44.9
- ▨ 45 to 89.9
- ■ 90 and over

203.2 million

23.2 million

1850    1970

Negro 15%

White 85%

1850 President Fillmore told Congress that he regarded the compromise measures as "a final settlement of the dangerous and exciting subjects which they embraced." And forty-four congressmen of both parties signed a pledge to respect the terms of the compromise and never to support a candidate for public office who threatened to disturb it.

***Franklin Pierce.*** The presidential election of 1852 gave further evidence of the widespread hope that the Compromise of 1850 would in fact be a "final settlement." The Democrats adopted a platform that endorsed the compromise without qualification and promised to resist "agitation of the slavery question, under whatever shape or color the attempt may be made." After many futile ballots the convention dropped the leading candidates—Douglas, Cass, and James Buchanan of Pennsylvania—and nominated another "dark horse," Franklin Pierce of New Hampshire. The Whig party, with its Northern and Southern wings now almost hopelessly divided, wrangled over a platform that unenthusiastically "acquiesced in" the compromise and therefore pleased almost no one. The convention rejected Fillmore and turned to

another military hero, General Winfield Scott of Virginia, whose friendship with Seward and whose failure to endorse the compromise made him suspect in the South. In the election, though Pierce's popular majority was not overwhelming, he carried twenty-seven states with 254 electoral votes, while Scott carried only four states with 42 electoral votes. The Barnburners had returned to the Democratic fold, and the Free-Soil party, with John P. Hale of New Hampshire as its candidate, polled only about half as many votes as it had four years earlier.

Pierce was a Jacksonian Democrat of amiable disposition, modest talent, and almost no capacity for executive leadership. His close ties with Southern Democrats, especially with his Secretary of War, Jefferson Davis, and his sympathy for their views on questions of public policy caused antislavery leaders to damn him as a "doughface"—"a northern man with southern principles." But his promise in his inaugural address that the provisions of the Compromise of 1850 would be "unhesitatingly carried into effect" suited the popular mood. In his first message to Congress, in December 1853, Pierce rejoiced that the recent compromise had "given renewed vigor to our institutions and restored a sense of repose and security to the public mind." With the country prospering, with the hope that sectional issues had been disposed of, some optimists went so far as to predict a new era of good feelings.

**Surviving sources of friction.** But very soon there were abundant signs that the truce would be short. The disintegration of the Whig party after its defeat in 1852 snapped another of the ties holding the Union together. The admission of California had upset the sectional balance in the Senate—prior to 1850 there had been fifteen slave and fifteen free states—and the admission of several more free states could not be long delayed. The immigrants who poured into the United States during the 1840s and 1850s (see p. 288) shunned the South and thus further increased the North's numerical majority, and railroad-building and industrial expansion gave the North an accelerating economic supremacy. Now secessionists could argue that the rights and interests of the minority South were at the mercy of a hostile and overbearing North.

To Southern-rights men the controversy that began at once over the enforcement of the new Fugitive Slave Act proved their point. This provision of the Compromise of 1850 was the one Southerners regarded as their principal gain and the one Northerners found most difficult to accept. It was a harsh measure that subjected alleged fugitives to summary hearings before federal commissioners without trial by jury or the right to testify in their own behalf. Since a commissioner received a fee of $10 if he ruled that a black prisoner was a slave but only $5 if he ruled that the Negro was free, abolitionists charged that the commissioners were being bribed to collaborate with kidnapers who sought to sell free Negroes into slavery. In the Northern strongholds of antislavery sentiment the new law simply could not be enforced; during the 1850s abolitionists executed a series of dramatic rescues of fugitives and sent them on to Canada and freedom. Moreover, various Northern states passed personal-liberty laws that nullified the Fugitive Slave Act or at least interfered with its enforcement. This was an assertion of state rights and a form of nullification that Southerners scarcely appreciated.

Above all, the Compromise of 1850 could not stop the pens or quiet the voices of the abolitionists. Less than two years after the compromise was passed the most eloquent and influential appeal in behalf of the slave ever to be written appeared in Harriet Beecher Stowe's justly celebrated novel, *Uncle Tom's Cabin.* Mrs. Stowe was the daughter of a New England clergyman, sister of seven others, and wife of still another. Her anger over the Fugitive Slave Act prompted her to declare: "I will write something. I

*Harriet Beecher Stowe: "I will write something"*

will if I live." First published serially in an antislavery weekly, her novel appeared in book form in March 1852. By the end of the year, three hundred thousand copies had been sold. Thereafter the novel, together with its various adaptations for the stage, won thousands of converts to the antislavery cause. *Uncle Tom's Cabin* has more than a few flaws as literature: its situations are contrived; its dialogue is unreal; its slaves are romanticized. Mrs. Stowe knew almost nothing of slavery firsthand, but she understood clearly its tragic aspects; moreover, she had the wisdom to direct her moral indictment against the institution itself rather than against the Southern men and women who were caught in its toils. Indeed, the chief villain of her plot, the cruel overseer Simon Legree, was Northern born. But these subtleties made the book no more attractive to Southern slaveholders than the cruder forms of abolitionist propaganda.

Slavery, then, still threatened the nation's peace and unity. On the eve of the Civil War Abraham Lincoln wrote to Alexander H. Stephens of Georgia: "You think slavery is right and ought to be extended, while we think it is *wrong* and ought to be restricted. That I suppose is the rub."

277

*The aftermath*

**WESTWARD TO THE PACIFIC**

Among the surveys of the westward movement, R. A. Billington, *Westward Expansion* (4th ed., 1974), is especially good on American penetration of the Far West. General coverage of the diplomacy of expansion is provided in S. F. Bemis, *A Diplomatic History of the United States* (5th ed., 1965); T. A. Bailey, *A Diplomatic History of the American People* (8th ed., 1969); J. W. Pratt, *A History of United States Foreign Policy* (1955, rev. ed., 1965); R. H. Ferrell, *American Diplomacy: A History* (1959, rev. ed., 1969); and Alexander De Conde, *A History of American Foreign Policy*\* (1963, rev. ed., 1971). The best book dealing comprehensively with expansion in this period is R. A. Billington, *The Far Western Frontier, 1830–1860*\* (1956). N. A. Graebner, *Empire on the Pacific* (1955), stresses the desire for Pacific ports as a motive for expansion. A. K. Weinberg, *Manifest Destiny*\* (1935), is an excellent analysis of the ideology of expansionism. Frederick Merk has written two important books on the motivation and rationalization of expansionism: *Manifest Destiny and Mission in American History: A Reinterpretation*\* (1963), and *The Monroe Doctrine and American Expansionism, 1843–1849* (1966). H. N. Smith, *Virgin Land*\* (1950), brilliantly analyzes the place of the West in American literature and thought.

The two basic works on the American occupation of Texas are E. C. Barker, *Mexico and Texas, 1821–1835* (1928), and W. C. Binkley, *The Texas Revolution* (1952). A good popular account of the Santa Fe trade is R. L. Duffus, *The Santa Fe Trail* (1930). The best introductions to the fur trade of the Far West are H. M. Chittenden, *The American Fur Trade of the Far West,* 3 vols. (rev. ed., 1935); R. G. Cleland, *This Reckless Breed of Men: The Trappers and Fur Traders of the Southwest* (1950); D. L. Morgan, *Jedediah Smith and the Opening of the West*\* (1953); P. C. Phillips, *The Fur Trade,* 2 vols. (1961); and G. G. Cline, *Exploring the Great Basin*\* (1963). Missionary activity in Oregon can be studied in two competent biographies: C. J. Brosnan, *Jason Lee: Prophet of the New Oregon* (1932), and C. M. Drury, *Marcus Whitman, M.D., Pioneer and Martyr* (1937). Two books on the overland trails, reliable and well written, are W. J. Ghent, *The Road to Oregon* (1929), and Jay Monaghan, *The Overland Trail* (1937). A superb contemporary account, Francis Parkman, *The California and Oregon Trail* (1849), is available in several modern editions under the title *The Oregon Trail*\*. The American occupation of Oregon is treated adequately in O. O. Winther, *The Great Northwest* (2nd ed., 1950), and D. O. Johansen and C. M. Gates, *Empire on the Columbia* (2nd ed., 1967). Early American interest in California is covered in two general histories: A. F. Rolle, *California: A History*\* (1963, rev. ed., 1969), and W. E. Bean, *California: An Interpretive History* (1968). Wallace Stegner, *The Gathering of Zion: The Story of the Mormon Trail*\* (1964), is an excellent account of the Mormon migration. The Mormon settlement in the Salt Lake basin is viewed from several perspectives in Nels Anderson, *Desert Saints: The Mormon Frontier in Utah*\* (1942); R. B. West, Jr., *Kingdom of the Saints* (1957); T. F. O'Dea, *The Mormons*\* (1957); and L. J. Arrington, *Great Basin Kingdom*\* (1958). Preston Nibley, *Brigham Young: The Man and His Works* (1936), is warmly sympathetic. S. P. Hirshson, *The Lion of the Lord: A Biography of Brigham Young* (1969), is more critical.

**POLK AND THE TRIUMPH OF MANIFEST DESTINY**

The authoritative study of the election of 1844 and the first two years of the Polk Administration is Charles Sellers, *James K. Polk: Continentalist, 1843–1846* (1966). Polk's presidential years can also be studied in E. I. McCormac, *James K. Polk* (1922), and in Allan Nevins, ed., *Polk: The Diary of a President, 1845–1849*\* (1952). A lively and readable introduction to the expansionism of the Polk era is Bernard De Voto, *The Year of Decision, 1846*\* (1943). Two books deal with negotiations for the annexation of Texas: J. H. Smith, *The Annexation of Texas* (1911), and J. W. Schmitz, *Texan Statecraft, 1836–1845* (1945). F. W. Merk, *Slavery and the Annexation of Texas* (1972), is critical of the proslavery propagandists and their fear of British intervention. M. C. Jacobs, *Winning Oregon* (1938), is a good summary of the Oregon dispute and its settlement. F. W. Merk, *The Oregon Question* (1967), is a collection of excellent interpretive essays. The standard works on the background of the Mexican War are J. S. Reeves, *American Diplomacy under Tyler and Polk* (1907), and G. L. Rives, *The United States and Mexico: 1821–1848,* 2 vols. (1913). D. M. Pletcher, *The Diplomacy of Annexation: Texas, Oregon, and the Mexican War* (1973), is detailed and comprehensive.

\*Available in a paperback edition.

**Expansion and sectional crisis**

Though dated and marred by its biases, the fullest and most authoritative work on the Mexican War is J. H. Smith, *The War with Mexico,* 2 vols. (1919). S. V. Conner and O. B. Faulk, *North America Divided: The Mexican War, 1846–1848* (1971), attributes responsibility to both belligerents but is mostly a defense of the United States. Three other books contribute few fresh interpretations but are brief and readable: A. H. Bill, *Rehearsal for Conflict: The War with Mexico, 1846–1848* (1947); R. S. Henry, *The Story of the Mexican War* (1950); and O. A. Singletary, *The Mexican War\** (1960). The military campaigns are traced in K. J. Bauer, *The Mexican War, 1846–1848* (1974), and in two excellent biographies: C. W. Elliott, *Winfield Scott* (1937), and Holman Hamilton, *Zachary Taylor: Soldier of the Republic* (1941). J. H. Schroeder, *Mr. Polk's War: American Opposition and Dissent, 1846–1848* (1973), explores the sources of antiwar sentiment.

## CRISIS AND COMPROMISE

Allan Nevins, *Ordeal of the Union,* 2 vols. (1947), contains a full, incisive, and well-written account of the issue of slavery expansion and of the Compromise of 1850. Among the most useful books for the politics of slavery expansion are T. C. Smith, *The Liberty and Free-Soil Parties in the Northwest* (1897); R. H. Shryock, *Georgia and the Union in 1850* (1926); J. T. Carpenter, *The South as a Conscious Minority* (1930); A. O. Craven, *The Growth of Southern Nationalism, 1848–1861* (1953); K. J. Brauer, *Cotton Versus Conscience: Massachusetts Whig Politics and Southern Expansion, 1843–1848* (1967); C. W. Morrison, *Democratic Politics and Sectionalism: The Wilmot Proviso Controversy* (1967); F. J. Blue, *The Free Soilers: Third Party Politics, 1848–1854* (1973); and R. S. Sewell, *Ballots for Freedom: Antislavery Politics in the United States, 1837–1860* (1976). Negrophobia as a motive for opposition to slavery expansion is stressed in E. H. Berwanger, *The Frontier Against Slavery: Western Anti-Negro Prejudice and the Slavery Extension Controversy\** (1967). J. G. Rayback, *Free Soil: The Election of 1848* (1970), is both scholarly and readable. The Taylor Administration is treated thoroughly in two good biographies: Brainerd Dyer, *Zachary Taylor* (1946), and Holman Hamilton, *Zachary Taylor: Soldier in the White House* (1951).

Of the many books on the California gold rush, the following are among the best: R. W. Paul, *California Gold: The Beginning of Mining in the Far West\** (1947); R. W. Paul, *Mining Frontiers of the Far West, 1848–1880\** (1963); J. W. Caughey, *Gold Is the Cornerstone* (1949); O. C. Coy, *The Great Trek* (1931); A. B. Hulbert, *Forty-Niners* (1931); and J. H. Jackson, *Anybody's Gold: The Story of California's Mining Towns* (1941).

The best study of the Compromise of 1850 is Holman Hamilton, *Prologue to Conflict: The Crisis and Compromise of 1850\** (1964). The crisis and compromise can also be studied through the numerous biographies of national political leaders. Among the most useful are: C. B. Going, *David Wilmot, Free-Soiler* (1924); W. Y. Thompson, *Robert Toombs of Georgia* (1966); G. G. Van Deusen, *William Henry Seward* (1967); F. B. Woodward, *Lewis Cass: The Last Jeffersonian* (1950); R. W. Johannsen, *Stephen A. Douglas* (1973); G. M. Capers, *Stephen A. Douglas: Defender of the Union* (1959); C. M. Fuess, *Daniel Webster,* 2 vols. (1930, 2nd ed., 1968); R. N. Current, *Daniel Webster and the Rise of National Conservatism\** (1955); G. G. Van Deusen, *The Life of Henry Clay\** (1937); G. G. Van Deusen, *Thurlow Weed: Wizard of the Lobby* (1947); J. H. Parks, *John Bell of Tennessee* (1950); Rudolph Von Abele, *Alexander H. Stephens: A Biography* (1946); and C. M. Wiltse, *John C. Calhoun: Sectionalist, 1840–1850* (1951).

*Available in a paperback edition.

# CHAPTER 12

# *America at mid-century*

From the Mexican War to the Civil War the major themes of American political history were sectional conflict and the gradual disintegration of the second American party system. Outside the realm of politics, however, this period was notable for its positive achievements—its industrial growth, railroad construction, agricultural expansion, and technological innovations. In spite of the mounting political crisis Americans in general were concerned most of the time with other affairs. They were occupied with ships and railroads and machines and farm implements, with the settlement and development of the West, and with geographic expansion and Manifest Destiny. Stephen A. Douglas, energetic and tough-minded, idol of a bumptious element in the Democratic party that called itself Young America, cared little for the moral issue of slavery and was impatient with those who did. In the early 1850s Douglas struck a popular note when he urged Americans to forget the sectional quarrel and turn to the main business of building a prosperous and powerful nation. Young America was, to be sure, concerned about its soul, but it was concerned even more about getting things done.

*Cincinnati waterfront, 1848*

*The genius of the United States is not best or most in its executives or legisla-
tures, nor in its ambassadors or authors or colleges or churches or parlors, nor
even in its newspapers or inventors ... but always most in the common people.
Their manners, speech, dress, friendships—the freshness and candor of their
physiognomy—the picturesque looseness of their carriage ... their deathless attachment to freedom—their aversion to anything indecorous or soft or mean—the
practical acknowledgment of the citizens of one state by the citizens of all other
states—the fierceness of their roused resentment—their curiosity and welcome of
novelty—their self-esteem and wonderful sympathy—their susceptibility to a
slight—the air they have of persons who never knew how it felt to stand in the
presence of superiors—the fluency of their speech—their delight in music, the
sure symptom of manly tenderness and native elegance of soul ... their good temper and openhandedness—the terrible significance of their elections—the President's taking off his hat to them not they to him—these too are unrhymed poetry.
It awaits the gigantic and generous treatment worthy of it.*

**From Walt Whitman, Preface to *Leaves of Grass*, 1855.**

# The emergence of an American literature

The 1850s were one of the most distinguished and
productive periods in the history of American literature. The decade was preceded, however, by many
years of literary dependence on Europe. As late as the
1820s American readers were buying more than twice
as many books by British as by American authors.

The first writers to win more than local recognition—Washington Irving (1783–1859) and James Fenimore Cooper (1789–1851)—had exploited American
themes, but they had spent much of their lives abroad
and had observed the conventions of Europe's men of
letters. Irving, after writing an amusing and popular
*History of New York* (1809) and *The Sketch Book*
(1819–20), which depicts village life in rural New
York through characters such as Ichabod Crane and
Rip Van Winkle, went off to Europe hoping to exchange "the commonplace realities of the present" for
"the shadowy grandeur of the past." Cooper used the
American frontier as the setting for his five *Leather-
stocking Tales* (1823–41), but it is a romantic, unrealistic frontier where the hero, Natty Bumppo, em-
bodies the courage, nobility, innocence, and
naturalness supposedly characteristic of men who live
in the wilderness. Though defending American democracy to Europeans, Cooper had little confidence
in the future of literature in his native land. "There is
scarcely an ore which contributes to the wealth of the
author, that is found, here, in veins as rich as in
Europe," he complained. "There are no annals for the
historian; no follies ... for the satirist; no manners

for the dramatist; no obscure fictions for the writers
of romance . . . nor any of the rich artificial auxiliaries of poetry." A third writer of extraordinary talent,
Edgar Allan Poe (1809–49), born in Boston but a Virginian by adoption, was too exotic a figure, too much
lost in a weird world of his own creation, too alienated from his optimistic, democratic countrymen, to
be the founder or precursor of an American literature.

Yet the call for a national literature as an essential
part of a genuine American independence was heard
soon after the Revolution and grew stronger with the
passing years. In 1815 a group of Boston intellectuals
began publishing a literary magazine, the *North
American Review*, but rather than breaking new
ground it soon became the chief spokesman for a
conservative, European-oriented, genteel literary tradition. It often spoke in terms of a cultural nationalism, but it did little in these early years to disturb the
local literary establishment. In 1830 William Ellery
Channing, in his "Remarks on National Literature,"
criticized these traditionalists, many of them his Unitarian coreligionists, by urging Americans to encourage their own scholars and cease depending "for intellectual excitement and enjoyment on foreign minds."
The true rulers of a country, he said, "are those who
determine its mind, its tastes, its principles, and we
cannot consent to lodge this sovereignty in the hands
of strangers."

Eventually several transcendentalist writers made
the first successful break with the traditionalists. One
of the milestones in this revolt was Emerson's Phi Beta
Kappa address at Harvard in 1837, titled "The American Scholar." Calling for a literature of democracy,
Emerson advised American writers to stop imitating

**Individualism: Thoreau**

**From Henry David Thoreau, *Essay on Civil Disobedience*, 1849.**

the "courtly muses of Europe" and to produce a distinctive literature of their own. "Our day of dependence, our long apprenticeship to the learning of other lands draws to a close," he exulted. "The millions that around us are rushing into life cannot always be fed on the sere remains of foreign harvests. Events, actions arise, that must be sung, that will sing themselves." The writer should look to the lives of the common people, who, Emerson believed, were the finest products of this new nation. Writers should turn away from "the great, the remote, the romantic" and "sit at the feet of the familiar, the low. . . . What would we really know the meaning of? The meal in the firkin; the milk in the pan; the ballad in the street; the news of the boat; the glance of the eye; the form and gait of the body."

In the 1840s and 1850s American writers began to heed Emerson's advice. Emerson's own essays, as well as those of Thoreau, marked a turning away from Europe, a trend still more apparent in the novels of Nathaniel Hawthorne (1804–64) and Herman Melville (1819–91) and in the poetry of Walt Whitman (1819–92). Their masterpieces—Hawthorne's *The Scarlet Letter* (1850), Melville's *Moby Dick* (1851), which many critics call the greatest American novel, Thoreau's *Walden* (1854), and the first edition of Whitman's *Leaves of Grass* (1855)—attracted a limited but appreciative audience of educated men and women. Both Hawthorne, fascinated with the Puritan tradition and with New England's history and legends, and Melville, drawing on his adventures on the high seas, were tormented by deep philosophical questions: the nature of man and the source of evil, which they

saw as a powerful and enduring force in the world.

Whitman, far more a buoyant transcendentalist than either Hawthorne or Melville, responded most heartily to Emerson's call. His poetry—sensuous, exuberant, unorthodox, unconcerned about rhyme or meter—was denounced by some as crude, vulgar, even immoral. When *Leaves of Grass* first appeared, Emerson found it a little shocking, because some of the poems dwelt on "the form and gait of the body" somewhat more than he had bargained for; nevertheless, he greeted Whitman "at the beginning of a great career." Drawing his themes from nature and the common people, Whitman called *Leaves of Grass* "the great psalm of the republic." In his preface he expressed the humane, democratic idealism that underlies his poetry: "Love the earth and sun and the animals, despise riches, give alms to everyone that asks . . . hate tyrants, argue not concerning God, have patience and indulgence toward the people, take off your hat to nothing known or to any man or number of men." In effect, Whitman took the ideas of the transcendentalists out of the study and gave them joyous, uninhibited life.

## Intimations of imperialism

During the 1850s America's politicians doubtless understood the spirit of the people at least as well as America's poets did, and the politicians were listened to more attentively. As in the 1840s, they found widespread support for proposals for national geographic expansion. In his inaugural address President Pierce served notice that the acquisition of Oregon, California, and New Mexico was not the complete fulfillment of his country's Manifest Destiny. There were other areas that circumstances might force the United States to acquire, and Pierce announced that his Administration would not shrink from further expansion because of "any timid forebodings of evil." In part he was expressing the continuing belief that eventually all or part of Canada and the rest of Mexico would be annexed to share the blessings of American democracy. But by mid-century some expansionists were looking beyond these adjacent territories to Cuba, Central America, and Hawaii, where commercial and strategic considerations outweighed the hunger for land. This was a sign that Manifest Destiny might very easily be converted into a doctrine of imperialism.

***Cuba.*** The Spanish colony of Cuba, a land of slaves and sugar plantations, interested Southerners who hoped to acquire it in order to increase their political and economic power. Cuba also attracted certain Northern commercial interests, especially a small but active group of business-speculators in New York. Moreover, its proximity to Florida and its commanding position at the mouth of the Caribbean Sea and the Gulf of Mexico gave it great strategic importance. The United States had always been apprehensive about the possibility that Cuba might pass from Spain to a stronger power. As early as 1810 President Madison had warned that his country "could not be a satisfied spectator" if Cuba were to fall to some European government "which might make a fulcrum of that position against the security and commerce of the United States."

Until the 1840s the chief aim of American diplomacy had been merely to keep Cuba out of the hands of Britain and France. After the Mexican War, however, proannexation sentiment became so strong that the government changed its policy. In 1848 James Buchanan, Polk's Secretary of State, instructed the American minister at Madrid to offer as much as $100 million for Cuba. The Spanish government responded with a cold refusal; indeed, the foreign minister vowed that he would sooner see the island sunk in the ocean than sold.

Failing to gain Cuba by diplomacy, some expansionists (mostly Southerners) were ready to try force. In 1848 General Narciso López, a Venezuelan adventurer, appeared in New Orleans to find arms and recruits for a filibustering expedition against Cuba. The next year, in spite of federal attempts to stop him, López invaded the island with two hundred fifty volunteers, mostly Mexican War veterans, but Spanish troops quickly repulsed them. In 1851 López tried again with a force of four hundred men, but once more he was defeated; this time Spanish authorities executed him and fifty other captives as pirates. Disappointed sympathizers in New Orleans retaliated by destroying the Spanish consulate, and the American and Spanish governments exchanged angry notes. Eventually the United States paid an indemnity for the damage committed by the New Orleans mob, and Spain pardoned the rest of the captured filibusters. But the government did not disavow its interest in Cuba; indeed, it rejected a British and French proposal for a tripartite agreement designed to assure the island's continued possession by Spain.

The Pierce Administration made the acquisition of Cuba one of its chief goals. It sent Pierre Soulé of Louisiana, a flamboyant French exile and ardent expansionist, as minister to Spain, and it gave him cause to believe that his mission was to acquire the island regardless of methods. Secretary of State William L. Marcy authorized Soulé to renew the attempt to purchase Cuba, this time for $130 million; failing in this, he might try to "detach" it from Spain by intrigue. Lacking the most elementary qualifications of a diplomat, the impetuous minister soon was embroiled in a bitter dispute with the Spanish government. In February 1854 an American merchant vessel, the *Black Warrior*, was seized at Havana for a technical violation of Spanish customs laws. Soulé promptly demanded a disavowal of the act and an indemnity; when he received no immediate reply, he renewed his demands in the form of a virtual ultimatum. The Spanish foreign minister simply ignored Soulé and negotiated a settlement directly with Washington and with the owners of the *Black Warrior*.

At this point Soulé might well have been replaced by a more skillful minister. Instead, Marcy showed no outward sign of disapproval and gave him an even more delicate assignment. Soulé was to confer with John Y. Mason, minister to France, and James Buchanan, minister to Great Britain, about methods of

*Inauguration of Pierce:
no timid forebodings*

acquiring Cuba and of dealing with possible British and French opposition. In October 1854 the three ministers met for a few days at Ostend and then for a week at Aix-la-Chapelle. They sent their recommendations to the Secretary of State in a confidential memorandum, but its contents were soon known to the public—and the document itself was quite inaccurately labeled the Ostend Manifesto. Largely the work of Soulé, the memorandum declared that the United States would benefit from the possession of Cuba, while Spain would be better off without it. Accordingly, it proposed that another effort be made to purchase the island. If Spain again refused to sell, the United States would have to consider whether Cuba was a threat to her internal peace. If it was found to be such a threat, "then by every law human and divine, we shall be justified in wresting it from Spain, if we possess the power."

The Ostend Manifesto delighted Southern expansionists and the Young America element in the Democratic party, and it played no small part in Buchanan's presidential nomination two years later. But the criticism from abroad and the indignation of antislavery Northerners forced the Pierce Administration to repudiate it. Marcy sent a strong rebuke to Soulé, and the shocked and humiliated minister resigned. But Cuba was not forgotten; the Democratic platform of 1856 favored annexation, and in three of his annual messages to Congress President Buchanan urged another attempt to purchase it. Cuba, however, had become a sectional issue, and any further action was impossible.

**Central America.** For centuries men had dreamed of joining the Atlantic and Pacific by cutting a canal through Panama or Nicaragua, but the United States did not become seriously interested in the idea until after the Mexican War and the acquisition of California. In 1848 the need for faster communication between the East and the Far West led to the signing of a treaty with New Granada (Colombia), which gave the United States transit rights through Panama in exchange for a guarantee of New Granada's sovereignty over this isthmian province. By 1855 a group of American promoters had built a railroad across Panama; until the completion of the first transcontinental railroad in 1869, this was the easiest route to the Pacific coast.

Meanwhile, American diplomats, speculators, and adventurers had become deeply involved in the affairs of the small and politically unstable Republic of Nicaragua, which seemed as promising a site for a canal as Panama. Here, however, the Americans met a formidable competitor in Great Britain, whose worldwide trade, large navy, and extensive colonial possessions gave it a keen interest in an isthmian canal.

Indeed, because of the enormous cost of such a project, many assumed that when a canal was built, British capitalists would finance and control it. The British government, watching American movements suspiciously, established a foothold at the mouth of the San Juan River (the probable eastern terminus of a Nicaraguan canal) and claimed a protectorate over the Mosquito Indians on the eastern coast of Nicaragua. This action alarmed the American government, and in the resulting diplomatic exchanges each country warned that it would not permit the other to have exclusive control over an isthmian canal. In 1850 the dispute was settled when Sir Henry Lytton Bulwer, the British minister to the United States, and John M. Clayton, President Taylor's Secretary of State, agreed to the terms of a treaty. It provided, first, that any canal built through Panama or Nicaragua was to be unfortified, neutral in time of war, and open to the ships of all countries on equal terms; second, that neither country was to colonize or establish dominion over any part of Central America.

The Clayton-Bulwer Treaty was approved by the Senate and remained in force for the next half-century, but it was unpopular from the start. Expansionists disliked the commitment not to acquire territory in Central America, which meant, they said, that the United States had voluntarily applied the Monroe Doctrine against itself. This concession, together with the implicit recognition that Britain had equal interests in Central America, provoked critics to accuse Clayton of having been outwitted by Bulwer— Buchanan suggested that Clayton ought to be rewarded with elevation to the British peerage. Resentment increased when the British government maintained that the treaty applied only to the future and was not an obligation to abandon its existing protectorate over the eastern coast of Nicaragua. Impulsive Southern expansionists applauded when, in 1855, William Walker, a Tennessean by birth, led a filibustering expedition into Nicaragua and seized control of its government. Walker was soon driven out, and when he tried to return in 1860 he was captured and executed.

In spite of the criticism, the Clayton-Bulwer Treaty was not a bad bargain for the United States, given the circumstances of the time. The British government removed one cause of complaint when in 1859 it voluntarily gave up its protectorate over the Mosquito Indians. Then and later the treaty avoided a race between the two countries for possessions in Central America. Above all, it assured the United States equal access to an isthmian canal at a time when the nation was in no position to ask for more.

**Hawaii.** Even before the acquisition of Oregon and California made the United States a Pacific power, some Americans had developed an interest in Hawaii. Merchantmen engaged in trade with the Far East, and whaling ships, had stopped there for supplies; by the 1830s missionaries had begun to arrive; other Americans had come in search of land or commercial opportunities. In those early years there was little talk of annexation, but the government was uneasy about the intentions of the British and the French. In 1849, when France seemed ready to seize the islands, Secretary of State Clayton, though denying that the United States desired to establish its sovereignty over them, warned that it "could never with indifference allow them to pass under the dominion or exclusive control of any other power." The Pierce Administration, however, pursued a more aggressive policy; in 1854 Secretary of State Marcy negotiated a treaty of annexation with the Hawaiian government. But British protests and Senate opposition caused Pierce to drop the matter. Thereafter, until the 1880s, the United States seemed content merely to keep Hawaii free from foreign control.

**The Gadsden Purchase.**  The only tangible result of the various expansionist schemes of the 1850s was the purchase from Mexico of another slice of land in the Southwest. In 1853 the War Department made a survey of possible routes for a transcontinental railroad. The survey revealed that if a line were to be built westward from a Southern city it would probably have to enter Mexican territory south of the Gila River. Realizing that this would be an effective argument for a Northern route, Secretary of War Jefferson Davis persuaded President Pierce to send James Gadsden, a Southern railroad-promoter, to negotiate with Mexico. When Gadsden arrived in Mexico City, he found Santa Anna back in power and in need of money. In 1853 they signed a treaty giving the United States a forty-five-thousand-square-mile strip of desert land below the Gila for $10 million. Except for Alaska, the Gadsden Purchase rounded out the continental frontiers of the United States.

# International trade

**Europe.**  After American merchants and shipowners recovered from the disasters they had suffered during the War of 1812, they were severely hurt again by the long depression following the Panic of 1837. By the mid-1840s however, economic recovery and several other favorable developments combined to encourage a revival of foreign trade. The repeal of the British Corn Laws in 1846 opened a large market for American wheat; the passage of the low Walker Tariff the same year (followed by a still lower tariff in 1857) encouraged the flow of European manufactured goods to the United States; and a spectacular rise in immigration kept American ships filled to capacity on the homeward voyage. As a result, the combined value of American exports and imports increased from $222 million in 1840 to $318 million in 1850; during the next decade they more than doubled, to reach $687 million in 1860.

More than two-thirds of this commerce was with Europe, and the most valuable part of it was the exchange of American cotton, wheat, and flour for the products of British factories. In 1860 finished manufactured goods constituted only 10 percent of United States exports but nearly half of her imports. As is typical of a still undeveloped country, the value of imports usually exceeded the value of exports—by $29 million in 1850. This unfavorable trade balance forced the United States to send to Europe a large part of the gold mined in California. Nevertheless, foreign trade was vital to the whole national economy. Though Americans still concentrated on their own internal development, they were bound to the outside world by important commercial ties.

**China.**  As late as 1860 scarcely more than 5 percent of American trade was with Asia. Ever since the late eighteenth century, however, many New York and New England merchants had been dazzled by the profits they anticipated, and often made, from the penetration of Far Eastern markets. As we have seen, their hope of developing this trade was related to the desire for ports on the Pacific coast. By the early nineteenth century, American merchant ships were stopping in the Philippines, Java, and India, and in 1833 the United States signed a trade treaty with Siam. But the center of activity was at Canton, the one Chinese port open to foreigners, where furs were traded for tea, spices, and nankeens.

Though the United States government never took the initiative in wringing commercial concessions from China, it always capitalized on opportunities afforded by the encroachments of others. When Britain, after the Opium War of 1839–42, forced open several additional Chinese ports and gained various other advantages, American merchants demanded that their government intervene in their behalf. President Tyler responded by sending Caleb Cushing of Massachusetts, a man of rare diplomatic talent, to negotiate with China. In the Treaty of Wanghia (1844) Cushing won access to the ports that had been opened to the British; he established the right of extraterritoriality, which enabled resident Americans accused of crimes to be tried in American rather than Chinese courts; and he obtained a promise of "most favored nation" treatment, whereby privileges granted to other powers would also be granted to the United States. In subsequent years, as the British and French forced China to make further concessions, American merchants were thus able to claim similar rights. Since the United States merely asked to be given what others had seized by force, however, relations with China remained friendly.

*Japan.* From the sixteenth century to the middle of the nineteenth century Japan's only contact with the outside world had been a limited trade with the Dutch East India Company through the port of Nagasaki. The military shoguns, who dominated the weak emperors, had excluded foreign merchants, missionaries, and diplomats in order to preserve a feudal society. But during the 1840s some Americans began to take an interest in Japan. The Pacific whaling industry needed a treaty to assure proper treatment of shipwrecked sailors cast up on Japanese shores; merchants engaged in the China trade hoped to make Japan a port of call; and textile-manufacturers were eager for a chance to exploit the Japanese market.

In 1852 pressure from these groups caused President Fillmore to send Commodore Matthew C. Perry to Japan with an imposing fleet of steam warships. Perry bore a letter and gifts to the emperor and an array of gadgets illustrating the wonders of Western civilization. In July 1853 he arrived at Yedo Bay, insisted that his letter be delivered to the emperor, and promised to return in the spring. Perry made his second visit early in 1854 and found Japanese officials conciliatory and ready to negotiate. By combining vague threats of war with skillful diplomacy, he secured a treaty of friendship that opened two small ports to American trade, permitted the establishment of a consulate at one of them, guaranteed the safety of shipwrecked sailors, and gave the United States "most favored nation" treatment. Other Western powers soon negotiated their own treaties and forced Japan to open other ports and make additional concessions.

The State Department sent Townsend Harris, a brilliant diplomat, to Japan as the first American consul. Pointing to the fate of China under foreign domination, Harris assured Japan that the United States had no territorial ambitions and urged it to protect itself by modernizing and Westernizing under American guidance. "If you accept my proposals," he predicted, "Japan will become the England of the Orient." His case was persuasive, and in 1858 he signed another treaty greatly enlarging the concessions that Perry had won. Ministers were now to be exchanged; American consuls could reside at the six ports then open to foreigners; American citizens could buy property and enjoy freedom of religion at the so-called treaty ports; and Japan could buy warships and merchantmen from the United States. In 1860 the first

*Perry at Yokohama, 1854*

Japanese diplomatic delegation visited Washington, and soon thereafter Japan began to make rapid strides toward catching up with the modern world.

*The clipper ships.* The recovery of American foreign trade was immensely aided by a series of dramatic changes in the design of the old three-masted packet ships (see p. 199), changes that produced a fleet of the swiftest and most beautiful sailing vessels ever to engage in ocean commerce. In 1845 the *Rainbow*, a seven-hundred-fifty-ton ship designed by John Griffith, a naval architect, was completed; it had a long, sleek hull with a concave bow, convex sides, and a rounded stern, and tall masts with an enormous spread of canvas. The launching of the *Rainbow*, a ship that incorporated the advances of several decades, marked the beginning of the era of the famed clipper ships.

Among the builders of clippers, Donald McKay, of Newburyport, Massachusetts, was the most successful; his yards produced scores of vessels, including the 1,783-ton *Flying Cloud*, the 2,421-ton *Sovereign of the Seas*, and the 4,000-ton *Great Republic*. Commanded by daring, hard-driving captains, these ships broke all records for speed. In 1851, on its maiden voyage, the *Flying Cloud* covered 374 miles in a day; then, on a voyage from New York to San Francisco, it made a run of 433 miles in a day to break its own record. The *Sovereign of the Seas* soon surpassed that with 495 miles in a day's run. Another clipper, the *Lightning*, set a record of thirteen and a half days for a voyage from New York to Liverpool; still another,

*The clipper* Rainbow:
*triumph of American practical art*

the *Oriental*, set a record of eighty-one days for a voyage from New York to Hong Kong.

From the mid-1840s to the mid-1850s the clippers gave the United States a larger share of the world's peacetime carrying trade than ever before, a share that briefly promised to surpass the British, especially in the long-distance trades. The new ships and their masters took a commanding position in the commerce of both Europe and the Far East. But the most spectacular role of the clippers came in the early 1850s in the growing trade between the Atlantic coast and California. The older sailing vessels had taken more than five months to make the voyage around the Horn, whereas the clippers made it in three.

The era of the clipper ships, however, soon ended, for by the mid-1850s advances in technology were making them obsolete. The opening of the Panama Railroad in 1855 deprived them of California passengers, who could reach San Francisco along the shorter route in five weeks. Meanwhile the clippers were losing out in the competition with British ironclad sailing ships, and then ironclad steam vessels, which were less beautiful in design but superior in speed and cargo space. American steamship companies had only indifferent success in their rivalry with the British, who now recaptured much of the ocean commerce they had lost to the clippers. Not until the First World War would the United States again hold the position in the carrying trade that it enjoyed for a decade in the mid-nineteenth century.

## Immigration

**The role of the immigrant.** Between 1830 and 1860 the population of the United States increased from 12,866,000 to 31,443,000. But in spite of this remarkable growth the country was still sparsely settled and short of manpower. The factories needed more and more hands to tend the machines. Revived programs of internal improvements following the depression of the early 1840s created another heavy demand for workers. Above all, the supply of arable land still seemed to be inexhaustible, and the Western states and territories eagerly welcomed new settlers. Depression created temporary unemployment in the Eastern industrial centers, but most of the time before the Civil War there were not enough men and women to meet the labor requirements of cities and farms.

The manpower problem would have been even more acute had it not been for a sharp increase in European immigration to the United States, for industrialization and urban growth had caused a decline in the birthrate among the native-born population. Until the mid-1840s immigrants had been arriving at a slowly accelerating annual rate—8,385 in 1820; 23,322 in 1830; and 84,066 in 1840—but in the decade before 1840 fewer than 600,000 had crossed the Atlantic. In the following decade, however, immigration increased to 1,713,000, and during the 1850s to 2,598,000. Each year between 1850 and 1854 the number of immigrants exceeded 300,000, reaching a peak of 428,000 in 1854—a figure that would not be surpassed until the 1870s.

The overwhelming majority of immigrants still came from northern and western Europe. During the 1850s slightly more than three hundred thousand migrated from Great Britain, about twenty-five thousand from the Scandinavian countries. But Germany and southern Ireland had now become the two principal sources. In addition to the usual incentives—technological unemployment in Europe, the lure of cheap land in America, and the vision of the United States as a country of opportunity, freedom, and social equality—several special conditions helped to bring in a tide of Irish and Germans. In Ireland the failure of the potato crop of 1845 began a succession of famine years that caused widespread misery and actual starvation. As a result, in the fifteen years after 1845 approximately a million and a half Irishmen, most of them in extreme poverty, crossed the Atlantic. In Germany the suppression of the liberal Revolution of 1848 brought many political refugees along with the majority who came in search of improved economic conditions. Between 1850 and 1860 nearly a million Germans arrived.

In the main these immigrants were not systematically recruited, and they were seldom subsidized by organized groups. The Mormon Church helped its converts, and an Irish Pioneer Emigration Fund, supported by British, Irish, and American leaders, paid the passage of a few. In addition, some immigrants helped friends or relatives to join them. But most came on their own. A minority of them were fairly well-to-do middle-class people whose motive for coming, according to one report, was "not want or oppression, but . . . a rage for speculation, or a desire to acquire wealth more rapidly." Usually, however, the immigrants were poor people who could afford to pay their way only because competing merchant ships, needing return cargoes, reduced fares to as low as $30. Immigrants were crowded into steerage quarters, where they suffered from poor food, inadequate sanitary facilities, and the ravages of smallpox, dysentery, and "ship fever."

Much of this immigrant stream poured into the country through New York, some of it through Boston, Philadelphia, Baltimore, and New Orleans. Since there was no public program to help these strangers find homes and jobs or to ease the difficult adjustment to a new environment, many of them at first had unhappy experiences. Although the state of New York, in 1855, gave immigrants some limited protection by establishing Castle Garden as a controlled landing place, they often fell victim to swindlers who cheated them with exorbitant charges for lodgings or transportation or with false promises of employment. Because the Irish seldom had the means to become farmers, they congregated in the slums of New York and Boston and in the factory towns of New England. A much larger proportion of the Germans arrived with enough money to move to the Middle West, where they acquired farms, became artisans, or established business enterprises in cities such as Cincinnati, St. Louis, Chicago, and Milwaukee. Fewer immigrants settled in the South. Most of them debarked at Northern ports, but even many of those who arrived at New Orleans took steamboats up the Mississippi to the free states. They were drawn north by their preference for the cooler climate, by their unwillingness to compete with slave labor, and, in the case of many Germans, by their opposition to slavery itself.

Though few immigrants found it easy to settle in a new land, though far too many lived in abject poverty in the cities of the East, in the long run most of them did manage to improve their lot, and their cultural, social, and economic contributions were incalculable. From the ranks of the immigrants in subsequent years came many of the country's distinguished leaders in politics, the professions, journalism, the fine arts, banking, industry, and transportation. The English and Germans augmented the short supply of skilled craftsmen; the Welsh and Cornish worked the coal mines of Pennsylvania and the lead mines of Missouri and Wisconsin; the Irish tended the machines in New England factories, built railroads, and dug canals; men and women from all the immigrant groups brought millions of acres of Western land under cultivation. Not the least of the immigrants' contributions was the richness and variety they gave to American society through the customs and amenities they brought with them from their old homes.

*Emigrants leave Hamburg:*
*nearly a million Germans arrived*

**Nativism.** Notwithstanding the value of the immigrants to a thinly settled country, their growing numbers began to alarm some Americans whose ancestors had arrived in earlier years. By the 1850s aliens constituted half the population of New York City and outnumbered the native-born Americans in Chicago, Milwaukee, and St. Louis. Such conditions helped to produce the first significant nativist, or antiforeign, movement in American history, a movement that briefly became a major force in both state and national politics.

The causes of nativism were several. A few racists feared that the Celts from southern Ireland would pollute the old American stock, and that the United States would cease to be predominantly an Anglo-Saxon nation. Some criticized the Irish and Germans for being clannish and for preserving Old World customs and habits of dress. Others were distressed by the prevalence of crime and pauperism in the immigrant slums, resented the burden that alien indigents put on public funds and private charity, and accused European governments of deliberately exporting their "undesirables" to the United States. Native workingmen disliked the immigrants as economic competitors whose low standard of living threatened to depress wages. Southerners were unhappy to find them adding to the North's majorities in population and congressional representation. Conservatives were concerned about the immigrants' political power, for many states permitted them to vote before they became naturalized citizens. Most immigrants supported the Democratic party as the party of the common man, and in the Eastern cities Democratic bosses used them to build political machines.

Though all these anxieties contributed to the nativist movement, the strongest force behind it was anti-Catholicism. In the early nineteenth century Roman Catholics were a small fraction of the population, but in the 1840s and 1850s nearly all of the Irish and many of the German immigrants were adherents of this faith. With the growth of the Catholic popula-

*Anti-Catholic riot, Philadelphia, 1844*

tion, there was a corresponding increase in the number of Catholic priests and bishops, convents and monasteries, schools and colleges. Anti-Catholic sentiment among American Protestants was old and deep rooted, having grown from a combination of bigotry and genuine disagreement over Christian doctrine. Frightened nativists viewed every Catholic immigrant as an agent of the pope sent to seize the government and destroy Protestantism. They believed the Church to be the ally of tyranny and reaction in Europe, the enemy of freedom and democracy in America. And their prejudices were confirmed by lurid accounts of immorality in the convents and among the priesthood.

Nativist agitation started in the 1830s. In New York the Reverend George Bourne edited an anti-Catholic weekly, *The Protestant*, while other clergymen organized a Protestant Association "to promote the principles of the Reformation" and to "unfold the true character of Popery." In 1834 Samuel F. B. Morse, portrait-painter and promoter of the telegraph, published an influential anti-Catholic book, *A Foreign Conspiracy Against the Liberties of the United States*, that went through numerous editions. Urging Protestants to unite against the Catholic menace, Morse advocated stricter immigration laws to "stop this leak in the ship through which the muddy waters from without threaten to sink us." Nativists incited anti-Catholic riots, stoned Catholic institutions, and, in 1834, burned the Ursuline Convent School in Charlestown, Massachusetts.

During the 1840s, when Catholic immigrants began to arrive in large numbers, a bewildering array of secret nativist societies sprang up: the Sons of '76, the Sons of America, the Druids, the Order of United Americans, and many others. Early in the 1850s most of these groups united to form a powerful national organization, the Order of the Star Spangled Banner. Because members were sworn to secrecy and refused to answer questions about their aims and activities, they were usually called the Know-Nothings. It soon became evident, however, that their purposes were to

defend Protestantism against Catholicism, to make immigration laws more restrictive, to increase the number of years required for naturalization, and to deprive aliens of the ballot.

Meanwhile, nativism had entered politics and had begun to score successes in local elections. After the presidential election of 1852, many former Whigs joined the movement as their own party disintegrated. Political nativism reached its peak in 1854 and 1855, when the Know-Nothings captured several state legislatures, elected numerous governors, and claimed the allegiance of at least seventy-five congressmen. Their most spectacular victory came in Massachusetts, where they controlled every state office and had an overwhelming majority in the legislature. In 1856 the nativists formed the American party, nominated Millard Fillmore for President, and polled about 25 percent of the popular vote.

Thereafter, nativism rapidly declined. In Massachusetts most of the Know-Nothing legislators proved to be incompetent, and they were able to write almost none of their demands into laws. Nationally the nativists soon lost their appeal as the country became increasingly absorbed in the conflict over slavery expansion—indeed, the American party itself split over this issue. Moreover, the religious bigotry and xenophobia of the Know-Nothings failed to destroy certain traditional American attitudes that soon began to reassert themselves: the belief in religious toleration, the idea of America as a refuge for the oppressed of the Old World, and a confidence that the United States could in time assimilate as many immigrants as came to its shores. Besides, nativism betrayed the Christian ideal of the brotherhood of man—as one critic observed, it "judges men by the accidents of their condition, instead of striving to find a common lot for all, with a common access to the blessings of life." Finally, nativist racism was refuted by a popular argument that held that the mixing of various nationalities was producing a new and unique individual, the American, superior to the old by the very fact of the mixing. As Herman Melville observed, "We are the heirs of all time, and with all nations we divide our inheritance."

## Economic development

**Domestic commerce.** The flourishing American foreign trade of the mid-nineteenth century required the movement of huge quantities of bulky raw materials and foodstuffs to the seaports on the Atlantic and Gulf coasts as well as the distribution of finished European goods to the markets of the interior. At the same time, internal trade expanded as the population

**Anxieties of the nativists**

grew and as the economies of the various regions became increasingly interdependent and somewhat more specialized. Much of this commerce continued to move along the country's excellent waterways. Coastal vessels carried cotton, tobacco, and sugar from Southern ports to New York and New England, while the glamorous Mississippi River steamboats, in spite of railroad competition, carried more freight and passengers in the 1850s than ever before.

The paths of inland water transportation were rapidly changing, however, for the canals were diverting a growing amount of business from the rivers to the Great Lakes. The Miami and Erie Canal through Ohio, and the Wabash and Erie Canal through Indiana both connected the Ohio River with Lake Erie at Toledo, while the Illinois and Michigan Canal united the Mississippi and Illinois rivers with Lake Michigan at Chicago. As trade shifted to the Great Lakes and the Erie Canal, New York replaced New Orleans as the chief outlet for Western commodities destined for Northeastern and European markets, and young cities on the lakes outgrew the older cities on the rivers. In the 1830s Chicago had been a small village; by 1860 it had a population of 109,000.

Meanwhile, all forms of water transportation were beginning to face serious competition from the railroads. The principle of running cars on wooden or iron rails had long been in use in the British mining districts for hauling coal, but until the early nineteenth century men or animals had always provided the power. Experiments with steam engines began soon after 1800, and in 1820 John Stevens of New Jersey demonstrated a steam locomotive that successfully pulled a train of cars over a short piece of track. Five years later a small British line, the Stockton and Darlington, became the first commercial railroad to utilize steam power.

This development was enough to stimulate feverish activity in the cities of the Eastern United States, where merchants had been seeking a way to compete with New York for the trade of the interior. In 1828 construction began on the Baltimore and Ohio, and by 1830 a thirteen-mile segment was open for business. A year later the Mohawk and Hudson established service over sixteen miles of track between Albany and Schenectady. In 1833 South Carolina's 136-mile Charleston and Hamburg line was completed and became for a time the longest railroad in the world. Philadelphia soon had a rail connection with the coal fields of eastern Pennsylvania, Boston with Worcester and other interior New England cities. By 1840 these and other lines had a combined trackage of 2,818 miles; by 1850 the trackage had grown to 9,021 miles and by 1860 to 30,627 miles.

Emerson once observed that "the Americans take to this little contrivance, the railroad, as if it were the cradle in which they were born." They took to it (after first showing considerable hostility) in spite of such early inconveniences as irregular schedules, frequent breakdowns, and the likelihood of being showered with sparks from the wood-burning locomotives. A major annoyance was the lack of a standard-gauge track—as late as 1860 there were still a dozen gauges in use—which made it impossible for the rolling stock of one railroad to use the tracks of another. Worse than the inconveniences were the disastrous wrecks resulting from soft roadbeds, broken rails, and collapsed bridges.

Construction engineers gradually increased the safety and efficiency of the railroads. They built solid roadbeds using crushed rock for ballast, substituted cast-iron "T" rails for the old wooden rails covered with iron straps, learned how to make curves and negotiate grades, erected sturdier bridges, and improved the design of locomotives and cars. By the 1850s, though accidents still occurred with painful frequency, technological advances had reduced the risks of travel by railroad to a point where they were not much greater than by steamboat. The speed of the railroads (twenty to thirty miles an hour by 1860), their ability to get through rough terrain and to tap remote markets, their serviceability in winter when the canals froze or in droughts when rivers were low, made them the ideal solution to the country's transportation needs.

During the 1850s, in addition to an enormous expansion of railroad mileage, considerable progress was made toward the consolidation of small, independent lines to form trunk lines. In the South, although both Norfolk and Charleston had established rail connections with the Mississippi River at Memphis, most lines continued to be short and to serve merely as feeders for river transportation. The railroad network that had emerged by 1860 was largely a system that united the Northwest with the Northeast. The Baltimore and Ohio had then reached the Ohio River at Wheeling, the Pennsylvania Railroad had connected Philadelphia and Pittsburgh, and several lines had given Boston access to the Erie Canal and the Great Lakes. Meanwhile, the Hudson River Railroad from New York to Albany, together with the New York Central, formed by the consolidation of seven lines between Albany and Buffalo, had given New York a through route to the West. A second

railroad, the Erie, had been built across southern New York State from Jersey City to Buffalo. Powerful corporations, controlled by railroad capitalists like Erastus Corning of Albany and John Murray Forbes of Boston, directed the construction and consolidation that produced the trunk lines. Most of the funds came from American and British investors, a little from state and local government subsidies.

In the West, where most of the railroad construction of the 1850s took place, various lines in Ohio, Indiana, and Illinois linked the Ohio and Mississippi rivers with the Great Lakes. The most important of these north-south lines was the Illinois Central, which by 1858 had given Chicago a connection with the rivers at Cairo. Other railroads ran eastward from Chicago, now the transportation hub of the West, to meet the Eastern trunk lines. By 1860 both the Erie and the New York Central either controlled or had agreements with a series of lines that gave them access to Chicago. Railroad bridges now spanned the Mississippi River, and new lines had penetrated as far west as Burlington, Iowa, and St. Joseph, Missouri.

Railroad-builders in the West, where traffic was initially lighter, depended on public support more than those in the East. State and local governments aided them with loans, subsidies, and stock subscriptions, and in 1850 Congress passed a momentous bill providing the first of many railroad land grants. This act, whose chief sponsor was Senator Stephen A. Douglas, was for the benefit of the Illinois Central; it gave the state of Illinois three square miles of land in alternate sections on both sides of the proposed line (six square miles for each mile of track), with the understanding that the land would be turned over to the company as the railroad was built. Southern support was obtained by making a similar grant for a line from the Ohio River to Mobile. By 1860 approximately 28 million acres from the public domain had been granted to various states for railroad construction.

After 1850 there was much talk of a transcontinental railroad to be built with a federal subsidy, but sectional disagreement over the location of the route delayed action until after the start of the Civil War. Meanwhile, in 1855 the firm of Russell, Majors & Waddell, aided by a government subsidy, established regular overland freight service by wagon train between Kansas and California. Three years later the Butterfield Overland Mail Company began to run subsidized semiweekly stagecoaches between St. Louis and San Francisco. In the spring of 1860 Russell, Majors & Waddell introduced the pony express, which carried mail from St. Joseph, Missouri, to Sacramento in ten days. But in less than a year and a half the pony express was put out of business by a device that was revolutionizing communication: the electric tele-

*Engine on the Baltimore and Ohio:
Americans took to this little contrivance*

The growth of the railroad network, 1850–60

graph. In 1844 Samuel F. B. Morse had demonstrated its practicality, and by 1860 the country had been tied together with fifty thousand miles of telegraph wire. In October 1861, when the Pacific Telegraph Company completed its line to San Francisco, communication between the Atlantic and Pacific coasts became a matter of minutes.

***Agriculture.*** The revolution in transportation, the rapid growth of industry, and advances in agricultural technology profoundly affected the life of the American farmer. In New England the rural population declined as many families, or at least the younger members, moved west in search of better land, or to the cities to find employment in factories. Farmland sold to sheep raisers made commercial wool production more feasible. In the 1850s a large proportion of the country's raw wool came from New England, while much wheat and corn were grown in New York and Pennsylvania. But farmers in the Northeast were rapidly turning from these crops to the production of fruits and vegetables, and to dairying for the growing cities nearby. Railroads enabled the owners of orchards, truck gardens, and dairy herds to make daily shipments to city markets, and in this highly specialized and commercialized form Eastern agriculture found new life and became a rewarding enterprise.

In the South the 1850s were generally prosperous years for the producers of the great staples (tobacco, rice, sugar, and cotton) with slave labor. By then the heart of the Cotton Kingdom had shifted from the Southeast to the Alabama-Mississippi Black Belt, the Mississippi Delta, the valleys of the Arkansas and Red rivers, and the prairies of eastern Texas. With cotton selling for 10 to 12 cents a pound, production rose from 2,469,000 bales in 1849 to 5,387,000 bales in 1859,

and the South came near to monopolizing world markets. Able-bodied young slaves sold for $1,500 in the New Orleans market. In eastern Virginia, where a generation earlier soil depletion had produced agricultural stagnation, conditions had greatly improved. The slave-plantation system gained new vitality from the introduction of fertilizers, improved methods of cultivation, and systems of crop rotation, but the sale of surplus slaves in the markets of the Southwest continued to be vital to the economy of the older plantation districts. Throughout the South the plantations, though highly commercialized agricultural enterprises, were less affected by technological changes than the farms of the Northeast and Northwest. Planters continued to cultivate the staples with gangs of slaves using simple hoes and plows. As for the mass of nonslaveholding yeoman farmers, they often planted a few acres in cotton or tobacco, but in the main they raised corn and hogs for their own subsistence and generally remained outside the market economy.

By 1860 the Old Northwest had become the center of wheat, corn, beef, and pork production. Responding to the growing demands of the East and of Europe, native-born farmers and German and Scandinavian immigrants had opened up the virgin lands of northern Illinois and Indiana, southern Michigan and Wisconsin, and eastern Iowa and Minnesota. With their help the corn crop had increased from 592 million bushels in 1849 to 839 million bushels in 1859, the wheat crop from 100 million bushels to 173 million bushels. Illinois and Indiana now led in hog production, Illinois in corn production, and Illinois, Indiana, and Wisconsin in wheat production.

Widening markets, the high cost of labor, and the abandonment of self-sufficient agriculture for specialized crops stimulated the improvement of farm im-

*Walk through the streets of any of our crowded cities; see how within stone's throw of each other stand the most marked and frightful contrasts! Here, look at this marble palace reared in a pure atmosphere and in the neighborhood of pleasing prospects. Its interior is adorned with every refinement that the accumulated skill of sixty centuries has been able to invent; velvet carpets, downy cushions, gorgeous tapestries, stoves, musical instruments, pictures, statues and books. For the gratification and development of its owner and his family, industry, science, and art have been tasked to their utmost capacity of production....*

*Look you, again, to that not far distant alley, where some ten diseased, destitute and depraved families are nestled under the same rickety and tumbling roof; no fire is there to warm them; no clothes to cover their bodies; a pool of filth sends up its nauseousness perhaps in the very midst of their dwelling; the rain and keen hail fall on their almost defenceless heads; the pestilence is forever hovering over their door-posts; their minds are blacker than night with the black mists of ignorance; ... the very sun-light blotted from the firmament and life itself turned into a protracted and bitter curse! Look you, at this, we say, and think that unless something better than what we now see is done, it will grow worse!*

**From Parke Godwin, Democracy, Constructive and Pacific, 1844.**

plements and mechanization. To cut through the tough prairie sod, Western farmers needed plows that were more efficient than the old ones made of wood or cast iron. In 1847 John Deere began to supply this need when he opened a factory at Moline, Illinois, to manufacture steel plows that cut deeper furrows. The fifties also saw the substitution of grain drills for hand planting and the introduction of mowers to harvest the hay crop. Most important for the wheat farmers was the invention of mechanical reapers to replace hand sickles and cradles. In 1831 Cyrus Hall McCormick, a Virginian, built a successful reaper, and in 1847 he moved to Chicago to begin manufacturing reapers on a large scale. The use of the reaper overcame the constraints of a short harvest period, reduced the risks of loss of a year's crop, and enlarged the production potential on a single-family farm. Mechanization advanced another step when threshing machines began to outmode the old method of flailing wheat by hand.

Having entered the market economy, a growing number of Western farmers thought of agriculture as a business enterprise rather than, in Jefferson's terms, as a way of life. Technological advances enabled them to cultivate more acres but also forced them to make heavier investments in implements and machinery. The railroads opened new markets to them but increased their dependence on the middlemen who financed, transported, stored, and marketed their crops. Specialization made them more efficient but increased their dependence on Eastern manufacturers for things they had once made for themselves. In short, the farmers were being caught up in the capitalist world of merchants, manufacturers, bankers, and railroad-operators, and by 1860 some of them were showing signs of dissatisfaction with their place in this world. Out of their discontent would grow the farmers' movements of the post-Civil War years.

**Industry.** In 1851, at London's Crystal Palace Exhibition, the products of American industry and technology were shown to the world. More than a hundred of them won prize medals, including the McCormick reaper, which attracted by far the greatest admiration. The success of the American exhibits was an indication of the rapid progress the country had made in manufacturing since the founding of the first textile mills in the early nineteenth century.

The industrial growth of the 1850s far surpassed that of any earlier decade. The capital investment of a half-billion dollars in 1849 had nearly doubled by 1859, the number of manufacturing establishments had increased from 123,000 to 140,000, and the annual value of their products had grown from $1,019 million to $1,886 million. Manufacturing was concentrated in the New England and Middle Atlantic states. The market was almost entirely a domestic one, with the Northeast exchanging its industrial surpluses for the foodstuffs and raw materials of the agricultural South and West.

Yet industry in the 1850s had certain characteristics indicating that the United States was still in the early stages of the Industrial Revolution. First, most of the manufacturing involved the processing of the

294

*McCormick's reaper: much admired*

products of American farms and forests. In 1860 the leading industry was the milling of flour and meal, whose value was about one-eighth of the total value of manufactures. Other important industries included lumber-milling, distilling, brewing, leather-tanning, and meatpacking. A second indication of industrial immaturity was the smallness of the typical manufacturing enterprises; on the average they employed fewer than ten workers and had a capital value of less than $7,500. Finally, as we have seen, the United States was still a large consumer of foreign manufactured goods and primarily an exporter of agricultural products.

Nevertheless, by 1860 the direction of American economic development was clear. Textile-manufacturing had already become the core of New England's economy: the investment in mills and machinery was more than $100 million, and the number of cotton spindles in operation had grown to 5,236,000—a 100 percent increase since 1840. In 1844 Charles Goodyear had patented a method of "vulcanizing" raw rubber to make it resist heat and cold, and a new rubber-goods industry was soon manufacturing hundreds of products. In 1846 Elias Howe had patented a sewing machine, and five years later Isaac Singer had begun to manufacture and market an improved model. During the 1850s these machines were used in hundreds of factories making shoes and ready-made clothing. The iron industry had expanded to supply the needs of the producers of farm machinery and at least some of the needs of the railroads. Between 1840 and 1860 pig-iron production rose from 321,000 tons to 920,000 tons a year. Originally the locomotives for American railroads had to be imported, but by the 1840s Pennsylvania iron-manufacturers were able to meet the domestic demand. Their rolling mills were still unable to turn out heavy rails, however, and the railroads continued to import them from Great Britain.

During the years of rapid industrial growth in the 1840s and 1850s, the chronic shortage of skilled workers and the relatively high cost of labor kept alive the American manufacturer's keen interest in increased efficiency and technological advances. As a result, by the 1850s the United States had outstripped all other industrial countries in turning out products whose

manufacture involved the use of precision instruments. A few industries began to apply the methods of modern mass production. The manufacturers of guns, clocks, sewing machines, and farm implements introduced assembly lines on which unskilled workers, performing standardized tasks, made the finished product from interchangeable parts. During the 1850s, two British commissions visited the United States to study manufacturing techniques, especially the remarkable progress of American technology. The British visitors were struck by the inventiveness of American artisans and by the fact that they seemed to be as fascinated by mechanical improvements as their employers.

Meanwhile, in America's growing industries the corporate form of business organization spread rapidly—during the 1850s the number of manufacturing corporations nearly doubled. Industry and the building and organizing of railroads were rivaling commerce as the road to wealth and economic power. Thus Amos and Abbot Lawrence of Boston, Phelps, Dodge & Company of New York, and many others got their start in mercantile enterprises but transferred their capital to manufacturing, railroads, and mining. The industrial entrepreneur had already become an important figure in the country's economic life.

By 1860 American factories were employing 1,311,000 workers, the mines and transportation a half-million more. Although skilled labor was still in great demand, each craft felt severely threatened by the steady encroachments of the machines and of mass production. Already the factories had made nearly obsolete several old and honorable crafts, notably those of the cordwainers, coopers, and ironsmiths. As the factories grew in size and the ranks of the unskilled were filled with recent immigrants, the relations of labor and capital became increasingly impersonal. Employers began to think of their workers less as human beings than as commodities to be bought at the lowest price. They paid their employees $6 a week or less for a working day of twelve to fifteen hours. They often ignored feeble state laws fixing maximum hours or regulating the labor of children. And they viewed with indifference the poor sanitary conditions

*New England mill, 1850*

and the high rate of industrial accidents in their factories. Conditions such as these touched the lives of only a small fraction of the population, but by the 1850s there had emerged in the factory slums of Eastern cities an unskilled, propertyless proletariat. The Industrial Revolution thus raised to prominence the problem of poverty in an affluent society.

Middle-class reformers who took an interest in the plight of the laboring population usually urged low-paid workers to form their own cooperative workshops or to go west and become farmers. They seldom approved of direct economic action through trade unions. This, however, was the means by which factory workers eventually improved their condition. The promising labor movement of the 1830s (see p. 201) had been destroyed by the depression following the Panic of 1837, and it took many years for another movement to get started. A formidable legal barrier was partially removed when the Massachusetts Supreme Court, in the case of *Commonwealth* v. *Hunt* (1842), ruled that trade unions were not in themselves conspiracies in restraint of trade, a rule that courts in other states soon accepted. But when workers resorted to strikes or boycotts they still ran into trouble with the courts, which continued to interpret such activities as violations of the old common-law doctrine of conspiracy. Trade unions were also handicapped by a hostile press, by generally unfavorable public opinion, and by the ability of employers to recruit strikebreakers.

In the 1850s, though conditions showed little improvement, only a few American workingmen belonged to trade unions. In 1852 the International Typographical Union was formed, and by the end of the decade the stonecutters, hat-finishers, iron-molders, and machinists had also established national organizations. The other skilled crafts were organized only locally, while the mass of unskilled workers had no unions at all. Strikes for higher wages or shorter hours occurred in the shoe and textile industries and on the railroads, but they usually failed. Though trade unionism had made a new beginning, a powerful labor movement would not emerge until after the Civil War.

# Economic discontent in the South

**The colonial South.** On the surface the economic conditions of the 1850s would seem to have given no cause for sectional conflict. Because of the growing demand for raw cotton in world markets, the South was prospering, and its economy appeared to be neatly complementary to that of the North—each section needed the products of the other. And yet, throughout the decade, there was in the South an undercurrent of economic discontent.

After the Panic of 1837 Southern cotton played a less dynamic role in the economic development of the country than it had before. Industry now played the role that cotton once played; and, with the growth of the West, Northeastern business interests were less dependent on the Southern market. In short, the South, though still flourishing and enjoying substantial economic growth, saw its economic power diminishing within the Union.

Far more than that of the Northeast, even more than that of the Northwest, the economy of the South was based on agriculture. In 1860 the eleven states that were to form the Southern Confederacy produced less than one-tenth of the country's manufactured goods; they contained about half as many manufacturing establishments as the Western states. Moreover, Northern ships carried Southern staples to European markets, and most Southern imports came indirectly via New York City. An Alabama editor complained,

> With us every branch and pursuit of life, every trade, profession, and occupation, is dependent upon the North. . . . In Northern vessels [the Southerner's] products are carried to market, his cotton is ginned with Northern gins, his sugar is crushed and preserved by Northern machinery; his rivers are navigated by Northern steamboats . . . his land is cleared with a Northern axe, and a Yankee clock sits upon his mantel-piece; his floor is swept by a Northern broom, and is covered with a Northern carpet; and his wife dresses herself in a Northern looking-glass.

Southerners resented this dependency and searched for ways to strengthen their economy. As early as 1837 a group of Georgians had sponsored a convention at Augusta "to attempt a new organization of our commercial relations with Europe." During the 1840s and 1850s a series of commercial conventions urged the establishment of direct trade between Southern and European ports. While some Southerners planned steamship lines, others favored the building of railroads to divert Western trade to Southern cities. Neither goal was achieved.

For a time there seemed to be a better prospect of improving the South's industrial position. During the depression years of the 1840s, when the price of raw cotton was low, interest in manufacturing increased in the older states of the Southeast, and a number of factories were built. William Gregg of South Carolina, a vigorous propagandist for industrialization, demonstrated its profitability at his highly successful cotton factory in Graniteville. In the 1850s, however, the revival of agricultural prosperity once again made it clear that the South's comparative economic advantage was in the production of staples, and Southern industry therefore found it difficult to compete for capital. Moreover, the Northern manufacturer was usually able to undersell his Southern competitor and to provide a superior product. As a result, the South's economy remained predominantly agricultural.

**Rumors of a Northern conspiracy.** The failure of these various efforts toward economic diversification was one of several factors, among which Negro slavery was the most important, producing a state of mind in the South that contributed to sectionalism and ultimately to disunion. Agriculture, Jefferson had taught and Southerners believed, was the most productive pursuit of man, and the man who worked the soil was the chief repository of human virtue. Yet the North had surpassed the South in wealth and population and, according to this widely held though highly inaccurate analysis, had reduced the region to a colonial status. This, said angry Southern sectionalists, was an evil and unnatural condition. Many of them seemed to think they were the victims of a sinister conspiracy planned by a close-knit body of Northern bankers, merchants, manufacturers, and their political agents. The chief haunts of the conspirators were New York and Washington; their distinguishing characteristics were their essential unproductiveness and their skill in amassing wealth from the labor of others. Their special field of operation was the South, from which they extracted a major portion of their profits.

Northern businessmen, according to this conspiracy theory, took advantage of the plain, homespun Southerner, who was no match for the artful Yankee in the techniques of chicanery. They were accused of exacting exorbitant middlemen's charges, of rigging prices, of manipulating the money market, and thus of causing much of the wealth produced in the South to flow steadily into their coffers. The price of Southern property, wrote an indignant Virginian, "is dependent upon the speculative pleasure of the Merchants, Bankers, and Brokers of New York. And why? Because Wall Street can depress the money market when it pleases." The South, said a Mississippian, had permitted itself to fall into a condition of "serfdom" and to become "the sport and laughing stock of Wall Street." A Southern editor described New York as "a mighty queen of commerce . . . waving an undisputed commercial scepter over the South." With an "avidity rarely equalled," she "grasps our gains and transfers them to herself."

But, according to this sectional indictment, Northern capitalists did not make their profits solely from their adroit maneuvers in a free economy. Rather, in advancing their conspiracy they had en-

*Cotton: the basis for agricultural prosperity in the South*

listed the support of the federal government. In November 1860 Senator Robert Toombs, in a speech before the Georgia legislature, described the political side of the alleged Northern conspiracy to prostrate the South. No sooner had the government been organized, he claimed, than "the Northern States evinced a general desire and purpose to use it for their own benefit, and to pervert its powers for sectional advantage, and they have steadily pursued that policy to this day." They demanded, and received, a monopoly of the shipbuilding business; they demanded, and received, a monopoly of the trade between American ports. The New England fishing industry obtained an annual bounty from the public treasury; manufacturers obtained a protective tariff. Thus, according to Toombs, through its policy of subsidizing "every interest and every pursuit in the North," the federal treasury had become "a perpetual fertilizing stream to them and their industry, and a suction-pump to drain away our substance and parch up our lands."

By the 1850s the notion that Northern profits were largely a form of expropriation of Southern wealth, that the South was "the very best colony to the North any people ever possessed," was having a powerful effect on Southern opinion. Much of this analysis of the antebellum economic relationship between North and South has been effectively challenged by modern economic historians. But what is important historically is not the inaccuracy of this economic analysis but the fact that most Southerners apparently believed it to be true. The attitudes they shared were characteristic of those held by nineteenth-century farmers and planters concerning the "middlemen" who financed, transported, and marketed agricultural commodities. Since they regarded the activities of middlemen as nonproductive and

*Economic discontent in the South*

parasitic, they were bound to consider marketing costs exorbitant. Sectional leaders exacerbated the existing resentment by using the concept of Northern exploitation as a rhetorical device to unify the South. Southerners had convinced themselves, remarked a Northerner, "that in some way or other, either through the fiscal regulations of the Government, or through the legerdemain of trade, the North has been built up at the expense of the South." Not even agricultural prosperity could banish this thought from the Southern mind.

When the sectional conflict was reopened in 1854, slavery transcended all other issues. Yet there is evidence that Northern attacks on slavery were sometimes intensified by sectional conflicts over federal economic policy, while Southern expressions of economic grievances may well have concealed deeper anxieties about the institution of slavery. As the historian Charles A. Beard once observed, it was not always easy to tell "where slavery as an ethical question left off, and economics—the struggle over the distribution of wealth—began."

## Suggestions for reading

### AMERICAN LITERATURE

The surveys of American intellectual history listed in the suggested readings for Chapter 10 all deal with American writers of the pre-Civil War years. The best special studies are F. O. Matthiessen, *American Renaissance** (1941), and Harold Kaplan, *Democratic Humanism and American Literature* (1972). Edmund Wilson, ed., *The Shock of Recognition: The Development of Literature in the United States Recorded by the Men Who Made It** (1943), is an excellent anthology. The biographies of individual writers should also be consulted: J. W. Krutch, *Henry David Thoreau** (1948); R. L. Rusk, *The Life of Ralph Waldo Emerson* (1949); Mark Van Doren, *Nathaniel Hawthorne** (1949); Newton Arvin, *Herman Melville** (1950); and G. W. Allen, *The Solitary Singer: A Critical Biography of Walt Whitman** (1955).

### EXPANSIONISM AND FOREIGN TRADE

American interests in Cuba, Central America, and the Far East are treated adequately in four general surveys of American foreign policy: S. F. Bemis, *A Diplomatic History of the United States* (5th ed., 1965); T. A. Bailey, *A Diplomatic History of the American People* (8th ed., 1969); J. W. Pratt, *A History of United States Foreign Policy,* (1955, rev. ed., 1965); and Alexander De Conde, *A History of American Foreign Policy** (1963, rev. ed., 1971). Several excellent monographs may also be consulted: M. W. Williams, *Anglo-American Isthmian Diplomacy, 1815–1915* (1916); Dexter Perkins, *The Monroe Doctrine, 1826–1867* (1933); and Basil Rauch, *American Interests in Cuba, 1848–1855* (1948). E. S. Wallace, *Destiny and Glory* (1957), is a vivid account of filibustering.

The most useful special studies of American-Far Eastern relations that deal with this period are: Tyler Dennett, *Americans in Eastern Asia* (1941); A. W. Griswold, *The Far Eastern Policy of the United States** (1938); P. J. Treat, *Diplomatic Relations Between the United States and Japan, 1853–1905,* 3 vols. (1932–38); F. R. Dulles, *China and America: The Story of Their Relations Since 1784* (1946); and L. H. Battistini, *The Rise of American Influence in Asia and the Pacific* (1960). Arthur Walworth, *Black Ships off Japan* (1946), is a readable account of the Perry mission to Japan. H. W. Bradley, *The American Frontier in Hawaii: The Pioneers, 1789–1843* (1942), is the best study of early American interest in Hawaii.

The standard works on the growth of American foreign trade are E. R. Johnson, *et al., History of Domestic and Foreign Commerce of the United States,* 2 vols. (1915), and J. H. Frederick, *The Development of American Commerce* (1932). The commerce of New England and New York City are the subjects of two distinguished books: S. E. Morison, *Maritime History of Massachusetts: 1783–1860** (1921), and R. G. Albion, *The Rise of New York Port, 1815–1860* (1939). The best books on the clipper ships are A. H. Clark, *The Clipper Ship Era* (1910); C. C. Cutler, *Greyhounds of the Sea* (1930); and Robert Carse, *The Moonrakers* (1961).

### IMMIGRATION AND NATIVISM

Several excellent surveys of immigration to the United States are valuable for this period: Carl Wittke, *We Who Built America** (1939, rev. ed., 1964); M. L. Hansen, *The Atlantic Migration, 1607–1860**

*Available in a paperback edition.

*America at mid-century*

(1940); and M. A. Jones, *American Immigration** (1960). Oscar Handlin, *The Uprooted** (1951, 2nd ed., 1973), and Philip Taylor, *The Distant Magnet: European Emigration to the U.S.A.** (1971), focus on the immigrants and their problems. Four specific immigrant groups are the subjects of individual volumes: T. C. Blegen, *Norwegian Migration to America,* 2 vols. (1931–40); R. T. Berthoff, *British Immigrants in Industrial America, 1790–1950* (1953); Carl Wittke, *Refugees of Revolution: The German Forty-Eighters in America* (1952), and *The Irish in America** (1956). The immigrant populations of two Eastern cities are studied in Oscar Handlin, *Boston's Immigrants** (1941), and Robert Ernst, *Immigrant Life in New York City, 1825–1863* (1949).

A perceptive account of mid-century nativism is in Allan Nevins, *Ordeal of the Union,* 2 vols. (1947). R. A. Billington, *The Protestant Crusade, 1800–1860** (1938), emphasizes the anti-Catholic aspect of the movement. I. M. Leonard and R. D. Parmet, *American Nativism, 1830–1860** (1971), is a study of the origins and political significance of nativism. Two special studies are also useful: Sister M. E. Thomas, *Nativism in the Old Northwest, 1850–1860* (1936), and W. D. Overdyke, *The Know-Nothing Party in the South* (1950).

### ECONOMIC DEVELOPMENT

All of the books on agriculture, industry, transportation, and technology listed in the suggested readings for Chapter 8 are useful for this period. There are also several good chapters on the American economy at mid-century in Nevins, *Ordeal of the Union,* cited above.

A good introduction to the history of the railroads is J. F. Stover, *The Life and Decline of the American Railroad* (1970). Problems of railroad promotion and finance can be studied in F. A. Cleveland and F. W. Powell, *Railroad Promotion and Capitalization in the United States* (1909); A. M. Johnson and B. E. Supple, *Boston Capitalists and Western Railroads: A Study in the Nineteenth Century Railroad Investment Process* (1967); L. H. Haney, *A Congressional History of Railways in the United States to 1850* (1908), and *A Congressional History of Railways in the United States, 1850–1877* (1910). An outstanding history of the New England railroads is E. C. Kirkland, *Men, Cities and Transportation,* 2 vols. (1948). Railroad promotion in the Southeast is described in U. B. Phillips, *A History of Transportation in the Eastern Cotton Belt to 1860* (1908). T. C. Cochran, *Railroad Leaders, 1845–1890* (1953), contains important material on early railroad promoters and their social attitudes. The following histories of individual railroads are useful: F. W. Stevens, *The Beginnings of the New York Central Railroad* (1926); P. W. Gates, *The Illinois Central Railroad and Its Colonization Work* (1934); Edward Hungerford, *The Story of the Baltimore and Ohio Railroad, 1827–1927,* 2 vols (1928), and *Men of Erie* (1946); and R. C. Overton, *Burlington West* (1941). Two books deal with the impact of the railroads on the American economy: R. W. Fogel, *Railroads and American Economic Growth** (1964), and Albert Fishlow, *American Railroads and the Transformation of the Ante-Bellum Economy* (1965).

In addition to the listings in the suggested readings for Chapter 8, the following books on industry and technology are worth consulting for this period: G. S. Gibb, *The Saco-Lowell Shops: Textile Machinery Building in New England* (1950); Waldemar Kaempffert, ed., *A Popular History of American Invention,* 2 vols. (1924); Allan Nevins, *Abram S. Hewitt: With Some Account of Peter Cooper* (1935); J. A. Kouwenhoven, *Made in America** (1948); D. J. Struik, *Yankee Science in the Making** (1948); and Mitchell Wilson, *American Science and Invention: A Pictorial History* (1954). The best book on labor in this period is N. J. Ware, *The Industrial Worker, 1840–1860** (1924). Hannah Josephson, *The Golden Threads* (1949), is excellent on the women textile-workers of New England. Two good general treatments are J. G. Rayback, *History of American Labor** (1959), and H. M. Pelling, *American Labor** (1960). R. H. Bremner, *From the Depths** (1956), deals with the emergence of the problem of poverty in America.

The causes of economic discontent in the South can be studied in R. R. Russel, *Economic Aspects of Southern Sectionalism, 1840–1861* (1924); J. G. Van Deusen, *The Ante-Bellum Southern Commercial Conventions* (1926); Herbert Wender, *Southern Commercial Conventions, 1837–1860** (1930); and Clement Eaton, *The Growth of Southern Civilization, 1790–1860** (1961).

*Available in a paperback edition.

# CHAPTER 13

# A decade of crisis

**B**etween the Compromise of 1850 and the outbreak of civil war lay ten years of mounting tension punctuated by outbursts of hostility between North and South. Each crisis hinged on the question of slavery and its role in the expansion of the nation or on the enforcement of the Fugitive Slave Act of the Compromise of 1850 (see pp. 272–75). Each brought the nation closer to war. By 1860 many Southerners believed that the North was bent not only on the containment of slavery where it then existed but on its ultimate extinction. Many Northerners, on the other hand, fearing the "slave power conspiracy," believed that the South would not rest until federal law protected slave property everywhere in the Union.

Those fears reflected valid concerns. Having lost equality in the Senate as a result of the compromise measures of 1850, the South soon insisted on an interpretation of the Constitution that would guarantee the survival of slavery, not only as the economic basis of society but as the only conceivable solution to the emotional question of race relations in the South. By 1860 Jefferson Davis, a United States senator who was soon to become president of the Confederacy, was demanding a slave code to govern and protect slave property in the territories. Believing that expansion was essential to the survival of slavery, William Lowndes Yancey of Alabama and a few extremists from each Southern state backed Davis' demand. These so-called fire-eaters met passionate resistance from the free farmers of the North, who were bent on carrying their own way of life into the new federal territories. The South's idea that the states retained their sovereignty under the Constitution and that the federal government must enforce Southern state laws on slavery in the federal territories was unacceptable to the large majority of Northerners, whether Democrats or Whigs.

At bottom, then, the Civil War resulted from the conflict over slavery, even though few Northerners hated it enough in 1860 to go to war for emancipation. Few Northerners believed blacks were equal to whites, and few would have willingly accorded them equal rights; but most believed by then that slavery was wrong, and that it should be allowed to spread no further. The successive crises of the 1850s strained the bonds of union ever more sharply until the end of the decade, when at last both North and South saw the sectional problem as a moral issue. By then a breach was unavoidable.

## The divisive issue

**The Kansas-Nebraska bill.**  The peace that followed the Compromise of 1850 was illusory. Although the Democrats had won the Presidency for Franklin Pierce, who campaigned for the acceptance of the compromise as final, the organization of new territories could not be delayed indefinitely (see p. 277). With the territorial question the slavery issue arose anew.

Early in January 1854 Senator Stephen A. Douglas, chairman of the Committee on the Territories, abruptly shattered the sectional truce by introducing a bill for the organization of the Kansas and Nebraska territories for statehood on the principle of "popular sovereignty." That principle had already been applied to New Mexico and Utah in the Compromise of 1850. Letting the people of a territory decide on the question of slavery seemed eminently reasonable to men like Douglas, the cocksure little senator from Illinois, whose motives for reopening the territorial question were unclear. Douglas certainly had presidential aspi-

*A Kansas Free State battery*

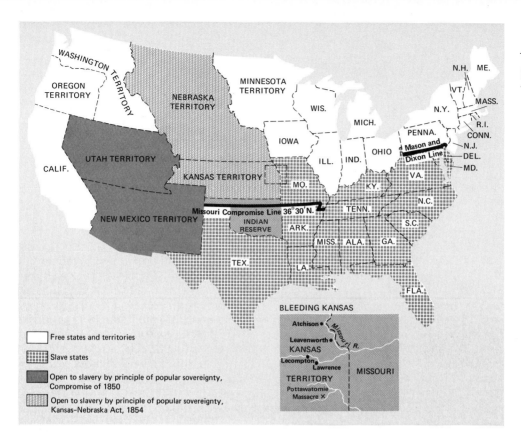

The Kansas-Nebraska Act, 1854

BLEEDING KANSAS

Free states and territories

Slave states

Open to slavery by principle of popular sovereignty, Compromise of 1850

Open to slavery by principle of popular sovereignty, Kansas–Nebraska Act, 1854

rations, and his critics promptly charged him with trying to appease Southern Democrats whose backing he needed for the nomination. Clearly the removal of the prohibition against slavery north of 36° 30′ would please many Southern leaders. Yet the presidential contest was still two years away, and few Southern senators were enthusiastic about organizing new territories ill adapted to slavery.

Probably the "Little Giant" from Illinois was acting primarily as a regional booster. "The tide of immigration and civilization must be permitted to roll onward," he declared. The country needed "a continuous line of settlements, with civil, political and religious institutions all under the protection of the law." Douglas was thinking of the eastern terminus of the projected transcontinental railway. If the "continuous line of settlements" should lead out from Chicago, it would benefit not only Illinois but all the Midwestern states. The South hoped for a terminus at New Orleans. Even while Douglas was readying his bill for action, Jefferson Davis of Mississippi, Pierce's Secretary of War, was concluding the Gadsden Purchase, which was essential to the southern route challenging Chicago's aspirations.

Douglas knew there was danger of reopening the slavery question whenever new territories were organized. He realized too that that question had potentialities for dividing the Democratic party. He took those

risks because he believed his divided party, just then squabbling over patronage, could reunite on a coherent program of western development, and because he wanted the Chicago terminus badly. Douglas was also under intense pressure from a group of senators led by tough-minded David Atchison of Missouri, whose interest in organizing Kansas was even stronger than that of Douglas. Further, Atchison had the power, sitting as president of the Senate, to remove Douglas from his cherished chairmanship of the Committee on Territories. Atchison bragged later about having persuaded the senator from Illinois to accept amendments to the bill that were anathema to the free-soil Democrats.

What Douglas failed to assess accurately was the extent to which slavery had become a moral issue. Opponents of slavery in the territories would not be satisfied with the mere probability that slavery would be turned down on the Kansas plains: they would take no chances. Free-soilers had an excellent argument. Because Kansas and Nebraska were north of the 36° 30′ parallel, passing Douglas' bill would endanger the rule of 1820, adopted in the Missouri Compromise, which prohibited slavery above that line in all lands secured by the Louisiana Purchase. Free-soil leaders therefore introduced an amendment explicitly reaffirming the Missouri prohibition. Quickly countering this move, Southern senators secured instead a

*A decade of crisis*

specific repeal of the Missouri prohibition. The final version of the Kansas-Nebraska bill included that inflammatory feature and called for the Platte River country to be divided into two territories (they had previously been treated as a unit), each to be organized immediately on the basis of popular sovereignty. Because the northern territory, Nebraska, was west of Iowa, a free state, few feared the development of slavery there. Kansas, to the south and immediately west of Missouri, a slave state, was another matter. Missouri seemed to think of Kansas as its own backyard. In final form the bill appalled the free-soil wing of the Democratic party as well as Northern antislavery Whigs, because it repealed the Missouri Compromise. With stunning perversity, Southerners abandoned their initial coolness to the Kansas-Nebraska bill and endorsed it as a measure "reasonable in its operation and effect" and fair to the South.

***A new political party.*** The outcry was loud and immediate. "The Appeal of the Independent Democrats," a pamphlet written by Salmon P. Chase of Ohio, voiced the outrage of free-soilers, but they could not dissuade President Pierce from endorsing the Kansas-Nebraska bill. On March 3 the Senate passed the controversial measure. After nearly three months, and after a heated and lengthy debate, the House did the same. On May 30, by a narrow margin of three votes and as a result of active pressure on the part of the President, the Kansas-Nebraska bill became law. New England and the Northwest exploded in angry demonstrations as "anti-Nebraska" people came together across party lines to denounce Douglas and his bill. Douglas declared that he could travel from Washington to Chicago in the light of his own burning effigies. Some of the strongest opponents of the act were Northern Democrats, who had divided evenly on the issue in the House of Representatives. The territorial issue had already severely damaged the Whigs. Now it threatened to divide the Democrats as well.

As early as February, in Ripon, Wisconsin, a gathering of anti-Nebraska Whigs and Democrats united to form a new party, and similar meetings took place elsewhere. Two weeks after President Pierce signed the Kansas-Nebraska bill one of these fusionist groups met at Jackson, Michigan, and adopted the name "Republican." This party was composed entirely of members from one section and was devoted to the containment of slavery within the states where it was already established. The new party stressed most its belief in the dignity of free labor; it held that the spread of slavery endangered not only the agrarian way of life idealized by Americans since Jefferson's day but the way of life of artisans and mechanics as well. Ever since the election of 1852, the Whig party

had been in disarray. Now the "conscience" Whigs began joining the new party, where they were met by numbers of Northern Democrats alienated by the Kansas-Nebraska Act.

By 1854 the Whig party was badly eroded, maintaining its organization intact in only a few states, but whether the Republicans would take their place as the chief party to oppose the Democrats was still uncertain. Democrats sustained heavy losses in the congressional elections that year, but it was hard to tell whether they lost to combinations of the various opponents of the Kansas-Nebraska Act or to the American party (see p. 290). That party was winning votes on the distrust of Catholics and foreign-born citizens so strong in urban areas, along the Middle Atlantic area, and in the entire border-state region. Because so many of the foreign-born were Catholics, and because many had no aversion to the use of alcohol, and because most were Democrats, a voter who chose to oppose the Democrats by voting for the Know-Nothings could be voting against the demon rum, Catholicism, and the "slave power conspiracy" as well. There was such hearty cooperation between the anti-Nebraska forces and the members of the American party that distinguishing the head from the tail of the victorious combination was not easy. But as the Pierce Administration began organizing the Kansas Territory, the attention of the country was riveted by a chaotic contest that worked to the benefit of the Republicans.

***The test in Kansas.*** Critics of "popular sovereignty" preferred to call it "squatter sovereignty." Once the policy had gone into effect in Kansas, its shortcomings seemed to merit that contemptuous phrase. Nobody expected trouble in Nebraska, and there was none. But in Kansas there was general and sustained disorder that discredited popular sover-

*Republicans at Jackson, Michigan*

eignty as a workable solution to the question of slavery in the territories. The customary lawlessness of the frontier was heightened by special causes of dispute. The government had permitted speculators to make claims in Kansas before legal titles had been acquired from the Indians, and early purchasers were making claims where they supposed towns would spring up and along the line of the anticipated transcontinental railroad. They were greedy, not for homesites, but for a rise in values. Speculators came from everywhere, but Missourians, on the scene early, apparently regarded Kansas as their rightful territory, their natural place to expand. Senator Atchison blustered that he preferred to see the new territory "sink in hell" rather than to have it organized as a free state.

Preparing to fight matters out on a popular-sovereignty basis, since that was now the law, free-soil forces determined to make themselves the more numerous party in Kansas. In Massachusetts an Emigrant Aid Society was formed under the leadership of Eli Thayer, a wealthy cotton-manufacturer, to give financial help to those willing to undertake the westward trek. To John Greenleaf Whittier, the poet of antislavery, the emigrants were crusaders, rearing "a wall of men . . . on freedom's southern line." All told, only 1,240 settlers came to Kansas under Thayer's auspices, and efforts to promote Kansas in the Southern states inspired even fewer emigrants. Most of the Kansas settlers came, as they usually did when new territories were opened, from neighboring states. Many were from Missouri, and though the slaveholders among them were few, even the nonslaveholders abhorred abolitionism. If abolitionism was unpopular, so were blacks; and the majority of the Kansas settlers (including Thayer's settlers) wanted to exclude free blacks as well as slaves. Blacks, free or slave, formed no part of their collective vision of Kansas' future, and even "free soil" was for whites only.

When Andrew C. Reeder, the Pennsylvanian chosen by Pierce to be the first territorial governor of Kansas, arrived there in the fall of 1854, he found several thousand settlers ahead of him. The first elections he called set the pattern for many Kansas elections to follow. The proslavery forces won overwhelmingly, electing a territorial delegate to Congress in the fall of 1854 and a proslavery legislature the following spring. Both elections were riddled with fraud. Encouraged by Senator Atchison to believe that their own security depended on getting a government set up in Kansas that would protect slave property, Missourians living in the counties adjacent to the border crossed the state line to cast illegal ballots. Governor Reeder threw out the most blatantly fraudulent returns but permitted the main result to stand. President Pierce, who should have called a new elec-

tion, vacillated and then did nothing. The new Kansas legislature, sitting at Shawnee Mission, drew up a territorial slave code so severe that it set the death penalty for anyone aiding a fugitive slave.

The free-soil forces denounced the actions of the "bogus" legislature, as they called it, and organized their own "shadow" government. They drew up the so-called Topeka constitution, which provided for the end of slavery by 1857; it also excluded free blacks from entry into Kansas. The free-soilers announced new elections for a state legislature and established a capital at Topeka. Now two governments, complete with capitals, governors, and legislatures, confronted each other: one was the product of fraud; the other lacked legal foundation.

For three weeks in late November armed bands of "border ruffians" from Missouri roamed the countryside. They claimed to be helping the legal government of Kansas restore order, but their real intent was to terrify the free-soil settlers. The free-state men met the invaders with "Beecher's Bibles," named for Henry Ward Beecher, a famous preacher who in an indiscreet moment had declared Sharps rifles a better force than Bibles for morality in Kansas. Finally the free-state "governor," Charles Robinson, struck a truce with Governor William Shannon, whom Pierce had sent out to replace Reeder. Shannon denied that he had sent for the Missourians, and Robinson explained that the free-state men had no intention of disobeying territorial laws.

The winter of 1855–56 was exceptionally severe in Kansas, and the settlers had all they could do to keep from freezing. With the spring thaw, trouble broke out again. In Leavenworth violence at a free-state election resulted in death and injury to several persons, including one particularly brutal murder of a free-state militia captain. A newspaper war followed, with the Missouri papers excusing atrocities against "abolitionists," as they wrongly labeled the free-soilers, and with the Eastern papers, particularly the New York *Tribune*, exaggerating the number of victims. Free-staters were justifiably indignant when President Pierce attributed the violence in Kansas to the emigrant aid societies and placed no blame on the raiders from Missouri. Pierce rejected the Topeka, or free-state, constitution as illegal, thus almost inviting an attack on the free-state capital at Lawrence. In May the attack occurred. A roving band of Missourians broke up the free-state printing press at Lawrence, burned out a hotel, intimidated the inhabitants, and rode off unscathed.

**"Bleeding Kansas."** One grim free-stater undertook a savage retaliation. The roving survivor of many failed enterprises, John Brown had come to Kansas in the fall of 1855 to settle down with his large tribe of

*A decade of crisis*

sons and their families in support of the free-state cause. An early advocate of armed resistance, Brown was outraged that nothing had been done to punish the border ruffians; after the Lawrence episode, he resolved to even the score himself. Leading a small band of his sons and followers in a midnight attack on the sleeping community of Pottawatomie Creek, Brown ordered them to kill five of the settlers with broadswords he had deliberately sharpened for the purpose and then made off with the victims' horses. Brown thought of himself as God's instrument of revenge. Although his victims were associated with the proslavery party, not one was a slaveholder, and none had done special services for the Missourians. The seemingly random character of those murders lent a special terror to the episode. Within days the whole of southeast Kansas was at war. John Brown went into hiding with his men, but the Missourians took revenge by burning the free-state town of Osawatomie and killing one of Brown's sons while seeking Brown himself.

A summer of guerrilla war followed. The death toll for the first year of settlement under popular sovereignty rose to over two hundred; property losses in barn-burnings, theft, and general destruction reached nearly $2 million. Pierce removed Shannon and sent yet another governor to replace him. In September 1856 Governor John Geary brought order to the territory with federal troops. Though he persuaded the Missourians to abandon hostilities, nobody believed that the question of slavery in the territories was settled.

Tempers in Congress soon matched those on the frontier. An ugly event on the floor of the Senate contributed to the fierce climate of politics. Just as the Missourians were burning the hotel in Lawrence, Senator Charles Sumner of Massachusetts, a famous antislavery orator, gave a ringing denunciation of the "Crime Against Kansas." In the course of a two-day speech during which he urged the admission of Kansas as a state under the Topeka constitution, he lashed the Administration for its alleged partiality to the proslavery settlers and defined the "crime" as the "rape of a virgin territory, compelling it to the hateful embrace of slavery." Pursuing his sexual metaphors, Sumner even insinuated that the aging Senator Andrew Butler of South Carolina had taken "slavery" as his mistress; then he referred to the "loose expectoration" of Butler's speech. That cruel reference to a partial paralysis caused by a stroke prompted the senator's young cousin, Congressman Preston Brooks, to walk into the Senate a few days later and cane Sumner into unconsciousness. Because of his injuries Sumner was not in the Senate again for several years, and his empty seat became a focus of antislavery sympathy. To Northern supporters the senator from

*The caning of Sumner: symbol of divisiveness*

Massachusetts was a martyr to Southern barbarism; but to Southerners he was a hyprocrite, and "Bully" Brooks' admirers sent Brooks complimentary walking canes. The polarization of sympathies in the Sumner-Brooks affair symbolized the hardening of attitudes on every issue touching on slavery in the territories.

***The election of 1856.*** The Pierce Administration had promised to reconcile the sections, but in the gamble to organize Kansas for statehood it had forced the slavery issue into open conflict. Now the country and the Democratic party drifted rudderless toward a crucial presidential election. Only the Republicans faced the future with confidence, for they had made important gains since the congressional elections two years earlier. In New York, where many Whigs had voted for Know-Nothings in 1855, Senator William H. Seward foresaw the destruction of his party and cast his influence for the Republicans. In Ohio, Salmon P. Chase, elected governor in 1855, announced his departure from the Democrats. He joined the Republicans at the same time his old Whig antagonist Benjamin Wade did. The two men disliked each other, but they disliked slavery even more. Other important public figures, including Abraham Lincoln, were co-operating with the Republicans while retaining their old party labels. By 1856 most state governments in the North were under the control of political leaders sympathetic to the Republicans. They reflected a growing popular conviction that only the new party could halt the aggressions of the "slave power conspiracy."

Even the Know-Nothing threat to Republican ascendancy disappeared in February before the presidential elections. At the American party convention

*The divisive issue*

one wing withdrew because it was unable to get an antislavery plank included in the platform. Hoping to win Republican support for their candidate, the antislavery Americans ended up endorsing the Republican choice.

In June the Republicans met in Philadelphia and adopted a strong free-soil platform. Denouncing the repeal of the Missouri Compromise, they asserted that Congress had the duty to prohibit slavery—"a relic of barbarism"—in the territories. Free-soil but not abolitionist, the platform did not condemn Kansas, or indeed the Midwestern states, for their policy of excluding free blacks. Many Republicans tacitly accepted the view that blacks could not be citizens. They aimed specifically to contain slavery where it already existed. Further, they made no effort to attract Southern votes, and they condemned the Ostend Manifesto as an imperialist design of the Administration to expand slave territory into the Caribbean (see p. 285). Former Whigs in the party applauded the call for internal improvements, particularly for federal aid to the construction of a Pacific railroad.

The Republicans chose John C. Frémont, a popular but weak figure, as their presidential candidate. Though thoroughly antislavery, the "Pathfinder of the West" had had no more political experience than William Henry Harrison and Zachary Taylor had had. But they had won. Frémont added to a soldier's glory the fame of an explorer, and he knew how to dramatize himself. Flamboyant and self-assured, he was married to Jesse Benton, the daughter of Thomas Hart Benton, who shared the personality traits of her husband; Frémont and his wife were an exceptionally "available" political couple. One of Frémont's detractors said of him that he had every qualification of genius except talent.

The Democrats nominated James Buchanan, one of the architects of the Ostend Manifesto, which had asserted that the United States would be justified in taking Cuba by force, if Spain refused to sell. An amiable but mediocre Pennsylvanian, he enjoyed the inestimable advantage of having been minister to the Court of St. James while troubles in Kansas were ruining the chances of abler men. Recognizing the destructive potential of the slavery question, the Democratic platform denied the authority of Congress to legislate on slavery in the territories and avoided the question of whether the population of a territory could exclude slavery before achieving statehood. The Democrats might well have lost to the Republicans had they been more explicit on this latter point, which raised the fine question of just when the people would become sovereign under the Democratic formula of popular sovereignty. Could they constitutionally vote to exclude slavery while still a territory? Or must they wait for statehood? The plat-

*James Buchanan: amiable mediocrity*

form also endorsed the Ostend Manifesto, which voiced a continuing belief that expansion would shore up the declining representation of the slave states in Congress.

Buchanan won the election handily with 174 electoral votes against 114 for Frémont; Millard Fillmore, the candidate of the marginal Whigs and Know-Nothings, got only the 8 votes of Maryland. In the popular vote, however, Buchanan had only 45 percent of the total. Without the South he would have lost the election, for Frémont carried all but five of the free states. Without even a single vote from the South, Frémont could have won had he been able to carry Pennsylvania and either Illinois or Indiana. If the Democrats could not either resolve or bury the slavery issue, they would go the way of the Whigs and the Know-Nothings, and they knew it.

# The house divided

**The Dred Scott decision.** During the campaign the Democrats had charged that the Republicans were a sectional party devoted to a single issue: the exclusion of slavery from the territories. Once reelected, the Democrats hoped to deprive their opponents of that issue and save their party. In his inaugural address, James Buchanan referred to a momentous case then pending before the Supreme Court that would settle the question of slavery in the territories. He urged the public to accept the verdict, whatever it might be, as final. Actually, Buchanan already knew that Southern

Democrats would be pleased with the Supreme Court decision in the case of Dred Scott.

Dred Scott was a black man, once the property of John Emerson, an army doctor who had bought him as a slave in Missouri and had then taken him into Illinois, a free state, and from there into Wisconsin Territory, north of the 36° 30′ line of the Missouri Compromise. After Dr. Emerson died, Scott sued in the state courts of Missouri for his freedom, on the grounds that he had lived in free territory. He won his case, but the decision was reversed on appeal. Meantime, Mrs. Emerson remarried, and under Missouri law, the executor of her estate—in this case, her brother John Sanford—could dispose of her property on behalf of the Emersons' daughter. Sanford was a citizen of New York, which gave Scott's lawyers the right to present his case in the federal courts, because Scott, if free, could claim to be a citizen of a different state from Sanford.

The Supreme Court faced two central questions: Did Dred Scott have a right to bring his case into the federal courts? This was another way of asking whether a Negro, even a free Negro, could be a citizen of the United States. Free blacks had been denied the right to enter claims to Western lands, and they had often been denied passports to travel abroad. Before ratification of the Fourteenth Amendment (1868), there was no constitutional definition of federal citizenship. The second main question for the Supreme Court was whether his sojourn in free territory had made Dred Scott a free man, and that question invited the Court to judge whether the Missouri Compromise of 1820 was constitutional.

Both questions were politically volatile, and the Court might have avoided them by following the formula already used in the Missouri courts: Scott's residence in free territory had not altered his slave status, because he had voluntarily returned to Missouri. The majority of the Supreme Court decided to undertake a broad decision, however, in part because they knew that the public had been expecting such a decision since 1850, and in part because three Justices were determined to get a decision on the Missouri Compromise. The Republican Justices, Benjamin R. Curtis and John McClean, who favored Scott's claim to freedom, would assume that the Missouri Compromise was constitutional, thus vindicating their party's position that Congress, not the people of the territories, had authority over slavery in the territories. Justice James Wayne of Georgia would argue that the compromise was unconstitutional because Congress was not explicitly empowered under the constitution to decide on the question.

Although each Justice followed his own line of argument, the Court ruled six to three against Scott's claim to freedom. Five concurred in the long, involved, but forceful opinion of Chief Justice Roger B. Taney of Maryland, who declared that Scott could not claim the rights of a United States citizen. Negroes, Taney pronounced, had been regarded for more than a century before the Constitution was adopted as "beings of an inferior order" with "no rights which any white man was bound to respect." That statement was not good history, as Justice Curtis pointed out in a brilliant dissent, for in four of the original states free blacks had been entitled to vote. If a majority of the Justices had followed Taney's exact line of reasoning, the Court might have avoided the second question—whether the Missouri Compromise was constitutional. But four Justices, while concurring that Scott's claim to freedom must be denied, did so for reasons different from Taney's and avoided a judgment on whether free blacks could be citizens. Therefore the Court had cast doubt on the first question without actually deciding it and then had proceeded to rule that the Missouri Compromise was unconstitutional. The Fifth Amendment, said Justice Taney, had denied Congress the right to deprive persons of property without due process of law, and therefore the Missouri Compromise prohibiting slavery north of the 36° 30′ had violated the Constitution. Slaves were property, and neither Congress nor the territorial governments could deprive citizens of property "without due process of law."

Even mildly antislavery Northerners were outraged by the harshness of Justice Taney's language. Republicans believed that Justice Curtis' powerful dissent had come closer to the truth in pointing out that Congress was given the power to "make all needful rules" for the government of the territories. They observed that most of the Justices were Democrats, many appointed by Andrew Jackson, and that the Northern Democrat, Justice Robert C. Grier of Pennsylvania, who sided with the Southern Justices, was a political associate of President Buchanan. Many Northerners wondered if the Supreme Court and the

*Dred Scott: he lost his case*

President were not in conspiracy to extend slavery throughout the nation.

All Democrats had hoped for a decision on the slavery question that would cut the ground from under the Republicans, but Douglas and the Northern Democrats quickly saw that the Dred Scott decision had troublesome implications for their own policy of popular sovereignty. That Congress could not rule on slavery in the territories reinforced the Kansas-Nebraska Act, which they had sponsored; but the decision also cast doubt on whether a territorial legislature had any more right than Congress had to exclude slavery. This seemed to mean that the people of a territory could take no action against slavery until after the territory was authorized to draw up a constitution in preparation for statehood. Many Northerners feared that slavery might be too deeply entrenched by that time to be abolished.

**Lecompton vs. Topeka.** By ruling against the Missouri Compromise the Supreme Court had cast doubt on the constitutionality of popular sovereignty; events in Kansas were making popular sovereignty appear ridiculous in practice. Two governments were operating there: the proslavery government, now at Lecompton, which enjoyed legitimacy; and the free-state government at Topeka, which commanded the support of the majority of actual settlers. The United States House of Representatives had approved the Topeka constitution, but the Senate would not, claiming that its ratification in Kansas had been irregular.

Soon after his inauguration, President Buchanan sent a fourth governor, Robert Walker, to the territory. Buchanan hoped Walker would be able to get a constitution adopted through a fair vote, so that Kansas could be admitted to statehood. A native Pennsylvanian who had moved to Mississippi and had risen in the Democratic party of his adopted state, Walker seemed qualified to bring harmony to the troubled territory. He undoubtedly counted on strong support from Buchanan in his effort.

Walker knew that, although the free-soil settlers were three times more numerous than the proslavery Northern settlers, the real abolitionists among the free-soilers were few. He hoped therefore to get the free-soilers to cooperate with the proslavery faction long enough to establish a legal government. To that end he called a constitutional convention. Because the proslavery legislature planned the election for delegates, however, the free-soilers refused to participate, claiming that the legislature had divided the voting districts unfairly. Even though they might have won, fraud notwithstanding, the free-soilers would not lend legitimacy to a rigged election. As a result the proslavery delegates dominated the constitutional convention,

which met in the village of Lecompton. They drew up a document that attempted to please free-soilers and proslavery voters alike by prohibiting the entry of free blacks into Kansas. Otherwise the Lecompton constitution was thoroughly unsatisfactory to the free-soilers. It included a clause establishing slavery in Kansas, and voters were given the opportunity to vote for the constitution with that clause or without it. There was no way for the people to vote for or against the general body of the constitution, a fact that infuriated those who wanted to be rid of current as well as future slave-holding in Kansas. This action thoroughly discredited popular sovereignty as a solution to the question of slavery in the territories. Again the free-state men declined to vote, and the Lecompton constitution was overwhelmingly ratified with the slavery clause.

Though disappointed, Governor Walker continued his efforts to secure free-soil participation. He persuaded the free-soilers to vote in the elections for the territorial legislature, and they handily won a large majority. The new legislature then called a referendum on the Lecompton constitution for January 4, 1858. This time the proslavery men refused to vote, and the constitution was rejected.

One month after the referendum, and against Governor Walker's wishes, President Buchanan asked Congress to admit Kansas to the Union under the Lecompton constitution. Walker had come east to persuade Buchanan to support him in his efforts to get a constitution acceptable to the majority of Kansas voters. Buchanan refused and Walker resigned. Buchanan had become increasingly submissive to his Cabinet, which was dominated by Southerners. Stephen Douglas was as annoyed with Buchanan as Walker was, for he recognized that the Northern Democrats would not tolerate another capitulation to the Southern wing of the party. Realizing that his own support came from Midwestern Democrats, Douglas defied the President and began building support in the Senate to oppose the Lecompton constitution.

Although Douglas lost his struggle in the Senate, the Republicans in the House of Representatives blocked the admission of Kansas under the Lecompton constitution. By a compromise, the constitution was then resubmitted to the voters of Kansas. It was again defeated, in August 1858, by a margin of nearly ten to one.

The question of admitting Kansas now receded, and only after much of the South had seceded did the territory achieve statehood. In the meantime, however, the rupture in the Democratic party had brought the country closer to war.

**The Panic of 1857.** The slavery question so thoroughly dominated politics that all other questions came to be seen in its light. In 1857 a sharp economic crisis promised briefly to distract the nation's attention from Kansas. Soon, however, sectional partisans, each trying to thrust the blame on the selfishness of the other, were discussing the panic by comparing the relative merits of the Northern and Southern economies. Understanding what had really happened was indeed challenging.

The failure of the New York branch of the Ohio Life Insurance and Trust Company triggered the panic, and within months foreclosures, bankruptcies, and unemployment spread through the Northeast. The nation slipped into a severe depression from which it did not fully recover for over two years. The fundamental causes of the crisis were complex, deriving from excessive investments in railroads that promised no immediate profits and from a feverish land boom. Speculators invested in lands along the lines of railroads yet to be built, and Americans borrowed as never before to cover investments promising no quick return. Eventually the flimsy credit institutions of the country collapsed under the strain. International conditions also contributed to the disaster. Basic to the new economic expansion, general throughout the industrialized countries of western Europe as well as the United States, was the discovery of rich new deposits of gold in California and Australia. This new wealth facilitated the flow of goods between nations, and America was becoming increasingly tied to international trade. During the 1850s the American West had benefited from the European demand for its agricultural products. The end of the Crimean War deflated this market, and Western farmers suffered accordingly. Only the market for cotton held firm.

Noticing that the South passed through the crisis relatively unscathed, the Northeast, where suffering was acute, sought explanations. Actually the industrialized economy of the Northeast was more sensitive to the conditions that produced the depression, but many aggrieved manufacturers blamed the low tariff supported by Southern politicians for their troubles. Had not the "slave power" once more sacrificed the nation's well-being to its own sectional interests? Many believed so. Others, who regarded the revenue-only Tariff of 1857 as the result of a conspiracy, joined the Republican party. Responding to these charges with infuriating smugness, Southern leaders boasted that their economy was superior in that it produced a commodity that Europe had to have and rested on a better organization of labor—namely, slavery.

Although the panic was relatively brief, few have had a greater political impact. The West clamored for homestead legislation to secure financial relief, and the East saw hope in a protective tariff. The Republicans, making these issues their own, attracted many workingmen and farmers who were little moved by the slavery issue. The South was further alarmed for its safety in the Union.

**The election of 1858.** The Democrats, faced with a congressional election during a depression, tried to dress ranks. It was no use, for President Buchanan and Stephen Douglas had broken irreparably over the Lecompton constitution, and the President had removed Douglas' patronage and purged his followers. Buchanan thought that only stern measures would convince the South of the devotion of the Democratic party. Though badly handicapped in his fight to retain his Senate seat, Douglas knew that his constituents in Illinois would tolerate no further surrenders to Southern pressure on the territorial question. In criticizing the handling of the Lecompton constitution as a perversion of popular sovereignty, Douglas believed that

New states, 1858–61

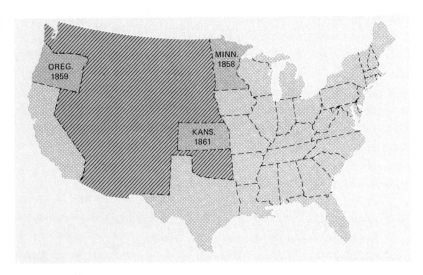

OREG. 1859

MINN. 1858

KANS. 1861

### The great debate: Lincoln

*I have stated upon former occasions ... what I understand to be the real issue in this controversy between Judge Douglas and myself. On the point of my wanting to make war between the Free and the Slave States, there has been no issue between us. So, too, when he assumes that I am in favor of introducing a perfect social and political equality between the white and black races. These are false issues.... The real issue in this controversy—the one pressing upon every mind—is the sentiment on the part of one class that looks upon the institution of slavery as a wrong, and of another class that does not look upon it as a wrong. The sentiment that contemplates the institution of slavery in this country as a wrong is the sentiment of the Republican party.... They look upon it as being a moral, social, and political wrong; and while they contemplate it as such, they nevertheless have due regard for ... the difficulties of getting rid of it in any satisfactory way and to all the constitutional obligations thrown about it. Yet ... they insist that it should, as far as may be, be treated as a wrong; and one of the methods of treating it as a wrong is to make provision that it shall grow no larger.*

**From Abraham Lincoln, Speech at Alton, Illinois, October 15, 1858.**

he was fighting not only for his own political life but for the survival of the Democratic party, one of the few trans-sectional institutions left in the country. Only on the basis of popular sovereignty could the party survive.

Douglas' challenger for his Senate seat was Abraham Lincoln, a lawyer from Springfield, Illinois, who two years before had abandoned a long and loyal attachment to the Whig party to join the Republicans. Lincoln was forty-nine years old, largely but splendidly self-educated. A person of many moods but great steadiness of character, Lincoln had an air of melancholy that was broken from time to time by bursts of rough frontier humor. Though Easterners knew little about him, he was no newcomer to Illinois politics. Lincoln had served a term in Congress during the Mexican War, which he strenuously opposed, and in 1852 he had nearly been elected senator. A superb politician, he could surprise and amuse his audiences, establishing his points with homely analogies drawn from the common experiences of the frontier farmers he knew so well. In a time when politicians sometimes doubled as traveling entertainers, even Lincoln's remarkable appearance, though it amused sophisticates, was an asset. People remembered him for his tall frame, his shambling carriage, his plain features. But most of all he impressed his hearers with his sincerity and common sense. Lincoln was not an abolitionist—indeed, he was no extreme advocate of any point of view—but he was deeply convinced that slavery should spread no further. Congress, he believed, had the right and the responsibility to prohibit slavery in the territories. This was the main issue of

the senatorial contest in Illinois in 1858, because Senator Douglas still spoke for letting the people decide.

**The Freeport Doctrine.** In a famous series of debates held at various towns over the state, Lincoln and Douglas discussed the great question of their time. Douglas was badly handicapped by Chief Justice Taney's decision in the case of Dred Scott that slave property could be brought into the territories on the same basis as any other property. When were the people to decide whether they wanted slavery? If a territory could not outlaw slavery until it had become a state, it might then be too late to exclude it. "Letting the people decide" was no longer so appealing a compromise to Northern Democrats as it had once been.

At Freeport, Illinois, Lincoln asked Douglas whether there was any lawful way for the inhabitants of a territory to exclude slavery before achieving statehood. Lincoln was trying to make Douglas state frankly how badly the Dred Scott decision had damaged popular sovereignty. Douglas' answer was not new, but for a presidential aspirant it was hazardous. Douglas pointed out that slavery was by its nature an institution that would dissolve unless protected by a slave code and by local police enforcement. Without these defenses slavery could not, Douglas insisted, last a day or even an hour. Therefore the opponents of slavery in a territory simply had to see to it that every effort to enact a slave code was defeated. That answer satisfied pragmatic Northern Democrats, but it antagonized the South. It did no more than state what most thoughtful Southern Democrats knew to be true, especially after the Kansas experience, but it seemed to

### The great debate: Douglas

**From Stephen A. Douglas, Speech at Alton, Illinois, October 15, 1858.**

render meaningless the South's constitutional triumph in the Dred Scott decision. Even the moral victory the decision represented was sullied. Douglas was saying, after all, that slavery couldn't be taken anywhere it wasn't wanted, and his opponents in the South would not forget.

In the campaign Lincoln and Douglas outlined their positions on slavery and race with painful frankness. Resorting to racist demagoguery, Douglas attempted to smear Lincoln as an abolitionist in areas where blacks were disliked and distrusted. Lincoln vigorously denied those charges, saying he did not believe in social or political equality and maintaining the white-supremacy argument. He nevertheless held to his belief that slavery was a social wrong that should be contained. Throughout their many debates Douglas evinced an insensitivity to the moral issue that slavery had become for an increasing number of Northern voters.

Lincoln did not win Douglas' seat in the Senate, nor did his party win control of the Senate. Lincoln ran well, however, and the Republicans came out of the election with more seats in the House of Representatives than any other party. New faces appeared in Washington—Republicans who would lead the nation in Civil War and through Reconstruction. The Democrats lost in every state except Illinois; the election was a rough rebuke to the Administration. The depression affected voter attitudes in many areas, especially in Buchanan's own state of Pennsylvania, where only anti-Lecompton Democrats survived. If they could win the cooperation of a handful of

Know-Nothings, the Republican party would have a majority.

Most significantly, the contest had established the reputation of Abraham Lincoln. He had given the principles of the Republican party their most forceful statement, and he had expressed the people's growing concern over the cost of slavery when he likened the nation to "a house divided." "I believe this government cannot endure permanently half *slave* and half *free*," he told the Republicans at their state convention, adding that he did not expect it to be divided. Douglas and Lincoln assumed positions in 1858 from which neither would retreat in 1860 as they faced each other in the contest for the Presidency of the United States.

By that time several crises had enhanced Lincoln's position that slavery must be contained. Those same crises had made Douglas' position, that slavery concerned only those who had a direct interest in it, seem irrelevant in the South and inadequate to the demands of the times in the North.

**Personal liberty laws.** As the South lost power in Congress, its leaders, as if insisting on a symbolic recompense, stridently demanded that the Fugitive Slave Law be systematically implemented. Numbers of slaves were returned, but every application of the law in the North aroused more people to the cruelty of slavery. Many citizens helped supposed fugitives to escape. More offensive to the South than those individual actions were the personal liberty laws passed in Northern states to impede the enforcement of the

Fugitive Slave Law. By reinforcing the rights of alleged slaves to proper legal defense, and by making illegal the use of state and local police and jails to detain them, angry state legislatures made "slave-catching" a difficult business. The South charged that the personal liberty laws were unconstitutional. In 1859 the Supreme Court endorsed the Southern view.

Early in 1859 tension mounted higher. A Southern commercial convention meeting in Vicksburg in May called for the reopening of the Atlantic slave trade. If even a handful of Southerners could voice such ideas in the middle of the nineteenth century, then slavery, many Northerners thought, had driven the South into collective madness. While the leading fire-eaters were campaigning ever more openly for secession, voters in Kansas went to the polls and ratified a constitution prohibiting slavery. Congress was not yet ready to act on the admission of Kansas to statehood, but it was evident that Kansas would soon become the nineteenth free state instead of the sixteenth slave state, which portended further decline in Southern representation in the Senate. Even worse fears were soon to surface.

## From debate to violence

**Harper's Ferry.** Ten days after the Kansas voters ratified the free-state constitution, John Brown carried his war on slavery into the South. After the Pottawatomie killings and the guerrilla fighting of the summer of 1856, Brown had escaped authorities and dropped from public view. He had not been idle. With the help of Gerrit Smith, a wealthy abolitionist from upstate New York, Brown secured the backing of a distinguished group of intellectual and financial leaders in the Boston area who called themselves the "Secret Six." With their help, Brown diverted contributions made to the relief of free-soil Kansas settlers to the purchase of guns and ammunition. On the night of October 16, 1859, he led a band of eighteen men from Maryland into Virginia, where he seized hostages among the citizens and occupied the fire-engine house of the federal arsenal at Harper's Ferry. He held the engine house for two days, in a state of siege, before surrendering to a small force of United States marines sent out from Washington under the command of Colonel Robert E. Lee. With many of his men killed and others wounded, John Brown waited quietly in the Charles Town jail, resisting all talk of efforts to rescue him and preparing his own defense.

Although Brown explicitly denied the charge at his trial, evidence indicates that he had intended to raise a slave insurrection. Once in Ralph Waldo Emer-

son's hearing he had stated that it would be better that every man, woman, and child then living should meet violent death than that "one word" of the Golden Rule or the Declaration of Independence "should be violated in this country." Emerson reflected comfortably that the old man must have been speaking "transcendentally," but he was wrong. Although Brown was sincere in his friendship for the oppressed slave, religious fanaticism best explains his actions from Pottawatomie Creek to Harper's Ferry. Whether that fanaticism extended to insanity, as his friends and relatives hoped to show in presenting his defense, is impossible to judge at this distance. They collected many affidavits attesting to widespread derangement among Brown's close relatives. Their obvious interest in saving Brown from execution cast suspicion on their efforts, however, and the victim himself would have none of that defense.

John Brown knew how to die. From the jail in Charles Town his words stirred many souls who had been impervious to abolitionist arguments. Brown's final appeal to the court expressed a great truth even though it obscured his real intentions: he reminded his hearers that what he had done would have been thought worthy of reward rather than punishment had it been done "in behalf of the rich, the powerful, the so-called great." In his captivity Brown was mag-

*John Brown: he thought he was God's avenger*

*A decade of crisis*

nanimous and cheerful, an altogether credible martyr. The parallels between the crucifixion of Christ and the execution of John Brown were abundant, not least in the conspicuous absence of the Secret Six, who with one exception agreed that Brown could best serve the cause of abolition by dying. In the end John Brown was a better prophet than revolutionary leader. He said on December 2, the day he died, that "the crimes of this guilty land: will never be purged *away*: but with Blood."

**Reactions North and South.** Although most sober-minded Northerners deplored Brown's actions, Southerners were unaware of that fact. They only heard the tolling bells and memorial services held throughout the North as numbers of citizens (many of them prominent) mourned a man who had tried to free the slaves and who had now become a martyr to the cause of freedom. To most Southerners Brown was no more than a madman who had intended to visit death and destruction upon guilty and innocent alike. The discovery of maps among his belongings showing likely points of assault deep in the southern Appalachians brought Virginia's fears into the Lower South. Edmund Ruffin, a vociferous Virginia fire-eater, distributed among Southern governors nine hundred captured pikes that Brown had had forged from bowie knives and iron staves. It required no paranoid imaginings to see that those crude but quiet weapons were better designed for midnight assassination than for a frontal assault against firearms. In many communities hysteria vented itself in attacks on persons who held unorthodox opinions on slavery. This outburst of hatred showed that the region deeply distrusted outsiders and that there lurked an abiding fear of what the slaves might do if a realistic possibility of freedom presented itself.

**The contest for the Speakership.** On the Monday following Brown's execution, Congress convened and set about the routine business of electing a Speaker of the House. This time the task required two months of extravagant recrimination and verbal abuse without precedent. By combining with Southern Know-Nothings and Whigs, the Democrats prevented the nomination of the Republican choice, John Sherman of Ohio, but they could not command enough votes to elect a Democrat. Sherman would have made an excellent Speaker, but Democrats opposed him because he had endorsed a controversial book about the South and slavery. Hinton Rowan Helper, the author of *The Impending Crisis of the South*, was a white man from North Carolina who charged that slavery was ruining the nonslaveholders, socially and economically. Helper likened slaveholding to throwing strychnine into a public well, so dangerous was it to the safety of white people. Though he called for immediate emancipation, Helper was not a friend of the blacks. Like many other Republicans, he recommended that emancipated slaves be exported from the country. His book touched a sensitive Southern problem, the economic impotence of nonslaveholders in a society dominated by the plantation system and by owners of slaves.

Although Sherman had not seen *The Impending Crisis* after its completion, he had carelessly allowed his name to be used in promoting it after glancing casually at the table of contents. Name-calling was not new in Congress, but there was no humor and no style or eloquence in the verbal duels that followed. Radical Southerners, insinuating that men like John Sherman had provoked Harper's Ferry, angrily renewed their threats to secede from the Union. The Republicans, though more restrained than the Democrats, goaded their opponents from the South by sneering at the threats of secession and by declaring that they would no longer be bluffed by such talk. In this charged atmosphere, members of Congress began to carry pistols to the stormy sessions. Never able to garner the votes needed to elect Sherman as Speaker, the Republicans at last fell upon a man of inferior talents, John Pennington of New Jersey, who had the necessary Know-Nothing support. In the troubles that lay ahead, the nation might well have used a man of John Sherman's ability as Speaker.

In early February, on the day after Pennington became Speaker of the House, Jefferson Davis introduced in the Senate a series of resolutions that defined the position of extreme Southern Democrats. Davis demanded a national slave code for the protection of slave property in the territories and a congressional declaration that personal liberty laws and attacks on slavery were unconstitutional. After many stormy sessions these resolutions were eventually passed on May 24, nearly four months later. Davis' purpose was to test the Northern Democrats' support of the South and to set forth the program Southern Democrats would insist on in return for party loyalty. Well before Davis' resolutions were adopted, however, the Democrats had tried and failed to nominate a presidential candidate. Their party was destroyed by the principles of Davis' resolutions.

**The election of 1860.** The Democrats who met in Charleston in April were divided even before they arrived. Senator Douglas was the favorite of most of the Northern Democrats. President Buchanan still opposed him, however, and Administration supporters at the convention found allies among the Southern fire-eaters—men like William Lowndes Yancey—who had come to Charleston to find an excuse for secession. For this reason they demanded the impossible: a

313

party platform calling for federal protection of slavery in the territories. Unfortunately for Douglas the convention took up the platform before nominating a candidate. The majority of the platform committee then brought in a document very like the Davis resolutions that were being debated in the Senate. Since Douglas clearly could not run on such a platform, his supporters had no choice but to fight for the adoption of a minority report. On grounds of principle and politics, they could not recede from the popular-sovereignty position. As H. B. Payne of Ohio warned, if the majority report was adopted, "you cannot expect one Northern electoral vote, or one sympathizing member of Congress from the free states." Without these men the Democrats could not win the Presidency.

After several days of struggle, a compromise was adopted in a vote boycotted by the Southern delegates. After a solemn speech by Yancey in which he detailed Southern grievances, the delegates of the Lower South withdrew. The remaining delegates defeated an effort to nominate Douglas and at last decided to go home and hold another convention in Baltimore in June.

Seizing on the opportunity presented by the split among Democrats, the Republicans convened in Chicago. On May 18, to a wild ovation, they nominated Abraham Lincoln, the rail-splitter of Sangamon County. Hannibal Hamlin of Maine was nominated as the vice-presidential candidate. Lincoln held firmly to the basic Republican principle that slavery must be contained, but his nomination over William H. Seward represented a victory for the more restrained statement of that principle. Seward's exposure during his career as Senator had given wide circulation to his views on the "irrepressible conflict" between slavery and freedom and to his advocacy of a "higher law" than the Constitution. But Lincoln was nominated

*Lincoln at Cooper Union*

largely because he had established himself as a national figure, even winning popularity in Seward's own state of New York. In February Lincoln had come east to speak at Cooper Union in New York City. There he had outlined with powerful simplicity the historical basis for Congress' right to exclude slavery from the territories. "There is a judgment and a feeling against slavery in this nation, which [has] cast at least a million and a half of votes." Destroying Republicans would not destroy that feeling. To striking workers in New England, he had spoken of the rights of free labor, saying he wished all men could quit work when they wished to quit. Lincoln also had a very practical political advantage over Seward. The former governor of New York, who had long fought the Know-Nothings of his state, could not hope to attract members of that party to the Republicans. And yet their votes were essential to victory, especially in Pennsylvania, a key state lost by the Republicans in 1856.

Lincoln campaigned on a platform broader than Frémont's had been. The platform adhered firmly to the basic Republican policy of containing slavery within the states where it existed, but it affirmed also the belief that it should not be disturbed there. It condemned John Brown's raid. The Republicans also gained by the addition of important economic issues. The Democrats, by frustrating Republican efforts to secure homestead legislation, the Pacific Railroad bill, and an elevation of the tariff, had alienated many voters who saw in those measures hope of economic recovery. The Republicans now built those issues into their platform. No longer could they be called the party of "one idea."

Halfway between the Democratic fiasco at Charleston and the Republican nomination of Lincoln in Chicago, the Constitutional Union party met in Baltimore. Here was an old party with a new name. Old border-state Whigs, known for their long service to the Union, hoped to head off secession by nominating John Bell of Tennessee, with Edward Everett of Massachusetts as his running mate. The Constitutional Union men declared for "the Constitution of the country, the union of the states, and the enforcement of the laws."

The Democrats, meeting in Baltimore in June, recognized their peril. They even saw the possibility of Southern secession if the Republicans won. Although Douglas would have withdrawn his candidacy in favor of a compromise, he would not retreat from popular sovereignty as the essential plank in the platform. Most Northern Democrats shared his conviction. The convention fell apart almost immediately over the question of accreditation. Bolters from the Charleston convention came to Baltimore and challenged the credentials of the more moderate delega-

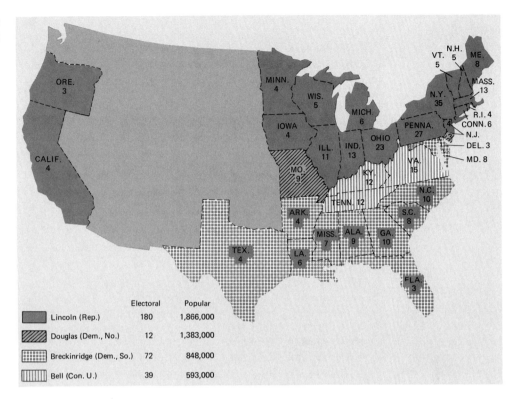

The election of 1860

| | | Electoral | Popular |
|---|---|---|---|
| | Lincoln (Rep.) | 180 | 1,866,000 |
| | Douglas (Dem., No.) | 12 | 1,383,000 |
| | Breckinridge (Dem., So.) | 72 | 848,000 |
| | Bell (Con. U.) | 39 | 593,000 |

tions their states had sent in their stead. Deep South delegates again seceded to a separate convention, and the Democratic rump nominated Douglas to run with Herschel V. Johnson of Georgia. The Southern Democrats nominated John C. Breckinridge of Kentucky, with Joseph Lane of Oregon as their vice-presidential candidate. They called for federal protection of slavery in the territories.

The stage was set for a fateful four-way contest. Whether the nation would move toward war or peace depended on its outcome. The Republicans, capitalizing on their many youthful supporters, organized smart marching bands calling themselves the "Wide Awakes." These bands demonstrated vigorously throughout the North for Lincoln, singing, "Ain't you glad you joined the Republicans?" The Republicans reaffirmed their stand against the extension of slavery into the territories, attacked the vulnerable record of the Democrats for eight years of bickering, corruption, and vacillation; and laid exceptional emphasis on a series of economic proposals, concentrating in each locality on the issue that would appeal most strongly. Protective tariffs were stressed in manufacturing states; homestead legislation, land-grant colleges, internal improvements, and a Pacific Railroad were stressed further west, where they were popular. The Republicans also reassured the foreign-born that they were in no danger from a Republican election. The strongest argument brought against the new party

was that a vote for the Republicans was a vote for disunion, that the South would secede if Lincoln was elected. Therefore the Republicans played down the sectional issue, claiming that Southern Democrats were once again crying "wolf" with their threats. Douglas knew better; he was the first presidential candidate to undertake a nationwide personal campaign. In the South he urged acceptance of popular sovereignty as the only possible way for the Democrats to save themselves and urged that the South not secede whatever the outcome of the election. He was in Selma, Alabama, when he learned that Lincoln had defeated him.

The Republicans won an overwhelming majority in the Electoral College. Concealed by that majority was a profound division of opinion in the country. Taking only 40 percent of the total ballots cast, the Republicans collected 180 electoral votes, as compared with only 12 for Douglas, 72 for Breckinridge, and 39 for Bell. In the popular vote Douglas won 1,382,713, no disgraceful showing compared with Lincoln's 1,865,593. The South knew that those figures rested on the great increase of population the Middle West had experienced since the last census. Clearly the die had been cast in the North, and the South's electoral votes had been only incidental to the result. With only a third of the total white population in the country, the states of the future Confederacy saw that decisions concerning slavery could now be made without them.

315

*The history of the ... Black Republican party of the North is a history of repeated injuries and usurpations, all having in direct object the establishment of absolute tyranny over the slave-holding States. And all without the smallest ... justification.... Every appeal and expostulation has only brought upon us renewed insults and augmented injuries. They have robbed us of our property ... they have set at naught the decrees of the Supreme Court, they have invaded our States and killed our citizens, they have declared their unalterable determination to exclude us altogether from the Territories, they have nullified the laws of Congress, and finally they have capped the mighty pyramid of unfraternal enormities by electing Abraham Lincoln ... on a platform and by a system which indicates nothing but the subjugation of the South and the complete ruin of her social, political and industrial institutions.*

**From the New Orleans *Daily Crescent*, November 13, 1860.**

*The secession of the Lower South.* Anticipating the outcome of the election, the South Carolina legislature had remained in session until the results were in and then called a state convention. On December 20 that convention, without a dissenting vote, passed an ordinance of secession. By February the entire Lower South had left the Union, and a convention of the seceded states met in Montgomery, Alabama, to form a new government. They called themselves the Confederate States of America.

The urge to secede had been growing steadily for many years, and the extremists who led the movement were seasoned politicians. In the crisis of 1860 such men as Robert Barnwell Rhett of South Carolina, Robert Toombs of Georgia, and even the soft-spoken fire-eater William Lowndes Yancey of Alabama seized the initiative over the Southern Unionists. Secession was very popular throughout the Lower South, and strongest wherever the plantation system and slavery were well developed. Unionism was strongest in the highlands, the upcountry, and the Upper South, where secession was held to be impractical but not illegal. What the Upper South would do if forced to choose between remaining in the Union and denouncing the constitutional right to secede remained to be seen.

*Failure of compromise.* The eight slave-holding states still within the Union were in a precarious situation. The election of a Republican President did not, they believed, require them to abandon the Union, and they distrusted the fire-eating leaders of secession. Yet any effort to coerce the Lower South would involve them; and if the Lower South were not coerced or persuaded to return, they would be left as a small minority in the depleted Union. A compromise that would restore peace and lead to the voluntary return of the seceding states was the best hope of the border-state leaders and of the Upper South generally.

On December 18, two days before South Carolina seceded, John J. Crittenden of Kentucky had introduced resolutions in the Senate that would have prohibited slavery north of the 36° 30' line of the old Missouri Compromise and that would have recognized it south of that line, even to protecting it with a federal slave code. The compromise Crittenden proposed called for a series of constitutional amendments to secure those objects and one other: he asked for an "unamendable" amendment that would guarantee slavery forever. The Republicans could not accept those proposals, because they were unwilling to return to the Missouri Compromise. Although few Republicans really feared that slavery would take root in the arid Southwest, they knew that some Southerners wanted to acquire slave territory in the Caribbean. While maintaining a perilous silence himself, Lincoln, the President-elect, warned his followers privately: "Entertain no proposition for a compromise in regard to the *extension* of slavery. The instant you do, they have us under again; all our labor is lost, and sooner or later must be done over. . . . Have none of it. The tug has to come, and better now than later." When it was clear that the Senate would not accept his resolutions, the venerable Crittenden proposed as a last resort that they be offered as a referendum to the people of the country. The Republicans prevented that step. The congressional plans to achieve compromise had failed.

In February the Virginia General Assembly took up the effort for compromise by inviting the delegates of all the states to Washington to seek a solution, but with no better result. Many states boycotted the meeting, including all the Lower South states. In several weeks of discussion the delegates proposed constitutional amendments similar to Crittenden's, but they could not get them adopted by the Senate. Hope for compromise faded.

By this time the Confederate government was established in Montgomery, and the Southern states were seizing federal arsenals and forts. In his annual message, President Buchanan had spoken in conciliatory tones of Southern grievances. He had denied the right of South Carolina to secede but then had disclaimed his own authority to prevent the state by force from doing so. Though rightly convinced that the secession threats were in earnest, Buchanan erred by delaying to take firm measures. He acted for peaceful ends but inadvertently encouraged the South to believe that secession could be accomplished without war. Buchanan abruptly changed his course early in the year. When the state-rights Southern members of his Cabinet withdrew, he replaced them with staunch Union men. In his last message to Congress, on January 8, 1861, the President referred to the Union as "a sacred trust" and declared that he would collect federal revenues and protect government property throughout the United States. Even before his annual message he had sent an unarmed merchant ship to Charleston Harbor with supplies for a small force at Fort Sumter under the command of Major Robert Anderson. The South Carolinians fired on the *Star of the West* before she entered the harbor, driving her off. Short on provisions, Fort Sumter became a symbol, along with Fort Pickens in Florida, of all that was left of federal authority in the seceded states. What the new President would do was the question uppermost in the North, where indignation mounted daily.

**Two new Presidents.** Lincoln's arrival in Washington on February 23 to take the helm of government was in painful contrast with the brilliant reception that had been accorded the President-elect of the Confederacy one week earlier. Informed of an assassination plot, Lincoln came into the city ahead of schedule after a secret ride through the night; he avoided stopping in Baltimore, a city unfriendly to Republicans. President Davis, riding a crest of enthusiasm, brought to his office a long record of public service and an awareness of popular approval. William Lowndes Yancey, introducing him to the crowd in Montgomery, declared, "The hour and the man have met." The leaders of the South were old acquaintances of their President, whereas Lincoln was largely

*Jefferson Davis: Confederate man of the hour*

*From debate to violence*

UNCLE TOM'S CABIN;
OR,
LIFE AMONG THE LOWLY.

BY
HARRIET BEECHER STOWE.

VOL. I.

BOSTON:
JOHN P. JEWETT & COMPANY.
CLEVELAND, OHIO:
JEWETT, PROCTOR & WORTHINGTON.
1852.

*Mr. Haley and Tom jogged onward in their wagon, each, for a time, absorbed in his own reflections. Now, the reflections of two men sitting side by side are a curious thing,—seated on the same seat, having the same eyes, ears, hands and organs of all sorts, and having pass before their eyes the same objects,—it is wonderful what a variety we shall find in these same reflections!*

*As, for example, Mr. Haley: he thought first of Tom's length, and breadth, and height, and what he would sell for, if he was kept fat and in good case till he got him into market. He thought of how he should make out his gang; he thought of the respective market value of certain supposititious men and women and children who were to compose it, and other kindred topics of the business; then he thought of himself, and how humane he was, that whereas other men chained their "niggers" hand and foot both, he only put fetters on the feet, and left Tom the use of his hands, as long as he behaved well; and he sighed to think how ungrateful human nature was, so that there was even room to doubt whether Tom appreciated his mercies. He had been taken in so by "niggers" whom he had favored; but still he was astonished to consider how good natured he yet remained!*

*As to Tom, he was thinking over some words of an unfashionable old book, which kept running through his head again and again, as follows: "We have here no continuing city, but we seek one to come; wherefore God himself is not ashamed to be called our God; for he hath prepared for us a city." These words of an ancient volume, got up principally by "ignorant and unlearned men," have, through all time, kept up, somehow, a strange sort of power over the minds of poor, simple fellows, like Tom. They stir up the soul from its depths, and rouse, as with trumpet call, courage, energy, and enthusiasm, where before was only the blackness of despair.*

**From Harriet Beecher Stowe, Uncle Tom's Cabin: or, Life among the Lowly, 1852.**

---

unknown to the men whose support he now urgently required. Unaware of Lincoln's matchless political skill, many Republicans thought he should take advice from men like Seward, his Secretary of State, whose leadership had been proved, or even Salmon P. Chase, Lincoln's new Secretary of the Treasury.

On the day of his inauguration, Lincoln suddenly dispelled the air of ineffectuality that had clung to him from the time of his inglorious arrival in Washington. He pledged that he would maintain the Union, that he would use his office "to hold, occupy, and possess property, and places belonging to the federal government." But he promised not to begin hostilities. The South must decide the "momentous issue of civil war." In a passionate appeal to the patriotism of old, Lincoln voiced his moving hope that "the mystic chords of memory . . . will yet swell the chorus of the Union, when again touched, as surely they will be, by the better angels of our nature." Though his speech was eloquent, and peaceful in intent, it was firm. As one historian has remarked, there was "a clank of metal" in it. The testing time was near.

**Fort Sumter.** On that same inauguration day, Lincoln learned for the first time that Major Anderson had nearly exhausted his supplies. Forced to choose in haste between surrendering the fort and sending supplies, Lincoln found himself with the initiative, despite his inauguration promise.

Lincoln's new Cabinet gave him advice that reflected the political past of its members. At first only Montgomery Blair, the new Postmaster General, and Salmon P. Chase, Secretary of the Treasury, favored sending supplies. Former Jacksonian Democrats, they undoubtedly remembered the old General's style of dealing with South Carolina in the nullification crisis (see p. 219). The counselors of caution were headed by Seward, who feared that forceful provisioning of Sumter would push the border states to secession. He had on his own authority promised Confederate commissioners in Washington that the government would not reinforce the garrison. Lincoln hesitated briefly, but Seward's view was declining in the Cabinet. The President hit upon his own formula.

Lincoln informed Governor F. W. Pickens of South Carolina that he would try to provision Fort

**A Southern editor on secession**

Sumter but that he would send no troops without notice, unless of course South Carolina attacked first. He had shifted the decision to Jefferson Davis. Also anxious to avoid bloodshed, Davis instructed General P. G. T. Beauregard, in command in Charleston, to ask Major Anderson to state when he would evacuate the fort and to fire only if Anderson refused to set a time.

Major Anderson replied, through three aides-de-camp Beauregard had sent to inquire, that he would leave Sumter by noon on April 15, "should I not receive prior to that time controlling instructions from my government or additional supplies." The aides-de-camp took action without reporting to Beauregard. At 4:30 on the morning of April 12, the Palmetto Guard

*Stars and Bars above Sumter*

of South Carolina opened fire on the fort. Forty hours of bombardment damaged Sumter badly; on April 13, with his ammunition gone, Anderson surrendered. His garrison left Charleston aboard the relief ships that had been powerless to assist during the engagement.

The Civil War had begun. It would be exactly four years before Anderson would again raise the United States flag, most ceremoniously, over Fort Sumter. But in April of 1861 no one could know how long the war would last or what toll in blood and treasure the conflict would exact.

## Suggestions for reading

### GENERAL

Probably the best introduction to the period covered in this chapter is the early part of J. G. Randall and David Donald, *The Civil War and Reconstruction* (2nd ed., 1961), a learned, judicious, and comprehensive work that is also valuable for its treatment of relevant bibliography. There is a longer account of the years 1854–61, distinguished for its clarity, scope, and the movement of its prose, in the latter part of Allan Nevins, *Ordeal of the Union*, 2 vols. (1947), and its sequel, *The Emergence of Lincoln*, 2 vols. (1950). Of equal importance for the period from 1856, and especially significant for its interpretation of politics and the political process, is R. F. Nichols, *The Disruption of American Democracy** (1948). There are other important points of view in A. O. Craven, *The Coming of the Civil War** (1942); H. H. Simms, *A Decade of Sectional Controversy* (1942); and D. L. Dumond, *Antislavery Origins of the Civil War in the United States** (1939). Bruce Catton, *The Coming Fury** (1961), is a spirited narrative.

### THE KANSAS-NEBRASKA ACT AND ITS AFTERMATH

A major concern of the general works cited above, the Kansas-Nebraska Act, receives special analysis in J. C. Malin, *The Nebraska Question, 1852–1854* (1953), and in a splendid essay, R. F. Nichols, "The Kansas-Nebraska Act: A Century of Historiography," *Mississippi Valley Historical Review*, XLIII, 2 (1956). On the aftermath of the act, P. W. Gates, *Fifty Million Acres: Conflicts Over Kansas Land Policy, 1854–1890** (1954), is of major significance, as are two studies of John Brown: J. C. Malin, *John Brown and the Legend of Fifty-Six* (1942), and the essay on that disturbed figure in C. V. Woodward, *The Burden of Southern History** (1960). The best modern biography of John Brown is Stephen Oates, *To Purge This Land with Blood** (1970). Two other recent works are Truman Nelson, *The Old Man: John Brown at Harper's Ferry* (1973), and R. O. Boyer, *The Legend of John Brown: A Biography and History* (1973). For the views of American blacks on Brown, see B. A. Quarles, *Allies for Freedom* (1974).

On Northern attitudes toward the operation of the Fugitive Slave Act, see S. W. Campbell, *The Slave Catchers** (1968). Eric Foner, *Free Soil, Free Labor, Free Men** (1970), is the best single analysis of the ideas of the Republican party. A. W. Crandall describes the birth and growth of the new party in *The Early History of the Republican Party, 1853–1861* (1947), and G. G. Van Deusen, *William Henry Seward* (1967), traces the development of Republicanism in New York State through the lives of individuals. The same is done for Massachusetts in M. B. Duberman, *Charles Francis Adams** (1961), and David Donald, *Charles Sumner and the Coming of the Civil War* (1960). The latter contains a brilliant analysis of Sumner and his controversial caning. For a study of the development of the new party in an area where ethno-cultural factors and local issues were more important than the slavery issue, see M. F. Holt, *Forging a Majority: The Republican Party in Pittsburgh, 1848–1860* (1969). J. H. Silbey, in *Transformation of American Politics, 1840–1860** (1967), and R. P. Formisano, in *The Birth of Mass Political Parties* (1971), emphasize local issues also. For background history of the Republicans in the Free Soil movement, see F. J. Blue, *Free Soilers: Third Party Politics, 1848–54* (1973), and J. G. Rayback, *Free Soil: The Election of 1848* (1970). For the racism of the free-soil impulse, consult Eugene Berwanger, *The Frontier Against Slavery** (1967), and Saul Sigelschiffer, *The American Conscience* (1973). On Stephen Douglas see Robert Johannsen, "Stephen A. Douglas and the South," *The Journal of Southern History*, XXXIII, i (1967); for a probing treatment of the Lincoln-Douglas debates see D. E. Fehrenbacher, *Prelude to Greatness: Lincoln in the 1850's** (1962) and Saul Sigelschiffer, *The American Conscience* (1973). Allan Nevins' work mentioned above also includes an

*Available in a paperback edition.

excellent treatment of Douglas. Allen Johnson, *Stephen A. Douglas* (1908), G. F. Milton, *The Eve of Conflict: Stephen A. Douglas and the Needless War* (1934), and G. M. Capers, *Stephen A. Douglas, Defender of the Union** (1959) are important studies of Douglas, but R. W. Johannsen, *Stephen A. Douglas* (1973), is now definitive.

### THE COURT, THE ECONOMY, THE ELECTION

The classic studies of the Dred Scott case appear in two books by C. B. Swisher, *Roger B. Taney* (1935) and *American Constitutional Development* (1943), which can be supplemented with Vincent Hopkins, *Dred Scott's Case** (1951), and, with special profit, relevant sections of the books by Nevins and Nichols cited above. Nevins also handles well the subject of G. W. Van Vleck, *The Panic of 1857: An Analytical Study* (1943). Lincoln's entire life has been studied many times, and all the general studies cited above assign him many pages. The best one to start with is the superb biography by B. P. Thomas, *Abraham Lincoln* (1952). Fehrenbacher's work, mentioned above, is especially helpful for the 1850s. A. J. Beveridge, *Abraham Lincoln, 1809–1858,* 2 vols. (1928), remains useful, and R. H. Luthin, *The First Lincoln Campaign* (1944), has instructive depth. The one-volume edition of Carl Sandburg, *Abraham Lincoln: The Prairie Years* (1929), is a beautiful interpretation of Lincoln the man.

### SECESSION AND WAR

Among the many accounts of secession, three of the best are Nevins, cited above; A. O. Craven, *The Growth of Southern Nationalism 1848–1861* (1953); and R. A. Wooster, *The Secession Conventions of the South* (1962). More recently, W. L. Barney has contributed two relevant works, *The Road to Secession** (1972) and *The Secessionist Impulse: Alabama and Mississippi in 1860* (1974). Also recent is W. C. Wright, *The Secession Movement in the Middle Atlantic States* (1973). Two older works are still admirable for their scope and form: D. L. Dumond, *The Secession Movement, 1860–1861* (1931), and U. B. Phillips, *The Course of the South to Secession** (1939). Of special significance is David Potter, *The South and the Sectional Conflict** (1969), the distillation of many years of study by one of the South's great historians. Of equal importance are two volumes of essays by C. V. Woodward, the one cited above and *American Counterpoint** (1971), which include many pieces of special interest to students of the South's movement toward independence. For an interpretation of the Southern position on the eve of the war, see Arthur Bestor, "State Sovereignty and Slavery: A Reinterpretation of Proslavery Constitutional Doctrine," *Journal of Illinois State Historical Society,* LIV (1961). Challenging, but important for complete understanding of the political struggle, is T. B. Alexander, *Sectional Stress and Party Strength: A Study of Roll-Call Voting Patterns in the United States House of Representatives 1836–1860* (1967). There are two very important and somewhat conflicting analyses of the secession winter of 1860–61 in David Potter, *Lincoln and His Party in the Secession Crisis 1860–61** (1942), and K. M. Stampp, *And the War Came: The North and the Secession Crisis, 1860–61** (1950). A lively account of Lincoln as President-elect is W. E. Baringer, *A House Dividing* (1945). On the Fort Sumter confrontation see R. N. Current, *Lincoln and the First Shot** (1963). For a spirited scholarly debate on the secession crisis, G. H. Knoles, ed. *The Crisis of the Union, 1860–61** (1965), is very good reading.

---

*Available in a paperback edition.

# CHAPTER 14

# Civil war

The Civil War tested the strength and exposed the weakness of Americans as nothing before or since has done. It was a savage contest between conflicting ideas of liberty and justice, waged with weapons far more advanced than were the means of defense against them. The rest of the world, appalled at what Americans were doing to one another, watched with fascination this modern war of ideals and technology.

Because the military contest was long and costly, fighting it severely challenged the resources of both North and South. One signal result of meeting that challenge was a great expansion of government, at all levels, in both nations. Raising enormous armies, paying, transporting, and equipping them, manufacturing munitions, controlling the press, suppressing disloyalty, and administering justice in the many areas where the war was unpopular, required large government. For just this reason, federal power grew more rapidly than that of the states, and precedents were laid for the evolution of the modern state, with its characteristic central authority in public finance and the administration of justice. This was not the result of grasping central authority, but a by-product of necessity. Yet many Northern citizens objected strenuously, resenting conscription of soldiers, the suspension of the habeas corpus privilege, and the expansion of federal judicial processes into local communities. In the Confederacy, where the state-rights philosophy was at the foundation of the government, such measures had severe effects on morale and the will to fight. But in both North and South the requirements of war chipped away at the old state-federal relationship, and a new nationalism grew in its place.

The signal social result of the war was the emancipation of four and a quarter million slaves, the largest such liberation undertaken by any government. Lincoln took this step under the war power,

and as an act of war, without the nobility of language that would better have pleased abolitionists of principle. The immediate condition of the freedmen was not greatly improved, and was even worse, in many instances, for some years after the war. Nowhere were the freedmen treated as equal citizens, and they were very poor. Could the emancipation then be called a social revolution? Even though the ultimate consequences of the step were slow in coming, blacks themselves were jubilant in their freedom from the start. The difference between freedom and slavery seemed a revolution indeed. For the South the economic effects were vast, and for the slave-owning class in particular the loss of their property had far-reaching consequences in political and social life as well as economic power.

Lincoln and the Congress had declared that the war would be fought only to preserve the Union, and that the "domestic institutions" of the states would not be disturbed. Others knew better from the beginning. James L. Pettigru, a staunch Unionist lawyer from Charleston, remarked on learning that South Carolina had fired on the *Star of the West* that slavery would not last five years. Many abolitionists shared that understanding, as did many blacks, both freemen and slaves. Even the followers of William Lloyd Garrison dropped their traditional pacifism and joined in hearty support of a war they believed must grow into a war on slavery.

In 1860 only a few realized a new nationalism and emancipation were to be the results of the war, for only a few foresaw how long the war would last. Northern leaders underestimated the commitment of the Southerners to their new nation, while Southern leaders underestimated the Northerners' attachment to the old Union and their economic and human resources as well. Only four years of fighting would banish those illusions.

*Union depot, City Point, Virginia*

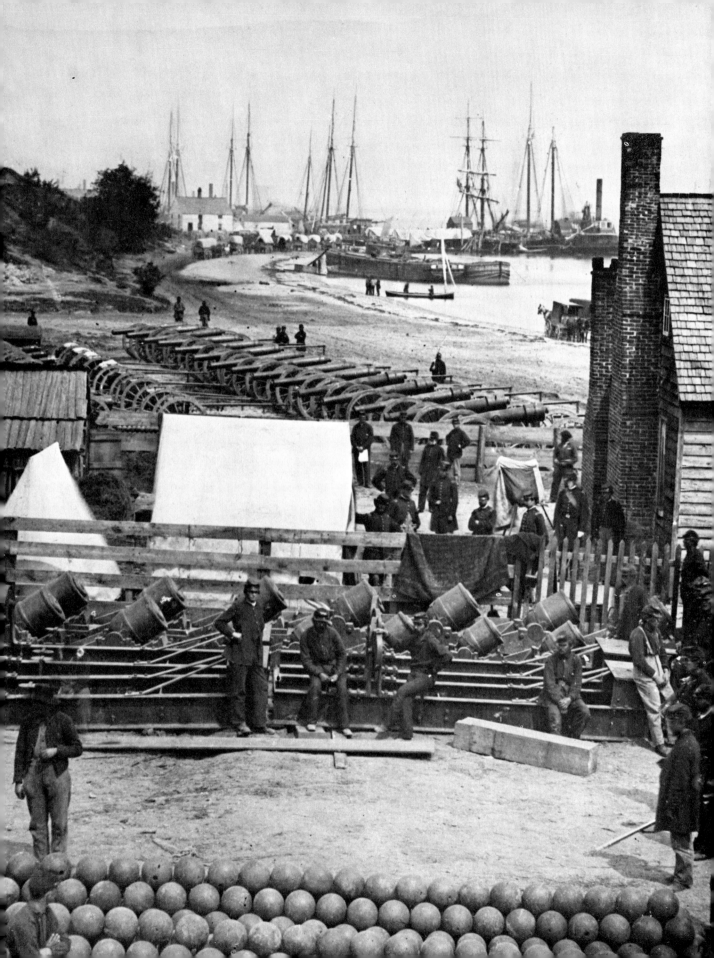

# The struggle for the border states

**The border states and the call to arms.** To most of the nation the strength of those conflicting commitments would be revealed only in battle. But in the vast border region that stretched from Delaware on the Atlantic westward to Missouri, approximately a third of the country then organized into states, it was tested within days after the attack on Fort Sumter. On April 15, 1861, President Lincoln called on the state governors to provide him with seventy-five thousand militiamen for ninety days' service, in order to enforce the law where it was opposed "by combinations too powerful to be suppressed" by ordinary judicial processes. What part would the border states choose to play in the suppression of these "combinations"? Within each of the border states there were historical forces working for union and forces working for secession. The most concrete and formidable on the side of secession was slavery.

The border states had to make their decisions in a cross fire of patriotic enthusiasm that swept the North and the Confederacy. As the South took up arms, the Confederate government sent emissaries to the border states to encourage them to secede. The governors and the people of the North sprang to the defense of the flag that had been fired on at Charleston. Most Northerners of both parties agreed with Lincoln's view that secession was illegal. "The central

idea pervading this struggle," Lincoln said, "is the necessity of proving that popular government is not an absurdity. We must settle this question now, whether, in a free government, the minority have the right to break up the government whenever they choose." Lincoln was to state that thought more eloquently two years later when he dedicated the Union cemetery on the battlefield at Gettysburg, Pennsylvania; it was his philosophical justification for the war.

For the moment, however, most people in the border states declined to take part in forcing the seceding states to return to the Union, and a second wave of secession followed. Virginia seceded on April 17, despite nearly unanimous opposition in the state's western counties. This reversal of an antisecessionist vote taken earlier influenced the decision of other border states; Arkansas, Tennessee, and North Carolina soon followed Virginia into the Confederacy. North Carolina based its action on the oldest American justification for war: the right of revolution. Only Delaware, of all the slave states, was safe for the Union.

**Maryland, Missouri, and Kentucky.** Everything now seemed to hang on the action of Maryland, Missouri, and Kentucky, which faltered between closely matched forces. Lincoln saved those states from secession by a combination of diplomacy and force that was more or less effective depending on how well he understood the Unionist leaders of the wavering states and on the kind of advice they gave him.

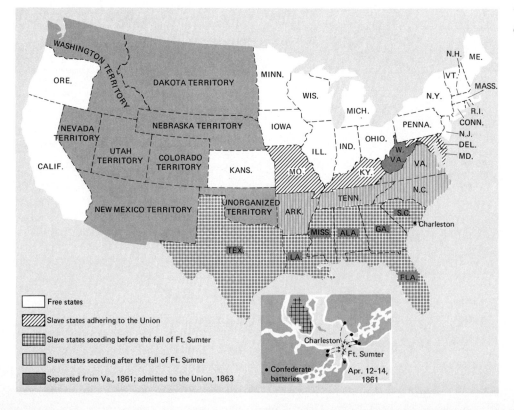

The alignment of states in 1861

Free states

Slave states adhering to the Union

Slave states seceding before the fall of Ft. Sumter

Slave states seceding after the fall of Ft. Sumter

Separated from Va., 1861; admitted to the Union, 1863

On April 19, only a week after Sumter, Maryland pitched directly into crisis. An angry mob in Baltimore, stirred up by pro-Confederate newspapers, attacked the troops of the Sixth Massachusetts Infantry as they changed trains on their way to Washington. Citizens and soldiers were killed in a riot. For more than a week the capital of the United States was set at defiance by a hostile city. On April 27, Lincoln instituted martial law in Baltimore, suspended the writ of habeas corpus, and jailed overt Confederate sympathizers. An ordinance of secession was then defeated in the Maryland legislature, partly because it convened in Frederick, in the northwest part of the state where Unionism was strong, and partly because the delegates from the southern counties en route to the session were impounded at Fort McHenry in Baltimore. Those delegates favored secession. In spite of the harsh measures taken, and in spite of the sympathy for the Confederacy that lived on in Maryland throughout the war, the state was stabilized for the Union within a few months.

Matters were not so well managed in Missouri, where secessionist sentiment was strong and where Unionist leaders precipitated a crisis before they could muster popular support. The secessionist governor, Claiborne Jackson, succeeded in getting a convention, but it refused to adopt an ordinance of secession. The state militia, which was under Governor Jackson's command, was stationed in St. Louis, the site of an important federal arsenal. Francis Blair, then a United States representative from Missouri, surmising that Jackson might attack the arsenal, persuaded Lincoln to let him create a "home guard" to defend the Union position in Missouri. Lincoln agreed, probably because Francis Blair's brother Montgomery, Lincoln's Postmaster General, had persuaded him that the step was essential. The home guard, composed largely of German immigrants, was thrown against Governor Jackson's militia by a hotheaded young captain in the regular army, Nathaniel Lyon. Caught by surprise, the militia surrendered without a fight. But the sight of the Germans marching the militiamen through the streets of St. Louis so enraged the populace that the home guard was mobbed, and many citizens and soldiers were killed in the ensuing melee. Those events alienated even staunch Unionists. Approximately thirty thousand Missourians ultimately fought for the South, and there were Missouri representatives in the Confederate Congress. Until the Battle of Pea Ridge in March 1862, Missouri was not reliable for the Union, and even afterward there was intermittent guerrilla warfare in the state. No state emerged from the war with deeper scars or more bitter memories. Greater patience would have permitted latent Union sentiment to develop among Missourians, and a painful heritage might have been

*Baltimore, an angry mob*

avoided that made Reconstruction in Missouri in some respects more difficult than in the former Confederate states themselves.

Lincoln understood better the Unionists of his native Kentucky. Sympathies in the state were hopelessly divided, even within families. Still, the Unionist leaders managed, with Lincoln's help, to scotch secession in spite of a pro-Confederate governor supported by nearly half the citizenry. The Kentucky Unionists simply called for neutrality, knowing that they would be defeated if they asked for firm support of the Union and cooperation with the Union effort to raise an army. A petition demanding neutrality signed by fourteen thousand Kentucky women was presented to the legislature.

Lincoln kept the federal recruiting offices on the Ohio side of the Ohio River and even permitted neutral trade between Kentucky and the South to flourish through the summer. Had Kentucky not been handled so tactfully the Union cause would have suffered; the state was astride a major thoroughfare into the heartland of the Confederacy.

***West Virginia.*** Lincoln capitalized immediately on the divided sympathies of Virginia. In the first months of the war he sent twenty thousand volunteers into western Virginia to secure the lines of the Baltimore & Ohio Railroad. Then, after the Confederates had been driven out of this transmontane region, the federal government began to encourage the separatist feelings of the people, who had long felt themselves neglected by the large landholders and slaveholders of the eastern counties. In November 1861 the western counties formed a government of their own and asked to be admitted to the Union as the state of West Virginia. Congress agreed in 1863. The urgency of securing a route from the East to the Ohio Valley quieted any qualms the members of Congress may have had about the legality of their unprecedented action.

Although Lincoln's border policy was not everywhere successful, he nevertheless retained for the Union by diplomacy or force the key states of Maryland, Missouri, and Kentucky. They were essential to military victory, for they provided easy communica-

*The struggle for the border states*

tions about the periphery of the Confederacy. Moreover, control of those states exposed Tennessee, whose geographic frontier was especially vulnerable, to Union penetration.

A hard economic fact may have counted for even more than Lincoln's tact. By 1860 a dense network of railroads had already developed binding the Middle West, indeed all the states on the Ohio River, with the Northeast. Only a few lines led southward. But secessionist leaders assumed mistakenly that access to the mouth of the Mississippi River was still as important to the trade of the Middle West as ever. Trade still came down the river in seemingly undiminished volume, but the production of raw agricultural products had increased sharply in the 1850s on both sides of the Ohio, and with every year more of those products were rolling eastward on rails, especially over the Chesapeake & Ohio and the Baltimore & Ohio. Even the slave states that remained in the Union benefited from access to the Eastern markets. They soon discovered, even though sympathy for the South remained strong, that being on the periphery of the Union was more profitable than being on the periphery of the Confederacy.

## Two nations prepare for war

**The two sides compared.**  When the war began, each section believed that its own peculiar advantages would bring swift victory. Victory had entirely different meanings for North and South, however, and different imperatives.

The North would have to invade, occupy, and hold hostile places and would have to destroy the armies of an enemy state, while the South would have to block such efforts until its enemies gave up trying. Northern confidence at the outset was based on a preponderance of people and on a superior economic potential for making the tools of war. The North also thought that Southern secession did not have wide popular support, that the majority of Southerners had been hustled out of the Union against their will by arrogant leaders. In that view, the Southern people would soon lose the will to fight.

Southerners, convinced that Northerners would not support a long and costly war to impose their will on an unoffending nation, thought that their independence would be recognized if they gave early evidence of stout determination to defend it in battle. In battle the South would have important advantages. Many of the country's high-ranking military officers were Southern-born, and most of them offered their services to their states. Moreover, the young men of the South could be counted on to fight valiantly in defense of their own soil.

But sober-minded leaders of the South were not relying on the imponderables of gifted military leadership or on the fighting qualities of Southern youth. They were relying instead on an economic advantage they believed to be paramount: the cotton export. As early as March 1858 James Henry Hammond of South Carolina had taunted Congress over the world's dependence on Southern cotton. "No power on earth dares make war upon it. Cotton *is* king." When the war came, the dogged confidence that prompted such bombast led Southerners into a diplomacy aimed at winning British recognition of the Confederacy. With recognition would come the financial aid and moral support that the rebellious colonies had received from France during the American Revolution. Surely France and England would see the advantages they would gain by Southern independence. Direct access to the South's cotton export would benefit mill-owners and workers alike. The British, anticipating free trade in Southern ports, could take the middlemen's profits and the carrying trade from Northern businessmen and shippers. Southern enthusiasts could point out that they were fighting for two ideals characteristic of nineteenth-century revolutions: national determination and liberty. In their view of liberty they forgot the slaves, of course; but so did the Northerners, who denied repeatedly, until September 1862, that emancipation was a goal of the war. What, asked the South, would deter Europe from recognizing the Confederacy?

**Northern advantages.**  With cotton and the spirit of nationalism on their side, Southern leaders tended to discount the North's formidable economic advantages. Four-fifths of the nation's manufacturing was located in the North, two-thirds of its railroad track, three-quarters of the wealth produced. The share of the wealth produced by the South was largely agricultural, but even that did not mean that the South would be better able to feed her armies. The Middle West had supplied the South with much hay and grain before the war, while the South concentrated on producing staple crops for export. Except for rice and corn, the North and West produced far more grain than the South. Although some Southerners had endeavored to diversify their agricultural output, the war caught them frantically importing stocks of bacon and pork from the North. Moreover, the Northern population was more than three times as large as the white population of the South in 1860. Finally, Southerners were primarily an agricultural people, unaccustomed to factory work. On the eve of the war William T. Sherman had warned a Southern friend that ". . . in all history no nation of mere agriculturalists ever made a successful war against mechanics." If the South failed to win victory before the Northern economy could be fully geared to wartime production, its troubles would multiply and all would be lost. But few expected the war would last that long.

**The South—a new nation.** To survive as a nation, the Confederacy had to create a viable new government with new institutions, and that government in turn had to persuade the people that it could dispense justice, secure internal peace, and fight a successful war for independence. The Constitution of the Confederate states imitated, in its main structure, the Constitution of 1787. Most Southerners respected the old Constitution and claimed that trouble had arisen not from basic flaws in it but from wrong interpretation of certain clauses. The signal departures of the new document from the old were designed to prevent such misinterpretation in the future. Those changes also showed that the new government was the product of a conservative revolt. Far from being reluctant to mention slavery, as the Founding Fathers had been, the Confederate constitution-makers, who met in February 1861 at Montgomery, gave the peculiar institution every conceivable guarantee short of the restoration of the Atlantic slave trade, which they forbade. The mobility of slave property within the Confederacy was assured through the right of sojourn and transit throughout the Confederacy. The Confederate Congress was obliged to secure the rights of slaveholders in the territories, and the dominant influence of slaveholders in the legislative branch was assured by the retention of the three-fifths ratio for congressional representation (see p. 126). The admission of new states was made more difficult; protective tariffs and appropriations for internal improvements were made unconstitutional. The President had power to veto individual parts of an appropriations bill, and there was no general-welfare clause. The new Constitution plainly recognized the sovereignty of the states, though it avoided an explicit endorsement of the right of secession.

**Jefferson Davis.** The Montgomery convention, composed largely of conservatives, not radical extremists, passed over fiery secessionists for the Presidency and chose Jefferson Davis of Mississippi instead. Although Davis represented the new West, where men could make a fortune and become gentlemen planters in a generation, and though he himself had been born of yeoman stock, he was an instinctive aristocrat. He was also sensitive to criticism, perhaps a lingering mark of his family's rapid rise in the world. Davis, the intellectual in politics, set about forming an ideal Cabinet in which all the states of the Confederacy would be represented. Though his intention was

to convince people of his fairness, he managed to create a curious assembly of modest talents who were not always cast in the roles they knew best. His Cabinet members were constantly changing; there were fourteen appointees in six posts over four years, including six Secretaries of War. The ablest and most trusted of all Davis' advisers, Judah P. Benjamin, held three offices in turn—Attorney General, Secretary of War, and Secretary of State.

A responsible public servant, Davis consulted regularly with his Cabinet members and supported them loyally when the press attacked them. Other assets included a great capacity for hard work and a strong background in military affairs. For Davis, as the chief of the losing side, it must be said that his character and abilities have often been judged unfairly and too freely regarded as a major cause of Confederate defeat. It could well be that no one had the ability to meet the challenge, and Davis had many of the personal qualities that his own society valued most. But it still must be said that the Confederacy did not reap the full benefit that Davis' experience in military matters seemed to promise. As the primary formulator of strategy, Davis must be held responsible for the army's defensive policy, which was maintained for the first two years of the war and changed only when it was too late. The policy had many advantages, and one insurmountable flaw. True, it is cheaper in men and materiel to fight a defensive war; and, in the instance of the Confederacy, a defensive war was better calculated to make the most, politically, of the sympathy that many Northerners felt for the South's simple wish to be left alone. And yet the fact remained that the South was conducting a revolutionary war, however conservative in its goals, and therefore required decisive victories quickly. Gambling that the North would decide to quit surely involved too grave a risk; for if the North decided not to quit, the South would be doomed to an extended contest with diminishing reserves against an established government that would grow in war-making power. In time Davis changed his strategy, but it was too late. Davis was also tardy in coordinating the command system of his army, and he never did it well. He left too much to the discretion of departmental commanders, assuming that they understood the local situation better. This indulgence seemed necessary at first, considering the vast expanse of the Confederacy, but it shortly caused problems by making it more difficult to make full use of interior lines in order to coordinate the armies. In other respects Davis seemed not to understand the problems of the western armies, or indeed the great vulnerability and importance of Tennessee to the Confederacy.

In politics Davis had grave problems. Although he was at first successful in getting his legislation

*Two nations prepare for war*

through Congress, he soon found himself hamstrung by the bickering lawmakers. His failures derived not from a lack of respect for Congress' privileges, but from a lack of tact in dealing with legislators and their greed for patronage. He gained little, therefore, by asking Congress to *permit* him to suspend the writ of habeas corpus, instead of suspending it on his own authority as Lincoln did, and by steadily respecting the constitutional rights of the states. But the war required nationalizing measures that were in grave conflict with state rights, and Davis often led the way, with Congress following reluctantly. Under the Conscription Act of 1862 a national army was raised, and the government used its authority to manipulate the economy by favoring certain enterprises with draft exemptions and government contracts. Under the War Department it even operated such essential manufacturing concerns as shoe factories, ordnance plants, power works, and mines. But there were limits, and Davis' opponents often combined to frustrate him on issues touching state rights. The Confederacy never developed political parties in the usual sense, but there was an anti-Davis party in Congress strong enough to mount vicious attacks in the press and to enact thirty-nine bills he felt obliged to veto. Lincoln vetoed only three.

Davis' opposition centered in the diminutive figure of Alexander H. Stephens, the Vice President, who had abandoned a career as a staunch Unionist to become a reluctant secessionist. Stephens, brilliant and acerb, finding that his talents were not absorbed by his weak office, turned them to obstructionism. It was ironic that the alleged violation of state rights, the ostensible philosophy of the secession, should have become the most potent argument of Stephens and his adherents in Congress in their running attack on the Davis Administration.

Had Davis understood the skillful deployment of patronage as well as Lincoln did, he too might have divided his enemies and developed support in Congress. Lacking it, only popularity with the people could have helped him rule. This, too, escaped him. To those who knew him well Davis was an ardent patriot, not cold and passionless. But he could not convey his love of country to the people of the Confederacy. "A crippling shyness . . . banked his passion," wrote one historian, "and left him forever a strangely muffled man."

**The South prepares for war.** Raising and maintaining the armies required by a modern war imposed grave pressures on the Confederacy's political philosophy of state rights, local liberties, and restraints on central authority. The Conscription Act of 1862, which drafted white men between eighteen and thirty-five for three years' service, passed the Confederate Congress by a substantial majority only because it was regarded as essential to victory. The draft age was subsequently extended to forty-five, and eventually, as the manpower shortage became acute, all males between seventeen and fifty were subject to the draft. Powerful voices spoke out against conscription

*The South prepares: Georgian Light Guards, 1861*

as a violation of personal freedom, and the inequitable terms of the act fed hostility to the draft as the war went on. Alterations and expansions of the law did not much improve it or placate its critics. The poor found it unjust that a man who could pay the price could send a substitute, and the long list of exemptions made it easy for all but the poorest and least powerful to avoid service altogether. The most demoralizing provision exempted from the draft one white man on a plantation that had twenty or more slaves. Though designed to defend the nation against insurrection and to ensure a steady supply of food, this exemption stirred up latent class antagonisms among whites. Actually very few men were exempted under its terms, but it came to be known among the common people as "the twenty-nigger law." Many a young soldier, deciding against "a rich man's war and a poor man's fight," deserted.

Probably three hundred thousand men, just under a third of all the men who served in the Confederate armies, joined because of the Conscription Act. Some of them were drafted, but many volunteered in order to avoid the onus of being drafted. The draft would have been more effective had it not been for the obstructionism of several governors who made a fetish of state rights. Georgia's Governor Joseph E. Brown, for one, enrolled ten thousand men in the state militia before they could be drafted, exempted from conscription large numbers of civil servants, and insisted that Georgia troops be officered by Georgians.

Despite the resistance of state righters, the armies of the Confederacy increased in size until the summer of 1863, when on the eve of the Gettysburg campaign 261,000 men were reported ready for action. Thereafter the Southern armies dwindled slowly, for there was no way of replacing casualties. To make matters worse, the Northern armies grew steadily until the end of the war, when they had a three-to-one advantage.

An enormous aid to the North was the quickening of immigration during the last two years of the war. New arrivals received strong inducements to enlist. The enrollment of black soldiers from 1863 on also contributed to the manpower of the Northern armies. The South consistently rejected this means of raising troops until the last days of the war, when provision was made for a draft "irrespective of color." That law stipulated, however, that emancipation would follow military service only with the approval of the slave's owner and the state legislature.

Financing the war exposed the weakness of the state-rights philosophy as surely as had the recruitment process. Beginning in 1861 without a treasury, the Confederate government promptly passed a direct tax on property. The tax could be paid by the states

themselves, however, and most state governments chose to do so by issuing and selling their own bonds. The tax produced a poor return of $18 million. Further, it did not reach individual property-holders, where it would have damped inflationary spending. Meanwhile the Confederate government was also issuing bonds.

Such practices would not have been crippling in a short war, but continual borrowing in preference to taxing boosted inflation to a perilous level by late 1863. The poor, whose income lagged behind the cost of food and other necessities, steadily lost enthusiasm for the war. The primary cause of inflation was the flood of paper money and treasury notes issued by the Confederate government, by individual states, and even by cities to pay interest on bonds, pay troops, and purchase needed supplies. As prices rose, flour sold at $300 a barrel and men's shoes at $125 a pair. The Confederate government was hardly more timid or cowardly about taxation than other new governments have been, and somehow it managed to feed and transport enormous armies against tremendous odds for four years. Still, the misery inflation engendered eroded the South's will to resist.

One effort to circumvent inflation and still feed the armies was the "tax in kind," which allowed military authorities to requisition foodstuff directly from the farmers and to pay them a price fixed by the government. Since this price usually was well below the open-market price, and since the practice was widely abused by officers making requisitions, farmers contrived to evade the tax.

Although many Southerners, perhaps half, had been reluctant to secede from the Union, they went to war with high morale. Believing secession constitutional even while questioning its wisdom, most were unified behind a war for independence after the North determined to put down secession as rebellion. Their ultimate disillusionment came, not through a change of heart, but with the lengthening casualty lists and the failure of their economy to support a long war against a burgeoning industrial power.

**The North prepares for war.** Abraham Lincoln, confident of his own judgment, appointed what was probably the ablest Cabinet ever assembled by any President. In making his selections he considered talent, but he was especially aware of the need to balance factions and to repay political debts. He knew he would have to make the members of his Cabinet function as a unit in a time of national peril. Few Presidents have understood the use of patronage as well as Lincoln did. Few have needed to, for the Republicans were a new party that had never been obliged to merge discrete factions into a united administration under the public gaze.

As his Secretary of State, Lincoln named William Seward, whom the Republicans had regarded as too radical to qualify as their presidential nominee in 1860; as a Cabinet member, however, Seward advised caution in interfering with slavery. For his Secretary of the Treasury, Lincoln picked Salmon P. Chase, a Democrat whose views on slavery had propelled him into the Republican party. Both Seward and Chase had served as state governors—and both had presidential ambitions. Lincoln recognized their ability, but he knew too that they brought to his Cabinet the potential for discord. Chase, convinced that he would have made a better chief executive than Lincoln, never became an altogether selfless follower of the President. Seward, after vainly trying to maneuver Lincoln into a foreign war that he believed would bring the South back to the old flag, surrendered to Lincoln's leadership and became an excellent subordinate.

To pay off a campaign debt, Lincoln installed Simon Cameron as Secretary of War. That was an error. Cameron proved inept and was even suspected of venality. Lincoln replaced him in 1862 with the eccentric and brilliant Edwin M. Stanton, who became one of the most dedicated of Lincoln's Cabinet members. Stanton, a hard-working wizard, deserved much of the credit for the eventual victory of Northern arms. Gideon Welles of Connecticut was Secretary of the Navy; Edward Bates, whom some Republicans had pushed as a presidential candidate, was Attorney General; and Montgomery Blair of Maryland was Postmaster General.

Despite their disputes and personal animosities, Lincoln elicited the best from his talented advisers. He averted several crises, usually involving Chase and Seward. But the only major shake-up occurred in 1864, when Lincoln at last accepted Chase's resignation and replaced him with William Pitt Fessenden. Chase became Chief Justice of the Supreme Court of the United States. To soothe Chase's radical supporters, Lincoln also permitted Montgomery Blair, a conservative on slavery and emancipation, to resign. The President's skill in balancing his Cabinet and in seeing that the patronage was distributed to the satisfaction of senators and congressmen was essential to the development of the Republican party and to the teamwork that won the war.

Raising the armies, putting the economy on a war footing, and determining how to pay for the war were the Administration's first tasks. There was some bungling at first because of the illusion that the war would be over soon. Fortunately for the Union, ample resources allowed time for trial and error, and many of the worst difficulties were resolved during the first summer and fall. Though clearly stronger than the South in human and material resources, the North at first squandered that advantage in confusion, dissension, delay, and greed. Inadequate organization complicated the problems of the senior military officers, who were on the whole second-rate men. Before the war ended the Union had found and developed great commanders—Grant, Thomas, Sheridan, and Sherman—but in the beginning the military leaders frittered away the energies of powerful armies in sorry and haphazard campaigns. Even sorrier was the behavior of war profiteers who overcharged the government for shoddy goods: blankets that disintegrated in the rain, unwholesome meat, inferior rifles, and ships with leaky bottoms.

The first year of the war was marked by conflicts of authority and initiative between the state governors and the Administration in Washington. When Lincoln called for the first seventy-five thousand militiamen to come to the defense of the capital, Northern governors threw themselves with energetic confusion into their traditional role of raising volunteers. The governor of Ohio sent so many troops to Washington so fast that he lost count. Raising troops in the first flush of patriotic enthusiasm was not difficult, but soon the governors had problems with recruiting. At first the War Department in Washington undertook to reimburse the governors for their expenses in equipping the soldiers, but this scheme, inefficient and subject to graft, had to be abandoned. With the best will in the world, the state governments failed to cope effectively with the demands of war, and many of their traditional responsibilities devolved upon the national Administration. The result was a shift of power away from the states, the very shift that the Confederate states, under the same pressures, resisted so stubbornly.

Realizing sooner than most of his advisers that the Union was in for a long war and that the seventy-five thousand volunteers who reported in April for three months' service would not suffice, Lincoln stretched his constitutional authority as commander in chief. He authorized an increase in the size of the regular army, a power reserved to Congress under the Constitution, and called for forty-two thousand volunteers for three years in the national service. When Congress reconvened in July, the President asked for indemnification for the action he had taken. Congress granted it promptly. By establishing that large volunteer armies would be enlisted for long-term service, Lincoln averted the immediate problem of being left without troops once the three-month militiamen had gone home.

The overwhelming majority of soldiers who served in the Union armies were volunteers encouraged to enlist by generous bounties paid by the federal government, state governments, and local communities. Those bounties were attractive to the poor and

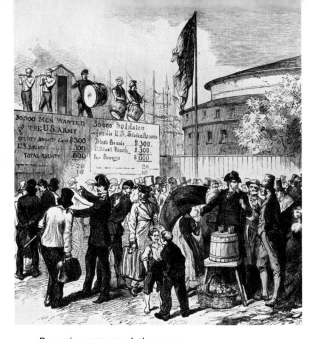

Bounties attracted the poor

the unemployed, especially during the first year of the war. But after the military setbacks of 1862 even generous bounties failed to attract enough volunteers, and in March 1863 the United States passed the first national draft law. Men between twenty and forty-five were subject to conscription for three years' service. There were a few occupational exemptions, and men who were the sole support of dependent families were not obliged to serve. The most detested feature of the law permitted a man to avoid service by hiring a substitute to serve in his stead or by paying a flat fee of $300 to the government. This class legislation was especially resented in areas where the war was unpopular. In July 1863, rioters protesting the draft law disrupted New York City for a week. The mob vented its vengeance on the unoffending blacks of the city, hating them most illogically for the government's adoption of emancipation as a war aim, and supposing there would otherwise be no need for a draft of soldiers. A Colored Orphan Home was burned, and hundreds of blacks were beaten, attacked, tormented, or otherwise wounded. Draft resistance, sometimes violent, was not limited to New York, but the outbreak there in July was the worst of all the domestic riots, for over 128 persons were killed, the overwhelming majority of them black.

Although only forty-six thousand men were actually drafted under the Conscription Act, the measure promoted volunteer enlistments, especially in communities anxious to avoid imposing the draft on a resentful populace. Each state was divided into enrollment districts and was assigned a certain draft quota from time to time. If those districts could provide their quota in volunteers, they could avoid the conscription process and the troubles Governor Seymour

of New York had encountered. In any case, soldiers preferred the status of volunteer to that of conscript, especially if they could pocket a good bounty. State governors and local authorities, eager to avoid recourse to the draft machinery, borrowed money to raise bounties as high as necessary to fill their quotas. In parts of Illinois the total bounty came to more than $1,000, and in New York a volunteer could get $375 over and above the federal bounty, which was $300 in 1864. Those fat sums led to an abuse known as "bounty-jumping," whereby a man would enlist, desert, reenlist in another district, and collect another bounty.

Yet another abuse followed from the Conscription Act's provision that granted state recruiters the right to go into occupied areas of the South to enlist black soldiers from among former slaves. Recruiting officers exploited that opportunity shamelessly. The poor health of many freedmen, their ignorance in dealing with recruiters, and their gullibility permitted the unscrupulous recruiters to carry people off from their plantations, pocket the "bounty" provided by their state, and give the freedmen over to the army.

**Northern finances.**  Although the North possessed the industrial wealth for fighting a modern war, the government was slow in discovering how to tap that wealth. The Lincoln Administration resorted to the same means of raising money that the Confederacy used: taxation, borrowing, and the issue of paper money. But the North, unlike the South, eventually succeeded with its financial experiments. The assumption that the war would be short at first led the government into the same errors the Confederacy made. The most serious mistake of Treasury Secretary Chase was failing to recommend high taxes to meet a substantial proportion of the government's bills. Such taxes would have lessened reliance on borrowing and printing money, in itself inflationary, and would have reduced the inflationary buying power of workers, farmers, and managers who were profiting from war-created demands. As it turned out, only a small fraction of the war bill was paid through taxes, and the North, like the South, was subjected to demoralizing inflation.

By far the largest source of money was borrowing. Bankers bought most of the bond issues, the mainstay of the war chest, driving the best bargain they could with Secretary Chase. Chase, however, disliked selling the government's bonds below par, or for long terms, or at high interest. As a result of his struggle with the bankers, bonds were issued from time to time with different dates of maturity and at different rates. In a significant innovation in public finance, Chase enlisted Jay Cooke, a wealthy Philadelphia banker, in a campaign to sell to the general public bonds redeemable in not less than five years or more than twenty—the famous "five-twenties." The Treasury Department had never before used the sale of government bonds to increase popular support of a war.

Early in 1862 the Treasury Department realized that a financial crisis was at hand. The war was costing the government nearly $1.75 million a day, Chase complained, and the Treasury was empty. While expenses were growing, dwindling imports reduced the government's intake from customs, formerly its main source of money. At last Secretary Chase reluctantly asked Congress to make the government's paper money legal tender for all debts, public and private. That request was a bitter step for a former Jacksonian Democrat with hard-money principles. Congress responded with the Legal Tender Act of 1862, which created the "greenbacks." That act was the first phase of a comprehensive plan for financing the war, a plan with far-reaching implications for state rights in the North as well as for the policy of hard money.

Making paper currency legal tender added to inflation, but it solved the immediate crisis by promptly putting money into the Treasury. Congress went further by passing the Internal Revenue Act, which imposed a tax on incomes over $800—the first income tax in United States history. The act also taxed manufactures and imposed sales taxes and license fees. Although the legislation met little of the cost of the war, it set a comprehensive precedent for a national system of taxation.

The National Banking Act of 1863, in part a further effort to stimulate the sale of war bonds, required all national banks chartered under the act to invest one-third of their capital in federal bonds and to deposit those bonds with the Treasury Department. The banks could then issue bank notes, which would serve as legal tender, up to 90 percent of the market value of the deposited bonds. The banks were also subjected to regular federal inspection to protect depositors. In 1865 Congress brought most of the banks chartered by the states into the national system by imposing a prohibitive 10 percent tax on their bank notes.

The net result of all those financial measures was to enhance the power of the national government at the expense of the state governments. The Legal Tender Act put into circulation $50 million and created the basis for a national currency.

## The course of arms

**The first offensive: Bull Run.** What strategy was Lincoln to follow in destroying the Confederate government and its armies? General Winfield Scott, the aging commanding general of the Union Army, had developed a long-range plan calling for a close blockade of the Confederate coastline and for "containment" of the Confederacy all along its land frontier. An amphibious expedition was to open up the Mississippi Valley, restoring the Middle West's traditional access to the ocean and cutting off Texas, Arkansas, and Louisiana from the rest of the Confederacy. Then separate armies were to strike inland from the Atlantic and the Gulf of Mexico, progressively fragmenting and ultimately destroying the Southern nation, as a giant serpent, the anaconda, might. General Scott was seventy-four, no longer well, but not unwise. Newspaper strategists eager for military action derided his plan for the slow, remorseless constriction of the enemy. Yet the formula for victory that Union generals eventually stumbled upon after many futile engagements coincided with General Scott's "Anaconda Plan" in all essential features except one: before victory, the Confederate armies had to be destroyed.

One part of General Scott's plan won immediate acceptance: on April 19, 1861, Lincoln declared a blockade of the Southern coastline. By taking that action, Lincoln implicitly recognized that a state of belligerency existed, even though he continued to hold that the war was merely an insurrection on the part of individuals. Clearly, a nation does not blockade its own coastline. And nobody knew how the British would react to a blockade that could not be enforced, whether they might choose to remind the United States of its former condemnation of paper blockades (see p. 165). The question was answered on May 13, when the British recognized the Confederates as belligerents. Lincoln's Administration, deeply disappointed, should not have been surprised. England's ruling classes sympathized with the South, and in any case English interests required a formula that would permit Confederate vessels to be treated as privateers rather than as pirates.

The United States proceeded rapidly with the blockade. Plans were laid for the seizure of forts at Cape Hatteras Inlet, controlling the North Carolina coast, and for the capture of the vulnerable and valuable Port Royal Sound, halfway between Charleston and Savannah. This haven, which had come into Union hands by November 1861, provided shelter for the South Atlantic Blockading Squadron in hurricane weather and a station for refueling and repairs. Within a year, owing to the energy of the navy under Gideon Welles' direction, all major Southern ports except Charleston, but including New Orleans, had been taken. The blockade was effective enough to cause the Confederacy considerable annoyance and to deprive it of needed supplies.

Major campaigns
of the Civil War

Union states

Confederate states

Union blockade of
Confederate shipping

Scott's plan to split
the Confederacy

Circled numbers ① are keyed to
detail maps in the pages which
follow. The following symbols are
used to designate Union and
Confederate forces:

Union advance

Union retreat

Confederate advance

Confederate retreat

Lincoln, rejecting other parts of General Scott's plan, decided to try for a quick victory over the army of P. G. T. Beauregard, who was located in northern Virginia not thirty miles from Washington. Lincoln hoped to defeat Beauregard and take Richmond, where the Confederate government had moved after Virginia seceded. On July 21, near a sluggish stream called Bull Run, General Irvin McDowell engaged Beauregard's army in the first major battle of the war. It was a battle of green armies, and McDowell did not even have a good map of the terrain. Although the Northern recruits fought well at first and had the initial advantage of numbers, they failed to carry the day against Confederate reinforcements brought out of the Shenandoah Valley from Joseph Johnston's army in one of the first major uses of railroads for troop transport. When McDowell attempted an orderly retreat, his demoralized men broke ranks and streamed back to Washington. The victors were too stunned by their triumph to give chase. Lincoln and his Cabinet now saw that the road to Richmond would be hard and long.

But Lincoln did not lose confidence in himself as a strategist. Instead he settled into the long process of training the new three-year volunteer army. For this task he picked George B. McClellan. Only thirty-four years old but a superb organizer and administrator, McClellan chose to undertake no new offensive until his troops were fully prepared for combat. Lincoln approved that policy, and throughout the summer and fall an uneasy quiet fell on the land war.

① The first Battle of Bull Run,
July 21, 1861

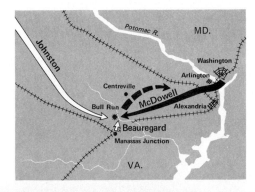

**The war opens in the West.** Meanwhile, in the West, military threats to Kentucky's proclaimed neutrality led to a campaign that revealed the Confederacy's soft spot (see p. 325). A large Union force was assembling at Cairo, Illinois, under the command of an obscure but tough young officer named Ulysses S. Grant. Major General Leonidas Polk, who watched this development anxiously from the Missouri side of the Mississippi, decided to get his Confederate army into a more strategic position with regard to Grant's force. On September 4, Polk crossed over into Kentucky and occupied high ground overlooking the Ohio River from the Kentucky side. General Grant, grasping the opportunity he had been waiting for, followed hard on Polk's heels with a large force of federal troops, in order, he declared, to defend the state from the Confederates. Thereafter the political standoff in Kentucky cleared with remarkable speed: Union candidates won in the 1861 fall elections, giving Grant and his army the local security they required to drive the Confederates out of Kentucky. Grant quickly gained control of the mouths of the Tennessee and Cumberland rivers as they flowed into the Ohio. Those great waterways, which looped through Kentucky and across the whole of Tennessee, provided a natural highway into the heartland of the Confederacy.

Recognizing the danger, Jefferson Davis appointed the man he regarded as his best officer, General Albert Sidney Johnston, to take command of the Confederate defense. There were now two Confederate armies in Kentucky: Johnston's at Bowling Green, facing a large Union army of eighty thousand under General Don Carlos Buell; and P. G. T. Beauregard's smaller force to the west, at Columbus. But the two armies were not strong enough to hold against the campaign that Grant now launched. Near the end of January 1862 the Union Army began to push the Confederates southward. Early in February, Grant took part of his army along the Tennessee River with a flotilla of gunboats and captured Fort Henry, which guarded the river just below the Kentucky border in Tennessee. This movement, which ruptured the communications of the extended Confederate line, caused General Johnston to withdraw to Nashville, leaving a small force of fifteen thousand to guard Fort Donelson on the Cumberland River. With help from General Henry W. Halleck, who had a small army in Missouri, Grant seized Fort Donelson and captured its garrison. One of the decisive achievements of Union arms, this

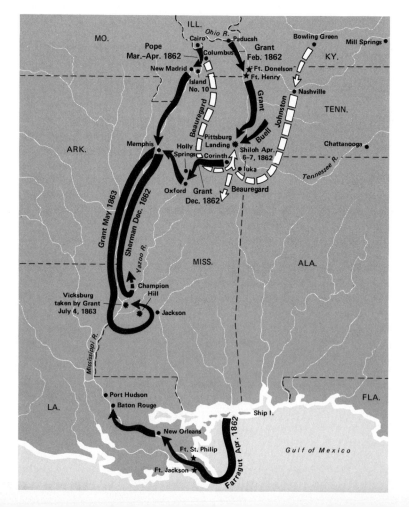

② Grant's campaigns in the Mississippi Valley, 1862–63

action cut Johnson's defensive lines and forced a general Confederate retreat back to northern Mississippi. With western Tennessee now secured, the way was open for a Union advance into the Deep South. In February, Lincoln promptly set up a Union government at Nashville and appointed Andrew Johnson, a Tennessee senator who had refused to secede, as governor.

**Shiloh.** Beauregard and Johnston reunited their armies near the Tennessee-Mississippi line. There they conceived a plan to stop Grant, who had pursued the line of the Tennessee River all the way to Pittsburg Landing in southern Tennessee. Aware that Grant's army was slightly smaller than the total fifty-five thousand men of his own troops combined with Beauregard's, Johnston made a surprise attack on April 6 in a tangle of woodlands and pasture near a country meetinghouse called Shiloh. Grant's army, taken by surprise, was nearly driven into the river the first day, but Johnston was killed in the action and reinforcements from Buell's command began arriving in the evening. On the following day the outnumbered Confederates, under Beauregard, had to retreat to Corinth, Mississippi. Shiloh, the greatest battle yet seen on the North American continent, left thirteen thousand Union casualties and more than ten thousand Confederate.

The Confederate gamble to prevent the concentration of the Union armies had been frustrated. It was now a simple matter for General Halleck, who emerged with more credit for the operations than he deserved, to gather his large army of 125,000 men and drive Beauregard out of Corinth, an important railroad center. Now northern Mississippi lay open to Halleck and the Confederate forces in the West were on the brink of disaster.

Support from the Union Navy had been indispensable in that development. Flag Officer David Farragut had pushed his way up the Mississippi to New Orleans and on April 25 had occupied that city. General Benjamin Butler followed to establish a military occupation of New Orleans and its environs and was soon in possession of Baton Rouge as well. Meanwhile, early in June, a fleet of federal gunboats came down the Mississippi and annihilated a Confederate fleet at Memphis, bringing that city into Union possession and opening the upper Mississippi. The Union Navy and Army together now controlled the whole length of the river except for a section between Vicksburg to the North and Port Hudson to the south.

**The Monitor and the Merrimac.** The technological advances of the first half of the nineteenth century contributed significantly to naval design. Steamships were already in common use by 1860, and screw

Shiloh:
twenty-three thousand casualties

propellers, rifled ordnance, and shell guns had been developed. During the war those innovations, widely used, marked the advent of a new era in naval warfare. Early in the war Navy Secretary Welles had contracted to have gunboats on the Mississippi armed with 2½ inches of iron plate, and several of these little ironclad vessels were launched in October and November of 1861. They were available to Grant on the Mississippi and Tennessee rivers in the spring campaign of 1862, and Flag Officer Farragut used ironclads in reducing the defenses of New Orleans.

Suddenly it appeared that armor was of even greater strategic importance for battleships than for gunboats. Just after Virginia seceded from the Union, federal authorities had decided, unwisely and precipitately, to abandon the Gosport Navy Yard near Portsmouth, Virginia. In doing so, they scuttled and burned a forty-gun warship named the *Merrimac*, which was then under repair. Confederate Secretary of the Navy Stephen Mallory, alert to the meaning of technology for naval warfare, had the *Merrimac* raised, reconditioned, stripped of its superstructure, and armed in four-inch iron plate made at the Tredegar works in Richmond. Nobody had seen anything like this amazing vessel before. Rechristened the *Virginia*, it appeared in Hampton Roads on March 8, 1862. There it sealed the doom of wooden warships. The ironclad vessel threatened to destroy the whole federal fleet around Fort Monroe. Impending disaster was avoided by the timely arrival the next day of the *Monitor*, an ironclad that had just been finished for the Union Navy.

The ability of the Confederates, who had had no navy at all at the outbreak of the war, to come so close to crippling the Union Navy exposed the conservatism of the Naval Board and Congress. Although Union authorities had had ample warning of what was afoot at the Gosport Yard, Secretary Welles had difficulty persuading Congress of the need for haste, and the Naval Board had been slow to see the virtues of ironclad vessels. Had it not been for the passionate

*The course of arms*

advocacy of a Swedish-born engineer named John Ericsson, the *Monitor* might not have appeared in time to challenge the *Merrimac* in its bid for control of the lower Chesapeake. Ericsson laid the keel of the *Monitor* on October 1, 1861, and it was completed just in time.

The *Monitor* and the *Merrimac* fought a wearing battle, demonstrating that warships without armor plate were obsolete. The *Monitor* gained no real advantage, for it was unable to destroy the Confederate ironclad. The *Merrimac* remained in the lower James River, barring the stream to federal shipping and posing a threat to any plan to take Richmond by invasion of the peninsula below the city. Two months later, on May 9, Union forces had occupied the sounds and capes of North Carolina and were threatening Norfolk. The Confederates abandoned the city and scuttled the *Merrimac* to keep it from Northern hands.

### McClellan's peninsular campaign.

For so young a general, George B. McClellan was painfully slow and methodical. Or so Lincoln and many of his best advisers thought. Yet McClellan did put his huge army of 150,000 men into good fighting shape during the winter of 1861–62. In the spring he convinced Lincoln that he should take the larger part of his army down the Potomac to the Chesapeake, put his men ashore at Fortress Monroe, and move on Richmond from the southeast. McClellan had "the slows," Lincoln complained. Even though his army outnumbered General Joseph E. Johnston's, which stood between his own and Richmond, McClellan frittered away precious weeks on siege tactics. Johnston quietly withdrew up the peninsula and reestablished himself less than ten miles from Richmond. In late May McClellan, having reached Johnston again, sent part of his army across the Chickahominy, a stream that divided the penin-

sula; he refused to attack until reinforcements came from Washington. Lincoln had agreed to send troops, provided Washington was not threatened. But by late May Washington appeared to be in danger of Confederate attack. Jefferson Davis and Robert E. Lee, who happened to be in Richmond, had worked out a deception to prevent Lincoln from sending McClellan his reinforcements. They instructed young Thomas J. Jackson, who had earned the nickname "Stonewall" for his stand at the Battle of Bull Run, to engage the enemy vigorously in the Shenandoah Valley and to create the illusion that an attack on Washington was imminent. Jackson carried out his assignment brilliantly. Then, on the last day of May, Johnston attacked McClellan's exposed right flank at Fair Oaks. The battle was indecisive, and Johnston was badly wounded.

Now General Robert E. Lee came out from Richmond to replace Johnston as commander of the Army of Northern Virginia, a post he would retain for the rest of the war. Lee had been a reluctant secessionist, forced, as he wrote a Northern girl who asked for his photograph on the eve of war, "to side either with or against my section or country. I cannot raise my hand," he added, "against my birthplace, my home, my children." He hated the choice he had made because it implied ingratitude to the United States army, which he loved and which had provided the opportunities that launched his career. Like John Brown, ironically, Lee foresaw a terrible war—a war that would be "a necessary expiation" for the sins of the country. A daring commander, Lee was at his best in adversity. Resolving to save Richmond, he called on Jackson to bring his troops swiftly east to join him. Jackson's seventeen thousand soldiers came out of the mountains and across the Piedmont at record speed, arriving just in time to help Lee drive the right wing of

*Bridging the Chickahominy*

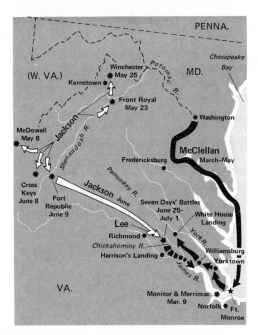

③ The peninsular campaign, 1862

the Union Army to the southeast in a series of engagements known as the Seven Days' Battle. Though outnumbered at all times, Lee managed, by skillful deployment of his men, to bring to each encounter a superior force. In those battles Lee lost twenty thousand men and McClellan fifteen thousand. Pushed back to Harrison's Landing on the James River, McClellan settled down again to wait for reinforcements. But Lee was determined not to lose the initiative he had gained.

**The second Battle of Bull Run.** In what must have seemed to McClellan a belated effort, Lincoln called Generals John Pope and Henry Halleck east, placing Halleck in general command of the war and sending Pope southward with his army to help McClellan catch Richmond in a pincer movement. Halleck, failing in his effort to coordinate the two Union armies, at last ordered McClellan to bring his troops north and join Pope. Lee, who had no intention of letting these armies meet, boldly divided his own army to send twenty-five thousand men under Jackson to attack Pope from the rear. On August 28 and 29 he maneuvered Pope into battle on the old field of Bull Run. Wholly undone by Lee's generalship, Pope was driven back to the fortifications around Washington. Lincoln removed Pope from command and asked McClellan to take over, hoping to replace the latter with a more combative general when time allowed.

Time did not allow, or rather Robert E. Lee did not. Lee had already achieved a remarkable reversal of the conflict, shifting the scene of action from the outskirts of Richmond to the banks of the Potomac.

Realizing better than most commanders that the Confederacy's survival depended on the destruction of the Union Army, he knew he could not afford to lose time. He struck across the Potomac River. By forcing McClellan to stand between the Confederate Army and Washington, Lee could draw the Union Army out of Virginia, allowing the farmers to harvest their crops in peace. If Lee could win a decisive victory on Northern soil, England and France might be convinced that the South could win independence. This, in turn, might persuade those powers to recognize the Confederacy.

# The war at crisis

**England and the Confederacy.** Neither the Union nor the Confederacy had been entirely satisfied with the official British attitude toward the war. The North was displeased that England had recognized the Confederates as belligerents; the South wanted full recognition of its independence. In the summer of 1862 the French too, apparently ready to recognize the Confederacy, waited only for a signal from England to do so. Lord John Russell, Britain's foreign minister, proposed to the British cabinet that the European powers offer to mediate the American dispute. If mediation was not accepted, Russell indicated, Britain would recognize the Confederacy. Those steps would have provoked war with the United States.

Public attitudes in England were mixed. The upper-class English saw in the Southern cause a defense of conservative values, and many of them would have welcomed the defeat of the world's most important exemplar of popular government. English liberals, especially antislavery reformers, pointed out that the South was defending slavery, which was generally disliked in England. But their conservative opponents replied that the federal government had taken pains to dissociate the war from the issue of slavery. The English working classes would have welcomed almost any solution that would have brought a return of plentiful cotton and full employment, but theirs was not the decisive influence. The need for cotton was not gaining for the Confederacy all that the advocates of "King Cotton diplomacy" had hoped.

There were other reasons for the failure of cotton as a basis for Confederate diplomacy. The rich cotton crop of 1860 had been sold in the Liverpool market before the outbreak of hostilities, and the Union blockade had had slight effect on the shipment of cotton during the first year of the war. Near the end of the summer of 1862 the stockpile was dwindling. By that time, however, England had developed alternative sources of supply in Egypt and India, thus breaking the Confederate monopoly. England had yet another problem to consider. Poor grain harvests in 1861 and 1862 had made grain purchased from the Northern states very important in feeding England's industrial population. So long as the United States refused to make emancipation an aim of the war, only the certainty that the Confederates were actually going to win their independence in battle could budge the British.

***England and the Union.*** The main objective of United States diplomacy was to prevent the British from recognizing the Confederacy. Avoiding hostile encounters that might pitch the British into the Confederate camp was essential.

Actually a dangerous confrontation had already occurred in November 1861, when James Wilkes, captain of the U.S.S. *San Jacinto*, stopped a British mail steamer named the *Trent* and removed two Confederate envoys, James Mason and John Slidell, who were on their way to England. Secretary of State William Seward should have acknowledged that breach of neutral rights promptly, for the United States had historically regarded such seizures as illegal and had in 1812 pointed to similar British actions as one reason for declaring war on England (see p. 166). Lord Palmerston, the prime minister, informed his nervous cabinet that he'd "be damned" if he would let the affront go unnoticed. The popular enthusiasm among Northerners for Wilkes' brash act made it hard for Seward to back down. Congress even voted Wilkes a medal. Demanding a return of the envoys and an apology, even while preparing troops to sail to Canada, the British seemed ready to go to war. The message they sent to Washington might have been even sharper had Queen Victoria and Prince Albert, who were disposed to be friends with the United States, not suggested a softening of the language. Much of the credit for averting hostilities belonged to two skillful diplomats, America's minister to England, Charles Francis Adams, and the British minister to Washington, Lord Lyons. Since neither nation wanted war, the only question was whether Seward and Lincoln could accept the graceful retreat the English opened up for them. By delaying tactics, the two ministers were able to draw out their negotiations until popular opinion in the United States had cooled. The federal government then released Mason and Slidell and issued an expression of regret to the British.

Tensions between the United States and England nevertheless remained high. With little regard for their duties as neutrals, the British allowed two cruisers built for the Confederacy to escape from Liverpool under British registry. Once on the high seas, the *Alabama* and the *Florida* seriously menaced Northern shipping; before the end of the war they had destroyed $15 million in ships and trade. The Confederacy hoped that these vessels would break the Union blockade, but they never succeeded in doing so.

More ominous plans were developing to break the blockade. Two huge ironclad rams, ships specially designed to attack blockade vessels, were on the ways in a Scottish shipyard, scheduled to be in the water by 1863. Minister Adams now set about preventing their delivery to the Confederacy. How sympathetically the British would listen to him depended in part on whether the United States could reverse the pattern of military defeat. With the British seriously considering mediation and ignoring what was happening in their shipyards, nothing seemed more important to President Lincoln in early September of 1862 than throwing Lee out of Maryland.

***The slavery question again.*** The President needed a victory for another reason. By mid-summer of 1862 he had decided to abandon his hands-off policy on slavery and to issue a proclamation freeing the slaves in the seceded states. He was waiting for a victory to make his announcement. Lincoln interpreted his war powers to include the right to emancipate the enemy's property, but he had hesitated long to do so. Lincoln's views on race were more ambivalent than his views on slavery, more difficult for historians to describe. While he had easy personal relations with individual blacks, never did he make a statement of belief in racial equality, though he made many statements evidencing distrust of equality. Then, there were political facts to consider. A merciful man, the President on more than one occasion had said that he wished all men could be free, but he had been unwilling to make enemies for the cause of the Union among the many Northern citizens who shared the South's view of racial distinctions even while condemning Southern slavery. The slaveholding border states that had stayed in the Union would, he feared, consider themselves betrayed. Looking for issues in the upcoming congressional elections of 1862, the Democrats would surely charge the government with encouraging a slave insurrection in the South, and few Northerners were willing to visit on the seceded states what they termed "the horrors of servile war."

As the casualty lists lengthened, however, and the war turned against the Union, some Northerners began to ask themselves if they were not enduring an unfair handicap by failing to use that weapon. The Confederate government had employed slaves to build their fortifications, and slave-labor on the plantations released many whites for military service. Scoffing at Lincoln's conservatism and his solicitude for the border-state slaveholders, Wendell Phillips asked, "How many times are we to save Kentucky and lose the war?" Abolitionists like Phillips, once hounded in the North, were enjoying a new popularity among staunch supporters of the war. Only lukewarm patriots showed them the old contempt. Had not abolitionists claimed from the first that slavery was the cause of the war? Northern inability to win victory short of emancipating slaves seemed a signal that they had been right all along.

***Fugitive slaves.*** There were other signs. Especially troublesome for Lincoln was the question of how army officers were to deal with fugitive slaves. In all sectors of the fighting, and from the very beginning of the war, blacks had come over into the Union lines. As long as emancipation was denied as an aim of the war, Southern sympathizers in the North, and all the border-state people, regarded failure to return runaways as hypocrisy. Other Northerners saw no good reason to return slaves who would strengthen the Confederacy.

General Benjamin F. Butler, a soldier-politician from Massachusetts, evolved a formula that served for a time. When Butler led his Massachusetts volunteers through Maryland in the first weeks of the war, he had offered his men to help put down a slave insurrection that was rumored to be imminent; and he had returned fugitive slaves to their masters. But his action had raised an immediate outcry in Massachusetts, and Butler, never slow to learn a political lesson, found a way to retain the fugitives and use them in the Union cause. He simply suggested that they be regarded as "contraband of war." Some officers followed his lead; some did not. Lincoln, tolerating latitude on the part of commanders who faced this dilemma, realized that their individual responses tended to match their political views.

Lincoln would not allow any officer, however, to make fundamental policy on this sensitive subject. When John C. Frémont, in command of the army in Missouri, proclaimed that the slaves of masters disloyal to the Union were emancipated, Lincoln made him retract the order and shortly removed him from his command. Frémont's order was very popular, nonetheless. Governor Andrew of Massachusetts said Frémont's action gave "the grandest character" to the Union effort, and antislavery people everywhere approved. The border slave states were getting to be, in the words of black abolitionist Frederick Douglass, "a millstone about the neck of the Government." Antislavery Northerners pledged themselves to convert the war into a crusade against slavery.

Time and events were on their side. Union defeats, especially McClellan's failures in the peninsular campaign against Richmond, made Northern citizens, abolitionists or not, less tolerant of the South's advantage in slave labor. Recognizing in the black man a potential Northern ally, they were beginning to ask why he should not be enlisted in Union armies.

The recruitment of blacks was directly related to the question of emancipation, for no one could expect black men to serve in the army as slaves. With the number of volunteers tapering off in the North, the need for manpower became more pressing. The vigorous new Secretary of War, Edwin M. Stanton, advocated an army of black regiments. Lincoln saw that the time had come for him to test the will of the public on emancipation. Therefore in March 1862 he pointed out to the border states that the war was bringing an end to slavery in areas where it was easy for slaves to run away and urged them to undertake voluntary emancipation with the expectation that Congress would compensate slave owners for their loss. The border states took no action and neither did Congress. At this point, however, Lincoln's own policy shifted subtly but positively. General David Hunter began to enlist black soldiers in the occupied districts of coastal South Carolina and then, in May 1862, issued a proclamation similar to Frémont's. Instead of removing Hunter from his command, Lincoln simply ordered him to retract his proclamation. It was clear from newspaper comment and from letters to political leaders that public opposition to emancipation and to the enlistment of black soldiers was rapidly diminishing. On July 17, 1862, Congress passed a Confiscation Act that freed the slaves of masters who served in the Confederate Army. It was almost impossible for fugitives to win freedom under this act, however, because they would somehow have to demonstrate that their master was disloyal to the Union. Moreover, the act made no provision for the enforcement of the emancipation clause. The fact that the Confiscation Act of 1862 was passed, however, suggested that Congress was becoming increasingly radical on the slavery question.

Horace Greeley, in a famous letter to the President known as "The Prayer of 20 Millions," urged Lincoln to enforce the Confiscation Act and to convert the war into a war on slavery. The President's answer was firm: he would continue to place the Union ahead of all else. He added that he would consider every possible means to save the Union, including the emancipation of slaves. Actually Lincoln had already decided to issue an emancipation proclamation. He had been working on the text in the privacy of the telegraph office, where he had hidden himself from office-seekers, and on July 22 he told his Cabinet of his decision. Persuaded by Seward that a proclamation on the heels of McClellan's poor showing in the peninsular campaign would be a demonstration of weakness, Lincoln agreed to await a Union victory.

Now Lincoln learned of Lee's invasion of Maryland. As Lincoln sent McClellan to stop Lee's army, much hung on the outcome. Only emancipation seemed likely to stop the English from thinking about mediation, and emancipation would have to wait upon McClellan's success.

**Antietam.** The Union and Confederate armies were groping toward one of the crucial encounters of the war. As Lee led his sixty thousand-man army into Maryland, he deployed part of it under General "Stonewall" Jackson to seize the federal arsenal at Harper's Ferry, Virginia. At this point McClellan had a stroke of incredibly good luck. One of his men happened to pick up three cigars wrapped in what turned out to be a lost dispatch from Lee revealing that his army was momentarily divided. McClellan moved promptly to bring Lee to battle, hoping to defeat him before Jackson could return. On September 17, at Antietam Creek near the small town of Sharpsburg, McClellan made several massive attacks on Lee's lines. In the course of one long ghastly day, three battles were fought on a single field. Very late, but just in time to save the Confederate Army from disaster, reinforcements arrived from Harper's Ferry. With one more attack McClellan might have defeated the Confederates conclusively, but he did not attack, and night fell upon a stalemate.

During that bloodiest day of the entire war, the Union Army of ninety thousand men had sustained thirteen thousand casualties, the Confederate Army nearly eleven thousand. His army was so weakened that Lee decided to abandon his drive into Maryland. Most unwisely, McClellan allowed him a whole day free of harassment, and Lee seized the opportunity to organize an orderly retreat across the Potomac. For McClellan's blunder Lincoln eventually removed him from his command, but for the moment Lincoln deemed the victory sufficient to justify release of the Emancipation Proclamation.

Fortunately the public was prepared for Lincoln's bombshell; Horace Greeley's letter and the President's reply to it had helped. Thousands who had once applauded Lincoln's caution were by now resigned to the idea of emancipation as a war measure. Other thousands were comforted to know that the sacrifices of war would advance freedom. Lincoln's timing was perfect, for a revolution was rising in public sentiment on emancipation. On September 23 Lincoln released the Emancipation Proclamation to the newspapers. In plain legal language, he stated that persons held as slaves in states that were still in rebellion on January 1, 1863, would be emancipated. He specifically exempted most areas occupied by federal troops, and he declared that the status of slaves in the Union slave states would be unaffected. His critics remarked that the proclamation freed slaves only in those areas where they could not be reached.

There were other objections that could be brought against the true significance of the proclamation. Many Americans resisted emancipation and hated blacks, it seemed, all the more because of it. Race riots broke out in the Middle West against blacks who fled the South. The fugitive slaves who came within the lines of the Union Army were often abused, and where large numbers of them congregated they were put to work on the plantations under circumstances that differed little from slavery. Throughout the Middle West, Democrats screamed that the Republicans' true colors were now showing and that they meant "to Africanize" their states. Recognizing the intensity of this hostility, Lincoln accompanied the Emancipation Proclamation with proposals that free blacks be colonized abroad. To the free blacks, whom he publicly urged to support their own colonization in Haiti, Lincoln explained that it would smooth the way for a wider emancipation, for "there is an unwillingness on the part of our people, harsh as it may be, for you free colored people to remain with us." Whether the President believed his project had any chance of succeeding is not known, but the immediate political effects were beneficial. The project failed miserably, and the survivors were brought back to the United States. Lincoln stopped talking about colonization once emancipation itself was more widely accepted by the voters.

But in spite of voter hostility and the hard fate of refugee blacks, the Emancipation Proclamation changed the meaning of the war. Territory occupied by federal troops after January 1 would be free territory, and the army was now an army of liberation,

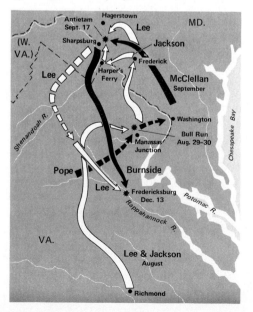

④ Virginia and Maryland, 1862

*I have ... thought a great deal about the relation of this war to Slavery: and ... several weeks ago, I read to you an Order I had prepared on this subject.... I have thought ... that the time for acting on it might very probably come. I think the time has come now. I wish it were a better time.... The action of the army against the rebels has not been quite what I should have best liked. But they have been driven out of Maryland, and Pennsylvania is no longer in danger of invasion. When the rebel army was at Frederick, I determined, as soon as it should be driven out of Maryland, to issue a Proclamation of Emancipation.... I made the promise to myself, and ... to my Maker.... I am going to fulfill that promise.... I do not wish your advice about the main matter.... What I have written is that which my reflections have determined me to say.... I know very well that many others might, in this matter, as in others, do better than I can; and if I were satisfied that the public confidence was more fully possessed by any one of them than by me, and knew of any Constitutional way in which he could be put in my place, he should have it.... But though I believe that I have not so much of the confidence of the people as I had some time since, I do not know that ... any other person has more; and ... I am here. I must do the best I can and bear the responsibility of taking the course which I feel I ought to take.*

**From the Diary of Salmon P. Chase, September 22, 1862.**

**Antietam and emancipation: Lincoln to his Cabinet**

however reluctant. The number of runaways increased rapidly wherever federal troops were deployed. The Proclamation served notice on the South that the war had become a social revolution; if the cause of secession should fail, the slave-based society of the South would also fail. The Confederacy now renewed its effort to win independence with the energy of desperation.

Emancipation helped the Northern war effort immediately in two important ways. It caused the English to postpone their decision on whether or not to step forward as mediators in the American war. Without the Emancipation Proclamation, the Battle of Antietam might have lent force to the mediationists' argument that the war had become a bloody stalemate. But emancipation ennobled the Northern war effort in the eyes of most Englishmen, and it would now be much harder for the British cabinet to abandon neutrality.

Black men also proved a valuable new source of recruits for the Union Army. By 1863 enlistments were falling off. Congress passed a general Conscrip-

*Black recruits for the Union Army*

tion Act in that year which encouraged localities to redouble their efforts to raise volunteers. But still more men were needed. Governor John Andrew of Massachusetts spearheaded the recruitment of black soldiers by raising the famous Fifty-fourth and Fifty-fifth Regiments of Massachusetts Volunteers. During 1863 a number of significant engagements proved even to the dubious that black troops made good soldiers. At Milliken's Bend, at Port Hudson in the West, and at Battery Wagner in the East, black troops fought valiantly and suffered heavy casualties. The nation learned to be grateful for their sacrifices. By the end of the war nearly 190,000 black soldiers had served in the Union Army.

**The election of 1862.** At first it was difficult to judge the impact of emancipation on the Northern people. Repeated defeats and ever lengthening casualty lists had provoked deep distrust of the Administration's handling of the war. In the struggle against disaffection at home and against subversion by the enemy, Lincoln's government, however reluctantly, had made arbitrary arrests and imprisonments, had suspended the writ of habeas corpus, and had censored the press. His severest critics saw Lincoln as a dictator. The "peace" Democrats, who opposed the war, claimed that the President had revealed his true colors by asking citizens to sacrifice their civil liberties in order to emancipate the enemy's slaves. Others too were asking what good was a war that threatened to destroy American freedom. In a mood of fear and despair, the voters handed the Republicans sharp reverses in the congressional elections of 1862.

The election could have gone worse for the Republicans. The government had not actually been defeated, as it might have been had the public had only the debacle of the second Battle of Bull Run, the futility of McClellan's peninsular campaign, and the unfulfilled promise of Antietam to consider. The Emancipation Proclamation, significant in itself, also gave the impression that the President was now totally committed to the war, ready to take every step necessary to win.

Lincoln dramatized that readiness by ridding himself of McClellan and other officers who were not only afflicted with "the slows" but who opposed emancipation. A new vigor seemed to infuse the people. The people of the North were at last accepting emancipation as a goal of the war. Some clearly accepted it for the ignoble reason that it would induce blacks to remain in the South, or return there. But, for whatever reasons, those who approved Lincoln's proclamation outnumbered those who opposed it. For its supporters, emancipation gave a noble meaning to the sacrifices demanded at home and the dreadful casualty lists from the field.

The sacrifices were far from over. By the end of the year both the Union and the Confederate armies were settling into a slow war of attrition. Lincoln gave command of the Army of the Potomac to General Ambrose E. Burnside, a dashing officer who had proved his mettle in the North Carolina coastal campaign. Knowing that he had been put in charge in order to give battle, Burnside astonished Generals Lee and Jackson by driving his troops across the Rappahannock River to attack the Confederates entrenched on Marye Heights above the little town of Fredericksburg, about halfway between Washington and Richmond. Burnside had a fault quite different from McClellan's. All day long on December 13 he threw assault after assault against the Confederates, but each time they turned him back with relative ease. At the end of the day a bewildered Burnside counted twelve thousand casualties in his futile exercise. The Confederates had lost half that many.

The two armies dug in for a wet, dreary winter, eyeing each other across the Rappahannock. The Confederates were low on food and clothing; the Union Army was demoralized. The Confederates had plenty of tobacco and no coffee; the Union soldiers had plenty of coffee and no tobacco. In spite of the savage fighting in the days just past, the men of the Army of Northern Virginia and the men of the Army of the Potomac adjusted the imbalance in those homely comforts by shuttling a small carved boat loaded with items in short supply back and forth across the river. Fraternization was a problem for the officers but not for the men; it was one of the most promising signs of what Lincoln sincerely hoped for, that this was "a war with peace in its belly." The two armies sat drinking their coffee and smoking their pipes, waiting for spring and a new campaign. In time, Lincoln appointed a new general, hoping that "Fighting" Joe Hooker would live up to his nickname.

**The Kentucky campaign.** The fall campaign of 1862 in the West was also indecisive. Confederate General Braxton Bragg conceived of a maneuver to recapture Kentucky. Rather than staying pinned down in northern Mississippi, he would strike north through Tennessee and Kentucky, aiming for Louisville. General Don Carlos Buell would have to follow him to defend the railroad junction at Louisville. En route Bragg could pick his own ground and force the Union Army into battle. It was a brilliant plan that came near succeeding, for Bragg did get his army between Buell and Louisville. All of Tennessee and most of Kentucky now seemed again safe for the Confederacy. But Bragg was afflicted by the same irresolution that blunted George McClellan's genius. Instead of challenging Buell he withdrew, giving Buell time to get into Louisville for reinforcements. Now it

342

*Civil war*

was Buell's turn to show reluctance to fight. After an inconclusive engagement at Perryville, Kentucky, in October, Bragg withdrew to Tennessee, followed at some distance by Buell. Buell too had "the slows," Lincoln concluded, and he replaced him with General William Rosecrans, who met Bragg's army in desperate battle at Murfreesboro, Tennessee, on the last day of 1862. After a second engagement, in which the Confederates came off badly, Bragg withdrew to winter quarters. In the West as in the East, the new year began in stalemate.

# Behind the lines

**Southern problems.** The wisest leaders, including both Lincoln and Davis, knew that the South had more to lose in a stalemate than the Union had. Medicine, salt to preserve meat, and leather for soldiers' shoes, wagon harness, and cavalry equipment became scarce early on. The South simply lacked the material resources to sustain a long war. Disaffection mounted with inflation, and unspeakable poverty, even hunger, dogged the families of soldiers conscripted from the poor.

The political system of the Confederacy now began to show strain under the demands of modern war. While the North was being transformed into a modern nation, the Confederacy, organized on the state-rights principle, fell victim to the jealousies of imperious state-right leaders. Without political parties to moderate their obstructionism, Southern leaders engaged in vicious factional disputes over the policies of Davis' Administration. Vice President Stephens sulked in Georgia, and the governors of several states blocked conscription (see p. 329). When the Confederate Congress convened in January 1863, President Davis spoke some homely truths. The South, he said, must not look abroad for help, and he observed that the Emancipation Proclamation had sparked the North with a new determination. He warned that sterner measures were needed to save the government. The Confederate people would have supported Davis if their leaders had asked them to do so and if they had felt that the burdens of war were fairly distributed. The Congress approved in principle a 10 percent tax in kind on farmers' produce and promised a more generous assessment of goods confiscated from the farmers than in previous impressments. Those steps were necessary, but the real wealth of the South was in slaves and cotton and land, and the tax bill that emerged from Congress scarcely touched those bulwarks of privilege. Inflation mounted, morale dipped, and by 1864 the women of Richmond were rioting for bread in the streets.

**The Northern war boom.** From 1863 on, the North gained steadily in material strength. Much of the amateurish experimentation of the first years of the war was distilled into useful knowledge. The North organized. The financial measures taken in 1862 began to show results; the army was paid promptly, and adequate supplies reached the front on time. General Herman Haupt, who was granted full authority to use the railroads to advance the war effort, emerged as a genius of organization. In naval power the Union had enjoyed supremacy even at the start of the war, with 42 effective vessels; by 1863 the figure had grown to a formidable 427.

By 1863 the North had already made its most painful adjustments to the war economy, and the last two years of the war were for the majority of Northerners a time of unprecedented prosperity. The wages of the working poor never quite kept pace with inflation. But for everyone else war contracts meant good jobs, and the enormously expanded production and export of Western grain assured good times for farmers. In almost every area of economic life new energy flowed: mining in copper, silver, and gold; railroad-building; the petroleum trade; and every kind of manufacturing, from iron to flour to woolen cloth. The leather-manufacturing establishments of Newark, New Jersey—once a great center of shoemaking for the slaves of the South—now made shoes for soldiers, and harness and saddles for the army. Immigration, which had slowed down early in the war, now recovered and surpassed prewar levels.

This exuberance was reflected in rampant speculative investment, much of it foolish. Corruption was widespread; employers and profiteers exploited the poor. With capital rapidly accumulating, a speculative psychology overtook the business world. Yet the economic boom, despite its bad features, contributed in manifold ways to Northern victory.

**New roles for women.** The war brought change to those on the home front, and woman's world expanded. Replacing the soldiers behind the plows was necessary everywhere; but in the South, where conscription soon swept the small farmers, young and old, off to war, farming was left largely to women. As horses and mules became scarce and were impressed by the army, women of the South found themselves not only stepping behind the plow. Sometimes they pulled it. Machinery of all kinds broke down or wore out, and women found themselves trying to raise food for their families under austere circumstances. Harassed by the impressment officer, who often took food as well as livestock for army use, making do with hardly enough to wear, Southern women experienced a distress that often crept into their letters to their soldier husbands, increasing the unhappiness of the troops over "the rich man's war" and quickening their willingness to desert. The women of the planter class perhaps suffered less as a group, but they often experienced a falling off in living standards and found themselves with many new burdens and responsibilities. Sometimes they organized the migration of large numbers of blacks and whites from the path of the enemy army and resettled them elsewhere. Learning how to manage plantations and the complexities of finance and an inflated economy, they attended for the first time to taxes and mortgage payments. In the Upper South, many women suffered the additional sorrow of sundered families, for husbands, sons, and fathers might be fighting on opposite sides.

Farming women of the Middle West experienced similar hardships, especially on the frontier, when garrisons were reduced or removed. In 1862 the Sioux Indians rose up in Minnesota, burning out white settlers and disrupting a wide territory of some twenty-three counties. But some ingenious frontier women managed to increase the value of their husbands' property in their absence. Some of them even homesteaded under the new Homestead Act, with only their children's help, taking advantage of the provision that one could win a farm by working it and building a cabin there.

In the East more and more women found jobs in new occupations. The first "government girls" came to Washington, appointed by Francis Spinner, United States Treasurer. Spinner hired 447 girls in Treasury at what must have been an unheard-of salary for a woman in those times, $600 per year! The idea caught fire, and soon other departments of government began hiring women as clerks and copyists. Reactions were mixed and predictable, ranging from loyal support from male colleagues to charges of distracting the men. Some women were accused of scandalous conduct. But civil service for women gained steadily in respectability, and by the end of the war women were too well established to be dislodged from their new occupations. The Confederate government also employed women, not only from poor and refugee families but from very prominent families, as the payrolls attest. Although these women were at first discriminated against in pay, before the war ended they were being paid equally with men.

Many industrial jobs previously closed to women opened up during the war. Perhaps one hundred thousand new jobs in factories and arsenals fell to women as the men went off to war and manufacturing concerns expanded to respond to rising demand. Many of these new working women were dreadfully exploited in pay. Those who excited the most sympathy were seamstresses, who received as little as four or five cents for sewing a shirt. They were victims of government contractors competing to produce sol-

diers' clothing at the lowest possible price, and of their own idea that sewing was one of the few "lady-like" jobs available to them. In any event, drawing sympathy from substantial citizens, they began to strike in protest. Organizing themselves in New York as the Workingwomen's Protective Union, they strove from 1863 to 1864 to improve their condition, even sending from Philadelphia a committee representing ten thousand seamstresses to call on Lincoln. The President intervened with the Quartermaster-General, but it was late in the war to improve their lot. No doubt the greatest benefit they derived was the experience of organizing.

Clara Barton, the pioneering nurse, claimed that women were fifty years ahead of where they would have been had the war not accelerated their advance. Although Barton was not referring only to nursing, that career became the most glamorous new opportunity for women, despite the blood and grime. Nursing had always been an approved activity for women, but the idea of women, particularly young ones, nursing soldiers in army hospitals and camps, possibly rude ones, excited the nineteenth-century mind fearfully. Dorothea Dix (see p. 240), who was appointed government Superintendent of Nurses, was mindful of those objections and incurred the wrath of more than one young woman, who grumbled that "Dragon Dix . . . won't accept the services of any pretty nurses." The minimum age was thirty, and only women "plain in appearance" were invited to apply. Once enrolled, the nurses wore somber, hoopless dresses, without adornments. The barriers to women nurses declined, North and South, as casualties mounted and as women proved their worth and their will to serve. The South did not officially recognize women nurses until September 1862 and then did not pay them adequately. The North set up specific requirements for nurses and a suitable program of training under the direction of Dr. Elizabeth Blackwell, who had already broken a barrier in becoming the first woman in the United States to graduate from medical college (see p. 242). Dr. Blackwell did a great deal of her important work through the Women's Central Relief Association of New York, an early volunteer organization that helped spur the War Department to organize the United States Sanitary Commission. That organization pulled together the volunteer services of many diverse groups and individuals under government supervision; it was the most famous example of the combination of private and public organization to grow out of the war effort. Under its auspices nursing help, medical supplies, and some small comforts were brought to soldiers in every sector of the fighting. One of the most dynamic and colorful of the Sanitary Commission's nurses was Mary Ann Bickerdyke, "Mother Bickerdyke," in her middle forties and very

*Workers at the Watertown Arsenal*

rough-spoken, who moved in her somber Quaker dress over nineteen battlefields in the course of the war, ordering officers of every rank about, all in the interest of better care for the wounded.

Another volunteer organization under the loose surveillance of government was the American Freedmen's Aid Commission, which had grown spontaneously among sympathetic Northern groups to do what they could for black refugees from slavery displaced by the war. Those groups sent hundreds of schoolteachers into the South as areas were opened up by the progress of Union armies to teach the black children and minister in other ways to a fugitive population lacking every human necessity. That story belongs more properly to the long saga of the blacks' reach toward freedom, reconstruction and beyond. But the women who came South came as concerned teachers mindful of the needs of the war's most innocent victims.

In nearly every walk of life women made forward strides; to an astonishing degree, they were able to maintain their gains after the fighting had ceased. The significance of those changes was not easy to measure, however, during the painful years of conflict.

## The decisive campaigns of 1863

***Chancellorsville.*** The military might of the Confederacy had reached its peak in 1862, though few recognized the fact at the time. The three great campaigns of 1863 put the South on the defensive and

ended Confederate hopes for military victory. In the East, Robert E. Lee once again carried the war into the North; in the West, Ulysses S. Grant pressed to reduce Vicksburg and gain control of the Mississippi; and in Tennessee, the Union at last moved energetically against the Confederate lines at Chattanooga. Those campaigns revealed that the North could achieve victory if it had the patience to push to its conclusion a slow war of attrition.

In Virginia the winter stalemate was broken when General Hooker crossed the Rappahannock River above Fredericksburg; his plan was to outflank Lee's army and force him either to retreat or be caught in a Union net. Once across the river, Hooker failed to move fast enough, a victim of his own irresolution. Lee then executed one of the most brilliant maneuvers of the war. Splitting his army, he sent "Stonewall" Jackson to attack Hooker's dangerously extended right wing. On May 3, near Chancellorsville, Jackson caught the federal forces by surprise and in smooth cooperation with Lee's diversionary offensive came close to destroying an army of 130,000 men with a force only half as large. The result was not so favorable to the South as it could have been, for the Union Army managed to withdraw north of the Rappahannock. Union losses were heavy and morale low, but the army was saved. The victory had been costly to Lee as well, for Jackson was mortally wounded the night after the battle by one of his own pickets who failed to recognize him in the darkness.

The extraordinary cooperation between Jackson and Lee, made possible by an absence of vanity surprising in high officers, had been worth regiments to the Confederate cause. With Jackson gone, the Army

345

of Northern Virginia would never be the same again. Even so, Lee began once more to ponder an invasion of the North. President Lincoln was pondering where he could find a general to match Lee's daring.

**Vicksburg and Gettysburg.** In the West, Union forces were at last gaining a clear advantage. The greatest fortified point on the Mississippi River still in Confederate control was Vicksburg, which commanded a bluff above a hairpin curve in the river and served as a vital connection between the eastern and western parts of the Confederacy. Late in 1862 Ulysses S. Grant set about reducing Vicksburg as well. After fruitless efforts to approach the city over the bayou country to the north, Grant hit on a better plan. He marched his troops down the west side of the Mississippi, ran his naval transports down the river under the Vicksburg batteries to pick the troops up, and brought his army across the river for an approach from the south. Sweeping eastward, Grant prevented reinforcements from reaching Confederate General J. C. Pemberton, who with a force of thirty thousand tried to defend Vicksburg against Grant's approach. Grant caught Pemberton within the defensive lines of Vicksburg and put the city under a six-week siege. The defending soldiers were exhausted, and the population of Vicksburg was reduced to near-starvation. Recognizing that no help could reach him, Pemberton surrendered on July 4, 1863. The fall of Vicksburg was

followed shortly by the capture of Port Hudson, the last Confederate strong point on the river. Those events marked the turning point of the war in the West. The Confederacy was now split in half.

Grant's strategy and determination brought about the fall of Vicksburg. It was also the result of a strategic decision made by Lee and Davis. To relieve pressure on the Western army under Pemberton they had to choose between two courses of action: either they could send divisions of Lee's army to aid Pemberton, or they could launch a second invasion of the North, which might persuade Lincoln to call part of Grant's army east. Lee and Davis decided that invasion of the North was now the best hope of the Confederacy. England might yet intervene, and the war-weary people of the North might give up their attempt to subjugate the South. In June, the Army of Northern Virginia, ragged but merry, swung into the Shenandoah Valley and again took the road north. This time they were heading for Harrisburg, Pennsylvania.

"Fighting" Joe Hooker followed, keeping his army between Lee and Washington and begging all the way for reinforcements. Actually Hooker seemed hesitant to engage Lee; he complained of petty problems and seized the first opportunity to resign his command. Lincoln, accepting the resignation with alacrity, gave the post to General George G. Meade, who reluctantly accepted. Meade was an able soldier with

Grant's army at Vicksburg

a good record for skillful deployment of troops. He was hot-tempered enough to earn the nickname "Old Snapping Turtle," but he had no stomach for a war of attrition.

On July 1 the two armies stumbled toward each other and fell almost by chance into the greatest battle of the war. The fighting began on the northern side of Gettysburg, Pennsylvania, not because either commanding officer had decided upon the spot but because some detached units happened to clash there. With a speed that astonished the Confederates, the new Union commander concentrated his army on a strong position along Cemetery Ridge, south of Gettysburg. Meade's line resembled an inverted fishhook, anchored at its eye by two rocky promontories called Round Top and Little Round Top. To the north the hook nearly encircled Culp's Hill. This was an extraordinarily strong defensive position.

On a line about a mile distant, across an open field, the Confederates held high ground on Seminary Ridge. Lee had to decide whether to risk breaking his lines to encircle the enemy's position or to launch a frontal assault on the Union lines. Confederate cavalry officer J. E. B. Stuart, whose men were the "eyes" of Lee's army, had been detached earlier on reconnaissance, and Lee had to make his decision without knowing what dangers an encircling movement might entail. Against the advice of General James Longstreet, now Lee's second in command, Lee decided on a frontal assault. Hoping Lee would change his mind, Longstreet dragged his feet and unwittingly gave the Union Army time to prepare. On July 3, the Confederates tried to soften the Union lines with the heaviest bombardment they could muster. Those who heard it on that hot, dry afternoon reported that the guns were as loud as any thunderstorm, and that there had never been anything like it in the entire war.

Then Lee made a grievous error of judgment. He launched fifteen thousand men under General George Pickett across the mile-wide field in a futile assault on the Union center. Pickett's Charge was a glorious restaging of the old warfare of legendary valor, flying banners, and disastrous bloodletting. Modern weaponry had made this kind of courage obsolete. In a devastating repulse, federal troops ended Lee's offensive power forever. After a day of mournful waiting for a counteroffensive that never came, the Army of Northern Virginia limped off down the Shenandoah Valley in a torrential rain. It was July 5, the day after the fall of Vicksburg. Lee had sustained nearly twenty-five thousand casualties in the battle.

The Union losses were as great as those of the Confederacy. Four months later, when President Lincoln dedicated the National Cemetery on the field at Gettysburg, he said of the brave Union dead that they had "nobly advanced" the cause of a new nationalism founded on liberty for all, and that it remained for the living to see that the nation would have "a new birth

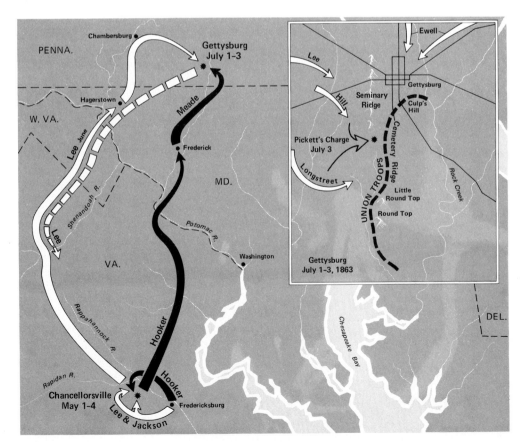

⑤ The war in the East, 1863

in freedom." Much hard fighting lay ahead, enough to discourage many patriots, but at Gettysburg the Union war effort had rounded a corner.

***The Tennessee campaign.*** In the West, the evenly matched armies of William Rosecrans and Braxton Bragg faced each other for six months. In spite of frantic urgings from the War Department that he go on the offensive, Rosecrans had delayed interminably. In September 1863 he suddenly sprang into action, and in a series of smart maneuvers he pressed Bragg southward and eastward into northern Georgia. On

⑥ Fighting around Chattanooga, 1863

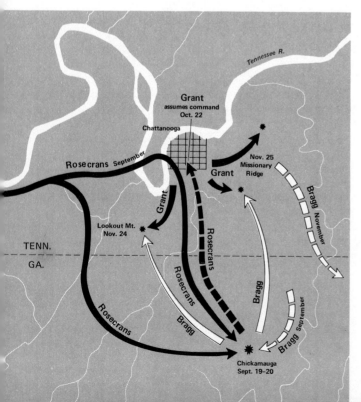

September 19 and 20, however, the Confederates caught their pursuers off guard and turned on them in one of the most savage engagements of the entire war. Between the two armies nearly thirty-eight thousand casualties were suffered at the Battle of Chickamauga Creek, and the Confederates routed the right flank of Rosecrans' army. Had it not been for the firm stand of General George Thomas, the Virginia-born commander of Rosecrans' left flank, the Union offensive might have been ruined. What the Union owed to Thomas, the victorious Confederates owed to General Longstreet, who had rushed the survivors of the Gettysburg campaign over rickety rails in time to reinforce Bragg's forces.

The Union forces, now under General Thomas, the "Rock of Chickamauga," withdrew to Chattanooga. Bragg followed slowly, supposing that a shortage of supplies would force Thomas to surrender. But late in October Grant arrived with fresh supplies and with Lincoln's commission to take over as supreme commander in the West. Grant infused vigor into the Tennessee campaign. In a tremendous feat of railroad warfare he brought twenty-three thousand troops from the East in two weeks' time. Thus strengthened, on November 24 and 25 Grant drove the Confederates back to the Georgia line and tightened his grip on Tennessee.

The year ended far better for the Union than it had begun. Lee's invasion of Pennsylvania had expended his offensive power; the Union now controlled the entire Mississippi; and Grant's army was poised near the Georgia line ready for further action. The Confederacy was being fragmented and crushed. General Scott's once-rejected "Anaconda Plan" had become the formula for victory.

Lincoln saw that the South was doomed. In the spring he sent for U. S. Grant, the general he had been

**A field nurse reports from Virginia**

looking for all along. An aggressive fighter, Grant could be relied on to press the enemy, however heavy the losses, to unconditional surrender. Lincoln named Grant to a newly created post, General of the Armies. The North was building a modern command system, and Grant would direct all theaters of the war. General Henry W. Halleck, called "Old Brains" by friend and foe alike, became the chief of staff, a new position created to clear communications between Grant, Lincoln, and the distant field commanders. Conducting the war from his field tent, Grant left the tactical details of the Virginia campaign to General Meade, his immediate subordinate, while he himself coordinated the strategy of the Eastern and Western sectors. Grant's plan was to destroy the two great armies of the South.

Both the Union and the Confederacy now shook up their field command. General William Tecumseh Sherman assumed the post Grant had vacated in the West, and Davis at last reinstated Joseph E. Johnston as commander of the Army of Tennessee. In the spring Sherman pressed into northern Georgia. His objective was Atlanta, a center of what was left of the

South's dwindling economic power. Grant launched his own offensive against Lee in the East.

Those dogged campaigns brought appalling casualties. The armies of Lee and Grant fought steadily and savagely from the first days of May into early June—from the Wilderness, to Spotsylvania Court House, to North Anna, and then to Cold Harbor. In just one month Grant sustained nearly sixty thousand casualties and Lee thirty thousand. Grant's efforts to

⑦ Grant's campaign around Richmond, 1864–65

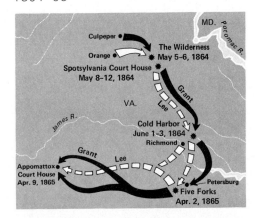

*Confederate fortifications at Atlanta*

encircle Lee's right flank were continually repulsed, with Lee showing uncanny skill in predicting the direction of Grant's next blow. Like his predecessors, Grant proved unable to destroy the Army of Northern Virgina, but unlike them he kept coming on despite grievous losses. After Cold Harbor, he passed below Richmond and put Petersburg, Virginia, under siege. This vital railroad center anchored Richmond to the Deep South, and Grant understood that without it Richmond would fall. Lee now had to stretch his army to protect the whole line between the two cities. Before it fell, Petersburg sustained a nine-month siege, the longest of the war.

Sherman's task was no easier than Grant's. Johnston fought a series of superb defensive engagements, and at Kennesaw Mountain, on June 27, he repulsed Sherman in a battle that cost the Union two thousand casualties. But Sherman was gaining ground, and Jefferson Davis once again lost faith in Johnston's generalship. In mid-July he gave the command to John B. Hood, who took the offensive. After two disastrous pitched battles, on July 20 and 22, Hood withdrew to Atlanta's entrenchments. The Union armies had invested the heart of the Confederacy.

**The election of 1864.** With the war in Grant's competent hands, Lincoln turned his attention to the fall elections. A Republican triumph seemed essential to military victory, because the Democrats were gaining strength from a peace movement of formidable proportions. Numbers of war-weary Northerners decided that the South would accept a negotiated peace if the slavery issue was abandoned; few realized that the end of the war was near. Northerners who read the ghastly casualty lists from the battles in Virginia called Grant a "butcher." When they reflected on Lincoln's curtailment of civil liberties, they asked if Lincoln himself was not heading a conspiracy to destroy American democracy. The Republicans, by naming a

*"Long Abraham: a little longer": the campaign of 1864*

war Democrat, Andrew Johnson of Tennessee, as Lincoln's running mate, hoped to neutralize criticism and win the election. Now they called themselves the Union party.

Lincoln faced disaffection even within his own party. Radical Republicans believed him too soft in his conduct of the war and too gentle in his plans for the readmission of former Confederate states to the Union. Lincoln had already begun his efforts to reconstruct occupied Louisiana, and as Union armies

**In the path of Sherman's army**

ploughed deeper into the South the question of how the former Confederate states were to be reorganized became a potent political issue. After hostilities ceased, Lincoln's plan would allow returning Southerners to participate in the political rehabilitation of their state if they would merely pledge allegiance to the United States, even though they had supported the Confederacy during the war. Once 10 percent of those in a state who had voted in 1860 had taken such a pledge, the state could, under Lincoln's plan, reorganize. Radical Republicans challenged Lincoln by passing the Wade-Davis bill, which would have limited voting in the Southern states to those who could pledge that they had always been loyal, who could say that they had never given aid or comfort to the Confederate government. Sponsored in the Senate by Benjamin Wade of Ohio and in the House of Representatives by Henry Winter Davis, the bill was a pattern for a harsh and thorough reconstruction of the South. Although Lincoln vetoed that bill, he could not still its sponsors. In a public manifesto denouncing the President's course, the Radical Republicans in Congress accused Lincoln of usurping congressional responsibility by beginning the reorganization of Louisiana on his own initiative. A number of Radicals,

challenging Lincoln's nomination, backed the candidacy of John C. Frémont. Lincoln was nervous about the election. "This morning as for some days past," he reflected on August 23, "it seems probable that this Administration will not be re-elected."

Fortunately for the Republicans, the Democrats tried to straddle the war issue. They denounced the war as a failure and proposed an armistice and peace negotiations. Yet they nominated the popular George McClellan, who denied that the war had failed. While criticizing the Republicans for making emancipation a goal of the war, McClellan also condemned Democrats who sought peace at the price of disunion.

It was good news from the front that reelected Lincoln. In late summer 1864, Rear Admiral Farragut captured Mobile Bay. Just before election time, Philip Sheridan routed the troops of General Jubal A. Early from the valley of Virginia. But best of all was the news that Hood had evacuated Atlanta on September 1. Northern spirits soared. Frémont retired from the campaign, and the Radicals closed ranks behind the President.

Lincoln won 55 percent of the popular vote and carried the Electoral College by two hundred twelve to twenty-one. He was supported by a strong coalition of middle-class professional men, farmers, skilled laborers, and conservative Union people who had voted for Bell in 1860. McClellan ran well in areas carried by Breckinridge in 1860, and the Democrats attracted most of the immigrant vote.

Lincoln had won a clear mandate for his policies. But the contest had engendered a profound bitterness that lived on into the decade of Reconstruction following the war. The Democrats, in an effort to fix blame for the lengthening casualty lists on Lincoln's emancipation policies, had coupled with their legitimate complaints a sordid appeal to racism. The Administration on its side had made a doubtful play for the soldier vote, allowing voting only in units where Republican sentiment was strong. Voting by voice made it difficult for soldiers in the field to oppose the general will. On the home front, military units were stationed in areas of strong peace sentiment to discourage Democrats from voting. The hatreds and partisanship of the war years had been raised to fever pitch before the polls even opened.

**The bitter end.** After the election Lincoln's generals moved quickly. Sherman, cutting loose from his supply base, let his army feed off the countryside. Leaving Atlanta behind, he headed southeast for Savannah. Lonely chimneys of burned homes and a charred, desolate landscape sixty miles wide marked the route of his famous journey to the sea. Behind his army followed a throng of black refugees seeking freedom.

But in the hearts and minds of the people of the South, this modern soldier left the strongest impression of all. The social system of the South could not withstand the economic might that Sherman's vast well-equipped and well-armed army represented, and after his passing the will to fight died. Hood's futile effort to distract Sherman from his march across Georgia ended in the destruction of Hood's army at the hands of General Thomas in the battle of Nashville. At Christmas Sherman telegraphed Lincoln the news of Savannah's fall.

The Confederacy had no armies left capable of doing harm. As Sherman pushed northward through

⑧ Sherman's Drive, 1864–65

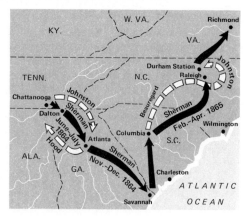

the Carolinas, Joseph Johnston confessed that he could "do no more than annoy him." In Virginia, Lee failed in a last desperate effort to break the Union lines and had to abandon Petersburg. Federal forces promptly occupied Richmond, and Lee's battered army moved westward. On April 9, at Appomattox Court House, Lee surrendered the Army of Northern Virginia to Grant. Johnston surrendered within a few days, and the remaining Confederate forces followed in short order. After four terrible years, the Civil War was over.

But the Union was not restored. The architects of peace would have to be statesmen, not soldiers. In his moving Second Inaugural Address, Lincoln had pledged to strive for a new Union based on human liberty and justice. The hopes of his countrymen were crushed on the night of April 14, at Ford's Theater in Washington, when a crazed actor, John Wilkes Booth, shot the President. He died the next morning. Gone was the leader who had planned for peace even in the agony of war, and gone with him were the prospects, never bright, that the nation might be reunited "with malice toward none; and charity for all."

*Lee's surrender*

**Suggestions for reading**

*GENERAL*

Here as in the preceding chapter the best introductory treatment, from the point of view of both its text and its extensive, critical bibliography, is J. G. Randall and David Donald, *The Civil War and Reconstruction* (2nd ed., 1961). A more extended treatment is found in Allan Nevins, *The War for the Union*, 4 vols. (1959–71). For a valuable short synthesis see R. F. Nichols, *The Stakes of Power** (1961), and, especially on military affairs, Bruce Catton, *This Hallowed Ground** (1956).

The literature of the Civil War abounds in good personal accounts. The outstanding Confederate diary is Mary Boykin Chesnut, *A Diary from Dixie** (1961), edited by B. A. Williams. Comparable in depth and grander in scope is R. M. Myers, ed., *The Children of Pride* (1972), the letters of a Georgia family caught in a social revolution. Thomas Wentworth Higginson, *Army Life in a Black Regiment** (1870), is a romanticized but fascinating account of the author's experience as leader of a black regiment; Suzie King Taylor, *Reminiscences of My Life in Camp* (1902), tells the story of a black laundress who taught black troops to read. For the impact of the war on writers, see Daniel Aaron, *The Unwritten War** (1973); on intellectuals, George Fredrickson, *The Inner Civil War** (1965); and on participants, Edmund Wilson's superb *Patriotic Gore** (1962).

*THE CONFEDERACY*

The outstanding study of the Confederacy is the judicious, trenchant Clement Eaton, *A History of the Southern Confederacy** (1954). E. M. Coulter, *The Confederate States of America, 1861–1865* (1950), is good social history, but less critical. A useful short account is C. P. Roland, *The Confederacy** (1960). Frank Vandiver, *Their Tattered Flags* (1970), is an accomplished short account of the Confederacy, enlivened by fine characterizations of the leaders. The causes of the South's defeat are the subject of a series of incisive essays in David Donald, ed., *Why the North Won the Civil War** (1960). On *The Confederate Congress* (1960) see W. B. Yearns' treatment, as well as T. B. Alexander and R. E. Beringer, *The Anatomy of the Confederate Congress* (1972). On Richmond, see Emory Thomas, *The Confederate State of Richmond: A Biography of the Capital* (1971). Among many special studies, one of the most engaging is B. J. Hendrick, *Statesmen of the Lost Cause* (1939), which examines Jefferson

*Available in a paperback edition.

Davis and his civilian associates. A more sophisticated treatment of the same subject is in R. W. Patrick, *Jefferson Davis and His Cabinet* (1944). T. L. Connelly and Archer Jones, in *The Politics of Command* (1973), describe Davis' arrival at strategic decisions in the political crossfire between Lee and the Western generals and leaders. Mary Ellison, *Support for Secession: Lancashire and the American Civil War* (1972), shows how the cotton-mill workers of England felt about the war. Two works of F. L. Owsley are of the first importance: *King Cotton Diplomacy* (1931) and *State Rights in the Confederacy* (1925). Emory Thomas, *The Confederacy as a Revolutionary Experience** (1971), shows the toll the war took on state rights. Among the many biographies of significance are Hudson Strode, *Jefferson Davis,* 2 vols. (1955), and R. M. McElroy, *Jefferson Davis: The Unreal and the Real,* 2 vols. (1937), as well as R. R. Von Abele, *Alexander H. Stephens: A Biography* (1946). Frank Vandiver's *Ploughshares into Swords* (1952) on Josiah Gorgas and Confederate ordnance is excellent. C. B. Dew, *Ironmaker to the Confederacy: Joseph R. Anderson and the Tredegar Iron-Works* (1966), is a unique account.

### LINCOLN AND THE UNION

The general studies cited above and the Lincoln studies listed here afford the appropriate points of departure for understanding the Union during the Civil War. Among additional important works, three bear upon significant diplomatic issues: E. D. Adams, *Great Britain and the American Civil War,* 2 vols. (1925); M. B. Duberman, *Charles Francis Adams** (1961); and the good biography of Seward in S. F. Bemis, ed., *The American Secretaries of State and Their Diplomacy,* 10 vols. (1927–29). See also G. G. Van Deusen's biography of William H. Seward (1967). F. L. Klement, *The Copperheads in the Middle West* (1960), explains the motivation of the group largely in economic terms, whereas disloyalty and danger are stressed by G. F. Milton, *Abraham Lincoln and the Fifth Column** (1942), and Wood Gray, *The Hidden Civil War: The Story of the Copperheads** (1942). The best general account of Lincoln's policies in the border states is E. C. Smith, *The Borderland in the Civil War* (1927). For a superb study of important agricultural developments P. C. Gates, *Agriculture and the Civil War* (1965), is best. For an overview of society in the Union states see E. D. Fite, *Social and Industrial Conditions in the North during the Civil War* (1910). A fine study of an important agricultural state is Frederick Merk, *Economic History of Wisconsin During the Civil War Decade* (1916). Sidney Ratner, *American Taxation* (1942), W. C. Mitchell, *Gold, Prices and Wages under the Greenback Standard* (1908), and R. P. Sharkey, *Money, Class and Party** (1959), treat the financial history of the Union. Indispensable on its subject is J. G. Randall, *Constitutional Problems under Lincoln** (1926). M. E. Massey, *Bonnet Brigades* (1966), recounts the amazing extent of woman's participation in the war, at home and on the front.

There is no end to Lincoln literature. The best short biography is Benjamin Thomas, *Abraham Lincoln* (1952). Among longer biographies, Carl Sandburg, *Abraham Lincoln: The War Years* [abridged version*], 4 vols. (1939), is distinguished for its passion, and J. G. Randall, *Lincoln the President,** 4 vols. (1945–55), completed by R. N. Current, for its depth and judgment. Among many anthologies, P. M. Angle, ed., *The Lincoln Reader** (1947), stands out for its readability. Two especially incisive collections of essays are David Donald, *Lincoln Reconsidered** (1956), and R. N. Current, *The Lincoln Nobody Knows** (1958). Truly interested students will want to consult R. P. Basler and others, *The Collected Works of Abraham Lincoln,* 9 vols. (1953–55), and the thorough Jay Monaghan, ed., *Lincoln Bibliography, 1839–1939,* 2 vols. (1945). There is a more selective and critical bibliography in P. M. Angle, *A Shelf of Lincoln Books* (1946), and a good selection of Lincoln writings in P. M. Angle and E. S. Miers, eds., *The Living Lincoln* (1955), and R. P. Basler, ed., *Abraham Lincoln: His Speeches and Writings* (1946). Especially significant on Lincoln as a politician are H. J. Carman and R. H. Luthin, *Lincoln and the Patronage* (1943); W. B. Hesseltine, *Lincoln and the War Governors* (1948); and T. H. Williams, *Lincoln and the Radicals** (1941). On Lincoln and military affairs, besides the books listed below, T. H. Williams, *Lincoln and His Generals** (1952), and R. V. Bruce, *Lincoln and the Tools of War* (1956), are particularly rewarding.

### BLACKS AND EMANCIPATION

The war almost immediately affected the status of blacks, and J. M. McPherson, *The Negro's Civil War** (1965), tells the story in a fine documentary history. *The Struggle for Equality** (1964) by the same author explains the abolitionists' drive for emancipation during the conflict. For an account of Lincoln's

*Available in a paperback edition.

views, see Benjamin Quarles, *Lincoln and the Negro* (1962), and his *The Negro in the Civil War** (1953), a pioneering work in its field. B. I. Wiley, *Southern Negroes, 1861–1865** (1938), is an outstanding early effort to cover a complex subject. For the limited nature of the North's commitment to black emancipation, see Louis Gerteis, *From Contraband to Freedman, Federal Policy toward Southern Blacks, 1861–1865* (1973). On the same topic see relevant essays in C. V. Woodward, *American Counterpoint: Slavery and Racism in the North-South Dialogue** (1971), as well as George Fredrickson's *The Black Image in the White Mind** (1971). J. P. Voegeli's *Free But Not Equal** (1967) is indispensible for Northern attitudes, while R. F. Durden's *The Gray and the Black* (1972) recounts the Confederate debate on the emancipation issue. Two works covering the transition of slaves to freedom in specific areas are J. W. Blassingame, *Black New Orleans, 1860–1880** (1973), and Peter Kolchin, *First Freedom: The Responses of Alabama's Blacks to Emancipation and Reconstruction* (1972). For the impact of the war on one South Carolina community of blacks see W. L. Rose, *The Port Royal Experiment** (1964). The outstanding work on the black man's military contribution is D. T. Cornish, *The Sable Arm** (1956). In *Armies of the Street* (1974) Adrian Cook gives the first thorough account of the New York draft riot of 1863, most of whose victims were blacks.

## MILITARY EVENTS

Just about every significant general, Union or Confederate, and just about every significant engagement at arms, has been the subject of at least one, and ordinarily of several, books or essays. The would-be specialist has no convenient terminus in his or her reading; the neophyte can begin profitably in any one of many places. For an exciting and informed start, an interested student might turn to the writings of Bruce Catton: *Mr. Lincoln's Army** (1951); *Glory Road** (1952); *A Stillness at Appomattox** (1954); *America Goes to War** (1958); *Banners at Shenandoah** (1965); *Centennial History of the Civil War,* 3 vols. (1961–63); *Grant Moves South* (1960); *This Hallowed Ground** (1956); *U. S. Grant and the American Military Tradition** (1954). See also E. S. Miers, *Web of Victory: Grant at Vicksburg* (1955), and F. D. Downey, *Storming the Gateway, Chattanooga, 1863* (1960). Jay Monaghan, *Civil War on the Western Border, 1854–1865* (1955), provides one of the good accounts available of the trans-Mississippi war, and the Northern navy absorbs several authors, among them R. S. West, Jr., *Mr. Lincoln's Navy* (1957), and C. E. Macartney, *Mr. Lincoln's Admirals* (1956)—both general accounts. John Niven's superb *Gideon Welles* (1973) should not be overlooked.

There is also an intriguing but more technical study in J. P. Baxter III, *The Introduction of the Ironclad Warship* (1933). The common soldier has had admirable attention from B. I. Wiley, *The Life of Johnny Reb** (1943) and *The Life of Billy Yank** (1952). Also good on that subject is the anthology, H. S. Commager, ed., *The Blue and the Gray: The Story of the Civil War as Told by Participants,* 2 vols.* (1950). *The Personal Memoirs of U. S. Grant,* 2 vols. (1885, 1886) are still an impressive testimony to the author's ability and humility, possibly the best of all Civil War memoirs, but W. T. Sherman, *Memoirs,* 2 vols. (1875), is also first rate; and both men have had talented biographers, in particular Lloyd Lewis in his memorable *Sherman, Fighting Prophet* (1932) and *Captain Sam Grant* (1950). James A. Ward, *That Man Haupt* (1973), is good on the gruff railroad engineer. On the Southern side, the literature, like the valor, balances that of the North, and D. S. Freeman stands out as one of the great historians of the conflict in his two classics, *R. E. Lee, A Biography,* 4 vols. (1934–35) and *Lee's Lieutenants,* 3 vols. (1942–44). On Lee's great lieutenant, Frank Vandiver, *Mighty Stonewall* (1957), and Lenoir Chambers, *Stonewall Jackson,* 2 vols. (1959), are readable accounts. The first Western battles of the Confederacy are covered splendidly in T. L. Connelly, *Army of the Heartland: The Army of the Tennessee, 1861–1862* (1967). Connelly's account of the South's western army concludes with *Autumn of Glory* (1971). See as well Robert L. Kerby, *Kirby Smith's Confederacy: The Trans-Mississippi South, 1863–65,* and Ludwell Johnson, *Red River Campaign: Politics and Cotton in the Civil War* (1958). Shelby Foote's three-volume study *The Civil War* (1958–1973) is narrative history at its best.

Finally, not even a list as brief and selective as this should omit mention of the atlases of the Civil War: the most authoritative, H. S. Commager, 1958 ed. of *Atlas to Accompany the Official Records of the Union and Confederate Armies* (1891–95); the more modern, in its design and use of symbols, V. J. Esposito, ed., *The West Point Atlas of American Wars,* 2 vols. (1959); and the motorists' handy J. B. Mitchell, *Decisive Battles of the Civil War** (1955).

*Available in a paperback edition.

# CHAPTER 15

# The aftermath of war

**T**he long war was over. Now the nation, still divided in spirit, plunged into a decade of political and social turmoil. Northern victory had preserved the Union and had ended slavery; the constitutional right of states to secede would never be argued again. But all else was confusion. The Constitution was as silent on how states could be readmitted to the Union as it was on their right to secede. Indeed if Lincoln was correct in holding that states could not secede, then the Southern states had not seceded. They would simply resume their former responsibilities and enjoy their old privileges. The Southern states hoped for just such a simple restoration, even though the bitterness of the war made it unlikely that the North would at once embrace them again.

Uncertainty too marked the future of the blacks emancipated by war. Would the Southern states relegate the freedmen to peonage, handicap them legally as they had handicapped free blacks before the war, or grant them full citizenship? That question would have to be resolved by the Southern people, ill equipped to do so, because they had been devastated materially and emotionally by the war. And, although many Southerners were slow to realize it, their answer would have to satisfy the Northern people.

Northerners faced dramatic changes of their own. Since the 1840s the North had been moving rapidly toward an industrial economy. The war had only diverted the demographic and social changes that accompany industrialism, and with the return of peace those changes sped forward once again. In 1863 immigration resumed its prewar pace, and after the war, for approximately ten years, an average of three hundred thousand new Americans arrived each year at the nation's ports. Every year more workers moved to the city, where they became increasingly dependent on industrial employment, and more vulnerable to cycles of trade. Unprecedented opportunities for wealth opened for businessmen. The distractions posed by a dynamic economy prevented Northerners from concentrating steadily on the problems of Southern Reconstruction. Then, too, the passions of war were slow to subside, and few politicians of either section could rise above partisanship to disinterested statesmanship. The war lasted four years; winning the peace required twelve.

357

*Charleston, South Carolina: the ruins of war*

# The problems of recovery

**The new nation.**  The South had seceded from a union of states. It returned to a nation forged by war and vindicated by victory. Although the new spirit of nationalism was evident in many ways, especially in the powers exercised by the President and Congress, it revealed itself most clearly in economic legislation enacted during the war years. The absence of traditional Southern opposition in Congress during the war had made it easy for Republicans to adopt a protective tariff and reduce foreign competition in industry, to create a national banking system, to put through a homestead act, and to start funding a transcontinental railroad. Those measures signaled a new era of expansion in industry, agriculture, and transportation—all under the favoring hand of the national government.

Prosperity fed a mood of confident materialism. Seizing the opportunities of wartime economic expansion and inflation, entrepreneurs concentrated in their own hands new wealth that they now sought to invest. They had not far to look. Technological advances, many inspired by the demands of war, opened thousands of new opportunities to put capital to work. The natural resources of the country, seemingly inexhaustible, were more available than ever; industrialists exploited them fully, often ruthlessly and wastefully. Such vital indexes of industrial growth as the production of pig iron and bituminous coal and the extent of railroad mileage climbed sharply.

The iron horse symbolized the age of energy. The forty thousand miles of railroad track laid in the decade after 1865 stimulated heavy industry and opened the further West to agriculture, supplying the food for an expanding army of industrial workers. Federal loans and land grants had sped the construction of the Central Pacific eastward from California and the Union Pacific westward across the plains. For every mile of track laid the railway company received 6,400 acres of free land. Congress made generous loans on second-mortgage bonds: $16,000 for each mile of level ground covered, $48,000 in the mountains, and $32,000 in the high plains. As the two roads raced for their share of the federal subsidies, they sacrificed quality to speed. Still their accomplishment was spectacular. The Union Pacific built 1,089 miles of track; the Central Pacific, 689. They met at Promontory Point, northwest of Ogden, Utah. At ceremonies there on May 10, 1869, the blows of a silver sledge drove in the golden spikes connecting the rails. Now only a week's journey separated the Atlantic Ocean from the Pacific.

Demobilization posed problems for the Northern economy. Eight hundred thousand Union veterans were released in six months, and the abrupt cancellation of war contracts threw a million men out of work. Secretary of the Treasury Hugh McCulloch picked this inopportune time to withdraw from circulation nearly $100 million of the greenbacks that had been issued during the war. Constricting the currency when so many were unemployed intensified a brief but sharp economic slump in 1867. Within a year, however, railroad construction and expansion of the industries that supplied railroads with essential equipment created new jobs for the unemployed. Until 1873, when a new depression struck, most Americans were optimistic about the future.

**The devastated South.**  In the South there was no such boisterous return to civilian pursuits. Agriculture, the region's economic bulwark, had been ruined wherever armies had clashed and passed. "The country between Washington and Richmond was . . . like a desert," wrote one observer. Another described the path of Sherman's march as "a broad black streak of ruin and desolation." Houses and outbuildings had been burned, crops destroyed, and livestock killed. Seed to plant new crops was often unavailable, and many farmers could not afford to buy it when they found it. Horses and mules to plow the land were even harder to find. Credit was almost unobtainable, and labor was scarce. A quarter of a million soldiers had lost their lives, and many freedmen were reluctant to work for their former masters. They believed, not without reason, that one-time masters would never treat one-time slaves as free people. The freedmen had other problems. Seeking relatives lost in slavery, returning to old homes, and looking for land and jobs, they were much on the road. They long remained a disorganized element in the work force the South required for economic recovery.

The cities fared no better than the countryside. Industry had been crippled or abandoned, financial institutions ruined, and resources for credit wiped out. At one stroke, emancipation had destroyed a credit base made up of billions of dollars invested in slaves. Land values slumped in response to the general devastation and lack of labor. The appearance of cities in the path of the armies was as dreary as the real condition of their industry and commerce. Charleston, South Carolina, was "a city of ruins, of desolation, of vacant houses, of widowed women, of rotting wharves." Columbia lay in ashes, as did most of Richmond.

Most Southerners, accepting defeat with fortitude and resignation, set about rebuilding their land. Many Southern whites expressed relief that slavery had come to an end but were at the same time uneasy about how the races would live together in the future. Long conditioned to rely on slavery as a means of controlling blacks, they were afraid of insurrections in the first year after the war, especially in regions where there were many freedmen. They could not even imagine political equality between the races. The freedmen had to face their own emotional hurdles. Learning to accept the responsibilities of family and self-support was not easy for men who had no land, no money, no education. When freedmen did manage to win some success, few understood the effort success required; when they failed, friend and foe alike were apt to explain it on grounds of inferiority.

The Northerners proved to be generous conquerors, as conquerors go. They executed no one for treason and briefly imprisoned only a few Confederates, one of them Jefferson Davis. They volunteered indispensable relief for the destitute of both races. In the last year of the war they had created the Bureau of Refugees, Freedmen, and Abandoned Lands, commonly known as the Freedmen's Bureau, to aid emancipated slaves. The Bureau frequently aided whites as well. After the war was over the Bureau sent supplies, seed, and rations to planters so farming could begin anew and freedmen could get work. It protected freedmen from exploitative planters and provided them with transportation to reach their families.

But poverty and daily reminders of defeat were hard for white Southerners to bear, and Northern bounty was not always graciously received. Women expressed their bitterness by shunning the army of occupation and by wearing on their gowns the insignia of the Confederacy in the form of buttons taken from the uniforms of husbands and sweethearts. Many young people of the defeated planter class had little hope for the future. "For the first time in my life I feel the pressure of want," wrote one young veteran, struggling vainly to conquer bitterness. "I have no country, no flag, no emblems, no public spirit. . . . I live now simply to live, and for my family." Experienced Southern leaders, however, were eager to reorganize their state governments and regain their lost political rights. They anxiously awaited reassuring signals from the North.

**The dilemma of Reconstruction.** Southerners aware of Lincoln's course during the war had reason

*Camp for freedmen*

to be optimistic. Although Lincoln had used military might to reestablish state governments, his plan was generous, its workings swift. As the Northern armies occupied Tennessee, Louisiana, and Arkansas, Lincoln had installed military governors and had sought the support of the loyal minority of citizens in establishing governments loyal to the Union. He had generously pardoned former Confederates who would take an oath of loyalty to the Constitution and the Union. In December 1863, by presidential proclamation, Lincoln outlined a plan for the full restoration of the Southern states to the Union. When in any state one-tenth of the citizens who had voted in the presidential election of 1860 had taken that oath, they could establish a government, without slavery, and the President would recognize it as the "true government." In 1864 Tennessee, Louisiana, and Arkansas had reorganized under Lincoln's "10 percent plan."

The Radical Republicans in Congress had challenged Lincoln's plan by passing the Wade-Davis bill. Moreover, Congress refused to seat congressional delegations from the states Lincoln had reorganized under his plan. In these actions the Radicals had strong support from moderate Republicans who agreed that Lincoln had usurped Congress' authority by taking over Reconstruction and who distrusted the loyalty of the Southern citizenry almost as deeply as the Radicals did (see p. 351). The harsh Wade-Davis bill provided that only after a majority of citizens in a state had taken an oath of loyalty to the United States could their state be reorganized. But only citizens able to take an ironclad oath of past loyalty could vote for representatives to the constitutional conventions. To deny former Confederate officials any role in the new governments, the bill provided that they could not be representatives to the conventions, and that new constitutions must disqualify them from voting and holding office. Lincoln vetoed the Wade-Davis bill, but Congress adamantly refused to seat delegates from the states Lincoln had reorganized. In the Wade-Davis Manifesto the Radicals rebuked Lincoln publicly, instructing him to execute the law and leave the making of it to Congress. The war ended with this conflict unresolved.

The Republicans in Congress faced a serious political problem. By an ironic twist, the late Confederate states stood to gain in defeat more representatives in Congress than they had had before the war. The elimination of slavery meant that blacks, only three-fifths of whom had been counted for purposes of congressional representation while they were slaves, would now be counted to their full number as freedmen. If the freedmen were enfranchised, Republicans might hope they would vote for the party that had emancipated them. To insist that the Southern states enfranchise freedmen before being readmitted to the

Union was politically dangerous, however, because even in the North only a few states (those with the fewest blacks) allowed blacks to vote. There was also the danger that Southern planters might use their economic power to influence the votes of their former slaves, thus strengthening the Democrats rather than the Republicans. Beyond these immediate concerns was the Constitution's guarantee that states had the right to regulate their own suffrage requirements, and no one supposed that any Southern state would voluntarily grant the vote to freedmen. Republicans saw no way around their problem. On one point they were firm, however: they had no intention of giving the Democrats the Southern votes they needed to win back their power in Congress. Lincoln himself had hoped to build Republican support among Southern whites, but even he had wavered when he saw Louisiana electing conservatives unwilling to compromise on the race issue.

Republicans seldom spoke openly about the dilemma posed by Southern congressional representation. They stressed instead their distrust of the former rebels and what they pictured as the disloyal behavior of Northern Democrats during the war. Many Republicans, perhaps a majority, believed that the safety of the Union rested on their party's staying in power. They suspected that a combination of former rebels and Northern "Copperheads"—their name for pro-Southern Democrats—might even persuade the federal government to assume the Confederate war debt. For these reasons the Republicans were determined to bar Southern representatives from Congress until the government of the Southern states rested securely in the hands of loyal Unionists, preferably Republicans.

**Johnson takes charge.** Lincoln might have untangled the political snarl in which his party was caught. He was a superb politician, deft in maneuver. But before he could devise a workable plan, an assassin's bullet put Andrew Johnson in the White House.

Born to poverty in North Carolina, Johnson moved to Tennessee as a young man and earned his living as a tailor. After he was married, his wife taught him to read and write. By dint of determination and hard work he overcame his background and rose in the politics of his adopted state, serving before the war in both houses of Congress. Johnson never outgrew the attitudes shaped by his harsh past. A belligerent man, he hated aristocrats and special privilege. And yet he had little regard for the freedmen, who in his view were instruments of planter privilege rather than oppressed chattels. Only the destruction of the planter class would, he believed, give power to the poor whites and yeoman farmers, the classes best equipped, in Johnson's mind, to make the South democratic and loyal. Johnson's struggle upward through the rough

politics of Tennessee had not taught him the need to compromise. A rigid man, devoted to the Constitution, he was unable to reconcile his literal interpretation of that document with the revolutionary demands of the times. He showed none of Lincoln's flexibility or capacity for growth.

With Congress in recess when the war ended, Johnson seized the initiative. On May 29 he issued two proclamations. The first granted amnesty to former Confederates who would take an oath of loyalty to the Constitution and the federal laws. Their property was to be restored to them, except for slaves and any lands and goods that were already in the process of being confiscated by federal authorities. Fourteen classes of persons were excepted from the general amnesty, however, including the highest-ranking civil and military officers of the Confederacy, all those who had deserted judicial posts or seats in Congress to serve the Confederacy, and persons whose taxable property was worth more than $20,000. Those men were to make individual applications for amnesty, though the President promised to judge each case fairly. In denying automatic pardon to the rich, Johnson seemed as reluctant as the most ardent Radicals to trust Reconstruction to the "bloated aristocrats" he deemed responsible for secession. Still, no one knew what criteria he would use in judging their pleas for amnesty.

The second proclamation, in which Johnson outlined his requirements for the reconstruction of North Carolina, foreshadowed the policy he would follow in future proclamations to other states. He appointed William W. Holden, a well-known Unionist, as provisional governor and directed him to call a convention for the purpose of amending the state constitution "to restore said State to its constitutional relations to the Federal government." Johnson stipulated that only those who had taken the loyalty oath could vote for delegates or serve in that capacity at the convention. Although he did not include the "10 percent" provision, Johnson believed he was following Lincoln's plan of Reconstruction. Indeed, he accepted the governments already established in Arkansas, Louisiana, Tennessee, and Virginia under Lincoln's plan. Only after a public outcry against the leniency of his terms did Johnson require the returning states to disavow their ordinances of secession, repudiate the Southern war debt, and ratify the Thirteenth Amendment. That amendment, which would end slavery forever in the United States, had been approved by Congress in January 1865. Because there were now thirty-six states, approval by some of the former Confederate states was needed to reach the three-fourths that was required for ratification.

The easy terms that Johnson set for the restoration of Southern states to the Union bothered many

Northerners. Southerners heightened that concern by voting into public office popular former-Confederates. Johnson might have helped by being more chary of his pardons to Confederate leaders, for without pardons they were not qualified to hold public office. The pardoning process was extremely cumbersome, however, demanding his attention to every case, and the harassed President fell into the habit of approving all the pardons requested by the provisional governors. Since those governors were Unionists, he followed their advice. Some, like Governor B. F. Perry of South Carolina, forwarded every petition they received. Others requested pardons to reward or to win political friends and withheld them to destroy political foes. Johnson, inundated with petitions, pardoned freely. All too often those he pardoned soon turned up as duly elected congressmen and officers of the restored state governments. Among them was the former Vice President of the Confederacy, Alexander H. Stephens, who was elected senator from Georgia. The stubborn loyalty of the Southern voters to their former leaders alarmed the North.

There were other signs of Southern obstinacy. Some states refused to repudiate the Confederate war debt. South Carolina merely "repealed" its ordinance of secession, thus refusing to admit that it had been unconstitutional. The Thirteenth Amendment was ratified, but without Mississippi's approval. Southern Unionists and freedmen complained that they were not safe under the Johnson governments.

Clearly Johnson was failing in his plan to transfer leadership to the yeoman farmers. By late summer of 1865 Governor Holden of North Carolina was complaining to the President that there was "much of a rebellion spirit" left in the state. He feared that Johnson's "leniency" had "emboldened" the enemies of the government. Privately Johnson counseled Southern leaders to avoid antagonizing the Radicals in Congress, but he was too stubborn to admit publicly that his plan had misfired. Trapped by his own lavish pardoning policy, he had bestowed political power on the very leaders he had once distrusted most.

## Reconstructing the South

***Congress acts.*** When Congress reconvened in December 1865, only the Democrats and a few Republicans were willing to admit the Southern delegates. The majority of Republicans feared that if they seated former champions of the Confederacy they would surrender control over the course of Reconstruction. And yet many of those who voted against admitting the Southern delegates still hoped that Johnson might cooperate with the moderates in Congress by adopting a stronger Southern policy. The moderates were not, in the winter of 1865–66, ready to adopt a radical plan of Southern Reconstruction.

The Radicals, though only a small minority in Congress, had one advantage over the moderates: they held strong opinions on Reconstruction and they knew what they wanted. They believed that, beyond the freedmen, there were few true Unionists in the South. To ensure the future of the Republican party and the safety of the Union they worked for the rapid advancement of the freedmen and the exclusion of the old Southern leaders from politics. Some Radicals were bent mainly on humiliating the South. But others were truly concerned for the safety of the blacks, most of whom had supported the North during the war, some by serving in the army. All the Radicals, however, wanted to protect Southern Unionists from the ex-Confederate leaders whom Johnson was now restoring to power.

Thaddeus Stevens, a rancorous but able congressman from Pennsylvania, exemplified this mixture of vindictiveness and idealism. He opposed black suffrage (though he was later to endorse it), because he feared that the Southern planters would use their economic power to control the freedmen's votes. Instead of the vote, he proposed to give the freedmen land. He would confiscate the holdings of former Confederates and divide it into small freeholds. "Forty acres . . . and a hut," he declared, would "be more valuable . . . than the . . . right to vote." In the coastal areas of South Carolina and Georgia freedmen were already farming land, under "possessory titles," that had been assigned them by the government on estates confiscated during the war. Stevens wanted this policy extended throughout the South.

Charles Sumner, on the other hand, pinned his hopes on suffrage. He called first for votes only for educated blacks and black veterans but soon moved for general black suffrage. He argued that freedmen required the vote for their own protection. Other Radicals, including Salmon P. Chase and Ben Wade, agreed with Sumner. But the moderates, still the majority of Republicans, hoped to discover a middle road short of suffrage, between Johnson's simple restoration and the Radicals' more sweeping plans. The moderates dominated the Joint Committee on Reconstruction, which was created in December 1865 to formulate a plan for the South.

As the Joint Committee began its work, signs of Southern intransigence multiplied. Radical congressmen received countless letters from Southern Unionists complaining that they were at the mercy of former rebels. The deepest suspicions were aroused when the Southern states began to pass laws defining the status of blacks. These new "black codes," which

**Thaddeus Stevens on black suffrage**

*There is more reason why colored voters should be admitted in the rebel States than in the Territories. In the States they form the great mass of the loyal men. Possibly with their aid loyal governments may be established in most of those States. Without it all are sure to be ruled by traitors; and loyal men, black and white, will be oppressed, exiled, or murdered. There are several good reasons for the passage of this bill. In the first place, it is just. I am now confining my argument to negro suffrage in the rebel States. Have not loyal blacks quite as good a right to choose rulers and make laws as rebel whites? In the second place, it is a necessity in order to protect the loyal white men in the seceded States. The white Union men are in a great minority in each of those States. With them the blacks would act in a body; and it is believed that in each of said States, except one, the two united would form a majority, control the States, and protect themselves. Now they are the victims of daily murder. They must suffer constant persecution or be exiled....*

*Another good reason is, it would insure the ascendency of the Union party.... I believe ... that on the continued ascendency of that party depends the safety of this great nation. If impartial suffrage is excluded in the rebel States, then every one of them is sure to send a solid rebel representative delegation to Congress, and cast a solid rebel electoral vote. They, with their kindred Copperheads of the North, would always elect the President and control Congress. While slavery sat upon her defiant throne, and insulted and intimidated the trembling North, the South frequently divided on questions of policy between Whigs and Democrats, and gave victory alternately to the sections. Now, you must divide them between loyalists, without regard to color, and disloyalists, or you will be the perpetual vassals of the free-trade, irritated, revengeful South.... I am for negro suffrage in every rebel State. If it be just, it should not be denied; if it be necessary, it should be adopted; if it be a punishment to traitors, they deserve it.*

**From Thaddeus Stevens, Speech to the United States House of Representatives, January 3, 1867.**

looked like the old slave codes, were actually more like the laws governing free blacks in antebellum times. Blacks could now own property, witness, sue and be sued in court, and contract legal marriages. In some states they could even serve on juries. Despite these seemingly liberal provisions, the thrust of the new codes revealed Southern determination to keep blacks in a separate and inferior position. Blacks were segregated; intermarriage was forbidden; in Mississippi blacks could not own land; in several states they had to pay a special license fee in order to engage in certain trades. Everywhere special punishments were prescribed for black vagrants and for those who broke labor contracts. In some states blacks who could show no means of support could be bound out by the courts as labor apprentices. The most severe codes, drawn up by Mississippi and South Carolina in 1865, reflected the fears of whites during the social chaos of the first six months of peace. Those that followed in the winter of 1865–66 were little better. All were based on the assumption that freedmen would never be anything but dependent farm-workers. Both Radicals and moderates quickly agreed that the black codes must go.

**The search for a middle course.** In order to counteract the black codes, Congress soon enacted two bills reported by the Joint Committee on Reconstruction. The first, passed in February 1866, extended the life and expanded the powers of the Freedmen's Bureau; the second, passed in April, made a sweeping guarantee of civil rights.

Moderates regarded the Bureau of Refugees, Freedmen and Abandoned Lands as the perfect means of safeguarding Southern Unionists and blacks. Basically a paternalistic agency, the Bureau had been set up in March 1865 primarily to help thousands of displaced persons—refugee white Unionists, and freedmen—get homes, jobs, food, and transportation. The original Freedmen's Bureau Act had empowered the agency to administer lands abandoned by Confederates or confiscated from them and had committed the government to grant freedmen homestead rights to those lands. Under the benevolent administration of Commissioner Oliver Otis Howard, the Bureau provided housing and transportation to Northern schoolteachers who came to the South to teach illiterate freedmen. The Bureau had its faults.

*Southern freedmen:
objects of the black codes*

The military officers who served as bureau agents sometimes seemed friendlier to the planters than to the freedmen, and a few of them were cruel and even venal. Some of the agents leased farms for themselves and worked them with their charges; others used their power to "enforce contracts" more in the interest of the planters than the freedmen.

On the whole, however, those who were concerned for the safety of the freedmen knew that the Bureau was indispensable. Only those unsympathetic to the fate of blacks accused the Bureau of "coddling" them. Though Johnson had rendered the land provision in the original act void by returning confiscated property to its owners, the Bureau still had substantial power. The new bill, extending the life of the Bureau, would grant local agents authority to see that free labor contracts were just and that they were enforced, to defend freedmen against unscrupulous employers, and even to conduct courts when they found that freedmen were not receiving justice.

President Johnson held that those provisions would lead to "military jurisdiction," which was unconstitutional in time of peace. Accused persons tried in the Bureau courts would be tried and even convicted, he stated, without benefit of jury, rules of evidence, or right of appeal. And so Johnston vetoed the bill. He used his veto message to rebuke Congress for continuing to exclude the Southern delegates. Although Johnson's observations on the dubious constitutionality of the Freedmen's Bureau bill had some merit, they irritated congressmen who knew that freedmen were not getting justice in Southern courts. Four days after vetoing the bill Johnson harangued a crowd gathered outside the White House to hear him deliver a Washington's Birthday greeting. In a rambling speech he denounced his opponents as traitors, suggested that they wanted to kill him, and compared himself to the crucified Christ. Johnson clearly saw himself as the martyred champion of the Southern states and constitutional liberty.

Furious, Congress turned to its civil-rights bill. That bill sought to grant freedmen the protection of federal citizenship, thus securing for them the same rights and protection as whites regardless of local statutes. Further, it authorized the use of troops to enforce its privileges and penalties. Again the President resorted to a veto. But this time Congress overrode him and voted the Civil Rights bill of 1866 into law. Heartened by their success, congressional leaders now put through a mildly amended version of the Freedmen's Bureau bill. Once again Johnson vetoed it, and once again Congress overrode his veto. Some Republican senators had sustained Johnson's veto of the first Freedmen's Bureau bill, but only three of them sustained his veto of the amended bill. The broad middle section of the Republican party had joined forces to guarantee civil rights for the freedmen. The President in his obstinacy had consolidated his adopted party in opposition.

**The Fourteenth Amendment.** In the case of Dred Scott (see p. 306) Chief Justice Roger B. Taney had given his opinion that no black, whether free or slave, could be regarded as a United States citizen or was entitled to the privileges the Constitution granted citizens. Many Republicans, remembering that decision, were afraid to depend on an act of Congress, which would be subject to Supreme Court review, to secure civil rights to the freedmen. They decided that

*School for freedmen, Vicksburg, Mississippi*

**Reconstructing the South**

only an amendment to the Constitution would safeguard the freedmen and secure a new electorate in the South loyal to the Union. The Fourteenth Amendment, proposed in April 1866 by the Joint Committee on Reconstruction, was subsequently passed by Congress on June 19. First it defined American citizenship: "All persons born or naturalized in the United States, and subject to the jurisdiction thereof, are citizens of the United States and of the State wherein they reside." The amendment then prohibited states from passing laws "which shall abridge the privileges or immunities of citizens of the United States," from depriving "any person of life, liberty, or property, without due process of law," and from denying "to any person within its jurisdiction the equal protection of the laws." Although the courts in time began to interpret the word "person" to include corporations (to protect them from state regulatory laws), the framers of the Fourteenth Amendment had only the freedmen in mind.

The second and third sections of the Fourteenth Amendment attempted to bring about a basic change in the Southern electorate. The second tried to force the states to grant Negro suffrage: either they enfranchised all male citizens or else they would lose seats in the House of Representatives proportionate to the number they excluded. Some Radicals would have preferred a specific guarantee of universal manhood suffrage. Practical politicians realized, however, that such a guarantee might have led to the defeat of the amendment in the North, for only a few New England states had enfranchised blacks. The third section disqualified from officeholding, state and federal, all who before the war had held public office requiring an oath to support the Constitution and who had subsequently supported the Confederacy. Only Congress could remove this disability. Other sections of the amendment disavowed the Confederate war debt, validated the United States war debt, and disallowed all claims for loss of property, including slaves.

**The battle joined.**   The upcoming congressional elections of 1866 caught the voters in a widening rift between President and Congress, with the Fourteenth Amendment as the central issue. The summer and fall witnessed the bitterest congressional election in national history. As with the Thirteenth Amendment, favorable action by some Southern legislatures was needed to secure ratification by the required three-fourths of the states. President Johnson opposed the Fourteenth Amendment and encouraged Southern legislatures to oppose it too. Of all the former Confederate states only Tennessee ratified the amendment. Vainly hoping to prompt other states to follow suit, Congress seated Tennessee's delegates.

Johnson continued to oppose Republican measures, especially the Civil Rights Act and the Freedman's Bureau Act, with all the weapons at his command. He used the patronage to reward his friends and hurt his enemies. As commander in chief he replaced military officers serving as agents in the Freedmen's Bureau who showed themselves too enthusiastic in the freedmen's cause. He interpreted acts of Congress passed over his veto so narrowly that he almost negated their intent. By cultivating the support of Democrats he angered all Republicans. Though Johnson claimed to be working for peace and reconciliation, he was actually trying to unite moderate and conservative Republicans with willing Democrats in a new National Union party. His purpose was to elect his own supporters to Congress in 1866.

The new party held a convention in Philadelphia in August, but the delegates could do no more than state grand principles. There was no real community of interest in the conglomeration of conservative Republicans, Democrats, and former Confederates who attended. Republicans grew skittish, moreover, at the reappearance of their old enemies, the "rebels" and the "Copperheads." At one point Governor Orr of South Carolina, a huge man, walked down the aisle arm-in-arm with Governor Couch of Massachusetts, a slight man. The scene symbolized the Republican fear that the Southerners were about to overpower the Unionists. The convention was a fiasco.

An even greater fiasco was the President's personal campaign to win support for conservative congressmen. In a "swing-around-the-circle" stump-speaking junket through the Middle West, he met hecklers on their own terms and sacrificed the dignity of his office at every whistlestop. The people grew angry, especially as the President revealed over and over his hostility to blacks. In recent outbreaks of racial violence in Memphis and New Orleans scores of blacks had been killed and hundreds wounded. The President deplored those events, as did most Southerners, but the voters could see nothing in Johnson's restoration policy to prevent them from recurring. In November the Democrats and most of Johnson's supporters were swept out of office. The Republican regulars had won a critical victory.

***Congressional Reconstruction.***   Although the election was more a rejection of Johnson than a mandate for extremists, the Radicals eventually gained most of their aims. The voters in calling for the Fourteenth Amendment as a basis of Reconstruction were endorsing a moderate measure, contemplating only essential changes. But securing enough Southern states to adopt so unpopular an amendment would require forcible measures. Thus a moderate victory became the avenue for a Radical triumph. Even Thaddeus Stevens, though disappointed that Southern estates would not be confiscated and turned over to the freedmen, was pleased with the stringency of the legislation Congress now passed.

On March 2, 1867, in its final hours and after long debate, the outgoing Thirty-ninth Congress drove through a bill "to Provide for the more efficient Government of the Rebel States." This Reconstruction Act returned the South, two years after the war, to military rule. The severity of the act was partly owing to the determination of the Radicals, but even more to the unwitting aid of the Democrats who had joined with them to defeat less harsh proposals offered by moderate Republicans. Johnson's veto, not unexpected, condemned the bill as "utterly destructive" to the "principles of liberty," but his veto was promptly overridden.

The new law divided the ten Southern states (Tennessee had already been readmitted to Congress) into five military districts, each under the command of an army general backed by troops and armed with full authority over police and over judicial and civil functions. Each commander's immediate task was to secure a new (and verifiably loyal) electorate in his district, to enroll blacks, and to eliminate all persons excluded under the Fourteenth Amendment. Those voters were to elect a constitutional convention, which would draw up a document granting universal manhood suffrage and excluding "such as may be disfranchised for participation in the rebellion." Although the conventions interpreted that requirement variously, most new state constitutions excluded former Confederate leaders from voting and office-holding, and some excluded any who had sympathized with the Confederacy. An estimated 150,000 whites were thus disfranchised. The Reconstruction Act further declared that after a state had presented an acceptable constitution to Congress and had ratified the Fourteenth Amendment, Congress would then admit that state's delegates.

Even after this impressive victory, congressional leaders feared that Johnson might use his authority as commander in chief to subvert their intentions. Some even suspected that he might attempt a military coup. So they passed two more measures to trim his power. The Army Appropriations Act directed the President and the Secretary of State to issue military orders through the General of the Army, U. S. Grant, who was required to maintain his headquarters in Washington. The Tenure of Office Act provided that any officeholder appointed by the President with the Senate's consent was to serve until the Senate had approved a successor. If the President replaced a Cabinet member while the Senate was out of session, the replacement would serve after the Senate reconvened only with its consent; otherwise, the former incumbent would resume his duties. The Tenure of Office Act was designed in general to keep Johnson from using the patronage to destroy those who opposed his views on Reconstruction, in particular to prevent his replacing Edwin Stanton, Secretary of War. Stanton was the only member left in the Cabinet who was friendly to the Radicals, and many Radicals, including Stanton himself, believed that the safety of the nation depended on his remaining in office. The Tenure of Office Act further provided that, unless the Senate approved a change, Cabinet members were to hold office "during the term of the President by whom they may have been appointed, and for one month thereafter." These two acts, the second of dubious constitutionality, were passed on March 2, the day on which the Reconstruction Act was passed.

The Radical program of Reconstruction was now as airtight as its sponsors could make it. In the following months Johnson and the Southern leaders exploited loopholes in the new laws, but Congress promptly closed them by passing three supplementary

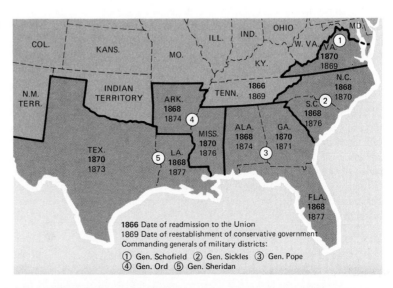

Reconstruction

1866 Date of readmission to the Union
1869 Date of reestablishment of conservative government
Commanding generals of military districts:
① Gen. Schofield ② Gen. Sickles ③ Gen. Pope
④ Gen. Ord ⑤ Gen. Sheridan

**Radical doctrine for Reconstruction**

*It is the opinion of your committee—*

*I. That the States lately in rebellion were, at the close of the war, disorganized communities, without civil government, and without constitutions or other forms, by virtue of which political relations could legally exist between them and the federal government.*

*II. That Congress cannot be expected to recognize as valid the election of representatives from disorganized communities, which, from the very nature of the case, were unable to present their claim to representation under those established and recognized rules, the observance of which has been hitherto required.*

*III. That Congress would not be justified in admitting such communities to a participation in the government of the country without first providing such constitutional or other guarantees as will tend to secure the civil rights of all citizens of the republic; a just equality of representation; protection against claims founded in rebellion and crime; a temporary restoration of the right of suffrage to those who had not actively participated in the efforts to destroy the Union and overthrow the government, and the exclusion from positions of public trust of, at least, a portion of those whose crimes have proved them to be enemies to the Union, and unworthy of public confidence.*

**From the Report of the Joint Committee on Reconstruction, 1866.**

---

acts. However unhappily, Johnson at last declared that he would execute the laws.

**The Republican South.** During the last half of 1867 most of the Southern states wrote acceptable constitutions under military supervision, called their new legislatures into session, and ratified the Fourteenth Amendment. All but three were readmitted to the Union in 1868. There was much foot-dragging over the disfranchisement of former Confederates, who were often the most popular leaders in their states. Endless discussions of this bitter point delayed the writing of constitutions in Virginia and Texas; in Mississippi the constitution was defeated because of it. It was 1870 before those three states won congressional approval of their constitutions and were permitted to reenter Congress. Georgia, admitted in 1868, was cast out again when its new legislature dismissed duly elected black delegates. Georgia, too, had to wait until 1870.

By this time one further requirement had been added for readmission: ratification of the Fifteenth Amendment, proposed by Congress in February 1869. This amendment forbade the states to deny the right to vote "on account of race, color, or previous condition of servitude." Its most immediate effect was to enfranchise Northern blacks; in the South, blacks were already enfranchised under the new state constitutions. Its sponsors hoped, however, that the amendment would prevent unfriendly legislatures from disfranchising freedmen in the future.

The new constitutions of the Southern states were in many respects better than their antebellum constitutions. The states now assumed responsibility for many social services that had formerly been left to local officials and private initiative. States without public-school systems now established them, along with institutions for the care of the indigent, homeless, and the physically handicapped. Tax systems were made more equitable, penal codes more humane, and the rights of women more comprehensive. For the first time in its history, South Carolina now had a divorce law. In states where planters had enjoyed advantages over upcountry farmers, districting for representation in the legislature was made fairer. The new constitutions also empowered state governments to undertake programs of economic recovery, especially for the rebuilding of the ruined railroads. Though not radical, the new constitutions were modern for their time, and they served the Southern states for several decades after the hated Republicans who initiated them had fallen from power.

Southern conservatives denounced the new governments, mainly because they detested the political coalition that had created them and that served in the first legislatures. They dubbed resident Northerners who held office in the new governments "carpetbaggers," suggesting that as transients they had no stake in Southern society. They denounced Southern whites who cooperated with the new regimes as "scalawags," a term suggesting at once disloyalty and a smallness of means and spirit. The spectacle of blacks

366

*The aftermath of war*

**Veto of the Radicals' plan**

voting for public officers shocked the white South. Although blacks never held office in proportion to their numbers, their very presence in government fostered resentment and complaints of "Negro rule."

The assumption behind all this criticism was that none of these groups had any right to participate in the governing of the South. Actually there was little truth in the stereotypes the conservatives fastened on the Republican coalition. Many scalawags were prominent and affluent leaders who found Republican economic policies not unlike the old Whig program. Small farmers sensed that their interests would be better protected than they had been before the war, and they voted accordingly. The carpetbaggers included all sorts of people who had business in the South after the war. Some were military personnel; some were professionals—teachers, ministers, and lawyers; some were planters; and some, of course, were adventuring businessmen and speculators. There were fewer carpetbaggers than there were scalawags and blacks, but their undoubted loyalty to the Union and their connections with the federal government gave them great influence. Working through local groups called "Loyal Leagues," they organized the black Republican vote in the South.

The great weakness of this Republican coalition was that it had come to power as a result of revolutionary drives generated outside the South. Members of the once-powerful class of planters, now excluded from public office, would always regard the Republican governments as fraudulent and alien.

Yet idealism and high purpose marked the early stages of the Republican effort to rebuild the South. Whether the three groups comprising the coalition could stand together against the stresses of biracial politics was uncertain. Uncertain too was the strength of individual Republicans to resist the temptation for easy wealth presented by the rich spending and borrowing programs that were now launched for economic recovery. The Republican leaders, who professed commitment to more genuine democracy than the South had ever known, were under special obligation to conduct themselves as virtuous public servants.

**The impeachment of Johnson.** Congress had been right in suspecting that Johnson would use his control of the army to weaken the Reconstruction acts. His behavior was technically correct. But by instructing district commanders not to question the past behavior of those who took an oath of allegiance, he permitted Southerners of doubtful loyalty to regain the vote. He eventually removed three generals who were sympathetic to the Radical program, and he rashly challenged Congress in his December message of 1867 by declaring that he would maintain his rights as President, "regardless of consequences."

Several times the Radicals in Congress had contemplated impeaching Johnson, but they could find no legal ground for action. Their opening came when Johnson resolved to test the constitutionality of the Tenure of Office Act. While Congress was in the 1867 summer recess, he dismissed Edwin Stanton and appointed Grant as temporary Secretary of War. When Congress reconvened, the Senate refused to consent to Stanton's removal. Grant withdrew in confusion, protesting that he had never agreed to join the President in breaking the law. Grant had spoiled Johnson's plan, and his critics suggested that he had done so after a hint from the Radicals that he might himself become a presidential candidate. Johnson, angry with Grant, now embarked on an *opéra-bouffe* search for a more cooperative general. As stand-in he finally produced General Lorenzo Thomas, but he had no success in installing his protégé in the War Department. Stanton, barricading himself in his office, cooked his own meals and regularly consulted with the Radical leaders. Removing Stanton was bad enough but trying to replace him with a pliable Secretary of War convinced even moderate Republicans that Johnson now intended to have a free hand in his use of the army to undo what the military Reconstruction Acts were bringing about in the South, and to do so in face of specific laws Congress had passed to prevent him. For moderate Republicans it was the last straw. Mindful of the fall elections when the voters had given the Radicals signs of displeasure over the extreme measures they had taken, the Republican moderates had in December blocked a vote of impeachment, but by February their patience was gone.

Confident that most citizens believed Johnson had broken the law, the Republican majority in the House of Representatives voted, unanimously, on February 24, 1868, to impeach Johnson for "high crimes and misdemeanors in office." The Radicals then drew up a list of specific charges, centering on his alleged violation of the Tenure of Office Act. The most significant was the charge that Johnson had been "unmindful of the high duties of his office . . . and of the harmony and courtesies which ought to exist . . . between the executive and legislative branches." He had attempted to bring Congress into "contempt and reproach." Essentially the House, by this charge, was accusing Johnson of disagreement with congressional policies. A conviction on that charge would have established a precedent for the removal of any President who could not command a majority in the House of Representatives on an important issue. In that event, the American system of balance of powers in government might have given way to the parliamentary system.

To convict the President, two-thirds of the Senate sitting as a court presided over by the Chief Justice would have to agree that Johnson had broken the law (with the implication that he had no right to test the constitutionality of an act of Congress) and that he was not "fit" to hold his office. Johnson's able legal defense had no trouble disposing of the first point. Whatever Johnson had done, he had not broken the Tenure of Office Act, because Stanton had been appointed by Lincoln and not by Johnson and had served beyond the term of the President who appointed him. Cautious senators were troubled by the magnitude of the changes that might follow the removal of a President on the political charge that he had not worked for "harmony" with Congress. By a margin of only one vote, the Senate acquitted Johnson. Chief Justice Chase, who presided at the trial, was in sympathy with the President's arguments, and additional Republican senators would have voted for acquittal had their votes been needed. Many of those who voted to acquit the President did so because they distrusted the radicalism of Benjamin Wade, acting President of the Senate, who would have become President if Johnson had been convicted. Wade's views on public finance, labor, and woman suffrage were fully as radical as his views on civil rights for blacks, and they were far more shocking to the moderate Republicans. After Johnson's narrow escape, Stanton resigned and the Senate adjourned. The defeat of the impeachment was an ominous sign for the future of the new Republican governments in the Southern states.

### The Supreme Court and Reconstruction.

During the war much of the power formerly held by the states had gravitated to the national government. It was not clear whether the executive or legislative branch would be the greater beneficiary of this shift. Then, after the war, the struggle over the military phase of Reconstruction severely upset the balance of powers within the federal government itself. Congressional power had reached a high point in the impeachment action against Johnson, but Johnson had won that contest. In another power struggle he failed: he never got a Supreme Court judgment on the Tenure of Office Act, which remained on the books for twenty years. Neither had he managed to get rulings on the two Reconstruction Acts. What was the role of the Supreme Court during this prolonged struggle between the President and the Congress?

The Court had started off boldly late in 1866. In the case of *Ex parte* Milligan it had ruled unanimously that neither Congress nor the President had the power to create military courts to try civilians in areas remote from war. That noteworthy decision liberated several men who had been condemned by such courts for military subversion in the North during the war. Still, the Milligan decision angered congressional Radicals because it cast doubt on the legality of the courts the Freedmen's Bureau was then sponsoring in Southern states. By passing the Reconstruction Acts in the spring of 1867, Congress delivered an overt challenge to the Court. Unsure of the Court's response, the Radicals began to talk of reducing its size, with some even urging that the Court be abolished. The Supreme Court grew cautious. By a five-to-four decision in the twin cases of *Cummings* v. *Missouri* and *Ex parte* Garland, heard in 1867, it invalidated the use of loyalty oaths, pronouncing them ex post facto and bills of attainder. In the same year, in the cases of *Georgia* v. *Stanton* and *Mississippi* v. *Johnson*, the Court was challenged to rule on the constitutionality of the Reconstruction Acts. In both instances it refused jurisdiction on technical grounds.

The Court's critics charged cowardice. The Justices, they suggested, were afraid that Congress would destroy the Court's power, if it ever elected to use that power, just as it had ridden over the President's prerogatives. But this was not the main reason for the Court's caution. The Court had not been popular in the years following the Dred Scott decision. But when Lincoln replaced the Southern Justices with staunch Unionists, it had grown much stronger in public esteem. By the time Congress and the President clashed, it had no reason to be fearful. Only a few Radicals wanted to destroy the Court. There were more compelling reasons for the Supreme Court's refusal to rule on the Reconstruction Acts: the Justices knew that the country was passing through a revolutionary period marked by questions on which the Constitution was either silent or not clear, and they realized that public opinion in the North demanded a rigorous Reconstruction of the South. Moreover, the Justices felt the public good would be best served by judicial restraint. After Radical Reconstruction waned, the Chase Supreme Court reemerged in the early 1870s with strong decisions that had a profound effect on American law for the rest of the century.

### Foreign affairs under Johnson.

Although Johnson's Southern policy was a disaster, his conduct of foreign relations under the able direction of Secretary of State William Seward was a credit to his record. During the war the French under Napoleon III had affronted the Monroe Doctrine by setting up a puppet government in Mexico under the pliant and ambitious Austrian Archduke Maximilian. Fully occupied with fighting the Confederacy, Lincoln and Seward had denounced the French action but had been unable to challenge Napoleon's bid to restore French imperial power in the Western Hemisphere. Seward lost no time once the war was over. In 1866 President Johnson sent fifty thousand veteran troops to the Mexican border, and Seward demanded the withdrawal of French forces. The French complied, and the Mexicans reestablished their independence.

A vigorous expansionist, Seward believed that trade with other countries would help convince the world of the superiority of American democracy. In 1868 he signed a treaty of friendship and commerce with China. In 1867 he negotiated a treaty to buy the Virgin Islands from Denmark for $7,500,000. The Senate rejected that treaty but at the same time approved one that Seward had arranged with Russia for the purchase of Alaska for $7,200,000. Many Americans joked about Seward's "icebox," for it seemed no more than a frozen wasteland. Time was to demonstrate the strategic value and the richness of Alaska.

**The election of 1868.** Johnson's able conduct of foreign affairs was overshadowed by the turbulent issue of Southern Reconstruction, which dominated the presidential contest of 1868. The Republicans, rejecting Johnson's leadership, nominated Ulysses S. Grant as their presidential candidate, with Speaker of the House Schuyler Colfax as his running mate. Grant had no political experience, but moderates in the party had long favored the candidacy of the popular war hero. While the Radicals preferred Benjamin Wade, they came around to Grant as an "available" candidate who had listened to their advice during the struggle with Johnson and had broken with the President over the Tenure of Office Act. Who better than this popular war leader could inspire voter confidence in the safety of the military Reconstruction measures?

The Democrats were thoroughly demoralized. They had yet to rid their party of the taint of disloyalty, and they had no leaders capable of replacing their prewar spokesmen. For President they nominated Horatio Seymour, a wealthy conservative who as war governor of New York had gained an undeserved reputation for disloyalty. His running mate, Francis P. Blair, though recognized as a staunch Unionist, added little allure to the ticket. The Democratic platform declared the questions of slavery and secession to be settled forever and denounced Republican Reconstruction policies. The party called for amnesty for former Confederates and restoration of the Southern states. Negro suffrage, the Democrats urged, was a matter for the states to settle, not the federal government. This position gained less for the Democrats than it might have, because the Republicans themselves agreed that in the North the suffrage question should be left to the states, while maintaining that black suffrage was essential in the South. The Democratic platform opened the party to the charge that it was soft on the South.

The Democrats' only hope for victory was to focus public attention on the question of money and the repayment of the war debt, which was under hot debate. During the war the government had issued some $450 million in greenbacks. The value of that currency had fluctuated over the years, but it was always below the value of coins and gold-backed currency. Between 1866 and 1868 the Treasury Department had retired some $100 million of greenbacks from circulation. Now the Democrats adopted the "Ohio Idea," sponsored by George H. Pendleton, congressman from that state, who demanded that the notes be reissued to redeem outstanding war bonds not explicitly requiring redemption in gold. This demand for cheap money appealed to debtors, especially farmers with long-term mortgages who stood to benefit from inflation. It appealed also to critics of the "bloated bondholders," the war-profiteers. The Re-

publicans, on the other hand, pledged themselves to the redemption of the national debt in gold. They knew that conservative financiers would approve this adherence to sound money, and they also understood that Western farmers, however much many of them might prefer cheap money, would, like other Northerners, still remember the passions of war vividly enough to distrust the Democrats' amnesty proposals for the South. The racial demagoguery of the Democratic campaign stirred that memory.

The Republicans worked to keep those passions alive. In the savage campaign of 1868, they concentrated on the alleged treason of the Democrats and waved the "bloody shirt" of war. They knew they could count on the support of the Southern states now dominated by carpetbaggers and on the backing of a multitude of federal officeholders. The Democrats lost whatever appeal they might have enjoyed from the Ohio Idea when their nominee, Horatio Seymour, repudiated that plank in the platform. Even with all their advantages, however, including the popularity of U. S. Grant, the Republicans just managed to win. Grant carried the Electoral College by 214 to 80 but received only 52.7 percent of the popular vote. Without the "bloody shirt" and the support of six Southern states safe in Republican hands, Grant would have lost the election. Of the former Confederate states, Seymour carried Louisiana and Georgia and showed strength in all the Border States. Mississippi, Virginia, and Texas had not been readmitted to the Congress, and their votes were not counted. The signs for future Republican victories were not auspicious, and it was plain that without the black votes of the South Grant's popular majority would have been a minority.

## The Grant era

**Government under Grant.** No President had ever come to office so poorly equipped in temperament, intellect, or political experience as Ulysses S. Grant. And it was Grant's fate to come to that office in trying times. The white South, increasingly restive under Republican rule, began to express that restiveness in violence; in the West, farmers were beginning to feel the pinch of a long decline in commodity prices; in the North, a spirit of greedy materialism fostered graft inside the government and out. Grant did not create those problems, but he lacked the statesmanship to meet the first two and the strength of character to resist the third. He had been a great general, with the soldier's virtues of judgment, courage, and loyalty to subordinates. As President he was rudderless and confused by circumstances. His judgment was valueless because it was uninformed. When he found the courage induced by frustration, he often vented it in the malignant persecution of honest critics. He took everything personally. Loyalty to his subordinates proved his undoing, for he was duped at every turn. His mediocre Cabinet included several rascals who helped themselves to public funds. He was so obtuse in his choice of friends, so easily flattered, that he accepted expensive gifts from favor-seekers and appeared in public as the guest of such notorious stock-market swindlers as Jay Gould and Jim Fisk.

Grant, who had a fatal talent for falling out with the few able men who found themselves in his constantly shifting Cabinet, thereby lost the services of those who might have saved his Administration from shame. The one exception was Hamilton Fish, Secretary of State, an able and conscientious man who conducted foreign affairs with dignity and success.

Through the Treaty of Washington, signed in 1871, Fish opened a new era of friendly relations with Great Britain. Among the many problems that had exacerbated Anglo-American relations in recent years, the most serious had arisen over the extensive damage done to American shipping by the *Alabama* and other raiders that the British had built for the Confederacy. Violent speeches had been made in the Senate by irate patriots like Charles Sumner, who demanded that England be made to pay for indirect damage to American shipping as well as for the actual destruction of property. All those problems were referred, under the Treaty of Washington, to international arbitration. The British expressed "regret" about the *Alabama* and agreed to abide by the decision of the arbitration commission. That decision turned out to be favorable to the United States. Although the commission did not allow the indirect claims, it found that Britain had not exercised "due diligence" over her shipyards and awarded the United States $15,500,000. This successful arbitration of a sore dispute advanced both Anglo-American understanding and international peace.

The President's friends could be proud of little else. In his last annual message, Grant sadly acknowledged the faults of his Administration, blaming many of them on his own inexperience. But he pointed out that his political appointments, disastrous as many turned out to be, had been made "upon recommendations of the representatives chosen directly by the people." The patronage system had failed the President, because those representatives were on the whole true products of their age. The gaudy materialism symbolized by the brightly patterned waistcoats and florid oratory of Senator Roscoe Conkling, the flashy idol of New York, had its counterpart in the cheerful abandon with which Congress disposed of public goods. Politicians ignored the plight of the poor and showered their favors on the wealthy. In 1872, Congress abolished the wartime income tax. Like the wealthy, the lobbies of industrial interests, particularly those of copper and steel, found Congress receptive to their urgings. In spite of a 10 percent reduction of duties to placate farmers in 1872, many tariff rates that stood at 25 percent in Henry Clay's time had climbed to 500 percent by that year. Still the industrialists were not satisfied.

Neither were the railroad men, nor the congressmen themselves. In the fall of 1872 newspaper-reporters disclosed that prominent congressmen had accepted stock at "token" rates in return for a promise not to investigate the construction company of the Union Pacific Railroad. The Crédit Mobilier's relation to the Union Pacific was wholly fraudulent. Its purpose was to divert the profits from building the Union Pacific to the pockets of the road's promoters. In this way the Union Pacific was relieved of some $23 million in securities appropriated by Congress. Though many were involved in the chicanery—including Vice President Schuyler Colfax and future President James A. Garfield—only one, Oakes Ames, representative from Massachusetts and organizer of the scheme, was censured.

Corruption in Congress was tame compared to the colorful swindles that were taking place elsewhere. Grant's friends, Fisk and Gould, conspired with the President's brother-in-law to corner the available supply of gold in the New York stock market. Assuming they had convinced Grant not to sell government gold, they drove its market price to dizzying heights. Because many transactions had to be made in gold, the nation's business was thrown into panic. At last Secretary of the Treasury George Boutwell destroyed the scheme by selling $4 million of government gold, bringing the market suddenly down to earth. When the crash came on "Black Friday," September 24, 1869, many innocents were ruined but the principal culprits escaped. Gould, probably on the basis of inside information from government bankers, had started selling early; Fisk escaped by the simple expedient of repudiating his debts and then hiring thugs to threaten his creditors.

In New York City, "Boss" William Marcy Tweed of Tammany Hall relieved the city of an estimated $200 million. That figure included the proceeds from fraudulent bond issues and the sale of franchises as well as graft collected from corrupt contractors and merchants dealing directly with the city government. Since the governor of New York was a Tweed henchman, the "Boss," though a Democrat himself, had little trouble silencing the Republican legislature with bribes. Control of the police, the courts, and the district attorney made Tweed almost invulnerable. At last, when the city was nearly bankrupt, Samuel J. Tilden successfully challenged Tweed for control of the Democratic organization in the city. Tilden gained a perhaps inflated reputation for having "smashed" the ring. Tweed's was only the most notorious of the party machines. Others operated in Philadelphia, Chicago, and Washington. In their heyday they had little trouble winning the cooperation of reputable public figures.

The South experienced the same blight. The corruption of the reconstructed Southern legislatures was particularly disastrous. Governments organized for the first time on the basis of racial equality were hopelessly discredited by association with railroad and printing swindles and eventually fell into bankruptcy. The ideal of political equality suffered in public esteem because it was supported by corruptionists. Bold efforts to rebuild the South's transportation system dissolved in the wholesale theft of railroad stock. In South Carolina even the Land Commission founded to help blacks buy farms ended up as a device for transferring state funds to the private accounts of unscrupulous assessors and their friends in high places. Florida's bill for printing costs in 1869 was more than the entire cost of running the state government in 1860. The list of scandals was long and the crooks were blithe. "Damn it," expostulated Henry Clay Warmoth, carpetbag governor of Louisiana and one of the worst spoilers, "everybody is demoralizing down here. Corruption is the fashion." He had a point. It takes two to make a deal, and many of those who bribed the legislature for favors were native Southerners and Democrats.

Blacks, seldom the beneficiaries of these schemes, were frequently the dupes of those wiser in the ways of the world. Nevertheless the presence of blacks in the legislatures and their loyalty to the carpetbag Republicans enabled disfranchised whites to condemn "Negro rule" and to blame corruption on this experiment in political equality. Even the performance of the honest and efficient Radical government of Mississippi, and of remarkable black leaders like Senator Hiram Revels of that state and South Carolina's Secretary of State Francis Cardozo changed few opinions. Political association with blacks and carpetbaggers became more unpopular as scandals multiplied. Scalawags found themselves ostracized by their neighbors. As one former Whig planter explained when he withdrew from the Republican party, a man with four marriageable daughters could do no less.

White resentment took a vicious turn with the appearance and rapid growth of the Ku Klux Klan. First organized in 1866, the white-hooded nightriders contented themselves for a time with playing pranks on freedmen to frighten them into "good" behavior. But soon the Klan, with its Grand Dragon, "Dens," and "Cyclopses," had spread over the South. Now an instrument of political terror, it attacked the Loyal Leagues, intimidated black voters, and destroyed the effectiveness of local black organizers. Nor did the Klan shun murder. Many able black leaders, including Wyatt Outlaw of North Carolina, lost their lives to the fury of the Klansmen. When the organization was officially disbanded in 1869, it went underground. After an elaborate investigation Congress passed the Ku Klux Klan Act of 1871, empowering the President to suspend the writ of habeas corpus in order to cope with the violence that regularly erupted at elections. The Republican governors were often forced to call on federal troops to keep peace, but critics of the Administration, north and south, abhorred the practice of using soldiers to supervise elections. The North was growing tired of the "autumnal outbreaks," indeed of Southern Reconstruction in general. Before Grant's first term was over, the Republican governments in the South, steeped in corruption and torn by violence, were doomed.

***The Liberal Republican movement.*** Few doubted that the Republicans would nominate Grant for a second term. In 1872, however, a revolt in the ranks of the party gave the regulars pause. Calling themselves "Liberal Republicans," the dissidents challenged the party regulars on three issues: corruption in government, Grant's financial policies (the high level of tariff protection and the continued use of greenback currency, which delayed resumption of specie payments), and the Radical Southern policy.

To eliminate corruption in government, they demanded a reform of the civil service. As early as 1870 Carl Schurz, a German immigrant and war hero, had led a Liberal Republican revolt in Missouri. There the Radical Republicans had all but proscribed party members who wanted to restore political rights to former Confederates in the state. The victorious Liberals took up the cause of the excluded faction and placed B. Gratz Brown in the governor's chair. Before 1872 the Missouri Liberals had merged with a group of prominent Eastern leaders to form a new party. A number of distinguished journalists who had had a hand in exposing scandal lent their talents; E. L. Godkin of the new reform paper, *The Nation*, and two young brothers, Boston patricians, Henry and Charles Francis Adams, were among them. Indeed many men of talent and idealism in the East were sympathetic to the movement, and many one-time abolitionists enrolled against Grant. Even Charles Sumner, who had fallen out with Grant over the President's stubborn but futile determination to annex Santo Domingo (see p. 491), joined the Liberals.

The party had its share of office-seekers, however, who at the 1872 convention in Cincinnati were able to kill the nomination of any of several men they

*The aftermath of war*

These men are not only armed, disciplined, oath-bound members of the Confederate army, but they work in disguise; and their instruments are terror and crime. Why, sir, we are already familiar, and perhaps too familiar, with the common description of these Ku-Klux Klans riding at night over a region of country, going from county to county, coming into a county town, and spreading terror all over a community; and not only that, but they endeavor to excite superstition. They pretended, I believe, in the outset to be the representative ghosts of the Confederate dead. That was the idea which they sought to give out; the ghosts of the Confederate dead were coming back to punish those who had been disloyal to the Confederate service; and they terrified men, women and children, white and black. They excited the superstition of the ignorant negroes of the South, endeavored to frighten them first by superstition, then by intimidation, by threats, by violence, and by murder.

Mr. President, I do not know anywhere an organization similar to this Ku-Klux Klan. I have thought of the Thugs of India. They murdered, and they murdered secretly; but they did not disguise themselves while they were in the act of murder. If any Senator now, in looking over the record of crime in all ages, can tell me of an association, a conspiracy, or a band of men who combined in their acts and in their purposes more that is diabolical than this Ku-Klux Klan I should like to know where it was. They are secret, oath-bound; they murder, rob, plunder, whip, and scourge; and they commit these crimes, not upon the high and lofty, but upon the lowly, upon the poor, upon feeble men and women who are utterly defenceless. They go out at night, armed and disguised, under color of superstitious forms, and commit their work. They go over vast regions of country, carrying terror wherever they go. In all the record of human crime—and God knows it is full enough—where is there an organization against which humanity revolts more than it does against this? I know there is not a Senator here but feels that this thing ought to be put down.

**From John Sherman, Speech in the United States Senate, March 18, 1871.**

feared might fight too well for reform. After a chaotic convention, the Liberals ended up nominating Horace Greeley, the quixotic editor of the New York *Tribune.* Though the Liberals opposed the tariff, Greeley was a protectionist. During his long, controversial career in journalism, the candidate had himself written the script for those who now attacked him for his contradictory statements on public issues. Greeley understood politics well, but not well enough to know that he was a poor candidate. With his wispy chin-whiskers and cherubic face, he looked anything but a President.

In short, the Liberals had failed to come up with an attractive alternative to Grant. The worst of the Grant Administration scandals were yet to be exposed, and the general's heroic image retained its luster. Few Republicans would abandon him to join hands with the hated Democrats. Moreover, the Democrats gave the kiss of death to the new party of dissident Republicans by weakly endorsing its candidates. Even so, the Democrats could not deliver all their party's potential votes to Horace Greeley, long-time Whig, staunch Republican, archfoe of Democrats in general, and anathema in the South. The "bloody shirt" was still a potent symbol, and Grant won a great victory. Greeley died a few weeks later, broken-hearted over his personal defeat and sad that corrupt government had won so thunderous an endorsement.

***The collapse.*** Even though they had lost the election, the Liberals had redefined the goals of most of the concerned and best-informed Northern citizens. Most of them were tired of Southern Reconstruction and embarrassed by the Radical governments in the Southern states. To them reform now meant clean government. Civil-service reform took precedence over civil rights for blacks, and the nation became more interested in economic questions than in supporting regimes in the South that regularly sent delegates to Washington to vote with the Radicals.

Republican sensitivity to the Liberals' criticism was demonstrated just before the election of 1872, when Congress passed the Amnesty Act. By its terms political rights were restored to all former Confederates except about five hundred of the most prominent leaders. In the South, Liberal Republican factions charged party regulars with misgovernment and made a bid for white conservative support in a cleanup campaign. They seldom succeeded, because the white conservatives, now rehabilitated politically, preferred a new political coalition to any form of Republicanism. Defecting scalawags promptly joined ranks. Sometimes the new coalition called themselves Democrats, and sometimes simply "conservatives."

Thoroughly factionalized, the Republican state governments in the South fell, one by one, over the next four years. Now Grant sent troops at election time only when he thought there was a strong chance that the Republicans could win. The triumphant conservatives claimed that they had "redeemed" their states from the Radicals. By the time of the 1876 presidential election, only three (South Carolina, Louisiana, and Florida) were still in Republican control.

Less than a year after Grant's second election political scandals and economic distress had destroyed the brittle reputation of his Administration. A congressional committee revealed that the newspaper-reporters had been right about the affairs of Crédit Mobilier. Worse yet, five of Grant's Cabinet officers were exposed as corruptionists. The most notorious was William W. Belknap, Secretary of War, who had accepted bribes from traders at Indian posts. Benjamin Bristow, Grant's new Secretary of the Treasury, uncovered the Whiskey Ring, a conspiracy of hundreds of distillers who had bribed Treasury officials in order to evade federal taxes. Grant's private secretary, Orville E. Babcock, was implicated in that corrupt adventure. Grant declared, "Let no guilty man escape," but he provided Babcock with a deposition that helped him evade punishment.

Economic disaster followed in the wake of public scandal. In September 1873 a rash of financial failures in New York dragged the country into the deepest depression it had known. The sudden withdrawal of European investments, prompted by the Franco-Prussian War and vast railroad-building abroad, triggered the panic. But American investment in concerns that produced no immediate or real profits, such as the railroads, rendered bankers unable to cope with the crisis. The failure of Jay Cooke & Co., one of the most respected banking firms in the country, set off a chain reaction. Cooke's firm was deeply involved in financing the ∙Northern Pacific Railroad. Eighty-nine railroads defaulted on their bonds, and eighteen thousand businesses failed in two years. Iron mills and furnaces fell idle, and by 1875 half a million men were out of work. Wages declined, and agricultural prices dropped so low that many farmers, unable to pay their mortgages, had to surrender their properties, their homes, their fondest dreams.

Hard times and scandal hurt the Republicans in the congressional elections of 1874. The Democrats elected a majority in the House of Representatives, improved their standing in the Senate, and won control in twenty-three states. Many dissatisfied groups were now blaming Republican financial measures for their problems. As exporters of agricultural products, the South and West disliked the protective tariff. In the West farmers wanted a freer circulation of paper money (the greenbacks issued as legal tender during the war) to ease their burden of debt and, so they presumed, to raise farm prices. But businessmen, with some exceptions, favored a retirement of greenbacks and a return to the gold standard, for they thought that these measures would stabilize the value of currency and thus reduce the uncertainty of commerce and exchange.

The legal status of greenbacks was in doubt. In 1870 the Supreme Court, under Chief Justice Chase, who had been, ironically, Secretary of the Treasury when greenbacks were issued, ruled that the Legal Tender Act was unconstitutional. Protesting that decision, Grant's advisers pointed out that it cast doubt on the validity of all contracts calling for payment in money that had been legal tender ever since 1862. They also feared that the abrupt removal of greenbacks would overly contract the supply of money. Grant, with the consent of the Senate, therefore expanded the Supreme Court by appointing two Justices whose views he knew in advance, and in 1871 the enlarged Court ruled that the government had been within its rights in issuing the paper currency. That opinion settled the legal question but left open the question whether the greenbacks should be kept in circulation.

In 1873, in order to relieve the deflation accompanying the panic, the Treasury Department reissued $26 million of the greenbacks it had retired earlier. But the Administration balked at a further expansion of the currency demanded by Congress the following year. It backed instead a bill designed by John Sherman to give the West and the South a a fairer share of the nation's banking facilities. That bill increased the number of national banks and allowed them to augment the amount of bank notes in circulation. It also provided that after January 1, 1879, the Treasury would, on demand, redeem all legal-tender notes in coin. The Specie Resumption Act became law in 1875. In the same year the Republicans, with the help of some Eastern Democrats, restored the protective-tariff duties that had been reduced three years earlier.

The Republicans were now adopting the twin principles of political economy that would become the party's articles of faith in the decades to come—

high tariffs and hard money. Those principles endeared the party to business and industry but rendered it increasingly suspect to farmers, debtors, and workers. Advocates of paper money severely criticized the Specie Resumption Act. Overlooking its constructive aspects, they predicted that resumption would precipitate a disastrous contraction. But nothing of the sort happened in 1879, when payments in specie were resumed, because of the coincidental return of prosperity. This accident convinced the Republicans of the merit of their "sound money" policy, but it was too late to mitigate the unpopularity the Grant regime had reaped from the depression, from corruption, and from its steady deference to the propertied interests of the country.

**The twilight of Reconstruction.** Scandal and depression during Grant's second term diverted the attention of Congress from the South. Grant, sensing the disenchantment of the public, grew less willing every year to support the toppling carpetbag regimes with troops. Moreover, with most of the older states of the Middle West now safe for the Republicans, a Republican South was no longer essential to their control of the federal government. With federal support withdrawn, the carpetbag governments could no longer withstand the onslaught of the white South. Openly now, without hoods or robes, conservatives organized to intimidate blacks who showed interest in politics, and the few surviving scalawags.

Congress made a last pathetic gesture to the blacks whose fate was at stake. Senator Charles Sumner had introduced a civil-rights bill in 1872 that was passed in 1875, after his death, in a much denatured form. Sumner had intended to assure full equality for the freedmen, including political rights, all civil liberties, and the elimination of social segregation. His purpose was frustrated by the ambiguous racial views of Republican moderates and by Northern opinion. The act, as it was finally passed, guaranteed equal accommodations in such public places as inns and theaters and forbade the exclusion of blacks from jury duty, but it provided no practicable means of enforcement. Moreover, school integration, which Sumner had proposed, was quietly dropped from the final bill. What little force the act carried was destroyed in 1883 when the Supreme Court declared invalid those parts of it designed to secure social equality. The Court also ruled that, although the Fourteenth Amendment prohibited the invasion of civil rights by the states, it did not prohibit the invasion of civil rights by individuals unaided by state authority. Blacks might be driven from the polls or otherwise abused by individuals, and the federal government would have no power to intervene.

Although the emasculation of Sumner's program revealed that Republicans were no longer committed to protecting blacks in their citizenship, the Civil Rights Act of 1875 established a significant precedent. In the next century a new generation of crusaders would rediscover the Civil Rights Acts of 1866 and 1875 and in the Fourteenth and Fifteenth Amendments their original purpose. A new Supreme Court would restore their original meaning. But for two generations blacks were to face a lonely struggle. Deprived of legal recourse to defend their freedom and abandoned by Northern public opinion, they were largely ignored by the federal government.

Reconstruction was a story of lost opportunity. Victory in war had opened the grand prospect of a country reunited on the principles of liberty. Sometimes with the best intentions, but often with greed and venom, the nation's leaders allowed the principles of liberty to be smirched by corruption. In restoring the South, they scarred it. In developing the economy, they abandoned power and granted privilege to a grasping few. In dealing with civil rights, they inspired blacks to reach for high goals and then left them to the mercy of demagogues and embittered whites. The fruits of victory were lost in the aftermath of war.

**Suggestions for reading**

GENERAL

There is a concise analysis of Reconstruction and critical discussion of the bibliography on that subject in J. G. Randall and David Donald, *The Civil War and Reconstruction* (2nd ed., 1961). That volume also covers the Grant years. Three recent and indispensable studies in the rapidly growing scholarship on Reconstruction are W. R. Brock, *An American Crisis** (1963); David Donald, *The Politics of Reconstruction** (1965); and K. M. Stampp, *The Era of Reconstruction** (1965). See also J. H. Franklin, *Reconstruction After the Civil War** (1962); Avery Craven, *Reconstruction: The Ending of the Civil War* (1969); and R. W. Patrick, *The Reconstruction of the Nation* (1967). Another general treatment of the period 1865–78, stressing social and economic conditions, is Allan Nevins, *The Emergence of Modern America, 1865–1878** (1927). The national politics of the period receive detailed but sometimes jaundiced treatment in Matthew Josephson, *The Politicos, 1865–1896** (1938). The national mood

*Available in a paperback edition.

concerns P. H. Buck, *The Road to Reunion, 1865–1900*\* (1937). J. G. Randall, *Constitutional Problems under Lincoln* (rev. ed., 1951), discusses wartime legal decisions that had an impact on postwar reorganization. Clement Eaton, *The Waning of the Old South Civilization*\* (1968), traces Southern reactions to defeat in war.

Lincoln's views on Reconstruction are discussed in W. B. Hesseltine, *Lincoln's Plan of Reconstruction* (1960), and R. N. Current, *The Lincoln Nobody Knows*\* (1958). See also Benjamin Quarles, *Lincoln and the Negro* (1962).

### JOHNSON, THE RADICALS, AND RECONSTRUCTION

H. K. Beale, *The Critical Year: A Study of Andrew Johnson and Reconstruction* (1930), provides a sympathetic treatment of the President, with an interpretation of the Radicals that emphasizes their economic motives. Johnson is criticized for his inept dealings with Congress in E. L. McKitrick, *Andrew Johnson and Reconstruction*\* (1960), an indispensable study. Two recent works of note on Johnson's impeachment are M. L. Benedict, *The Impeachment and Trial of Andrew Johnson*\* (1973), and H. L. Trefousse, *Impeachment of Andrew Johnson* (1975). W. A. Dunning's older study, *Reconstruction, Political and Economic, 1865–1877*\* (1907), is still useful for its concise account of events, though its interpretation is marred by the author's assumptions on race. E. M. Coulter, *The South During Reconstruction, 1865–1877* (1947), has been faulted on the same score, but it provides strong chapters on cultural life. W. E. B. DuBois, in his beautifully written *Black Reconstruction*\* (1935), imposes a Marxist interpretation on the period, without much success.

The two most famous Radical leaders have excellent biographies, in Fawn Brodie, *Thaddeus Stevens, Scourge of the South*\* (1959), and D. H. Donald, *Charles Sumner and the Rights of Man*\* (1970). More generally, H. L. Trefousse treats *The Radical Republicans*\* (1969). David Montgomery, *Beyond Equality: Labor and the Radical Republicans 1862–1872* (1967), discusses the relationship between Northern labor and the Radical goals for Southern blacks. A general survey is Robert Cruden, *The Negro in Reconstruction*\* (1969), as are the relevant chapters in J. H. Franklin, *From Slavery to Freedom* (3rd ed. rev., 1966), and August Meier and E. M. Rudwick, *From Plantation to Ghetto: An Interpretive History of American Negroes* (1966). Peggy Lamson, *The Glorious Failure: Black Congressman Robert Brown Elliott and the Reconstruction of South Carolina*\* (1973), and J. R. Lynch's own *Facts of Reconstruction*\* (1913), provide insights on the position of black leaders in the South.

Alone on its subject is J. E. Sefton, *The United States Army and Reconstruction, 1865–1877* (1967), but related, and of great significance, are two studies of the Freedmen's Bureau: G. F. Bentley, *A History of the Freedmen's Bureau* (1955), and W. S. McFeely, *Yankee Stepfather: General O. O. Howard and the Freedmen*\* (1968). What the Bureau was up against in the South may be overstated in Allen Trelease's powerful *White Terror: The Ku Klux Klan Conspiracy and Southern Reconstruction*\* (1971), but Otto Olsen's *Carpetbagger's Crusade: Albion Winegar Tourgeé*\* (1965) shows that the problems were great. John W. Blassingame, *Black New Orleans, 1860–1880* (1973), deals splendidly with a famous black community in transition, and Peter Kolchin, *First Freedom: The Responses of Alabama's Blacks to Emancipation and Reconstruction* (1972), ably treats a more typical world of farming freedmen. V. L. Wharton, *The Negro in Mississippi, 1865–1890*\* (1947), was a pathbreaking work, now a classic, while Joel Williamson, *After Slavery*\* (1965), records the South Carolina experience. An early contributor to the story of blacks in Reconstruction was A. A. Taylor, whose *Negro in South Carolina during Reconstruction* (1924), *The Negro in the Reconstruction of Virginia* (1926), and *The Negro in Tennessee* (1941) are still useful. W. L. Rose records the experience of blacks and their relationship with the federal government and Northern abolitionists in *Rehearsal for Reconstruction*\* (1964), also about South Carolina. Carol Bleser, *The Promised Land: The History of the South Carolina Land Commission, 1869–1890* (1969), writes of the use and abuse of the one state commission founded to gain for the freedmen what they most wanted. H. L. Swint, *The Northern Teacher in the South, 1862–1870* (1941), is a general treatment of its theme, still useful, and J. M. McPherson, *The Struggle for Equality: Abolitionists and the Negro in the Civil War and Reconstruction*\* (1964), stresses the humanitarian motivation of the abolitionist wing of the Republicans' support. LaWanda and J. H.

\*Available in a paperback edition.

Cox, *Politics, Principle, and Prejudice, 1865–1866*\* (1963), also stress civil rights as the basic issue of political reconstruction, but a number of newer works have questioned the depth of the North's commitment to implementing civil equality for blacks. Louis Gerteis, *From Contraband to Freedman: Federal Policy Toward Southern Blacks* (1973), is illustrative of the trend in interpretation, as is C. V. Woodward, "Seeds of Failure in Radical Race Policy," from the *Proceedings* of the American Philosophical Society, 110(1966), 1. F. G. Wood, *Black Scare: The Racist Response to Emancipation and Reconstruction*\* (1968), also stresses limits. Michael Perman, *Reunion without Compromise* (1973), stresses Southern politicians' skill in resistance.

Among the many reliable state and local studies of Reconstruction in the South are: J. G. Taylor, *Louisiana Reconstructed* (1974); E. S. Nathans, *Losing the Peace: Georgia Republicans and Reconstruction (1865–1871)* (1968); W. M. Evans, *Ballots and Fence-Rails: Reconstruction on the Lower Cape Fear*\* (1967); F. B. Simkins and R. H. Woody, *South Carolina During Reconstruction* (1932); and T. B. Alexander, *Political Reconstruction of Tennessee* (1950). Also of interest on special topics are Richard Current, *Three Carpetbag Governors* (1967), O. A. Singletary, *The Negro Militia and Reconstruction* (1957), and J. W. DeForest's own account of his experiences, *A Union Officer in Reconstruction*, edited by J. W. Croushore and David Potter (1948).

On the Fourteenth Amendment, see J. B. James, *The Framing of the Fourteenth Amendment*\* (1956), and Jacobus ten Broek, *The Antislavery Origins of the 14th Amendment*\* (1951). On the Fifteenth Amendment, see W. R. Gillette, *The Right to Vote*\* (1969). On pardons, see J. T. Dorris, *Pardon and Amnesty under Lincoln and Johnson* (1953). On the role of the courts, see S. I. Kutler, *Judicial Power and Reconstruction Politics* (1968). For a broad general study of the judicial process in the period consult H. J. Hyman, *A More Perfect Union* (1973). For a very detailed history of the Supreme Court, see Charles Fairman, *Reconstruction and Reunion 1864–1888* (1971). Part One, which is Volume VI of the Oliver Wendell Holmes Devise *History of the Supreme Court of the United States.* For wartime thinking in Washington about the constitutional issues of Reconstruction, see Herman Belz, *Reconstructing the Union: Theory and Policy during the Civil War* (1969). (General and special literature on the South and its postwar problems through 1900 is listed in connection with Chapter 16; on American business, consult the listing following Chapter 18.)

### THE GRANT ERA
There is a dearth of truly satisfactory books on this period. W. B. Hesseltine is best on Grant, *U. S. Grant, Politician* (1935). A good general study of business is contained in T. C. Cochran and William Miller, *The Age of Enterprise: A Social History of Industrial America*\* (1942), which also touches intelligently on public policy. Rendigs Fels, *American Business Cycles, 1865–1897* (1959), is authoritative on the Panic of 1873. Glenn Porter is helpful on *The Rise of Big Business 1860–1910*\* (1973). For the currency question, see Irwin Unger, *The Greenback Era* (1964), and for a balanced and significant analysis of public policy on money and the general economic picture of the period, see R. P. Sharkey, *Money, Class and Party* (1959). Postwar diplomacy has had able attention, especially in Dexter Perkins, *The Monroe Doctrine, 1876–1907*\* (1937), and Allan Nevins, *Hamilton Fish: The Inner History of the Grant Administration* (1936), which also provides the best account of the topic described by its subtitle. See specifically Adrian Cook's *The Alabama Claims: American Politics and Anglo-American Relations, 1865–1872* (1975). On the scandals of Grant's time and on the responses to them, three worthy studies are D. G. Loth, *Public Plunder: A History of Graft in America* (1938); C. R. Fish, *The Civil Service and the Patronage* (1904); and E. D. Ross, *The Liberal Republican Movement* (1919). There is a first-rate analysis of Grant and the Liberals in the beginning chapters of E. F. Goldman, *Rendezvous with Destiny*\* (1955). J. G. Sproat, *The Best Men*\* (1968), describes the liberal reformers of the Gilded Age. See also C. M. Fuess, *Carl Schurz: Reformer* (1932), and G. G. Van Deusen, *Horace Greeley: Nineteenth Century Crusader*\* (1952). For a delightful contemporary exposure of Grant era scandals, see C. F. Adams and Henry Adams, *Chapters from Erie (1866)*. On the Tweed Ring see A. B. Callow, *The Tweed Ring*\* (1966), and Seymour Mandelbaum, *Boss Tweed's New York*\* (1965). For a cartoonist's observations of the Grant era's heroes and villains, see Morton Keller, *Art and Politics of Thomas Nast*\* (1968).

\*Available in a paperback edition.

# Appendix

# The Declaration of Independence*

THE UNANIMOUS DECLARATION OF THE THIRTEEN UNITED STATES OF AMERICA,

WHEN in the Course of human events it becomes necessary for one people to dissolve the political bands which have connected them with another, and to assume among the Powers of the earth, the separate and equal station to which the Laws of Nature and of Nature's God entitle them, a decent respect to the opinions of mankind requires that they should declare the causes which impel them to the separation.

We hold these truths to be self-evident, that all men are created equal, that they are endowed by their Creator with certain unalienable Rights, that among these are Life, Liberty and the pursuit of Happiness. That to secure these rights, Governments are instituted among Men, deriving their just Powers from the consent of the governed. That whenever any Form of Government becomes destructive of these ends, it is the Right of the People to alter or to abolish it, and to institute new Government, laying its foundation on such principles and organizing its Powers in such form, as to them shall seem most likely to effect their Safety and Happiness. Prudence, indeed, will dictate that Governments long established should not be changed for light and transient causes; and accordingly all experience hath shewn, that mankind are more disposed to suffer, while evils are sufferable, than to right themselves by abolishing the forms to which they are accustomed. But when a long train of abuses and usurpations, pursuing invariably the same Object evinces a design to reduce them under absolute Despotism, it is their right, it is their duty, to throw off such Government, and to provide new Guards for their future security. Such has been the patient sufferance of these Colonies; and such is now the necessity which constrains them to alter their former Systems of Government. The history of the present King of Great Britain is a history of repeated injuries and usurpations, all having in direct object the establishment of an absolute

Tyranny over these States. To prove this, let Facts be submitted to a candid world.

He has refused his Assent to Laws, the most wholesome and necessary for the public good.

He has forbidden his Governors to pass Laws of immediate and pressing importance, unless suspended in their operation till his Assent should be obtained; and when so suspended, he has utterly neglected to attend to them.

He has refused to pass other Laws for the accommodation of large districts of people, unless those people would relinquish the right of Representation in the Legislature, a right inestimable to them and formidable to tyrants only.

He has called together legislative bodies at places unusual, uncomfortable, and distant from the depository of their Public Records, for the sole Purpose of fatiguing them into compliance with his measures.

He has dissolved Representative Houses repeatedly, for opposing with manly firmness his invasions on the rights of the People.

He has refused for a long time, after such dissolutions, to cause others to be elected; whereby the Legislative Powers, incapable of Annihilation, have returned to the People at large for their exercise; the State remaining in the mean time exposed to all the dangers of invasion from without, and convulsions within.

He has endeavoured to prevent the Population of these States; for that purpose obstructing the Laws for Naturalization of Foreigners; refusing to pass others to encourage their migrations hither, and raising the conditions of new Appropriations of Lands.

He has obstructed the Administration of Justice, by refusing his Assent to Laws for establishing Judiciary Powers.

He has made Judges dependent on his Will alone, for the tenure of their offices, and the amount and payment of their salaries.

He has erected a multitude of New Offices, and sent

*Reprinted from the facsimile of the engrossed copy in the National Archives. The original spelling, capitalization, and punctuation have been retained. Paragraphing has been added.

hither swarms of Officers to harrass our People, and eat out their substance.

He has kept among us, in times of peace, Standing Armies without the Consent of our legislatures.

He has affected to render the Military independent of and superior to the Civil Power.

He has combined with others to subject us to a jurisdiction foreign to our constitution, and unacknowledged by our laws; giving his Assent to their Acts of pretended Legislation:

For Quartering large bodies of armed troops among us:

For protecting them, by a mock Trial, from Punishment for any Murders which they should commit on the Inhabitants of these States:

For cutting off our Trade with all parts of the world:

For imposing Taxes on us without our Consent:

For depriving us in many cases, of the benefits of Trial by Jury:

For transporting us beyond Seas to be tried for pretended offences:

For abolishing the free System of English Laws in a neighbouring Province, establishing therein an Arbitrary government, and enlarging its Boundaries so as to render it at once an example and fit instrument for introducing the same absolute rule into these Colonies:

For taking away our Charters, abolishing our most valuable Laws, and altering fundamentally the Forms of our Governments:

For suspending our own Legislatures, and declaring themselves invested with Power to legislate for us in all cases whatsoever.

He has abdicated Government here, by declaring us out of his Protection, and waging War against us.

He has plundered our seas, ravaged our Coasts, burnt our towns, and destroyed the lives of our people.

He is at this time transporting large Armies of foreign Mercenaries to compleat the works of death, desolation and tyranny, already begun with circumstances of Cruelty and perfidy scarcely paralleled in the most barbarous ages, and totally unworthy the Head of a civilized nation.

He has constrained our fellow Citizens taken Captive on the high Seas to bear Arms against their Country, to become the executioners of their friends and Brethren, or to fall themselves by their Hands.

He has excited domestic insurrections amongst us, and has endeavoured to bring on the inhabitants of our frontiers, the merciless Indian Savages, whose known rule of warfare, is an undistinguished destruction of all ages, sexes and conditions.

In every stage of these Oppressions We have Petitioned for Redress in the most humble terms: Our repeated Petitions have been answered only by repeated injury. A Prince, whose character is thus marked by every act which may define a Tyrant, is unfit to be the ruler of a free People.

Nor have We been wanting in attentions to our Brittish brethren. We have warned them from time to time of attempts by their legislature to extend an unwarrantable jurisdiction over us. We have reminded them of the circumstances of our emigration and settlement here. We have appealed to their native justice and magnanimity, and we have conjured them by the ties of our common kindred to disavow these usurpations, which, would inevitably interrupt our connections and correspondence. They too have been deaf to the voice of justice and of consanguinity. We must, therefore, acquiesce in the necessity, which denounces our Separation, and hold them, as we hold the rest of mankind, Enemies in War, in Peace Friends.

WE, THEREFORE, the Representatives of the UNITED STATES OF AMERICA, in General Congress, Assembled, appealing to the Supreme Judge of the world for the rectitude of our intentions, do, in the Name, and by Authority of the good People of these Colonies, solemnly publish and declare, That these United Colonies are, and of Right ought to be FREE AND INDEPENDENT STATES; that they are Absolved from all Allegiance to the British Crown, and that all political connection between them and the State of Great Britain, is and ought to be totally dissolved; and that, as Free and Independent States, they have full Power to levy War, conclude Peace, contract Alliances, establish Commerce, and to do all other Acts and Things which Independent States may of right do. And for the support of this Declaration, with a firm reliance on the protection of divine Providence, we mutually pledge to each other our Lives, our Fortunes and our sacred Honor.

# The Constitution of the United States of America*

**We the People** of the United States, in Order to form a more perfect Union, establish Justice, insure domestic Tranquility, provide for the common defence, promote the general Welfare, and secure the Blessings of Liberty to ourselves and our Posterity, do ordain and establish this Constitution for the United States of America.

## Article. I.

Section. 1. All legislative Powers herein granted shall be vested in a Congress of the United States, which shall consist of a Senate and House of Representatives.

Section. 2. The House of Representatives shall be composed of Members chosen every second Year by the People of the several States, and the Electors in each State shall have the Qualifications requisite for Electors of the most numerous Branch of the State Legislature.

No Person shall be a Representative who shall not have attained to the Age of twenty five Years, and been seven Years a Citizen of the United States, and who shall not, when elected, be an Inhabitant of that State in which he shall be chosen.

Representatives and direct Taxes† shall be apportioned among the several States which may be included within this Union, according to their respective Numbers, which shall be determined by adding to the whole Number of free Persons, including those bound to Service for a Term of Years, and excluding Indians not taxed, three fifths of all other Persons.‡ The actual Enumeration shall be made within three Years after the first Meeting of the Congress of the United States, and within every subsequent Term of ten Years, in such Manner as they shall by Law direct. The Number of Representatives shall not exceed one for every thirty Thousand, but each State shall have at Least one Representative; and until such enumeration shall be made, the State of New Hampshire shall be entitled to chuse three; Massachusetts eight; Rhode Island and Providence Plantations one; Connecticut five; New York six; New Jersey four; Pennsylvania eight; Delaware one; Maryland six; Virginia ten; North Carolina five; South Carolina five; and Georgia three.

When vacancies happen in the Representation from any State, the Executive Authority thereof shall issue Writs of Election to fill such Vacancies.

The House of Representatives shall chuse their Speaker and other Officers; and shall have the sole Power of Impeachment.

Section. 3. The Senate of the United States shall be composed of two Senators from each State, chosen by the Legislature thereof, for six Years; and each Senator shall have one Vote.*

Immediately after they shall be assembled in Consequence of the first Election, they shall be divided as equally as may be into three Classes. The Seats of the Senators of the first Class shall be vacated at the Expiration of the second Year, of the second Class at the Expiration of the fourth Year, and of the third Class at the Expiration of the sixth Year, so that one third may be chosen every second Year; and if Vacancies happen by Resignation, or otherwise, during the Recess of the Legislature of any State, the Executive thereof may make temporary Appointments until the next Meeting of the Legislature, which shall then fill such Vacancies.†

No Person shall be a Senator who shall not have attained to the Age of thirty Years, and been nine Years a Citizen of the United States, and who shall not, when elected, be an Inhabitant of that State for which he shall be chosen.

The Vice President of the United States shall be President of the Senate, but shall have no Vote, unless they be equally divided.

The Senate shall chuse their other Officers, and also a

---

*From the engrossed copy in the National Archives. Original spelling, capitalization, and punctuation have been retained.

† Modified by the Sixteenth Amendment.

‡ Replaced by the Fourteenth Amendment.

*Superseded by the Seventeenth Amendment.

† Modified by the Seventeenth Amendment.

President pro tempore, in the Absence of the Vice President, or when he shall exercise the Office of President of the United States.

The Senate shall have the sole Power to try all Impeachments. When sitting for that Purpose, they shall be on Oath or Affirmation. When the President of the United States is tried, the Chief Justice shall preside: And no Person shall be convicted without the Concurrence of two thirds of the Members present.

Judgment in Cases of Impeachment shall not extend further than to removal from Office, and disqualification to hold and enjoy any Office of honor, Trust or Profit under the United States: but the Party convicted shall nevertheless be liable and subject to Indictment, Trial, Judgment and Punishment, according to Law.

Section. 4. The Times, Places and Manner of holding Elections for Senators and Representatives, shall be prescribed in each State by the Legislature thereof, but the Congress may at any time by Law make or alter such Regulation, except as to the Places of chusing Senators.

The Congress shall assemble at least once in every Year, and such Meeting shall be on the first Monday in December, unless they shall by Law appoint a different Day.*

Section. 5. Each House shall be the Judge of the Elections, Returns and Qualifications of its own Members, and a Majority of each shall constitute a Quorum to do Business; but a smaller Number may adjourn from day to day, and may be authorized to compel the Attendance of absent Members, in such Manner, and under such Penalties as each House may provide.

Each House may determine the Rules of its Proceedings, punish its Members for disorderly Behaviour, and, with the Concurrence of two thirds, expel a Member.

Each House shall keep a Journal of its Proceedings, and from time to time publish the same, excepting such Parts as may in their Judgment require Secrecy; and the Yeas and Nays of the Members of either House on any question shall, at the Desire of one fifth of those Present, be entered on the Journal.

Neither House, during the Session of Congress, shall, without the Consent of the other, adjourn for more than three days, nor to any other Place than that in which the two Houses shall be sitting.

Section. 6. The Senators and Representatives shall receive a Compensation for their Services, to be ascertained by Law, and paid out of the Treasury of the United States. They shall in all Cases, except Treason, Felony and Breach of the Peace, be privileged from Arrest during their Attendance at the Session of their respective Houses, and in going to and returning from the same; and for any Speech or Debate in either House, they shall not be questioned in any other Place.

No Senator or Representative shall, during the Time for which he was elected, be appointed to any civil Office under the Authority of the United States, which shall have been created, or the Emoluments whereof shall have been encreased during such time; and no Person holding any Office under the United States, shall be a Member of either House during his Continuance in Office.

Section. 7. All Bills for raising Revenue shall originate in the House of Representatives; but the Senate may propose or concur with Amendments as on other Bills.

Every Bill which shall have passed the House of Representatives and the Senate shall, before it become a Law, be presented to the President of the United States; If he approve he shall sign it, but if not he shall return it, with his Objections to that House in which it shall have originated, who shall enter the Objections at large on their Journal, and proceed to reconsider it. If after such Reconsideration two thirds of that House shall agree to pass the Bill, it shall be sent, together with the Objections, to the other House, by which it shall likewise be reconsidered, and if approved by two thirds of that House, it shall become a Law. But in all such Cases the Votes of both Houses shall be determined by yeas and Nays, and the Names of the Persons voting for and against the Bill shall be entered on the Journal of each House respectively. If any Bill shall not be returned by the President within ten Days (Sundays excepted) after it shall have been presented to him, the Same shall be a Law, in like Manner as if he had signed it, unless the Congress by their Adjournment prevent its Return, in which Case it shall not be a Law.

Every Order, Resolution, or Vote to which the Concurrence of the Senate and House of Representatives may be necessary (except on a question of Adjournment) shall be presented to the President of the United States; and before the Same shall take Effect, shall be approved by him, or being disapproved by him shall be repassed by two thirds of the Senate and House of Representatives, according to the Rules and Limitations prescribed in the Case of a Bill.

Section. 8. The Congress shall have Power To lay and collect Taxes, Duties, Imposts and Excises, to pay the Debts and provide for the common Defence and general Welfare of the United States; but all Duties, Imposts and Excises shall be uniform throughout the United States;

To borrow Money on the credit of the United States;

To regulate Commerce with foreign Nations, and among the several States, and with the Indian Tribes;

To establish an uniform Rule of Naturalization, and uniform Laws on the subject of Bankruptcies throughout the United States;

To coin Money, regulate the Value thereof, and of foreign Coin, and fix the Standard of Weights and Measures;

To provide for the Punishment of counterfeiting the Securities and current Coin of the United States;

To establish Post Offices and post Roads;

To promote the Progress of Science and useful Arts, by securing for limited Times to Authors and Inventors the exclusive Right to their respective Writings and Discoveries;

*Superseded by the Twentieth Amendment.

To constitute Tribunals inferior to the supreme Court;

To define and punish Piracies and Felonies committed on the high Seas, and Offences against the Law of Nations;

To declare War, grant Letters of Marque and Reprisal, and make Rules concerning Captures on Land and Water;

To raise and support Armies, but no Appropriation of Money to that Use shall be for a longer Term than two Years;

To provide and maintain a Navy;

To make Rules for the Government and Regulation of the land and naval Forces;

To provide for calling forth the Militia to execute the Laws of the Union, suppress Insurrections and repel Invasions;

To provide for organizing, arming, and disciplining, the Militia, and for governing such Part of them as may be employed in the Service of the United States, reserving to the States respectively, the Appointment of the Officers, and the Authority of training the Militia according to the discipline prescribed by Congress;

To exercise exclusive Legislation in all Cases whatsoever, over such District (not exceeding ten Miles square) as may, by Cession of particular States, and the Acceptance of Congress, become the Seat of the Government of the United States, and to exercise like Authority over all Places purchased by the Consent of the Legislature of the State in which the Same shall be, for the Erection of Forts, Magazines, Arsenals, dock-Yards, and other needful Buildings;—And

To make all Laws which shall be necessary and proper for carrying into Execution the foregoing Powers, and all other Powers vested by this Constitution in the Government of the United States, or in any Department or Officer thereof.

Section. 9. The Migration or Importation of such Persons as any of the States now existing shall think proper to admit, shall not be prohibited by the Congress prior to the Year one thousand eight hundred and eight, but a Tax or duty may be imposed on such Importation, not exceeding ten dollars for each Person.

The Privilege of the Writ of Habeas Corpus shall not be suspended, unless when in Cases of Rebellion or Invasion the public Safety may require it.

No Bill of Attainder or ex post facto Law shall be passed.

No Capitation, or other direct, Tax shall be laid, unless in Proportion to the Census or Enumeration herein before directed to be taken.

No Tax or Duty shall be laid on Articles exported from any State.

No Preference shall be given by any Regulation of Commerce or Revenue to the Ports of one State over those of another: nor shall Vessels bound to, or from, one State, be obliged to enter, clear, or pay Duties in another.

No Money shall be drawn from the Treasury, but in Consequence of Appropriations made by Law, and a regular Statement and Account of the Receipts and Expenditures of all public Money shall be published from time to time.

No Title of Nobility shall be granted by the United States: And no Person holding any Office of Profit or Trust under them, shall, without the Consent of the Congress, accept of any present, Emolument, Office, or Title, of any kind whatever, from any King, Prince, or foreign State. Section. 10. No State shall enter into any Treaty, Alliance, or Confederation; grant Letters of Marque and Reprisal; coin Money; emit Bills of Credit; make any Thing but gold and silver Coin a Tender in Payment of Debts; pass any Bill of Attainder, ex post facto Law, or Law impairing the Obligation of Contracts, or grant any Title of Nobility.

No State shall, without the Consent of the Congress, lay any Imposts or Duties on Imports or Exports, except what may be absolutely necessary for executing its inspection Laws: and the net Produce of all Duties and Imposts, laid by any State on Imports or Exports, shall be for the Use of the Treasury of the United States; and all such Laws shall be subject to the Revision and Controul of the Congress.

No State shall, without the Consent of Congress, lay any Duty of Tonnage, keep Troops, or Ships of War in time of Peace, enter into any Agreement or Compact with another State, or with a foreign Power, or engage in War, unless actually invaded, or in such imminent Danger as will not admit of delay.

## Article. II.

Section. 1. The executive Power shall be vested in a President of the United States of America. He shall hold his Office during the Term of four Years, and, together with the Vice President, chosen for the same Term, be elected, as follows:

Each State shall appoint, in such Manner as the Legislature thereof may direct, a Number of Electors, equal to the whole Number of Senators and Representatives to which the State may be entitled in the Congress: but no Senator or Representative, or Person holding an Office of Trust or Profit under the United States, shall be appointed an Elector.

The Electors shall meet in their respective States, and vote by Ballot for two Persons, of whom one at least shall not be an Inhabitant of the same State with themselves. And they shall make a List of all the Persons voted for, and of the Number of Votes for each; which List they shall sign and certify, and transmit sealed to the Seat of the Government of the United States, directed to the President of the Senate. The President of the Senate shall, in the Presence of the Senate and House of Representatives, open all the Certificates, and the Votes shall then be counted. The Person having the greatest Number of Votes shall be the President, if such Number be a Majority of the whole Number of Electors appointed; and if there be more than one who have such Majority, and have an equal Number of Votes, then the House of Representatives shall immediately chuse by Ballot one of them for President; and if no Person have a Majority, then from the five highest on the List the said House shall in like Manner chuse the President. But in chusing the President, the Votes shall be taken by States, the Representation from each State having one Vote; A quorum for this Purpose shall consist of a Member or Members from two thirds of the States, and a Majority of all the States shall be necessary to a Choice. In every Case, after the Choice of the President, the Person having the greatest Number of Votes of the Electors shall be the Vice President. But if there should remain two or more who have equal Votes, the Senate shall chuse from them by Ballot the Vice President.*

The Congress may determine the Time of chusing the Electors, and the Day on which they shall give their Votes; which Day shall be the same throughout the United States.

No Person except a natural born Citizen, or a Citizen of the United States, at the time of the Adoption of this Constitution, shall be eligible to the Office of President; neither shall any Person be eligible to that Office who shall not have attained to the Age of thirty five Years, and been fourteen Years a Resident within the United States.

In Case of the Removal of the President from Office, or of his Death, Resignation, or Inability to discharge the Powers and Duties of the said Office, the Same shall devolve on the Vice President, and the Congress may by Law provide for the Case of Removal, Death, Resignation or Inability, both of the President and Vice President, declaring what Officer shall then act as President, and such Officer shall act accordingly, until the Disability be removed, or a President shall be elected.†

The President shall, at stated Times, receive for his Services, a Compensation, which shall neither be encreased nor diminished during the Period for which he shall have been elected, and he shall not receive within that Period any other Emolument from the United States, or any of them.

Before he enter on the Execution of his Office, he shall take the following Oath or Affirmation:—"I do solemnly swear (or affirm) that I will faithfully execute the Office of President of the United States, and will to the best of my Ability, preserve, protect and defend the Constitution of the United States."

Section. 2. The President shall be Commander in Chief of the Army and Navy of the United States, and of the Militia of the several States, when called into the actual Service of the United States; he may require the Opinion, in writing, of the principal Officer in each of the executive Departments, upon any Subject relating to the Duties of their respective Offices, and he shall have Power to grant Reprieves and Pardons for Offences against the United States, except in Cases of Impeachment.

He shall have Power, by and with the Advice and Consent of the Senate, to make Treaties, provided two thirds of the Senators present concur; and he shall nominate, and by and with the Advice and Consent of the Senate, shall appoint Ambassadors, other public Ministers and Consuls, Judges of the supreme Court, and all other Officers of the United States, whose Appointments are not herein otherwise provided for, and which shall be established by Law; but the Congress may by Law vest the Appointment of such inferior Officers, as they think proper, in the President alone, in the Courts of Law, or in the Heads of Departments.

The President shall have Power to fill up all Vacancies that may happen during the Recess of the Senate, by granting Commissions which shall expire at the End of their next Session.

Section. 3. He shall from time to time give to the Congress Information of the State of the Union, and recommend to their Consideration such Measures as he shall judge necessary and expedient; he may, on extraordinary Occasions, convene both Houses, or either of them, and in Case of Disagreement between them, with Respect to the Time of Adjournment, he may adjourn them to such Time as he shall think proper; he shall receive Ambassadors and other public Ministers; he shall take Care that the Laws be faithfully executed, and shall Commission all the Officers of the United States.

Section. 4. The President, Vice President and all civil Officers of the United States, shall be removed from Office on Impeachment for, and Conviction of, Treason, Bribery, or other high Crimes and Misdemeanors.

## Article. III.

Section. 1. The judicial Power of the United States, shall be vested in one supreme Court, and in such inferior Courts as the Congress may from time to time ordain and establish. The Judges, both of the supreme and inferior Courts, shall hold their Offices during good Behaviour, and shall, at stated Times, receive for their Services, a Compensation, which shall not be diminished during their Continuance in Office.

Section. 2. The judicial Power shall extend to all Cases, in Law and Equity, arising under this Constitution, the Laws of the United States, and Treaties made, or which shall be made, under their Authority;—to all Cases affecting Ambassadors, other public Ministers and Consuls;—to all Cases of admiralty and maritime Jurisdiction;—to Controversies to which the United States shall be a Party;—to Controversies between two or more States;—between a State and Citizens of another State;*—between Citizens of different States,—between Citizens of the same State

*Superseded by the Twelfth Amendment.
† Modified by the Twenty-fifth Amendment.

*Modified by the Eleventh Amendment.

claiming Lands under Grants of different States, and between a State, or the Citizens thereof, and foreign States, Citizens or Subjects.

In all Cases affecting Ambassadors, other public Ministers and Consuls, and those in which a State shall be Party, the supreme Court shall have original Jurisdiction. In all the other Cases before mentioned, the supreme Court shall have appellate Jurisdiction, both as to Law and Fact, with such Exceptions, and under such Regulations as the Congress shall make.

The Trial of all Crimes, except in Cases of Impeachment, shall be by Jury; and such Trial shall be held in the State where the said Crimes shall have been committed; but when not committed within any State, the Trial shall be at such Place or Places as the Congress may by Law have directed.

Section. 3. Treason against the United States, shall consist only in levying War against them, or in adhering to their Enemies, giving them Aid and Comfort. No Person shall be convicted of Treason unless on the Testimony of two Witnesses to the same overt Act, or on Confession in open Court.

The Congress shall have Power to declare the Punishment of Treason, but no Attainder of Treason shall work Corruption of Blood, or Forfeiture except during the Life of the Person attainted.

## Article. IV.

Section. 1. Full Faith and Credit shall be given in each State to the public Acts, Records, and judicial Proceedings of every other State. And the Congress may by general Laws prescribe the Manner in which such Acts, Records and Proceedings shall be proved, and the Effect thereof.

Section. 2. The Citizens of each State shall be entitled to all Privileges and Immunities of Citizens in the several States.

A Person charged in any State with Treason, Felony, or other Crime, who shall flee from Justice, and be found in another State, shall on Demand of the executive Authority of the State from which he fled, be delivered up, to be removed to the State having Jurisdiction of the Crime.

No Person held to Service or Labour in one State, under the Laws thereof, escaping into another, shall, in Consequence of any Law or Regulation therein, be discharged from such Service or Labour, but shall be delivered up on Claim of the Party to whom such Service or Labour may be due.

Section. 3. New States may be admitted by the Congress into this Union; but no new State shall be formed or erected within the Jurisdiction of any other State, nor any State be formed by the Junction of two or more States, or Parts of States, without the Consent of the Legislatures of the States concerned as well as of the Congress.

The Congress shall have Power to dispose of and make all needful Rules and Regulations respecting the Territory or other Property belonging to the United States; and nothing in this Constitution shall be so construed as to Prejudice any Claims of the United States, or of any particular State.

Section. 4. The United States shall guarantee to every State in this Union a Republican Form of Government, and shall protect each of them against Invasion; and on Application of the Legislature, or of the Executive (when the Legislature cannot be convened) against domestic Violence.

## Article. V.

The Congress, whenever two thirds of both Houses shall deem it necessary, shall propose Amendments to this Constitution, or, on the Application of the Legislatures of two thirds of the several States, shall call a Convention for proposing Amendments, which, in either Case, shall be valid to all Intents and Purposes, as Part of this Constitution, when ratified by the Legislatures of three fourths of the several States, or by Conventions in three fourths thereof, as the one or the other Mode of Ratification may be proposed by the Congress; Provided that no Amendment which may be made prior to the Year One thousand eight hundred and eight shall in any Manner affect the first and fourth Clauses in the Ninth Section of the first Article; and that no State, without its Consent, shall be deprived of its equal Suffrage in the Senate.

## Article. VI.

All Debts contracted and Engagements entered into, before the Adoption of this Constitution, shall be as valid against the United States under this Constitution, as under the Confederation.

This Constitution, and the Laws of the United States which shall be made in Pursuance thereof; and all Treaties made, or which shall be made, under the Authority of the United States, shall be the supreme Law of the Land; and the Judges in every State shall be bound thereby, any Thing in the Constitution or Laws of any State to the Contrary notwithstanding.

The Senators and Representatives before mentioned, and the Members of the several State Legislatures, and all executive and judicial Officers, both of the United States and of the several States, shall be bound by Oath or Affirmation, to support this Constitution; but no religious Test shall ever be required as a Qualification to any Office or public Trust under the United States.

## Article. VII.

The Ratification of the Conventions of nine States, shall be sufficient for the Establishment of this Constitution between the States so ratifying the Same.

*done* in Convention by the Unanimous Consent of the States present the Seventeenth Day of September in the Year of our Lord one thousand seven hundred and Eighty seven and of the Independence of the United States of America the Twelfth. *In witness* whereof We have hereunto subscribed our Names,

*Articles in Addition to, and Amendment of, the Constitution of the United States of America, Proposed by Congress, and Ratified by the Legislatures of the Several States, Pursuant to the Fifth Article of the Original Constitution.*

## Amendment I*

Congress shall make no law respecting an establishment of religion, or prohibiting the free exercise thereof; or abridging the freedom of speech, or of the press; or the right of the people peaceably to assemble, and to petition the Government for a redress of grievances.

## Amendment II

A well regulated Militia, being necessary to the security of a free State, the right of the people to keep and bear Arms shall not be infringed.

## Amendment III

No Soldier shall, in time of peace, be quartered in any house, without the consent of the Owner, nor in time of war, but in a manner to be prescribed by law.

## Amendment IV

The right of the people to be secure in their persons, houses, papers, and effects, against unreasonable searches and seizures, shall not be violated, and no Warrants shall issue, but upon probable cause, supported by Oath or affirmation, and particularly describing the place to be searched, and the persons or things to be seized.

## Amendment V

No person shall be held to answer for a capital or otherwise infamous crime, unless on a presentment or indictment of a Grand Jury, except in cases arising in the land or naval forces, or in the Militia, when in actual service in time of War or public danger; nor shall any person be subject for the same offence to be twice put in jeopardy of life or limb; nor shall be compelled in any criminal case to be a witness against himself, nor be deprived of life, liberty, or property, without due process of law; nor shall

private property be taken for public use, without just compensation.

## Amendment VI

In all criminal prosecutions, the accused shall enjoy the right to a speedy and public trial, by an impartial jury of the State and district wherein the crime shall have been committed, which district shall have been previously ascertained by law, and to be informed of the nature and cause of the accusation; to be confronted with the witnesses against him; to have compulsory process for obtaining witnesses in his favor, and to have the Assistance of Counsel for his defence.

## Amendment VII

In suits at common law, where the value in controversy shall exceed twenty dollars, the right of trial by jury shall be preserved, and no fact tried by a jury, shall be otherwise reexamined in any Court of the United States, than according to the rules of the common law.

## Amendment VIII

Excessive bail shall not be required, nor excessive fines imposed, nor cruel and unusual punishments inflicted.

## Amendment IX

The enumeration in the Constitution, of certain rights, shall not be construed to deny or disparage others retained by the people.

## Amendment X

The powers not delegated to the United States by the Constitution; nor prohibited by it to the States, are reserved to the States respectively, or to the people.

## Amendment XI*

The Judicial power of the United States shall not be construed to extend to any suit in law or equity, commenced or prosecuted against one of the United States by Citizens of another State, or by Citizens or Subjects of any Foreign State.

## Amendment XII†

The Electors shall meet in their respective States and vote by ballot for President and Vice-President, one of whom, at least, shall not be an inhabitant of the same

---

*The first ten amendments were passed by Congress September 25, 1789. They were ratified by three-fourths of the states December 15, 1791.

*Passed March 4, 1794. Ratified January 23, 1795.
†Passed December 9, 1803. Ratified June 15, 1804.

State with themselves; they shall name in their ballots the person voted for as President, and in distinct ballots the person voted for as Vice-President, and they shall make distinct lists of all persons voted for as President, and of all persons voted for as Vice-President, and of the number of votes for each, which lists they shall sign and certify, and transmit sealed to the seat of the government of the United States, directed to the President of the Senate;—The President of the Senate shall, in the presence of the Senate and House of Representatives, open all the certificates and the votes shall then be counted;—The person having the greatest number of votes for President, shall be the President, if such number be a majority of the whole number of Electors appointed; and if no person have such majority, then from the persons having the highest numbers not exceeding three on the list of those voted for as President, the House of Representatives shall choose immediately, by ballot, the President. But in choosing the President, the votes shall be taken by states, the representation from each state having one vote; a quorum for this purpose shall consist of a member or members from two-thirds of the states, and a majority of all the states shall be necessary to a choice. And if the House of Representatives shall not choose a President whenever the right of choice shall devolve upon them, before the fourth day of March next following, then the Vice-President shall act as President, as in the case of the death or other constitutional disability of the President.—The person having the greatest number of votes as Vice-President, shall be the Vice-President, if such number be a majority of the whole number of Electors appointed, and if no person have a majority, then from the two highest numbers on the list, the Senate shall choose the Vice-President; a quorum for the purpose shall consist of two-thirds of the whole number of Senators, and a majority of the whole number shall be necessary to a choice. But no person constitutionally ineligible to the office of President shall be eligible to that of Vice-President of the United States.

## Amendment XIII*

SECTION 1. Neither slavery nor involuntary servitude, except as a punishment for crime whereof the party shall have been duly convicted, shall exist within the United States, or any place subject to their jurisdiction.

SECTION 2. Congress shall have power to enforce this article by appropriate legislation.

## Amendment XIV†

SECTION 1. All persons born or naturalized in the United States, and subject to the jurisdiction thereof, are citizens of the United States and of the State wherein they reside.

No State shall make or enforce any law which shall abridge the privileges or immunities of citizens of the United States; nor shall any State deprive any person of life, liberty, or property, without due process of law; nor deny to any person within its jurisdiction the equal protection of the laws.

SECTION 2. Representatives shall be apportioned among the several States according to their respective numbers, counting the whole number of persons in each State, excluding Indians not taxed. But when the right to vote at any election for the choice of electors for President and Vice-President of the United States, Representatives in Congress, the Executive and Judicial officers of a State, or the members of the Legislature thereof, is denied to any of the male inhabitants of such State, being twenty-one years of age, and citizens of the United States, or in any way abridged, except for participation in rebellion, or other crime, the basis of representation therein shall be reduced in the proportion which the number of such male citizens shall bear to the whole number of male citizens twenty-one years of age in such State.

SECTION 3. No person shall be a Senator or Representative in Congress, or elector of President and Vice-President, or hold any office, civil or military, under the United States, or under any State, who, having previously taken an oath, as a member of Congress, or as an officer of the United States, or as a member of any State legislature, or as an executive or judicial officer of any State, to support the Constitution of the United States, shall have engaged in insurrection or rebellion against the same, or given aid or comfort to the enemies thereof. But Congress may by a vote of two-thirds of each House, remove such disability.

SECTION 4. The validity of the public debt of the United States, authorized by law, including debts incurred for payment of pensions and bounties for services in suppressing insurrection or rebellion, shall not be questioned. But neither the United States nor any State shall assume or pay any debt or obligation incurred in aid of insurrection or rebellion against the United States, or any claim for the loss or emancipation of any slave; but all such debts, obligations, and claims shall be held illegal and void.

SECTION 5. The Congress shall have the power to enforce, by appropriate legislation, the provisions of this article.

## Amendment XV*

SECTION 1. The right of citizens of the United States to vote shall not be denied or abridged by the United States or by any State on account of race, color, or previous condition of servitude—

SECTION 2. The Congress shall have power to enforce this article by appropriate legislation.

*Passed January 31, 1865. Ratified December 6, 1865.
†Passed June 13, 1866. Ratified July 9, 1868.

*Passed February 26, 1869. Ratified February 2, 1870.

## Amendment XVI*

The Congress shall have power to lay and collect taxes on incomes, from whatever source derived, without apportionment among the several States, and without regard to any census or enumeration.

## Amendment XVII†

The Senate of the United States shall be composed of two Senators from each State, elected by the people thereof, for six years; and each Senator shall have one vote. The electors in each State shall have the qualifications requisite for electors of the most numerous branch of the State legislatures.

When vacancies happen in the representation of any State in the Senate, the executive authority of such State shall issue writs of election to fill such vacancies: *Provided,* That the legislature of any State may empower the executive thereof to make temporary appointments until the people fill the vacancies by election as the legislature may direct.

This amendment shall not be so construed as to affect the election or term of any Senator chosen before it becomes valid as part of the Constitution.

## Amendment XVIII‡

SECTION 1. After one year from the ratification of this article the manufacture, sale, or transportation of intoxicating liquors within, the importation thereof into, or the exportation thereof from the United States and all territory subject to the jurisdiction thereof for beverage purposes is hereby prohibited.

SECTION 2. The Congress and the several States shall have concurrent power to enforce this article by appropriate legislation.

SECTION 3. This article shall be inoperative unless it shall have been ratified as an amendment to the Constitution by the legislatures of the several States, as provided in the Constitution, within seven years from the date of the submission hereof to the States by the Congress.

## Amendment XIX§

The right of citizens of the United States to vote shall not be denied or abridged by the United States or by any State on account of sex.

Congress shall have power to enforce this article by appropriate legislation.

*Passed July 12, 1909. Ratified February 3, 1913.
†Passed May 13, 1912. Ratified April 8, 1913.
‡Passed December 18, 1917. Ratified January 16, 1919.
§Passed June 4, 1919. Ratified August 18, 1920.

## Amendment XX*

SECTION 1. The terms of the President and Vice-President shall end at noon on the 20th day of January, and the terms of Senators and Representatives at noon on the 3d day of January, of the years in which such terms would have ended if this article had not been ratified; and the terms of their successors shall then begin.

SECTION 2. The Congress shall assemble at least once in every year, and such meeting shall begin at noon on the 3d day of January, unless they shall by law appoint a different day.

SECTION 3. If, at the time fixed for the beginning of the term of the President, the President elect shall have died, the Vice-President elect shall become President. If a President shall not have been chosen before the time fixed for the beginning of his term, or if the President elect shall have failed to qualify, then the Vice-President elect shall act as President until a President shall have qualified; and the Congress may by law provide for the case wherein neither a President elect nor a Vice-President elect shall have qualified, declaring who shall then act as President, or the manner in which one who is to act shall be selected, and such person shall act accordingly until a President or Vice-President shall have qualified.

SECTION 4. The Congress may by law provide for the case of the death of any of the persons from whom the House of Representatives may choose a President whenever the right of choice shall have devolved upon them, and for the case of the death of any of the persons from whom the Senate may choose a Vice-President whenever the right of choice shall have devolved upon them.

SECTION 5. Sections 1 and 2 shall take effect on the 15th day of October following the ratification of this article.

SECTION 6. This article shall be inoperative unless it shall have been ratified as an amendment to the Constitution by the legislatures of three-fourths of the several States within seven years from the date of its submission.

## Amendment XXI†

SECTION 1. The eighteenth article of amendment to the Constitution of the United States is hereby repealed.

SECTION 2. The transportation or importation into any State, Territory, or possession of the United States for delivery or use therein of intoxicating liquors, in violation of the laws thereof, is hereby prohibited.

SECTION 3. This article shall be inoperative unless it shall have been ratified as an amendment to the Constitution by conventions in the several States, as provided in the Constitution, within seven years from the date of the submission hereof to the States by the Congress.

*Passed March 2, 1932. Ratified January 23, 1933.
†Passed February 20, 1933. Ratified December 5, 1933.

## Amendment XXII*

No person shall be elected to the office of the President more than twice, and no person who has held the office of President, or acted as President, for more than two years of a term to which some other person was elected President shall be elected to the office of the President more than once.

But this Article shall not apply to any person holding the office of President when this Article was proposed by the Congress, and shall not prevent any person who may be holding the office of President, or acting as President, during the term within which this Article becomes operative from holding the office of President or acting as President during the remainder of such term.

## Amendment XXIII†

SECTION 1. The District constituting the seat of Government of the United States shall appoint in such manner as the Congress may direct:

A number of electors of President and Vice President equal to the whole number of Senators and Representatives in Congress to which the District would be entitled if it were a State, but in no event more than the least populous State; they shall be in addition to those appointed by the States, but they shall be considered, for the purposes of the election of President and Vice President, to be electors appointed by the State; and they shall meet in the District and perform such duties as provided by the twelfth article of amendment.

SECTION 2. The Congress shall have power to enforce this article by appropriate legislation.

## Amendment XXIV‡

SECTION 1. The right of citizens of the United States to vote in any primary or other election for President or Vice President, or for Senator or Representative in Congress, shall not be denied or abridged by the United States or any State by reason of failure to pay any poll tax or other tax.

SECTION 2. The Congress shall have power to enforce this article by appropriate legislation.

## Amendment XXV§

SECTION 1. In case of the removal of the President from office or of his death or resignation, the Vice President shall become President.

SECTION 2. Whenever there is a vacancy in the office of the Vice President, the President shall nominate a Vice President who shall take office upon confirmation by a majority vote of both Houses of Congress.

SECTION 3. Whenever the President transmits to the President pro tempore of the Senate and the Speaker of the House of Representatives his written declaration that he is unable to discharge the powers and duties of his office, and until he transmits to them a written declaration to the contrary, such powers and duties shall be discharged by the Vice President as Acting President.

SECTION 4. Whenever the Vice President and a majority of either the principal officers of the executive department or of such other body as Congress may by law provide, transmit to the President pro tempore of the Senate and the Speaker of the House of Representatives their written declaration that the President is unable to discharge the powers and duties of his office, the Vice President shall immediately assume the powers and duties of the office of Acting President.

Thereafter, when the President transmits to the President pro tempore of the Senate and the Speaker of the House of Representatives his written declaration that no inability exists, he shall resume the powers and duties of his office unless the Vice President and a majority of either the principal officers of the executive department or of such other body as Congress may by law provide, transmit within four days to the President pro tempore of the Senate and the Speaker of the House of Representatives their written declaration that the President is unable to discharge the powers and duties of his office. Thereupon Congress shall decide the issue, assembling within forty-eight hours for that purpose if not in session. If the Congress, within twenty-one days after receipt of the latter written declaration, or, if Congress is not in session, within twenty-one days after Congress is required to assemble, determines by two-thirds vote of both Houses that the President is unable to discharge the powers and duties of his office, the Vice President shall continue to discharge the same as Acting President; otherwise, the President shall resume the powers and duties of his office.

## Amendment XXVI*

SECTION 1. The right of citizens of the United States, who are eighteen years of age or older, to vote shall not be denied or abridged by the United States or by any State on account of age.

SECTION 2. The Congress shall have power to enforce this article by appropriate legislation.

---

* Passed March 12, 1947. Ratified March 1, 1951.
† Passed June 16, 1960. Ratified April 3, 1961.
‡ Passed August 27, 1962. Ratified January 23, 1964.
§ Passed July 6, 1965. Ratified February 11, 1967.

* Passed March 23, 1971. Ratified July 5, 1971.

# Presidential elections (1789–1840)

| Year | Number of states | Candidates | Parties | Popular vote | Electoral vote | Percentage of popular vote |
|------|------|------------|---------|--------------|----------------|----------------------------|
| 1789 | 11 | GEORGE WASHINGTON | No party designations | | 69 | |
| | | John Adams | | | 34 | |
| | | Minor Candidates | | | 35 | |
| 1792 | 15 | GEORGE WASHINGTON | No party designations | | 132 | |
| | | John Adams | | | 77 | |
| | | George Clinton | | | 50 | |
| | | Minor Candidates | | | 5 | |
| 1796 | 16 | JOHN ADAMS | Federalist | | 71 | |
| | | Thomas Jefferson | Democratic-Republican | | 68 | |
| | | Thomas Pinckney | Federalist | | 59 | |
| | | Aaron Burr | Democratic-Republican | | 30 | |
| | | Minor Candiates | | | 48 | |
| 1800 | 16 | THOMAS JEFFERSON | Democratic-Republican | | 73 | |
| | | Aaron Burr | Democratic-Republican | | 73 | |
| | | John Adams | Federalist | | 65 | |
| | | Charles C. Pinckney | Federalist | | 64 | |
| | | John Jay | Federalist | | 1 | |
| 1804 | 17 | THOMAS JEFFERSON | Democratic-Republican | | 162 | |
| | | Charles C. Pinckney | Federalist | | 14 | |
| 1808 | 17 | JAMES MADISON | Democratic-Republican | | 122 | |
| | | Charles C. Pinckney | Federalist | | 47 | |
| | | George Clinton | Democratic-Republican | | 6 | |
| 1812 | 18 | JAMES MADISON | Democratic-Republican | | 128 | |
| | | DeWitt Clinton | Federalist | | 89 | |
| 1816 | 19 | JAMES MONROE | Democratic-Republican | | 183 | |
| | | Rufus King | Federalist | | 34 | |
| 1820 | 24 | JAMES MONROE | Democratic-Republican | | 231 | |
| | | John Quincy Adams | Independent Republican | | 1 | |
| 1824 | 24 | JOHN QUINCY ADAMS | Democratic-Republican | 108,740 | 84 | 30.5 |
| | | Andrew Jackson | Democratic-Republican | 153,544 | 99 | 43.1 |
| | | William H. Crawford | Democratic-Republican | 46,618 | 41 | 13.1 |
| | | Henry Clay | Democratic-Republican | 47,136 | 37 | 13.2 |
| 1828 | 24 | ANDREW JACKSON | Democratic | 647,286 | 178 | 56.0 |
| | | John Quincy Adams | National Republican | 508,064 | 83 | 44.0 |
| 1832 | 24 | ANDREW JACKSON | Democratic | 687,502 | 219 | 55.0 |
| | | Henry Clay | National Republican | 530,189 | 49 | 42.4 |
| | | William Wirt | Anti-Masonic | 33,108 | 7 | 2.6 |
| | | John Floyd | National Republican | | 11 | |
| 1836 | 26 | MARTIN VAN BUREN | Democratic | 765,483 | 170 | 50.9 |
| | | William H. Harrison | Whig | | 73 | |
| | | Hugh L. White | Whig | 739,795 | 26 | 49.1 |
| | | Daniel Webster | Whig | | 14 | |
| | | W. P. Mangum | Whig | | 11 | |
| 1840 | 26 | WILLIAM H. HARRISON | Whig | 1,274,624 | 234 | 53.1 |
| | | Martin Van Buren | Democratic | 1,127,781 | 60 | 46.9 |

Candidates receiving less than 1 percent of the popular vote have been omitted. For that reason the percentage of popular vote given for any election year may not total 100 percent.

Before the passage of the Twelfth Amendment in 1804, the Electoral College voted for two presidential candidates; the runner-up became Vice President.

Figures are from *Historical Statistics of the United States, Colonial Times to 1957* (1961), pp. 682–83; and the U.S. Department of Justice.

# Presidential elections (1844–1900)

| Year | Number of states | Candidates | Parties | Popular vote | Electoral vote | Percentage of popular vote |
|------|------------------|------------|---------|--------------|----------------|----------------------------|
| 1844 | 26 | JAMES K. POLK | Democratic | 1,338,464 | 170 | 49.6 |
|      |    | Henry Clay | Whig | 1,300,097 | 105 | 48.1 |
|      |    | James G. Birney | Liberty | 62,300 | | 2.3 |
| 1848 | 30 | ZACHARY TAYLOR | Whig | 1,360,967 | 163 | 47.4 |
|      |    | Lewis Cass | Democratic | 1,222,342 | 127 | 42.5 |
|      |    | Martin Van Buren | Free Soil | 291,263 | | 10.1 |
| 1852 | 31 | FRANKLIN PIERCE | Democratic | 1,601,117 | 254 | 50.9 |
|      |    | Winfield Scott | Whig | 1,385,453 | 42 | 44.1 |
|      |    | John P. Hale | Free Soil | 155,825 | | 5.0 |
| 1856 | 31 | JAMES BUCHANAN | Democratic | 1,832,955 | 174 | 45.3 |
|      |    | John C. Frémont | Republican | 1,339,932 | 114 | 33.1 |
|      |    | Millard Fillmore | American | 871,731 | 8 | 21.6 |
| 1860 | 33 | ABRAHAM LINCOLN | Republican | 1,865,593 | 180 | 39.8 |
|      |    | Stephen A. Douglas | Democratic | 1,382,713 | 12 | 29.5 |
|      |    | John C. Breckinridge | Democratic | 848,356 | 72 | 18.1 |
|      |    | John Bell | Constitutional Union | 592,906 | 39 | 12.6 |
| 1864 | 36 | ABRAHAM LINCOLN | Republican | 2,206,938 | 212 | 55.0 |
|      |    | George B. McClellan | Democratic | 1,803,787 | 21 | 45.0 |
| 1868 | 37 | ULYSSES S. GRANT | Republican | 3,013,421 | 214 | 52.7 |
|      |    | Horatio Seymour | Democratic | 2,706,829 | 80 | 47.3 |
| 1872 | 37 | ULYSSES S. GRANT | Republican | 3,596,745 | 286 | 55.6 |
|      |    | Horace Greeley | Democratic | 2,843,446 | * | 43.9 |
| 1876 | 38 | RUTHERFORD B. HAYES | Republican | 4,036,572 | 185 | 48.0 |
|      |    | Samuel J. Tilden | Democratic | 4,284,020 | 184 | 51.0 |
| 1880 | 38 | JAMES A. GARFIELD | Republican | 4,453,295 | 214 | 48.5 |
|      |    | Winfield S. Hancock | Democratic | 4,414,082 | 155 | 48.1 |
|      |    | James B. Weaver | Greenback-Labor | 308,578 | | 3.4 |
| 1884 | 38 | GROVER CLEVELAND | Democratic | 4,879,507 | 219 | 48.5 |
|      |    | James G. Blaine | Republican | 4,850,293 | 182 | 48.2 |
|      |    | Benjamin F. Butler | Greenback-Labor | 175,370 | | 1.8 |
|      |    | John P. St. John | Prohibition | 150,369 | | 1.5 |
| 1888 | 38 | BENJAMIN HARRISON | Republican | 5,477,129 | 233 | 47.9 |
|      |    | Grover Cleveland | Democratic | 5,537,857 | 168 | 48.6 |
|      |    | Clinton B. Fisk | Prohibition | 249,506 | | 2.2 |
|      |    | Anson J. Streeter | Union Labor | 146,935 | | 1.3 |
| 1892 | 44 | GROVER CLEVELAND | Democratic | 5,555,426 | 277 | 46.1 |
|      |    | Benjamin Harrison | Republican | 5,182,690 | 145 | 43.0 |
|      |    | James B. Weaver | People's | 1,029,846 | 22 | 8.5 |
|      |    | John Bidwell | Prohibition | 264,133 | | 2.2 |
| 1896 | 45 | WILLIAM McKINLEY | Republican | 7,102,246 | 271 | 51.1 |
|      |    | William J. Bryan | Democratic | 6,492,559 | 176 | 47.7 |
| 1900 | 45 | WILLIAM McKINLEY | Republican | 7,218,491 | 292 | 51.7 |
|      |    | William J. Bryan | Democratic; Populist | 6,356,734 | 155 | 45.5 |
|      |    | John C. Wooley | Prohibition | 208,914 | | 1.5 |

*Greeley died shortly after the election; the electors supporting him then divided their votes among minor candidates.
Candidates receiving less than 1 percent of the popular vote have been omitted. For that reason the percentage of popular vote given for any election year may not total 100 percent.

# Presidential elections (1904–1956)

| Year | Number of states | Candidates | Parties | Popular vote | Electoral vote | Percentage of popular vote |
|------|------------------|------------|---------|--------------|----------------|---------------------------|
| 1904 | 45 | THEODORE ROOSEVELT | Republican | 7,628,461 | 336 | 57.4 |
|      |    | Alton B. Parker | Democratic | 5,084,223 | 140 | 37.6 |
|      |    | Eugene V. Debs | Socialist | 402,283 | | 3.0 |
|      |    | Silas C. Swallow | Prohibition | 258,536 | | 1.9 |
| 1908 | 46 | WILLIAM H. TAFT | Republican | 7,675,320 | 321 | 51.6 |
|      |    | William J. Bryan | Democratic | 6,412,294 | 162 | 43.1 |
|      |    | Eugene V. Debs | Socialist | 420,793 | | 2.8 |
|      |    | Eugene W. Chafin | Prohibition | 253,840 | | 1.7 |
| 1912 | 48 | WOODROW WILSON | Democratic | 6,296,547 | 435 | 41.9 |
|      |    | Theodore Roosevelt | Progressive | 4,118,571 | 88 | 27.4 |
|      |    | William H. Taft | Republican | 3,486,720 | 8 | 23.2 |
|      |    | Eugene V. Debs | Socialist | 900,672 | | 6.0 |
|      |    | Eugene W. Chafin | Prohibition | 206,275 | | 1.4 |
| 1916 | 48 | WOODROW WILSON | Democratic | 9,127,695 | 277 | 49.4 |
|      |    | Charles E. Hughes | Republican | 8,533,507 | 254 | 46.2 |
|      |    | A. L. Benson | Socialist | 585,113 | | 3.2 |
|      |    | J. Frank Hanly | Prohibition | 220,506 | | 1.2 |
| 1920 | 48 | WARREN G. HARDING | Republican | 16,143,407 | 404 | 60.4 |
|      |    | James N. Cox | Democratic | 9,130,328 | 127 | 34.2 |
|      |    | Eugene V. Debs | Socialist | 919,799 | | 3.4 |
|      |    | P. P. Christensen | Farmer-Labor | 265,411 | | 1.0 |
| 1924 | 48 | CALVIN COOLIDGE | Republican | 15,718,211 | 382 | 54.0 |
|      |    | John W. Davis | Democratic | 8,385,283 | 136 | 28.8 |
|      |    | Robert M. La Follette | Progressive | 4,831,289 | 13 | 16.6 |
| 1928 | 48 | HERBERT C. HOOVER | Republican | 21,391,993 | 444 | 58.2 |
|      |    | Alfred E. Smith | Democratic | 15,016,169 | 87 | 40.9 |
| 1932 | 48 | FRANKLIN D. ROOSEVELT | Democratic | 22,809,638 | 472 | 57.4 |
|      |    | Herbert C. Hoover | Republican | 15,758,901 | 59 | 39.7 |
|      |    | Norman Thomas | Socialist | 881,951 | | 2.2 |
| 1936 | 48 | FRANKLIN D. ROOSEVELT | Democratic | 27,752,869 | 523 | 60.8 |
|      |    | Alfred M. Landon | Republican | 16,674,665 | 8 | 36.5 |
|      |    | William Lemke | Union | 882,479 | | 1.9 |
| 1940 | 48 | FRANKLIN D. ROOSEVELT | Democratic | 27,307,819 | 449 | 54.8 |
|      |    | Wendell L. Willkie | Republican | 22,321,018 | 82 | 44.8 |
| 1944 | 48 | FRANKLIN D. ROOSEVELT | Democratic | 25,606,585 | 432 | 53.5 |
|      |    | Thomas E. Dewey | Republican | 22,014,745 | 99 | 46.0 |
| 1948 | 48 | HARRY S. TRUMAN | Democratic | 24,105,812 | 303 | 49.5 |
|      |    | Thomas E. Dewey | Republican | 21,970,065 | 189 | 45.1 |
|      |    | J. Strom Thurmond | States' Rights | 1,169,063 | 39 | 2.4 |
|      |    | Henry A. Wallace | Progressive | 1,157,172 | | 2.4 |
| 1952 | 48 | DWIGHT D. EISENHOWER | Republican | 33,936,234 | 442 | 55.1 |
|      |    | Adlai E. Stevenson | Democratic | 27,314,992 | 89 | 44.4 |
| 1956 | 48 | DWIGHT D. EISENHOWER | Republican | 35,590,472 | 457 | 57.6 |
|      |    | Adlai E. Stevenson | Democratic | 26,022,752 | 73 | 42.1 |

Candidates receiving less than 1 percent of the popular vote have been omitted. For that reason the percentage of popular vote given for any election year may not total 100 percent.

# Presidential elections (1960–1972)

| Year | Number of states | Candidates | Parties | Popular vote | Electoral vote | Percentage of popular vote |
|------|------|------|------|------|------|------|
| 1960 | 50 | JOHN F. KENNEDY | Democratic | 34,227,096 | 303 | 49.9 |
|      |    | Richard M. Nixon | Republican | 34,108,546 | 219 | 49.6 |
| 1964 | 50 | LYNDON B. JOHNSON | Democratic | 43,126,506 | 486 | 61.1 |
|      |    | Barry M. Goldwater | Republican | 27,176,799 | 52 | 38.5 |
| 1968 | 50 | RICHARD M. NIXON | Republican | 31,785,480 | 301 | 43.4 |
|      |    | Hubert H. Humphrey | Democratic | 31,275,165 | 191 | 42.7 |
|      |    | George C. Wallace | American Independent | 9,906,473 | 46 | 13.5 |
| 1972 | 50 | RICHARD M. NIXON | Republican | 47,169,911 | 520 | 60.7 |
|      |    | George S. McGovern | Democratic | 29,170,383 | 17 | 37.5 |

Candidates receiving less than 1 percent of the popular vote have been omitted. For that reason the percentage of popular vote given for any election year may not total 100 percent.

# Admission of states

| Order of admission | State | Date of admission | Order of admission | State | Date of admission |
|---|---|---|---|---|---|
| 1 | Delaware | December 7, 1787 | 26 | Michigan | January 26, 1837 |
| 2 | Pennsylvania | December 12, 1787 | 27 | Florida | March 3, 1845 |
| 3 | New Jersey | December 18, 1787 | 28 | Texas | December 29, 1845 |
| 4 | Georgia | January 2, 1788 | 29 | Iowa | December 28, 1846 |
| 5 | Connecticut | January 9, 1788 | 30 | Wisconsin | May 29, 1848 |
| 6 | Massachusetts | February 7, 1788 | 31 | California | September 9, 1850 |
| 7 | Maryland | April 28, 1788 | 32 | Minnesota | May 11, 1858 |
| 8 | South Carolina | May 23, 1788 | 33 | Oregon | February 14, 1859 |
| 9 | New Hampshire | June 21, 1788 | 34 | Kansas | January 29, 1861 |
| 10 | Virginia | June 25, 1788 | 35 | West Virginia | June 30, 1863 |
| 11 | New York | July 26, 1788 | 36 | Nevada | October 31, 1864 |
| 12 | North Carolina | November 21, 1789 | 37 | Nebraska | March 1, 1867 |
| 13 | Rhode Island | May 29, 1790 | 38 | Colorado | August 1, 1876 |
| 14 | Vermont | March 4, 1791 | 39 | North Dakota | November 2, 1889 |
| 15 | Kentucky | June 1, 1792 | 40 | South Dakota | November 2, 1889 |
| 16 | Tennessee | June 1, 1796 | 41 | Montana | November 8, 1889 |
| 17 | Ohio | March 1, 1803 | 42 | Washington | November 11, 1889 |
| 18 | Louisiana | April 30, 1812 | 43 | Idaho | July 3, 1890 |
| 19 | Indiana | December 11, 1816 | 44 | Wyoming | July 10, 1890 |
| 20 | Mississippi | December 10, 1817 | 45 | Utah | January 4, 1896 |
| 21 | Illinois | December 3, 1818 | 46 | Oklahoma | November 16, 1907 |
| 22 | Alabama | December 14, 1819 | 47 | New Mexico | January 6, 1912 |
| 23 | Maine | March 15, 1820 | 48 | Arizona | February 14, 1912 |
| 24 | Missouri | August 10, 1821 | 49 | Alaska | January 3, 1959 |
| 25 | Arkansas | June 15, 1836 | 50 | Hawaii | August 21, 1959 |

# Population of the United States (1790–1975)

| Year | Total population (in thousands) | Number per square mile of land area (continental United States) | Year | Total population (in thousands) | Number per square mile of land area (continental United States) |
|---|---|---|---|---|---|
| 1790 | 3,929 | 4.5 | 1837 | 15,843 | |
| 1791 | 4,056 | | 1838 | 16,264 | |
| 1792 | 4,194 | | 1839 | 16,684 | |
| 1793 | 4,332 | | 1840 | 17,120 | 9.8 |
| 1794 | 4,469 | | 1841 | 17,733 | |
| 1795 | 4,607 | | 1842 | 18,345 | |
| 1796 | 4,745 | | 1843 | 18,957 | |
| 1797 | 4,883 | | 1844 | 19,569 | |
| 1798 | 5,021 | | 1845 | 20,182 | |
| 1799 | 5,159 | | 1846 | 20,794 | |
| 1800 | 5,297 | 6.1 | 1847 | 21,406 | |
| 1801 | 5,486 | | 1848 | 22,018 | |
| 1802 | 5,679 | | 1849 | 22,631 | |
| 1803 | 5,872 | | 1850 | 23,261 | 7.9 |
| 1804 | 5,065 | | 1851 | 24,086 | |
| 1805 | 6,258 | | 1852 | 24,911 | |
| 1806 | 6,451 | | 1853 | 25,736 | |
| 1807 | 6,644 | | 1854 | 26,561 | |
| 1808 | 6,838 | | 1855 | 27,386 | |
| 1809 | 7,031 | | 1856 | 28,212 | |
| 1810 | 7,224 | 4.3 | 1857 | 29,037 | |
| 1811 | 7,460 | | 1858 | 29,862 | |
| 1812 | 7,700 | | 1859 | 30,687 | |
| 1813 | 7,939 | | 1860 | 31,513 | 10.6 |
| 1814 | 8,179 | | 1861 | 32,351 | |
| 1815 | 8,419 | | 1862 | 33,188 | |
| 1816 | 8,659 | | 1863 | 34,026 | |
| 1817 | 8,899 | | 1864 | 34,863 | |
| 1818 | 9,139 | | 1865 | 35,701 | |
| 1819 | 9,379 | | 1866 | 36,538 | |
| 1820 | 9,618 | 5.6 | 1867 | 37,376 | |
| 1821 | 9,939 | | 1868 | 38,213 | |
| 1822 | 10,268 | | 1869 | 39,051 | |
| 1823 | 10,596 | | 1870 | 39,905 | 13.4 |
| 1824 | 10,924 | | 1871 | 40,938 | |
| 1825 | 11,252 | | 1872 | 41,972 | |
| 1826 | 11,580 | | 1873 | 43,006 | |
| 1827 | 11,909 | | 1874 | 44,040 | |
| 1828 | 12,237 | | 1875 | 45,073 | |
| 1829 | 12,565 | | 1876 | 46,107 | |
| 1830 | 12,901 | 7.4 | 1877 | 47,141 | |
| 1831 | 13,321 | | 1878 | 48,174 | |
| 1832 | 13,742 | | 1879 | 49,208 | |
| 1833 | 14,162 | | 1880 | 50,262 | 16.9 |
| 1834 | 14,582 | | 1881 | 51,542 | |
| 1835 | 15,003 | | 1882 | 52,821 | |
| 1836 | 15,423 | | 1883 | 54,100 | |

Figures are from *Historical Statistics of the United States, Colonial Times to 1957* (1961), pp. 7, 8; *Statistical Abstract of the United States: 1974,* p. 5; Census Bureau for 1974 and 1975.

| Year | Total population (in thousands) | Number per square mile of land area (continental United States) | Year | Total population (in thousands)* | Number per square mile of land area (continental United States) |
|---|---|---|---|---|---|
| 1884 | 55,379 | | 1930 | 122,775 | 41.2 |
| 1885 | 56,658 | | 1931 | 124,040 | |
| 1886 | 57,938 | | 1932 | 124,840 | |
| 1887 | 59,217 | | 1933 | 125,579 | |
| 1888 | 60,496 | | 1934 | 126,374 | |
| 1889 | 61,775 | | 1935 | 127,250 | |
| 1890 | 63,056 | 21.2 | 1936 | 128,053 | |
| 1891 | 64,361 | | 1937 | 128,825 | |
| 1892 | 65,666 | | 1938 | 129,825 | |
| 1893 | 66,970 | | 1939 | 130,880 | |
| 1894 | 68,275 | | 1940 | 131,669 | 44.2 |
| 1895 | 69,580 | | 1941 | 133,894 | |
| 1896 | 70,885 | | 1942 | 135,361 | |
| 1897 | 72,189 | | 1943 | 137,250 | |
| 1898 | 73,494 | | 1944 | 138,916 | |
| 1899 | 74,799 | | 1945 | 140,468 | |
| 1900 | 76,094 | 25.6 | 1946 | 141,936 | |
| 1901 | 77,585 | | 1947 | 144,698 | |
| 1902 | 79,160 | | 1948 | 147,208 | |
| 1903 | 80,632 | | 1949 | 149,767 | |
| 1904 | 82,165 | | 1950 | 150,697 | 50.7 |
| 1905 | 83,820 | | 1951 | 154,878 | |
| 1906 | 85,437 | | 1952 | 157,553 | |
| 1907 | 87,000 | | 1953 | 160,184 | |
| 1908 | 88,709 | | 1954 | 163,026 | |
| 1909 | 90,492 | | 1955 | 165,931 | |
| 1910 | 92,407 | 31.0 | 1956 | 168,903 | |
| 1911 | 93,868 | | 1957 | 171,984 | |
| 1912 | 95,331 | | 1958 | 174,882 | |
| 1913 | 97,227 | | 1959 | 177,830 | |
| 1914 | 99,118 | | 1960 | 178,464 | 60.1 |
| 1915 | 100,549 | | 1961 | 183,672 | |
| 1916 | 101,966 | | 1962 | 186,504 | |
| 1917 | 103,414 | | 1963 | 189,197 | |
| 1918 | 104,550 | | 1964 | 191,833 | |
| 1919 | 105,063 | | 1965 | 194,237 | |
| 1920 | 106,466 | 35.6 | 1966 | 196,485 | |
| 1921 | 108,541 | | 1967 | 198,629 | |
| 1922 | 110,055 | | 1968 | 200,619 | |
| 1923 | 111,950 | | 1969 | 202,599 | 57.5† |
| 1924 | 114,113 | | 1970 | 203,875 | |
| 1925 | 115,832 | | 1971 | 207,045 | |
| 1926 | 117,399 | | 1972 | 208,842 | |
| 1927 | 119,038 | | 1973 | 210,396 | |
| 1928 | 120,501 | | 1974 | 211,894 | |
| 1929 | 121,770 | | 1975 | 213,631 | |

*Figures after 1940 represent total population including Armed Forces abroad, except in official census years.
†Figure includes Alaska and Hawaii.

# Presidents, Vice Presidents, and Cabinet members (1789–1841)

| President | Vice President | Secretary of State | Secretary of Treasury | Secretary of War |
|---|---|---|---|---|
| George Washington 1789–97 | John Adams 1789–97 | Thomas Jefferson 1789–94<br>Edmund Randolph 1794–95<br>Timothy Pickering 1795–97 | Alexander Hamilton 1789–95<br>Oliver Wolcott 1795–97 | Henry Knox 1789–95<br>Timothy Pickering 1795–96<br>James McHenry 1796–97 |
| John Adams 1797–1801 | Thomas Jefferson 1797–1801 | Timothy Pickering 1797–1800<br>John Marshall 1800–01 | Oliver Wolcott 1797–1801<br>Samuel Dexter 1801 | James McHenry 1797–1800<br>Samuel Dexter 1800–01 |
| Thomas Jefferson 1801–09 | Aaron Burr 1801–05<br>George Clinton 1805–09 | James Madison 1801–09 | Samuel Dexter 1801<br>Albert Gallatin 1801–09 | Henry Dearborn 1801–09 |
| James Madison 1809–17 | George Clinton 1809–13<br>Elbridge Gerry 1813–17 | Robert Smith 1809–11<br>James Monroe 1811–17 | Albert Gallatin 1809–14<br>George Campbell 1814<br>Alexander Dallas 1814–16<br>William Crawford 1816–17 | William Eustis 1809–13<br>John Armstrong 1813–14<br>James Monroe 1814–15<br>William Crawford 1815–17 |
| James Monroe 1817–25 | Daniel D. Tompkins 1817–25 | John Quincy Adams 1817–25 | William Crawford 1817–25 | George Graham 1817<br>John C. Calhoun 1817–25 |
| John Quincy Adams 1825–29 | John C. Calhoun 1825–29 | Henry Clay 1825–29 | Richard Rush 1825–29 | James Barbour 1825–28<br>Peter B. Porter 1828–29 |
| Andrew Jackson 1829–37 | John C. Calhoun 1829–33<br>Martin Van Buren 1833–37 | Martin Van Buren 1829–31<br>Edward Livingston 1831–33<br>Louis McLane 1833–34<br>John Forsyth 1834–37 | Samuel Ingham 1829–31<br>Louis McLane 1831–33<br>William Duane 1833<br>Roger B. Taney 1833–34<br>Levi Woodbury 1834–37 | John H. Eaton 1829–31<br>Lewis Cass 1831–37<br>Benjamin Butler 1837 |
| Martin Van Buren 1837–41 | Richard M. Johnson 1837–41 | John Forsyth 1837–41 | Levi Woodbury 1837–41 | Joel R. Poinsett 1837–41 |

| Secretary of Navy | Postmaster General | Attorney General |
|---|---|---|
| | Samuel Osgood 1789–91 Timothy Pickering 1791–95 Joseph Habersham 1795–97 | Edmund Randolph 1789–94 William Bradford 1794–95 Charles Lee 1795–97 |
| Benjamin Stoddert 1798–1801 | Joseph Habersham 1797–1801 | Charles Lee 1797–1801 |
| Benjamin Stoddert 1801 Robert Smith 1801–09 | Joseph Habersham 1801 Gideon Granger 1801–09 | Levi Lincoln 1801–05 John Breckinridge 1805-07 Caesar Rodney 1807–09 |
| Paul Hamilton 1809–13 William Jones 1813–14 Benjamin Crowninshield 1814–17 | Gideon Granger 1809–14 Return Meigs 1814–17 | Caesar Rodney 1809–11 William Pinkney 1811–14 Richard Rush 1814–17 |
| Benjamin Crowninshield 1817–18 Smith Thompson 1818–23 Samuel Southard 1823–25 | Return Meigs 1817–23 John McLean 1823–25 | Richard Rush 1817 William Wirt 1817–25 |
| Samuel Southard 1825–29 | John McLean 1825–29 | William Wirt 1825–29 |
| John Branch 1829–31 Levi Woodbury 1831–34 Mahlon Dickerson 1834–37 | William Barry 1829–35 Amos Kendall 1835–37 | John M. Berrien 1829–31 Roger B. Taney 1831–33 Benjamin Butler 1833–37 |
| Mahlon Dickerson 1837–38 James K. Paulding 1838–41 | Amos Kendall 1837–40 John M. Niles 1840–41 | Benjamin Butler 1837–38 Felix Grundy 1838–40 Henry D. Gilpin 1840–41 |

# Presidents, Vice Presidents, and Cabinet members (1841-77)

| President | Vice President | Secretary of State | Secretary of Treasury | Secretary of War |
|-----------|----------------|--------------------|-----------------------|------------------|
| William H. Harrison 1841 | John Tyler 1841 | Daniel Webster 1841 | Thomas Ewing 1841 | John Bell 1841 |
| John Tyler 1841–45 | | Daniel Webster 1841–43<br>Hugh S. Legaré 1843<br>Abel P. Upshur 1843–44<br>John C. Calhoun 1844–45 | Thomas Ewing 1841<br>Walter Forward 1841–43<br>John C. Spencer 1843–44<br>George M. Bibb 1844–45 | John Bell 1841<br>John C. Spencer 1841–43<br>James M. Porter 1843–44<br>William Wilkins 1844–45 |
| James K. Polk 1845–49 | George M. Dallas 1845–49 | James Buchanan 1845–49 | Robert J. Walker 1845–49 | William L. Marcy 1845–49 |
| Zachary Taylor 1849–50 | Millard Fillmore 1849–50 | John M. Clayton 1849–50 | William M. Meredith 1849–50 | George W. Crawford 1849–50 |
| Millard Fillmore 1850–53 | | Daniel Webster 1850–52<br>Edward Everett 1852–53 | Thomas Corwin 1850–53 | Charles M. Conrad 1850–53 |
| Franklin Pierce 1853–57 | William R. King 1853–57 | William L. Marcy 1853–57 | James Guthrie 1853–57 | Jefferson Davis 1853–57 |
| James Buchanan 1857–61 | John C. Breckinridge 1857–61 | Lewis Cass 1857–60<br>Jeremiah S. Black 1860–61 | Howell Cobb 1857–60<br>Philip F. Thomas 1860–61<br>John A. Dix 1861 | John B. Floyd 1857–61<br>Joseph Holt 1861 |
| Abraham Lincoln 1861–65 | Hannibal Hamlin 1861–65<br>Andrew Johnson 1865 | William H. Seward 1861–65 | Salmon P. Chase 1861–64<br>William P. Fessenden 1864–65<br>Hugh McCulloch 1865 | Simon Cameron 1861–62<br>Edwin M. Stanton 1862–65 |
| Andrew Johnson 1865–69 | | William H. Seward 1865–69 | Hugh McCulloch 1865–69 | Edwin M. Stanton 1865–67<br>Ulysses S. Grant 1867–68<br>John M. Schofield 1868–69 |
| Ulysses S. Grant 1869–77 | Schuyler Colfax 1869–73<br>Henry Wilson 1873–77 | Elihu B. Washburne 1869<br>Hamilton Fish 1869–77 | George S. Boutwell 1869–73<br>William A. Richardson 1873–74<br>Benjamin H. Bristow 1874–76<br>Lot M. Morrill 1876–77 | John A. Rawlins 1869<br>William T. Sherman 1869<br>William W. Belknap 1869–76<br>Alphonso Taft 1876<br>James D. Cameron 1876–77 |

| Secretary of Navy | Postmaster General | Attorney General | Secretary of Interior |
|---|---|---|---|
| George E. Badger 1841 | Francis Granger 1841 | John J. Crittenden 1841 | |
| George E. Badger 1841 Abel P. Upshur 1841–43 David Henshaw 1843–44 Thomas Gilmer 1844 John Y. Mason 1844–45 | Francis Granger 1841 Charles A. Wickliffe 1841–45 | John J. Crittenden 1841 Hugh S. Legaré 1841–43 John Nelson 1843–45 | |
| George Bancroft 1845–46 John Y. Mason 1846–49 | Cave Johnson 1845–49 | John Y. Mason 1845–46 Nathan Clifford 1846–48 Isaac Toucey 1848–49 | |
| William B. Preston 1849–50 | Jacob Collamer 1849–50 | Reverdy Johnson 1849–50 | Thomas Ewing 1849–50 |
| William A. Graham 1850–52 John P. Kennedy 1852–53 | Nathan K. Hall 1850–52 Sam D. Hubbard 1852–53 | John J. Crittenden 1850–53 | Thomas McKennan 1850 A. H. H. Stuart 1850–53 |
| James C. Dobbin 1853–57 | James Campbell 1853–57 | Caleb Cushing 1853–57 | Robert McClelland 1853–57 |
| Isaac Toucey 1857–61 | Aaron V. Brown 1857–59 Joseph Holt 1859–61 Horatio King 1861 | Jeremiah S. Black 1857–60 Edwin M. Stanton 1860–61 | Jacob Thompson 1857–61 |
| Gideon Welles 1861–65 | Horatio King 1861 Montgomery Blair 1861–64 William Dennison 1864–65 | Edward Bates 1861–64 James Speed 1864–65 | Caleb B. Smith 1861–63 John P. Usher 1863–65 |
| Gideon Welles 1865–69 | William Dennison 1865–66 Alexander Randall 1866–69 | James Speed 1865–66 Henry Stanbery 1866–68 William M. Evarts 1868–69 | John P. Usher 1865 James Harlan 1865–66 O. H. Browning 1866–69 |
| Adolph E. Borie 1869 George M. Robeson 1869–77 | John A. J. Creswell 1869–74 James W. Marshall 1874 Marshall Jewell 1874–76 James N. Tyner 1876–77 | Ebenezer R. Hoar 1869–70 Amos T. Akerman 1870–71 G. H. Williams 1871–75 Edwards Pierrepont 1875–76 Alphonso Taft 1876–77 | Jacob D. Cox 1869–70 Columbus Delano 1870–75 Zachariah Chandler 1875–77 |

# Presidents, Vice Presidents, and Cabinet members (1877–1923)

| President | Vice President | Secretary of State | Secretary of Treasury | Secretary of War | Secretary of Navy |
|---|---|---|---|---|---|
| Rutherford B. Hayes 1877–81 | William A. Wheeler 1877–81 | William M. Evarts 1877–81 | John Sherman 1877–81 | George W. McCrary 1877–79 Alexander Ramsey 1879–81 | R. W. Thompson 1877–81 Nathan Goff, Jr. 1881 |
| James A. Garfield 1881 | Chester A. Arthur 1881 | James G. Blaine 1881 | William Windom 1881 | Robert T. Lincoln 1881 | William H. Hunt 1881 |
| Chester A. Arthur 1881–85 | | F. T. Frelinghuysen 1881–85 | Charles J. Folger 1881–84 Walter Q. Gresham 1884 Hugh McCulloch 1884–85 | Robert T. Lincoln 1881–85 | William E. Chandler 1881–85 |
| Grover Cleveland 1885–89 | T. A. Hendricks 1885 | Thomas F. Bayard 1885–89 | Daniel Manning 1885–87 Charles S. Fairchild 1887–89 | William C. Endicott 1885–89 | William C. Whitney 1885–89 |
| Benjamin Harrison 1889–93 | Levi P. Morton 1889–93 | James G. Blaine 1889–92 John W. Foster 1892–93 | William Windom 1889–91 Charles Foster 1891–93 | Redfield Procter 1889–91 Stephen B. Elkins 1891–93 | Benjamin F. Tracy 1889–93 |
| Grover Cleveland 1893–97 | Adlai E. Stevenson 1893–97 | Walter Q. Gresham 1893–95 Richard Olney 1895–97 | John G. Carlisle 1893–97 | Daniel S. Lamont 1893–97 | Hilary A. Herbert 1893–97 |
| William McKinley 1897–1901 | Garret A. Hobart 1897–1901 Theodore Roosevelt 1901 | John Sherman 1897–98 William R. Day 1898 John Hay 1898–1901 | Lyman J. Gage 1897–1901 | Russell A. Alger 1897–99 Elihu Root 1899–1901 | John D. Long 1897–1901 |
| Theodore Roosevelt 1901–09 | Charles Fairbanks 1905–09 | John Hay 1901–05 Elihu Root 1905–09 Robert Bacon 1909 | Lyman J. Gage 1901–02 Leslie M. Shaw 1902–07 George B. Cortelyou 1907–09 | Elihu Root 1901–04 William H. Taft 1904–08 Luke E. Wright 1908–09 | John D. Long 1901–02 William H. Moody 1902–04 Paul Morton 1904–05 Charles J. Bonaparte 1905–06 Victor H. Metcalf 1906–08 T. H. Newberry 1908–09 |
| William H. Taft 1909–13 | James S. Sherman 1909–13 | Philander C. Knox 1909–13 | Franklin MacVeagh 1909–13 | Jacob M. Dickinson 1909–11 Henry L. Stimson 1911–13 | George von L. Meyer 1909–13 |
| Woodrow Wilson 1913–21 | Thomas R. Marshall 1913–21 | William J. Bryan 1913–15 Robert Lansing 1915–20 Bainbridge Colby 1920–21 | William G. McAdoo 1913–18 Carter Glass 1918–20 David F. Houston 1920–21 | Lindley M. Garrison 1913–16 Newton D. Baker 1916–21 | Josephus Daniels 1913–21 |
| Warren G. Harding 1921–23 | Calvin Coolidge 1921–23 | Charles E. Hughes 1921–23 | Andrew W. Mellon 1921–23 | John W. Weeks 1921–23 | Edwin Denby 1921–23 |

| Postmaster General | Attorney General | Secretary of Interior | Secretary of Agriculture | Secretary of Commerce and Labor | |
|---|---|---|---|---|---|
| David M. Key 1877–80 Horace Maynard 1880–81 | Charles Devens 1877–81 | Carl Schurz 1877–81 | | | |
| Thomas L. James 1881 | Wayne MacVeagh 1881 | S. J. Kirkwood 1881 | | | |
| Thomas L. James 1881 Timothy O. Howe 1881–83 Walter Q. Gresham 1883–84 Frank Hatton 1884–85 | B. H. Brewster 1881–85 | Henry M. Teller 1881–85 | | | |
| William F. Vilas 1885–88 Don M. Dickinson 1888–89 | A. H. Garland 1885–89 | L. Q. C. Lamar 1885–88 William F. Vilas 1888–89 | Norman J. Colman 1889 | | |
| John Wanamaker 1889–93 | W. H. H. Miller 1889–93 | John W. Noble 1889–93 | Jeremiah M. Rusk 1889–93 | | |
| Wilson S. Bissel 1893–95 William L. Wilson 1895–97 | Richard Olney 1893–95 Judson Harmon 1895–97 | Hoke Smith 1893–96 David R. Francis 1896–97 | J. Sterling Morton 1893–97 | | |
| James A. Gary 1897–98 Charles E. Smith 1898–1901 | Joseph McKenna 1897–98 John W. Griggs 1898–1901 Philander C. Knox 1901 | Cornelius N. Bliss 1897–98 E. A. Hitchcock 1898–1901 | James Wilson 1897–1901 | | |
| Charles E. Smith 1901–02 Henry C. Payne 1902–04 Robert J. Wynne 1904–05 George B. Cortelyou 1905–07 George von L. Meyer 1907–09 | Philander C. Knox 1901–04 William H. Moody 1904–06 Charles J. Bonaparte 1906–09 | E. A. Hitchcock 1901–07 James R. Garfield 1907–09 | James Wilson 1901–09 | George B. Cortelyou 1903–04 Victor H. Metcalf 1904–06 Oscar S. Straus 1906–09 | |
| Frank H. Hitchcock 1909–13 | G. W. Wickersham 1909–13 | R. A. Ballinger 1909–11 Walter L. Fisher 1911–13 | James Wilson 1909–13 | Charles Nagel 1909–13 | |
| | | | | **Secretary of Commerce** | **Secretary of Labor** |
| Albert S. Burleson 1913–21 | J. C. McReynolds 1913–14 T. W. Gregory 1914–19 A. Mitchell Palmer 1919–21 | Franklin K. Lane 1913–20 John B. Payne 1920–21 | David F. Houston 1913–20 E. T. Meredith 1920–21 | W. C. Redfield 1913–19 J. W. Alexander 1919–21 | William B. Wilson 1913–21 |
| Will H. Hays 1921–22 Hubert Work 1922–23 Harry S. New 1923 | H. M. Daugherty 1921–23 | Albert B. Fall 1921–23 Hubert Work 1923 | Henry C. Wallace 1921–23 | Herbert C. Hoover 1921–23 | James J. Davis 1921–23 |

# Presidents, Vice Presidents, and Cabinet members (1923–63)

| President | Vice President | Secretary of State | Secretary of Treasury | Secretary of War | Secretary of Navy |
|---|---|---|---|---|---|
| Calvin Coolidge 1923–29 | Charles G. Dawes 1925–29 | Charles E. Hughes 1923–25 Frank B. Kellogg 1925–29 | Andrew W. Mellon 1923–29 | John W. Weeks 1923–25 Dwight F. Davis 1925–29 | Edwin Denby 1923–24 Curtis D. Wilbur 1924–29 |
| Herbert C. Hoover 1929–33 | Charles Curtis 1929–33 | Henry L. Stimson 1929–33 | Andrew W. Mellon 1929–32 Ogden L. Mills 1932–33 | James W. Good 1929 Patrick J. Hurley 1929–33 | Charles F. Adams 1929–33 |
| Franklin Delano Roosevelt 1933–45 | John Nance Garner 1933–41 Henry A. Wallace 1941–45 Harry S Truman 1945 | Cordell Hull 1933–44 E. R. Stettinius, Jr. 1944–45 | William H. Woodin 1933–34 Henry Morgenthau, Jr. 1934–45 | George H. Dern 1933–36 Harry H. Woodring 1936–40 Henry L. Stimson 1940–45 | Claude A. Swanson 1933–40 Charles Edison 1940 Frank Knox 1940–44 James V. Forrestal 1944–45 |
| Harry S Truman 1945–53 | Alben W. Barkley 1949–53 | James F. Byrnes 1945–47 George C. Marshall 1947–49 Dean G. Acheson 1949–53 | Fred M. Vinson 1945–46 John W. Snyder 1946–53 | Robert P. Patterson 1945–47 Kenneth C. Royall 1947 | James V. Forrestal 1945–47 |
| | | | | **Secretary of Defense** | |
| | | | | James V. Forrestal 1947–49 Louis A. Johnson 1949–50 George C. Marshall 1950–51 Robert A. Lovett 1951–53 | |
| Dwight D. Eisenhower 1953–61 | Richard M. Nixon 1953–61 | John Foster Dulles 1953–59 Christian A. Herter 1959–61 | George M. Humphrey 1953–57 Robert B. Anderson 1957–61 | Charles E. Wilson 1953–57 Neil H. McElroy 1957–61 Thomas S. Gates 1959–61 | |
| John F. Kennedy 1961–63 | Lyndon B. Johnson 1961–63 | Dean Rusk 1961–63 | C. Douglas Dillon 1961–63 | Robert S. McNamara 1961–63 | |

| Postmaster General | Attorney General | Secretary of Interior | Secretary of Agriculture | Secretary of Commerce | Secretary of Labor | Secretary of Health, Education and Welfare |
|---|---|---|---|---|---|---|
| Harry S. New 1923–29 | H. M. Daugherty 1923–24 Harlan F. Stone 1924–25 John G. Sargent 1925–29 | Hubert Work 1923–28 Roy O. West 1928–29 | Henry C. Wallace 1923–24 Howard M. Gore 1924–25 W. M. Jardine 1925–29 | Herbert C. Hoover 1923–28 William F. Whiting 1928–29 | James J. Davis 1923–29 | |
| Walter F. Brown 1929–33 | J. D. Mitchell 1929–33 | Ray L. Wilbur 1929–33 | Arthur M. Hyde 1929–33 | Robert P. Lamont 1929–32 Roy D. Chapin 1932–33 | James J. Davis 1929–30 William N. Doak 1930–33 | |
| James A. Farley 1933–40 Frank C. Walker 1940–45 | H. S. Cummings 1933–39 Frank Murphy 1939–40 Robert Jackson 1940–41 Francis Biddle 1941–45 | Harold L. Ickes 1933–45 | Henry A. Wallace 1933–40 Claude R. Wickard 1940–45 | Daniel C. Roper 1933–39 Harry L. Hopkins 1939–40 Jesse Jones 1940–45 Henry A. Wallace 1945 | Frances Perkins 1933–45 | |
| R. E. Hannegan 1945–47 Jesse M. Donaldson 1947–53 | Tom C. Clark 1945–49 J. H. McGrath 1949–52 James P. McGranery 1952–53 | Harold L. Ickes 1945–46 Julius A. Krug 1946–49 Oscar L. Chapman 1949–53 | C. P. Anderson 1945–48 C. F. Brannan 1948–53 | W. A. Harriman 1946–48 Charles Sawyer 1948–53 | L. B. Schwellenbach 1945–48 Maurice J. Tobin 1948–53 | |
| A. E. Summerfield 1953–61 | H. Brownell, Jr. 1953–57 William P. Rogers 1957–61 | Douglas McKay 1953–56 Fred Seaton 1956–61 | Ezra T. Benson 1953–61 | Sinclair Weeks 1953–58 Lewis L. Strauss 1958–61 | Martin P. Durkin 1953 James P. Mitchell 1953–61 | Oveta Culp Hobby 1953–55 Marion B. Folsom 1955–58 Arthur S. Flemming 1958–61 |
| J. Edward Day 1961–63 John A. Gronouski 1963 | Robert F. Kennedy 1961–63 | Stewart L. Udall 1961–63 | Orville L. Freeman 1961–63 | Luther H. Hodges 1961–63 | Arthur J. Goldberg 1961–62 W. Willard Wirtz 1962–63 | A. H. Ribicoff 1961–62 Anthony J. Celebrezze 1962–63 |

# Presidents, Vice Presidents, and Cabinet members, (1963–    )

| President | Vice President | Secretary of State | Secretary of Treasury | Secretary of Defense | Postmaster General* | Attorney General |
|---|---|---|---|---|---|---|
| Lyndon B. Johnson 1963–69 | Hubert H. Humphrey 1965–69 | Dean Rusk 1963–69 | C. Douglas Dillon 1963–65 Henry H. Fowler 1965–68 Joseph W. Barr 1968–69 | Robert S. McNamara 1963–68 Clark M. Clifford 1968–69 | John A. Gronouski 1963–65 Lawrence F. O'Brien 1965–68 W. Marvin Watson 1968–69 | Robert F. Kennedy 1963–65 N. deB. Katzenbach 1965–67 Ramsey Clark 1967–69 |
| Richard M. Nixon 1969–74 | Spiro T. Agnew 1969–73 Gerald R. Ford 1973–74 | William P. Rogers 1969–73 Henry A. Kissinger 1973–74 | David M. Kennedy 1969–70 John B. Connally 1970–72 George P. Shultz 1972–74 William E. Simon 1974 | Melvin R. Laird 1969–73 Elliot L. Richardson 1973 James R. Schlesinger 1973–74 | Winton M. Blount 1969–71 | John M. Mitchell 1969–72 Richard G. Kleindienst 1972–73 Elliot L. Richardson 1973 William B. Saxbe 1974 |
| Gerald R. Ford 1974– | Nelson A. Rockefeller 1974– | Henry A. Kissinger 1974– | William E. Simon 1974– | James R. Schlesinger 1974–75 Donald H. Rumsfeld 1975– | | William B. Saxbe 1974–75 Edward H. Levi 1975– |

*On July 1, 1971, the Post Office became an independent agency. After that date, the Postmaster General was no longer a member of the Cabinet.

| Secretary of Interior | Secretary of Agriculture | Secretary of Commerce | Secretary of Labor | Secretary of Health, Education and Welfare | Secretary of Housing and Urban Development | Secretary of Transportation |
|---|---|---|---|---|---|---|
| Stewart L. Udall 1963–69 | Orville L. Freeman 1963–69 | Luther H. Hodges 1963–65 John T. Connor 1965–67 Alexander B. Trowbridge 1967–68 C. R. Smith 1968–69 | W. Willard Wirtz 1963–69 | Anthony J. Celebrezze 1963–65 John W. Gardner 1965–68 Wilbur J. Cohen 1968–69 | Robert C. Weaver 1966–68 Robert C. Wood 1968–69 | Alan S. Boyd 1966–69 |
| Walter J. Hickel 1969–71 Rogers C. B. Morton 1971–74 | Clifford M. Hardin 1969–71 Earl L. Butz 1971–74 | Maurice H. Stans 1969–72 Peter G. Peterson 1972 Frederick B. Dent 1972–74 | George P. Shultz 1969–70 James D. Hodgson 1970–73 Peter J. Brennan 1973–74 | Robert H. Finch 1969–70 Elliot L. Richardson 1970–73 Caspar W. Weinberger 1973–74 | George W. Romney 1969–73 James T. Lynn 1973–74 | John A. Volpe 1969–73 Claude S. Brinegar 1973–74 |
| Rogers C. B. Morton 1974–75 Stanley K. Hathaway 1975 Thomas D. Kleppe 1975– | Earl L. Butz 1974– | Frederick B. Dent 1974–75 Rogers C. B. Morton 1975 Elliot L. Richardson 1975– | Peter J. Brennan 1974–75 John T. Dunlop 1975–76 W. J. Usery 1976– | Caspar W. Weinberger 1974–75 Forrest D. Mathews 1975– | James T. Lynn 1974–75 Carla A. Hills 1975– | Claude S. Brinegar 1974–75 William T. Coleman 1975– |

# Source of illustrations

232: Northern Natural Gas Company Collections, Joslyn Art Museum, Omaha, Nebraska
235: The Bettmann Archive
236: The Bettmann Archive
238: The Bettmann Archive
239: Brown Brothers
241: Historical Pictures Service, Inc.
242: Library of Congress
243: Brown Brothers
247: The New-York Historical Society
248: Library of Congress
249: Brown Brothers
250: New York Public Library
254: The Bettmann Archive
258: Historical Pictures Service, Inc.
259: George Eastman House
261: New York Public Library
265: Granger Collection
267: The Bettmann Archive
270: The Metropolitan Museum of Art, Gift of I. N. Phelps Stokes and the Hawes Family, 1937
271: History Division, Los Angeles County Museum of Natural History
272: The New-York Historical Society
273: The New-York Historical Society
274: (*top*) Brown Brothers; (*bottom*) The Metropolitan Museum of Art, Gift of I. N. Phelps Stokes, Edward S. Hawes, Alice Mary Hawes, Marion Augusta Hawes, 1937
277: Brown Brothers
280: Public Library of Cincinnati and Hamilton County
282: Brown Brothers
283: Concord Free Public Library
284: Culver Pictures
287: Brown Brothers
288: Historical Pictures Service, Inc.
289: New York Public Library
290: The Bettmann Archive
292: Brown Brothers
295: (*top*) Brown Brothers; (*bottom*) George Eastman House
297: Brown Brothers
301: Kansas State Historical Society
303: Culver Pictures
305: The Bettmann Archive
306: The Bettmann Archive
307: Library of Congress
310: Library of Congress
311: Library of Congress
312: Library of Congress
314: Culver Pictures
317: Library of Congress
318: Library of Congress
319: National Archives
323: U.S. Signal Corps in the National Archives
325: Historical Pictures Service, Inc.
328: Georgia Department of Archives and History
331: The New-York Historical Society
335: Historical Pictures Service, Inc.
336: Library of Congress
341: (*top*) The Bettmann Archive; (*bottom*) Library of Congress
345: The Bettmann Archive
346: *Detail,* anonymous painting, pencil and watercolor. 20 x 32¼ in. M. and M. Karolik Collection, 61.362,

Courtesy Museum of Fine Arts, Boston
350: (*left*) National Archives; (*right*) Culver Pictures
353: The Bettmann Archive
356: U.S. War Department in the National Archives
359: Historical Pictures Service, Inc.
362: Culver Pictures
363: (*both*) Library of Congress
366: Historical Pictures Service, Inc.
367: Library of Congress
373: Historical Pictures Service, Inc.
379: Library of Congress
380: Brown Brothers
381: Brown Brothers
383: Granger Collection
384: Brown Brothers
385: Brown Brothers
386: Brown Brothers
387: Library of Congress
388: Brown Brothers
393: Brown Brothers
395: Brown Brothers
396: Brown Brothers
398: U.S. Department of Agriculture
400: Library of Congress
403: The Bettmann Archive
404: The Bettmann Archive
407: The Montana State Historical Society, Helena
409: Culver Pictures
413: The Oklahoma Historical Society
416: Nebraska State Historical Society
418: Courtesy Amon Carter Museum, Fort Worth, Texas
421: Union Pacific Railroad Museum Collection
424: Minnesota Historical Society
426: Culver Pictures
427: Culver Pictures
432: Brown Brothers
434: Brown Brothers
435: Brown Brothers
439: AFL-CIO News
442: Culver Pictures
445: The Bettmann Archive
446: Museum of the City of New York
451: Culver Pictures
453: The Bettmann Archive
454: Photo by Jacob A. Riis. The Jacob A. Riis Collection. Museum of the City of New York
458: Photoworld, Inc.
459: Chicago Architectural Photographing Company
460: Culver Pictures
461: The Bettmann Archive
464: The Bettmann Archive
468: The Bettmann Archive
471: (*top*) The Smithsonian Institution; (*bottom*) Brown Brothers
472: Library of Congress
475: The Bettmann Archive
478: Historical Pictures Service, Inc.
480: Brown Brothers
481: Kansas State Historical Society
483: Library of Congress
484: Culver Pictures
485: Culver Pictures
486: (*top*) The Bettmann Archive; (*bottom*) Library of Congress

490: National Archives
492: Rocky Mountain News, Denver
494: Brown Brothers
495: The Bettmann Archive
496: New York Public Library
499: New York Public Library
502: Harper's Weekly
504: The Bettmann Archive
505: The Bettmann Archive
506: (*top*) U.S. Navy photo; (*bottom*) Library of Congress
509: Brown Brothers
512: Library of Congress, photo by Lewis W. Hine
513: Photo by Byron, The Byron Collection, Museum of the City of New York
514: Culver Pictures
515: Brown Brothers
516: (*top*) Tamiment Library, New York University; (*bottom*) Library of Congress
517: Addison Gallery of American Art, Phillips Academy, Andover, Massachusetts
518: Brown Brothers
519: Brown Brothers
521: Brown Brothers
522: Library of Congress
523: Hazleton Area Public Library
527: Culver Pictures
528: The Mariner's Museum, Newport News, Virginia
529: New York Globe
531: Culver Pictures
536: United Press International
538: (*top*) Brown Brothers; (*bottom*) The World, New York
540: The Bettmann Archive
541: Culver Pictures
542: United Press International
544: The Bettmann Archive
545: Brown Brothers
548: Library of Congress
550: (*top*) National Archives; (*bottom*) Culver Pictures
552: National Archives
554: Brown Brothers
555: Brown Brothers
557: Granger Collection
558: New York Public Library
560: Historical Pictures Service, Inc.
562: (*top*) Culver Pictures; (*bottom*) USSC, National Archives
563: Imperial War Museum, London
564: USSC, National Archives
566: National Archives
568: Culver Pictures
570: National Archives
572: Photo Trends
573: Library of Congress
575: Musée de la Guerre, Paris, American Heritage
579: (*top*) United Press International; (*bottom*) Chicago Historical Society
580: The Bettmann Archive
581: United Press International
582: Brown Brothers
585: Culver Pictures
587: Alley in the Memphis Commercial Appeal
588: Culver Pictures

880

*Source of illustrations*

# Index

phy, 652, 656; and progressive reforms, 526–27; and speculation, 224, 343, 605–07, 616. *See also* Business; Industry; Laissez-faire policy; Trusts
Capone, Al, 598
Cardozo, Benjamin N., 648
Cardozo, Francis L., 372
Caribbean, 3, 32, 81, 140, 269, 284, 491, 492, 495, 502, 540, 549; and international interests, 530; naval bases in, 674. *See also* Latin America
Carlisle, Lord, 107, 108
Carlyle, Thomas, 235
Carmichael, Stokely, 782, 833
Carnegie, Andrew, 428–29, 434, 455, 503
*Caroline,* 229
Carpetbaggers, 366, 367, 372, 378, 383, 389, 390
Carranza, Venustiano, 549, 550, 551
Carter, James C., 484
Carter, James, 484
Carteret, Sir George, 35, 36
Cartier, Jacques, 7–8
Carver, John, 20
Casablanca Conference (*1943*), 700
Cass, Lewis, 270, 276
Castle Garden, 289
Castro, Cipriano, 530
Castro, Fidel, 748, 753, 754, 768, 784
Catchings, Waddill, 609
Cathay Company, 10
Catherine of Aragon, 9
Catholic Worker Movement, 841
Catholics. *See* Roman Catholic Church
Catt, Carrie Chapman, 452, 514
Cattle-raising, 408–11, 526
Caucus, 207
Cavelier, Robert (Sieur de la Salle), 70
Cavendish, Thomas, 12
Censorship, 567, 571, 841
Central America. *See* Caribbean; Latin America
Central Intelligence Agency (CIA), 726, 748, 752, 754, 755, 757, 764, 765, 784, 803, 809, 814
Central Pacific Railroad, 358, **421**, 422
Central Treaty Organization (CENTO), **748,** 951
Cerro Gordo, Battle of, 266, **268**
Cervera, Pascual, 500, 501
Chamberlain, Neville, 663, 668, 669, 670, 671
Chambers, Whittaker, 741
Champlain, Samuel de, 8, 70
Chancellorsville, Battle of, 345, **347**
Chandler, Zach, 467, 468
Channing, William Ellery, 235, 239, 282
Chaplin, Charlie, 601
Charity Organization Society, 450
Charles I (king of England), 18, 21, 23, 25, 30–31, 36, 42, 86
Charles II (king of England), 31, 32, 33, 36, 37, 40, 41, 42, 43, 44
*Charles River Bridge* v. *Warren Bridge,* 227–28
Charleston, S.C., **356–57**
Charlestown, 21; bombardment of, 97, 105
Charter of Liberties (*1701*), 35, 41
Chase, Salmon P., 271, 303, 305, 318,

330, 331, 332, 341, 361, 368–69, 374
Chase, Samuel, 158
Chattanooga, Battle of, 348
Chauncey, Charles, 65
Chautauqua movement, 455
Chavez, Cesar, 837, 838
Cheever, John, 842
Chemical defoliation, 796
Chennault, Claire, 725
Cherokee Indians, 71, 92, 215
Cherokee Outlet, 414
Chesapeake & Ohio Railroad, 326
Cheves, Langdon, 167
Cheyenne Indians, 402, 403
Chiang Kai-shek, 623, 667, 668, 697, 698, 701, 703, 704, 717, 725, 726, 747, 750, 752, 798
Chicago anarchists, 439
Chicanos, 837
Chickamauga, Battle of, 348
Chief Joseph's Rebellion, 402
Child Labor Act (*1916*), 547
Chile, 495, 550, 803, 822
China, 469, 494, 502, 504–05, 532, 533, 540, 548, 574, 657, 679, 697–98; alliance with Russia, 503; Japanese imperialism in, 623–24, 666, 678; revolution in, 725–26; and Second World War, 687, 694–97; and U.S. trade, 286–87, 369, 666; and Washington Conference, 583. *See also* China, Communist; China, Nationalist
China, Communist, 697, 725–26, 749, 761, 794–97; and Formosan Straits, 747, 752; and Korean War, 728; and peaceful coexistence, 754, 762; and Vietnam, 749–50
China, Nationalist, 697, 699, 701, 703, 704, 715, 717, 725, 726, 728, 747, 750, 752, 798
Chinese Eastern Railway, 623
Chisholm, Shirley, 833
*Chisholm* v. *Georgia,* 150
Chisum, John, 410
Chivington, John M., 402
Chivington massacre, **402**
Choate, Joseph H., 485
Chou En-lai, 798, 799
Chouart, Médart (Sieur de Groseilliers), 71
Christian Science. *See* Church of Christ, Scientist
Christian Socialists, 487
Church, 63–66, 745, 841; and reform, 234, 452–54; and state, 113. *See also* Religion; *individual denominations*
Church of Christ, Scientist, 453
Church of England, 9, 10, 19, 21, 454. *See also* Anglican Church; Episcopal Church
Church of Jesus Christ of Latter Day Saints, 238
Churchill, Winston, 668, 671, 672, 673, 674, 679, 688–89, 690, 691, 697, 701, 705, 712, 714, 716, 720; and Atlantic Charter, 677–78, 699–700; and Yalta Conference, 702–04
Cincinnati, 178–79
Cities, 829–32; black ghettos in, 781, 783, 837; disorders in, 781, 783, 805; economic origins of, 60–62; growth of,

191, 289, 291, 357, 443–48, 511; and machine politics, 371–72, 448, 449–50; population in, 781, 829; and schools, 454, 832; and slums, 447–48, 773. *See also* Government, municipal
Citizenship, 306, 307, 363
Civil liberties, 149–50, 375, 567, 568, 580, 685; and Supreme Court, 744; and Truman, 730, 731
Civil rights, 362, 363, 375, 742–43, 772, 781, 783, 833, 835; and L. B. Johnson, 772, 783; and Kennedy, 770–71; and Truman, 722–23
Civil Rights Act: (*1866*), 363, 364, 384; (*1875*), 375, 384; (*1957*), 743; (*1964*), 772
*Civil Rights Cases,* 384
Civil service, 207, 212, 380, 450, 468. *See also* Spoils system
Civil Service Commission, 471, 472, 473
Civil Service Act (*1883*), 467, 471–72
Civil War, 277, 300, 320, 322–52, 378, 495; alignment of states, **324;** campaigns of, 332–43, 345–53; casualties during, 796; demobilization after, 358; economic consequences of, 357–58, 418, 419–20; and Emancipation Proclamation, 340–42; and England, 332, 337–38; financing of, 331–32; and Mexico, 369; mobilization for, 326–32; naval operations of, 335–36; and reelection of Lincoln, 351–52; and slavery issue, 338–39. *See also* Confederacy; Secession; Union
Civilian Conservation Corps (CCC), 653
Clark, Champ, 543
Clark, George Rogers, 162
Clark, J. Reuben, 621
Clark, James Freeman, 235
Clark, William, 162, 259
Clarke, Arthur C., 845
Classes, social, 200, 205, 251; and distribution of wealth, 433–36; divisions among, 200, 458; middle class, 450, 520, 521, 655, 806–07; mobility of, 68–69, 113, 205, **206;** and progressivism, 518, 521
Clay, Henry, 167, 212, 214, 216, 219, 223, 371; "American System" of, 179–80, 181, 184, 186, 208, 209, 210, 216, 222, 228, 263; and Compromise of *1850,* 273, 274; and compromise tariff, 219; and election of *1844,* 262; and Latin American revolutions, 185; and Missouri Compromise, 197; and National Republicans, 205; and Treaty of Ghent, 174; and War of *1812,* 168, 174, 175
Clay, Lucius, 721
Clayton, John M. 285, 286
Clayton Act (*1914*), 547, 586
Clayton-Bulwer Treaty (*1850*), 285
Cleaver, Eldridge, 783, 840, 841
Clemenceau, Georges, 571, 573
Clemens, Samuel L., 407, 460–61, 503, 712
Cleveland, Grover, 472–73, 503; Administration of, 425, 440, 464, 473–74, 481–84, 485–86, 492, 495–96, 496–97, 498
Clifford, Clark, 722, 777, 779

Corruption in government, 371–72, 374, 449–50; 468, 517, 587, 731, 744, 808–13, 814. *See also* Politics, machine; Spoils system
Corso, Gregory, 785
Cortelyou, George B., 524
Cortez, Hernando, 5–**7**
Corwin, Thomas, 266
Costigan, Edward P., 625
Cotton, 192, 193, 198, 216, 293, 296, 337–38, 394, 497
Cotton, John, 23
Couch, Darius, 364
Coughlin, Charles E., 642, 647, 685
Council of Economic Advisors, 722, 769
Council of Foreign Ministers, 714
Council for Mutual Economic Assistance (COMECON), 720
Council of National Defense, 565
Council for New England, 18, 20, 21, 24, 44
Counterculture, 786–87
Country Life Commission, 526
Court of Commerce, 538, 539
Courts, federal district, 134, 152, 158
Cowley, Malcolm, 608, 628
Cox, Archibald, 810, 811
Cox, James M., 577, 582
Coxe, Tench, 142
Coxey's Army, 483
Cozzens, James Gould, 842
Crawford, William H., 182, 207–08, 209, 210
Crédit Mobilier, 371, 374
Creek Indians, 3, 71, 140, 168, 172, 209
Creel, George, 567, 571
CREEP, 808, 809
*Creole,* 239
Crick, F. H. C., 845
Crime, 731; and growth of cities, 448, 830; organized, 598, 830; women involved in, 835
"Crime of 1873," 470, 482
Crime Investigation Committee (Senate), 731
Crittenden, John J., 316
Croker, Richard, 449, 451
Croly, Herbert, 543, 566
Cromwell, Oliver, 31–32, 37, 42, 85
Crummell, Alexander, 389
Crystal Palace Exhibition, 294
Cuba, 82, 185, 186, 269, 491, 492, 502, 504, 661, 748, 761, 803; and campaign of *1898,* 498–501; and nineteenth-century imperialism, 497, 498; rebel invasion of, 764; revolution of, 753; and Soviet Union, 754, 755, 767–68; and Spanish-American War, 497–501; U.S. protectorate of, 529
Cubans, 837
Cullen, Countee, 609
Cullom, Shelby M., 425
Cumberland Road. *See* National Road
Cummings, Homer, 648
*Cummings* v. *Missouri,* 369
Currency Act (*1764*), 84
Curtis, Benjamin R., 307
Curtis, Charles, 628
Curtis, Edwin U., 450
Curtis, George William, 450, 468, 471, 472, 473
Cushing, Caleb, 286

Custer, George A., **403,** 404
Cutting, Bronson, 620
Cybernetics, 832
Czechoslovakia, 573, 669, 670, 715, 720, 721, 797, 803

DNA (deoxyribonucleic acid), 845
D-Day, 691
Dakota Indians, 404
Daladier, Edouard, 669
Dale, Thomas, 15
Dana, Richard H., 261
Daniels, Josephus, 676
Darlan, Jean François, 690, 698, 700
Darrow, Clarence, 599, 638
Dartmouth, Lord William, 93, 96
*Dartmouth College* v. *Woodward,* 185
Darwin, Charles, 434, 598
Darwinism, social, 434, 435, 436, 452, 493, 518
Daugherty, Harry M., 587
Daughters of the American Revolution (DAR), 653
Davenport, James, 64
Davie, William R., 149
Davis, Angela, 785
Davis, David, 381–82
Davis, Elmer, 731
Davis, Henry G., 468
Davis, Henry Winter, 351
Davis, James H., 480
Davis, Jefferson, 286, 300, 302, 313, 314, 359, 380; and Confederacy, 317–20, 327–28, 336, 343, 346, 349, 350
Davis, John W., 599, 600
Davis, Norman, 663
Davis, Richard Harding, 499, 500
Dawes, Charles G., 584, 603, 625
Dawes Act (*1887*), 404
Dawes Plan, 603
Day, Dorothy, 841
Dean, James, 746
Dean, John, 809, 810, 811
Deane, Silas, 108
Dearborn, Henry, 156, **170,** 171
Debs, Eugene V., 439, 440, 487, 505, 516, 567
Decker, Sarah Platt, 513
Declaration of Independence, **99,** 100, 108, 112, 114, 124, 243, 247, 251; bicentennial of, 826
Declaration of Lima, 669
Declaration of Moscow, 701
Declaration of Sentiments and Resolutions, 242
Declaratory Act (*1766*), 87
Deep Throat, 810
Deere, John, 294
De Gaulle, Charles, 672, 690, 700, 767, 798
Degler, Carl N., 654
Deism, 65, 234
De La Warr, Lord, 14, 15
Delaware, colony of, 39, 41, 116
Deloria, Vine, Jr., 838, 839
Democracy: and egalitarianism, 113, 114, 206; participatory, 773, 784; and representative government, 62–63, 67, 86, 90, 95, 519–20; and Stalinism, 717,

751. *See also* Jacksonian democracy; Jeffersonian democracy; New Deal; Populism; Progressivism; Reform movement
Democratic National Committee, 808
Democratic party, 223, 226, 227, 262, 263, 266, 268, 270, 272, 276, 289, 303, 305, 306, 313, 364, 365, 370, 380, 381, 466, 467, 470, 473, 474, 484, 599, 628; and agrarian movement, 479; and black support, 653, 723; and Civil War, 338, 351; early expansionist aims of, 285; in First World War, 568; and labor support, 779; Locofoco faction of, 225, and *n;* and New Deal, 650, 651; and *1968* convention, 779, 784, 785; origin of, 205, 213; and Peace Democrats, 342, 350; and progressive movement, 539, 543, 547; in Second World War, 672, 687, 699; and slavery, 313, 314; and tariff, 466; and Treaty of Versailles, 575–77; and *'29* depression, 619, 625; and Vietnam War, 778, 779; and voting pattern, **466;** Young America faction of, 285. *See also* Conservative party, Southern Democratic; Elections; Whig party
Dempsey, Jack, 600
Denmark, 412, 721; and Second World War, 671
Dependent Pension Act (*1890*), 476
Dependent Pension bill (*1887*), 473
Depression: post-Revolutionary, 114; of *1857,* 308–09; of *1873,* 374, 380; of *1879,* 469; of *1893,* 439, 481–83; of *1907,* 526, 546; of *1929,* 616–21, 624–28, 652. *See also* Hoover, Herbert C.; New Deal; Roosevelt, Franklin D.
Desegregation. *See* Civil rights; Segregation
Desert Land Act (*1877*), 411
De Soto, Hernando, 6, **7**
Destroyer-naval base agreement, 674, 675
Détente, 768, 799–801, 803
Dewey, George, 499, 501, 530
Dewey, John, 518, 609, 610
Dewey, Thomas E., 672, 698, 699, 723, 724
Dewson, Molly, 653
Diaz, Bartholomeu, 4
Dickens, Charles, 200, 244
Dickinson, Emily, 460
Dickinson, John, 90, 98
Diem, Ngo Dinh, 750, 751, 765, 775, 809
Dies, Martin, 651, 730
Dillingham, William Paul, 533, 596
Dillon, Douglas, 754, 769
Dingley, Nelson, 488
Dingley Tariff (*1897*), 488, 506, 537, 538
Dinwiddie, Robert, 79
Diplomacy. *See* Foreign policy
Disarmament, 662–63; and Kennedy Administration, 766; naval, 583–84; and outlawing war, 604; F. D. Roosevelt proposals for, 662. *See also* Nuclear weapons
Disfranchisement, 386
Divorce, 827
Dix, Dorothea, 240, **241,** 242, 344
Dixiecrats. *See* States Rights Democratic party

887

*Index*

Powers, J. F., 842
Powhatan Confederacy, 3, 70
Pragmatism, 518
Presbyterians, 19, 21, 63, 92, 234, 237, 452
President, U.S., 126, 132–33, 467, 587, 811, 813–14, 815; and electoral system, 126, 144–45; extension of powers of, 358, 727, 729, 738, 793, 806; Kennedy on, 739; prohibition of third term for, 722; role of, 132, 138; Truman on, 738
President's Committee on Civil Rights, 722
President's Committee on Farm Tenancy, 645
Press, 487, 571, 807, 811; freedom of, 68, 249; and jingoism, 495–96, 497, 498; penny, 244; religious, 502; and yellow journalism, 497. *See also* Newspapers
Prevost, Sir George, 172, 174
Price-wage guidelines, 769, 804
*Prigg* v. *Pennsylvania*, 248
Princeton, Battle of, 106
Private enterprise. *See* Capitalism; Laissez-faire policy
Proclamation of *1763,* 92
Proctor, Redfield, 498
Progressive party, 542, 547; and election of *1912,* 545; and election of *1916,* 556–57. *See also* Progressivism
Progressive party (*1924*), 599
Progressive party (*1948*), 723
Progressivism, 508–34, 536–59, 582, 609; character of, 520; in cities and states, 519–20; origin of, 508; resurgence of, 545; and T. Roosevelt, 521–25, 532; and Taft, 537; and Wilson, 543, 547. *See also* New Deal; Populism
Prohibition movement, 240–41, 514, 568, 597–98, 630, 635
Propaganda: in First World War, 567; in Second World War, 676
Protectionists. *See* Tariff
Protestant Reformation, 9–10
Protestantism, 113, 234, 237–39, 290, 452, 453. *See also* individual denominations
Providence *Gazette,* 89
Psychoanalysis, 608
Public Contracts Act (*1935*), 644
Public land. *See* Frontier, land policy; Railroads, federal grants to
Public opinion, 167; and election of *1948,* 723–24; in First World War, 567–71; in Spanish-American War, 495–96; in Vietnam War, 777
Public services, 830
Public spending, 646, 650, 684, 773
Public utilities, 445–46, 449, 468, 610, 640–41, 645, 653, 740
Public Utilities Holding Company Act (*1935*), 645, 647, 648
Public Works Administration (PWA), 637, 644, 699
Puerto Ricans, 837–38
Puerto Rico, 185, 492, 501, 502, 837
Pujo, Arsène P., 546
Pulitzer, Joseph, 497
Pullman, George M., 439, 440
Pullman strike, 439–40, 483, 486, 524
Punta del Este Conference (*1961*), 764

Pure Food and Drug Act (*1906*), 525, 785
Puritanism, 18–19
Puritans, 10, 18, 19, 21, 22–24, 25, 56, 63, 70, 85
Put-in-Bay, Battle of, **170,** 171
Puzo, Mario, 842

Quakers, 35–36, 38–39, 45, 63, 237, 244; and antislavery crusade, 193, 245; settlement of, in Pennsylvania, 40
Quartering Acts (*1765* and *1774*), 85, 90, 95
Quay, Mathew, 468, 474
Quebec, 8, 70, 81, 94
Quebec Act (*1774*), 93–94
Quebec conferences, 700, 701, 714
Queen Anne's War, 71
Quincy, Josiah, 172–73
Quint, H. H., 606

RFC. *See* Reconstruction Finance Corporation
ROTC. *See* Reserve Officers Training Corps
Race prejudice, 54, 248, 360, 362, 372, 375, 404, 452, 493, 494, 513, 579, 581, 596–97, 686–87, 742–44, 781, 835, 836. *See also* Blacks; Nativism; Segregation; Slavery
Race riots, 579, 687, 781, 783
Radical Republicans, 370; and Civil War, 350–51; and impeachment of Johnson, 367–69; and Lincoln's reelection, 350–51; and Reconstruction, 359, 361, 362, 364–65
Radisson, Pierre, 71
Railroads, 190, 224, 374, 412–13, 420–27, 577, 578; and agriculture, 412; and banker control, 426–27; competition among, 424–25, 427; consolidation of, 424; European investment in, 292, 422; federal grants to, 292, 358, 371, 412, 422; and First World War, 566; and growth of empire, 281, 286, 291–92, **293,** 393–94, 395, 420–23; regulation of, 425–26, 538–39, 522, 525; standardization of, 424; and strikes, 439–40, 722; and towns, 413; transcontinental, 358, 420–23
Railton, George, 453
Railway Labor Board, 585
Railway Union, 487
Rajk, Laszlo, 715
Raleigh, Sir Walter, 12–13
Randolph, A. Philip, 686
Randolph, Edmund, 123, 125, 127, 128, 133, 140, 141, 146
Randolph, Edward, 42, 44, 45, 47
Randolph, John, 163, 166, 167, 169, 180, 182, 208
Rappites, 245
Raskob, John J., 611
Rauschenbusch, Walter, 454, 517
Rayburn, Samuel, 738
Readjusters, 390
Reagan, Ronald, 800
Rearmament, 662, 669, 729
Recession, 650, 740, 744
Reconstruction, 356–67, 378; failure of,

375; and Lincoln's 10 percent plan, 351, 359, 360; and military districts, 365; problems of, 350–51, 359, 361–63; and state constitutions, 366; and Supreme Court, 369
Reconstruction Act (*1867*), 365, 367, 368, 369
Reconstruction Finance Corporation (RFC), 625, 626, 634, 731
Red Cloud, Chief, 402
Red power, 838
Red River War, **402**
Red scare, 579–81, 730–31, 740–42, 744
Redeemers. *See* Conservative party, Southern Democratic
Reed, Thomas Brackett, 475, 503
Reeder, Andrew C., 304
Reform movement, 232–51; and abolitionism, 242, 243, 245–50; agrarian, 468, 476–88; catalyst of, 239–40; and churches, 452–54; and education, 243–45; and humanitarianism, 240, 450–51, 514; and labor, 295–96; for peace, 244–45; religious background of, 234–39; and social critics, 239–40, 435–36, 449, 450, 460, 503, 515, 517–19, 746; and temperance, 240–41, 514; for women's rights, 241–43, 451–52, 513–15, 832–35. *See also* New Deal; Populism; Progressivism
Reformation. *See* Protestant Reformation
Regulators movement, 92, 116
Reich, Charles, 786
Reid, Whitelaw, 481
Religion: American pattern of, 63, 66, 113; and anti-immigration agitation, 289; and bigotry, 404; in colonial period, 18–21, 22–24; contemporary, 841–42; and Enlightenment, 67–68; in *1950*s, 745–46; freedom of, 40, 41, 113, 126; and reform movements, 234–39, 452–54
Rembrandt van Rijn, 33
Remington, Frederick, 499
Remington Arms Company, 431–32
Remond, Charles Lenox, 246
Reno, Milo, 626
Rensselaer, Kiliaen van, 34
Rensselaer Polytechnic Institute, 200
Republican party, 180, 303, 305, 306, 313, 314, 359, 380–82, 384, 425, 465–66, 467, 470, 473, 474, 497, 554–55, 582, 595, 611, 647, 648, 723; and Civil War, 329, 342, 350; and conservatism, 738; contemporary, 807, 808; in First World War, 562, 567, 568, 570; and internationalism, 672; liberal movement in, 372–74; and Lincoln, 310, 311, 330; and monetary policy, 374–75, 469–70; during New Deal, 647–48; Old Guard of, 522, 524, 525, 526, 537, 538, 540, 541, 556; origin of, 303; Readjusters faction of, 390; during Reconstruction, 364, 366–67, 368, 370; and Second World War, 672, 687; and slavery issue, 313; and tariff, 358, 465, 466, 537–38; and Treaty of Versailles, 575–77; and '29 depression, 616; and voting pattern, 465, **466;** Wide Awakes faction of, 315. *See also* Election; Radical Republicans;

Spruance, Raymond A., 695, 696
Stabilization Act (*1942*), 684
Stagflation, 804
Stalin, Joseph, 677, 700, 702, 703, 704, 706, 714, 715, 718, 723, 725, 726, 749, 754; and Big Three, 700, 702
"Stalwarts," 380, 466, 470
Stamp Act (*1765*), 85, 86, 87, 90, 91, 95
Stamp Act Congress (*1765*), 86, 98, 121
Standard Oil Company, 394, 429–30, 431, 517, 522, 541
Stanton, Edwin M., 330, 339, 365, 367, 368, 369
Stanton, Elizabeth Cady, 242, 243, 452
Stanton, Frank, 745
Stark, John, **107**
State and Local Fiscal Assistance Act (*1972*), 804
State rights, 134, 135, 150–51, 163, 167, 184, 185, 209, 213, 217, 543; under Articles of Confederation, 116, 124–25; under Constitution, 126; and desegregation, 742–43. *See also* Compromise of *1850;* Government, state; Kansas-Nebraska Act; Kentucky Resolutions; Missouri Compromise; Virginia Resolutions
States, admission of, **142, 180, 309, 406, 539, 757;** and Reconstruction, **365**
States Rights Democratic party, 723
Steamboat, 189–90, 198, 291
Steelworkers Union, 769
Steffens, Lincoln, 517, 519
Stein, Gertrude, 608
Stephens, Alexander H., 277, 328, 343, 361
Stephenson, David, 597
Steuben, Friedrich von, 109
Stevens, John, 291
Stevens, John L., 496
Stevens, Robert, 742
Stevens, Thaddeus, 243, 361, 362, 365
Stevenson, Adlai E. (*1835–1914*), 481, 506
Stevenson, Adlai E. (*1900–65*), 481*n*, 731–32, 733, 744, 747, 761, 767
Stewart, Potter, 744
Stiles, Ezra, 121
Stilwell, Joseph W., 697, 698
Stimson, Henry L., 602, 615, 621, 622, 624, 672, 676, 690, 706
Stimson Doctrine (*1932*), 623, 659, 666
Stoddard, John L., 455
Stoddert, Benjamin, 148
Stone, Harlan Fiske, 591, 648
Stone, Lucy, 242, 452
Story, Joseph, 183
Stowe, Harriet Beecher, 277, 318
Strategic Arms Limitation Talks (SALT), 799
Street people, 785, 786
Strikes. *See* Labor; Unions, labor
Strip mining, 817
Strong, Josiah, 454, 493, 494
Strong, William L., 451
Stuart, House of, 99
Stuart, J. E. B., 347
Student Nonviolent Coordinating Committee, 770, 782, 833
Students for a Democratic Society (SDS), 784

Stuyvesant, Peter, 34
Styron, William, 842
Sublette, Milton, 259
Suburbia, 829, **830**
Subversive Activities Control Board, 731
Sudan, 494
Suez Canal, 476, 752
Suez crisis of *1956*, 752–53
Suffolk Resolves (*1774*), 94
Suffrage: manhood, 206, 359–60, 361, 362, 364, 365, 366, 385, 386, 743, 770, 772, 836; woman, 241–43, 452, 514–15, 568
Sugar Act (*1764*), 84, 85, 86, 91
Sullivan, John, 121
Sullivan, Louis H., 459, 460
Summit conferences, 754, 755
Sumner, Charles, 248, 275, 305, 361, 371, 372, 375
Sumner, William Graham, 434, 436, 503
Supreme Court, 134, 150, 152, 158, 215, 221, 227–28, 248, 330, 374–75, 386, 435, 478, 743, 783, 807, 813, 814, 827, 832, 836, 841; antitrust legislation, 431, 522, 525, 541; under Chase, 368–69, 374; and civil liberties, 744; and civil rights, 742–43; *Civil Rights Cases*, 384; and contracts, 184, 185, 227–28; and corporations, 227, 435; and desegregation, 742–44; and Dred Scott, 307, 310, 369; and "Gospel of Wealth," 435; and income tax, 483, 484, 485; Insular cases, 529; and judicial review, 227; and labor, 440, 586; and legislative apportionment, 832; under Marshall, 183–85, 227; and New Deal legislation, 638; and railroads, 425; and Reconstruction, 369; and state rights, 150, 184, 227–28; under Taney, 227–28; on the Union, 217; under Vinson, 743; under Warren, 744
Sutter, John A., 261
Sutter's Fort, 261, 271
*Swann* v. *Charlotte-Mecklenburg Board of Education,* 836
Sweden, 8–9, 34, 413, 571
Swedenborg, Emanuel, 239
*Sweezy* case, 744
Switzerland, 571
Sylvis, William H., 438
Symbionese Liberation Army, 839
Syria, 752, 801

TVA. *See* Tennessee Valley Authority
Taft, Robert A., 672, 675, 676, 719, 722, 729, 731, 737, 739
Taft, William Howard, 522, 587; Administration of, 537–42; election of, 534; foreign policy under, 540–41, 549; as governor of Philippines, 529; and T. Roosevelt's reforms, 539; and War Labor Board, 566
Taft-Hartley Act (*1947*), 722, 739
Taiwan, 696, 701, 726, 798
Talleyrand, 147, 148, 160
Tallmadge, James, Jr., 196
Talmage, T. DeWitt, 453

Tammany Hall, 371, 381, 472, 542, 599, 628
Taney, Roger B., 212, 227; and Dred Scott case, 307, 310
Tangku Truce (*1933*), 666
Tanner, James, 476
Tappan, Arthur, 238–39, 246
Tappan, Lewis, 238–39, 246, 248
Tarawa, 695, 696
Tarbell, Ida M., 517
Tariff, 134, 170, 180, 201, 216, 218, 219, 228, 263, 286, 358, 371, 374, 465, 466, 468, 472, 474, 483, 488, 537–38, 540, 545–46, 568, 585, 615–16, 659
Tariff Act (*1870*), 474
"Tariff of abominations" (*1828*), 209
Tate, Sharon, 786
Taxation, 126, 134, 135, 143, 151, 170, 390, 436, 472, 477, 568, 577, 584, 592, 610, 645, 684, 685, 772. *See also* Income tax; Navigation Acts; Stamp Act
Taylor, Edward, 66
Taylor, Frederick W., 593
Taylor, John, 163, 185
Taylor, Maxwell, 765
Taylor, Zachary, 264, 266, **268;** Administration of, 271–72, 274, 285, 780; career of, 270–71
Taylor Society, 593
Tea Act (*1773*), 93
Teamsters Union, 699
Teapot Dome Scandal, 587
Technology, growth of, 197–99, 281, 358, 817, 832, 844–46. *See also* Industry
Tecumseh, Chief, 168, 170, 171, 175
Teheran Conference (*1943*), 701
Television, 745, 756, 770, 807, 841; effect of, on politics, 756, 844
Teller, Henry M., 485, 499
Temperance movement, 240–41, 514
Temporary National Economic Committee (*1938*), 646
Tenneco, 820
Tennent, Gilbert, 64
Tennessee, statehood of, 142, 159
Tennessee Coal and Iron Company, 389, 526, 820
Tennesse Valley Authority (TVA), 640–41, 673, 740, 772
Tenskwatawa (the Prophet), 168
Tenure of Office Act (*1867*), 365, 367, 368, 369, 370
"Tertium Quids," 163
Tesla, Nikola, 433
Texas, 254, 256–58; annexation of, 257, 263; and Louisiana Purchase, 176; Republic of, 257–58; settlement of, 257–58; statehood of, 263
Texas and Pacific Railroad, 383, 422, 423
Thailand, 750
Thames, Battle of the, **170,** 171, 226
Thayer, Eli, 304
Theater, 843
Thieu, Nguyen Van, 775, 792, 795
Third International, 579
Third World, 725, 751, 761, 763–64, 796, 797, 802, 822
Thomas, George, 330, 348, 352

A 6
B 7
C 8
D 9
E 0
F 1
G 2
H 3
I 4
J 5